Communications
in Computer and Information Science　　　1705

Rationale

The CCIS series is devoted to the publication of proceedings of computer science conferences. Its aim is to efficiently disseminate original research results in informatics in printed and electronic form. While the focus is on publication of peer-reviewed full papers presenting mature work, inclusion of reviewed short papers reporting on work in progress is welcome, too. Besides globally relevant meetings with internationally representative program committees guaranteeing a strict peer-reviewing and paper selection process, conferences run by societies or of high regional or national relevance are also considered for publication.

Topics

The topical scope of CCIS spans the entire spectrum of informatics ranging from foundational topics in the theory of computing to information and communications science and technology and a broad variety of interdisciplinary application fields.

Information for Volume Editors and Authors

Publication in CCIS is free of charge. No royalties are paid, however, we offer registered conference participants temporary free access to the online version of the conference proceedings on SpringerLink (http://link.springer.com) by means of an http referrer from the conference website and/or a number of complimentary printed copies, as specified in the official acceptance email of the event.

CCIS proceedings can be published in time for distribution at conferences or as post-proceedings, and delivered in the form of printed books and/or electronically as USBs and/or e-content licenses for accessing proceedings at SpringerLink. Furthermore, CCIS proceedings are included in the CCIS electronic book series hosted in the SpringerLink digital library at http://link.springer.com/bookseries/7899. Conferences publishing in CCIS are allowed to use Online Conference Service (OCS) for managing the whole proceedings lifecycle (from submission and reviewing to preparing for publication) free of charge.

Publication process

The language of publication is exclusively English. Authors publishing in CCIS have to sign the Springer CCIS copyright transfer form, however, they are free to use their material published in CCIS for substantially changed, more elaborate subsequent publications elsewhere. For the preparation of the camera-ready papers/files, authors have to strictly adhere to the Springer CCIS Authors' Instructions and are strongly encouraged to use the CCIS LaTeX style files or templates.

Abstracting/Indexing

CCIS is abstracted/indexed in DBLP, Google Scholar, EI-Compendex, Mathematical Reviews, SCImago, Scopus. CCIS volumes are also submitted for the inclusion in ISI Proceedings.

How to start

To start the evaluation of your proposal for inclusion in the CCIS series, please send an e-mail to ccis@springer.com.

Fabián R. Narváez · Fernando Urgilés ·
Teodiano Freire Bastos-Filho ·
Juan Pablo Salgado-Guerrero

Editors

Smart Technologies, Systems and Applications

3rd International Conference, SmartTech-IC 2022
Cuenca, Ecuador, November 16–18, 2022
Revised Selected Papers

 Springer

Editors
Fabián R. Narváez ⓘ
Universidad Politécnica Salesiana
Quito, Ecuador

Fernando Urgilés ⓘ
Universidad Politécnica Salesiana
Cuenca, Ecuador

Teodiano Freire Bastos-Filho ⓘ
Universidade Federal do Espírito Santo
Vitória, Brazil

Juan Pablo Salgado-Guerrero ⓘ
Universidad Politécnica Salesiana
Cuenca, Ecuador

ISSN 1865-0929   ISSN 1865-0937 (electronic)
Communications in Computer and Information Science
ISBN 978-3-031-32212-9   ISBN 978-3-031-32213-6 (eBook)
https://doi.org/10.1007/978-3-031-32213-6

This Springer imprint is published by the registered company Springer Nature Switzerland AG
The registered company address is: Gewerbestrasse 11, 6330 Cham, Switzerland

Preface

This volume contains the papers presented at the Third International Conference on Smart Technologies, Systems and Applications (SmartTech-IC 2022) held on November 16–18, 2022 in Cuenca, Ecuador. The SmartTech-IC conference aims to attract researchers, scientists and technologists from some of the top companies, universities, research groups, and government agencies from Latin America and around of the world to communicate their research results, inventions and innovative applications in the area of smart science and the most recent smart technological trends. SmartTech-IC 2022 was organized by the Universidad Politécnica Salesiana, a private institution of higher education with social purposes, nonprofit and co-financed by the Ecuadorian State. The SmartTech-IC conference was conceived as an academic platform to promote the creation of technical and scientific collaboration networks. The goal of the conference is to address relevant topics related to smart technologies, smart systems, smart trends and applications in different domains in the field of computer science and information systems that represent innovation in current society.

We would like to express our gratitude to all the authors who submitted papers to SmartTech-IC 2022, and our congratulations to those whose papers were accepted. There were 121 submissions. Each submission was reviewed by at least three qualified reviewers chosen from our Program Committee (PC) based on their qualifications and experience. The papers were selected by Program Chairs and their selection was based on a series of criteria including the reviewer's average score and comments provided by the Program Committee members. Finally, the Program Chairs decided to accept 37 full papers.

We would also like to thank the PC members, who reviewed the manuscripts in a timely manner and provided valuable feedback to the authors.

November 2022

Fabián R. Narváez
Fernando Urgilés
Teodiano Bastos
Juan P. Salgado-Guerrero

Organization

Honorary Committee

Juan Cárdenas	Universidad Politécnica Salesiana, Ecuador
Fernando Pesantez	Universidad Politécnica Salesiana, Ecuador
Fernando Moscoso	Universidad Politécnica Salesiana, Ecuador
Angela Flores	Universidad Politécnica Salesiana, Ecuador
Juan Pablo Salgado	Universidad Politécnica Salesiana, Ecuador

Organizing Committee

Fernando Urgilés Ortiz	Universidad Politécnica Salesiana, Ecuador
Fabián R. Narváez E.	Universidad Politécnica Salesiana, Ecuador
Ana Cecilia Villa	Universidad Politécnica Salesiana, Ecuador
Pablo Cevallos	Universidad Politécnica Salesiana, Ecuador
Christian Salamea	Universidad Politécnica Salesiana, Ecuador

Program Chairs

Smart Technologies

César Ferri	Universidad Politécnica de Valencia, Spain
Patricia Acosta Vargas	Universidad de Las Américas, Ecuador
Vladimir Robles Bykbaev	Universidad Politécnica Salesiana, Ecuador

Smart Systems

Teodiano Bastos	Universidade Federal do Espírito Santo, Brazil
Mauro Callejas	Universidad Pedagógica y Tecnológica, Colombia
Ismael Minchala	Universidad de Cuenca, Ecuador

Smart Applications

Antoine Manzanera	ENSTA-ParisTech, France
Vinicio Sanchez	Universidad Politécnica Salesiana, Ecuador
Gloria Díaz	Instituto Tecnológico Metropolitano, Colombia

Program Committee

Alberto López Delis	Medical Biophysics Center, Cuba
Alexander Águila	Universidad Politécnica Salesiana, Ecuador
Alexandre Pino	Universidad Federal do Rio de Janeiro, Brazil
Alvaro D. Orejuela	Universidad del Rosario, Colombia
Antoine Manzanera	ENSTA - ParisTech, France
Andrés Felipe Ruiz Olaya	Universidad Antonio Nariño, Colombia
Ana Cecilia Villa	Universidad Politécnica Salesiana, Ecuador
Ángel Cruz Roa	Universidad de Los Llanos, Colombia
Angélica Ramírez	Universidad Militar Nueva Granada, Colombia
Carlos Calderón	Universidad Técnica Particular de Loja, Ecuador
Carlos Novo	Universidad Tecnológica del Uruguay, Uruguay
Carlos Mera	Instituto Tecnológico Metropolitano, Colombia
Carmen Carrión	Universidad de Castilla - La Mancha, Spain
César Ferri	Universidad Politécnica de Valencia, Spain
Christian Cifuentes	Universidad de los Andes, Colombia
Christian Salamea	Universidad Politécnica Salesiana, Ecuador
Cristian David Gerrero	Universidade Federal do Espirito Santo, Brazil
Daniel González Montoya	Instituto Tecnológico Metropolitano, Colombia
David Romo	Univeridad Industrial de Santander, Colombia
David Ojeda	Universidad Técnica del Norte, Ecuador
Derfrey Duque Quintero	Universidad Pascual Bravo, Colombia
Denis Delisle	Universidad de Oriente, Cuba
Diego Carrión	Universidad Politécnica Salesiana, Ecuador
Diego Almeida	Yachay Tech University, Ecuador
Diego Vallejo	Universidad Politécnica Salesiana, Ecuador
Eduardo Pinos	Universidad Politécnica Salesiana, Ecuador
Edwin Carrasquero	Universidad Estatal de Milagro, Ecuador
Enrique Arias	Universidad de Castilla - La Mancha, Spain
Erick Reyes	Instituto Tecnológico Metropolitano, Colombia
Estefania Coronado	Fundazione Bruno Kessler FBK, Italy
Fausto García Márquez	Universidad de Castilla - La Mancha, Spain
Fabián Narváez E.	Universidad Politécnica Salesiana, Ecuador
Fabio Martínez	Universidad Industrial de Santander, Colombia

Fernando Urgiles	Universidad Politécnica Salesiana, Ecuador
Fernando Villalba	Yachay Tech Universidad, Ecuador
Gabriel León	Universidad Politécnica Salesiana, Ecuador
Germán Corredor	Case Western Reserve University, USA
Gloria M. Díaz	Instituto Tecnológico Metropolitano, Colombia
Hiram Ponce Espinosa	Universidad Panamericana, Mexico
Hugo Franco	Universidad Central, Colombia
Ismael Minchala	Universidad de Cuenca, Ecuador
Israel Pineda	Yachay Tech University, Ecuador
Jack Bravo Torres	Universidad Politécnica Salesiana, Ecuador
Javier Cabrera	Universidad Católica de Cuenca, Ecuador
John Villarejo	Universidad Federal do Paraná, Brazil
José Ignacio Huertas	Tecnológico de Monterrey, Mexico
José Sampietro	CELEC EP, Ecuador
José Raúl Castro	Universidad Técnica Particular de Loja, Ecuador
Jorge E. Camargo	Universidad Antonio Nariño, Colombia
Juan Inga	Universidad Politécnica Salesiana, Ecuador
Juan Pablo DÁmanto	Universidad Nacional UNICEN, Argentina
Juan Sebastián Botero	Instituto Tecnológico Metropolitano, Colombia
Juan David Martínez	Instituto Tecnológico Metropolitano, Colombia
Juan C. Caicedo	Broad Institute of MIT and Harvard, USA
Juan C. Santillán	Universidad Politécnica del Chimborazo, Ecuador
Julio Proaño Orellana	Universidad Politécnica Salesiana, Ecuador
Leony Ortiz	Universidad Politécnica Salesiana, Ecuador
Nitish Thakor	Johns Hopkins University, USA
Manuel Quiñones	Universidad Técnica Particular de Loja, Ecuador
Marco Carpio	Universidad Politécnica Salesiana, Ecuador
Marcelo García	Universidad Politécnica Salesiana, Ecuador
María Blanca Caminero	Universidad de Castilla-La Mancha, Spain
María Constanza Torres	Instituto Tecnológico Metropolitano, Colombia
Mariela Cerrada	Universidad Politécnica Salesiana, Ecuador
M. Carmen Juan Lizandra	Universidad Politécnica de Valencia, Spain
María Gabriela Baldeón	Universidad San Francisco de Quito, Ecuador
Mauro Callejas-Cuero	Universidad Pedagógica y Tecnológica, Colombia
Milton Ruiz	Universidad Politécnica Salesiana, Ecuador
Miguel Zúñiga	Universidad de Cuenca, Ecuador
Lenin V. Campozano	Escuela Politécnica Nacional, Ecuador
Leonardo Bueno	Universidad Politécnica Salesiana, Ecuador
Lucía Rivadeneira	University of Manchester, UK
Oscar Acosta	Université de Rennes 1, France
Oscar Rueda	Centro de Pesquisas de Energia Elétrica, Brazil
Pablo Cevallos	Universidad Politécnica Salesiana, Ecuador

Pablo Salamea	Universidad Politécnica Salesiana, Ecuador
Patricia Acosta Vargas	Universidad de Las Américas, Ecuador
Paula Rodríguez	Universidad Nacional de Colombia, Colombia
Paulina Morillo	Universidad Politécnica Salesiana, Ecuador
Ricardo Flores	Universidad San Francisco de Quito, Ecuador
Ricardo Gutiérrez	Universidad Militar Nueva Granada, Colombia
Roberto Macoto	Universidad Federal do Rio de Janeiro, Brazil
Rubén D. Fonnegra	Universidad Pascual Bravo, Colombia
Santiago Gonzáles	Universidad de Cuenca, Ecuador
Sergio Luján	Universidad de Alicante, Spain
Silvio Simani	University of Ferrara, Italy
Sri Krishnan	Toronto Metropolitan University, Canada
Teodiano Bastos	Universidade Federal do Espírito Santo, Brazil
Tuesman Castillo	Universidad Técnica Particular de Loja, Ecuador
Vladimir Robles	Universidad Politécnica Salesiana, Ecuador
Vicente Rojas	Universidad Politécnica Salesiana, Ecuador
Villie Morocho	Universidad de Cuenca, Ecuador
Walter Orozco	Universidad Politécnica Salesiana, Ecuador
Wilson Pavón	Universidad Politécnica Salesiana, Ecuador
Ximena López	Universidad de San Marcos, Perú

Local Organizing Committee

Paola Ingavelez	Universidad Politécnica Salesiana, Ecuador
Pablo Salamea	Universidad Politécnica Salesiana, Ecuador
John Calle	Universidad Politécnica Salesiana, Ecuador
Maria Tocachi	Universidad Politécnica Salesiana, Ecuador
Sara Sarmiento	Universidad Politécnica Salesiana, Ecuador
Juan José Narváez Z.	Universidad Politécnica Salesiana, Ecuador

Sponsoring Institutions

http://www.ups.edu.ec

Contents

Smart Trends and Applications

Smart Technologies

Demand Forecasting of Fast-Moving Consumer Goods by Deep Learning-Based Time Series Analysis

José Nicolás Valbuena Godoy, Roberto Arias, and Hugo Franco[✉]

Faculty of Natural Sciences and Engineering, Universidad Central, Bogotá, Colombia
hfrancot@ucentral.edu.co

Abstract. Demand forecasting plays an essential role in the ability of certain companies to meet future customer requirements. Current research is focused on the construction of models intended to reduce forecasting error. However, most Colombian companies using demand forecasting tools mostly apply traditional regression models to project their demands, so they obtain and employ coarse estimations. This paper presents a performance comparison between stochastic time series models (SARIMA-MLR) and Recurrent Neural Networks (RNN) for demand forecasting of a group of Fast Moving Consumer Goods (FMCG) in the beauty and make-up sector (nail varnish). A set of demand projection models based on SARIMA-MLR and RNN (LSTM) are evaluated using forecast error measures. According to the results in this work, RNN with two LSTM layers presents the highest forecasting performance for four selected goods.

Keywords: Demand Forecasting · Fast Moving Consumer Goods (FMCG) · SARIMA-MLR · Recurrent Neural Networks (RNN) · Long Short-Term Memory (LSTM)

1 Introduction

Organizations use demand forecasting models to support decisions on production, logistics, and inventories of goods and services. Specifically, based on the prediction of the behavior of customer requirements, according to different estimations on the amount of produced units and the market trends. Taking into account the production resources and costs within a specific company, these models allow the proper planning of machines, raw materials, production lines, and workforce employed to meet the demand of the target market. Similarly, different models for production and inventory management in the supply chain require demand forecasting information to minimize costs and time. Nonetheless, inadequate forecasting leads to unnecessary inventory costs, wasted time, and even the inability to meet customer demand.

In this field, predictive demand modeling research has become more prevalent in recent years. New markets, technologies, and online trading tools imply faster

F. R. Narváez et al. (Eds.): SmartTech-IC 2022, CCIS 1705, pp. 3–17, 2023.
https://doi.org/10.1007/978-3-031-32213-6_1

product life cycles [1]. New methods have also been developed to facilitate the application of the models and/or to improve the projection margins of error, including several aspects of the corresponding time series and the incorporation of random and deterministic variables [2]. Consequently, current research has focused on adapting models for Fast Moving Consumer Goods (FMCG) due to their high turnover rate, high consumer demand, seasonal behaviors, and short product life cycles compared to other goods [1,3].

However, new methods to determine the appropriate models in different emerging markets (e.g., the Colombian ones) are scarce in industrial applications, and frequently rely on data mining, market knowledge modeling, and linear predictive models. Non-linear models and recent approaches, such as Neural Networks are practically unused in this scope [5].

2   Literature Review

2.1   SARIMA-MLR Model

SARIMA-MLR combines the SARIMA (Seasonal Autoregressive Integrated Moving Average) approach and Multiple Linear Regression models. Linear Regression determines the dependence of a variable Y on one or more explanatory variables x_i [6]. This model has been formulated as a linear combination of all independent (explanatory) variables x_i and their corresponding partial coefficients β_i, plus an intercept (β_0) and an observational error u, related to uncontrolled variables. The result is the expected value of the dependent variable Y, also denoted as $E(Y|x_i)$, which minimizes the sum of the squares of the residuals u for all the observations j. In time series analysis, j represents the time or period (Eq. 1).

$$E(Y|x_i) = \beta_0 + \beta_1 x_{1j} + \beta_2 x_{2j} .... + \beta_i x_{ij} + u_j \tag{1}$$

To estimate the value of the partial coefficients β_i, the method of least squares of the residuals is applied, considering that the first-order partial derivatives with respect to each of the parameters x_i cancel out [7], obtaining Eq. 2:

$$\beta = (X^t X)^{-1} X^t Y \tag{2}$$

Thus, a forecasting model $\hat{Y}$ is created, aiming for the lowest estimation error for Y (Eq. 3), while the residual u_j corresponds to the difference between the real and the predicted value for each of the observations j [7]. Such regression model must comply with the assumptions of Linearity, Collinearity, Homoscedasticity, Normality, and residual Independence [6]:

$$\hat{Y} = \beta_0 + \beta_1 x_{1j} + \beta_2 x_{2j} .... + \beta_i x_{ij} = X\beta \tag{3}$$

The SARIMA approach consists of finding a mathematical expression representing and explaining the behavior of a time series from past observations and forecast errors [8,9]. This family of models is based on the ARMA family, which is built upon an autoregressive (AR) part, with order p, and a moving average (MA) part, with order q, using a stochastic component a_t [10]. ARMA models can only be applied to stationary time series, where the mean and variance of the time series are constant and do not exhibit a trend (i.e., the time series does not have heteroscedasticity) [10]. Thus, the application of ARMA models to real problems depends on trend elimination methods in mean and variance. Since there are no effective univariate homoscedasticity tests, time series transformations are used to eliminate or mitigate the trend in variance (e.g. logarithmic and Box-Cox transformations) [11]. To eliminate the trend in the mean, it is necessary to apply successive differences to the time series $\triangle Y_t$, as many times as required (parameter d of the model). Correspondingly, the ARIMA (Autoregressive Integrated Moving Average) model is created as an adaptation of the ARMA model, tackling both the trend of the data and the seasonality conditions (Eq. 4).

$$\triangle^d Y_t = [\phi_1 \triangle^d Y_{t-1} + ... + \phi_p \triangle^d Y_{t-p}] + [\theta_1 a_{t-1} + ... + \theta_q a_{t-q}] + a_t \qquad (4)$$

where the series is differentiated d-times (order d) and the autoregressive coefficients of order p and moving average of order q are maintained. In this way, taking into account the lag operator B, the equation can also be expressed as:

$$\phi_p(B) \, \nabla^d Y_t = \theta_q(B) a_t \qquad (5)$$

ARIMA models have multiple applications in the analysis and forecasting of time series exhibiting different behaviors. However, for high-frequency periodical data series, the treatment of seasonality plays a central role in the modeling process to improve the forecasting results [12]. Once the frequency main of the time series is determined, the ARIMA (p, d, q) model is transformed into the seasonal ARIMA (p, d, q) $\times$ SARIMA (P, D, Q) [S], where the values P, D, Q refer to the autoregressive model, difference, and moving average model orders, for S periods, i.e., the season length (Eq. 6):

$$\phi_p(B)\Phi_P(B) \, \nabla^d \, \nabla^D Y_t = \theta_q(B)\Theta_Q(B) a_t \qquad (6)$$

SARIMA models are practical in many demand forecasting situations, yet the behavior of a target time series usually depends on one or more independent variables [13]. SARIMAX models [14] incorporate exogenous variables x_i into the original model and are appropriate for time series exhibiting higher fluctuations (Eq. 7):

$$\phi_p(B)\Phi_P(B) \, \nabla^d \, \nabla^D Y_t = \theta_q(B)\Theta_Q(B) a_t + \sum_{i=1}^{n} \beta_i(x_i)_t \qquad (7)$$

where β_i are the coefficients of the polynomial including the exogenous variables in the model, over time t. However, the computational cost of taking into account such exogenous variables could be quite expensive in multiple applied scenarios. To address such a drawback, the SARIMA-MLR approach uses a SARIMA model on the target variable, and its result is included as a new variable into the multiple linear regression model that considers the exogenous variables [15]:

$$\text{SARIMA}: \qquad \phi_p(B)\Phi_P(B)\,\nabla^d\,\nabla^D Z_t = \theta_q(B)\Theta_Q(B)a_t \qquad (8)$$

$$\text{SARIMA} - \text{MLR}: \qquad \hat{Y} = \beta_0 + [\beta_1 x_{1t} + \beta_2 x_{2t}.... + \beta_i x_{it}] + \beta_z Z_t \qquad (9)$$

where Z_t represents the values of the SARIMA and β_z is the regression coefficient that accompanies these values; the SARIMA-MLR must comply with the regression assumptions.

2.2   Recurrent Neural Networks and LSTM Cells

The uncertainties and complex relationships within the market in which a particular good is placed lead to uncertain demand values, making it difficult to extract accurate information on sales behavior. Artificial Neural Networks are known to properly adapt to complex behaviors in the target variables and are able to adapt to changing external factors [16].

Historical demand data are sequential in nature. To use neural network approaches in time series analysis, it is necessary to consider the impact of the complexity of the underlying dynamical process in order to properly train non-linear models. The RNNs allow the storage of historical information through a hidden state or layer, by means of activation functions allowing adequate information between past, present, and future states of the system [19]. Among others, LSTM (Long Short Term Memory) units are used to update the hidden state and forget unnecessary information along the network training process, assigning the proper relevance to recent and early values of the time series [20]. This type of units (neurons) can be used in single or multiple learning layers throughout the neural network, where the first layer can be fed by one or more variables. Finally, the network construction generally uses a dense output layer, which uses a single neuron to predict the desired value, or multiple neurons to predict a sequence [21].

One of the main issues when using a RNN model is the memory loss at different time steps due to the transformations the data undergoes across the neural network layers. Consequently, LSTM units enhance the long-term learning of sequences [21] by dividing their state into a vector h_t (short-term state) and a vector c_t (long-term state). LSTM units have a more complex behavior than those used by other ANN models; their training converges faster and allows them to detect long-term dependencies [21]. The internal structure of an LSTM cell is shown in Fig. 1.

Thus, the state c_{t-1} passes through a *forgetting gate* to delete some values before passing through an *input gate* to add new memorized values. The resulting data becomes the new state c_t, and a copy is made to pass through a hyperbolic tangent function (tanh) and a filter based on an *exit gate*, in order to create the new state h_t. The input vector x_t and the state h_{t-1} are passed to four *sublayers*, where:

– The main layer g_t keeps the most important parts in the state c_t and discards the other parts.

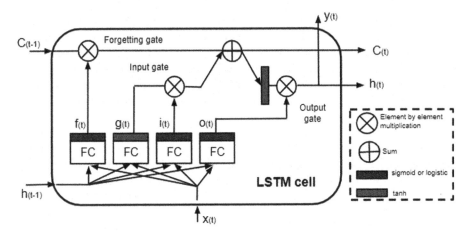

Fig. 1. LSTM cell structure [21].

- Layer f_t is the forgetting gate controller with logistic or *sigmoid* activation function and controls the parts to be deleted from state c_t.
- Layer i_t is the controller of the input gate with logistic or *sigmoid* activation function and controls the parts of g_t to be added to state c_t.
- Layer o_t is the output gate driver with logistic or *sigmoid* activation function and controls the parts of state c_t to be read to generate the output.

To determine each of the states and outputs, the following expressions are evaluated for each unit:

$$i_t = \sigma(W_{xi}^T \, x_t + W_{hi}^T \, h_{t-1} + b_i) \tag{10}$$

$$f_t = \sigma(W_{xf}^T \, x_t + W_{hf}^T \, h_{t-1} + b_f) \tag{11}$$

$$o_t = \sigma(W_{xo}^T \, x_t + W_{ho}^T \, h_{t-1} + b_o) \tag{12}$$

$$g_t = tanh(W_{xg}^T \, x_t + W_{hg}^T \, h_{t-1} + b_g) \tag{13}$$

$$c_t = f_t \otimes c_{t-1} + i_t \otimes g_t \tag{14}$$

$$y_t = h_t = o_t \otimes \tanh(c_t) \tag{15}$$

2.3   Time-Series Analysis in Demand Forecasting

Both stochastic and ANN approaches are used in the recent literature to address the problem of FMCG forecasting. In order to improve product demand forecasts in Chilean supermarkets, Aburto and Weber [22] developed a sequential comparison system of ARIMA models with Neural Networks to reproduce the time series combination techniques and the advantages of each of the SARIMAX and MLP (Multi Layered Perceptron) models. By applying this approach, they found a significant improvement compared to traditional models and described new applications for joint forecasting systems, using SARIMAX results as input of neural networks, going from an Normalized Mean Square Error (NMSE) of 0.609 to 0.354. In Hong Kong, Au et al. [23] proposed a Neural Network evolutionary computation approach compared with the SARIMA for forecasting retail fashion items. Their results were useful for forecasting demands with low seasonal trends, reducing the error to half its original value using Neuronal Network models.

On the other hand, Arunraj & Ahrens [15] adjusted a SARIMA model, combining it with demand-related factors through Multiple Linear Regression analysis (SARIMA-MLR) and Quantile Regression (SARIMA-QR), looking for a reduction in the waste of perishable food in Germany. They report a reduction in the Mean Absolute Percentage Error (MAPE) from 28.78 to 24.18 and 23.47, respectively. To improve sale forecasts among oral care product supply chains in the city of Mumbai, Vhatkar & Dias [24] used a Multilayer Perceptron on sales information from the entire commercial chain to evaluate the error reported for different goods. The forecast results were accurate, with an average Mean Square Error (MSE) of 4.9 and a model that can fit future FMCG. To reduce warehouse space per unit in inventory, Hodzić et al. [25] designed a RNN with LSTM layers to forecast daily demands for consumer goods. The network results were compared to those from an Adaptive Means algorithm, concluding that the RNN-LSTM exhibits the highest accuracy MAPE of 84.37% to 71.14%. Wang et al. [26] and Weng et al. [27] implemented models based on RNN, Back Propagation (BP) network, Support Vector Machine (SVM), and ARIMA, to forecast sales of edible and agricultural goods. The performance of the methodologies was very good for all cases, especially with the (RNN) model, with a Mean Absolute Error (MAD) of 0.3.

3   Materials and Methods

For the construction and evaluation of the models, the data set is described, specifying the FMCG of the study and the variables of the models. Subsequently, the methodology for the construction of the SARIMA and the RNN is explained, taking into account the characterization of the time series, the assumptions of the regression models, and the configuration of each of the training layers and hyper-parameters in the neural networks. Finally, to evaluate the performance of the models, the forecast error measures are described.

3.1   Dataset Description

Both internal and external variables were used to improve the learning performance of the models under study. Given the data usage agreement established with the company (nail varnish producer), the daily demand dataset for all the goods of the organization was provided as a CSV file from January 2015 to May 2019, including 5,516,317 records with the following information:

- Order date: Day/Month/year
- Regional: order origin, city of Colombia or abroad.
- Channel: chains and supermarkets, Exports, Professional or Retail.
- Product management group.
- Name and identification of the product.
- Requested quantity (units).

Additionally, the records of macroeconomic indicators in Colombia were used as external variables for the construction of the models. This information is publicly accessible, allowing the use of historical data of the country's main macroeconomic data series, within the time period of the study, from the web portal of the *Banco de la República de Colombia*, and the currency exchange data series from the SET-FX system of the *Superintendencia Financiera de Colombia* [28]. The resulting data, in CSV format, consists of the following variables:

- COLCAP value: reflects the variations in the prices of the 20 most liquid shares on the Colombian Stock Exchange (BVC) [28].
- Colombian peso in terms of the dollar.
- TRM Market Representative Rate: expresses the daily average value of the exchange rate between the Colombian peso and the US dollar [28].
- Monetary Policy Intervention Rate: minimum interest rate that the *Banco de la República de Colombia* charges financial institutions for the loans it makes to them through open market operations (OMA) [28].
- Colombian peso average per UVR: The unit of real value (UVR) is certified by the *Banco de la República de Colombia* and reflects the purchasing power based on the variation of the consumer price index (CPI) during the calendar month immediately prior to the month. From the beginning of the calculation period [28].

For the present work, the training dataset is conformed by the time series from the first week of 2015 to the last week of 2018 (90% historical data) and the test set from week 1 to week 21 of 2019 (10% historical data), given that, for the construction of the SARIMA-MLR, the 2015 data must be discarded since the independent variables the same year and require the largest amount of data for model building. Such a training set is appropriate for constructing the time steps of the input data matrix for the RNN.

Selection of FMCG: The selection of the FMCG for this study was performed in collaboration with the company staff, taking into account the most representative goods according to demand and the interests of the *Management Group*. Thus, the percentage of goods belonging to each category was established, identifying that the category with the largest number of goods is *Nail Polish*. Thus, for purposes of future applications according to the organization's perspectives on the market, the four nail polish with the highest number of demands to date (FMCG 1, FMCG 2, FMCG 3, and FMCG 4) were selected and used for the construction and evaluation of different demand forecasting models.

Model Variables: For the model formulation, variables contributing to explaining the demand behavior for each of the four FMCG were included. The first set of variables was the demand for goods in the category of *Nail polish*. As a consequence, the demand information for 994 goods was found, eliminating the nail polishes that were discontinued or were new in the market, for a total of 34 variables to be introduced in the model. Finally, the second set of variables were the five macroeconomic variables from the *Banco de la republica de Colombia*, for a total of 39 variables. For model-building purposes, each of these variables was assigned an X_i. In the same way, the training and test sets were kept separate when the models were built and tested.

3.2   SARIMA-MLR

For the construction of the SARIMA-MLR, a basic SARIMA model was obtained from the data, with the objective of using its information as an additional input variable of the regression model. Initially, a time series was created from the training data, with an S frequency based on the seasonality of the variable, and the evaluation of seasonality with the Dickey-Fuller and Phillips-Perron hypothesis tests. Subsequently, a Box-Cox transformation was performed on the data set, in order to guarantee the minimum trend in mean and variance. Thus, different combinations of SARIMA (p, d, q) x (P, D, Q) $[S]$ models were obtained, starting from the trend of the data and the required value for d and/or D (iterative differentiation). Then, each of the models was evaluated using the Akaike Information Criterion, AIC (Eq. 16), and Bayesian Information Criterion, BIC (Eq. 17), selecting the model with their lowest values [29]. Where $\widehat{L}$ represents the maximum value of the model's likelihood function, k is the number of free parameters to be estimated, and T is the length of the data series.

$$AIC = -2 \ln \widehat{L} + 2\,(p + q + P + Q + k + 1) \qquad (16)$$

$$BIC = -2 \ln \widehat{L} + \ln(T)\,(p + q + P + Q + k + 1) \qquad (17)$$

Once the model with the lowest AIC and BIC was identified, the respective SARIMA was constructed. Next, in order to comply with the model and white noise assumptions, the independence and normality of the residuals were verified by means of the Autocorrelation Function, the Q-Q plot, and the adjusted Z_t value obtained through the corresponding equation. Finally, the values of the SARIMA were incorporated as an input variable for the construction of a Multiple Linear Regression model. So, the SARIMA-MLR was constructed using a group of X_i variables plus the Z_t variable. Likewise, each of the regression assumptions and the evaluation method were taken into account:

- Collinearity: Correlation Matrix.
- Linearity of the variables: Trend graphs.
- Homoscedasticity: White's test.
- Normality: Q-Q plot and Kolmogorov-Smirnov test.
- Independence: Residual plots and Durbin-Watson test.

The transformations of the variables, the dimensionality reduction of the model using the Backward method, and the elimination of outliers were also performed to meet the required regression assumptions. On the other hand, The formulation of the SARIMA-MLR took into account the logarithmic transformations of the independent variables and the Box-Cox transformation of the dependent variable. Likewise, Z_t variable is accompanied by β_z, and Y was cleared from the equation.

3.3   Recurrent Neural Networks

For the construction and training of the neural network, the training and test sets were separated and normalized in the range $(0, 1)$. For the training and test set, an input matrix (X) and a target vector (Y) were constructed, given the size of the historical dataset (time-step) to produce the forecast and the seasonal behavior of the time series. Then, the network was constructed by defining the number of layers, the number of neurons and the activation functions (*sigmoid* and *hyperbolic tangent* for LSTM layers, and *linear* for Dense layers). Thus, the model was trained with a compiler `RMSProp` and a loss function (`MeanSquaredError` or `MeanAbsoluteError`), while the number of *epochs* and the size of the gradient calculation ("batch-size") were defined according to the loss function of the training and validation data to avoid model overfitting. Starting from the seasonal behavior of the time series and the RNN used by Hodžić and Wang, where the maximum number of LSTM layers was two, the hyperparameters, three particular models were selected for evaluation (Fig. 2).

RNN 3 works by learning z multiple variables, including the predicted variable and highly correlated (above 0.9) exogenous variables [30]. Thus, considering the architecture of each RNN under evaluation, RNN 1 has 50961 parameters, while RNN 2 requires 76805 parameters, independently of the FMCG. Finally, according to the z variables used for each of the FMCG, RNN 3 has different numbers of parameters, as shown in Table 1.

Table 1. Variables and total parameters of the RNN 3 for each of the FMCG.

	Variables	Total Parameters
FMCG 1	FMCG 1; x12; x13; x18; x23; x30	78885
FMCG 2	FMCG 2; x24; x27; x32	78053
FMCG 3	FMCG 3; x6; x13; x15; x22	78469
FMCG 4	FMCG 4; x12; x23; x24	78053

3.4   Forecast Error Measures

The predictive ability of the models was evaluated by calculating the following forecast error measures, according to their representation at the production unit level:

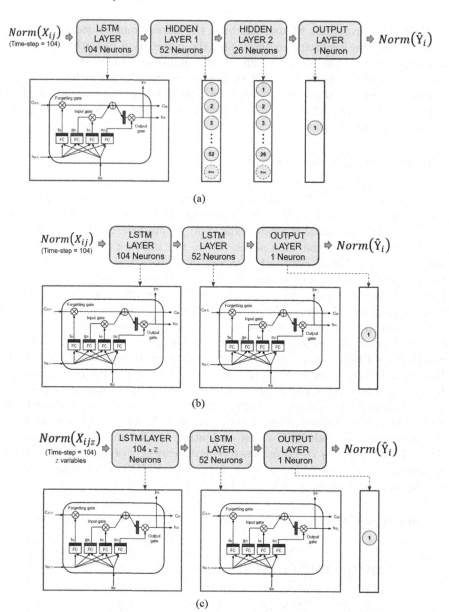

Fig. 2. RNN architecture: (a) RNN 1: one LSTM layer, two dense hidden layers and one dense output layer, (b) RNN 2: two LSTM layers and one dense output layer, (c) RNN 3: two LSTM layers, one dense output layer and multiple variable learning.

- Mean Square Error (MSE): Average square units in stock.
- Mean Absolute Deviation (MAD): Average absolute units in stock.
- Cumulative Sum of Forecast Errors (CFE): Total units in stock.
- Tracking Signal (TS): CFE to MAD ratio (Total units/Average units).
- Mean Absolute Percentage Error (MAPE): Difference degree in the behavior or movement of the forecast series in a percentage measure.

4   Results and Discussion

4.1   SARIMA-MLR Equations

For the formulation of the SARIMA-MLR models, transformations on the independent and dependent variables were performed, in order to meet the assumptions for regression and the assumption of time series stationarity. Thus, for the four goods under study, the dependent variable underwent a BoxCox transformation, and the last four macroeconomic variables underwent a logarithmic transformation (Eq. 18).

$$\hat{Y}_t = \sqrt[\lambda]{\left(\beta_0 + \sum_{i=1}^{35} \beta_i(x_i)_{t-52} + \sum_{i=36}^{39} \beta_i(\log(x_i)_{t-52})) + \beta_Z Z_t\right)\lambda + 1} \quad (18)$$

where, the Zt value represents the values projected with the SARIMA for each of the FMCG, such that:

- FMCG 1 - SARIMA(2, 0, 2)(0, 0, 1) [52]

$$Z_t = \mu + \phi_1\left(\frac{(Y_{t-1})^\lambda - 1}{\lambda}\right) + \phi_2\left(\frac{(Y_{t-2})^\lambda - 1}{\lambda}\right) + \theta_1 a_{t-1} + \theta_2 a_{t-2} + \Theta_1 a_{t-52} + a_t \quad (19)$$

- FMCG 2 - SARIMA(0, 0, 0)(1, 0, 0) [52]

$$Z_t = \mu + \Phi_1\left(\frac{(Y_{t-52})^\lambda - 1}{\lambda}\right) + a_t \quad (20)$$

- FMCG 3 - SARIMA(0, 1, 1)(1, 0, 0) [52]

$$\Delta Z_t = \theta_1 a_{t-1} + \Phi_1 \Delta\left(\frac{(Y_{t-52})^\lambda - 1}{\lambda}\right) + a_t \quad (21)$$

- FMCG 4 - SARIMA(0, 1, 4)(1, 0, 0) [52]

$$\Delta Z_t = \theta_1 a_{t-1} + \theta_2 a_{t-2} + \theta_3 a_{t-3} + \theta_4 a_{t-4} + \Phi_1 \Delta\left(\frac{(Y_{t-52})^\lambda - 1}{\lambda}\right) + a_t \quad (22)$$

All of the time series presented a seasonal behavior of 52 weeks. FMCG 1 and FMCG 2 have a constant behavior, while FMCG 3 and FMCG 4 presented a decreasing trend.

By means of Student's-t test, it was found that each of the FMCG depends on the demand behavior of different combinations of the 34 goods used, considering the characteristics of tonality and use in the market. On the other hand, goods 19 and 28 exhibited a high frequency of use and contribution to the forecasting of the study goods, as well as the variable Z_t. Finally, the Monetary Policy Intervention Rate was the macroeconomic variable with the highest contribution to the forecast.

4.2   Model Performance Comparison and Assessment

Each model performance was evaluated according to the forecast error obtained for the first 21 weeks of 2019, according to the metrics MSE, MAD, CFE, TS, and MAPE. Table 2 reports these errors using normalized values, highlighting the lowest error values.

Table 2. Forecast error measures of the FMCG models.

FMCG	Model	MSE	MAD	CFE	TS	MAPE
1	SARIMA-MLR	0.074	0.202	−0.548	−2.72	61.67%
	RNN 1	0.072	0.201	−1.028	5.104	82.14%
	RNN 2	0.07	**0.185**	−0.08	**−0.435**	87.54%
	RNN 3	**0.061**	0.201	−2.809	13.97	**43.8%**
2	SARIMA-MLR	0.109	0.268	−3.622	−13.53	98.61%
	RNN 1	0.068	0.202	−0.444	−2.2	82.61%
	RNN 2	**0.061**	**0.193**	−0.318	−1.65	**79.04%**
	RNN 3	0.078	0.225	**0.02**	**0.09**	88.14%
3	SARIMA-MLR	0.057	0.194	−0.719	−3.708	89.16%
	RNN 1	0.06	0.184	−0.413	−2.25	112.9%
	RNN 2	0.064	0.199	0.047	0.234	114.2%
	RNN 3	**0.043**	**0.169**	**−0.022**	**−0.13**	**75.82%**
4	SARIMA-MLR	0.134	0.273	−4.059	−14.88	101.4%
	RNN 1	0.082	0.23	**−0.088**	**−0.381**	86.85%
	RNN 2	**0.053**	**0.18**	1.733	9.603	70.22%
	RNN 3	0.065	0.207	2.858	13.8	**57.82%**

Thus, the RNN with two LSTM layers yield the lowest error value for most of the cases. On the other hand, Deep Learning models bring improved forecastings, in comparison to linear and autoregressive moving average models, such as

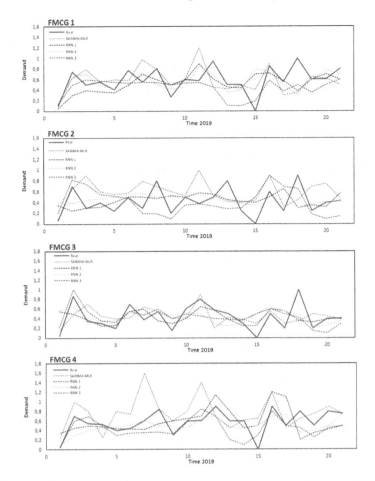

Fig. 3. Forecast plots of the models: FMCG 1, FMCG 2, FMCG 3 and FMCG 4

SARIMA-MLR approaches. The forecast plots of the models for the 4 FMCG are shown in Fig. 3.

From the evaluation of the proposed models, the RNN with two LSTM layers was the best approach for FMCG demand forecasting in this study. These results are consistent with those described in the recent literature. On the other hand, the weekly time series of the four goods have very noisy, given their high sales variability, hindering the representation of the time series behavior by classical and stochastic demand models. Incorporating seasonal factors and autoregressive moving averages into the regression models did not significantly improve the forecasting performance in most cases since the demand for FMCG depends to a great extent on the behavior of internal and external variables of the company.

Additionally, demand behavior for goods with similar properties is highly correlated with the demand for FMCG in this study. Similarly, the monetary policy intervention rate was the macroeconomic variable with the highest impact on the linear model performance. The RNN models exhibit a higher predictive ability for univariate and multivariate learning cases. Incorporating a second LSTM layer decreased the forecast error in most experimental configurations. Additionally, training the RNN with multiple variables enhanced the treatment of noise or time shifts in raw data.

4.3   Conclusions and Future Work

The reported results provide a basis for designing predictive demand models beyond the type of goods (or services) involved. Regression and Autoregressive Moving Average models could be helpful approaches for low-cost demand forecasting processes in small companies. Nevertheless, exploring Neural Network models is recommended, using model selection techniques under exhaustive experimental setups. Finally, such models should be evaluated periodically to be adapted for production and supply chain planning in real-life scenarios.

References

1. Thain, G., Bradley, J.: FMCG: The Power of Fast-Moving Consumer Goods, 1st edn. Design Publishing, Sarasota (2014)
2. Green, K.C., Armstrong, J.S.: Demand Forecasting: Evidence-based Methods. SSRN Electron. J. **24**(5) (2005)
3. Vértice, E.: Política de producto, 1st edn. Publicaciones Vértice SL, Barcelona (2007)
4. Contrera, G., Arango, O.: Planeación y optimización de la demanda: Componente retador dentro de todo proyecto detransformación digital. Sinnetic News **1**(19), 1–2 (2017)
5. Cadena, L., Ariza, G., Palomo, Z.: La gestión de pronóstico en las decisiones empresariales: un análisis empírico. Espacios **1**(39) (2018)
6. Gujarati, D.N., Guerrero, D.G., Medina, G.A.: Econometría, 5th edn. McGraw-Hill, New York (2010)
7. Sabadías, A.V.: Estadística descriptiva e inferencial. Universidad de Castilla-La Mancha, Ciudad Real (1995)
8. Chatfield, C.: The Analysis of Time Series: An Introduction, 6th edn. CRC Press, Boca Raton (2016)
9. Jiménez, J.F., Gázques, J.C., Sánches, R.: Mercadeo Básico. Rev. Eur. Dirección Econ. Empresa **15**(1), 185–189 (2006)
10. Valencia-Cárdenas, M., Díaz-Serna, F.J., Correa-Morales, J.C.: Multi-product inventory modeling with demand forecasting and Bayesian optimization. DYNA (Colombia) **83**(198), 236–244 (2016)
11. Ruppert, D.: Statistics and Data Analysis for Financial Engineering. Springer, New York (2010)
12. Kotler, P., Armstrong, G.: Fundamentos de marketing, 11th edn. Pearson Educación, Mexico (2013)
13. Chase, C.W.: Demand-Driven Forecasting: A Structured Approach to Forecasting, 1st edn. Wiley, New Jersey (2013)
14. Bisht, D.C.S., Ram, M.: Recent Advances in Time Series Forecasting, 1st edn. CRC Press, Boca Raton (2021)

15. Arunraj, N.S., Ahrens, D.: A hybrid seasonal autoregressive integrated moving average and quantile regression for daily food sales forecasting. Int. J. Prod. Econ. **170**(1), 321–335 (2015)
16. Díez, R.P., Gómez, A.G., de Abajo Martínez, N.: Introducción a la inteligencia artificial: sistemas expertos, redes neuronales artificiales y computación evolutiva, 1st edn. Servicio de Publicaciones, Universidad de Oviedo (2001)
17. López, R.F. and Fernández, J.M.F: Las Redes Neuronales Artificiales. 1st edn. Servicio de Publicaciones, Netbiblo, La Coruña (2008)
18. Fonseca, M.R.: Simulación de redes neuronales como herramienta Big Data en el ámbito sanitario. Lulu, Morrisville (2016)
19. Maass, W., Joshi, P., Sontag, E.D.: Computational Aspects of Feedback in Neural Circuits. PLoS Comput. Biol. **156**(3) (2007)
20. Schmidhuber, J., Wierstra, D., Gagliolo, M., Gomez, F.: Training recurrent networks by evolino. Neural Comput. **19**(3), 757–779 (2007)
21. Géron, A.: Hands-On Machine Learning with Scikit-Learn, Keras, and TensorFlow: Concepts, Tools, and Techniques to Build Intelligent Systems, 2nd edn. O'Reilly Media, Sebastopol (2019)
22. Aburto, L., Weber, R.: Improved supply chain management based on hybrid demand forecast. Appl. Soft Comput. **4571**(1), 136–144 (2007)
23. Au, K.-F., Choi, T.-M., Yu, Y.: Fashion retail forecasting by evolutionary neural networks. Int. J. Prod. Econ. **114**(2), 615–630 (2008)
24. Vhatkar, S., Dias, J.: Oral-care goods sales forecasting using artificial neural network model. Procedia Comput. Sci. **79**(1), 238–243 (2016)
25. Hodžić, K., Hasić, H., Cogo, E., Jurić, Ž.: Warehouse demand forecasting based on long short-term memory neural networks. In: 2019 XXVII International Conference on Information, Communication and Automation Technologies (ICAT), pp. 1–6 (2019)
26. Wang, J., Liu, G.Q., Liu, L.: A selection of advanced technologies for demand forecasting in the retail industry. In: 2019 4th IEEE International Conference on Big Data Analytics, ICBDA 2019, pp. 317–320 (2019)
27. Weng, Y., Wang, X., Hua, J., Wang, H., Kang, M., Wang, F.-Y.: Forecasting horticultural products price using ARIMA model and neural network based on a large-scale data set collected by web crawler. IEEE Trans. Comput. Soc. Syst. **6**(3), 547–553 (2019)
28. Banco de la República de Colombia Homepage. http://www.banrep.gov.co/es/estadisticas. Accessed 22 Aug 2020
29. Montesinos López, A.: Estudio del aic y bic en la selección de modelos de vida con datos censurados. Centro de investigación en matemáticas (2011)
30. Brownlee, J.: Machine Learning Mastery With Python: Understand Your Data, Create Accurate Models, and Work Projects End-to-End, 1st edn. Machine Learning Mastery, Melbourne (2016)

Data Mining Application for the Generation of User Profiles in Serious Games Aimed at Attention and Memory Training

Juan-Sebastian Toledo⬤, María-Inés Acosta-Urigüen(✉)⬤, and Marcos Orellana⬤

Laboratorio de Investigación y Desarrollo en Informática - LIDI, Universidad del Azuay,
Cuenca, Ecuador
{jstoledo,macosta,marore}@uazuay.edu.ec

Abstract. Serious games designed for cognitive stimulation have proven to be effective for training skills such as attention, memory, and reaction time. As with any other highly interactive system, serious games generate large amounts of data, which directly reflect the player's decisions. Therefore, it is possible to evaluate users' performance and customize training according to their progress to provide a cognitive challenge appropriate to their abilities. One of the possible approaches to enabling personalized training and increasing user engagement is the identification of player profiles. This study aims to reveal the influence of player characteristics (demographic, socioeconomic, and behavioral) on performance and identify the most significant attributes to generate profiles. For this purpose, a data mining model based on the CRISP-DM methodology was developed. The results showed that the variables age, daily physical activity time, and computer use time directly influence the cognitive performance of the game users'. Finally, four-player profiles were discovered: 1) High Cognitive Performance, 2) Average Cognitive Performance, 3) Low Cognitive Performance I, and 4) Low Cognitive Performance II.

Keywords: Serious game · Game analytics · Data mining · Player profiles

1 Introduction

It is now known that older people can suffer cognitive impairment due to aging; however, in some cases, the impact is more significant than expected, with deficits in attention, memory, and reasoning ability [1]. Fortunately, extensive research demonstrates the brain's susceptibility to neuronal and cognitive plasticity, making it possible to reduce the effects of structural alterations through daily cognitive training [2].

In this context, the scientific community has seen the need to find modern and scalable tools that can be used over extended periods to detect sudden changes in cognitive status, stimulate psychological well-being, and successfully adjust to ordinary demands in older adults [3]. Serious games play a fundamental role in these tasks, complementing existing therapy methods and providing the specialist with an effective support tool for cognitive training [4–6], such as attention and memory [7].

© The Author(s), under exclusive license to Springer Nature Switzerland AG 2023
F. R. Narváez et al. (Eds.): SmartTech-IC 2022, CCIS 1705, pp. 18–32, 2023.
https://doi.org/10.1007/978-3-031-32213-6_2

As with any other highly interactive system, serious games generate large amounts of data, which directly reflect players' actions and decisions. Data mining techniques widely used today in various fields, such as education, medicine, manufacturing, and finance [8], can be applied to the vast amount of data derived from users' interaction with serious games [9]; therefore, it is possible to discover patterns and extract knowledge. Nevertheless, despite these benefits, the application of serious games is still limited [10]. Among the existing barriers, we highlight the fact that specialists in charge of conducting the training sessions do not have information about what is happening in the game; instead, games act as a black box. Therefore, it becomes difficult to evaluate users' performance and adjust the parameters according to their progress in order to provide a cognitive, emotional, or physical challenge appropriate to their abilities. One of the possible strategies to enable personalized training and increase user engagement is the identification of player profiles.

This paper aims to propose a data mining methodology to 1) explore and discover the relationship between player characteristics (demographic, socioeconomic, and behavioral) with those variables that denote the performance during each session (score and duration time). 2) Explore the existence of groups of players and analyze their representative characteristics to generate player profiles associated with cognitive performance. Furthermore, this study seeks to provide a starting point for the customization of serious games based on the specific needs of different patient profiles in the context of mental health.

The paper is organized as follows: Sect. 2 describes the related works for serious games and data mining techniques. Section 3 details the methodology implemented for generating player profiles. Section 4 presents the main results and their interpretation. Section 5 offers a discussion of the achievements of this work. Finally, the conclusions are given in Sect. 6.

2 Related Work

Serious games can be defined as digital applications or simulation tools whose main objective is not to entertain but to improve players' abilities and performance through training and education [7, 11]. According to Wiemeyer & Kliem [12], serious games can be classified by their "characterizing goals" (e.g., perception, emotional control, attention, reaction time) into one or several domains of competence, e.g., emotion and volition, sensory-motor control, personal characteristics, social attitudes, media use, and cognition and perception.

In this context, Chi et al. [7] developed Smart Thinker, a set of four serious games aimed at training cognitive skills (attention and memory) in older adults. The games included are "High-Low," which consists of a series of mathematical puzzles designed to improve memorization and reasoning skills; the "Colors Game," which aims to improve attention span; "Find Me," designed to strengthen short-term memory; and the "Rock, Paper, Scissors" game focused on enhancing attention and reaction time skills. In the study, the researchers evaluated 59 participants for six weeks, 20 of whom did not play Smart Thinker. All participants were assessed by Mini-Mental State Examination (MMSE) method; the study revealed a significant improvement in cognitive skills in the group that played Smart Thinker compared to the control group.

In some studies, researchers have chosen to use specialized computational methods and data mining techniques in order to discover valuable patterns within a data set. Sun et al. [13] conducted a study where they proposed a methodology that starts from designing a serious game to the mining and analysis of data in order to determine detailed player decision patterns. Through this approach, they developed VistaLights, a serious simulation game based on the supply chain of a port entity, where the player oversees making decisions that maximize the economic score. In order to determine patterns in decision-making under various circumstances and scenarios, the researchers performed a coarse-grained and fine-grained analysis, followed by a cluster analysis whose result was used to predict the probability of success in the designated task, allowing to compare the actions of the players with the expected results.

Depending on the game design and the purpose of the research, data can be collected through various mechanisms, such as web-based logging, tracking engines, sensors such as eye trackers, location tracking and motion detectors, or even electroencephalogram (EEG) technology [14]. As in the case of the study conducted by [15], here the researchers explain the integration of a serious game controlled by EEG signals that allows attention training while classifying the received data with a support vector machine (SVM) model in order to detect people who have Attention Deficit Hyperactivity Disorder (ADHD), the results reveal an accuracy of 98% with a standard uncertainty of 0.16% in the detection of ADHD patients.

The literature offers several methods to measure player performance and generate behavioral profiles. According to [11], data mining techniques (supervised and unsupervised) and behavior categorization can be used to analyze user-generated actions in search of patterns to identify and develop player (behavioral) profiles. Among the techniques used are: clustering, decision trees, linear discriminant analysis, and correlation techniques [9, 11]. Concerning player segmentation, Benmakrelouf et al. [16] present a study in which they propose using data mining techniques to determine player profiles. For this purpose, they used a dataset from the serious game "Game for Science" and the application of clustering, particularly the K-means algorithm, to identify common characteristics among groups of players. The study reveals three profiles according to their level of participation: beginner, intermediate and advanced.

Although there are studies that use data mining techniques in the cognitive and perceptual areas, no research analyzes data from serious games for the cognitive training of attention and memory for the generation of player profiles. Therefore, the present work is based on the application of supervised and unsupervised techniques that allow determining a relationship between demographic, socioeconomic, and behavioral variables, with those variables that denote the player's performance during each session, such as score and gaming duration. As a result, it is intended to determine player profiles associated with performance and problem-solving.

3   Methodology

The approach we propose analyzes the data collected from a serious game oriented to attention and memory training, aiming to identify a relationship between player characteristics and performance. The existence of groups with similar characteristics will allow the generation of player profiles. For this purpose, a methodology based on CRISP-DM [17] was developed. The Software & Systems Process Engineering Metamodel (SPEM2.0) specification [18] was used to represent each process phase (Fig. 1).

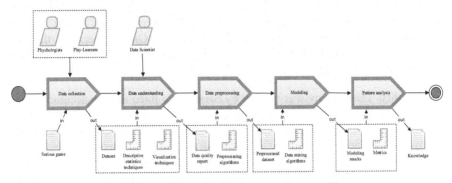

Fig. 1. Methodology used to generate player profiles.

3.1 Data Collection

Serious Game Description. Picture Pairing is an online game developed by psychologists and students from the University of Azuay, intending to reinforce skills associated with the cognitive area (attention and memory). The game consists of finding the pair of each image; for this, the images are shown for a specific time and then hidden so that the player remembers the initial position. Four levels must be overcome to complete the game, each with increasing difficulty (two more pairs for each level). The player's performance is determined by the time taken to complete each level and the final score (penalized for each mistake) with a maximum of 2000 points.

Dataset. The data collected correspond to sessions recorded from May 2022 to June 2022 and are divided into two categories. 1) Those acquired through a single user registration, in which demographic, socioeconomic, and behavioral data are requested. 2) Data generated during the execution of the game directly denote the user's interaction with the system (game time, score). A total of 228 people from two provinces (Azuay and Loja) of Ecuador participated in the study, 119 men and 109 women.

3.2 Data Understanding

This phase aims to acquire a better understanding of the initial state of the data and to provide essential knowledge for treating the data in the preprocessing stage. For this purpose, two sub-processes were performed 1) data exploration and 2) data quality verification.

Data Exploration. This process involved the application of descriptive statistics (measures of central tendency and dispersion of the data) and exploratory visualization techniques (scatter plots, quantile plots, histograms). Thus, it was possible to expose the structure and distribution of the data, the presence of outliers, and identify the interrelationships within the data set. We can highlight that there is an equal distribution concerning the gender of the players, 52.19% and 47.81%, male and female, respectively. However, 75% of the players are under 29 years old. On the other hand, the final score presents a symmetrical distribution, with a mean of 1725 points. Finally, outliers have been detected, which will require special treatment.

Data Quality. Data quality was verified by considering three factors: accuracy, completeness, and consistency. First, incorrect data regarding the date of birth was determined, where some players entered the current date at the time of registration. Although the dataset does not have null records, inconsistencies were detected related to the requested unit of measure and the one entered by the user in the weight and height text fields. There are also inconsistencies concerning the school location and the current level of education; in some cases, the user indicates that they did not complete secondary education but did have higher education studies.

3.3 Data Preprocessing

Applying preprocessing techniques before data mining modeling can increase the efficiency of the process and improve the quality of the patterns found. However, commonly, the collected data are not in an optimal state. Therefore, they must be treated considering the observations detected in the previous phase [19].

Data Sampling. The records were selected using non-probabilistic methods based on two criteria: 1) players aged 20 years and older and 2) the second attempt recorded for each player (the first attempt does not demonstrate the player's actual performance due to the time needed to become familiar with the dynamics of the game). A total of 95 records were obtained.

Data Cleaning. Data cleaning can be applied to correct inconsistencies in the data, remove noise and deal with outliers. In this context, data optimization was performed by correcting 1) incorrect time and measurement units corresponding to the attributes: "Weight," "Height," "Computer use," and "Physical activity." 2) Expressions containing characters (e.g., "approx," "h," "cm") in numeric fields.

Data Derivation. Techniques were applied to generate new attributes from existing ones. For example, the age of the players was derived from the date of birth. Additionally, the body mass index (weight in kilograms divided by the square of the height in meters) was calculated; studies have shown that BMI can influence cognitive abilities [20].

Remove Outliers. Outliers or anomalies are numerically distant observations from the rest of the data. Therefore, an outlier is always defined in the context of the other objects in the dataset [21]. In this step, it is necessary to identify the presence of outliers as they require special treatment. For this purpose, we used the Local Outlier Factor (LOF) technique [22]. According to Wang et al. [23], an outlier will be assigned a LOF score far away from 1. On the contrary, objects in a uniformly distributed area will obtain a LOF score close to 1. However, there is no specific threshold value above which an object is defined as an outlier; rather, it depends on the data set and the field of application. Therefore, all records with a LOF score > 1.5 were discarded for our study. The resulting data set consists of 81 records.

Data Transformation and Discretization. In this step, the data are transformed or consolidated into forms appropriate for mining so that the resulting process may be more efficient, and the patterns found may be easier to understand [19].

Table 1. BMI adult categories.

BMI	Weight Status
Bellow 18.5	Underweight
18.5 – 24.9	Healthy Weight
25.0 – 29.9	Overweight
30.0 and above	Obesity

It is known that normalization in preprocessing can improve results when clustering is applied [24]. 1) Transformation: the data were normalized using the Z-score normalization, so each resulting feature has zero mean and unit variance [25]. 2) Discretization: the BMI values were categorized using World Health Organization cut-off points, as shown in Table 1.

Drop Non-Relevant Data. As a first step, a statistical-based method called "Low variance" was used. Features whose variance score is below a predefined threshold (0.05) were eliminated. The purpose of this filter is to remove features with minimal variation or that consist only of noise [26, 27]. It was also verified that the variables comply with the assumption of independence of the observations (useful for regression models); for this purpose, the presence of multicollinearity among the independent variables (player characteristics) was analyzed using the Variance Inflation Factor (VIF), which determines the degree to which the variance increases. According to [28], there are three intervals to interpret the VIF value $\{1, 1 < VIF \leq 5, VIF > 5\}$, and they are classified as {Not correlated, Moderately correlated, Highly correlated} respectively. Highly correlated variables (VIF > 5) were eliminated.

3.4 Modeling

Modeling Techniques. Choosing the correct data mining technique for modeling is not a simple task. However, Alonso et al. [9] found that among the most used supervised

Table 2. Selected player's features.

Characteristics	Age, Gender, COVID-19, Educational stages, Financial income, Computer use, Physical activity, BMI
Performance	Game time, Final score

methods in serious game analytics are linear/logistic regression and decision trees, and for the unsupervised ones, correlation and clustering techniques. Depending on the purpose of the research, it is necessary to use different techniques to achieve the desired results. For example, some researchers [29, 30] have used statistical model quality indicators to determine the most relevant attributes and select the appropriate variables. On the other hand, to determine players' performance and generate user profiles [31, 32] recommend using clustering algorithms.

Multiple linear regression (MLR), a statistical approach used to describe the simultaneous associations of several variables with a continuous outcome [33], was applied to reveal the influence of player characteristics on cognitive performance. In addition, mutual information regression (MI) was used to complement the analysis, a method that allows the detection of any relationship or dependence between random variables [34]. To extract groups of players and identify the most representative characteristics of each cluster, we used the k-means clustering algorithm, an exclusive partitioning method whose algorithmic approach is based on prototypes, where the dataset is divided into k-clusters, and each group is represented by an object called centroid [21].

Test Design Generation. A test plan was generated to determine the model's quality and validity.

Multiple Linear Regression. The quality indicators used for the regression analysis:

- **P-value:** The probability of finding a test statistic as extreme as the value measured on the sample if the null hypothesis (H_0: $\beta_1 = \beta_2 = ... = \beta_{p-1} = 0$) is true. To reject the null hypothesis and consider the test results significant, the *p-value* must be less than the threshold $\alpha = 0.05$ (*p-value* $< \alpha$).
- **F-statistic:** This indicator was used to measure the overall significance of the regression model. The null hypothesis is rejected if its *p-value* $< \alpha$.
- **Coefficient of determination (R^2):** Explains how much the independent variables explain variability in the dependent variable. R^2 takes values from 0 through 1, but it can be negative in the case of particularly bad models. On the other hand, model fit is better when the R^2 is close to 1 [33].

Mutual Information. MI between two random variables is a non-negative value, which measures the dependency between variables. MI is zero if two random variables are strictly independent: the higher the value, the more significant the dependency. Because this method uses a nearest-neighbor entropy estimator, it is necessary to set the k parameter. According to [34], the estimator consistently gives good results when k is set to a low integer. For our model, k = 3 was used, as suggested by [35]. The three variables with the highest MI were selected.

K-means. According to [36], the most critical factors impacting the performance and outcome of k-means clustering are 1) the initial values of the centroids and 2) the number of k clusters. The optimized k-means + + algorithm has been chosen for the first factor, which increases the probability of achieving a global solution by initializing distant centroids [37]. For the second factor, the silhouette score is used as a quality indicator, calculated as the average silhouette coefficient of all the objects belonging to a cluster. The silhouette coefficient can be between $[-1, 1]$. A score close to 1 means that the object is close to its cluster (intra-cluster distance) and distant from other clusters (inter-cluster distance), while a coefficient close to -1 means that the object has been assigned to the wrong cluster [38]. From 3 to 10 clusters were evaluated, and the best silhouette score was 0.33 for k = 4.

Building the Model. The approach we propose consists of three stages: 1) MLR and MI to reveal the influence of the player's characteristics on cognitive performance and select the most significant. For this purpose, we selected player characteristics as predictor variables and those representatives of game performance (score and game time) as response variables. 2) Group players with similar characteristics by generating clusters with the most significant attributes selected in the previous stage. 3) Analyze the centroids of each cluster and generate user profiles.

Model Assessment. The model was validated to ensure that it met the expectations set, and the results were corroborated with the evaluation metrics established for each algorithm.

3.5 Pattern Analysis

The analysis was conducted in two stages: 1) statistical analysis of the multiple linear regression model, using the quality indicators (*p-value*, *F-test* and R^2) presented in detail in the previous Sect. 2) Analysis of the mutual information model, using a bar chart that allowed us to visualize and determine the degree of similarity between the independent and dependent variables. For cluster analysis, the procedure suggested by Bauckhage et al. [32] was followed, and visualization techniques such as Scatterplots and Radar charts were also used to facilitate the detection of patterns in the centroid behavior [36].

4 Results

4.1 Performance Analysis

Multiple Linear Regression. The results were obtained using the variables in Table 2 by multiple linear regression models.

For clarity and readability, we present in Table 3 the estimated coefficients of X and their respective *p-value*, *F-stat* and their *p-value,* and R^2. In addition, each model was named MLR_GTime and MLR_Score, respectively. From the quality indicators shown in Table 3, we can highlight the following:

Table 3. Multiple linear regression models of Game Time and Score.

Dep. Variables: Game Time, Score	MLR_GTime			MLR_Score		
	R^2:	F-statistic:	p − value:	R^2:	F-statistic:	p − value:
	0.364	5.144	4.34E-05	0.217	2.491	0.019
Ind. Variables	Coeff	t	p − value	Coeff	t	p − value
Age	**0.912**	**2.978**	**0.004**	**-4.052**	**11.235**	**0.036**
Computer use	-0.305	-0.339	0.736	-5.048	-2.135	0.368
COVID-19	-0.179	-0.038	0.97	5.337	-0.905	0.856
Gender	-5.862	-1.214	0.229	38.366	0.182	0.204
Educational stages	-2.216	-0.320	0.750	-21.667	1.281	0.615
Physical activity	**-10.391**	**-3.210**	**0.002**	**45.975**	**-0.505**	**0.025**
BMI	-1.395	-1.481	0.143	4.310	2.290	0.463
Financial income	-2.975	-0.904	0.369	20.894	0.738	0.310

- For MLR_GTime, the coefficient of determination is $R^2 = 0.364$, and for MLR_Score, $R^2 = 0.217$, which indicates 36.4% and 21.7% of the variation in the dependent variables of each model can be explained by the independent variables, respectively.
- The *p-value* of both models is significant, less than the established significance level $\alpha = 0.05$ ($p < \alpha$). Therefore, we can reject the null hypothesis $H_0: \beta_1 = \beta_2 = ... = \beta_{p-1} = 0$ (no independent variable influences the dependent variable).

The estimated coefficients in each model represent the influence of the independent variables on the variation of the dependent variables. In this context, it can be highlighted that in both models, age and average physical activity time present a significant relationship ($p < 0.05$) with total playing time and final score. Specifically, it was found that 1) In MLR_GTime, for a one-year increase in age, the expected total playing time increases by 0.911 s. However, for one hour of daily physical activity increase, the total game time decreases by 10.391 s. 2) In MLR_Score, the analysis of the coefficients tells us that due to the increase of one year in age, the final score decreases by 4.052, and due to the increase of one hour of physical activity, the expected final score increases by 45.975 points.

Mutual Information. As previously mentioned, the MI method allowed us to measure the uncertainty reduction (entropy) between the independent and dependent variables, that is, to know the statistical dependence between both variables. With MI, it was possible to detect nonlinear dependencies and thus complement the MLR analysis.

Figure 2 shows the values obtained for each independent variable. In both cases, the variables Physical activity, Computer use, and age share the first three positions in terms of the highest MI value, and two (physical activity and age) are common in terms of significance with the results of the MLR model analysis. Based on the analysis

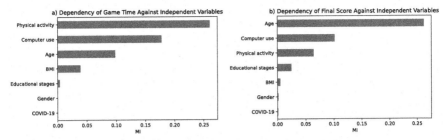

Fig. 2. Analysis of dependence between variables.

of results, age, physical activity, and computer use are the attributes that denoted the most significant influence on the cognitive performance of attention and memory in the Picture Pairing game.

4.2 Clustering Analysis

Clusters were generated using the dependent variables, Game Time and Total Score, and three influential independent variables (Age, Physical activity, and Computer use) based on the results of MLR and MI models.

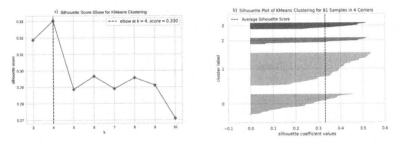

Fig. 3. Selecting the number of clusters k using the silhouette score.

Figure 3, part a) shows the optimal number of clusters $k = 4$ with a silhouette score of 0.33. While part b) shows the associated silhouette diagram where a knife-shaped figure represents each cluster. The shape's height indicates the number of instances the cluster contains and its width, the sorted silhouette coefficients of the instances in the cluster. The vertical dashed line indicates the mean Silhouette coefficient.

In k-means, each cluster is represented by a central object called a centroid or prototype. The centroids are the most significant representation of all the objects belonging to the cluster [21].

Figure 4 shows the result of the clustering process with k-means. The analysis seeks to discover patterns associated with player performance and its relationship with demographic and behavioral characteristics. The radial graph shows the specific behavior of the players in each cluster, the most relevant aspects of which are highlighted below.

High performance in the game characterizes players belonging to cluster 1, i.e., a higher score and a lower total time to finish the game, another characteristic that stands

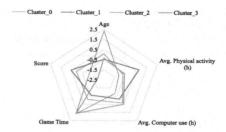

Fig. 4. Analysis of centroids generated by k-means.

out in their centroid is the high commitment of the players to daily physical activity (0.787 deviations above the mean), higher than the other centroids. In contrast, cluster_0 represents players with a performance close to the mean (0), both for the overall score (0.064) and the total time (−0.080). The centroids corresponding to clusters 2 and 3 are characterized by a lower performance than the other centroids, with an overall score of − 1.955 and − 1.075, respectively; however, both centroids have evident characteristics that differentiate them. On the one hand, cluster_3 groups older players (2.352) as well as those with a lower rate of time spent using the computer (−0.808) and physical activity (−1.103). On the other hand, cluster_2 groups players with the highest computer time index (0.501); even though the centroid of this cluster shows that players took less time to solve the game than cluster_3, the score obtained is considerably lower, which could indicate a lack of engagement with the game (see Table 4).

Table 4. Centroids of clustering.

Features	Cluster_0 Avg. Cognitive performance (ACP)	Cluster_1 High Cognitive Performance (HCP)	Cluster_2 Low Cognitive Performance (LCP_1)	Cluster_3 Low Cognitive Performance (LCP_2)
Age	0.088	− 0.460	− 0.326	2.352
Avg. Physical activity (h)	− 0.722	0.787	− 0.579	− 1.103
Avg. Computer use (h)	0.322	− 0.140	0.501	− 0.808
Game Time	− 0.080	− 0.609	1.619	1.673
Score	0.064	0.566	− 1.955	− 1.075

In conjunction with k-means, the dimensionality reduction technique PCA is a powerful method for visualizing high-dimensional data, where coherent patterns associated with cluster density and distance can be detected more clearly.

From Fig. 5, we can see that ACP and HCP clusters are similar in density, contrary to LCP_1 and LCP_2, which have greater intra-cluster dispersion and inter-cluster distance due to the dissimilarity in terms of their demographic and behavioral characteristics. It

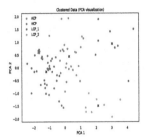

Fig. 5. Clustered data. The black marks represent the centroids for each group.

is also observed that HCP has a greater inter-cluster distance with LCP_1 and LCP_2, separated by ACP.

5 Discussion

The MLR and MI models showed that age, daily physical activity, and computer use significantly influence players' game time and score. While in the cluster analysis, it was possible to identify four groups of players, each categorized according to the level of performance associated with the cognitive ability of attention and memory in the picture pairing game. The most relevant aspects according to each profile are detailed below.

- **Low Cognitive Performance I:** Players with the lowest performance index and whose average use time of electronic devices is higher than the others. They show little commitment to the game and seek to finish the training session in the shortest time possible, making several mistakes.
- **Low Cognitive Performance II:** This profile corresponds to older players who have little interaction with electronic devices and do little or no physical activity. They also stand out for requiring a longer time to complete the game.
- **Average Cognitive Performance:** Players who do not have a daily physical activity habit. Their performance is within the expected values.
- **High Cognitive Performance:** Players with the highest physical activity index. Capable of solving the game in a shorter time and making few mistakes, they are also the youngest players in the study.

6 Conclusions

The present study analyzed data collected from a serious game to reveal the influence of player characteristics (demographic, socioeconomic, and behavioral) on performance and identify the most significant attributes to generate behavior and cognitive performance profiles. It was found that the most influential characteristics for the players' performance are age, average daily physical activity time, and average computer use time. Specifically, players with regular physical activity habits demonstrate higher performance than other players; on the contrary, players with lower cognitive performance are characterized by belonging to the older age group or having a low physical activity habit. Furthermore, the clustering process revealed the presence of four groupings that were categorized according to the level of performance associated with cognitive ability.

The main contribution of this work focuses on providing a better understanding of the data mining process applied to serious games aimed at attention and memory for identifying relevant variables and analyzing players' profiles. Furthermore, this study provides a starting point for customizing serious games according to each profile's needs in the context of mental health.

A data visualization model suitable for serious games will be developed in future work to allow experts to analyze the results and decision-making.

References

1. Rodriguez-Fortiz, M.J., et al.: Serious games for the cognitive stimulation of elderly people. In: 2016 IEEE Int. Conf. Serious Games Appl. Heal. SeGAH 2016. (2016). https://doi.org/10.1109/SeGAH.2016.7586261
2. Kalbe, E., et al.: Computerized cognitive training in healthy older adults: baseline cognitive level and subjective cognitive concerns predict training outcome. Health (Irvine. Calif) **10**, 20–55 (2018). https://doi.org/10.4236/health.2018.101003
3. Rienzo, A., Cubillos, C., Soto, G.: Gamification elements in digital applications for the evaluation and cognitive training of older adults. In: 2021 IEEE Int. Conf. Autom. Congr. Chil. Assoc. Autom. Control. ICA-ACCA 2021 (2021). https://doi.org/10.1109/ICAACCA51523.2021.9465207
4. Abd-Alrazaq, A., et al.: The Effectiveness and Safety of Serious Games for Improving Cognitive Abilities Among Elderly People With Cognitive Impairment: Systematic Review and Meta-Analysis (2022)
5. Mezrar, S., Bendella, F.: A Systematic Review of Serious Games Relating to Cognitive Impairment and Dementia. J. Digit. Inf. Manag. **20**, 1 (2022). https://doi.org/10.6025/jdim/2022/20/1/01-09
6. Manera, V., et al.: Recommendations for the use of serious games in neurodegenerative disorders: 2016 Delphi Panel. Front. Physiol. **8**, 1 (2017). https://doi.org/10.3389/fpsyg.2017.01243
7. Chi, H., Agama, E., Prodanoff, Z.G.: Developing serious games to promote cognitive abilities for the elderly. In: 2017 IEEE 5th Int. Conf. Serious Games Appl. Heal. SeGAH 2017 (2017). https://doi.org/10.1109/SeGAH.2017.7939279
8. Kumar, D., Bhardwaj, D.: Rise of Data Mining: Current and Future Application Areas Dharminder. **8**, 256–260 (2011)
9. Alonso-Fernández, C., Calvo-Morata, A., Freire, M., Martínez-Ortiz, I., Fernández-Manjón, B.: Applications of data science to game learning analytics data: A systematic literature review. Comput. Educ. **141**, 103612 (2019). https://doi.org/10.1016/j.compedu.2019.103612
10. Alonso-Fernandez, C., Calvo-Morata, A., Freire, M., Martinez-Ortiz, I., Manjon, B.F.: Data science meets standardized game learning analytics. IEEE Glob. Eng. Educ. Conf. EDUCON. 2021-April, 1546–1552 (2021). https://doi.org/10.1109/EDUCON46332.2021.9454134
11. Loh, C.S., Sheng, Y., Dirk, I.: Serious Games Analytics (2015)
12. Wiemeyer, J., Kliem, A.: Serious games in prevention and rehabilitation—a new panacea for elderly people? European Review of Aging and Physical Activity **9**(1), 41–50 (2011). https://doi.org/10.1007/s11556-011-0093-x
13. Sun, Y., Liang, C., Sutherland, S., Harteveld, C., Kaeli, D.: Modeling player decisions in a supply chain game. IEEE Conf. Comput. Intell. Games, CIG. 0 (2016). https://doi.org/10.1109/CIG.2016.7860444

14. Hauge, J.B., et al.: Implications of learning analytics for serious game design. In: Proc. - IEEE 14th Int. Conf. Adv. Learn. Technol. ICALT 2014, pp. 230–232 (2014). https://doi.org/10. 1109/ICALT.2014.73

15. Alchalabi, A.E., Shirmohammadi, S., Eddin, A.N., Elsharnouby, M.: FOCUS: Detecting ADHD patients by an EEG-based serious game. IEEE Trans. Instrum. Meas. **67**, 1512–1520 (2018). https://doi.org/10.1109/TIM.2018.2838158

16. Benmakrelouf, S., Mezghani, N., Kara, N.: Towards the identification of players' profiles using game's data analysis based on regression model and clustering. In: Proc. 2015 IEEE/ACM Int. Conf. Adv. Soc. Networks Anal. Mining, ASONAM 2015, pp. 1403–1410 (2015). https:// doi.org/10.1145/2808797.2809429

17. Wirth, R., Hipp, J.: CRISP-DM: towards a standard process model for data mining. In: Proceedings of the Fourth International Conference on the Practical Application of Knowledge Discovery and Data Mining, pp. 29–39 (2000)

18. Object Management Group: Software & Systems Process Engineering Metamodel SPEM2.0, https://www.omg.org/spec/SPEM/2.0

19. Han, J.: Data Mining Concepts and Techniques. Elsevier Inc (2012)

20. Lentoor, A.G.: Obesity and neurocognitive performance of memory, attention, and executive function. NeuroSci. **3**, 376–386 (2022). https://doi.org/10.3390/neurosci3030027

21. Kotu, V., Deshpande, B.: Data Science: Concepts and Practice (2019)

22. Breunig, M.M., Kriegel, H.-P., Ng, R.T., Sander, J.: LOF: identifying density-based local outliers. ACM SIGMOD Rec. **29**, 93–104 (2000). https://doi.org/10.1145/335191.335388

23. Wang, C., Liu, Z., Gao, H., Fu, Y.: Applying anomaly pattern score for outlier detection. IEEE Access. **7**, 16008–16020 (2019). https://doi.org/10.1109/ACCESS.2019.2895094

24. Suarez-Alvarez, M.M., Pham, D.T., Prostov, M.Y., Prostov, Y.I.: Statistical approach to normalization of feature vectors and clustering of mixed datasets. Proc. R. Soc. A Math. Phys. Eng. Sci. **468**, 2630–2651 (2012). https://doi.org/10.1098/rspa.2011.0704

25. Fukunaga, K.: Introduction to Statistical Pattern Recognition. Elsevier Science (2013)

26. Siti Ambarwati, Y., Uyun, S.: Feature selection on magelang duck egg candling image using variance threshold method. In: 2020 3rd Int. Semin. Res. Inf. Technol. Intell. Syst. ISRITI 2020, pp. 694–699 (2020). https://doi.org/10.1109/ISRITI51436.2020.9315486

27. Li, J., et al.: Feature Selection. ACM Comput. Surv. **50**, 1–45 (2018). https://doi.org/10.1145/ 3136625

28. Daoud, J.I.: Multicollinearity and regression analysis. J. Phys. Conf. Ser. 949 (2018). https:// doi.org/10.1088/1742-6596/949/1/012009

29. Cornforth, D.J., Adam, M.T.P.: Cluster Evaluation, Description, and Interpretation for Serious Games. In: Loh, C.S., Sheng, Y., Ifenthaler, D. (eds.) Serious Games Analytics. AGL, pp. 135– 155. Springer, Cham (2015). https://doi.org/10.1007/978-3-319-05834-4_6

30. Wallner, G.: Sequential analysis of player behavior. CHI Play 2015 - Proc. 2015 Annu. Symp. Comput. Interact. Play. pp. 349–358 (2015). https://doi.org/10.1145/2793107.2793112

31. Loh, C.S., Sheng, Y.: Measuring Expert Performance for Serious Games Analytics: From Data to Insights. In: Loh, C.S., Sheng, Y., Ifenthaler, D. (eds.) Serious Games Analytics. AGL, pp. 101–134. Springer, Cham (2015). https://doi.org/10.1007/978-3-319-05834-4_5

32. Bauckhage, C., Drachen, A., Sifa, R.: Clustering game behavior data. IEEE Trans. Comput. Intell. AI Games. **7**, 266–278 (2015). https://doi.org/10.1109/TCIAIG.2014.2376982

33. Hayes, A.F.: Multiple Linear Regression. Stat. Methods Commun. Sci. **404**, 310–365 (2020). https://doi.org/10.4324/9781410613707-13

34. Ross, B.C.: Mutual information between discrete and continuous data sets. PLoS One **9** (2014). https://doi.org/10.1371/journal.pone.0087357

35. Kraskov, A., Stögbauer, H., Grassberger, P.: Estimating mutual information. Phys. Rev. E - Stat. Physics, Plasmas, Fluids, Relat. Interdisc. Top. **69**, 16 (2004). https://doi.org/10.1103/ PhysRevE.69.066138

36. Aggarwal, C.C., Reddy, C.K.: Data Clustering. Chapman and Hall/CRC (2014)
37. Arthur, D., Vassilvitskii, S.: K-means++: The advantages of careful seeding. Proc. Annu. ACM-SIAM Symp. Discret. Algorithms. 07–09-Janu, 1027–1035 (2007)
38. Géron, A.: Hands-on Machine Learning with Scikit-Learn , Keras & TensorFlow. O'Reilly Media, Inc. (2019)

Automatic Class Extraction from Spanish Text of User Stories Using Natural Language Processing

Miguel Ángel Tovar Onofre[✉] and Jorge E. Camargo[✉]

UnSecure Lab Research Group, Universidad Nacional de Colombia, Bogotá, Colombia
{matovaro,jecamargom}@unal.edu.co

Abstract. During the software development process, one of the most important stages is the requirements analysis, since in this stage the requirements supplied by the client or end user are analyzed and the system structure is defined, which is essential for the design stage. However, it is a process in which multiple inconsistencies can occur due to misunderstanding of the requirements or excessive time in understanding them. This paper presents an approach in the use of Natural Language Processing for the automatic extraction of classes of a software from the user stories in Spanish language for its design and the comparison of the results obtained against the classes obtained manually. Finally, it is proposed for a future work, the extraction of more characteristics of the classes with the objective of improving their classification, as well as the construction of a dataset focused on the Spanish language to reduce the possible noise in the results.

Keywords: Class diagram · Software engineering · UML · NLP · User stories

1 Introduction

During the last years, software engineering has had a constant growth, driven by new technologies and the adaptation of systems to them. In response to this, software design and development techniques have been strengthened to keep pace with this progress and to be able to count on more complete tools every day, which cover the needs and/or desires of the users.

For this reason, requirements analysis and software design are essential stages in software development since they are used to analyze the user's desires or needs and to build the system structure with which it will be developed. During this process, the requirements provided by the customer are taken and analyzed in detail to extract the components that structure the system and their viability, according to the need, consistency and integrity of these against the other components [1]. The components obtained are represented through unified modeling language (UML) diagrams, which allow having a greater perspective of

© The Author(s), under exclusive license to Springer Nature Switzerland AG 2023
F. R. Narváez et al. (Eds.): SmartTech-IC 2022, CCIS 1705, pp. 33–47, 2023.
https://doi.org/10.1007/978-3-031-32213-6_3

the system and the necessary resources to be able to implement it [2]. However, performing this process manually entails some risks that can seriously affect the future stages of the software development project.

Among these risks, there is the excess of time used, since each requirement is carefully analyzed and often must be reanalyzed to re-evaluate its feasibility against other requirements, leading to the use of more time than planned and creating delays that may affect the development stages and even represent an increase in project costs [3]. Likewise, the ambiguity of terms can be a frequent problem in the analysis process, as there are often cases in which a word or phrase can have different interpretations and be confusing [4,5], causing inconsistencies to be created in the requirements and therefore, costly errors in the structure of the software that will be reflected in the development stage. This can be mitigated by continuous communication with the user [6], but even so, it would be prone to exceed the established times.

Based on these aspects, multiple works have been carried out with the aim of mitigating these risks, focusing mainly on the English language as is the case of [12], where patterns established by experts are used for the identification of classes and relationships from descriptions in natural language or [13], where deep learning is used to train recurrent networks to extract the necessary components for the construction of a class diagram, through the textual specification of the software. It is worth mentioning the system developed in [20], where patterns are established for the extraction of classes, attributes, and the relationships between them from user stories in English. Despite this, there have not been many (or any) efforts to apply these systems to the Spanish language, maintaining the risks mentioned when working with descriptions and user stories generated in this language and possibly, generating systems structured in an erroneous way because of this.

This paper presents the development methodology of a system oriented to the automatic extraction of classes to support the construction of UML diagrams according to user stories in Spanish language. A hyper-set of 33 sets of user stories was used, which describe the requirements of several software systems and were manually analyzed to obtain the classes, methods and attributes that are later used to evaluate the results obtained by the system. This system will receive the set of user stories that describe the software and through pattern rules determined and adapted for the Spanish language in conjunction with NLP tools such as Spacy, NLTK and Stanza, extracts the possible classes that can structure the software to be built. The system performs an analysis of the different user stories received, their structure, the relationships between each word and their frequency within the requirements document, to determine the possible classes that may be involved and cover the requirements supplied. For the evaluation of results, the precision and recall metrics are used, starting from the objects obtained through the manual analysis. Among the results obtained, it can be seen that although the system detects more classes than a human expert (leading to a decrease in accuracy), the Recall remains at high values, ensuring that among the classes detected by the system, there are many (if not all) of the classes detected by the human expert.

This paper is organized as follows: Sect. 2 contains *Materials and Methods*, which describes the dataset used, the data collection process and data preprocessing. Section 3 contains *Experiments and Results*, which explains the process of applying patterns and the treatment of the results to visualize them at the end of the section. Finally, Sect. 4 contains *Conclusions and Future work*.

1.1   Related Work

During the last years, different systems have been developed with the aim of automating the process of extracting components for the generation of UML diagrams, mainly focused on the use of NLP (Natural Language Processing), a field of artificial intelligence oriented to the understanding of human language, involving computation, linguistics and logic theory.

In [7–9], the use of grammar rules and TreeParser was implemented to extract the classes, attributes and methods for the generation of class diagrams from the components extracted through specific rules applied on the requirements in free format and English language.

In [20], this same methodology is applied to user stories, adapting pattern rules to their structure in English. In this work, the classes, attributes and relationships between classes are extracted based on the existing relationships between nouns, as well as the methods that are determined taking into account the relationship of the verbs with the classes found.

In [10] a similar approach was applied by using heuristic rules in conjunction with *WordNet* (online database of English words developed by a team of psychologists and linguists at Princeton University [11]), in order to obtain the classes, attributes, methods and relations for the construction of class diagrams from texts with simple sentences.

In [12], the pattern rules used were established by experts based on their experience to extract and classify the different objects that will compose the class diagram, however, it presents problems of redundancy or confusion of terms.

In [13], a new approach is taken by integrating deep learning in the detection of classes and their attributes. In this work, a recurrent neural network model was trained in order to detect the classes, attributes, methods and relations present in a free-format text in the English language. However, it may present drawbacks with words that have multiple representations.

As can be seen, there have been multiple works focused on detection in the English language. However, little or nothing has been done for the detection of these objects in the Spanish language, limiting the Spanish-speaking developers to perform the manual analysis of requirements, exposing themselves to the exposed risks or translating the requirements to the English language in order to make use of the exposed tools, although this translation could change the meaning or the context of the requirements and lead to the incorrect structuring of the system. For this reason, it is necessary to develop an element detection system for the construction of UML diagrams based on descriptions or user stories in Spanish, contributing to the advancement of this field within the analysis and development of software.

2   Material and Methods

For this work, several sets of user stories were collected, processed with NLP and then pattern rules were applied to them in order to extract the classes. For data visualization, a comparison was made between the classes obtained by this process and the classes obtained from the manual generation of diagrams from these sets of user stories. Figure 1 describes the entire process and the following subsections will detail each of its stages.

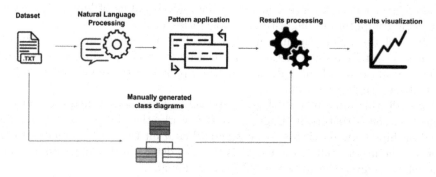

Fig. 1. Method process overview

2.1   Dataset

For this work, we searched for different datasets in which we could find a enough number of user stories that could provide the necessary information about the system they describe. However, it was not possible to find a Spanish language dataset that met this condition and due to time constraints, there was not enough capacity to generate an appropriate dataset for the work. Because of this, we opted for the use of two datasets of user stories in English. The first dataset is part of the project "Ambiguity detection with the REVV-Light tool" [14], it consists of 22 text files in English language and each one contains more than 50 user stories in which a specific system is described. The second dataset belongs to the project "Extraction of Conceptual Models: User Stories vs. Use Cases" [15] and consists of 15 groups of files where user stories or detailed use cases are specified for 3 particular software: Hospital Management System, Urban Traffic Simulator and International Football Association portal. All user stories contained in these datasets comply with the format:

As [Actor], I want [Action], so that [Benefit]

Preprocessing. The second dataset was reduced to the files in which the software requirements are described by user stories, which were found in 11 of the original 15 sets of files. Since both datasets are originally in English, each set of user stories is translated into Spanish language using Google Translate machine translator, similar to [22] and [23], since it has minimal translation bias and its results are very similar to those obtained by transformer-based machine translation [21]. The translation of each set of user stories is saved in a text file, which will have an alias as name in order to recognize the set of stories more easily when analyzing the user stories. Finally, 20 sets of stories were taken from the first dataset and 10 sets from the second dataset, for a total of 30 sets of user stories in Spanish.

Manually Generated Class Diagrams. Different students belonging to curricula related to software engineering were asked to analyze one of the sets of user stories and from this process, generate the class diagram corresponding to the requirements described. The students are in different percentages of progress in their respective career. As a result of the analysis, each student had to deliver a list of entities that are present in the requirements, a use case diagram and a class diagram, built from the requirements provided.

The collected datasets, the translated text files and the manually generated diagrams can be consulted through the Github[1] platform.

2.2   Natural Language Processing

At the same time, natural language processing was applied to each of the stories in order to observe their structure, the relationships between the words that compose them and the main characteristics of each of the terms. This process was carried out using the Python language, making use of the *Stanza* library. Stanza is a library implemented by Stanford NLP Group, focused on the analysis of texts in human natural language to transform them into lists of sentences, extract their morphological characteristics and Part of Speech [16]. For the analysis of the user stories we used the pre-trained model *Ancora*, which is provided by Stanza and it was trained for Spanish language terms.

Each user story of the different sets obtained was processed through Stanza to obtain its characteristics. For this work, the most relevant features are:

- *Word*: The original word in user story
- *Upos*: Part of Speech tag.
- *Feats*: Characteristics of the word. In this feature there are different properties depending on the word, as it indicates if it is plural, if it is a possessive or its gender.
- *Lemma*: The most basic form of the word.

---

[1] https://github.com/matovaro/PyUNML-DataSet.

In order to optimize the analysis of the results, the product of the processing of each story is stored in a database in the FireBase[2] cloud service, grouped by dataset and story set identifier.

3   Experiments and Results

3.1   Pattern Application to Extract Class Entities

In the process of applying patterns, the corresponding classes are extracted according to certain patterns in the structure of the user stories and the frequency of the results obtained within the whole set of stories. For this process, two tools were used: NLTK and Sklearn.

NLTK (Natural Language Toolkit) is a tool developed to work with human language data, providing a comprehensive set of libraries for tokenization, stemming, tagging, parsing and semantic reasoning [17]. Sklearn is Scikit-learn's opensource machine learning library for supervised and unsupervised learning, which also provides tools to process data or evaluate the results of machine learning models [18].

Extraction of Possible Classes. For this step, the NLTK library was used through its *RegexpParser* function, which receives a list of rules or patterns and builds a parser with which it will search for those structures or user history fragments that comply with the patterns, giving priority according to their order, that is, if it finds a fragment that complies with more than one pattern, it will assign it to the one that is before in the list of patterns. As a result, it returns a list corresponding to the tokens of the analyzed history. Those structures in which one of the mentioned patterns is found are labeled with the identifier of the respective pattern. The patterns used in this work are:

$$R1: \{<NOUN><ADJ><DET>?<NOUN>*\}$$
$$R2: \{<NOUN>*\}$$

These patterns were the result of the adaptation of the rules established in [5,20], which determine the structure or cases in which a noun can be a candidate for class according to the grammatical rules of the English language. For the adaptation of these rules, an analysis of the grammatical rules applicable in the Spanish language was carried out to cover the cases mentioned in the related works in the English language and thus adapt the rules established to cover the same cases in the Spanish language.

NOUN represents nouns, ADJ represents adjectives and DET represents determiners. In R1, we seek to extract the compound nouns from the user stories. In R2, simple nouns are extracted.

Since some classes may contain highly technical terms of the system that are not included in the class structure or that do not contribute significant

---

[2] firebase.google.com.

information to the results, a set of nouns or words that should be removed from the results should be created in order to clean the data. The words to be omitted are:

$$IGNORED = [\text{`base\_de\_datos'}, \text{`base\_de\_dato'}, \text{`base\_dato'}, \text{`registro'},$$
$$\text{`sistema'}, \text{`información'}, \text{`organización'}, \text{`detalle'}, \text{`cosa'}]$$

Likewise, there are nouns that represent the attributes of the system but not its classes, so they must also be taken into account when extracting the information. These attributes are:

$$ATTR = [\text{`número'}, \text{`no'}, \text{`codigo'}, \text{`fecha'}, \text{`tipo'}, \text{`volumen'}, \text{`nacimiento'}, \text{`id'},$$
$$\text{`dirección'}, \text{`nombre'}]$$

Both the ATTR set and the STOP set were detected based on the rules established in [5] and the ignored terms for class detection in the English language. These terms were adapted to the Spanish language and refined in order to cover possible cases of words that did not provide adequate information to the results but could cause noise in the results.

Subsequently, the trees obtained through the parser are collected and analyzed to verify that they do not contain IGNORED or ATTR terms within them and that if they do, they are removed. During this process, a transformation process is also applied on terms, replacing those nouns that are in plural by their respective singular form, making use of the features extracted by Stanza for each noun. If among the characteristics is that it is a plural, the noun is replaced by its corresponding lemma, allowing us to have the singular form of this and thus, to abstract the nouns to their singular form to avoid inconsistencies for nouns that are the same but differ in terms of their grammatical number.

Once the verification has been performed, a single term is constructed for the nouns found. As mentioned before, the parser returns a tree for each structure that complies with one of the determined patterns, so each one represents a compound or simple noun. The verified trees are converted into a string, where the different parts they contain are joined by a " _ ". Ex: "desarrollador_software".

This procedure is performed for each of the user stories of a set of stories. Once we have all the possible classes of a set, they are concatenated through an empty space (" "), in order to build a document with all the extracted classes.

This document is received by Sklearn through the *CountVectorizer* function, which is a library that allows us to know the frequency of the terms that compose a document. CountVectorizer analyzes how many times each term appears in a series of documents and returns a matrix with the calculated frequency. As a result of this analysis for the set of stories, it returns a matrix with the frequency of each class in the document obtained previously. Through this matrix, the total occurrence percentage of each class is calculated. This information is stored together with the possible classes detected and organized by frequency, leaving the most frequent ones in the first places. In this way, we can determine the main classes of the target system according to the frequency with which they appear in the document.

3.2 Processing Results

In order to be able to make a direct comparison of the results of the system versus the manually generated classes, the class diagrams obtained were converted to JSON format, which has the following format:

```
Clases: {
    Clase 1 : {
        'Atributos':[
            Atributo 1,
            Atributo 2,
            Atributo 3,
            ...
        ],
        'Metodos':[
            Metodo 1,
            Metodo 2,
            ...
        ]
    },
    Clase 2 : {
    ...
    }
}
```

In this way, you can easily traverse the manually obtained classes.

In order to perform a more accurate analysis of the results, special characters were removed and all capital letters were replaced by lowercase letters both in the manual classes and in the classes obtained by the system, so that the classes obtained through the patterns would be as similar as possible to the classes obtained manually for each set of stories.

Subsequently, a similarity comparison was made between each class obtained by the software versus each class obtained by manual generation. To determine the similarity between both terms, the similarity tool provided by the *Spacy* library [19] was used, based on its model *es_core_news_lg*, which is the most extensive model for the Spanish language of the tool.

In order to analyze the results, the following criteria were established:

- TP (True positive) represents the classes detected by the system that were also detected manually.
- FP (False positive) represents those classes that were detected by the software but are not found in the manually detected set.
- FN (False negative) represents those classes that were obtained in the manual process but were not detected by the software.

The steps described in Algorithm 1 were applied to determine the similarity between the manual classes and the classes generated by the system; and to extract the values of these criteria:

Algorithm 1. Algorithm for comparison of results vs. datasets

---

Require: results, N (Number of words to take from the results), dataset_classes
  (Classes obtained in the dataset)
1: *system_classes* ← *results*[0 : N]
2: **for each** *system_class* ∈ *system_classes* **do**
3:    **for each** *dataset_class* ∈ *dataset_classes* **do**
4:       *similarity* ← *similarity*(*system_class*, *dataset_class*)
5:       **if** *similarity* ≥ *threshold* **then**
6:          *TP*[] ← *system_class*
7:          *OW*[] ← *dataset_class*
8:       **else**
9:          *manual_compound_noun* ← *separate*(" _ ", *dataset_class*)
10:          *similarity* ← *similarity*(*system_class*, *manual_compound_noun*[0])
11:          **if** *similarity* ≥ *threshold* **then**
12:             *TP*[] ← *system_class*
13:             *OW*[] ← *dataset_class*
14:          **end if**
15:       **end if**
16:    **end for**
17:    *system_compound_noun* ← *separate*(" _ ", *system_class*)
18:    **if** *system_class* ∉ *TP* ∧ *system_compound_noun*[0] ∉ *TP* **then**
19:       *FP*[] ← *system_class*
20:    **end if**
21: **end for**
22: **for each** *dataset_class* ∈ *dataset_classes* **do**
23:    **if** *dataset_class* ∉ *TP* ∧ *dataset_class* ∉ *OW* **then**
24:       *FN*[] ← *dataset_class*
25:    **end if**
26: **end for**

In lines 2 and 3, and for each one, a run over the classes obtained from the system is performed to compare both classes. In line 4, the similarity calculation between the two classes (manual and system) is applied and stored in the *similarity* variable. Between line 5 and 7, if the value of *similarity* is greater than or equal to a given threshold, it is taken to mean that both classes are similar and stored in a list composed of the True Positive. If *similarity* does not exceed the threshold (between lines 8 and 14), the manually generated class is separated into the possible nouns that compose it (in case it is a compound noun) and the first noun is taken to perform the comparison again since it is the main noun. E.g.: if the name of the manual class is *usuario_principal*, the noun *usuario* will be taken to perform the comparison again.

The similarity comparison between the main noun of the manual class and the system class is performed to assign the new similarity value to *similarity* variable. If the new *similarity* value exceeds the threshold value, it is taken as that both classes are similar and stored in a list composed by the True Positive. Between lines 17 and 20, the generated classes of the system are traversed, and it is checked which of them are not in the list composed by the True Positive and those that fulfill this condition, are stored in a list composed by the False Positive. Between line 22 and 26, the manually generated classes are traversed and it is checked which of them are not in the True Positive and those that fulfill this condition are stored in a list composed by the False Negative.

Another important factor is the number of classes to be taken from the results obtained through the software, establishing a number N of classes to be taken from the first places of the results (i.e., the most frequent classes).

Once the criteria have been extracted, we can estimate the precision, accuracy and recall of the results obtained against the manual data. The metrics used in this work were calculated as follows:

$$Precision = \frac{TP}{TP + FP} \tag{1}$$

$$Recall = \frac{TP}{TP + FN} \tag{2}$$

$$Accuracy = \frac{TP}{TP + FN + FP} \tag{3}$$

$$F1 - Score = 2 * \frac{Precision * Recall}{Precision + Recall} \tag{4}$$

$$OverGeneration = \frac{FP}{TP + FN} \tag{5}$$

Performance Evaluation. To evaluate the performance of the proposed model, the calculation of each of the metrics mentioned above was performed, varying both the similarity threshold and the number of terms taken from the results, establishing the following ranges:

```
range_n_words = [25, 50, 75, 100]
range_thresholds = [0.5,0.55,0.6,0.65,0.7,0.75,0.8,0.85,0.9,0.95]
```

The results can be seen in Figs. 2 and 3.

3.3   Discussion

As can be seen in the images, as the similarity threshold increases, each of the metrics tends to decrease until it stabilizes at the 0.75 threshold. This decrease is due to the fact that with the increase of the similarity threshold, the number of similar classes found decreases and with this, the evaluation metrics decrease.

With respect to recall, it determines how many of these terms are found among the manually detected classes, therefore, the greater the number of possible classes, the higher the value of Recall. Therefore, as the number of possible classes obtained by the system (n_words) increases, the stabilization of the Recall tends to be higher, due to the increase in the possibilities of similarity

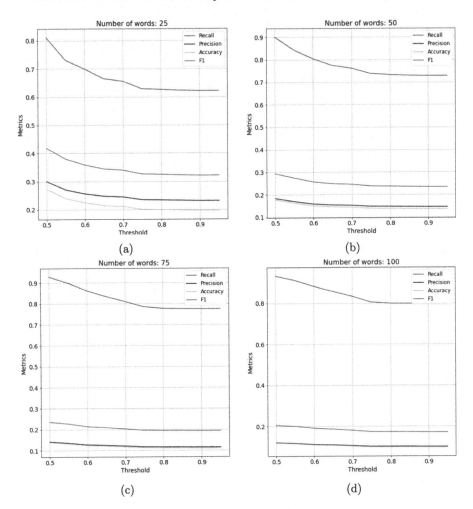

Fig. 2. Precision, accuracy, recall and f1-score graphs of the results according to the number of words taken.

between the system classes and the manually obtained classes, because among the new classes taken, there may be manual classes or their similarities that had not been obtained with a smaller set of possible classes.

On the other hand, the accuracy determines how many of the elements detected by the software are among the manually detected classes. In this calculation, all the elements detected by the software are included. In our case, the higher the number of similar terms, the higher the precision value. However, the precision, accuracy and F1 in the results tend to stabilize at lower and lower values as the number of n_words increases, starting with values close to 0.3 with the lowest threshold and reaching values close to 0.1 with the highest threshold. This is based on the large number of terms detected by the software as possible

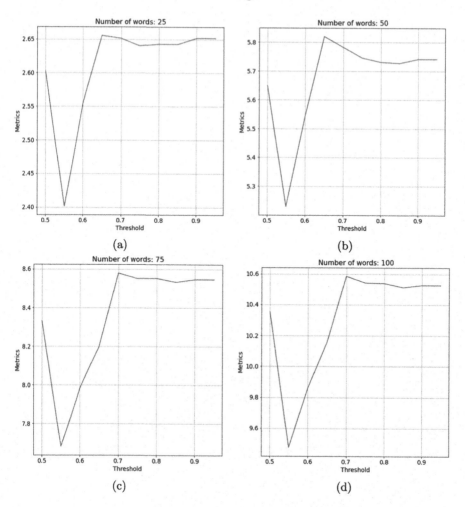

Fig. 3. OverGeneration graphs of the results according to the number of words taken.

classes based on the analyzed requirements, when in fact they are entities used to establish certain behaviors within the system operation, but they do not define a structure within the system. These entities are difficult to exclude from the results because of their grammatical similarity with the classes and the absence of characteristics that provide more information to determine more clearly the classes, therefore, the implemented patterns fail to establish a clear difference between classes and entities in order to exclude them.

Since there is an appreciable difference between recall and precision of the results, F1 was used to find a value at which these two metrics would be combined, giving equal importance to both. With this metric, we can observe that the best result is presented when 25 terms are taken from those detected by the system (2a), since it reaches values above 0.4 at the lowest thresholds and manages to stabilize above 0.3 at the highest values, indicating that despite the fact that in the terms taken from the system a lower amount of similarities is found compared to taking a greater amount of terms, this is compensated to some extent by the increase in the precision of the results due to a lower amount of False Positive in the evaluation of results.

Based on this and the decrease of F1 in the graphs, we can deduce that the higher the number of terms taken, the lower the quality of the system results due to the OverGeneration of terms by the system (Fig. 3), which increases with the increase of the thresholds and the number of terms taken from the system, as evidenced in the graphs.

4   Conclusions and Future Work

The use of patterns in the structure of the user stories offers a viable solution for the automatic detection of classes, obtaining good results in terms of the number of terms correctly detected by the software, since the software manages to detect a large part of the classes obtained manually and, as the number of terms taken from the system increases, the number of correct classes increases, even at high thresholds in which the recall exceeds 0.8. However, it presents an excess of detected terms, many of which are erroneous and lead to the accuracy being drastically affected by the OverGeneration, being reduced to almost 0.1. This is due to the large number of entities that can be found in the sets of stories, and which cannot be excluded through the use of patterns since they share a grammatical structure very similar to the classes, so that in certain cases, it is not possible to establish clarity between what constitutes an entity and what constitutes a class for its detection.

To improve the results, it is necessary to implement filtering mechanisms of possible classes applied on the totality of detected terms, determining characteristics and criteria that allow a better identification of terms, reducing the OverGeneration and improving the performance metrics analyzed above. It is also important to note that the translation process was performed through an automatic translation system, which may pose a threat to the validity of the experiments performed and the results obtained.

For future work, the attributes and methods of the possible classes could be detected, as well as the existing relationships between them, allowing the removal of all terms that are not connected or that do not add value to the UML model. Likewise, the construction of a proprietary dataset of user stories in Spanish is being considered in order to mitigate the risks to the validity of the experiments. This could reduce the noise caused by the excess of terms and increase the performance metrics with the optimization of the model.

References

1. Kassab, M.: The changing landscape of requirements engineering practices over the past decade. In: Proceedings of the 5th International Workshop on Empirical Requirements Engineering, EmpiRE 2015, pp. 1–8 (2015). https://doi.org/10.1109/EmpiRE.2015.7431299

2. Batool, A., et al.: Comparative study of traditional requirement engineering and Agile requirement engineering. In: International Conference on Advanced Communication Technology, ICACT, May 2017, pp. 1006–1014 (2013)

3. Vemuri, S., Chala, S., Fathi, M.: Automated use case diagram generation from textual user requirement documents. In: Canadian Conference on Electrical and Computer Engineering (2017). https://doi.org/10.1109/CCECE.2017.7946792

4. Narawita, C.R., Vidanage, K.: UML generator - use case and class diagram generation from text requirements. Int. J. Adv. ICT Emerg. Reg. (ICTer) **10**(1), 1 (2018). https://doi.org/10.4038/icter.v10i1.7182

5. Btoush, E.S., Hammad, M.M.: Generating ER diagrams from requirement specifications based on natural language processing. Int. J. Database Theory Appl. **8**(2), 61–70 (2015). https://doi.org/10.14257/ijdta.2015.8.2.07

6. Wang, X., Zhao, L., Wang, Y., Sun, J.: The role of requirements engineering practices in Agile development: an empirical study. In: Zowghi, D., Jin, Z. (eds.) Requirements Engineering. CCIS, vol. 432, pp. 195–209. Springer, Heidelberg (2014). https://doi.org/10.1007/978-3-662-43610-3_15

7. Bajwa, I.S., Choudhary, M.: Natural language processing based automated system for UML diagrams generation. In: 18th National Conference on Computer Application (18th NCCA), April (2006)

8. Herchi, H., Abdessalem, W.B.: From user requirements to UML class diagram (2012). https://arxiv.org/abs/1211.0713

9. Osman, C.-C., Zalhan, P.-G.: From natural language text to visual models: a survey of issues and approaches. Informatica Economica **20**(4/2016), 44–61 (2016). https://doi.org/10.12948/issn14531305/20.4.2016.05

10. More, P., Phalnikar, R.: Generating UML diagrams from natural language specifications. Int. J. Appl. Inf. Syst. **1**(8), 19–23 (2012). https://doi.org/10.5120/ijais12-450222

11. Miller, G.A., Beckwith, R., Fellbaum, C., Gross, D., Miller, K.J.: Introduction to wordnet: an on-line lexical database. Int. J. Lexicography **3**(4), 235–244 (1990). https://doi.org/10.1093/ijl/3.4.235

12. Karaa, W.B.A., Azzouz, Z.B., Singh, A., Dey, N., Ashour, A.S., Ghazala, H.B.: Automatic builder of class diagram (ABCD): an application of UML generation from functional requirements. Softw. Pract. Exp. **39**(7), 701–736 (2015). https://doi.org/10.1002/spe

13. Rigou, Y., Lamontagne, D., Khriss, I.: A sketch of a deep learning approach for discovering UML class diagrams from system's textual specification. In: 2020 1st International Conference on Innovative Research in Applied Science, Engineering and Technology, IRASET 2020 (2020). https://doi.org/10.1109/IRASET48871.2020.9092144

14. Dalpiaz, F.: Requirements data sets (user stories). Mirror of Mendeley Data. Dataset (2018). https://doi.org/10.17632/7zbk8zsd8y.1

15. Dalpiaz, F., Sturm, A., Gieske, P.: Extraction of Conceptual Models: User Stories vs. Use Cases. Zenodo. Dataset (2020). https://doi.org/10.5281/zenodo.4121935

16. Stanza. https://stanfordnlp.github.io/stanza/. Accessed 14 May 2022

17. NLTK. https://www.nltk.org/. Accessed 14 May 2022
18. Scikit-learn. https://scikit-learn.org/stable/. Accessed 14 May 2022
19. Spacy. https://spacy.io. Accessed 14 May 2022
20. Nasiri, S., Rhazali, Y., Lahmer, M., Chenfour, N.: Towards a generation of class diagram from user stories in Agile methods. Procedia Comput. Sci. **170**, 831–837 (2020). https://doi.org/10.1016/j.procs.2020.03.148
21. Elbasha, S., Elhawil, A., Drawil, N.: Multilingual Sentiment Analysis to Support Business Decision-making via Machine learning models (2021)
22. Névéol, A., Dalianis, H., Velupillai, S., Savova, G., Zweigenbaum, P.: Clinical Natural Language Processing in languages other than English: opportunities and challenges. J. Biomed. Semant. **9**, 12 (2018). https://doi.org/10.1186/s13326-018-0179-8
23. Suhaimin, M.S.M., Hijazi, M.H.A., Alfred, R., Coenen, F.: Natural language processing based features for sarcasm detection: an investigation using bilingual social media texts. In: 2017 8th International Conference on Information Technology (ICIT) (2017). https://doi.org/10.1109/icitech.2017.8079931

A Tuning Approach Using Genetic Algorithms for Emergency Incidents Classification in Social Media in Ecuador

Joel Garcia-Arteaga[1], Jesus Zambrano-Zambrano[1],
Jorge Parraga-Alava[1(✉)], and Jorge Rodas-Silva[2]

[1] Universidad Técnica de Manabí, Portoviejo, Ecuador
{jgarcia5169,jzambrano1217,jorge.parraga}@utm.edu.ec
[2] Universidad Estatal de Milagro, Milagro, Ecuador
jrodass@unemi.edu.ec

Abstract. The social media are an excellent opportunity to extract data of almost any topic and perform different kind of analysis and design of artificial intelligence models, nevertheless, researchers need to consider different kind of relevant issues such as low quality data or the hyperparameter tuning complexity, that can affect the performance of an classification model. Twitter is a very popular social network that allows to researchers to get historical and real time data of any topic. In this paper, we proposed an approach based on a genetic algorithm to perform the hyperparameter tuning for classification models. The CRISP-DM methodology was used with six stages: problem understanding, data collection, data understanding, modeling, testing and deploy. Results show a good overall performance when a genetic algorithm was used to fit the best hyperparameters combination for a certain number of classification models, scoring more than 0.90 for all the tested models. The LSVC (Linear Support Vector Classifier) was the model that performed the best for the extracted data (+170k tweets), with a Matthews correlational coefficient (MCC) of 0.97 and 0.96 for multi-class and binary classification, respectively. From the obtained results, we can conclude that using a genetic algorithm for hyperparameter tuning of classification models was a successful alternative, and with this, a classifier model was implemented for emergency event classification for Spanish tweets from Ecuador.

Keywords: Ecuador · Emergency text classification · Social Media · Genetic Algorithms · Machine Learning

1 Introduction

Nowadays an important number of people are using Twitter to post a wide range of content, including emergency related issues. This makes it an important source of information to identify and analyze various kind of disasters and

F. R. Narváez et al. (Eds.): SmartTech-IC 2022, CCIS 1705, pp. 48–63, 2023.
https://doi.org/10.1007/978-3-031-32213-6_4

emergency events [1]. In the last version of the Twitter API (V2) researchers can access to historical data and extract up to 1M (one million) of tweets per month using the official academic research product track. This huge amount of data is useful to train machine learning (ML) models and help humanitarian response organizations to get a better situational awareness and take better decisions to determine which emergency to assist first. According to [2], in Ecuador the use of Twitter during COVID-19 pandemic affected the response taken by the government, it was so since nowadays the news do not necessarily come from a journal or TV channel but currently they are also spread by social media platforms like Twitter through users posts. This is an important factor since users can get a big picture of what is happening from these posts. The problem for humanitarian response entities comes because not only official institutions make posts of these events, but an important number of people also publish content about this [3], and even when they help to spread the information about these events faster, these data may be of poor quality as they have bad information or irrelevant content.

The quality of data is an important pre-requisite when building ML models in a accurate and trustworthy way [4]. This can be a problem when Twitter data are used, since the poor quality content and irrelevant data. The researchers should put additional effort trying to handle poor quality datasets to build useful machine learning models. The researchers usually have to deal with another problem as well, that is the hyperparameters tuning process on ML models, which consists in exploring a vast range of architectures and hyperparameters before getting the best one that maximizes the performance metrics [5] score and, fits the best for the problem to be resolved. Popular approaches to parameterize models consists in the use of *evolutionary computing algorithms* (ECA), being *differential evolution (DE), covariance matrix adaptation evolution strategy (CMAES)*, and *genetic algorithms (GA)* the most popular models of this family [6].

There are some works analyzing the problems described above, such as [7,8] that analyzed and evaluated how the quality of the dataset significantly affects the performance of both traditional machine learning and deep learning algorithms. Considering the problem of the complexity of parameterizing ML models there are also some works that analyzed and solved the problem, as is the case of [5] that uses a cloud infrastructure to efficiently search for the best parameters for a ML model or [9] that exploits parallelism and aggressive early-stopping approaches; however, even when these approaches are good optimizing architectures, a cloud infrastructure with the required computational power to handle all these distributed processes is not a cheap option. There are some works that tested the effectiveness of evolutionary algorithms against other classical approaches, being the last one mentioned a little faster than GA but not ensuring to find the best combination of hyperparameters [10].

In this paper, we propose a simple method to search for the best hyperparameters of a ML model which is used to classify emergency events based on data extracted from Twitter regardless if there is a high quality dataset or not.

Our main contribution is to improve, using a simple GA, the performance of ML classifiers for the Twitter emergency event prediction problem. The paper is organized as follows. Section 2 presents the description for the used workflow to develop an approach for a classifier model using an hyperparameter tuning algorithm. In Sect. 3 we present the evolutionary configuration for the hyperparameter optimizer model and results obtained as well as the statistical tests and discussions. The conclusions are exposed in Sect. 4.

2   Methods

This paper uses the *CRISP-DM (CRoss Industry Standard Process for Data Mining)* methodology [11]. This methodology is following a workflow of six stages as Fig. 1 shows.

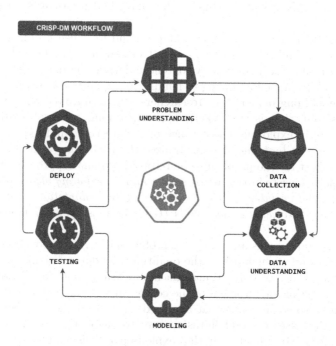

Fig. 1. *CRISP-DM* workflow used in this research.

2.1   Problem Understanding

In Ecuador, to the best knowledge of the authors, does not exist an automated process to extract and classify emergency issues from social media like Twitter and extract valuable insights from it, and since the data is coming from a social network, there is a high probability of getting a low quality dataset.

The techniques to ensure quality of the data are expensive in terms of time and computational power, so a solution to classify and handle poor data automatically with a low computational cost, but still getting a good performance when classifying tweets, is needed.

2.2   Data Collection

For the data collection, an auto-encoder proposed in [12] was used, which has keywords as output used as a reference for the extraction of tweets. Note the dataset used to train the models of this work was built using some kind of reinforcement learning approach, being the labelled data supervised by a human to check if it was correct, and then the auto-encoder was trained again with the new data in the next iteration, increasing the quality of the dataset with every single iteration. In total, more than 170k tweets related or not with emergency events, were collected to be used in the computational experiments.

2.3   Data Understanding

To understand the data we performed a simple Exploratory Data Analysis (EDA). First at all, the main class distribution was analyzed to determine the nature of the data and decide which model fits the most for that distribution, discovering some relevant information such as the imbalanced data present on the dataset (i.e., tweet labeled as "emergencia" or "no-emergencia", has about 20% and 80% of cases, respectively).

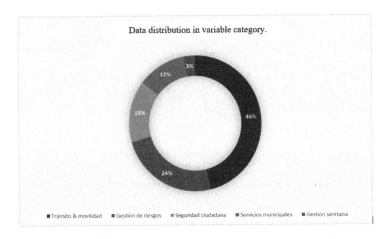

Fig. 2. Data distribution in variable category for Twitter emergency data in Spanish in Ecuador.

As showed in Fig. 2, the data are imbalanced in the variable of *category* which tries to identify the responsible institution for the emergency, here, "Tráfico &

movilidad" is the most common trend followed by "Gestión de riesgos", which is about earthquakes, floods, fires, and more. The category with the fewest tweets is "Gestión sanitaria" which is related with the emergency medical services (EMS).

The final dataset has only three columns: *text*, *class* and *category*, referring to the tweet itself, the class it belongs to ("*emergencia*" or "*no-emergencia*"), and the institution that must deal with the emergency[1]. Some other processes were applied to ensure the correct structure of the dataset for the ML models: the elimination of blank spaces, accents, special characters, stop words, hyperlinks, and emojis, in addition to transforming the verbs to their base form, so the model can performs the task of classification easier.

2.4   Modeling

A genetic algorithm to find the best combination of hyperparameters for five ML tested models was designed. Every tested model has its own distribution of genes and chromosome size, but the main architecture of the genetic algorithm remains the same for all the cases regardless if it is binary or multi-class classification. The main architecture for chromosomes is showed in Fig. 3.

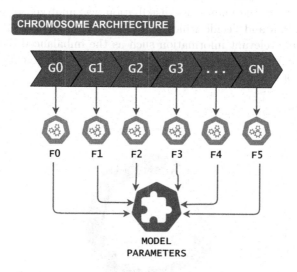

Fig. 3. Genetic Algorithm chromosome architecture.

Here, the number of genes depends on the number of parameters to tune in the ML model, and every single gene has associated a transformation function f_i to parse its value into a valid input for the corresponding parameter. This way, if we take as an example the parameter corresponding to *regularization*, which usually is one of two possible values (*L1, L2*), there will be a categorical

---

[1] https://www.ecu911.gob.ec/instituciones-articuladas/.

vector $\bar{V}$ with those two values ($\bar{V} = [L1, L2]$) and, the gene associated to this parameter is going to take a real value α_i (in the Fig. 3 is referred as "G"). So if α_i is below a minimum threshold value θ_i then it will be 0, otherwise it will be 1. This output is going to be the index of $\bar{V}$, which is the element to use in the parameter of regularization. So mathematically the value for the regularization parameter is defined as $p_i = f_i(\alpha_i)$, where f_i is the transformer for the ith gene in the chromosome, in this case defined as Eq. 1 shows.

$$f_i(\alpha_i) = \bar{V}_k, \; k = \begin{cases} 0 & \alpha_i \leq \theta_i \\ 1 & otherwise \end{cases} \tag{1}$$

Table 1 shows a summary of the genetic algorithm parameters. Here, the columns: *Parameter*, *Description* and *Value*, show the name, description and possible values for each parameter of the algorithm.

Table 1. Genetic Algorithm operators used in this paper.

Parameter	Description	Value
Optimization	What is the approach to face	Maximization
Population size	How many individuals per generation	200
Generations	The max number of generations	200
Chromosome type	Data type of the genes in chromosome	float
Hall of fame size	Top K individuals to preserve	5
Elitism	If architecture uses elitism or not	Yes
Crowding factor	Number of similar chromosomes to merge	1 out of 10
Selection	The selection strategy	Tournament
Crossover	Crossover strategy	SBX

The **selection strategy** that we choose is the *tournament selection*, this technique will create random subsets of N individuals of the whole population and then select the winner from every single tournament to be passed to the next generation. This strategy will preserve diversity since the groups for the tournament are generated randomly, so there could be groups of N individuals.

The **crossover strategy** that we chose is the *Simulated Binary Bounded (SBX)* [13], which simulates the operation of a *single-point binary crossover (BX)* on real variables. The way BX works is showed in Fig. 4, where there are two parents (center chromosomes), lets say A and B, and two children (top and bottom chromosomes). The parents are split in a strategic point to get two sets of genes, lets say i and j, so now to get the children A_i and B_j are going to be crossed and build the first child, and B_i with A_j are also crossed to build the second child. This behavior is the one that SBX wants to simulate, but to achieve that a set of properties must be analyzed and defined properly. This crossover technique is used together with a crowing factor, which will merge similar chromosomes so new chromosomes are created and diversity is preserved as well. The SBX does something similar, but the two offspring are created using the next two formulas: the Eq. 2 for the first offspring, and Eq. 3 for the second offspring. Here *beta* is a random number referred as the *spread factor*.

$$offspring_1 = \frac{1}{2}[(1 + \beta)parent_1 + (1 - \beta)parent_2] \tag{2}$$

$$offspring_2 = \frac{1}{2}[(1 - \beta)parent_1 + (1 + \beta)parent_2] \tag{3}$$

Finally, as the **mutation strategy** we chose the polynomial bounded one [14], that works well on real distribution values as is the case of the chromosomes chosen for this paper. The target function can be defined by the user, but we use the *Matthews correlation coefficient (MCC)* since other metrics such as *F1-Score* or *Accuracy* have problems with true positive values and or are extremely sensible to be biased by imbalanced classes [15]. Because of this, MCC is a suitable metric to measure performance over imbalanced data [16–18].

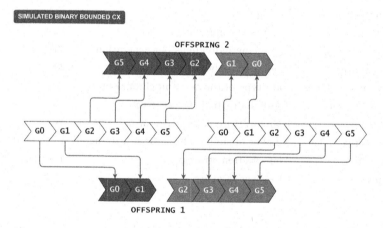

Fig. 4. Binary Crossover (BX) process.

The classifier models considered in this study are: 1) random forest classifier (RFC), 2) linear support vector classifier (LSVC), 3) decision tree classifier (DTC), 4) logistic regression (LR), and 5) K-nearest neighbor (KNN). Tables 4-9 show more detailed information about each model. Each table consists of four columns: 1) *hyperparameter* that refers to the name of the hyperparameter of the model, 2) *default value* of each parameter, 3) *binary*, which refers to the value provided by the GA for the binary class problem, and finally 4) *multi-class*, which represents the value obtained with the GA but for the multi-class problem. Note that for each classifier model there are two tables, in order to represent the scenarios using a low and high quality dataset. A high quality dataset is the one with manually labelled tweets. On the other hand, a low quality dataset is the one with predicted labels without human supervision.

Table 2. Hyperparameters to optimize in RFC with low quality dataset.

Low quality			
hyperparameters	default value	binary	multi-class
n_estimators	100	81	76
criterion	gini	entropy	entropy
max_depth	None	19	21
min_samples_split	2	0.2359	0.1356
max_features	sqrt	log2	log2

Table 3. Hyperparameters to optimize in RFC classifier with high quality dataset.

High quality			
hyperparameters	default value	binary	multi-class
n_estimators	100	81	74
criterion	gini	entropy	entropy
max_depth	None	25	20
min_samples_split	2	0.1071	0.1110
max_features	sqrt	log2	log2

Table 4. Hyperparameters to optimize in LSVC with low quality dataset.

Low quality			
hyperparameters	default value	binary	multi-class
penalty	l2	l2	l2
C	1.0	82.0540	84.0876
loss	squared_hinge	squared_hing	squared_hing
tol	1e-4	1.9033	1.4568
multi_class	ovr	crammer_singer	crammer_singer

Table 5. Hyperparameters to optimize in LSVC with high quality dataset.

High quality			
hyperparameters	default value	binary	multi-class
penalty	l2	l2	l2
C	1.0	0.02284	0.0260
loss	squared_hinge	squared_hing	squared_hing
tol	0.0001	2013.7381	0.5788
multi_class	ovr	crammer_singer	crammer_singer

Table 6. Hyperparameters to optimize in DTC classifier with low quality dataset.

Low quality			
hyperparameters	default value	binary	multi-class
criterion	gini	entropy	entropy
max_depth	None	56	71
min_samples_split	2	0.7890	1.3432
min_samples_leaf	1	0.1876	0.1123

Table 7. Hyperparameters to optimize in DTC classifier with high quality dataset.

High quality			
hyperparameters	default value	binary	multi-class
criterion	gini	entropy	entropy
splitter	best	best	best
max_depth	None	16	35
min_samples_split	2	0.5644	3.8971
min_samples_leaf	1	0.1948	0.1234

Table 8. Hyperparameters to optimize LR classifier with low quality dataset.

Low quality			
hyperparameters	default value	binary	multi-class
penalty	l2	l2	l2
tol	0.0001	2.4367	1.9087
C	1.0	5.5091	6.9081
fit_intercept	True	True	True
solver	lbfgs	lbfgs	lbfgs

Table 9. Hyperparameters to optimize LR classifier with high quality dataset.

High quality			
hyperparameters	default value	binary	multi-class
penalty	l2	l2	l2
tol	0.0001	3.2795	2.1146
C	1.0	3.1186	3.7610
fit_intercept	True	True	True
solver	lbfgs	lbfgs	lbfgs

Table 10. Hyperparameters to optimize KNN classifier with low quality dataset.

Low quality			
hyperparameters	default value	binary	multi-class
n_neighbors	5	5	7
weights	uniform	distance	distance
algorithm	auto	auto	auto
leaf_size	30	34	55
p	2	3	4

Table 11. Hyperparameters to optimize KNN classifier with high quality dataset.

High quality			
hyperparameters	default value	binary	multi-class
n_neighbors	5	7	7
weights	uniform	uniform	uniform
algorithm	auto	ball_tree	ball_tree
leaf_size	30	33	35
p	2	3	3

2.5 Testing

To evaluate the performance of the GA architecture when searching for the best hyperparameters set we used *Matthews Correlation Coefficient (MCC)*, which is widely used as a performance metric and can be used for imbalanced classes problems [17] as well as to optimize ML models when datase present or not high quality (it includes imbalanced data cases). This metric is defined by Eq. 4, where TP means the number of true positives predictions, TN the number of true positives, FN the number of false negatives, and FP the number of false positives predictions. In this work, the positive class makes reference to the tweets labelled as an emergency. MCC can be interpreted as a summary for the confusion matrix of the predictive process, being only high if the classifier is doing well on both the negative and the positive elements.

$$MCC = \frac{TN \times TP - FN \times FP}{\sqrt{(TN + FN)(FP + TP)(TN + FP)(FN + TP)}} \quad (4)$$

2.6 Deploy

The tool was development considering the architecture as showed in Fig. 5. The GADAE model mentioned in the image corresponds to a keywords identifier proposed in [12] in order to extract more relevant content from Twitter and minimize the noise in the data. All the processes begin with the *tweet extraction*

API, which will start an stream connection with Twitter to extract tweets based on keywords received from GADAE model. This tweets are preprocessed and stored in a database. After that, they are read by the *emergency issues classifier*, that is a model with optimized hyperparameters by our genetic algorithm. The genetic algorithm will train and find the best hyperparameters for a set of models mentioned in previous subsection and then the one with the best performance will be used as the *emergency issue classifier*.

The deployed tool was made using *Python 3* [19] and *Distributed Evolutionary Algorithms in Python (DEAP)* library [20]. The tool only needs a set of hyperparameters with their respective transformers, the model to parameterize, and the target function. The source code can be downloaded from here.

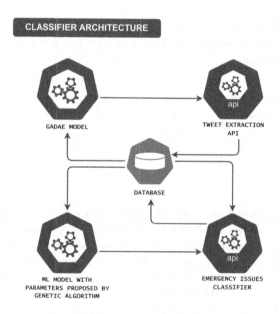

Fig. 5. Emergency classification architecture.

3   Results and Discussions

3.1   Performance

The performance of the models was measured using *MCC* for both binary and multi-class cases, using *micro averaging* [21] approach to calculate the score when using more than two classes. The performance of the five tested classifiers and the overall performance of the genetic algorithm architecture is exposed, using Google Colab, to measure the execution time. Tables 12-13 show a summary of the performance of all the tested model in multi-class and binary cases. Here, columns with *AG* implies that it is the result achieved when the classifier is optimized with the genetic algorithm, while that *default* corresponds to the use of the classifier without the optimization based on the genetic algorithm.

Table 12. MCC values over five tested classifiers for multi-class and binary, low quality dataset.

Classifier	multi-class/AG	binary/AG	multi-class/default	binary default
RFC	0.88057	0.86285	0.74561	0.67764
LSVC	0.85023	0.87863	0.84653	0.81124
DTC	0.84065	0.86056	0.77985	0.81412
LR	0.86035	0.84277	0.80144	0.70214
KNN	0.83684	0.79654	0.75659	0.66123

Table 13. MCC values over five tested classifiers for multi-class and binary, high quality dataset.

Classifier	multi-class/AG	binary/AG	multi-class/default	binary default
RFC	0.98057	0.89285	0.92365	0.89499
LSVC	0.97331	0.95863	0.96547	0.90123
DTC	0.89564	0.90124	0.88654	0.84654
LR	0.96035	0.94277	0.91245	0.90142
KNN	0.89456	0.90041	0.88451	0.79456

As it is showed on the Table 12, the *RFC* model achieved the highest performance over multiclass classification over low quality datasets, wih *0.88057*. The *LSVC* was not the best in this case but it got a good performance with the base parameters, so the model appears to perform well over low quality datasets, and also it got the highest score over binary classification and was the second one without the use of the default hyperparameters. *LSVC* is the one with the best performance over low quality datasets in all the tested scenarios.

The Table 13 also shows the *LSVC* as the one with the best performance over all the tested scenarios on high quality datasets, being the best in multiclass classification even with the default hyperparameteres, and getting the highest average performance over binary classification.

In Figs. 6 and 7 is showed the optimization process for the five models over a multi-class and binary dataset, being in horizontal axis the number of generations and in the vertical axis the maximum and average score of the model for the *MCC* metric. The blue line means the score of the elitism individuals (the average of the ones in the hall of fame) while the orange one corresponds to the average score of all the individuals, including the ones in the hall of fame.

As it is showed in Fig. 6, the AG architecture achieved a good result on LSVC for binary classification, getting a convergence over the *100th* generation using elitism but still getting good results on average, with a score of *0.96* for the best individual. Something similar occurs in the Fig. 7, where the model also converges over the *100th* generation.

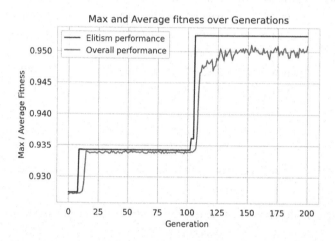

Fig. 6. Genetic algorithm optimization process on LSVC for binary classification.

3.2 Statistical Test

To detect whether the classifier models operate similarly or not from statistical point of view, considering the scenarios of multi-class and binary classification for high and low quality datasets, we carried out the One-Way ANOVA followed of a post-hoc test. The *ANOVA* test results show that there are a significant difference between the models score for all the evaluated scenarios because it gives *p-values* smaller than the level of significance of 0.05 (all of them got less than 2×10^{-16}). To determine which pair of models have significant differences we ran a *Tukey's Honestly Significant Difference (Tukey's HSD) post-hoc test* [22] for pairwise comparison over the *ANOVA* results we got in the previous stage. After running this test, not all the models have significant differences (p < 0.05) on the different tested scenarios, as is the case of the pair *KNN* and *DTC* when using a multi-class dataset and an enhanced binary one for classification, so these models are statistically equivalent; the same occurs for *RFC and DTC* when using a binary dataset for classification.

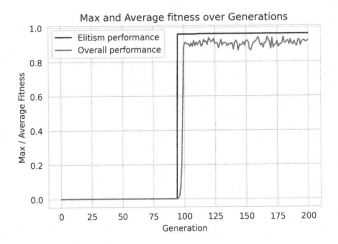

Fig. 7. Genetic algorithm optimization process on LSVC for multi-class classification.

4   Conclusion

In this paper, we proposed a tuning approach using genetic algorithms for emergency incidents classification in social media in Ecuador. Using the LSVC classifier along with the genetic algorithm the best performance was obtained. It allowed carried out the classification the tweets into diverse levels. For binary case, i.e., tweet labeled as "emergency" or "non-emergency" a Matthews correlational coefficient of 0.96, meanwhile for multi-class case, i.e., eight response institution, the same coefficient achieve a value of 0.97. This means that almost 10 out of 10 tweets are assigned the correct emergency label.

Our approach showed that even when working with low-quality datasets, the genetic algorithm is capable of setting the ideal value of the hyperparameters and thereby achieving almost perfect classification values.

Acknowledgement. The authors thank the project "Geospatial Patterns Recognition in Urban Emergency Service Events Data". Project reference code YTAUTO1889-2018-IINV0002, II-UTM.

Authors' note. The authors declare that there is no conflict of interest regarding the publication of this article. Authors confirmed that the paper was free of plagiarism.

References

1. Martínez-Rojas, M., del Carmen Pardo-Ferreira, M., Rubio-Romero, J.C.: Twitter as a tool for the management and analysis of emergency situations: a systematic literature review. Int. J. Inf. Manag. **43**, 196–208 (2018)
2. Luque, A., Francesco, M., Fernando, C., Jorge, G.-G.: Transmedia context and twitter as conditioning the ecuadorian government's action. the case of the "guayaquil emergency" during the covid-19 pandemic. Tripodos. Blanquerna School of Communication and International Relations-URL, **2**(47), 47–68 (2020)
3. Abedin, B., Babar, A.: Institutional vs. non-institutional use of social media during emergency response: a case of twitter in 2014 australian bush fire. Inf. Syst. Front. **20**(4), 729–740 (2018)
4. Bellini, V., Montomoli, J., Bignami, E.: Poor quality data, privacy, lack of certifications: the lethal triad of new technologies in intensive care. Intensive Care Med. **47**(9), 1052–1053 (2021)
5. Ranjit, M.P., Ganapathy, G., Sridhar, K., Arumugham, V.: Efficient deep learning hyperparameter tuning using cloud infrastructure: Intelligent distributed hyperparameter tuning with bayesian optimization in the cloud. In: 12th International Conference on Cloud Computing (CLOUD). IEEE, pp. 520–522 (2019)
6. Turner, R., et al.: Bayesian optimization is superior to random search for machine learning hyperparameter tuning: analysis of the black-box optimization challenge 2020. In: Escalante, H.J., Hofmann, K., (Eds.) Proceedings of the NeurIPS 2020 Competition and Demonstration Track, vol. 133, pp. 3–26. PMLR (2021)
7. Rodrigues, T.: The good, the bad, and the ugly in chemical and biological data for machine learning. Drug Discov. Today: Technol. **32–33**, 3–8 (2019)
8. Ding, J., Li, X.: An approach for validating quality of datasets for machine learning. In: IEEE International Conference on Big Data (Big Data), vol. 2018, pp. 2795–2803 (2018)
9. Li, L.: Massively parallel hyperparameter tuning (2019)
10. Liashchynskyi, P.: Grid search, random search, genetic algorithm: a big comparison for NAS. CoRR, vol. abs/1912.06059 (2019)
11. Wirth, R., Hipp, J.: CRISP-DM: towards a standard process model for data mining. In: Proceedings of the 4th International Conference on the Practical Applications of Knowledge Discovery and Data Mining, vol. 1, pp. 29–40 (2000)
12. Garcia-Arteaga, J., Zambrano-Zambrano, J., Parraga-Alava, J., Rodas-Silva, J.: An effective approach for identifying keywords as high-quality filters to get emergency implicated twitter Spanish data. under review (2022)
13. Deb, K., Agrawal, R.B., et al.: Simulated binary crossover for continuous search space. Complex Syst. **9**(2), 115–148 (1995)
14. Wirsansky, E.: Hands-On Genetic Algorithms with Python. Packt Publishing Ltd, Birmingham (2020)
15. Chicco, D., Jurman, G.: The advantages of the matthews correlation coefficient (mcc) over f1 score and accuracy in binary classification evaluation. BMC Genomics **21**(1), 1–13 (2020)
16. Yao, J., Shepperd, M.: Assessing software defection prediction performance: Why using the matthews correlation coefficient matters, pp. 120–129 (2020)
17. Boughorbel, S., Jarray, F., El-Anbari, M.: Optimal classifier for imbalanced data using matthews correlation coefficient metric. PloS One **12**(6), 1–17 (2017)
18. Chicco, D., Tötsch, N., Jurman, G.: The matthews correlation coefficient (mcc) is more reliable than balanced accuracy, bookmaker informedness, and markedness in two-class confusion matrix evaluation. BioData Min. **14**(1), 1–22 (2021)

19. Van Rossum, G., Drake, F.L.: Python 3 Reference Manual. CreateSpace, Scotts Valley (2009)
20. De Rainville, F.-M., Fortin, F.-A., Gardner, M.-A., Parizeau, M., Gagné, C.: Deap: a python framework for evolutionary algorithms. In: Proceedings of the 14th Annual Conference Companion on Genetic and Evolutionary Computation, GECCO'12, pp. 85–92 (2012)
21. Yang, Y.: An evaluation of statistical approaches to text categorization. Inf. Retrieval **1**(1), 69–90 (1999)
22. Tukey, J.W.: Comparing individual means in the analysis of variance. Biometrics, 99–114 (1949)

Software Hope Design for Children with ASD.

Mónica R. Romero[1](✉) ⒾD, Estela M. Macas[2] ⒾD, Nancy Armijos[3] ⒾD, and Ivana Harari[1]

[1] Faculty of Computer Science, National University of La Plata, LINTI, Calle 50 y 120, La Plata, Buenos Aires, Argentina
`monica.romerop@info.unlp.edu.ar`
[2] International Ibero-American University, UNINI MX, Calle 15 y 36, Campeche, Mexico
[3] Internacional University of Ecuador UIDE, Loja, Ecuador

Abstract. This article describes the analysis, design, implementation, and evaluation of a software called Hope to help children with autism spectrum disorder (ASD) to express themselves through dance. The proposed software is based on augmented reality and allows strengthening teaching learning processes that include aspects related to imitation, perception, gross and fine motor skills, and visual coordination. The design process conducted in an interactive way, centered on the human being, with the participation and guidance of a multidisciplinary team. The characteristics considered to design and implement the software are explained, which was tested in a Ludic Place Therapeutic Center with children with ASD, in addition, a pedagogical intervention proposal was built where parameters for evaluation are defined; the start-up of Hope required constant interaction, participatory design methods, likewise the software was improved with the recommendations of the participants, some students from the therapeutic center tried the application, they did so initially accompanied by their caregivers and progressively they achieved individual use of the system, Hope was assessed by 5 children with ASD, in addition to 5 parents, 5 IT specialists, followed by 5 experts (teachers, psychologists, therapists, doctors). In the end, encouraging results achieved that included recognition of the body, nonverbal dialogue, less directive, structured expressions, and the ability to create and make the participants' thinking more flexible.

Keywords: Autism Spectrum Disorder (ASD) · Dance · Teaching Learning · Hope Project · Special Educational Needs (NEE; Software; User centered design (DCU)

1 Introduction

Autism Spectrum Disorder, hereinafter ASD, is defined as a serious disturbance, [1–4] that affects several areas of development and has no cure [5], is diagnosed in children from a very early age and presents, according to its severity, problems in communication, empathy, and the internalization of knowledge [6].

On the other hand, Augmented Reality, hereinafter AR, is a technology that al-lows the combination of virtual objects with real environments [7–9]; which enriches the context. AR is used in the academic field, in the short time it has been used [10–13], it

© The Author(s), under exclusive license to Springer Nature Switzerland AG 2023
F. R. Narváez et al. (Eds.): SmartTech-IC 2022, CCIS 1705, pp. 64–76, 2023.
https://doi.org/10.1007/978-3-031-32213-6_5

has strengthened and improved teaching processes and has become a key piece when used for children with ASD since it allows better control of activities, and the experience of new and varied learning [14–16].

However, the implementation of products for children with ASD represents a real challenge [17], not only because of the complexity of starting them up, but also because for a product to be useful, it must work in an integrated manner with its stakeholders [18, 19], then we speak of teachers, tutors, caregivers, parents, medical staff. Aware of that, the present investigation describes the steps that conducted for the implementation of the software that teaches dance to children with ASD called Hope, this software built with the participation of a multidisciplinary team through user centered design from now on DCU from the initial stage with ideas that allowed the product to perfected over time.

The research structured as follow: Sect. 1 explains the Esperanza Project, and the user centered design processes. Section 2 explains the materials and methods used in the investigation. Section 3 presents the results, finally Sect. 4 establishes the discussion and the main conclusions, in Sect. 5 future work and limitations established.

1.1 Project Hope – Analytics

The Hope Project developed in the LINTI New Computer Technologies Re-search Laboratory, of the National University of La Plata UNLP, Argentina as part of a doctoral research. The main objective was to analyze, investigate, develop, and implement a software called Hope through DCU, supporting its actions through AR [20].

Hope is a software that complements educational activities for children diagnosed with ASD [21]. It allows to reinforce some teaching learning processes both individually and jointly, processes such as: imitation, perception, fine and gross motor skills, as well as allowing visual motor communication in the participants [5].

This project has been developed over several years and managed to integrate a multidisciplinary team: tutors of children with ASD, teachers, technology professionals, psychologists, child neurologists, educational psychologists, early child-hood education specialists, engineers specializing in UX user experience, accessibility experts and usability who have actively participated from the conceptualization, development, implementation, experimentation, and improvement of the product [22].

1.2 User Centered Design

The first step was to know and understand our user, to understand the limitations that he presents when diagnosed with ASD, unlike other users, children with ASD are not alone, they are highly dependent on their family circle (guardian, father, mother), of the educational center they attend (teachers, integrative teachers, pedagogues), therapy center (psychologists, speech therapist and medical personnel) [23–25].

Essentially, we focus on reviewing the problems associated with the cognitive field, we analyse how these children learn, their limitations and weaknesses when assimilating new knowledge, how they perceive signals [26]. The DCU consisted of placing the child as the center of our study a child with ASD presents certain characteristics, depending on the medical diagnosis and severity, thus needing help from: minor, medium and high scales, obeying a highly constant help chart; Therefore, according to the characteristics of the children with ASD who participated in the study, we began by identifying the tastes, affinities, inconveniences associated with the disorder [13, 28].

Next, the stages and original ideas of a product development prototype were defined and conceptualized, the same ones that have evolved over time, the product has been built using DCU and interactively [28], as the concept tests were carried out, the prototype was fed back, seeking to satisfy the needs of a user who has specific characteristics.

In each interaction we verify and perform tests with the user, so the software design was modified many times, and has been conceived through several approaches adjusting to modifiable versions based on the needs from low scales to reaching specify the software in a functional and operational way, all this thanks to the will and the participation of children with ASD supported by a multidisciplinary team.

- *Context of use:* the product designed to strengthen certain teaching and learning processes, for children with moderate and severe ASD from 4 to 8 years old, the product, initially approved in a therapy center in scheduled sessions and after that in the home of the kids.
- *Requirements:* this product developed as a playful space, it allowed the user to interact through emerging technology, specifically AR, taking accessibility attributes through a friendly interface.
- *Solution Development:* phases marked for the development of the product, SDK vuforia used as a programming language in addition to conditioning a Kinect that through its infrared cameras allowed to measure the depth and movement of children.
- *Evaluation and Evolution of the design:* this project evaluated as it built, this allowed for prototyping and product evolution.

Next, the stages where the original ideas of a Hope Software prototype defined and conceptualized described, the same ones that evolved over time. These meetings planned to conduct the following stages:

- *Initial Stage:* call, preparation, presentation of the Hope prototype.
- *User research stage:* a multidisciplinary team summoned to conduct the field research.
- *Evaluation stage of the Human Computer Interface (HCI):* in each interaction of the models defined for the prototype, usability testing conducted observing the interaction between the children with ASD summoned and the multidisciplinary group. That participated as an observer, guide, or support. It should note that in this project three of the first prototypes eliminated for not meeting user expectations, these experiences strengthened the research project.
- *Reflection and debate stage*: after the practical experience, changes made to the initial prototype, which allowed the project to be assertively consolidated.

2   Material and Method

This research presents a mixed, quantitative, and qualitative approach, the type of study framed in a descriptive, documentary, and propositional investigation. In this project there was a population of twenty people, five parents, five children with ASD, in addition to ten professionals, five IT specialists and five medical and academic team (teachers, therapists, psychologists, pedagogues, doctor).

Five children with autism, three boys: Eidan (E), Matias (M), Santiago(S) and two girls Valeria (V) and Ana (A) with an average age = 6 participated in the experiments. All children with ASD have confirmed the diagnosis through the Ministry of Public Health and the Ecuadorian Social Security Institute. deep observation.

2.1   Work Plan

The work plan was developed in the first quarter of 2021, in which the following participated: the medical and academic team of the children with ASD, their parents previously signed the permission for their children to participate in the experiment, we had a teacher who defined a curricular plan, the psychologist who expressed the guidelines of the approach and intervention with the software and the pedagogue who defined an adequate strategy for the evaluation of the cognitive indicators. The intervention conducted in three phases: diagnosis, intervention, evaluation.

Before using the software: we defined a diagnostic baseline of the children who would participate, Preschool Language Scales 5 (PLS 5) and the Battelle Developmental Inventory were used, the teaching learning processes were rated on a scale of 1 to 5, with 1 being the smallest and 5 the largest to address the intervention process individually, the central idea was to. Mark the processes that would address; Likewise, this evaluation conducted through scales that seek to identify the level of performance of the child in various cognitive aspects that are the basis of learning and school performance. For purposes of approaching the project, the following skills evaluated: intelligence, attention, memory, in process as imitation, motor skills, and visual motor coordination.

Before using the software: the purpose was to contrast the results obtained in the diagnostic evaluation with those obtained after the process. To obtain the necessary information to capture the results of the intervention of children with ASD with the Hoope Software.

Use of the software: for the intervention phase, strategies proposed to conduct a playful activity mediated by technology using the Hope system. This system allowed the child to interact alone or with the help of the professional during previously planned sessions. The activities that have conducted have a defined order, each session seeks an objective and aspects have previously considered: place where the activity would take place, time of the sessions, team collaboration, necessary hardware, software. Under the premise of man computer iteration, Hope software has allowed a mediated approach through technology to the characteristics and particularities of a user (child diagnosed with ASD), the intention was to know and adapt the product to the needs, this process It has been carried out through several proofs of concept, which were tested in real environments in therapy centers for children with special abilities. A form validated by expert judgment (Educational Technology Research Group of the University of Murcia) used. The descriptive sheet of the most relevant data of the activity using the Hope Software that is based on augmented reality shown below in Table 1.

Table 1. Descriptive sheet of augmented reality.

Basic reference data	Therapy center	Ludic Place
	Web page	https://www.facebook.com/ludicplace/
	City	Quito, Ecuador
	Educational stage	Initial I, Initial II, Elementary Basic
	Cycles	Period from September to July 2021
Activity data	Information sources about the activity	Primary source
	Venues of the activity	Floriana Island and Seymour
	Date of the activity	First semester of 2021 January to March
	Sessions per week	3
	Total number of sessions	36
ASD population	Total number of children involved in conducting the activity	5 (3 boys and two girls) For data confidentiality we will identify the children by initials (M. E, S, V, A)
ICT Strategy	Utilization from innovative technologies	Innovative technologies. Emerging technologies augmented reality
Software	Software Name	Hope version 1.5
Hardware	Necessary equipment	Kinect, television, computer, support
Multidisciplinary team	Participant data	5. Therapy Center: Therapist, psychologist, pedagogue, early childhood education teacher, nursery school specialist in special educational needs
Investigator	PhD student in computer science	1

(*continued*)

Table 1. (*continued*)

Observers	Parents	5
ICT support staff	Systems engineer Accessibility expert UX engineer Designer	4
Description of the activity: Evaluation Methodology	Goals	Conduct testing tests of the Hope software in children with ASD, with the collaboration of a multidisciplinary team Use the software to reinforce teaching learning processes such as imitation, coordination, fine and gross motor skills for children with ASD

The evaluation of these sessions conducted through observation and the expert judgment of the specialists who conducted the sessions, the bearable work lasted three months, planning the interventions three times a week and in each one of them activities

Fig. 1. Below is a member of the multidisciplinary team working with ASD children at the diagnostic stage.

had to completed. of teaching learning, the sessions conducted progressively, that is, at the beginning the children accompanied by their therapist who conducted the sessions, to later use the software and conduct the proposed activities individually in the last month. For each session, actions conducted so that children with ASD reinforce the processes defined in advance; This is how the software allowed to strengthen: imitation, gross and fine motor skills, visual coordination, motor movement (see Fig. 1).

3 Results

Under the premise of man computer iteration, Hope software has allowed a mediated approach through technology to the characteristics and particularities of a user (child diagnosed with ASD), the intention was to know and adapt the product to the needs, this process It has been carried out through several proofs of concept, which were tested in real environments in therapy center for children with special abilities.

The evaluation of these sessions conducted through observation and the expert judgment of the specialists who conducted the sessions, the bearable work lasted three months, planning the interventions three times a week and in each one of them activities had to completed. of teaching learning, the sessions conducted progressively, that is, at the beginning the children accompanied by their therapist who conducted the sessions, to later use the software and conduct the proposed activities individually in the last month. For each session, actions conducted so that children with ASD reinforce the processes

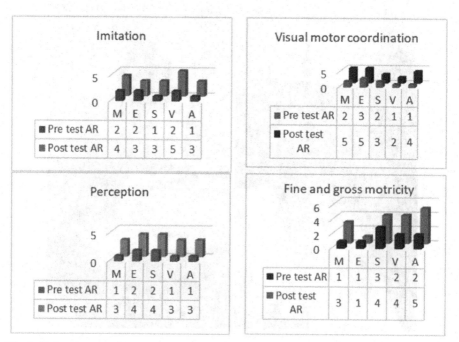

Fig. 2. Below is a graph that represents the analysis of the current situation of the processes (pretest) and after the interventions conducted using the Hope system (post-tests).

defined in advance; This is how the software allowed to strengthen: imitation, gross and fine motor skills, visual coordination, motor movement The multidisciplinary team kept a record with a baseline of each process, so at the end of this exercise the progress that the children showed after the intervention was evaluated, in Fig. 2 the results of the intervention carried out on children with ASD in the different processes, marking a score at the beginning and a subsequent evaluation at the end of the 36 sessions.

Additionally, the evaluation conducted on the Hope system shown, in three stages, the evaluation of the system created by reviewing various attributes, in addition to the experimentation conducted with children with ASD, and finally the curricular evaluation, through the indicative, rarely a better explanation, the results exposed in the Table 3 below:

4 Discussion

An investigation of techniques related to user centered design conducted, additionally we explore attributes of usability and accessibility for children with ASD. The methodology used consisted of a series of phases that allowed us to analyse, develop and implement the Hope Software, which reinforces learning processes in children with ASD.

The DCU, constituted a fundamental element to be able to define and refine the Hope System, in this process the system was modified several times, in which options were added and the parameterization of functions was allowed, specifically the activation or not of music for the sessions, the feasibility of choosing the scenarios, the way of evaluating each activity, completion of the activity, number of attempts, the choice of time for each activity. In this process, we held work meetings with professionals that allowed constant feedback as well as suggestions to improve the software, this allowed a constant refinement of the product.

To use the software, some rounds of training were previously carried out for the professionals of children with ASD, since they are the ones who accompany the child during the intervention, it is necessary and timely to carry out a training process, both in the operation of the technological equipment that intervene, as well as the Hope software, the intention is to clear any doubt of the participants.

We can indicate that the teaching learning process in the children improved, however, it is no less true that a sustainable fieldwork needed that conducted for 3 months, where thirty-six sessions conducted with each child with ASD, we believe that this has a direct impact on all processes presenting considerable progress.

After the planned interventions using the Hope software, we have verified that augmented reality reinforces the teaching learning processes in children with ASD, they present a special affinity with this type of technology, the children present a significant advance in all the processes, the most effective process turned out to be visual motor coordination, followed by fine and gross motor skills, then perception and finally imitation (see Fig. 3).

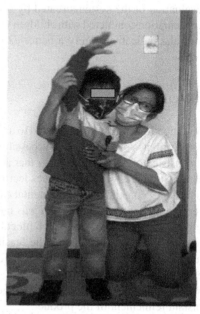

Fig. 3. The team of professionals shown below accompanying the child with ASD in the first sessions, so that he becomes familiar with the Hope software.

For the development of the activities, the ideal place was defined in the therapy center for this process to be carried out, a room with a large space for the child to move freely, in the same way a field of action was defined for the operation the system, the hardware that was used for the start-up is a television, a laptop, a Kinect and a support.

The success of interventions mediated through innovative technologies in children with ASD highly depends on the involvement of different professionals committed to a common goal, precise planning, clear objectives as well as evaluation mechanisms and an ethical approach to each session. Next, the children are presented using the Hope software, on the left a child with ASD is shown with the support of his therapist in the role of guide where the session is accompanied, on the right we observe the same child in one of the final sessions where he is no longer accompanied by the professionals and carries out the activities individually, in these sessions the multidisciplinary team carried out the observation of the actions carried out by the participants (see Fig. 4).

Fig. 4. Child with ASD in the sessions, finals doing the activities individually using the Hope software.

5 Conclusions

However, it can also be indicated that in addition to this there was a better performance in other processes that are intrinsic and that were manifested during the time of use of the Hope Software, we can indicate that the children maintained verbal and nonverbal communication with the therapists especially in the first phase in which they were the ones who accompanied the child in the process.

We can affirm that the results have been favourable since there was a multidisciplinary team, which actively participated in the sessions and was previously trained for the correct intervention with RA using the Hope software, in addition, it is necessary to establish an initial diagnostic line to carry out a measurement., it must be taken into account that each child learns differently from another, however these children have some similar characteristics, they all belong to the same therapeutic center, they have generated empathy with their treating team, they are children who have attended therapy for several years, they are in a formative process, they all present problems with their cognitive development, they present problems in the social aspect.

We use the Preschool Language Scales 5 (PLS 5) and test, Battelle Development Inventory (BDI), it can be determined that the patient's development is higher than expected in the teaching learning processes defined at the beginning of this investigation.

The therapists in their reports indicated that they used the clinical observation conducted, where the acceptable response that children have when working with applications and technology evidenced, in their conclusions they indicated that the behaviour, conduct, mood and disposition of the participants improved remarkably after using the Hope software.

During the sessions using the Hope software, the children were enthusiastic about the sensory stimuli they saw and heard, responding positively to behaviours such as coordination and fine and gross motor skills. From the results of the children who participated in this activity we can indicate that all teaching learning processes reinforced by Hope, thus establishing that it is possible to use innovative technologies for this disorder as a reinforcer in various cognitive processes, the same as previously they must review and analysed from a professional and ethical perspective.

Additionally, the children were enthusiastic when the sessions began, even of the professionals reported that the children asked and expected the intervention with RA. After using the applications, the acceptance to perform the tasks increased significantly and there was a decrease in stress.

Limitations
The limitation of this study is determined by the characteristics of ASD, it is risky to establish a generalization, however, this study provides an approach strategy that can be used in children with ASD, however, each child presents one or more associated problems Therefore, it is always necessary that prior to determining the use of new technologies, their use can be discussed with the medical and academic team.

Future Work
As a future line of research, it would be important to use this software in children with mild ASD, to find out if the results achieved in this research are even better than those initially achieved in children with moderate and severe ASD, and the intervention can also be extended to adolescents with ASD that present difficulties in the cognitive aspect. It is valid to note that the DCU in children with special abilities is a field that needs urgent academic attention, since it is complex to conduct research where you collaborate with multidisciplinary teams that must participate holistically in search of a common goal.

Emphasis should place on field work, if children have few intervention sessions with innovative technologies, it is unlikely that a significant advance will see, so we motivate professionals to generate strategies, methodologies and products that satisfy real needs of its user and that the DCU used from the very conception of the product to implement.

Acknowledgment. We are grateful to the LINTI New Computer Technologies Research Laboratory of the National University of La Plata -Argentina, the National Secretary of Higher Education, Science and Technology SENESCYT- Ecuador, as well as the Ludic Place therapeutic Centre where this project conducted.

References

1. Botto-Tobar, M., Zambrano Vizuete, M., Torres-Carrión, P., Montes León, S., Pizarro Vásquez, G., Durakovic, B.: In: Applied Technologies First International Conference, ICAT 2019, Quito, Ecuador, December 3–5, 2019, Proceedings, Part II (2020)

2. Málaga, I., Lago, R.B., Hedrera-Fernández, A., Álvarez-álvarez, N., Oreña-Ansonera, V.A., Baeza-Velasco, M.: Prevalence of autism spectrum disorders in USA, Europe and Spain: Coincidences and discrepancies. Medicina (B. Aires) **79**(1), 4–9 (2019)
3. Zheng, Z., Sarkar, N., Swanson, A., Weitlauf, A., Warren, Z., Sarkar, N.: CheerBrush: a novel interactive augmented reality coaching system for toothbrushing skills in children with autism spectrum disorder. ACM Trans. Access. Comput. **14**(4), 1–20 (2021)
4. Thevin, L., Rodier, N., Oriola, B., Hachet, M., Jouffrais, C., Brock, A.M.: Inclusive adaptation of existing board games for gamers with and without visual impairments using a spatial augmented reality framework for touch detection and audio feedback. Proc. ACM Hum.-Comput. Interact. **5**(ISS), 1–33 (2021)
5. Romero, M., Harari, I., Diaz, J., Ramon, J.: Augmented reality for children with autism spectrum disorder. A systematic review. In: International Conference Intelligent Systems Computer Vision, ISCV 2020, vol. 5 (2020)
6. Koumpouros, Y., Toulias, T.: User centered design and assessment of a wearable application for children with autistic spectrum disorder supporting daily activities. In: ACM International Conference Proceeding Series, pp. 505–513 (2020)
7. Láinez, B., Chocarro de Luis, E., Héctor Busto Sancirián, J., López Benito, J.R.: Aportaciones de la Realidad Aumentada en la inclusión en el aula de estudiantes con Trastorno del Espectro Autista Contributions of Augmented Reality in inclusive education with students with Autism Spectrum Disorders. Rev. Educ. Mediática y TIC 7(2), 120–134 (2018)
8. Putnam, C., Mobasher, B.: Children with autism and technology use: a case study of the diary method. In: Conference on Human Factors in Computing Systems Proceedings, vol. 1–8 (2020)
9. Baixauli-fortea, I., Gómez-garcía, S., Puig, M.D.E.: A proposal of intervention for children with autism spectrum disorder through dialogical reading. vol. **46110**, 135–150 (2019)
10. Fernández-Ordóñez, J.M., Jiménez, L.E.M., Torres-Carrión, P., Barba-Guamán, L., Rodríguez-Morales, G.: Experiencia Afectiva Usuario en ambientes con Inteligencia Artificial, Sensores Biométricos y/o Recursos Digitales Accesibles: Una Revisión Sistemática de Literatura. RISTI - Rev Ibérica Sist. e Tecnol. Informação **35**, 35–53 (2019)
11. Khowaja, K., et al.: Augmented reality for learning of children and adolescents with autism spectrum disorder (ASD): a systematic review. IEEE Access **8**, 78779–78807 (2020)
12. Romero, M., Macas, E., Harari, I., Diaz, J.: Eje integrador educativo de las TICS : Caso de Estudio Niños con trastorno del espectro autista. SAEI, Simp. Argentino Educ. en Informática Eje, pp. 171–188 (2019)
13. Rixen, J.O., Colley, M., Askari, A., Gugenheimer, J., Rukzio, E.: Consent in the age of AR : investigating the comfort with displaying personal information in augmented reality (2022)
14. Zheng, Z.K., Sarkar, N., Swanson, A., Weitlauf, A., Warren, Z., Sarkar, N.: CheerBrush: a novel interactive augmented reality coaching system for toothbrushing skills in children with autism spectrum disorder. ACM Trans. Access. Comput. **14**(4), 1–20 (2021)
15. Checa Cabrera, M.A., Freire Cadena, M.A.: Mobile applications as digital support material for the inclusion of students with special educational needs. In: Botto-Tobar, M., Zambrano Vizuete, M., Díaz Cadena, A. (eds.) Innovation and Research. CI3 2020. Advances in Intelligent Systems and Computing, vol. 1277, Springer, Cham. (2021)
16. Romero, M., Macas, E., Harari, I., Diaz, J.: Is it possible to improve the learning of children with asd through augmented reality mobile applications? In: Communications Computer Information Science, vol. 1194 CCIS, pp. 560–71 (2020)
17. Romero, M., Harari, I.: Uso de nuevas tecnologías TICS -realidad aumentada para tratamiento de niños TEA un diagnóstico inicial. CienciAmérica Rev. Divulg. científica la Univ. Tecnológica Indoamérica, vol. 6, no. 1, pp. 131–137 (2017) [Online]. Available: https://dialnet.unirioja.es/descarga/articulo/6163694.pdf

18. Romero, M., Díaz, J., Harari, I.: Impact of information and communication technologies on teaching-learning processes in children with special needs autism spectrum disorder. XXIII Congreso. Argentino Ciencias la Comput. pp. 342–353 (2017) [Online]. Available: https://www.researchgate.net/publication/341282542

19. Romero, M., Harari, I., Diaz, J., Macas, E.: Proyecto Esperanza: Desarrollo de software con realidad aumentada para enseñanza danza a niños con transtorno del espectro autista. Rev. Investig. Talent. **9**(1), 99–115 (2022)

20. Krause, M., Neto, M.A.C.: Systematic mapping of the literature on mobile apps for people with autistic spectrum disorder. ACM Int. Conf. Proceeding Ser. **5**, 45–52 (2021)

21. Zheng, Z.K., Sarkar, N., Swanson, A., Weitlauf, A., Warren, Z., Sarkar, N.: CheerBrush: a novel interactive augmented reality coaching system for toothbrushing skills in children with autism spectrum disorder. ACM Trans. Access. Comput. **14**(4), 1–20 (2021)

22. Thevin, L., Rodier, N., Oriola, B., Hachet, M., Jouffrais, C., Brock, A.M.: Inclusive adaptation of existing board games for gamers with and without visual impairments using a spatial augmented reality framework for touch detection and audio feedback. Proc. ACM Hum.-Comput. Interact. **5**(ISS), 1–33 (2021)

23. Putnam, C., Mobasher, B.: Children with autism and technology use: a case study of the diary method. In: Conference Human Factors Computing Systems - Proceedings, pp. 1–8 (2020)

24. López, F.A.: La Accesibilidad en Evolución: La Adaptación Persona-Entorno y su Aplicación al Medio Residencial en España y Europa. p. 319 (2016) [Online]. Available: https://www.tdx.cat/bitstream/handle/10803/385208/fal1de1.pdf?sequence=1

25. Lee, I.J.: Kinect-for-windows with augmented reality in an interactive roleplay system for children with an autism spectrum disorder. Interact. Learn. Environ. **29**, 1–17 (2020)

26. Harari, I., Diaz, F., Baldassarri, S.: Aplicaciones Google Y Adultos Mayores: Un Testeo De Usabilidad Sobre Gdocs Y Gdrive (2019)

27. Romero, M., Harari, I., Diaz, J., Macas, E.: Hoope project: user-centered design techniques applied in the implementation of augmented reality for children with ASD. In: International Conference Human-Computer Interact, pp. 277–290. Springer, Cham. (2022)

28. Koumpouros, Y., Toulias, T.: User centered design and assessment of a wearable application for children with autistic spectrum disorder supporting daily activities. In: ACM International Conference Proceeding Series, pp. 505–513 (2020)

Performance Analysis of Emotion Recognition Prediction on Mobile Devices

Jonathan Fabricio Pillajo Pilaguano, Pamela Elizabeth Tello Arévalo[✉],
and Flavio Vinicio Changoluisa Panchi

Universidad Politécnica Salesiana, Quito, Ecuador
{jpillajop2,ptelloa}@est.ups.edu.ec, fchangoluisa@ups.edu.ec

Abstract. Artificial Intelligence (AI) has had a boom in recent years thanks to technological development, it is increasingly used in various fields of research and many of these use mobile devices. Emotion recognition is one of them, as it helps in neuroscience, computer science, and medical applications. There is information where applications that are developed on mobile devices for emotion recognition, but none considers the performance of the algorithm used. The purpose of this article was to evaluate how it affects the performance of a mobile application based on Artificial Intelligence (AI) for emotion recognition according to the properties of mobile devices of different ranges. For this purpose, two different Convolutional Neural Network (CNN) architectures are evaluated, which will be analyzed according to the following metrics: response time, RAM, CPU usage, and accuracy. The results show that a deep layered CNN has better performance and lower computational cost compared to a conventional CNN on mobile devices.

Keywords: Emotion recognition · Convolutional Neural Networks · MobileNet · Fer-2013

1 Introduction

Nowadays most of the applications are based on Artificial Intelligence (AI) to help people by providing better efficiency in various fields and situations [1], one of them is emotion recognition using dynamic and static images by using classification algorithms [2].

Emotions are a very important aspect in people because they convey information about how we feel and at the same time through them we can understand the feelings of others [3], they are usually accompanied by behavior in the body, but specifically, they are denoted by facial expressions [4]. Facial expressions are an effective form of nonverbal communication and provide a clue about people's emotional states and intentions [5]. Dr. Ekman, a psychologist specializing in the study of human emotions, defined 6 basic expressions: happy, sad, anger, surprise, disgust, and fear, and states that they are characteristically universal [6].

Emotion recognition has had great potential in neuroscience, computer science, and medical applications [7]. In medicine, for example, it helps people with Autism Spectrum

F. R. Narváez et al. (Eds.): SmartTech-IC 2022, CCIS 1705, pp. 77–90, 2023.
https://doi.org/10.1007/978-3-031-32213-6_6

Disorder (ASD), who have difficulty perceiving facial expressions [8]. People with ASD find interventions with this type of technology interesting, as it helps them in social environments [9].

Although there are researches where applications are developed on mobile devices for emotion recognition, such as [10], which generally describes the performance of a smartphone when detecting facial expressions using three different models, comparing them with the metrics established in the work, however, none of them analyze the performance between algorithms on devices considering the range of the mobile device. Other investigations such as [11] and [12] analyze the performance of executable algorithms with extensive computational resources, while [13] describes a comparison between various architectures of CNN. Therefore, this research aims to know the influence of the diversity of model architectures on the performance of emotion recognition prediction in mobile devices of different ranges.

This article is structured as follows: the second section describes the related work, the third section describes the materials and methods, the fourth section describes the results obtained by applying the proposed methodology, and finally, the importance of the findings is discussed.

2 Related Works

In [10] shows a general description of three methods for the detection of facial expressions that use SVM, CNN, and MS-API using a smartphone, which exposes the comparison of the performance in precision, inference time, CPU usage, and RAM consumption.

In [11] the performance of Support Vector Machine (SVM), CNN, and Artificial Neural Network (ANN) for face recognition on a computer using Bag of Words (BoW), Histogram of Oriented Gradients (HOG), and Image Pixels (IP) feature extractors is presented. The results show that for good face recognition accuracy it is better to use ANN with IP.

The article presented in [12] shows an analysis of the performance when using four types of deep convolutional neural networks for semantic segmentation performed on a computer, where the results show that ERFNet has better accuracy, ESPnet v2 has lower execution time, MobileNet v2 has low memory footprint. On the other hand, Enet had the lowest accuracy and the largest memory footprint.

In [13] for the courier services market, the development of a subway logic system to identify damaged boxes by means of a computer using the following Convolutional Neural Networks; MobileNet, VGG16, and ResNet50 is presented. For the evaluation of the algorithm, the accuracy, test time, disk space, and the parameters of the models are used, resulting in MobileNet being superior to the other image classification models.

3 Methods

3.1 Mobile Devices

Three mobile devices were chosen for the research: Samsung J7 Prime, Huawei P20 Lite, and Xiaomi Redmi Note 9, Table 1 shows the characteristics of each of them extracted from [14–16].

Table 1. Characteristics of mobile devices

Features		Mobile devices		
		Samsung Galaxy J7 Prime	Huawei P20 Lite	Xiaomi Redmi Note 9
CPU	Processor	Exynos 7870	HiSilicon Kirin 65x	MediatekHelio G85
	Structure	8 × Cortex-A53	4 × Cortex-A53 4 × Cortex-A53	6 × Cortex-A55 2 × Cortex-A75
	Frequency	8 × 546 – 1586 MHz	4 × 1402 – 2362 MHz 4 × 480 – 1709 MHz	2 × 850 – 2000 MHz 6 × 500 – 1800 MHz
RAM	Type	LPDDR3 933 MHz	LPDDR3 933 MHz	LPDDR4X 1800 MHz
	Capacity	3 GB	4 GB	6 GB
Camera	Image	13 MP f1.9	16 MP f2.2	48 MP f1.8
	Video	1080p 30fps	1080p 30fps	1080p 120fps

They are categorized into low-end Samsung, mid-range Huawei, and high-end Xiaomi, considering the processor, since it is one of the most important components in a device and analyzes how fast it uses the information to accomplish the tasks [17] and the camera because it is the means by which the data is acquired.

3.2 Data Base

The Fer-2013 database was used for algorithm training, it was created in 2013 from the compilation of images from a Google search distributing them into different classes such as happiness, surprise, sadness, fear, anger, disgust, and neutrality, thus having a total of 35887 grayscale images with a format of 48 × 48 pixels. The given pixel values of each image are stored in cells per row in a spreadsheet [18].

3.3 Algorithms

Convolutional Neural Networks (CNN) are algorithms that take an image or video as input, process it by extracting features, and based on this they are able to differentiate some images from others [19]. For the research, CNNs have been used, since it is considered one of the best tools for image classification by machine learning [20], in Fig. 1 the scheme of a CNN is visualized.

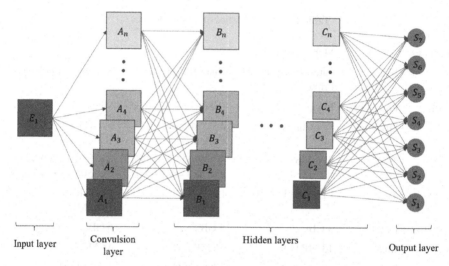

Fig. 1. Convolutional Neural Network Diagram

The two architectures that were used are detailed below.

Architecture 1. MobileNet is a model hosted by Tensorflow [21]. One of the main advantages of this model is that compared to a conventional CNN it requires less computational effort making it suitable for working on low performance computers and especially on mobile devices [22]. A model extracted from [23] was used which has an architecture as shown in Table 2, having an input layer of a 48×48 matrix and 13 blocks of hidden layers that perform the processing to train the model.

To create the model, a learning rate of 0.001 and 150 epochs were used, obtaining the training, validation, and test values shown in Table 3, and the total time it took to train the model was 1 h and 32 min. From here on the model will be referred to as M1.

Table 2. Architecture 1

Blocks	N° layers	Name of the layers
Input	1	InputLayer
Blocks 1	1	Conv2D
	1	BatchNormalization
	1	DepthwiseConv2D
	1	BatchNormalization
	1	Conv2D
	1	BatchNormalization
Blocks 2,4,6,12	1	ZeroPadding2D
	1	DepthwiseConv2D
	1	BatchNormalization
	1	Conv2D
	1	BatchNormalization
Blocks 3,5,7,8,9,10,11,13	1	DepthwiseConv2D
	1	BatchNormalization
	1	Conv2D
	1	BatchNormalization
Output	1	Reshape
	1	Dense
# Parameters	3,235,463	

Table 3. Values obtained when training M1

Training	0.8320
Validation	0.7510
Test	0.8154

Architecture 2. This CNN is proposed by [24], Table 4 shows the architecture of this network which is constituted by the input layer, 5 blocks formed by: two convolutional layers and batch normalization, a Pooling layer, a Dropout layer, and the fifth block has an additional flat layer, finally, there is the output layer.

Table 4. Architecture 2

Blocks	N° layers	Name of the layers
Input	1	InputLayer
Block 1	2	Conv2D y BatchNormalization
	1	MaxPooling2D
	1	Dropout
Block 2	3	Conv2D y BatchNormalization
	1	MaxPooling2D
	1	Dropout
Block 3	4	Conv2D y BatchNormalization
	1	MaxPooling2D
	1	Dropout
Block 4	4	Conv2D y BatchNormalization
	1	MaxPooling2D
	1	Dropout
Block 5	4	Conv2D y BatchNormalization
	1	MaxPooling2D
	1	Dropout
	1	Flatten
Output	1	Dense
# parameters	13,111,367	

A learning rate of 0.001 and 90 epochs was used to create the model, the training, validation, and test values are shown in Table 5, and the elapsed time of the trained model was 2 h and 38 min. From here on the model will be referred to as M2.

Table 5. Values obtained when training M2

Training	0.8260
Validation	0.6970
Test	0.7805

3.4 System Description

The emotion recognition application is described in two stages as shown in Fig. 2: The first stage consists of training the models in Google Colab with the Fer-2013 database, to later convert them into ".tflite" files and export them to Android Studio for use in the classification. The second stage describes the mobile application where the data acquisition is done by the camera in real time, for the detection of the faces the Mobile Vision API is used, which uses the subpackage "Face Detector" and thus extract the features and transform them into a pixel format to grayscale to classify them with the exported model obtaining, as a result, the label of the recognized emotion.

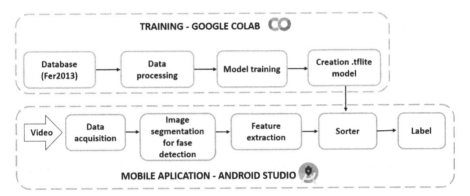

Fig. 2. Block diagram

3.5 Metric

To analyze the performance in predicting emotion recognition on mobile devices, the following metrics will be taken into account:

Response Time. It refers to the time elapsed from the time a request is requested until that request is executed and is a factor to consider for the user to have a good experience [25]. This metric will allow us to observe the time it takes for the application on each mobile device to recognize the emotion when detecting a face.

RAM. It is where data is stored temporarily and this determines the operations that will be performed simultaneously on the device [26]. Essentially, the consumption is measured after the application has been fully started [25].

CPU Usage. The amount of CPU used in a specific time interval is described as a percentage. Applications that consume excessive CPU on mobile devices tend to negatively affect other processes running on the device [25].

Accuracy. It allows us to evaluate the performance of the algorithm on the devices represented by the percentage of emotions correctly achieved [27] in the recognition during a time interval, taking the highest accuracy percentage of that interval.

3.6 System Performance Tests

For this stage, a concept test was considered with 5 participants, who were asked to make the following expressions: anger, happy, sad, surprise, fear, disgust, and neutral. In case the participant required help with any of them, he/she was shown guide images to perform the expression.

Participants performed a test on each mobile device with each model. An interval of 5 s was taken for the recognition of emotions and the same time was taken for the change between expressions, giving approximately 1 min and 10 s for the 7 expressions.

3.7 Usability

The application must allow the user to use it, understand it and control it easily, for this it is based on the ISO/IEC 25010 Usability standards, in these, there are characteristics that make the application can comply with the above mentioned. The characteristics are the following [28]:

- Ability to recognize its suitability.
- Ability to be used.
- Aesthetics of the user interface.
- Accessibility.

4   Results

For this research, the Android Studio project of [23] was used, however, the project was modified to adapt the two mentioned models and obtain the accuracy of all emotions when doing the recognition and thus acquire data for analysis, as shown in Fig. 3.

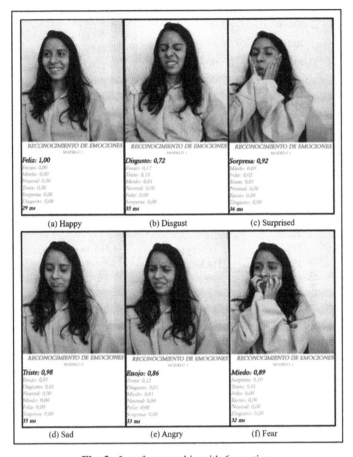

Fig. 3. Interface graphic with 6 emotions

To evaluate performance, the following metrics are considered: response time, RAM, CPU usage, and accuracy. This is done for the different mobile devices with each model.

The device with the shortest response time is the high-end device with 15.37 ms in M1, surpassing the low and medium ones, while, the device with the longest time is the low end device with 673 ms in M2 as visualized in Fig. 4.

The low-end device in M1 with 120.98 MB has the lowest RAM consumption among the two models, in contrast, the high-end device with 210.79 MB in M2 has the highest consumption in this metric, as shown in Fig. 5.

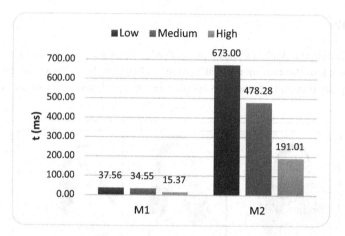

Fig. 4. Response time bar chart

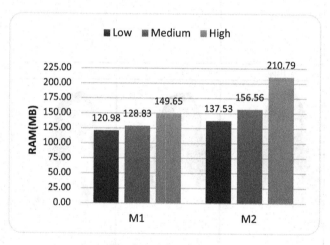

Fig. 5. RAM bar chart

For this metric, the device with the lowest CPU usage is the low-end device with 14.94% in M1, on the contrary, the high-end device in M2 has the highest consumption with 17.09%, as shown in Fig. 6.

Figure 7 shows that the mobile device with the best result in accuracy is the high-end device with 81.83% in M1, on the other hand, the low-end device in M2 is the one that showed the lowest accuracy obtaining 72.86%.

From the previous figures, Table 6 shows the following: in the average response time, the M1 model stands out notably from the M2 model, being the fastest with the shortest time. Regarding the average RAM consumption, M2 is the one with the highest consumption. In the average CPU usage, there is a minimal difference between the two models, even so, M2 is still the one with a higher CPU usage than M1. Finally, in average accuracy M1 shows better results in this metric than M2.

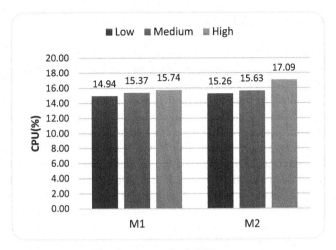

Fig. 6. Bar graph of CPU usage

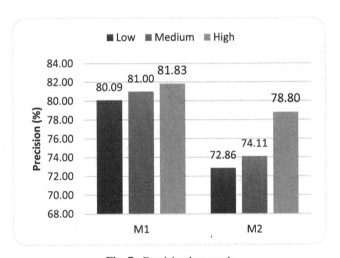

Fig. 7. Precision bar graph

Table 6. Average values with their standard deviation of the metrics with each model

MÉTRIC	M1	M2
Average response time	29,16 ms ± 12,04	447,43 ms ± 242,47
Average RAM	133,15 MB ± 14,82	168,29 MB ± 38,01
Average CPU utilization	15,35% ± 0,40	15,99% ± 0,97
Average accuracy	80,97% ± 0,87	75,26% ± 3,13

5 Discussion and Conclusions

The results of this research indicate the impact on response time, RAM consumption, CPU usage, and accuracy when evaluating the performance of a mobile application for emotion recognition according to the range of mobile devices.

The results obtained by training the models show that the M1 model obtained better training and test accuracy than the M2 model, as observed in Tables 3 and 5. These results are due to the fact that M1 has deep convolution layers [11, 29] unlike M2.

With respect to response time, the results in Fig. 4 show that M1 is considerably faster than M2. This result indicates that using an architecture as detailed in Table 2 of M1 which is composed of depth separable 2D convolution layers (DepthwiseConv2D), gives a higher speed, as mentioned in [30], unlike M2 which only has 2D convolution layers as in Table 4. As indicated in [31] CNN's are based on matrix multiplication, the fewer parameters in the model the fewer multiplications and less computational time it will have, this is corroborated in Tables 3 and 5, since M1 has less training time than M2.

On the other hand, with the RAM metric, it is observed in Fig. 5 that between the two models there is a difference, being M1 the one that consumes less, given that the model is designed for a lower computational effort [22]. The same happens with the CPU usage, however, the average difference value between models is 0.64%, being a very small value, as shown in Fig. 6.

Figure 7 shows the accuracy achieved after performing the tests on the subjects, they indicate that M1 has higher accuracy than M2, also because of the fact that the more depth there is in the layers, the better the accuracy [11].

In the performance of the mobile devices, the high-end device was the one that obtained a better response time leaving a big gap between mid-range and low-end as visualized in Fig. 4, since as mentioned in [32], with more RAM storage, the processing speed will be faster, and as shown in Table 1, this device is the one with the best characteristics.

Regarding the metrics of the two models, M1 shows better work in mobile devices, because of its architecture and the layers that constitute it, allows it to be a faster model, occupies less RAM, has lower CPU usage, and has high accuracy, however, if you have a device with better features it will have better performance. Demonstrating that using an efficient model such as M1 in a low-end device, will still be more accurate than a high-end device using a conventional model such as M2. This is shown in Fig. 7.

Future articles in this area could evaluate the prediction performance of facial microexpression recognition in mobile devices since they are a field that has not been explored in depth, as one of the reasons is due to the difficult access to a database of microexpressions.

This work contributes with an intelligent technological tool that can help in early intervention for people with ASD through a mobile device, achieving that they identify and improve the understanding of emotional states, having significant progress in social interaction.

References

1. Lu, Y.: Artificial intelligence: a survey on evolution, models, applications and future trends. J. Manage. Analyt. **6**(1), 1–29 (2019). https://doi.org/10.1080/23270012.2019.1570365
2. Zhao, X.M., Zhang, S.Q.: A review on facial expression recognition: feature extraction and classification. IETE Tech. Rev. **33**(5), 505–517 (2016). https://doi.org/10.1080/02564602.2015.1117403
3. Matsumoto, D., Hwang, H.S., López, R.M., Pérez-Nieto, M.Á.: Lectura de la expresión facial de las emociones: investigación básica en la mejora del reconocimiento de emociones, p. 9
4. Gogate, U., Parate, A., Sah, S., Narayanan, S.: Real time emotion recognition and gender classification. In: 2020 International Conference on Smart Innovations in Design, Environment, Management, Planning and Computing (ICSIDEMPC), pp. 138–143 (2020). https://doi.org/10.1109/ICSIDEMPC49020.2020.9299633
5. Michael Revina, I., Sam Emmanuel, W.R.: A survey on human face expression recognition techniques. J. King Saud Univ. Comput. Inf. Sci. **33**(6), 619–628 (2021). https://doi.org/10.1016/j.jksuci.2018.09.002
6. Ekman, P., Oster, H.: Expresiones faciales de la emoción. Estudios de Psicología **2**(7), 115–144 (2014). https://doi.org/10.1080/02109395.1981.10821273
7. Islam, M., et al.: Emotion recognition from EEG signal focusing on deep learning and shallow learning techniques. IEEE Access **9**, 94601–94624 (2021). https://doi.org/10.1109/ACCESS.2021.3091487
8. Li, J., Bhat, A., Barmaki, R.: A two-stage multi-modal affect analysis framework for children with autism spectrum disorder. (2021). http://arxiv.org/abs/2106.09199. Accedido 14 de abril de 2022
9. Jaliaawala, M.S., Khan, R.A.: Can autism be catered with artificial intelligence-assisted intervention technology? A comprehensive survey. Artif. Intell. Rev. **53**(2), 1039–1069 (2019). https://doi.org/10.1007/s10462-019-09686-8
10. Shu, J., Chiu, M., Hui, P.: Emotion sensing for mobile computing. IEEE Commun. Mag. **57**(11), 84–90 (2019). https://doi.org/10.1109/MCOM.001.1800834
11. Islam, K.T., Raj, R.G., Al-Murad, A.: Performance of SVM, CNN, and ANN with BoW, HOG, and image pixels in face recognition. In: 2017 2nd International Conference on Electrical & Electronic Engineering (ICEEE), pp. 1–4 (2017). https://doi.org/10.1109/CEEE.2017.8412925
12. Orozco, O.A.S., Saenz, A.D.C., González, C.E.R., Quintana, J.A.R.: Análisis del desempeño de redes neuronales profundas para segmentación semántica en hardware limitado. Recibe, Revista Electrónica de Computación, Informática, Biomédica y Electrónica **8**(2), C6-1-C6-21 (2019). https://doi.org/10.32870/recibe.v8i2.142
13. Kim, M., Kwon, Y.J., Kim, J., Kim, Y.M.: Image classification of parcel boxes under the underground logistics system using CNN MobileNet. Appl. Sci. **12**(7), 3337 (2022). https://doi.org/10.3390/app12073337
14. Galaxy J7 Prime|SM-G610MZKATCE|Samsung México. *Samsung mx.* https://www.samsung.com/mx/smartphones/others/galaxy-j7-prime-g610m-sm-g610mzkatce/. Accedido 16 de abril de 2022
15. HUAWEI P20 lite: Manual del usuario, Preguntas frecuentes, software|HUAWEI Soporte España. https://consumer.huawei.com/es/support/phones/p20-lite/. Accedido 16 de abril de 2022
16. Redmi Note 9. https://www.mi.com/global/redmi-note-9/specs/. Accedido 16 de abril de 2022
17. MediaTek, MediaTek News, *MediaTek* (2022). https://corp.mediatek.com.es/news-events/press-releases/para-qu%C3%A9-sirve-el-procesador-de-mi-tel%C3%A9fono-y-c%C3%B3mo-elegir-el-adecuado. Accedido 16 de abril de 2022

18. Kusuma, G.P., Jonathan, J., Lim, A.P.: Emotion recognition on FER-2013 face images using fine-tuned VGG-16. Adv. Sci. Technol. Eng. Syst. J. **5**(6), 315–322 (2020). https://doi.org/10.25046/aj050638
19. Moreno-Díaz-Alejo, L.: Análisis comparativo de arquitecturas de redes neuronales para la clasificación de imágenes (2020). https://reunir.unir.net/handle/123456789/10008. Accedido: 16 de abril de 2022
20. Albawi, S., Mohammed, T.A., Al-Zawi, S.: Understanding of a convolutional neural network. In: 2017 International Conference on Engineering and Technology (ICET), Antalya, pp. 1–6 (2017). https://doi.org/10.1109/ICEngTechnol.2017.8308186
21. Gavai, N.R., Jakhade, Y.A., Tribhuvan, S.A., Bhattad, R.: MobileNets for flower classification using TensorFlow. In: 2017 International Conference on Big Data, IoT and Data Science (BID), pp. 154–158 (2017). https://doi.org/10.1109/BID.2017.8336590
22. Srinivasu, P.N., SivaSai, J.G., Ijaz, M.F., Bhoi, A.K., Kim, W.J., Kang, J.J.: Classification of skin disease using deep learning neural networks with MobileNet V2 and LSTM. Sensors **21**(8), 2852 (2021). https://doi.org/10.3390/s21082852
23. Andres, E.: EliotAndres/tensorflow-2-run-on-mobile-devices-ios-android-browser (2021). https://github.com/EliotAndres/tensorflow-2-run-on-mobile-devices-ios-android-browser. Accedido: 16 de abril de 2022
24. Facial Emotion Detection Using CNN. Analytics Vidhya (2021). https://www.analyticsvidhya.com/blog/2021/11/facial-emotion-detection-using-cnn/. Accedido 16 de abril de 2022
25. Willocx, M., Vossaert, J., Naessens, V.: A quantitative assessment of performance in mobile app development tools. In: 2015 IEEE International Conference on Mobile Services, pp. 454–461 (2015). https://doi.org/10.1109/MobServ.2015.68
26. Kayande, D., Shrawankar, U.: Performance analysis for improved RAM utilization for Android applications. In: 2012 CSI Sixth International Conference on Software Engineering (CONSEG), pp. 1–6 (2012). https://doi.org/10.1109/CONSEG.2012.6349500
27. Zhang, X., Li, W., Chen, X., Lu, S.: MoodExplorer: towards compound emotion detection via smartphone sensing. Proc. ACM Interact. Mobile Wearable Ubiquit. Technol. **1**(4), 1–30 (2018). https://doi.org/10.1145/3161414
28. Debnath, N., et al.: Digital Transformation: A Quality Model Based on ISO 25010 and User Experience, pp. 1-11. https://doi.org/10.29007/1gnk
29. Elhassouny, A., Smarandache, F.: Trends in deep convolutional neural networks architectures: a review. In: 2019 International Conference of Computer Science and Renewable Energies (ICCSRE), pp. 1–8 (2019). https://doi.org/10.1109/ICCSRE.2019.8807741
30. Howard, A.G., et al.: MobileNets: Efficient Convolutional Neural Networks for Mobile Vision Applications (2017). http://arxiv.org/abs/1704.04861. Accedido 17 de abril de 2022
31. Junejo, I.N., Ahmed, N.: A multi-branch separable convolution neural network for pedestrian attribute recognition. Heliyon **6**(3), e03563 (2020). https://doi.org/10.1016/j.heliyon.2020.e03563
32. De qué manera la memoria de acceso aleatorio (RAM) afecta el rendimiento|Dell Honduras. https://www.dell.com/support/kbdoc/es-hn/000129805/how-random-access-memory-ram-repercusi-oacute-n-performance. Accedido 17 de abril de 2022

Android Mobile Application for Cattle Body Condition Score Using Convolutional Neural Networks

Sebastián Montenegro[1], Marco Pusdá-Chulde[1] [ORCID], Víctor Caranqui-Sánchez[1] [ORCID],
Jorge Herrera-Tapia[2] [ORCID], Cosme Ortega-Bustamante[1] [ORCID],
and Iván García-Santillán[1(✉)] [ORCID]

[1] Facultad de Ingeniería en Ciencias Aplicadas, Universidad Técnica del Norte, Ibarra, Ecuador
{dsmontenegroa,mrpusda,vmcaranqui,mc.ortega,idgarcia}@utn.edu.ec
[2] Facultad de Ciencias Informáticas, Universidad Laica Eloy Alfaro de Manabí, Manta, Ecuador
jorge.herrera@uleam.edu.ec

Abstract. The livestock sector is the set of activities related to raising cattle to take advantage of reproduction, dairy production, and beef benefits. In this sector, a vital factor is a cattle's body condition, considered a nutritional indicator since the subcutaneous body fat level found in certain anatomical points determines the animal's thinness or fatness levels. Therefore, it is a clue in defining nutritional deficiencies, a common problem in the livestock industry. Providing a timely cattle body condition assessment may prevent nutritional issues that improve cattle's health, reproduction processes, and dairy production. This study aims to develop an Android mobile app assessing Bos Taurus cattle body condition through computer-vision techniques and Deep Learning. The app was developed following the XP agile methodology and the Flutter, TensorFlow, and Keras frameworks. For this end, three CNN models were trained: Yolo, MobileNet, and VGG-16, for different tasks within the App. Models were evaluated using quantitative metrics such as Confusion Matrix, ROC Curve, CED Curve, and AUC. The ISO/IEC 25022 standard and USE questionnaire were used to assess the mobile app quality in use. The mobile app achieved an accuracy of 0.88 between the manual body condition score (BCS) and the one predicted. Results proved that this application enables anyone to adequately assess cattle's body condition using a conventional mobile device, contributing to the innovation of the livestock sector.

Keywords: Android mobile app · Body condition score · Deep Learning · CNN · Yolo · MobileNet · VGG-16 · ISO 25022

1 Introduction

1.1 Problem Statement

The livestock sector is the set of activities related to raising beef cattle to take advantage of reproduction and milk and meat production. *Bos Taurus* cattle type is the scientific name for a bull or cow usually considered a dairy breed [1]. In Ecuador, livestock activity

F. Narváez et al. (Eds.): SmartTech-IC 2022, CCIS 1705, pp. 91–105, 2023.
https://doi.org/10.1007/978-3-031-32213-6_7

has a great impact on the economy, while the dairy sector produces around 5 million liters of milk a day, 50% are products like cheese, cream, etc. The other 50% of production is the direct consumption of pure unpasteurized milk [2].

An important factor is cattle's body condition which is performed by assessing subcutaneous body fat in certain anatomical points. An animal's nutritional level indicator ranges from level 1, including the thinnest or undernourished cows, to level 5, those considered obese. Such thinness or fatness level may be a clue to determining nutritional deficiencies [3], health problems, or cattle inadequate management. Provided the body's condition assessment is carried out regularly, it may solve nutritional issues and, at the same time, enhance cattle's health, reproduction, and dairy production.

Cattle's body assessment may be performed visually to the touch by a veterinary, depending on the level of expertise, determining an approximate range under the scale from 1–5. Most times, data gathered is manually kept on paper or in an electronic sheet, limiting data analysis for timely pre-production, reproduction, and health action plan, especially in cattle with either low-fat levels (1) or high (5) body condition scores. Cattle scoring excellent grades – between 3 and 4 – is profitable for the livestock industry.

Thus, the objective of this study is to develop an Android mobile app for *Bos Taurus* cattle's body condition assessment through computer vision techniques and Deep Learning, which have been properly used in several application contexts [4–6]. The used frameworks are Flutter [7], TensorFlow 2.5 [9] with Python 3.9 [8], and Keras 2.5 [10]. The XP [11] methodology is applied to develop the 4-phase mobile App: exploration, planning, development, and testing.

This mobile app contributes to the livestock sector innovation since the body condition score (BCS) is performed based on the five nutritional levels 1–5 [12]. The idea emerges from the *BCS Cowdition* mobile app (available in Google Play) from the Bayer company [13], which performs such assessment but semi-automatically. The user captures two images from the lateral and back parts of the animal, then manually selects key points in the hip to estimate the body condition. In our work, these key points are automatically suggested to the user by using deep learning algorithm (regression task). It depicts the main contribution in this study as well as the release of the dataset created to train the deep learning models. Besides, results from Bayer's app are kept in a private server database. As far as we know, studies of this kind have never been performed in Ecuador, not to mention its free distribution. Therefore, the development of this free, easy-to-use mobile app is necessary for the livestock sector through a conventional mobile device.

1.2   Related Works

The following existing studies in the literature that helped as a foundation for the development of this project are:

Yukun et al. [14] who developed an automatic monitoring system for the body condition assessment of milk cows using neuronal networks and lineal regression techniques, resulting in a high-performance system with more than 0.94 accuracy levels between manual BCS (body condition score) and the one predicted by the model.

Liu et al. [15] developed an automatic monitoring system for the body condition assessment of milk cows from deep imaging using an ensemble model that obtains the subcutaneous level of fat that cows possess as energy reserves. The model achieved 56% mean accuracy with 0,125-deviation points, 76% with 0,25-deviation points and 94% mean accuracy with 0,5 deviation points.

Song et al. [16] developed an automatic monitoring system for the body condition scoring of milk cows using tri-dimensional cameras by extracting tri-dimensional characteristics of multiple body areas from 3 viewpoints (top, side, and back) in 8 select regions of the cattle's body. Favorable results were obtained, achieving a sensibility of 0,72 using the 10-folk cross-validation.

Martins et al. [17] performed in Matlab a body weight assessment system (BW), the body's condition score (BCS), and milk cows features (TDT) using 3D cameras with 14 images from the back of the cow and 13 from the side.

The rest of the document is organized as follows: Sect. 2 presents the methodology and tools used in the development of the study, while Sect. 3 presents the results obtained using several performance metrics. Section 4 discusses other research, and finally, conclusions, and future work in Sect. 5

2 Materials and Methods

The proposed solution consists of an Android Mobile app capturing a lateral view of the animal's body through the device camera. Next, the body condition score (BCS) is performed, and the nutritional score level (1–5 scale) is reported, as seen in Fig. 1.

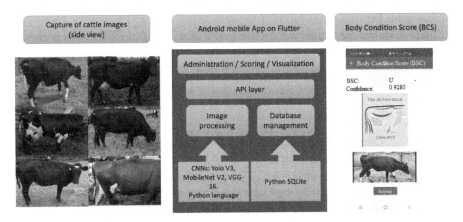

Fig. 1. Proposed solution diagram of the Android mobile app

The following topics are described below: Cattle body condition, the used dataset to train CNNs, and the development of the mobile app.

2.1 Cattle Body Condition

Body condition score ranges from 1 to 5, being 1 the skinniest cow and 5 the fattest. The scoring system has 0.25 increase degrees obtained by analyzing cattle's hip from

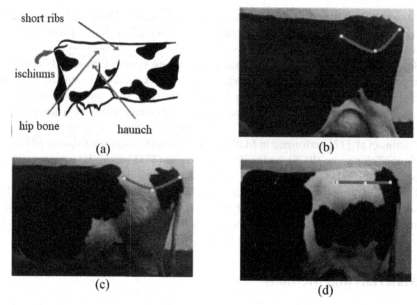

Fig. 2. (a) Hip sideview assessment area [12] considering 3 key points to evaluate the BCS; (b) Range V – 1 to 2.75; (c) Range U – 3 to 3.75; (d) Range L – 4 to 5.

the lateral area according to the produced shape formed by 3 key points such as V, U, L, as observed in Fig. 2

Table 1 shows the range and a description of a specific condition in a certain evaluation.

Table 1. Body Condition Scoring (BCS) Levels from 1 to 5

Level	Tag	Description
1	V	Cattle is too thin and shows malnutrition symptoms, ranging between 1 to 2.75—tag V due to the shape formed in the hip, as seen in Fig. 2(b)
3	U	Cattle have a normal and acceptable nutrition level, and the score range varies between 3 to 3.75—tag U due to the shape formed in the hip—Fig. 2(c)
5	L	Obese cattle showing fatty parts of the body, score range may be between 4 and 5—tag L (straight line) due to the shape formed in the hip—Fig. 2(d)

2.2 Data Set

Dataset used is formed by cow's lateral view having a body condition from 2–4 levels. The remaining ranges (1 and 5) are not considered because the livestock industry COPREGA SA., where the study took place (Imbabura, Ecuador), does not guest this type of cattle to prevent nutritional deficiencies and obesity. As far as we know, it is difficult to obtain good images of cows with scores of 1 to 5 from the Web that can be used for this study. Application *LabelMe* [18] was used for manual image annotation: Animal ID, BCS score assigned in V (range from 1 to 2.75) and U (range from 3 to3.75), as well as three key points located in the cattle's hip helping visual confirmation of the assigned score (Fig. 3) based on the given shape U, V, L (Fig. 2). This information was saved in Json files. The dataset contains in total 380 images from different lateral view cattle. This annotation task was performed with the help of a veterinary who knows cattle anatomy. The dataset is publicly available for academic purposes at https://bit.ly/3UpVtq8.

Fig. 3. Examples of dataset containing annotated cattle, including the 3 key points on cow hip. (Color figure online)

Python 3.9 programming language [8] was used for the training and testing of 3 convolutional neural networks or CNN [19], using *TensorFlow 2.5* [9] and *Keras* 2.5 [10] Frameworks. The CNNs are YOLO in charge of cattle's location (bounding box) at the image input, *MobileNet V2* in charge of BCS score within V, U, and VGG-16 in charge of 3 location key points in a cow's hip for visual confirmation of the BCS. Three different architectures were used here for experimentation purposes only regarding accuracy, model size, and inference speed. These findings will be considered in future works. The 3 networks are detailed as follows:

2.3 YOLO V3 Network

Pre-trained Yolo V3 network [20] in dataset COCO [21] was selected to locate the entire cattle in lateral view within an image (green rectangles in Fig. 3). Only one cattle is identified. The architecture is observed in Fig. 4 comprises a resized image input of $448 \times 448 \times 3$ pixels, 24 convolutional layers, and an output of 2 points (4 neurons) defining a cattle's bounding box in lateral view. The accuracy metric used for validation was *Intersection Over Union (IoU)*. Precision refers to the percentage of the correctly predicted bounding boxes (IoU > 0.5 generally) out of all predicted bounding boxes.

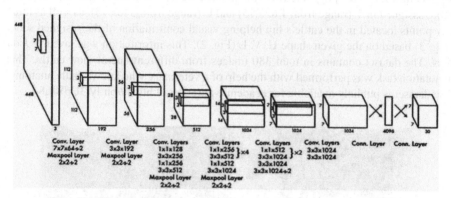

Fig. 4. YOLO v3 architecture [19] used in this proposal for cow detection

2.4 MobileNet V2 Network

MobileNet V2 [22] is a light neuronal network applied to scoring cattle's (classification task) between range V and U (see Table 1) depending upon the body's condition. Moreover, the architecture comprises a resized image input of $224 \times 224 \times 3$, 6-convolutional layers, and one output layer, as indicated in Fig. 5. Input to this network is the cattle previously located in the Yolo V3 network, and output has two neurons – cattle classification in range V and U (Fig. 2b and c). The data augmentation technique for dataset expansion was applied during training since it has a limited number (380 images in total). This technique applied 5 inline operations over each training sample (80% for the training set): brightness, channel shift, rotation, and zoom. The training was performed with 300 epochs using two learning rates—$1e{-}3$ (200 epochs) and $1e{-}4$ (100 epochs). A fixed number of epochs was used trying to avoid over/under fitting. The loss function used was *binary cross-entropy,* while the activation function in the final layer was *sigmoid*.

The metrics used to measure this network's performance were confusion matrix, Accuracy, Precision, Sensitivity, F1 score, ROC curve, and AUC (area under the curve).

2.5 VGG-16 Network

VGG-16 [23] is a model used for regression tasks locating cattle's three lateral viewpoints from the hip (Fig. 3), which determined the body condition score for the visual validation according to the given shape U, V, L. Input to this network is also the previously Yolo network v3 de $448 \times 448 \times 3$ located cattle, whereas the output is 3 points (6 neurons) with their respective coordinates (x, y). The architecture is shown in Fig. 6, consisting of 13 convolutional layers and three dense layers. Training had 300 epochs. The validation

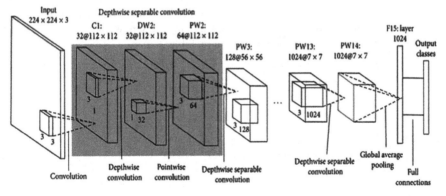

Fig. 5. *Mobilenet v2* architecture [22] used in this proposal for classification task

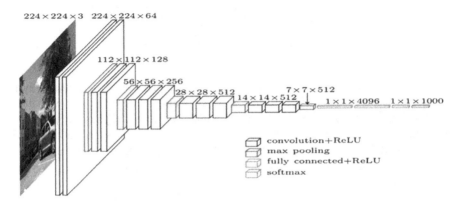

Fig. 6. VGG-16 architecture [23] used in this proposal for regression task

metrics are *Normalized Mean Error (NME), Cumulative Error Distribution (CED) curve and AUC.*

The Yolo v3 y VGG-16 network training was performed using a desktop computer equipped with AMD Ryzen 5600G processor with Radeon Graphics, 3.90 GHz, 16 GB in RAM.

2.6 Android Mobile App

The Android mobile app (Fig. 1) determines a cattle's body condition score based on a scale from 1–5 (Table 1). This mobile app was developed by applying the framework Flutter [7], which creates interfaces easily through a Toolkit based on the MVC (model, view, controller) software architecture pattern, which separates the data, business logic, and graphical interface of an application. The app was developed using the XP Methodology [11] with four phases: exploration, planning, development, and testing. Each stage contains iterations for analyzing, designing, developing, and testing [24].

The exploration phase refers to requirement checking, software selection, and frameworks used in application development.

During the planning phase, requirements for the development are determined through user history with standardized times in weeks and days. Users were created to use the app with different tasks to be fulfilled, as seen in Table 2.

Table 2. Users configured in mobile application

Users	Roles
Veterinary (System Administrator)	User Administration Cattle Creation States Creation Performing cattle's body score
Helper	Performing cattle's body score Record body score Note and record photographic evidence Upload cattle sheet records Generate body score reports

In the development phase, seven user histories were implemented: login, user record, farm record, farm's management, cattle record, body condition evaluation, and evaluation report—implemented in the Flutter framework. Finally, in the testing phase, all proposed requirements were tested in the application, and the quality of use was evaluated [24, 25] based on ISO/IEC 25022 [26] standards using SUS (System Usability Scale) satisfaction survey [27]. The database used in the mobile application was SQLite [28].

3 Results

3.1 Data Set

For the training of CNNs (*MobileNet and VGG-16*), 380 images were manually annotated containing 182 body conditions in U and 198 in V. Dataset was randomly divided, 80% for training and 20% for model validation.

3.2 Yolo V3 Network

As previously noted, this pre-trained CNN was used to locate the cattle through a bounding box. This model was pre-trained using dataset COCO [21] (*Common Objects in Context*), containing over 80 classes, including the *cow class*. The *IoU* metric [29] was used for its validation which measures the accuracy of an object detector on a particular dataset. This metric was calculated using a threshold of 0.6 (60% or more overlap) obtaining 0.718, considered an acceptable prediction in a cattle's location.

3.3 MobileNet V2 Network

As previously stated, this network is used for cattle body condition scoring (U and V classification in Table 1). Some metrics obtained from the confusion matrix (Fig. 7) are observed in Table 3. Overall, the model achieved an accuracy of 0.88 between the manual BCS (body condition score) and the one predicted.

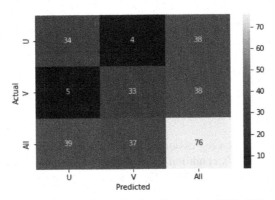

Fig. 7. Confusion matrix obtained on the test set (20%, 76 images)

Table 3. *MobileNet v2* metrics

Accuracy	0.88
Precision in V:	0.87
Precision in U:	0.89
Sensibility in V:	0.89
Sensibility in U:	0.87
F1 Score in V:	0.88
F1 Score in U:	0.88

The ROC curve is shown in Fig. 8, and UAC value obtained was 0.92.

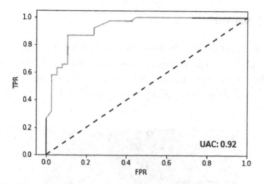

Fig. 8. ROC curve for classification task in U and V score

3.4 VGG-16 Network

This network was used as a regression task to locate 3-keypoints on the cattle hip to visually confirm the body's condition score (based on the given shape: U, V, L as in Fig. 2). Normalized mean error (NME), Eq. 1, was applied to evaluate the performance of this network [30].

$$NME = \frac{1}{L} \sum_{i=1}^{L} \frac{\left\| Yi - \hat{Y}i \right\|^2}{d} \tag{1}$$

L is the number of points located in the cattle's body, Yi is the actual (x, y)-coordinates whereas $\hat{Y}i$ the predicted ones. The normalizing factor of NME is d, which is the width and height of the cattle bounding box.

The NME average was 0.064 on the validation image. Next, CED curve was obtained (Cumulative Error Distribution), which gives an overall idea of the distribution of errors over a given dataset (Fig. 9). The horizontal axis of CED plot indicates the target NME (ranging between 0 and the pre-defined threshold), and the CED value at the specific point means the rate of samples whose NME values are smaller than the specific target NME. In our case, this graphic has the NME error in the x-axis as cattle's bounding box fraction, and the y-axis contains all tested images (76 images ~ 20%). Thus, the CED curve corresponds to the percentage of test images of which the error is less than 30%. We set the threshold as 0.30 in the experiment. The Area-Under-the-Curve (AUC) from the CED curve was 0.7688. The value of AUC is between 0 and 1, the closer we get to 1, the better.

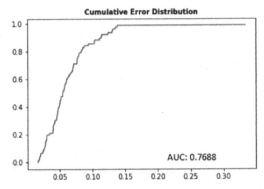

Fig. 9. CED curve obtained from the VGG-16 network

3.5 Android Mobile App

Figure 10 shows the process for cattle body condition scores using the mobile app developed with Flutter, including authentication, cattle image acquisition, body condition evaluation (BSC), and results from the report. The BSC estimation is performed locally on the mobile device.

Fig. 10. Body condition score (BCS) process using the Android mobile app

The mobile app was tested on Samsung S10+ (2019) with 8 GB RAM, processor Snapdragon 855 2.84 GHz and Android 12. On average, the application execution took about 12 s including the cow detection, the evaluation of the BSC, and the location of the 3 points on the hip of the cow.

The evaluation of the quality in use of the mobile app was performed using the ISO 25022 standard [24, 25, 26, 31] (usability characteristics) and the SUS (System Usability Scale) questionnaire [32]. La ISO 25022 provides measures, including associated measurement functions for the quality characteristics in use. The SUS model consists of 10 questions and five answers each (Likert scale) and 1–5 score depending on user satisfaction being 5 the highest (totally agree) and 1 (totally disagree).

Table 4 indicates that the app complies with the required satisfaction level, achieving 7.13%, namely, an acceptable satisfaction range.

Table 4. Mobile app satisfaction metric based on ISO 25022

Characteristic	Sub characteristic	Metric	Pondering	Measure	Valor
Satisfactory	Utility	Satisfaction	30	0,17	7,13
		Reliability	40	0,92	
		Comfortability	30	0,99	

4 Discussion

In this research, an Android mobile app is developed to determine *Bos Taurus* cattle body condition score through Deep Learning. This app helps assess cattle body condition so that the right nutritional plan is made for them to capitalize the animal's body better to benefit the livestock sector.

In this context, the Bayer company [12, 13] has a similar App, although a fee is paid. However, the difference is that this app does not use Deep Learning techniques to perform the body condition score (BCS) described in this study. Specifically, to automatically suggest to the user the 3 key points on the hip of cattle which are necessary to confirm the BCS. Likewise, authors Yukun et al. [14] designed a cow monitoring system thorough body condition estimation based on body fat thickness using ultrasound equipment, achieving an accuracy of 0.94. However, specialized equipment means higher cost, transport, and calibration services (due to vibrations), which represent drawbacks compared to this study in which a conventional portable, easy-to-install and operate the mobile device is required, although reaching a lower accuracy of 0.88. On the other hand, Song and Bokkers [16] designed an application for dairy cows' body recognition by tridimensional imaging screenshots obtaining satisfactory results but having the same drawbacks previously described related to cost, transport, equipment, and maintenance.

On the other hand, this project has some limitations like CNN training for the recognition and analysis of the rear area of the cow, which may enhance accuracy in cattle's body condition evaluation. Besides, in this project, levels 1 and 5 (skinny and obese) were not considered because the company COPREGA SA where this study was carried out does not have these types of cattle to avoid nutritional-related illnesses and a negative economic impact. Therefore, it was not possible to obtain these types of images (levels 1 and 5) to train and test the CNNs. As we mentioned before, these specific images are difficult to obtain and annotate from the Web.

5   Conclusions and Future Work

In this study, a new mobile Android app for scoring type *Bos Taurus* cattle's body condition through Deep Learning techniques is developed, enabling almost anyone who needs to perform this task using a conventional mobile device.

This application is mainly comprised of 3 CNNs: *Yolo v3* whose main task is to locate the cattle inside the image, obtaining IoU = 0.718 (Sect. 3.2). *MobileNet v2,* whose main mission is to score the cattle's body condition within range V and U, getting an accuracy of 0.88 (Table 3) and AUC = 0.92 (Fig. 8). And *VGG-16* who yields 3 key points in the cattle's hip to visually confirm (based on the given shape: U, V, L) the score previously obtained, achieving an AUC value from CED curve of 0.7688 (Fig. 9). Standard ISO/IEC 25022 evaluates mobile application quality in use through satisfaction characteristics, achieving 7,13% (Table 4).

In future work, it is suggested to increase the image dataset including 1 and 5 scores and analyze the back area of cattle for more accurate body condition scoring. Then, a comparison of the effectiveness of our proposal and the existing applications on the market (such as the Bayer App) could be desired, as well as to determine the influence of different mobile devices and their cameras on algorithm performance. The current proposal could be developed using a single lightweight CNN architecture instead of 3 considering a balance between some parameters such as precision, model size and time inference. Finally, publishing the mobile app to a public repository is also required, as well as the estimation of the BSC is performed on an external server to decrease the complexity of the model and the application.

References

1. iNaturalistEc: Ganado Vacuno Bos Taurus. https://ecuador.inaturalist.org/taxa/74113-Bos-taurus. Accessed 11 Mar 2022
2. INEC, E.: Encuesta de Superficie y Producción Agropecuaria Continua 2020 Contenido (2021)
3. Wildman, E.E., Jones, G.M., Wagner, P.E., Boman, R.L., Troutt, H.F., Lesch, T.N.: A dairy cow body condition scoring system and its relationship to selected production characteristics. J. Dairy Sci. **65**, 495–501 (1982). https://doi.org/10.3168/JDS.S0022-0302(82)82223-6
4. Chacua, B., et al.: People identification through facial recognition using deep learning. In: 2019 IEEE Lat. Am. Conf. Comput. Intell. LA-CCI 2019 (2019). https://doi.org/10.1109/LA-CCI47412.2019.9037043
5. Herrera-Granda, I.D., et al.: Artificial neural networks for bottled water demand forecasting: a small business case study. In: Lect. Notes Comput. Sci. (Including Subser. Lect. Notes Artif. Intell. Lect. Notes Bioinformatics). 11507 LNCS, pp. 362–373 (2019). https://doi.org/10.1007/978-3-030-20518-8_31
6. Pusdá-Chulde, M.R., Salazar-Fierro, F.A., Sandoval-Pillajo, L., Herrera-Granda, E.P., García-Santillán, I.D., De Giusti, A.: Image analysis based on heterogeneous architectures for precision agriculture: a systematic literature review. Adv. Intell. Syst. Comput. **1078**, 51–70 (2020). https://doi.org/10.1007/978-3-030-33614-1_4
7. Google: Flutter documentation. https://docs.flutter.dev/. Accessed 05 May 2022
8. Python Software Foundation: The Python Tutorial – Python 2.7.18 Documentation. https://docs.python.org/2.7/tutorial/index.html. Accessed 07 Feb 2022

9. Abadi, M., et al.: TensorFlow: Large-Scale Machine Learning on Heterogeneous Distributed Systems. www.tensorflow.org. Accessed 05 May 2022
10. Nain, A., Sayak, P., Maynard, R.M.: Keras.io. www.keras.io. Accessed 13 June 2022
11. Sagheb-Tehrani, M., Ghazarian, A.: Software development process : strategies for handling business rules and requirements. Comput. Eng. Dept. Softw. Eng. Notes **27**, 58–62 (2002). https://doi.org/10.1145/511152.511162
12. García Quiza, C.: Efecto de la somatotropina bovina en la producción y calidad de la leche y su influencia sobre la condición corporal e índice de mastitis (2001). https://doi.org/10.4067/S0301-732X2006000100005
13. Bayer, E.: BCS CowDition by Elanco on the App Store
14. Yukun, S., et al.: Automatic monitoring system for individual dairy cows based on a deep learning framework that provides identification via body parts and estimation of body condition score. J. Dairy Sci. **102**, 10140–10151 (2019). https://doi.org/10.3168/jds.2018-16164
15. Liu, D., He, D., Norton, T.: Automatic estimation of dairy cattle body condition score from depth image using ensemble model. Biosyst. Eng. **194**, 16–27 (2020). https://doi.org/10.1016/j.biosystemseng.2020.03.011
16. Song, X., Bokkers, E.A.M., van Mourik, S., Groot Koerkamp, P.W.G., van der Tol, P.P.J.: Automated body condition scoring of dairy cows using 3-dimensional feature extraction from multiple body regions. J. Dairy Sci. **102**(5), 4294–4308 (2019). https://doi.org/10.3168/jds.2018-15238
17. Martins, B.M., et al.: Estimating body weight, body condition score, and type traits in dairy cows using three dimensional cameras and manual body measurements. Livest. Sci. **236**, 104054 (2020). https://doi.org/10.1016/j.livsci.2020.104054
18. Russell, B.C., Torralba, A., Murphy, K.P., Freeman, W.T.: LabelMe: a database and web-based tool for image annotation. Int. J. Comput. Vis. **77**, 157–173 (2008)
19. Zhang, X., Zou, J., He, K., Sun, J.: Accelerating very deep convolutional networks for classification and detection. IEEE Trans. Pattern Anal. Mach. Intell. **38**, 1943–1955 (2016). https://doi.org/10.1109/TPAMI.2015.2502579
20. Redmon, J., Divvala, S., Girshick, R., Farhadi, A.: You only look once: Unified, real-time object detection. In: Proceedings of the IEEE Computer Society Conference on Computer Vision and Pattern Recognition, pp. 779–788. IEEE Computer Society (2016). https://doi.org/10.1109/CVPR.2016.91
21. Lin, T.-Y., et al.: Microsoft COCO: common objects in context. In: Fleet, D., Pajdla, T., Schiele, B., Tuytelaars, T. (eds.) ECCV 2014. LNCS, vol. 8693, pp. 740–755. Springer, Cham (2014). https://doi.org/10.1007/978-3-319-10602-1_48
22. Sandler, M., Howard, A., Zhu, M., Zhmoginov, A., Chen, L.C.: MobileNetV2: inverted residuals and linear bottlenecks. In: Proc. IEEE Comput. Soc. Conf. Comput. Vis. Pattern Recognit., pp. 4510–4520 (2018). https://doi.org/10.1109/CVPR.2018.00474
23. Liu, S., Deng, W.: Very deep convolutional neural network based image classification using small training sample size. In: Proc. 3rd IAPR Asian Conf. Pattern Recognition, ACPR 2015, pp. 730–734 (2016). https://doi.org/10.1109/ACPR.2015.7486599
24. Guevara-Vega, C., Hernández-Rojas, J., Botto-Tobar, M., García-Santillán, I., Basantes Andrade, A., Quiña-Mera, A.: Automation of the municipal inspection process in Ecuador applying mobile-D for android. Adv. Intell. Syst. Comput. **1066**, 155–166 (2020). https://doi.org/10.1007/978-3-030-32022-5_15
25. Juma, A., Rodríguez, J., Caraguay, J., Naranjo, M., Quiña-Mera, A., García-Santillán, I.: Integration and evaluation of social networks in virtual learning environments: a case study. Commun. Comput. Inf. Sci. **895**, 245–258 (2019). https://doi.org/10.1007/978-3-030-05532-5_18
26. ISO/IEC: ISO/IEC 25022. https://www.iso.org/standard/35746.html. Accessed 16 June 2022

27. Brooke, J.: SUS: A 'Quick and Dirty' usability scale. In: Jordan, P.W., Thomas, B., McClelland, I.L., Weerdmeester, B. (eds.) Usability Evaluation In Industry, pp. 207–212. CRC Press (1996). https://doi.org/10.1201/9781498710411-35
28. SQLite: Abour SQLite. https://www.sqlite.org/about.html. Accessed 07 Feb 2022
29. Rosebrock, A.: Intersection over Union (IoU) for object detection – PyImageSearch. https://pyimagesearch.com/2016/11/07/intersection-over-union-iou-for-object-detection/. Accessed 03 June 2022
30. Wang, W., Chen, X., Zheng, S., Li, H.: Fast head pose estimation via rotation-adaptive facial landmark detection for video edge computation. IEEE Access **8**, 45023–45032 (2020). https://doi.org/10.1109/ACCESS.2020.2977729
31. ISO 25010. https://iso25000.com/index.php/normas-iso-25000/iso-25010?start=3. Accessed 13 June 2022
32. Lewis, J., Sauro, J.: Item Benchmarks for the System Usability Scale. J. User Exp. 158–167 (2018)

Automatic Selection of Reference Lines for Spectrometer Calibration with Recurrent Neural Networks

Angel Zenteno(ID), Adriana Orellana(ID), Alex Villazón(✉)(ID),
and Omar Ormachea(ID)

Universidad Privada Boliviana (UPB), Cochabamba, Bolivia
{angelzenteno1,adrianaorellana1,avillazon,oormachea}@upb.edu

Abstract. Instrument calibration is a critical but time-consuming process in many scientific fields. In this paper, we present an approach using recurrent neural networks (RNNs) for automatically detecting reference lines required to calibrate a spectrometer with well-known wavelengths of mercury and neon spectra. RNNs are a type of neural network that is best suited for processing sequential data. We collect a dataset of spectral images by taking images with cameras of different resolutions to train the neural network. Moreover, we prove that RNNs can learn to predict spectra lines in the calibration process with high precision. We match spectrometer measurements to their corresponding wavelengths by fitting a polynomial with these predicted reference lines. We validate our method using a 3D-printed spectrometer and compare the results with the NIST Atomic Spectra Database. The automatic selection of neon or mercury reference lines helps the calibration procedure to become faster, thus avoiding any manual selection. Our proposed technique is suitable for spectrometry applications where the speed is critical and the calibration process needs to be performed frequently.

Keywords: Wavelength calibration · Spectrometer · Recurrent Neural Networks

1 Introduction

Spectrometers have a wide application in several fields such as medicine [1], analytic chemistry [2], and education [3]. They are used in research and industry to detect certain substances in food or medical samples [1,4], monitor the environment [5,6], and in education to teach optics and physics principles [3].

There is a wide variety of commercial spectrometers, but most of them are rather costly devices and require proprietary software, thus limiting their use in developing countries. In contrast, there are low-cost alternative spectrometers, that can be 3D-printed or even built with cardboard and paper [7,8]. Although these solutions are low-cost, portable, and compact, they also need specialized software to visualize spectra images [8,9]. The software is typically implemented

F. R. Narváez et al. (Eds.): SmartTech-IC 2022, CCIS 1705, pp. 106–121, 2023.
https://doi.org/10.1007/978-3-031-32213-6_8

on a smartphone or a Raspberry Pi single-board computer, and the spectral images are captured with the device's camera [10].

In all cases, spectrometers need to be calibrated to obtain accurate results of the spectra measurements. Wavelength calibration is the process of determining the wavelength of the light captured by a spectrometer. This is usually done by comparing the spectrometer's measurements to the known wavelengths of spectral lines from a calibration source such as a mercury lamp [8], LEDS [11], or a laser beam [12]. Methods to map pixels to wavelength include fitting low-order polynomials to the selected reference lines [13]. The first crucial step is to choose these known reference lines, usually done manually, to apply the calibration algorithm. Automating this selection step can offer benefits in terms of convenience, speed, and accuracy. On the one hand, for accuracy, automating can help to ensure that the reference lines are correct. On the other hand, for speed and convenience, it can be a time-saver for those who would otherwise have to perform the calibration process manually.

Recurrent neural networks (RNNs) [14] are a type of artificial neural network that is well-suited for processing sequential data. This makes them ideal for the automatic selection of reference lines. RNNs can learn to identify patterns in the data and automatically identify the reference lines for each measurement. We apply this learning algorithm to neon and mercury spectra, then use the predicted lines to calibrate our previously developed spectrometer [8], and compare the results to an atomic spectra database.

The contributions of this paper include:

- an object detection model trained to select the area of interest in the captured spectra image while being capable to differentiate between neon and mercury spectra,
- an RNN-based model that outputs the reference lines used to calibrate the spectrometer, and
- a reference implementation of the automatic selection of reference lines for the calibration integrated into a smartphone spectrometry app.

The rest of the paper is structured as follows: Section 2 shortly describes the principles of a spectrometer, our low-cost spectrometer, and the typical calibration process; Sect. 3 describes our approach using object detection and RNNs; Sect. 4 depicts the results and discusses our findings; and Sect. 5 concludes the paper.

2 Background

In this section, we shortly describe the principle of a baseline spectrometer, our 3D-printed low-cost spectrometer, and the typical calibration process.

2.1 Basic Spectrometer Principle

A spectrometer is a scientific instrument used to analyze the light properties of a luminous object, reflected or transmitted light. The instrument measures these properties of light over a specific section of the electromagnetic spectrum.

A conventional optical spectrometer is composed of the following fundamental components (see Fig. 1):

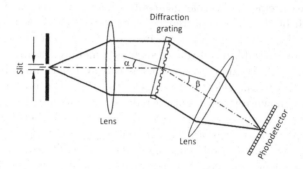

Fig. 1. Basic components of a spectrometer.

Entrance slit: The entrance slit within the spectrometer is important as it determines the amount of light that is able to enter the instrument to be measured, also the optical resolution; the smaller the slit size, the better its resolution. Light passing through a narrow opening like a slit has the natural behavior to become divergent. By transmitting the divergent beam onto a convergent lens, the light beam becomes collimating, i.e., all rays of light are directed parallel towards the diffraction grating.

Diffraction Grating: The grating is used to disperse the wavelengths of light. Properties of the grating do not only include its dispersion range but also influence the optical resolution by the number of grooves. Once the light hits the diffraction grating each wavelength of light is reflected under a different angle (similar to a prism). Different diffraction gratings can be used to identify different wavelength ranges. As also this beam is divergent because of the grating's behavior, a second convergent lens is used to focus light rays of each wavelength towards specific pixels of the photodetector.

Photodetector: The photodetector is used in spectrometers to measure the light intensity from the light source. Photodetectors have wide spectral responses from ultraviolet to visible and from visible to near-infrared.

Depending on the technology used in the spectrometer, the photosensor can be either a photodiode array (used in commercial spectrometers) or the CMOS sensor of a digital camera (used in low-cost spectrometers). In this paper, we focus on the second type of photosensor.

2.2 3D-Printed Low-Cost Spectrometer

Our 3D-printed low-cost optical device [8], is a transmission grating spectrometer. Figure 2(a) shows the 3D-printed parts that are composed of ① an input slit of approximately 200 µm; ② a sliding tube that regulates the distance between the slit and the collimation lens ③ to generate a parallel beam; and a support structure ④ to assemble all the previously mentioned parts with a diffraction grating with a period of 1000 lines/mm. The device includes a clip ⑤ that couples the spectrometer to any smartphone independently of the camera position, thus easing the mounting procedure. All these 3D-printed parts are assembled as shown in Fig. 2(b). Figure 3 shows the spectrometer attached to the smartphone running the spectrometry app with the spectral lines captured by the smartphone camera sensor.

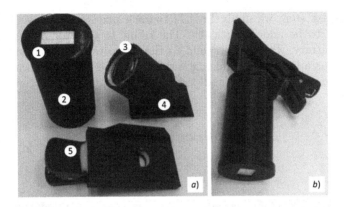

Fig. 2. The 3D-printed spectrometer: (a) the parts of the spectrometer; (b) the fully assembled spectrometer.

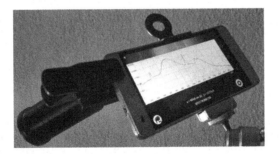

Fig. 3. The 3D-printed low-cost spectrometer attached to the smartphone running the spectrometry app.

2.3   Manual Calibration Process

To correctly collect the spectral data, the digital camera lens must be aligned with the output of the spectrometer. Once the spectrometer is correctly coupled and aligned, the camera sensor will start capturing a spectrum image. The image can be represented by a matrix of RGB (red, green, blue) pixels. These values need to be pre-processed for being represented on two axes, X to pixels position and Y to the intensity of the spectrum lines.

To accomplish this, the first step is to get the intensity of each pixel. We use the Y'UV color model, which is composed of Y' (luminance), U (blue projection), and V (red projection) [15]. The brightness (Y') is obtained from an RGB color image by giving weights to these values as shown in Eq. (1).

$$Y' = (0.257 \times R) + (0.504 \times G) + (0.098 \times B) + 16 \tag{1}$$

As the next step, we apply Eq. (1) to each pixel, and the values of each column have to be added vertically. The result is a vector of size n, whose units are arbitrary, which correspond to the intensities of the spectrum curve when shown as a line chart or histogram. Equation (2) expresses the procedure previously described, where i and j refer to the index of rows and columns, respectively.

$$intensity_j = \sum_{i=1}^{n} Y'_{i,j} \tag{2}$$

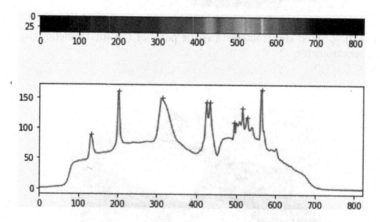

Fig. 4. On the top, is the image obtained from a fluorescent compact lamp containing mercury with the spectrometer. On the bottom, is the corresponding histogram of intensities. The X axis corresponds to the position of the pixels (i.e., not calibrated), and the Y axis is the intensity in arbitrary units.

Once the intensity vector is calculated we can display both the spectral image and the corresponding intensity as a histogram. Figure 4 shows on the top the spectrum of a light bulb lamp containing mercury, and on the bottom of the image, the corresponding intensity histogram or spectral curve. We clearly see that the X axis (representing only the pixel position in the image) does not have the correct values that must match the spectrometer wavelengths. Therefore, we require to correctly calibrate the spectrometer.

In our approach, we use the spectral lines of two different elements commonly available in different light sources: mercury or neon. We define our reference wavelengths as follows: for mercury 435.83 nm (blue line) and 546.07 nm (green line), and for neon 585.25 nm (yellow line) and 640.2 nm (red line).

Finally, the wavelength calibration procedure requires the following steps:

1. **Peaks detection:** Apply a peak detection algorithm on the intensity histogram or spectrum curve. This helps users to visualize and choose the reference lines. It is also recommended smooth the spectral curve with a Gaussian filter before peak detection.
2. **Selection of reference lines:** The user selects at least two lines (well separated and with a high intensity, i.e., peaks), which correspond to the established reference wavelengths. This step is usually done manually (e.g., by clicking or selecting the peak on a touch screen).
3. **Calibration**: We fit a first-order polynomial (*a straight line*) using the two selected reference lines to calibrate the wavelength axis. Finally, we use this slope to calibrate the wavelength axis of the entire spectrum. In Eq. (3), y_1 is the first smallest reference value and y_2 is the second reference value, whereas x_1 and x_2 are the pixels positions of the selected reference lines.

$$y = y_1 + (y_2 - y_1) \times \frac{x - x_1}{x_2 - x_1} \tag{3}$$

Once these steps are performed, the spectrometer is fully calibrated, and the correct wavelengths correspond to the pixel position on the X axis.

For example, when using mercury as the reference element for peak detection, Fig. 4 highlights with a red cross mark all the peaks detected from the spectrum. For the selection of reference lines, in our approach, we use recurrent neural networks to automate this process, so that no manual selection is needed. Finally, for the calibration, we use the corresponding reference values in Eq. (3) with $y_1 = 435.83$ and $y_2 = 546.07$. A similar process can be done for neon, with the corresponding reference lines.

3   Methodology

In this section, we describe the procedures performed to automatically calibrate the spectrometer. We extended and modified the spectrometry software used in the low-cost 3D-printed smartphone-based spectrometer from [8]. The original calibration process was fully manual, forcing the user to obtain the spectrum, choose the area of interest in the spectral image, and select the reference lines on the smartphone touchscreen. Our new implementation automates these tasks, making the calibration process more convenient.

Figure 5 shows sequentially the procedures necessary to achieve automatic calibration. First, the spectral images obtained by the spectrometer and our software are used as input for an object detection algorithm (based on convolutional neural network - CNN). In our case, this is used to detect and crop the area of interest of the spectra image. Then, this image with the detected spectrum is pre-processed and fed to a recurrent neural network (RNN) to automatically detect the spectral reference lines in it. Finally, the location, measured in pixels, of these lines is fitted to a low-order polynomial to match from pixels to wavelength. This last step is called the polynomial wavelength calibration method [16]. In the following, we describe each of these procedures in detail.

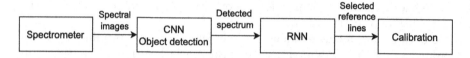

Fig. 5. Procedures performed to automatically calibrate the spectrometer.

3.1   Object Detection

Object detection is a field of computer vision for identifying objects in images. Convolutional neural networks (CNNs) are particularly effective at this task, and to train these models a dataset of images containing the objects is required. CNNs are a type of neural network especially used for image recognition and processing.

We applied object detection in two different parts of the calibration process. The first one is to detect the position of the rectangular region where the spectral image is captured, and the second one is to detect the spectrum of the element itself.

The reason for the first use of object detection is that the spectrometer we use, has a conventional collimating lens to generate a parallel beam, but this can produce curved images due to spherical aberrations. To reduce this problem, we use object detection to identify the rectangular region of the area of interest to be cropped from the captured image. Figure 6 shows the spectrum of a fluorescent lamp containing mercury, that was cropped to reduce the spherical aberration (we can observe that the image does not follow a straight line).

For the second use of object detection, we collected 90 spectral images of three different light sources: a tiny neon light bulb, a compact light bulb with mercury, and an RGB LED, in different positions. Considering that the extended spectrometry software runs on mobile devices and inference time is critical, we chose a pre-trained EfficientDet [17] object detection model to apply transfer learning with this new dataset. The main advantage is that it does not require a big dataset to achieve high performance. Figure 7 shows the resulting neon detected by EfficientDet in a spectral image, with a 91% of confidence.

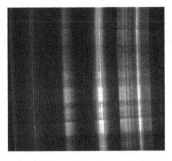

Fig. 6. Spectrum of a compact fluorescent lamp containing mercury.

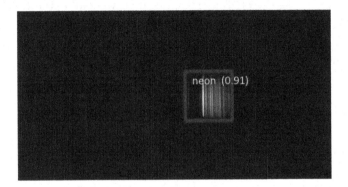

Fig. 7. Neon spectrum detected with object detection in a spectral image, with 91% of confidence.

3.2   Reference Lines Dataset Collection

To train our recurrent neural network, we collected 170 neon and mercury spectral images using smartphone cameras with different resolutions. Then, we increase the dataset size using data augmentation by applying transformations such as changes in brightness, rotation, and position. We also added noise to avoid overfitting and to increase the model's robustness. The images were also cropped to a smaller size according to the object detection model. Finally, we manually labeled two reference lines for each image, that are used for the spectrometer calibration. Figure 8 shows an example of the different variations of the images of the reference dataset (before labeling) for neon and mercury captured with the spectrometer.

A common step before feeding the neural network with the dataset is to scale the data between 0 and 1 (i.e., to normalize it). After processing the spectral image into the intensity curve and running the peak detection algorithm, we represent each peak as its pixel RGB values (ranging between 0–255) and the intensity level. To scale these features we apply Min-Max normalization as shown in Eq. (4).

Fig. 8. Variations of neon (on the left) and mercury (on the right) images captured with the spectrometer, used in the training dataset.

$$x_{scaled} = \frac{x - x_{min}}{x_{max} - x_{min}} \tag{4}$$

The input fed to the neural network is a 30×4 array of float values, where 30 are the first peaks detected in the spectral curve, and 4 (the R, G, B, and intensity values) are each peak's features.

3.3 Recurrent Neural Networks - RNNs

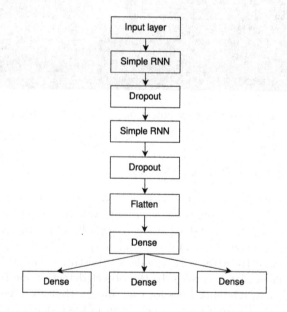

Fig. 9. Neural network architecture of the proposed RNN.

RNNs are a type of neural network that is best suited for processing sequential data, i.e., data where the order is important. In our case, the leftmost peak corresponds to smaller wavelengths, while the rightmost peak corresponds to larger wavelengths.

Figure 9 shows the model architecture, consisting of two layers of RNN, followed by a dense layer. A dropout layer is used to avoid overfitting the training data by randomly dropping out some units. The choice of hyperparameters in this architecture is discussed in more detail in Sect. 4. The output layer contains three dense layers (two for the first and second reference lines), with thirty units used to classify each of the first thirty input peaks. The activation function of this last layer is the *softmax function*, which converts the output of the dense layer into a probability distribution. To make a prediction, we choose the peak with the highest probability of being the reference peak. The third output layer is a single unit, with the *sigmoid function* as activation, which predicts the probability that the input spectra correspond to neon or mercury.

The labels are encoded as the peak index between 1 and 30, i.e. if the first reference line is the third peak, then the annotated label is 3. We use the multiclass cross-entropy function L to measure the classification loss between the real y_i and the predicted label $\hat{y}_i$ (see Eq. (5)).

$$L(y_i, \hat{y}_i) = - \sum_{i=1}^{30} y_i * log(\hat{y}_i) \tag{5}$$

4 Results and Discussion

In this section, we present and discuss the results of our experiments. This includes the performance of our proposed method and a comparison between our calibrated 3D-printed spectrometer and NIST Atomic Spectra Database.

4.1 Experiments

We trained our RNN with spectral data for both neon and mercury. The RNN was trained using Google Colab[1] free GPU for 100 epochs, achieving accuracy in the test set of 96.97% for the first reference line and 87.88% for the second line. The learning curves presented in Fig. 10 show a lower cross-entropy loss as the model improves in each epoch.

Predictions samples for both neon and mercury spectra are depicted in Figs. 11 and 12. In the compact fluorescent lamp containing mercury, the predicted blue line is 435.83 nm, whereas the green line is 546.07 nm. While in the neon sample, the yellow line is 585.25 nm and the red line is 640.20 nm. These predicted lines match the previously selected reference lines. Thus, we can proceed to the spectrometer calibration without human intervention. Note that in the plot X axis we now have wavelength measured in nanometers. We can also observe in Fig. 11 that the green line is very close to another peak. The model correctly selects the higher peak learned from the training dataset.

Tables 1 and 2 show the wavelengths measured after calibration compared to the NIST Atomic Spectra Database [18] reported lines. Note that we used a 3D-printed spectrometer without any optical filters or other hardware for the measures. For neon spectra, the root mean squared error (RMSE) was 0.3919,

---

[1] https://colab.research.google.com/.

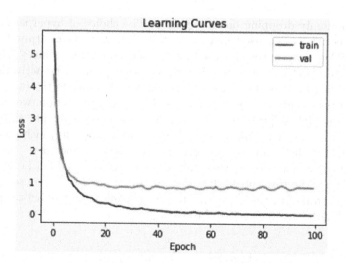

Fig. 10. Learning curve comparing training and validation loss.

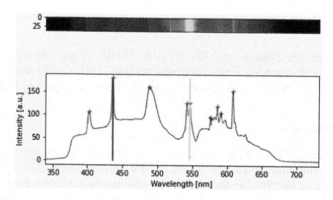

Fig. 11. Predicted mercury reference lines as blue and green lines. (Color figure online)

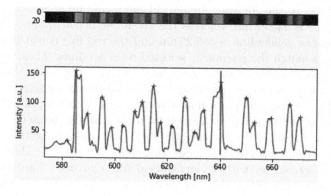

Fig. 12. Predicted neon reference lines as yellow and red lines. (Color figure online)

the mean absolute error (MAE) was 0.3010, and mean absolute percentage error (MAPE) was 0.048%. For mercury spectra, the RMSE was 0.1869, the MAE was 0.1442, and MAPE was 0.029%. This means that, on average, our measurements have an error of about 0.3 nm for neon and 0.14 nm for mercury.

Table 1. Mercury NIST spectra wavelength database compared to predicted wavelengths.

NIST reference wavelength [nm]	Predicted wavelength [nm]	Error
402.5950	402.2786	0.3164
435.8335*	435.8335*	0.0000
488.2999	488.5534	0.2535
546.0750*	546.0750*	0.0000
585.9254	585.8522	0.0732
591.8496	591.6039	0.2457
608.9794	608.8588	0.1206

*Reference line

4.2   Hyperparameter Tuning

When training a neural network, hyperparameters should be tuned to improve learning speed and final performance. These hyperparameters are the number of units for recurrent layers, dense units, the activation function, dropout probability, and the learning rate. The number of neurons in each dense layer varied from 16 to 512, activation function *tanh* and *ReLU*, and the number of recurrent layer units varied from 5 to 30. Finally, the learning rate was varied between 0.01 and 0.0001. We used random search to explore the hyperparameter space, which uses a parameter grid and a random sampling algorithm to find the best combination of parameters for this architecture. The best values for each of the parameters we found are reported in Table 3.

4.3   Discussion

The standard method for factory wavelength calibration used in commercial spectrometers is the polynomial method [16]. Smartphone-based low-cost spectrometers also apply the polynomial method [8,12,19,20], but require to be calibrated each time that the spectrometer is attached to the smartphone. Unfortunately, none of the aforementioned calibration processes, for both commercial and low-cost spectrometers, are automated.

In this work, we successfully applied object detection and RNNs to extend the polynomial method, by automatically detecting and selecting reference lines for spectrometer calibration. Our approach largely simplifies the tedious and

Table 2. Neon NIST spectra wavelength database compared to predicted wavelengths.

NIST reference wavelength [nm]	Predicted wavelength [nm]	Error
581.6622	581.9245	0.2623
585.2488*	585.2488*	0.0000
589.8329	589.5256	0.3072
594.4834	594.9098	0.4264
598.7907	598.7104	0.0804
602.9997	602.9860	0.0137
607.4338	607.5784	0.1446
609.6163	610.4288	0.8125
614.3063	614.5461	0.2398
617.2816	617.2382	0.0434
621.7281	621.5138	0.2143
626.6495	626.2646	0.3850
630.4789	630.0651	0.4138
633.4428	633.7073	0.2646
640.2248*	640.2248*	0.0000
650.6528	649.7014	0.9513
652.6030	652.8686	0.2656
659.8953	659.3612	0.5340
666.6892	666.3290	0.3602

* Reference line

Table 3. Best hyperparameters found for the calibration RNN model.

Hyperparameter	Value
Activation function	*tanh*
Recurrent layer units	20
Dense layer units	192
Learning Rate	0.001
Dropout probability	0.2

error-prone manual calibration process. We integrated the trained model into the spectrometry software for smartphone that is used with the 3D-printed spectrometer. Both the object detection algorithm and RNN model were implemented in Python using TensorFlow[2]. Once both the object detection algorithm and RNN model were validated, we integrated them into the smartphone app

---

[2] https://www.tensorflow.org/.

(implemented in Flutter[3]), using TensorFlow Lite[4]. We also successfully tested the software in a Raspberry Pi 3 micro-computer with a Pi Camera v2, obtaining similar accuracy.

One limitation that we observed when using the spectrometer, is that depending on the exposition of the smartphone camera, the RNN model may fail to correctly identify the lines (due to the camera's sensor over saturation). One possibility to reduce this effect is to limit the exposition parameter of the camera, which requires access low-level camera parameters through software. In the case of a low level of saturation, increasing the training dataset could also help.

Finally, we tested our approach in a spectrometry remote laboratory [21], i.e., an environment that requires frequent re-initialization and therefore automatic calibration of the spectrometer. Thanks to the use of the RNN model, remote users do not have to manually calibrate the spectrometer. All the calibration process is done automatically, and the spectrometry remote laboratory is ready for the next user, without any operator interacting with the device. This highly simplifies the process, avoids errors in the values obtained in the experiments, reduces the time to get the spectrometer to be ready to use, and can be available 24/7.

5   Conclusion

In this paper, we develop an approach that automates the selection of reference lines for calibrating a spectrometer using recurrent neural networks. We tested our technique and compared the obtained results with NIST Atomic Spectra Database. Our results demonstrate that we are able to accurately detect reference lines. Moreover, our technique allows users to reduce errors and save time by performing automatic calibration using different light sources (e.g., neon and mercury). We believe that our approach can be useful for different applications like real-time spectroscopy. Additionally, this method suits scenarios that demand remote control as remote laboratories or applications in which calibration is done frequently. Future work includes expanding the atomic elements to which our method can be applied and including more reference lines to the calibration, which would make the calibration process more reliable.

Acknowledgements. This work was partially funded by the Erasmus+ Project "EUBBC-Digital" (No. 618925-EPP-1-2020-1-BR-EPPKA2-CBHE-JP).

---

[3] https://flutter.dev/.
[4] https://www.tensorflow.org/lite/.

References

1. Lesani, A., et al.: Quantification of human sperm concentration using machine learning-based spectrophotometry. Comput. Biol. Med. **127**, 104061 (2020)
2. Kokilambigai, K.S., Lakshmi, K.S.: Utilization of green analytical chemistry principles for the simultaneous estimation of paracetamol, aceclofenac and thiocolchicoside by UV spectrophotometry. Green Chem. Lett. Rev. **14**(1), 99–107 (2021)
3. Noor, A.M., Norali, A.N., Zakaria, Z., Fook, C.Y., Cahyadi, B.N.: An open-source, miniature UV to NIR spectrophotometer for measuring the transmittance of liquid materials. In: Md. Zain, Z., Sulaiman, M.H., Mohamed, A.I., Bakar, M.S., Ramli, M.S. (eds.) Proceedings of the 6th International Conference on Electrical, Control and Computer Engineering. Lecture Notes in Electrical Engineering, vol. 842, pp. 407–416. Springer, Singapore (2022). https://doi.org/10.1007/978-981-16-8690-0_37
4. Tsotsou, G.E., Potiriadi, I.: A UV/Vis spectrophotometric methodology for quality control of stevia-based extracts in the food industry. Food Control **137**, 108932 (2022)
5. Zhang, Y., Zhang, T., Li, H.: Application of laser-induced breakdown spectroscopy (LIBS) in environmental monitoring. Spectrochim. Acta, Part B **181**, 106218 (2021)
6. Post, C., et al.: Application of laser-induced, deep UV Raman spectroscopy and artificial intelligence in real-time environmental monitoring-solutions and first results. Sensors **21**(11), 3911 (2021)
7. Young-Gu, J.: Fabrication of a low-cost and high-resolution papercraft smartphone spectrometer. Phys. Educ. **55**(3), 035005 (2020)
8. Ormachea, O., Villazón, A., Escalera, R.: A spectrometer based on smartphones and a low-cost kit for transmittance and absorbance measurements in real-time. Optica Pura y Aplicada **50**(3), 239–249 (2017)
9. Muñoz-Hernández, T.C., Valencia, E.G., Torres, P., Ramírez. D.L.A.: Low-Cost Spectrometer for Educational Applications using Mobile Devices. Optica Pura y Aplicada, **50**(3), 221–228 (2017)
10. McGonigle, A., et al.: Smartphone spectrometers. Sensors **18**(2), 223 (2018)
11. Wang, L.-J., Chang, Y.-C., Sun, R., Li, L.: A multichannel smartphone optical biosensor for high-throughput point-of-care diagnostics. Biosens. Bioelectron. **87**, 686–692 (2017)
12. Dutta, S., Saikia, K., Nath, P.: Smartphone based LSPR sensing platform for bioconjugation detection and quantification. RSC Adv. **6**(26), 21871–21880 (2016)
13. Liu, D., Hennelly, B.M.: Improved wavelength calibration by modeling the spectrometer. Appl. Spectrosc. **76**, 1283–1299 (2022)
14. Rumelhart, D.E., Hinton, G.E., Williams, R.J.: Learning representations by back-propagating errors. Nature **323**(6088), 533–536 (1986)
15. Podpora, M., Korba's, G., Kawala-Janik, A.: YUV vs RGB - choosing a color space for human-machine interaction. Ann. Comput. Sci. Inf. Syst. **3**(29–34), 09 (2014)
16. Liu, K., Feihong, Yu.: Accurate wavelength calibration method using system parameters for grating spectrometers. Opt. Eng. **52**(1), 013603 (2013)
17. Tan, M., Pang, R., Le, Q.V.: Efficientdet: scalable and efficient object detection. In: 2020 IEEE/CVF Conference on Computer Vision and Pattern Recognition (CVPR), pp. 10778–10787 (2020)
18. Kramida, A., and the NIST ASD Team. NIST Atomic Spectra Database (ver. 5.9). https://physics.nist.gov/asd [2022, August 12]. National Institute of Standards and Technology, Gaithersburg, MD (2021)

19. Jian, D., et al.: Sunlight based handheld smartphone spectrometer. Biosens. Bioelectron. **143**, 111632 (2019)
20. Markvart, A., Liokumovich, L., Medvedev, I., Ushakov, N.: Continuous hue-based self-calibration of a smartphone spectrometer applied to optical fiber fabry-perot sensor interrogation. Sensors **20**(21), 6304 (2020)
21. Villazon, A., Ormachea, O., Zenteno, A., Orellana, A.: A low-cost spectrometry remote laboratory. In: Auer, M.E., El-Seoud, S.A., Karam, O.H. (eds.) Artificial Intelligence and Online Engineering. REV 2022. Lecture Notes in Networks and Systems, vol. 524, pp. 198–208 Springer, Cham (2023)

Virtual Learning Environment for Children with Down Syndrome Through Leap Motion and Artificial Intelligence

René Chauca⬡, Andrea Simbaña⬡, Carmen Johanna Celi⬡, and William Montalvo$^{(\boxtimes)}$ ⬡

Universidad Politécnica Salesiana, UPS, 170146 Quito, Ecuador
{jchaucar,asimbanaa1}@est.ups.edu.ec, {cceli, wmontalvo}@ups.edu.ec

Abstract. The implementation of virtual and immersive environments has increased significantly in recent years, due to their ease of remote interaction, feedback provided, and learning acquired autonomously. This article is focused on the educational area, mainly math, for children with Down Syndrome and proposes the development of two applications as immersive environments full of visual stimuli and kinesthetic interaction, for learning and reinforcement of the basic topics required for preschool levels. The design and implementation were conducted using virtual reality (VR) tools in conjunction with the Leap Motion Controller (LMC) sensor Software Development Kit (SDK), in addition to having a supervised learning of artificial intelligence. The data for training the neural network, was obtained by creating and connecting a bidirectional local server. The neural network, was programmed using the Matlab artificial neural network toolbox, considering the local server to obtain data and feedback. The results are presented the same ones that are interesting.

Keywords: Leap Motion · Down Syndrome · Virtual Environment

1 Introduction

According to the United Nations, the estimated incidence of Down Syndrome (DS) worldwide is between 1 in 1,000 and 1 in 1,100 newborns [1]. In Ecuador, SD occurs in 1 of every 550 live births, an average much higher than the world rate of 1 of every 700 [2], that is why the need arises to improve the educational field, with the aim of achieving improvements, when children acquire knowledge. The approach that was considered is math; due to two reasons, it is an exact science, which can be easily measured in terms of results and that has foundations in the initial stages of learning. It is the subject that causes problems in later stages of learning, where the faults usually appear. The processing of visual information is a strong point in children, due to this several researchers have decided to explore the incorporation of teaching systems that make full use of visual images, to accurately represent the objectives required in the subject [3]. Fine motor skills are a latent deficiency, this stimulation is essential for the correct development and

F. R. Narváez et al. (Eds.): SmartTech-IC 2022, CCIS 1705, pp. 122–133, 2023.
https://doi.org/10.1007/978-3-031-32213-6_9

development; especially the movement of fingers and hands [4]. Currently technology and education were intertwined by the substantial number of tools that exist. Virtual environments are known for their advantages in optimizing resources and space. In the area of education, this tool is being widely used due to its accessibility, remote and autonomous use.

When talking about virtual environments, reference was made to educational spaces that are hosted within the web, software, or applications. They deal with a set of tools that facilitate learning and make up a space in which student and teacher can interact remotely [5]. In these environments, the use of TICs in education were reflected and contributes to modifying thinking strategies, thus adapting them to current needs and the needs of each student. Students have freedom and flexibility in schedules, in addition to guiding their autonomous learning and not depending solely on the role played by the teacher in the classroom [6].

Based on visual stimuli, it is necessary to develop a teaching system that makes full use of these stimuli, for which, the development of a virtual educational environment, with images and animation, would be suitable. On the other hand, the kinesthetic stimulus was immersed in the user's interaction using the Leap Motion Controller (LMC). Considering the background, this study aims to develop a Virtual Environment (VE) controlled by Leap Motion (LM) for children with DS focused on education, allowing the innovation of mathematics within the field of education. A didactic VE with stimulation, both visual and kinesthetic; it would be useful in learning, since children with DS, as they need all possible positive stimuli for greater retention of the different knowledge acquired.

2 Methodology

2.1 Design

In this study, an educational approach was proposed, developing two applications with Virtual Reality (VR) and immersive environments, controlled by LMC, which are interactive and attractive for children, where users will have access to two applications: geometric figures and numbers.

Geometric Figures the main purpose is to get the user to recognize and classify geometric figures, in addition to improving fine motor skills through interaction with LM. It was executed considering the operating scheme shown in Fig. 1 in which the user has a computer and the LM device. Once the application runs within the Unity environment, user interaction was managed by the LM SDK. Once finished, it receives a positive or negative feedback, which is programmed in C# language within the VE.

Numbers the main purpose is to get the user to perform and recognize the numbers from 1 to 10 using their hands to interact with the environment. It was executed considering the operating scheme shown in Fig. 2, in which the user has a computer and the LMC device. Once the application is started, the user interacts within Unity, however, the data obtained from the SDK is sent through a shared local server that works bidirectionally

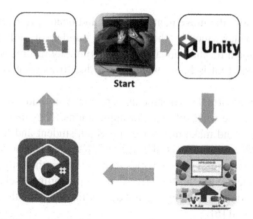

Fig. 1. Application process diagram of geometric figures.

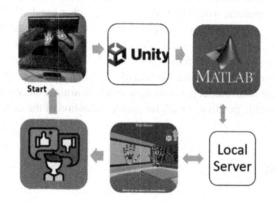

Fig. 2. Application process diagram of numbers.

with Matlab, where, thanks to the training of a neural network, they identify the numbers from 1 to 10 made by the user and show a response about their interaction.

2.2 Creating the Virtual Environment and Configuring the Leap Motion Sensor

The VE seen in Fig. 3 was developed for both applications in the Blender software, which has an .fbx export format for compatibility and opening in Unity 3D.

After the import in Unity, the connection with the LMC is configure by using the SDK, considering each application the sensor is place differently, as shown in Fig. 4.

The SDK allowed the use of three packages: Core, Interaction Engine and Hands.

Core allows to visualize and configure the LMC, mainly the hemispherical area of coverage that it has and its angle of vision.

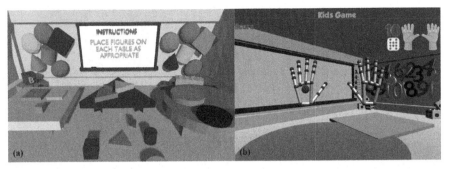

Fig. 3. (a) Geometric figures application virtual environment (b) Numbers application virtual environment.

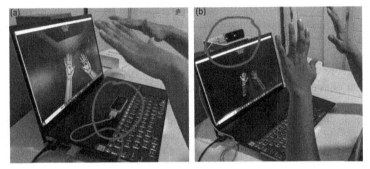

Fig. 4. (a) Leap Motion Sensor location in geometric figures app (b) Leap Motion Sensor location in numbers app.

Interaction Engine allows the configuration of the objects in the environment, considering that they have collision in all their walls, have gravity and interact according to the characteristics they have.

Hands allows you to configure the properties of the sensor, such as: scale, position, graphics, interaction properties, in addition to the VE and physical.

2.3 Visual Feedback

The feedback was elaborated, using the Unity script with the C# programming language. A script was configured for each table, which identifies each figure and produces a color change on the table. As seen in Fig. 5, when an object of the same figure was placed, the table changes its color to green which corresponds to positive feedback; whereas, if the object has a different shape, the table turns red showing negative feedback.

Feedback was done visually, considering that thanks to neural predictive mechanisms, visual stimuli are better captured and assimilated by children.

Fig. 5. Figure app feedback.

2.4 Data Acquisition and Processing

The sensor data processing was done for the application of numbers, since artificial intelligence was integrated to identify the numbers from 1 to 10. As an input, the signal provided by the position and orientation of the fingers of the user's hand was considered; considering the phalanges of the fingers and the angle they form. Through a graphic environment in Unity visualized in Fig. 6, the movements of the hands were detected, keeping a data record and a graph of the signal obtained by the sensor.

The data obtained from each record made in the training is saved in a local host, which saves an array with forty-two data for each number that you want to identify. Each value depends on the number that is being made, from 1 to 5 only one hand is used, for which twenty-one data have a value of zero and twenty-one data have varied values, from number 6 to 10, 2 hands are used, for which the forty-two data have different values.

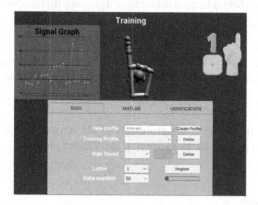

Fig. 6. Training environment.

2.5 Neural Network

The neural network is performed in Matlab, taking into account the following aspects:

Reading of the Database with the Values of the Matrix and Neuron Training

Through the use of Matlab and XAMPP, a connection bridge between the database and the Matlab environment is configured, using database explorer, within the DNS of the system, the data acquired in the training is read. Using a pass instead of TCPI/IP communication allows data to be editable and manageable without quantity restriction. Editing the values within the training data allows you to delete, replace or correct data that is far from the most representative.

When training the neural network, a Multilayer Perceptron (MLP) was used, which is configured with an input of forty-two rows ten columns, one hidden layer with ten neurons and ten outputs. The training of the neuron was done through the training of nntool, in Matlab.

Real-Time Reading of the Values Obtained from the Sensor and Detection

For real-time detection, two previous steps carried out bidirectionally, sample acquisition and network training, are considered for each number. After these steps, we proceed to the detection of numbers, through the training environment, using the same data acquisition configurations. Once the training environment correctly detects the desired values, the verification was conducted in real time together with the application and a response is sent, as shown in Fig. 7.

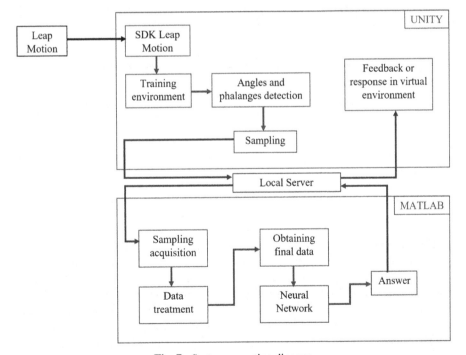

Fig. 7. System operation diagram.

3   Results

3.1   Leap Motion Recognition

For the location of the sensor in the environment, the type of interaction that was required is considered, in the case of the first application, a proper and ideal operation is achieved by placing it on a flat surface since the user interacts dynamically. On the other hand, the second application was placed in front of the computer, to ensure that they learn the gestures of numbers correctly and have better direct vision by the user.

The detections obtained after the distance tests were shown in Table 1, verifying that the sensor has an optimal detection in the range of ±10 cm of distance in all its coordinates, for an ideal detection.

Table 1. Coordinate axis for detection.

Distance	X (Y = 0, Z = 0)	Y (X = 0, Z = 0)	Z (X = 0, Y = 0)
−20 cm	No detected	Detected	No detected
−15 cm	No detected	Detected	No detected
−10 cm	Detected	Detected	Detected
−5 cm	Detected	Detected	Detected
0 cm	Detected	Detected	Detected
5 cm	Detected	Detected	Detected
10 cm	Detected	Detected	Detected
15 cm	No detected	Detected	No detected
20 cm	No detected	Detected	No detected

3.2   Obtaining Signals

Using the training in Matlab, the values of the signals were obtained graphically, as shown in Fig. 8, where 100 signals, obtained after tracking numbers one and six are plotted. The graph allows you to manage and observe the data in a better way, compared to a table that shows 4200 data at the same time, for each number.

In taking of each sample, different values are generated, so by superimposing all the signals, we can observe the trend of the graph, when each number is realize. The signal is blue in certain sections, because the samples obtained were mostly the same; on the other hand, the side where various signal colors are seen, the samples varied more and were less accurate. However, this does not affect training as each signal is within the required range.

After identification, data processing is an essential part when obtaining good results, since it allows eliminating or replacing those that contained errors or were completely out of range. This with the objective of improving the input values to the perceptron and achieving a correct training for the correct and real-time identification of each number.

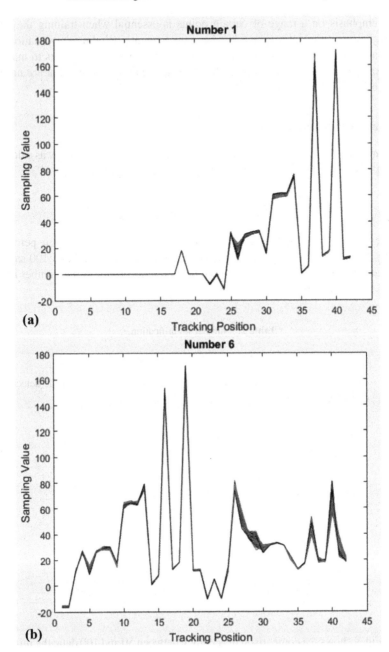

Fig. 8. (a) Data obtained graphically from the number one (b) Data obtained graphically from the number six.

The emphasis on a range of certain points is essential when training the neural network, however, the entire signal is taken into account, including the variations that it may have outside the range of interest. Since it is impossible for users to make the signal exactly the same all the time and variations are always found that are not very significant.

3.3 Number Recognition

The accuracy at the time of identifying the different numbers in real time was calculated using Eq. (1).

$$Acurracy = \frac{Correctly\ identified\ positions}{Number\ of\ identified\ positions} * 100\% \tag{1}$$

Table 2 shows the number of correct detections by number and their percentage applying the equation. The values obtained were separated from 50 and 100 samples, to compare the difference that exists in the detection according to the number of data obtained in the training.

Table 2. Number identification.

Number	50 data		50 data	
	Successful detections	Percentage detected	Successful detections	Percentage detected
1	22/30	73%	23/30	77%
2	20/30	67%	25/30	83%
3	21/30	70%	25/30	83%
4	20/30	67%	26/30	87%
5	17/30	57%	27/30	90%
6	21/30	70%	28/30	93%
7	19/30	63%	23/30	77%
8	15/30	50%	28/30	93%
9	20/30	67%	24/30	80%
10	19/30	63%	26/30	87%

The Fig. 9 shows the comparison in accuracy between 50 and 100 data; the minimum precision value with fifty data was 50% and the maximum value 73%, considering an unacceptable range within learning, since not all numbers were correctly identified in each test. However, for one hundred data, the minimum value is 77% and the maximum value is 93%, considering an acceptable learning range, since most of the numbers are identified correctly in each test.

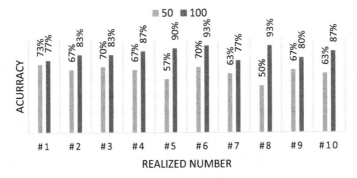

Fig. 9. Data obtained graphically from number one and six.

Comparing both ranges, it is observed that the maximum precision value with 50 samples is only 4% less than the minimum value with 100 samples. The lowest percentages were obtained due to the variation of the data in the points that are not of interest, due to this, despite being a low percentage, real-time identification is successful most of the time.

3.4 Final Results

Table 3 shows the results after 10 detections carried out on 5 children with and without DS, the age range of the children is 5–7 years, of which 3 were girls and 2 boys. The tests were limited, due to the difficult access to work with children with down syndrome. It was found that within the figure environment there is 86% correct detection in both cases; on the other hand, in the environment of numbers, children with DS have 78% correct detections and children without DS have 84%. The difference that exists in the number environment is due to the speed with which each child made the signal, but not to the attention paid during the interaction with the environment.

Table 3. Tests in children.

Number	3D figure environment		3D number environment	
	Down Syndrome Kids	Non-Down Syndrome Kids	Down Syndrome Kids	Non-Down Syndrome Kids
	Successful detections	Successful detections	Successful detections	Successful detections
1	9/10	9/10	8/10	9/10
2	8/10	10/10	7/10	10/10
3	9/10	9/10	8/10	8/10
4	9/10	7/10	7/10	7/10
5	8/10	8/10	9/10	8/10

4 Discussion

According to [7], learning through games is a promising field in the future of education, therefore it proposes an application focused on mental calculation with ten levels of difficulty that allows students to interact with the environment to find the response to a random operation. Although the focus is speed, many times the player becomes frustrated because they are under time pressure and do not understand correctly how to control the game. Similarly, [8] proposes a tool for experimentation and learning, focused on two areas, robotics, and dentistry. In the field of robotics, the movement of the robot is mainly carried out with the palms, so the detected movements are more abrupt compared to the use of the fingers, causing unwanted control in the robot. Within dentistry, an application was presented that simulates the creation of prostheses, however, the lack of haptics (science of transferring realistic sensations through touch) prevents the feedback that the user needs. In this work, the main focus is to achieve learning, which is why there is no time limit, allowing the user freedom of control, without the sense of competition that time trials generally cause. On the other hand, when detecting the numbers, the main characteristics that were considered are the fingers and the angle formed between them, since they do not vary drastically when the hand is moved. In addition, the feedback is visual in both cases, so the user does not require sensory stimuli to know if he is getting the results he wants.

5 Conclusions

The development of educational applications in immersive virtual environments allows a better way of learning and revision, optimizing resources and implementing various forms of learning at the same time. In turn, if these environments were supported by state-of-the-art technological resources such as the LMC sensor for their interaction, it is possible to maximize the results when capturing the user's attention and achieving a high concentration index.

The applications were developed, considering visual learning (shapes, figures, colors) and kinesthetic learning (experiences, sensations, movements), since they are a fundamental part of long-term memory. Allowing children with Down Syndrome deeper learning and better retention of information.

By using the Leap Motion Controller sensor, the motor development required by preschool children was considered, so they learn beyond the necessary mathematical foundations corresponding to their age. A great advantage of the Leap Motion Controller sensor is the null use of a keyboard or mouse, since in most cases, since they are preschool children, they still do not know how to use them, and they need help from an adult, which can interfere with correct learning. It was highlighted that, using these tools, learning can evolve and improve exponentially, especially if more electronic elements are added, such as virtual reality glasses or Kinect devices. Unity software offers endless possibilities for both virtual reality and augmented reality environments, creating immersive environments for users.

The information obtained through the training interface was transferred bidirectionally between the database, the graphical interface, and the artificial intelligence, using a local server. The procedure allows training the neural network, acquiring results and achieving detection in real time, always considering the connection and communication between all environments. The results obtained from the detection accuracy (Fig. 10), show that the reliability of the system is high with a greater number of analyzed values, since, when analyzing fifty values, a difference of 20% is obtained compared to when analyzing fifty values one hundred.

It was decided to use one hundred samples, because the application is mainly aimed at children, and they cannot always sign in the same way and in a specific range. The specific advantages with children are based on autonomous learning, which allows them to develop their own skills while playing. The memorization and practice of mathematical concepts necessary as foundations for future development. In addition, motor skills are practiced which provide a plus to their development.

References

1. U. Nations: Día Mundial del Síndrome de Down. 21 de marzo 2019. https://www.un.org/es/observances/down-syndrome-day. Accessed 14 Nov 2021
2. Proaño, K.: La tasa de Síndrome de Down en Ecuador es mayor que el promedio mundial. 21 de marzo 2019. https://www.edicionmedica.ec/secciones/salud-publica/la-tasa-de-sindrome-de-down-en-ecuador-es-mayor-que-el-promedio-mundial-93840. Accessed 12 Sep 2021
3. Trujillo, J.M., Fernández, C.R., Rodríguez, C.: The relevance of physical education to working the social skills of Down syndrome children in the second stage of infantile education. Educ. Sport Health Phys. Activity **3**(3), 384–400 (2019)
4. Toasa Cobo, J.E.: La importancia de la estimulación temprana en el desarrollo psicomotriz de los niños de 0 a 5 años que acuden a la consulta pediátrica en el hospital general Puyo. Universidad Técnica de Ambato (2015)
5. Belloch, C.: Las Tecnologías de la Información y Comunicación en el Aprendizaje. Departamento de Métodos de Investigación y Diagnostico en Educación (2012)
6. Hisham, B., Hamouda, A.: Arabic Sign Language Recognition using Microsoft Kinect and Leap Motion Controller. SSRN Electron. J. (2019)
7. Ebner, M., Spot, M.: Game-based learning with the leap motion controller. In: Handbook of Research on Gaming Trends, vol. 12, pp. 555–565 (2015)
8. Păvăloiu, I.-B.: Leap motion technology in learning. In: The European Proceedings of Social and Behavioural Sciences, Edu World, 7th International Conference (2017)

Building a Knowledge Graph
from Historical Newspapers: A Study
Case in Ecuador

Victor Saquicela[1]([envelope]) [ORCID], Luis M. Vilches-Blázquez[2] [ORCID], and Mauricio Espinoza[2] [ORCID]

[1] Department of Computer Science, University of Cuenca, Cuenca, Ecuador
victor.saquicela@ucuenca.edu.ec
[2] Centro de Investigación en Computación, Instituto Politécnico Nacional, Mexico City, Mexico
lmvilches@cic.ipn.mx, mauricio.espinoza@ucuenca.edu.ec

Abstract. History shows that different events occur every day in the world. In the past, knowledge of these events could only be orally transmitted from generation to generation due to a lack of appropriate technology. Currently, vast amounts of valuable historical information rests in deteriorated historical newspapers, which result very difficult to deal with. In this work, we use text digitization, text mining, and Semantic Web technologies to generate a knowledge graph comprising events occurred in Ecuador in the XIX-XX centuries.

Keywords: Historical newspapers · Meteorological events · Text mining · Knowledge graph

1 Introduction

Libraries have traditionally worked on making information resources available to the public. However, the way such information is being published, as well as how access to it is provided has changed in the current digital scenario. Nowadays, the ubiquity of the Web has made it possible to deliver electronically enormous amounts of resources to readers [1]. Therefore, digital resource collections are more easily reachable since digital libraries may be accessed over the Internet [3]. Among these collections, it is increasingly common to find digital versions of historical newspapers. These resources can provide valuable information on how environmental, administrative, economic, and social phenomena evolved, perceived, and spread across different countries [4,6] and plays an increasingly important role in collecting vast amounts of *hidden* data.

According to [4], newspapers are among the most valuable sources for scholars interested in researching about public opinion and how it has been shaped over time. Nevertheless, working with historical newspapers entail many technical challenges due to the distinctive characteristics of these information resources, which has complicated the application of text processing and layout recognition technologies for a long time.

F. R. Narváez et al. (Eds.): SmartTech-IC 2022, CCIS 1705, pp. 134–145, 2023.
https://doi.org/10.1007/978-3-031-32213-6_10

From a technical point of view, newspapers can be seen as very complex documents intended to keep readers up to date on the matters they report [2]. In this sense, using digital newspaper collections in research is relatively a novelty. However, some of the problems and possibilities connected to these information resources are quite old [5] and digitized collections present some issues [9]. Optical Character Recognition (OCR) errors, conservation quality, newspaper structure, and lack of complete collections remain among the main problems. A detailed review of existing issues in historical Latin-American newspapers is described in [30].

This current scenario brings suggests the necessity of a re-orientation of the library perspective on information interoperability which would facilitate the access to this content on the Web, carry out more complex queries, and connect existing resources with external data sources. Following this line of work, Semantic Web technologies have been increasingly utilized to address some issues found in libraries [3,10]. More recently, knowledge graphs have appeared as an extension of Semantic Web practices and been embraced by diverse companies such as Google, IBM, Facebook and Microsoft [29]. Moreover, knowledge graphs promote the creation, reuse, and recovery of human and machine-readable structured data about real-world objects using a graph-based representation [7].

The main contribution of this ongoing work focuses on extracting information from historical newspapers and describing them using semantic technologies to generate a knowledge graph with historical meteorological events that happened during the XIX-XX centuries in Ecuador.

The remainder of this paper is organized as follows: First, we present in Sect. 2 the motivation for this research. Section 3 provides some related work. Section 4 describes the implemented process, which is described and analyzed in detail. Finally, we include some conclusions and future work.

2   Related Work

The interest in meteorological events dates back to the beginning of Humanity. The efforts to understand and predict such events date back to the earliest times of those who have written witnesses testimonies [13]. In this sense, the digital preservation of the archives of antique newspapers pursue the salvation of information in peril of extinction and the creation of digital databases that enable knowledge extraction for decision-making through the use of current technologies [12].

Several research papers have addressed problems related to the processing of data from physical documents, particularly newspapers [12,14,15], and [16]. In [5], an OCR-based approach that allows the detection of newspaper columns and blocks of text is described. This approach shows good results though it does not consider the difficulties inherent in old newspapers (bias, deformations, etc.). Authors of [12], [?,?], presented different ways to approach problems such as processing historical newspapers, obtaining the identification of segments of the pages as title, texts, and images coming from several sources through the use of diverse techniques combined with OCR.

An approach to rescue and digitize data over a specific city regarding meteorological information, is presented in [17]. This work utilizes pressure data recorded on paper from 1864 to analyze the city's climate, improve decision-making, recommendations, research, data quality, etc. Moreover, the author describes the importance of current technologies for recovering, processing, and exploiting this type of information.

Hulme [18] analyzes meteorological data from the early twentieth century of the county of Norfolk-England. The author considered different historical events mainly focusing on heat waves. The collected information is analyzed using data mining techniques to achieve a different story compared with other entities described previously, providing accurate and truthful information about those events. Other works such as [19,20] and [21] also present interesting approaches based on the analysis of old newspapers data related to meteorological events, whose main objective is to perform the creation of databases to decision-making related to the weather.

As it is described in [22], it is important to implement integration processes and publish data in open formats of the web, allowing information to be reusable and interoperable for the community. In [23–25], different approaches are presented on processes of transformation of meteorological data to RDF[1] formats aiming to create free repositories and standardized access for Web users. However, to the best of our knowledge, existing works have not addressed events digitization, knowledge extraction, and knowledge graph generation from historical newspapers to illustrate the ancient meteorological phenomena in Ecuador.

3   Issues in Our Historical Newspaper Corpus

In this work, we deal with historical newspapers belonging to the National digital newspapers and periodical libraries in Ecuador, called *Casa de la Cultura Ecuatoriana*[2], which can be read in English as *Home of Ecuadorian culture*. This organization has a collection of 15,679 records associated with antique newspapers, each one having an image of the newspapers in PDF format and corresponding associated metadata. These information resources are available on a public website[3].

We chose two historical newspapers *El Tiempo* from Guayaquil and *El Comercio* from Quito, dating between 1860 and 1920. These newspapers present some specific characteristics. On the one hand, some digitized historical newspapers do not have a structure or sections. Therefore, news appear without titles; in the best cases, diverse news are separated from others using hyphens. On the other hand, newspaper collections are often incomplete and present relevant conservation problems due to poor preservation conditions and related to characteristics of the printing material used back in the days. Moreover, the digitization of these

---

[1] https://www.w3.org/RDF.

[2] http://repositorio.casadelacultura.gob.ec//.

[3] http://repositorio.casadelacultura.gob.ec/community-list.

historical newspapers has different quality issues associated with the aforementioned conservation problems, lack of awareness, and human and technological resources. These issues entail that historical newspapers are digitized as images, and when an OCR software is used, the output displays noise.

In addition, newspapers report information generated at the local, national, and international levels. Therefore, searching for information related only to Ecuador becomes a challenging research problem.

We envision that different processes of analysis and detection of information can be carried out on our newspaper corpus. In this sense, we are currently working to discover and characterize meteorological events that occurred in past centuries. Thus, we search for information related to words, organizations, dates, or locations related to the meteorological events in specific dates of interest.

4   Building a Knowledge Graph from Historical Newspapers

Taking into account the aforementioned challenges in our newspaper corpus, it is clear that a change in the National digital newspaper and periodical libraries practices on information interoperability is **necessary**. In this sense, we have considered the recent progress in knowledge graphs and text mining. Thereby, we work with digitized historical newspapers, which are automatically manipulated in order to be ready for further processing. Afterward, we process news content to generate and publish a knowledge graph of news related to meteorological events.

This section presents an overview of the approach we propose to build a knowledge graph from historical newspapers. We employ an example as a basis to explain the whole process using a specific newspaper of *EL GRITO DEL PUEBLO: Diario radical de la mañana*. A description of the system architecture is shown in Fig. 1.

4.1   Data Extraction and Storage

As we mentioned before, historical newspapers are available in a digital repository. Thus, we implement a process to extract the metadata content of each historical newspaper record using the OAI-PMH[4] protocol. It is important to note that the newspapers' PDF files cannot be downloaded using the OAI-PMH protocol. Thus, records extraction is followed by a scrapping process aimed to obtain the URL of the PDF files to download the newspapers. Each PDF file represents an a newspaper issue comprising several pages.

Next, each record's data is stored in a temporary database, and the downloaded PDFs are stored in a directory. In addition, each PDF is assigned a name that links it to the metadata extracted from each record. We found that the extraction process is delayed due to the different sizes of the PDFs, moreover

---

[4] https://www.openarchives.org/pmh/.

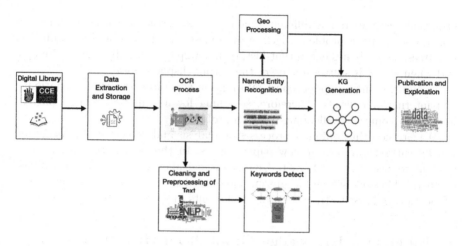

Fig. 1. An overview of the developed approach for handling historical newspapers.

and due to security issues in the extraction process through scraping, we faced a blocking caused by the high number of requests made from the same IP address to the server where historical newspapers are stored.

As a result of the process describe above, 15,670 records out of 15,679 were retrieved automatically. Subsequently, the scrapping process is executed to obtain the PDF files.

4.2 OCR Process

OCR transforms a two-dimensional image of text that can contains machine-printed or handwritten text from its image representation into machine-readable text. OCR tools such as [26] have shown to be effective in the recognition processes within the images. OCR software processes the images to find some events, entities, and more elements.

In our experiment, we used Tesseract[5] as our preferred OCR tool, an open-source engine developed by Hewlett-Packard [27]. We discovered that Tesseract presented some issues, such as confusion interpreting columns in the images, problems recognizing punctuation marks, extremely high processing time, and simply, incorrect results. In spite of these issues, Tesseract was chosen based on the scientific community's reviews of the most used libraries in the open-source world.

To process the downloaded files in PDF format, it is necessary to transform each of these files into an image, which is processed by the OCR algorithm. Each PDF has multiple pages in this case, so the image conversion process is performed on all downloaded files and for each page. Also, we followed the recommendation from different research works and existing libraries that suggests that

---

[5] https://github.com/tesseract-ocr/.

it is convenient to carry out image processing aimed to improve images quality before running the OCR algorithm[6]. As a result of processing each image with the Tesseract library, a text is obtained for each image.

4.3   Cleaning and Pre-processing

Texts extracted from historical newspapers have a form that can be understood and manipulated by computers. Pre-processing is a term used for our different activities to get our documents ready to be analyzed. We may only use a few pre-processing techniques or decide to use a wide array, depending on our documents, the kind of text available, and analyses to be performed. In this case, we used pre-processing methods to transform original texts into lowercase letters, remove punctuation, numbers, stop words, and strip white-space steps.

Results are shown to be better when entity detection is executed directly on each extracted text rather than when this phase is carried out in advance. We will analyze this problem and perform experiments more deeply in the near future.

4.4   Named Entity Recognition

Named Entity Recognition (NER) corresponds to the problem of locating and categorizing relevant nouns and proper nouns in a text. For example, identifying names of persons, organizations, and locations are typically important [28] in news stories.

As we previously mentioned, the OCR process generates a text for each image. Therefore, the entity detection process is applied to each text, and the Entity package[7] in R language is used. This corresponds to a wrapper for Natural Language Processing (NLP) and Apache openNLP that facilitates the extraction of named entities. All detected entities are then related to each record retrieved from the digital library and stored in a database for further processing.

It is necessary to indicate that since text is not structured, prior to the application of an NLP algorithm, the text is represented in the form of a vector space for its subsequent treatment. However, the software package we use performs all text preprocessing before applying the entity detection algorithm.

As a result of the entity detection process in the example we have considered in this ongoing work, we obtained examples of person entities (proper names), such as "Calixto Garcia," "Luis Quirola," "Medardo Alfaro," "Captain Domingo," etc. In the case of organization entities, we collected several entities, such as "Diario Radical de la Mañana," "Cable Teen LSE," "OFIDA," "República," "SE Linea Ferrea," etc. Regarding localization entities, we discovered some cases, such as "Madrid," "Buenos Aires," "Argentina," "Ecuador," "Chile," "Santiago," "Las Peñas," etc. Finally, some dates were also identified, retrieving "1896," "1881," "1893," etc. As it can be seen, the obtained results

---

[6] https://tesseract-ocr.github.io/tessdoc/ImproveQuality.html.

[7] https://github.com/trinker/entity.

are promising and will be used for different information extraction processes in the future.

4.5   Geospatial Processing

As part of this workflow, next we proceed with the geolocation of places retrieved through the entity recognition process. The geolocation process is carried out using the Google API[8]. This enrichment process allows improving original location entities by adding accurate information related to latitude and longitude. This step facilitates displaying meteorological events discovered in our newspaper corpus on a digital map and contributes to identify relationships with the newspapers in which the entity is found for subsequent processing.

4.6   Keywords Detection

Recognition is based on a set of meteorological keywords considered in [31]. In that previous work, different keywords are considered regarding the mentioned domain, such as rain, drought, weather epidemics, landslides, winter, sewers, overflows, tremors, or earthquakes. These keywords are the input parameters of the tools.

Keywords are searched in the texts previously obtained through the OCR process, in this case and as an example, words related to meteorological events were used: rain, winter, winter, rivers, frosts, droughts, storms, floods, storms, floods, earthquake temperature, heat, tremor, landslide, downpour, summer, cold, or lightning (in Spanish: *lluvias, invierno, ríos, heladas, sequías, temporal, crecientes, tempestad, inundaciones, temperatura sismo, calor, temblor, derrumbe, aguacero, verano, frío, or rayos.*).

As a result of the word detection process in the texts from the scanned newspaper shown in Fig. 2, the simple search process, that is, total word matching, several words were found by our algorithm. The specific case of page 2 shown in Fig. 2 detected the words: *invierno, temperatura, temblor, aguacero, and relámpago*, corresponding to winter, temperature, earthquake, downpour and thunder. It is essential to note that finding words does not necessarily imply that they correspond to meteorological events in Ecuador since the words can refer to other topics and places outside Ecuadorian territory. In this case, it is only shown as an example of the process carried out. As we point out in the future work section, it is intended to add a new stage to our approach where context is taken into account to precise whether what has been retrieved is effectively what we are looking for.

4.7   Knowledge Graph Generation

The knowledge graph generation [8] involves the process of extracting information from different data sources, analysis of domain entities and online rep-

---

[8] https://developers.google.com/maps/documentation/geocoding.

Fig. 2. An example of an Ecuadorian historical newspaper

resentations, the definition of a vocabulary based on restricting and extending semantic vocabularies, domain specifications and mapping to the semantic vocabularies, annotation development and deployment, evaluation and analysis of the annotation.

Data analysis provided us an idea of the vocabulary used in the newspaper and the resources we need to develop the knowledge graph for this work.

To this end, we searched for existing ontologies available at the Linked Open Vocabularies[9] (LOV).

Considering the information collected from newspapers (keywords, metadata, entities, etc.), we decided to reuse the following vocabularies: FOAF[10] to annotate the entities of people; The Organization Ontology[11] to note the organizations; Time Ontology[12] in OWL to record the dates, and Geonames Ontology[13] to record the locations found.

Once we developed our semantic vocabulary, we performed a manual process to establish the mappings between the data extracted from newspapers and the concepts of the selected ontologies. Afterward, the knowledge graph was created automatically using the LOD-GF tool [11]. The generated graph is then stored in a semantic database on which queries can be executed to recover historical events and related information.

4.8   Explotation

The generated knowledge graph needs to be exploited to ensure that the performed process is helpful. In this sense, we deployed a web-based application to visualize the spatial distribution of the collected meteorological events (see Fig. 3). We can execute several queries to validate our approach and show events of diverse types.

5   Conclusions and Future Work

There is valuable information on meteorological events found in vintage newspapers. Processing of such information will definitely contribute to reconstruct meteorological history of any country and support future decision-making and severe weather prevention policy.

During the generation process, we concluded that the best way to extract data from a digital repository is through the standard OAI-PMH protocol and scrapping techniques.

One of the steps remaining to be implemented is to exploit the information obtained, primarily through the date field, since this allows comparing events occurred in the past with those in present time, and to be analyzed over time.

Knowledge graph generation of the historical newspaper from a digital repository opens up new possibilities for students and researchers by facilitating the visibility and access to digital newspaper material as well as by easing information discovery based on the relationships between digital content, contributors, topics, and other entities of interest for the user.

---

[9] http://lov.okfn.org/dataset/lov/details/vocabularySpaceLibrary.html.
[10] http://xmlns.com/foaf/0.1/.
[11] https://www.w3.org/TR/vocab-org/.
[12] https://www.w3.org/TR/owl-time/.
[13] http://www.geonames.org/ontology/documentation.html.

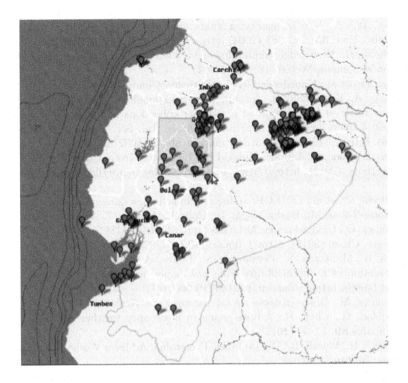

Fig. 3. Entities found

Also, it is intended to analyze the possibility of using the context of the text that allows one to better identify the events, for this, the use of thesauri or ontologies related to the subject becomes of the utmost importance and must be taken into account.

References

1. Golovchinsky, G., Chignell, M.: The newspaper as an information exploration metaphor. Inf. Process. Manag. **33**, 663–683 (1997). https://www.sciencedirect.com/science/article/pii/S0306457397000241. Electronic News
2. Cabo, M., Llavori, R.: An approach to a digital library of newspapers. Inf. Process. Manag. **33**, 645–661 (1997). https://www.sciencedirect.com/science/article/pii/S030645739700023X. Electronic News
3. Hallo, M., Lujan-Mora, S., Mate, A., Trujillo, J.: Current state of linked data in digital libraries. J. Inf. Sci. **42**, 117–127 (2016)
4. Neudecker, C., Antonacopoulos, A.: Making Europe's historical newspapers searchable. In: 2016 12th IAPR Workshop On Document Analysis Systems (DAS), pp. 405–410 (2016)
5. Wijfjes, H.: Digital humanities and historical newspaper research. Tijdschrift Voor Mediageschiedenis **20**, 4–24 (2017)

6. Gesler, W.: A place in history: a guide to using GIS in historical research. J. Interdisc. Hist. **35**, 283–283 (2004). https://doi.org/10.1162/0022195041742436

7. Paulheim, H.: Knowledge graph refinement: a survey of approaches and evaluation methods. Semant. Web **8**, 489–508 (2017)

8. Fensel, D., et al.: Knowledge Graphs. Springer, Cham (2020)

9. Järvelin, A., Keskustalo, H., Sormunen, E., Saastamoinen, M., Kettunen, K.: Information retrieval from historical newspaper collections in highly inflectional languages: a query expansion approach. J. Assoc. Inf. Sci. Technol. **67**, 2928–2946 (2016). https://onlinelibrary.wiley.com/doi/abs/10.1002/asi.23379

10. Baker, T., Isaac, A.: Library Linked Data Incubator Group Charter. W3C Incubator Activity (2011). https://www.w3.org/2005/Incubator/lld/charter. Electronic News

11. Saquicela, V., et al.: LOD-GF: an integral linked open data generation framework. In: Botto-Tobar, M., Barba-Maggi, L., González-Huerta, J., Villacrés-Cevallos, P., S. Gómez, O., Uvidia-Fassler, M.I. (eds.) TICEC 2018. AISC, vol. 884, pp. 283–300. Springer, Cham (2019). https://doi.org/10.1007/978-3-030-02828-2_21

12. Gatos, B., Mantzaris, S., Perantonis, S., Tsigris, A.: Automatic page analysis for the creation of a digital library from newspaper archives. Int. J. Digit. Libr. **3**, 77–84 (2000). https://doi.org/10.1007/PL00021477

13. Palomares, M.: Breve Historia De La Meteorologia. Aemet

14. Rundblad, G., Chen, H.: Advice-giving in newspaper weather commentaries. J. Pragmatics **89**, 14–30 (2015)

15. Gonzalez, R., Woods, R.: Digital Image Processing. Addison-Wesley Longman Publishing, Boston (1992)

16. Hebert, D., Palfray, T., Nicolas, S., Tranouez, P., Paquet, T.: Automatic article extraction in old newspapers digitized collections. In: Proceedings Of The First International Conference On Digital Access To Textual Cultural Heritage, pp. 3–8 (2014)

17. Le Blancq, F.: Rescuing old meteorological data. Weather **65**, 277–280 (2010)

18. Hulme, M.: Telling a different tale: literary, historical and meteorological readings of a Norfolk heatwave. Clim. Change **113**, 5–21 (2012)

19. Garnier, E., Ciavola, P., Spencer, T., Ferreira, O., Armaroli, C., McIvor, A.: Historical analysis of storm events: case studies in France, England, Portugal and Italy. Coast. Eng. **134**, 10–23 (2018)

20. Corella, J., Benito, G., Rodriguez-Lloveras, X., Brauer, A., Valero-Garcés, B.: Annually-resolved lake record of extreme hydro-meteorological events since AD 1347 in NE Iberian Peninsula. Quat. Sci. Rev. **93**, 77–90 (2014)

21. Boussalis, C., Coan, T., Poberezhskaya, M.: Measuring and modeling Russian newspaper coverage of climate change. Glob. Environ. Change **41**, 99–110 (2016)

22. Santipantakis, G., et al.: SPARTAN: semantic integration of big spatio-temporal data from streaming and archival sources. Future Gener. Comput. Syst. **110**, 540–555 (2018)

23. Novillo, R., Mejía, J., Cumbe, J., Galarza, V.: Una ontología para representar la información geográfica en el dominio hídrico Ecuatoriano. XV Congreso Internacional De Información Info'2018 (2018)

24. Atemezing, G., et al.: Transforming meteorological data into linked data. Semant. Web **4**, 285–290 (2013)

25. Lefort, L., Bobruk, J., Haller, A., Taylor, K., Woolf, A.: A linked sensor data cube for a 100 year homogenised daily temperature dataset. In: Proceedings Of The 5th International Conference On Semantic Sensor Networks, vol. 904, pp. 1–16 (2012)

26. Mori, S., Suen, C., Yamamoto, K.: Historical review of OCR research and development. Proc. IEEE **80**, 1029–1058 (1992)
27. Smith, R.: An overview of the tesseract OCR engine. In: Ninth International Conference on Document Analysis and Recognition (ICDAR 2007), vol. 2, pp. 629–633 (2007)
28. Mohit, B.: Named entity recognition. Nat. Lang. Process. Semitic Lang. 221–245 (2014). https://doi.org/10.1007/978-3-642-45358-8_7
29. Noy, N., Gao, Y., Jain, A., Narayanan, A., Patterson, A., Taylor, J.: Industry-scale knowledge graphs: lessons and challenges: five diverse technology companies show how it's done. Queue **17**, 48–75 (2019). https://doi.org/10.1145/3329781.3332266
30. Comesaña, D., Vilches-Blázquez, L.M.: Un estudio de la prensa latinoamericana entre los siglos XIX y XX con un enfoque en eventos meteorológicos. Revista de historia de América 156, 29–59. (2019). https://doi.org/10.35424/rha.156.2019.233
31. Vilches-Blázquez, L.M., Comesaña, D., Arrieta Moreno, L.J.: Construcción de una red de ontologías sobre eventos meteorológicos a partir de periódicoshistóricos. Transinformação **32**, e180077 (2020). https://doi.org/10.1590/1678-9865202032e180077

Smart Systems

Colombian Sign Language Classification Based on Hands Pose and Machine Learning Techniques

Anny Vera[1,2], Camilo Pérez[1,2], Juan José Sánchez[2],
and Alvaro D. Orjuela-Cañón[1(✉)] (iD)

[1] School of Medicine and Health Sciences, Universidad del Rosario, Bogotá, D.C., Colombia
alvaro.orjuela@urosario.edu.co
[2] Escuela Colombiana de Ingeniería Julio Garavito, Bogotá, D.C., Colombia

Abstract. New technologies can improve the inclusion of deaf (and hearing loss) people in different scenarios. In the present work, a classification of the Colombian sign language alphabet was implemented. For this, the employment of the mediapipe hands pose tool was used to feature extraction process. Then, three machine learning models: support vector classifiers, artificial neural networks and random forest, were trained to determine the best proposal. Results show how a neural network with one hidden layer obtained the best performance with 99.41%. The support vector classifier reached an accuracy of 99.12%, and the worse result was achieved by the random forest model with 96.67% in the classification. The proposal can contribute with advances in the sign language recognition in the Colombian context, which has been worked in different approaches with more complex models to do similar classifications.

Keywords: Deafness and hearing loss · Hands pose · Machine learning · Support vector classifier · Artificial neural networks · Random forest

1 Introduction

Deafness and hearing loss represent a difficult for around 430 million people that need rehabilitation, according to the World Health Organization [1]. It is estimated that for 2050 one out ten people will have disabling related to hearing loss. This disease can have causes associated to genetic issues, infectious in the childhood and adolescence or due to the degeneration given by the adulthood [2].

Impacts of the deafness can be seen in aspects as education, employment, social isolation, cognition and communication. This condition generates different consequences for this kind of people [3, 4], which have been increased in the current pandemic given by COVID-19 [5]. Furthermore, different approaches have been implemented to improve solutions to the problematic associated to deafness community [6, 7]. For example, an intelligent system to support healthcare based on sound [8], design assistance with parameters of functionality [9], and technologies developed employing artificial intelligence (AI) related to education [10, 11].

F. R. Narváez et al. (Eds.): SmartTech-IC 2022, CCIS 1705, pp. 149–160, 2023.
https://doi.org/10.1007/978-3-031-32213-6_11

Sign language (SL) is a method where a natural language that has linguistic properties based on movements of the hands and face allows to communicate any person to deafness and hearing loss people. Different methods have been produced to enhancethe translation between spoken language and SL. Most of these applications are based on image and vision processing [12, 13], but it has been a long way that implemented from haptic sensors located in gloves [14], leap motion technologies [15], skeleton with multi-modal information [16], and interdisciplinary approaches [17, 18].

Analyzing details of the employment of AI techniques for sign language recognition systems, most of them are based on artificial neural networks (ANN), specifically those that work by using pose models. There, it is possible to find some works that do the translation applied to words [19] and different expressions [20, 21]. However, from the first methodologies, the analysis of the alphabet remain of the more important. For this, interesting approaches take into account previous pose-models as in [22], which employs the media-pipe model. In addition, other machine learning (ML) approaches have allowed to determine what kind of models have better performance for alphabet sign classification [23].

In spite of the advances in the area, most of works have been oriented to American SL, having some approaches for Indian [24], Vietnamese [25], Arabic [26], and Japanese [27] languages, just to mention some of them. However, the SL changes according to the world region, making that one model could not be used in other countries. For the Colombian case, some proposals have been treated based on images [28–31], and sensors as accelerometers and electromyography signals processing [32], mainly. Approaches in delimitated scenarios as vowels recognition also have been determined [33, 34]. This topic continues open according to many questions associated to SL as performance, speed processing, and portability, among others.

According to the mentioned background, this paper shows a proposal for an alphabet identification for static signs [35], employing a pose-model and machine learning models for the Colombian SL (see Fig. 1, according to the INSOR, from Spanish *Instituto Nacional para Sordos*). This approach pretends to provide more perspectives for the SL translation for a local application that allows to improve the current advances in this area with the limitations associated to this.

2 Materials and Methods

The present proposal is based on hand-pose models applied to static signs from the Colombian SL alphabet. Figure 2 visualizes the methodology, where in a first step the image is converted into a vector with distances. Then, three different ML techniques were modelled to classify the signs. Each stage is detailed in next subsections.

2.1 Dataset

Images from three healthy people were taken representing the signs of the Fig. 1. These images were captured by different cameras as described in Table 1. For this acquisition a media-pipe hands interface was employed. Approximately ten images per sign were included, employing left and right hands. This allowed to have in average 70 images per sign. Static signs were taken into account due to letters as "J" and "Z" need movements for its representation. These letters were excluded of the dataset of images. Finally, a set with 1702 images was established after do not consider bad representation of some signs.

Fig. 1. Colombian Sign Language. Taken from https://www.educacionpasto.gov.co/

Fig. 2. Methodology employed for the classification

Table 1. Properties of cameras employed in the image's acquisition

Camera	Sensor Type	Resolution
1	CMOS	1080p
2	CMOS	720p
3	CMOS	460p

2.2 Feature Extraction

For employing ML models, it is necessary to determine what features must be utilized in the input. For this, it was used the media-pipe hands application program interface. This is a development from Google, which obtains information from 21 points associated to joints in the hands from an RGB image [36]. The tool provide the coordinates X, Y and Z from these points.

As information of the coordinates can be modified according to the proximity to the camera and the location on the screen, it was necessary to extract features from the 21 points associated to the hand. For this, the point's information was transformed using the Euclidean distance in the mode:

$$d(x, y, z) = \sqrt{(x_2 - x_1)^2 + (y_2 - y_1)^2 + (z_2 - z_1)^2} \tag{1}$$

where x, y and z are the coordinates of each point. Expression (1) was used the compute the distance between each pair of points, according to the information of the media-pipe interface. In this way, the vector was composed by 21 measures of the distance between the points according to the Table 2 and Fig. 3.

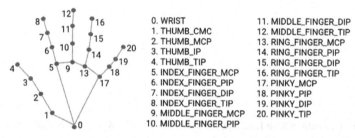

Fig. 3. Hand landmarks using Media-pipe hands. Taken from [36].

Table 2. Measures employed to build the input vector of ML models

Distance's name	Points considered in the measure
WT0	THUMB_CMC - WRIST
WT1	THUMB_MCP - THUMB_CMC
WT2	THUMB_ IP - THUMB_MCP
WT3	THUMB_TIP - THUMB_IP
WI0	INDEX_FINGER_MCP – WRIST
WI1	INDEX_FINGER _PIP - INDEX_FINGER _MCP
WI2	INDEX_FINGER _DIP - INDEX_FINGER _PIP
WI3	INDEX_FINGER _TIP - INDEX_FINGER _DIP
WP0	PINKY_MCP – WRIST
WP1	PINKY _PIP - PINKY _MCP

(continued)

Table 2. (*continued*)

Distance's name	Points considered in the measure
WP2	PINKY _DIP - PINKY _PIP
WP3	PINKY _TIP - PINKY _DIP
M0	MIDDLE _FINGER _PIP - MIDDLE _FINGER _MCP
M1	MIDDLE _FINGER _DIP - MIDDLE _FINGER _PIP
M2	MIDDLE _FINGER _TIP - MIDDLE _FINGER _DIP
R0	RING _FINGER _PIP - RING _FINGER _MCP
R1	RING _FINGER _DIP - RING _FINGER _PIP
R2	RING _FINGER _TIP - RING _FINGER _DIP
TI1	MIDDLE_FINGER_MCP - INDEX_FINGER_MCP
IM1	RING _FINGER_MCP - MIDDLE_FINGER_MCP
MP1	PINKY_FINGER_MCP - RING _FINGER_MCP

2.3 Machine Learning Techniques

From the vector of features obtained by hands-pose tool and distance computation, three ML models were employed for the classification of 24 signs. First, a support vector classifier (SVC) based on traditional theory of the support vector machines was trained. In this case, the classification hyperplane is important, which is carried out by the use of training data and a maximization of the margin of separation (C). For classification of data points that demand nonlinear functions, kernels provide better options when this kind of approaches is necessary [37]. For analysis of this aspect in the SVC models, different types of kernel were employed in the training: linear, polynomial and sigmoid.

Exploration of the values associated to the described kernels were computed based on data in the training set. Additionally, another hyperparameter was explored at the same time, the C parameter, which is associated to a penalty value based on the training error in the optimization process. This value was modified between 0.1 and 10000.

The second model employed for the classification was the random forest (RF) strategy, where different sets of classification trees are articulated to do the general classification [38]. There, it is necessary to determine the number of trees, nodes and leaves, and the number of the levels through the forest. For training of these models, the exploration of hyperparameters was based on two parameters: *i)* the metric to calculate the information in the nodes: Gini and Entropy criteria, and *ii)* the number of trees employed in the forest for the classification. It is important to note that RF models are preferable due to the best results in terms of generalization provided by the local compensation given by the trees [39].

Finally, the third model employed was an ANN, specifically the multilayer perceptron (MLP) [40]. Arrays of neurons are built to connect in each layer in a feedforward mode. The architecture of the MLP was defined by an input, which holds a vector with the 21 points of distances. The output contains 24 units, according to the number of target signs, and a hidden layer with a number of units to determine. In this case, two hyperparameters were explored: *i)* the activation function of the neurons: relu, identity, logistic, and hyperbolic tangent, and *ii)* the number of units in the hidden layer, testing values between two and thirty.

For hyperparameter's finding, the grid search strategy was implemented. There, the hyperparameters were varied according to mentioned values and the best election is saved for each final model. For comparison of the obtained models, accuracy metric was employed to evaluate the model's performance. This metric compute a classification rate, taking into account the hits in the output vector.

In terms of exploration of the training and validation sets, the cross-validation technique was implemented. The entire dataset was divided into five folds, remaining four subsets for training and one for validation, in a simultaneous manner for all employed models. All computational experiments were carried out by application of Python programing language with libraries as *pandas*, *numpy* and *scikit-learn* for ML modeling.

3   Results and Discussion

Table 2 lists the results for the three ML models. Mean and standard deviation were included to compare the performance of the SVC, RF and ANN. As the subsets provided in the cross-validation were the same for all models, these results can contribute to determine details for the models in the Colombian SL alphabet classification. In this specific application, the ANN obtained best results, followed by the SVC and RF models.

Figure 4 exhibits the comparison of the violin plot for the three ML models. Violin plot includes information the traditional boxplot and the kernel density, showing the peaks of results. It is possible to see how the ANN reached the best performance and less dispersion for the implemented folds. Figures 5, 6 and 7 show how the confusion matrixes were for three models. There, the letters with classes with denoted values out of diagonal, mainly, evinced errors in the classification. These misclassifications show where the models have problems to do the right classification (Fig. 7).

Table 3. Results for targeting signal sequences

Folds Number	ML Model		
	SVC	*ANN*	*RF*
1	**0.9912**	0.9912	0.9296
2	0.9765	0.9853	0.9413
3	0.9882	**0.9941**	**0.9676**
4	0.9647	0.9764	0.9117
5	0.9823	0.9882	0.9264
Mean ± std	0.980 ± 0.094	**0.987 ± 0.006**	0.935 ± 0.018

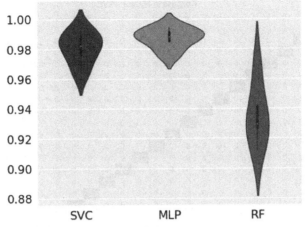

Fig. 4. Accuracy for the ML models.

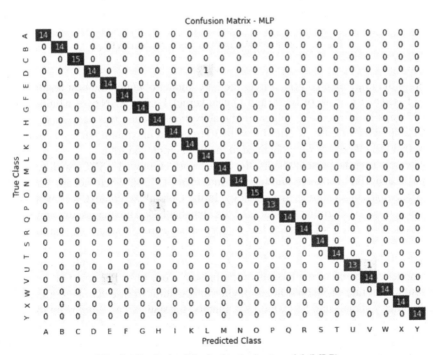

Fig. 5. Confusion Matrix for the best model (MLP).

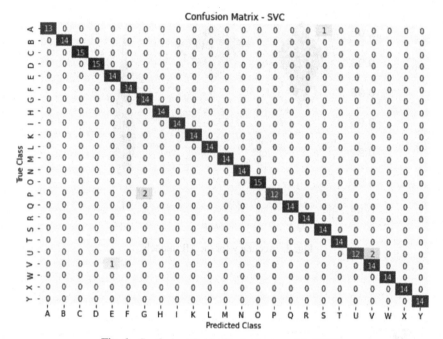

Fig. 6. Confusion Matrix for the best model (SVC).

From the implemented grid search, the SVC model obtained the best result with a model based on a C value of 10000 and a linear kernel. For the ANN case, a hidden layer with 25 units and hyperbolic tangent in the activation function was necessary. The RF model employed the entropy criterion with 30 trees and maximum ten levels of depth. These two last classifiers were obtained in the third employed fold.

At comparing the present results, the closer work employed a SVCs with values of C of 100 and 1000 for three datasets of American SL [22], where accuracy reached 98.56%, employing a similar methodology. In the Colombian context, a convolutional ANN was used to determine the letters of the alphabet based on images, obtaining 75% as classification rate [30], and six facial expressions were classified with an accuracy of 89.05% [41]. Analogous classifications, as Spanish vowels were achieved with an accuracy of 95.69% with a SVC of polynomial kernel, which represents a more complex model compared to the models in the present work [33]. Pereira et al., obtained a classification rate of 96.66% at employing information from electromyography and accelerometry signals and SVC, too [32]. Finally, for static signs, employing the same model and a combination from images and sensors, an accuracy classification of 94% was obtained in [31].

Limitations of present study are related to the built dataset, which it did not include the "J" and "Z" letters due to movement present in its representation. However the scope of the work was the classification of static signs related to the Colombian case. This could be improved with an updated alphabet because the employed for the present case is related to a specific region of the country and holds similarities with the ASL.

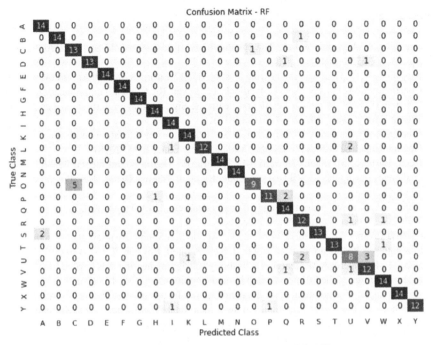

Fig. 7. Confusion Matrix for the best model (RF).

Furthermore, a more general national alphabet could be used in the future applications. Finally, more models could be tested, but in the light of the present results the reached accuracy was comparable with previous works in the area, where the MLP was preferable used.

4 Conclusions and Future Works

This paper presents the use of the media-pipe tool for pose hands and machine learning models for classification of alphabet letters for the Colombian sign language. Results show that an artificial neural network with a hidden layer and 25 units could classify 24 letters with an accuracy of 99.41% in the present case.

As future work, the increment of the dataset must be necessary and the inclusion of letter with movement associated to its representation. It is important to see how the media-pipe supported the feature extraction process.

Acknowledgements. Authors acknowledge the support of the Universidad del Rosario and *Semillero en Inteligencia Artificial en Salud – SemillIAS* those were relevant for the development of this work.

References

1. Sheffield, A.M., Smith, R.J.H.: The epidemiology of deafness. Cold Spring Harb. Perspect. Med. **9**, a033258 (2019)
2. Kushalnagar, R.: Deafness and hearing loss, pp. 35–47. Springer, In Web Accessibility (2019)
3. Chatzidamianos, G., Fletcher, I., Wedlock, L., Lever, R.: Clinical communication and the "triangle of care" in mental health and deafness: Sign language interpreters- perspectives. Patient Educ. Couns. **102**, 2010–2015 (2019)
4. Mishra, A., Nagarkar, A.N., Nagarkar, N.M.: Challenges in Education and Employment for Hearing Impaired in India. J. Disabil. Manag. Spec. Educ. **1**, 35 (2018)
5. Recio-Barbero, M., Sáenz-Herrero, M., Segarra, R.: Deafness and mental health: Clinical challenges during the COVID-19 pandemic. Psychol. Trauma Theory, Res. Pract. Policy 12, S212 (2020)
6. Khan, S.A.: Causes, prevention and effects of deafness. IJSA **3**, 6–11 (2022)
7. Welsh, W.: The economic impact of deafness (2021)
8. da Rosa Tavares, J.E., Victória Barbosa, J.L.: Apollo SignSound: An intelligent system applied to ubiquitous healthcare of deaf people. J. Reliab. Intell. Environ. **7**, 157–170 (2021)
9. Marti, P., Recupero, A.: Is deafness a disability? designing hearing aids beyond functionality. In: Proceedings of the 2019 on Creativity and Cognition, pp. 133–143 (2019)
10. Zdravkova, K.: The potential of artificial intelligence for assistive technology in education. In: Handbook on Intelligent Techniques in the Educational Process, pp. 61–85. Springer (2022)
11. Liu, Z., Pang, L., Qi, X.: MEN: mutual enhancement networks for sign language recognition and education. IEEE Trans. Neural Networks Learn. Syst. (2022)
12. Bantupalli, K., Xie, Y.: American sign language recognition using deep learning and computer vision. In: Proceedings of the 2018 IEEE International Conference on Big Data (Big Data), pp. 4896–4899 (2018)
13. Rahman, M.M., Islam, M.S., Rahman, M.H., Sassi, R., Rivolta, M.W., Aktaruzzaman, M.: A new benchmark on american sign language recognition using convolutional neural network. In: Proceedings of the 2019 International Conference on Sustainable Technologies for Industry 4.0 (STI), pp. 1–6 (2019)
14. Ahmed, M.A., Zaidan, B.B., Zaidan, A.A., Salih, M.M., Lakulu, M.M.: bin a review on systems-based sensory gloves for sign language recognition state of the art between 2007 and 2017. Sensors **18**, 2208 (2018)
15. Chong, T.-W., Lee, B.-G.: American sign language recognition using leap motion controller with machine learning approach. Sensors **18**, 3554 (2018)
16. Jiang, S., Sun, B., Wang, L., Bai, Y., Li, K., Fu, Y.: Skeleton aware multi-modal sign language recognition. In: Proceedings of the Proceedings of the IEEE/CVF Conference on Computer Vision and Pattern Recognition, pp. 3413–3423 (2021)
17. Bragg, D., et al.: Sign language recognition, generation, and translation: an interdisciplinary perspective. In: Proceedings of the The 21st international ACM SIGACCESS conference on computers and accessibility, pp. 16–31 (2019)
18. Camgoz, N.C., Koller, O., Hadfield, S., Bowden, R.: Sign language transformers: joint end-to-end sign language recognition and translation. In: Proceedings of the Proceedings of the IEEE/CVF conference on computer vision and pattern recognition, pp. 10023–10033 (2020)
19. Li, D., Rodriguez, C., Yu, X., Li, H.: Word-level deep sign language recognition from video: a new large-scale dataset and methods comparison. In: Proceedings of the Proceedings of the IEEE/CVF Winter Conference on Applications of Computer Vision (WACV) (2020)
20. Kumar, P., Roy, P.P., Dogra, D.P.: Independent bayesian classifier combination based sign language recognition using facial expression. Inf. Sci. (Ny).**428**, 30–48 (2018)

21. Mukushev, M., Sabyrov, A., Imashev, A., Koishibay, K., Kimmelman, V., Sandygulova, A.: Evaluation of manual and non-manual components for sign language recognition. In: Proceedings of the Proceedings of The 12th Language Resources and Evaluation Conference (2020)

22. Shin, J., Matsuoka, A., Hasan, M.A.M., Srizon, A.Y.: American sign language alphabet recognition by extracting feature from hand pose estimation. Sensors (Basel).21 (2021). https://doi.org/10.3390/s21175856

23. Cheok, M.J., Omar, Z., Jaward, M.H.: A review of hand gesture and sign language recognition techniques. Int. J. Mach. Learn. Cybern. **10**(1), 131–153 (2017). https://doi.org/10.1007/s13042-017-0705-5

24. Singh, A., Singh, S.K., Mittal, A.: A review on dataset acquisition techniques in gesture recognition from indian sign language. Adv. Data Comput. Commun. Secur. 305–313 (2022)

25. Vo, A.H., Pham, V.-H., Nguyen, B.T.: Deep learning for vietnamese sign language recognition in video sequence. Int. J. Mach. Learn. Comput. **9**, 440–445 (2019)

26. Mustafa, M.: A study on Arabic sign language recognition for differently abled using advanced machine learning classifiers. J. Ambient. Intell. Humaniz. Comput. **12**(3), 4101–4115 (2020). https://doi.org/10.1007/s12652-020-01790-w

27. Yabunaka, K., Mori, Y., Toyonaga, M.: Facial expression sequence recognition for a japanese sign language training system. In: Proceedings of the 2018 Joint 10th International Conference on Soft Computing and Intelligent Systems (SCIS) and 19th International Symposium on Advanced Intelligent Systems (ISIS), pp. 1348–1353 (2018)

28. Ortiz-Farfán, N., Camargo-Mendoza, J.E.: Computational model for sign language recognition in a colombian context. TecnoLógicas **23**, 191–226 (2020)

29. Betancourt, F.R., Arbulú, M.: others A gesture recognition system for the Colombian sign language based on convolutional neural networks. Bull. Electr. Eng. Informatics **9**, 2082–2089 (2020)

30. Arrieta-Rodr\'\iguez, E., Monterroza-Barrios, R.E., Torres-Alvarez, P.L., Castro-Lozano, G.E.: Recognition of colombian alphabeth in sign language using deep learning techniques. In: Proceedings of the IOP Conference Series: Materials Science and Engineering, vol. 1154, p. 12003 (2021)

31. Triviño-López, I.C., Rodr\'\iguez-Garavito, C.H., Martinez-Caldas, J.S.: Hand gesture recognition using computer vision applied to colombian sign language. In: Proceedings of the International Conference on Computer Aided Systems Theory, pp. 207–214 (2019)

32. Pereira-Montiel, E., et al.: Automatic sign language recognition based on accelerometry and surface electromyography signals: A study for Colombian sign language. Biomed. Signal Process. Control **71**, 103201 (2022)

33. Botina-Monsalve, D.J., Domínguez-Vásquez, M.A., Madrigal-González, C.A., Castro-Ospina, A.E.: Automatic classification of vowels in Colombian sign language. TecnoLógicas **21**, 103–114 (2018)

34. Jiménez, G., Moreno, E., Guzman, R., Barrero, J.: Automatic method for recognition of colombian sign language for vowels and numbers from zero to five by using SVM and KNN. In: Proceedings of the 2019 Congreso Internacional de Innovación y Tendencias en Ingenieria (CONIITI), pp. 1–6 (2019)

35. Wadhawan, A., Kumar, P.: Deep learning-based sign language recognition system for static signs. Neural Comput. Appl. **32**(12), 7957–7968 (2020). https://doi.org/10.1007/s00521-019-04691-y

36. Bazarevsky, V., Zhang, F.: On-device, real-time hand tracking with mediapipe. Google AI Blog (2019)

37. Anam, K., Al-Jumaily, A.: Evaluation of extreme learning machine for classification of individual and combined finger movements using electromyography on amputees and non-amputees. Neural Netw. **85**, 51–68 (2017)

38. Bergstra, J., Bengio, Y.: Random search for hyper-parameter optimization. J. Mach. Learn. Res.13 (2012)
39. Bergstra, J., Yamins, D., Cox, D.: Making a science of model search: Hyperparameter optimization in hundreds of dimensions for vision architectures. In: Proceedings of the International conference on machine learning, pp. 115–123 (2013)
40. Haykin, S.: In: Hall, P. (ed.) Neural Networks and Learning Machines, 3ra ed. Pearson (2009). ISBN 9780131471399
41. Rincon Vega, A.M., Vasquez, A., Amador, W., Rojas, A.: Deep learning for the recognition of facial expression in the colombian sign language. Ann. Phys. Rehabil. Med. **61**, e96 (2018). https://doi.org/10.1016/j.rehab.2018.05.204

Spanish Stylometric Features to Determine Gender and Profession of Ecuadorian Twitter Users

César Espin-Riofrio[1]([✉]) [ID], María Pazmiño-Rosales[1] [ID], Carlos Aucapiña-Camas[1] [ID], Verónica Mendoza-Morán[1] [ID], and Arturo Montejo-Ráez[2] [ID]

[1] University of Guayaquil, Guayaquil 090510, Ecuador
{cesar.espinr,maria.pazminor,carlos.aucapinac,
veronica.mendozam}@ug.edu.ec
[2] University of Jaén, 23071 Jaén, Spain
amontejo@ujaen.es

Abstract. Few studies on group authorship attribution have been conducted in Ecuador. The aim of this article is to analyze the importance of stylometric characteristics to determine the gender and profession of Twitter users in Ecuador using Machine Learning (ML) techniques for authorship attribution. The project corresponds to a quantitative-bibliographic type of research, with experimental design conducted to evaluate various stylometric features and classification algorithms. Its development consists of extracting tweets from users in Ecuador that will be divided for training and testing. For the preprocessing of the information, phraseological and word frequency features are implemented. Subsequently, the classifier methods Random Forest (RF), Decision Tree (DT), Logistic Regression (LR), Multi-Layer Perceptron (MLP) and Gradient Boosting (GB) are trained, and their performance is evaluated using the Cross Validation technique and metrics to choose the best classifier for gender and profession prediction. Finally, the results are presented in observable and measurable behaviors. Random Forest with an f1 of 0.7419 was determined as the best classifier for predicting gender and the MLP method with f1 of 0.8969 for profession, outperforming the other classifiers. It was possible to determine the gender and profession of Ecuadorian Twitter users from short texts published in Spanish using stylometric characteristics and frequently used words together with machine learning methods. This research is of great interest because it applies current technological methods and provides optimal solutions in authorship attribution of short texts.

Keywords: Stylometry · Natural Language Processing · Authorship Attribution · Machine Learning

1 Introduction

Authorship Attribution (AA) is responsible for answering the question of who the author of a text is [1]. For a long time, classification works have given good results for long texts, however, for short texts, there are fewer investigations. Thus, in this research work

F. R. Narváez et al. (Eds.): SmartTech-IC 2022, CCIS 1705, pp. 161–172, 2023.
https://doi.org/10.1007/978-3-031-32213-6_12

we propose an analysis of stylometric characteristics of phraseological type and word frequency in conjunction with ML techniques, to determine the gender and profession of 120 users of the social network Twitter in Ecuador. It is said that style is something that comes from the subconscious, for this reason everyone has their own style. This is the basis of stylometry, known to be the statistical analysis of literary texts at different levels.

The foundations of stylometry were established in the 19th century by [2], in his book "Principles of Stylometry". [3] was one of the first to identify an author based on stylometric techniques [4]. Decided to employ statistical methods based on the number of words in a text, giving rise to different approaches based on machine learning or, as [5] defines it, the science of algorithms that give meaning to data.

In the early 1960s, Rev. A.Q. Morton performed a computer analysis of the fourteen epistles attributed to St. Paul, which showed that they belonged to six different authors [6]. However, with the passage of time and practice, researchers and scholars have refined their methods, which today yield much more accurate results. One of the first successes was the resolution of the controversial authorship of twelve of the Federalist Papers, written by Frederick Mostellar and David Wallace [7]. This 1964 publication, Inference and Disputed Authorship, which made the cover of Time magazine, attracted the attention of academics and the public alike for its use of statistical methodology to resolve one of the most notorious questions in American history. It applies mathematics, including the controversial Bayesian analysis, the study of frequently used words in texts.

The evolution of Machine Learning techniques has resulted in their applicability to different fields, not only in the IT area, but also in areas such as medicine, engineering, literature, biology, etc.

Machine learning techniques are also applied in the field of stylometry, for this we must go back to its beginnings and mainly know its roots, since this tool is a derivation of artificial intelligence. In 1943, the mathematician Walter Pitts and the neurophysiologist Warren McCulloch [8] released their work focused on what we know today as artificial intelligence. In 1950, Alan Mathison Turing, a scientist, mathematician, philosopher, and sportsman, was able to create the well-known "Turing Test", whose purpose was to measure how intelligent a computer was [9]. In mid-1979 an algorithm capable of recognizing patterns was developed, the main tool of artificial intelligence that gave rise to machine learning, since by giving a machine the ability to learn patterns it could anticipate an effective response or solution [10].

Machine learning problems can be divided into supervised and unsupervised learning. Particularly supervised learning uses classification methods whose purpose is to identify to which category an object belongs. Among those selected for this study is Logistic Regression (LR), a method developed by [11] that allows estimating the probability of a binary qualitative variable as a function of a quantitative variable. Decision Tree (DT), originated in the studies conducted by Sonquist and Morgan [12] in 1964, was one of the first methods to demonstrate the relationship between each condition and the group of permissible actions associated with it. Multilayer Perceptron (MLP) originated in 1969 by Minsky and Papert [13], who demonstrated that the method is a universal approximator. Gradient Boosting (GB) [14], was introduced in 1999, this algorithm is used for the many predictions based on the boosting method. At the beginning of the 21st century, [15] developed Random Forest (RF), a supervised learning technique that generates multiple decision trees on a training data set where the results obtained are combined to obtain a single model more robust compared to the results of each tree separately.

For the training of Machine Learning algorithms and methods, stylometric characteristics of phraseological type, word length and word frequency were established. This is a linguistic classification method that has become very popular in recent years, although its origins date back to the mid-1960s. It is based on the idea that the author of a text always imprints a stylistic or authorial imprint on his creations, a style of his own that can be traced by means of quantitative methods [16].

Its execution aims to provide the necessary information for its due analysis following the guidance of relevant scientific articles. Machine Learning techniques such as Cross Validation are used for validation and, of classification, such as Logistic Regression, Random Forest Classifier, Decision Tree Classifier, MLP Classifier, Gradient Boosting Classifier, these different algorithms, and strategies with supervised learning approach using a dataset for training methods for the prediction of gender and profession.

1.1 Related Work

Nowadays, stylometry provides us with analysis tools that allow us to review the attribution of authorship with the objectivity provided by the quantification obtained by macroanalysis.

The different research and articles that we can find detail how these techniques give very concrete results. Throughout this research we see how the prediction of these techniques helps us to implement the determination of authorship in the text fields.

Already in the current era of the field of stylometry, we came across a deeper analysis where, to confirm this finding, lexical similarities of a tetralogy called My Brilliant Friend were compared, these similarities were close between Domenico Starnone and Elena Ferrante. In 2017 the goal was achieved when the nearest neighbor (k-NN) approach was applied on the whole vocabulary reaching the conclusion that Domenico Starnone is the real author behind the pseudonym Elena Ferrante [17]. For the years 2017 and 2021, a project ETSO (Estilometría aplicada al Teatro del Siglo de Oro) [18] was launched, managing to gather more than 2700 plays of the Spanish aurisecular period. After the application of stylometric analysis is shedding light on the authorship of dozens of plays of the Golden Age theater, thanks to stylometry can find out, in one of its most useful features, which texts have frequencies in lexicon, when the author uses the words in different proportions, so that the works are usually related according to their authorship.

There are references of AA work on Twitter using the mentioned classifiers [19]. Worked with Random Forest to classify unknown documents based on extracted features, their approach scored 75% accuracy. [20] performed tests with a Logistic Regression classifier to identify the author's gender and the linguistic variety of tweets, they experimented with a corpus obtained from Twitter of more than 11 thousand authors. The proposed model achieved an accuracy of 64% for the genre identification task. [21] succeeded in profiling the genre of an author to recognize whether the text was written by a bot or a human by applying the Multilayer Perceptron method for tweet classification.

PAN[1] is a series of scientific events and shared tasks on digital text forensics and stylometry. IberLEF[2], is a shared evaluation campaign for Natural Language Processing (NLP) systems in Spanish and other Iberian languages. SemEval[3] is a series of international Natural Language Processing (NLP) research workshops. They propose tasks focused on authorship verification such as gender and profession identification.

2 Method

The project is based on a type of experimental research, which in turn corresponds to a type of quantitative research since it is considered that, to determine the behavior of the object of study, it is necessary to apply evaluation metrics.

It is proposed to use an appropriate and understandable programming language, in this case Python in the Google Colab test environment, the corresponding libraries were selected for the extraction of data, which are processed and structured and, with the techniques of stylometry of phraseological type, frequency of use of words to obtain the vector of characteristics, followed by the entry to the chosen classification algorithms with which the training and learning was performed, in order to determine the gender and profession of the users. Figure 1 shows the model used.

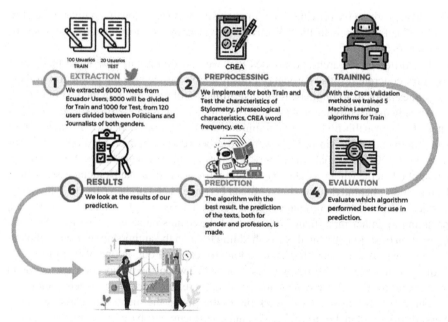

Fig. 1. Project development process

---

[1] "PAN." https://pan.webis.de/.

[2] "IberLEF 2022" https://sites.google.com/view/iberlef2022/home.

[3] "SemEval" https://semeval.github.io/.

2.1 Dataset

The Tweepy[4] library was used to extract tweets, used to access the Twitter API. Users were chosen from among politicians and journalists in Ecuador who were involved in their respective careers and in the social network, organizing them with the Panda library tool.

We extracted 6000 tweets from Ecuadorian users, including politicians and journalists of both genders. The dataset consists of 50 tweets from 120 users, it was divided into 100 training users and 20 users that will serve for prediction, as shown in Fig. 2.

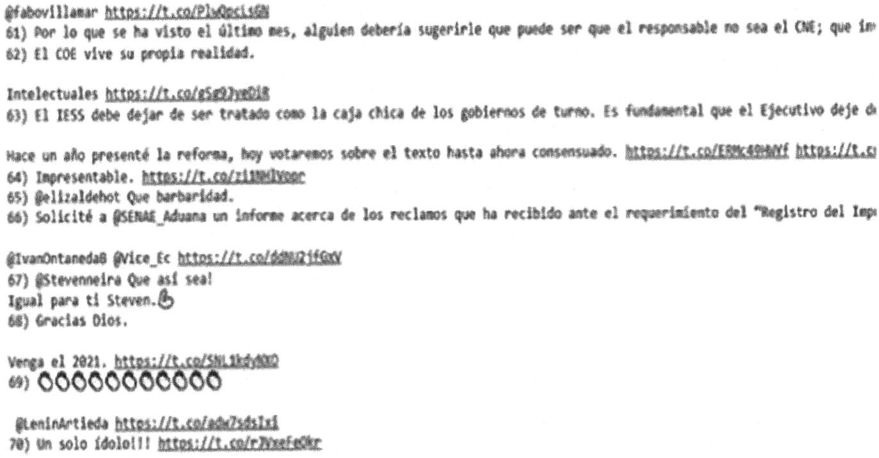

@fabovillamar https://t.co/PlwQpcisGN
61) Por lo que se ha visto el último mes, alguien debería sugerirle que puede ser que el responsable no sea el CNE; que im
62) El COE vive su propia realidad.

Intelectuales https://t.co/gSg9JveDiR
63) El IESS debe dejar de ser tratado como la caja chica de los gobiernos de turno. Es fundamental que el Ejecutivo deje d

Hace un año presenté la reforma, hoy votaremos sobre el texto hasta ahora consensuado. https://t.co/ERMk49HWYf https://t.c
64) Impresentable. https://t.co/ri1NWlVopc
65) @elizaldehot Que barbaridad.
66) Solicité a @SENAE_Aduana un informe acerca de los reclamos que ha recibido ante el requerimiento del "Registro del Imp

@IvanOntaneda8 @Vice_Ec https://t.co/d6NU2jfGxV
67) @Stevenneira Que así sea!
Igual para ti Steven.👏
68) Gracias Dios.

Venga el 2021. https://t.co/SNL1kdyNXO
69) 🥚🥚🥚🥚🥚🥚🥚🥚🥚🥚

@LeninArtieda https://t.co/adw7sdsIxi
70) Un solo ídolo!!! https://t.co/r7VxeFeQkr

Fig. 2. Tweets extracted without processing

These data served for training the ML algorithms. During the extraction, characters of little relevance were found, so techniques were implemented to clean the texts, eliminating unnecessary data such as emoticons, retweets, links, empty tweets, thus training and predicting with greater accuracy, as these could alter the results. Figure 3 shows the cleaned dataset.

Being politicians and journalists known in the media, the base labeling for supervised learning was performed. It was also important to identify them anonymously (Fig. 4).

2.2 Feature Extraction

Phraseological type features are part of the stylometric features, they are used to collect data that will be used by ML algorithms for training and prediction. The features selected in this research are: Lexical Diversity, Mean Word Len, Mean Sentence Len, Stdev Sentence Len, Mean Paragraph Len, Document Len. For this purpose, we used the library created by Jeff Potter [22] taken from his GitHub repository, whose purpose is to apply the study of the linguistic style of written language.

---

4 "Tweepy Documentation", https://docs.tweepy.org/en/v3.2.0/.

```
        Username Twitter                            Nombre GÃ©nero ProfesiÃ³n
0          @ottosonnenh    Otto RamÃ³n Sonnenholzner Sper    male  Politico
1          @ottosonnenh    Otto RamÃ³n Sonnenholzner Sper    male  Politico
2          @ottosonnenh    Otto RamÃ³n Sonnenholzner Sper    male  Politico
3          @ottosonnenh    Otto RamÃ³n Sonnenholzner Sper    male  Politico
4          @ottosonnenh    Otto RamÃ³n Sonnenholzner Sper    male  Politico
..                  ...                            ...        ...       ...
115       @GuillermoCeli   Guillermo Alejandro Celi Santos   male  Politico
116       @GuillermoCeli   Guillermo Alejandro Celi Santos   male  Politico
117       @GuillermoCeli   Guillermo Alejandro Celi Santos   male  Politico
118       @GuillermoCeli   Guillermo Alejandro Celi Santos   male  Politico
119       @GuillermoCeli   Guillermo Alejandro Celi Santos   male  Politico

                                                                   Tweet
0     En Manta, compartÃ con estudiantes y docentes...
1     Muy doloroso lo ocurrido en el Cristo del Cons...
2     @berecordero @ecuadortienevoz Una tragedia que...
3     En Milagro participÃ© de un encuentro con jÃ³v...
4     Desde hace dos aÃ±os he denunciado el uso frau...
..                                                  ...
115   En Cotopaxi seguimos SUMAndo con CÃ©sar Umajin...
116   @mariuxi_news Solidario contigo apreciada Mari...
117   Celebrar a #Guayaquil con hechos, llena el cor...
118   Pregunta serÃa: cÃ³mo se llama el platillo ma...
119   Los manabitas se siguen SUMAndo a la UNIDAD, e...
```

Fig. 3. Dataset of concatenated and cleaned tweets

	label	Género	Profesión	Tweet
0	@user001	male	journalist	los narcos comienzan por apoderarse de los gob...
1	@user002	female	journalist	pronta recuperacion [SEP] momento historico? l...
2	@user003	female	journalist	se amplio el plazo pon atencion a esta convoca...
3	@user004	male	journalist	excelente analisis de jorge alvear sobre la in...
4	@user005	male	journalist	mas de 2 horas duro mi comparecencia en la aud...
5	@user006	male	journalist	covid: pruebas de antigenos en farmacias? invi...
6	@user007	female	journalist	@quimeradann ni idea. [SEP] @quimeradann @silr...
7	@user008	male	journalist	les recomiendo mi articulo sobre los intentos ...
8	@user009	male	Politician	mientras saquicela se dedica a inoportunos hom...
9	@user010	female	Politician	comision de educacion	analizamos las #reform...
10	@user011	female	Politician	#envivosesion nro. 062	ceppinnarevision y ap...
11	@user012	female	Politician	entre 2020 y 2022, la fortuna de la cupula pol...
12	@user013	female	Politician	los mentirosos siempre fueron ellos! [SEP] los...
13	@user014	female	Politician	@bruningfernando @franciamarquezm [SEP] @lirad...
14	@user015	female	Politician	basta de gobernar con medidas jurisdiccionales...
15	@user016	female	Politician	gracias alejandro ! los ciudadanos de #duran t...

Fig. 4. Labeled dataset

On the other hand, for the characteristics of frequently used words, the first 1000 words were chosen from the CREA[5] list (Corpus de Referencia del Español Actual)

---

5 "CREA", https://corpus.rae.es/lfrecuencias.html.

taken from the Real Academia Española (RAE) which presents a list of the most used words in the Spanish language ordered according to frequency of use (Fig. 5).

Orden	Frec.absoluta		Frec.normalizada
1.	de	9,999,518	65545.55
2.	la	6,277,560	41148.59
3.	que	4,681,839	30688.85
4.	el	4,569,652	29953.48
5.	en	4,234,281	27755.16
6.	y	4,180,279	27401.19
7.	a	3,260,939	21375.03
8.	los	2,618,657	17164.95
9.	se	2,022,514	13257.31
10.	del	1,857,225	12173.87
11.	las	1,686,741	11056.37
12.	un	1,659,827	10879.95
13.	por	1,561,904	10238.07
14.	con	1,481,607	9711.74
15.	no	1,465,503	9606.18
16.	una	1,347,603	8833.36
17.	su	1,103,617	7234.06
18.	para	1,062,152	6962.26
19.	es	1,019,669	6683.79
20.	al	951,054	6234.03
21.	lo	866,955	5682.77
22.	como	773,465	5069.96
23.	más	661,696	4337.33
24.	o	542,284	3554.60
25.	pero	450,512	2953.04

Fig. 5. Sample list of frequently used Spanish words CREA

2.3 Training and Evaluation

As part of the training, the dataset of 100 users was used and the classifier methods were applied with the algorithms of the Scikit-Learn library [23], this library contains many tools for the study of machine learning, it is easy to understand thanks to the documentation provided. Random Forest, Logistic Regression, Decision Tree, Multi-Layer Perceptron and Gradient Boost classifiers were used. These methods are used in most similar works of authorship attribution and are also suitable according to the size of the dataset used.

Next, the Cross-validation technique [24] was used to evaluate the training of the classifiers. Cross-validation segments the dataset into different quantities for training and testing, evaluating in each process. Thus, it allowed us to know the performance and reliability of the classifiers for gender and profession prediction, as shown in Fig. 6.

```
def eval_classifiers(X_train, y_train):
    clfs = [('Logistic regression', LogisticRegression(max_iter=1000, random_state=45)),
            ('Decision tree', DecisionTreeClassifier(random_state=45)),
            ('RandomForest', RandomForestClassifier(n_estimators=20, random_state=45)),
            ('MLP', MLPClassifier(max_iter=1000, random_state=45)),
            ('GBT', GradientBoostingClassifier(n_estimators=100, learning_rate=1.0, max_depth=1, random_state=0))
            ]

    # Vamos devolver los resultados como una tabla
    # Cada fila un algoritmo, cada columna un resultado
    metrics = ['accuracy', 'balanced_accuracy', 'precision', 'recall', 'f1']
    results = pd.DataFrame(columns=metrics)
    for alg, clf in clfs:
        scores = cross_validate(clf, X_train, y_train, cv=10, scoring=metrics) # por defecto, es estratificado
        results.loc[alg,:] = [scores['test_'+m].mean() for m in metrics]
```

Fig. 6. Evaluation of classifiers by cross validation

2.4 Prediction

For prediction, we used the classifiers that performed best during the training phase. In the case of gender, the Random Forest method is used and in profession the MLP classifier method, here we use the test dataset with the tweets of 20 users intended for prediction. Figure 7 shows how these methods assign the prediction of gender and profession labels to each user.

	user	Genero	Profesion
0	@user001	femenino	periodista
1	@user002	masculino	periodista
2	@user003	femenino	politico
3	@user004	femenino	periodista
4	@user005	femenino	politico
5	@user006	femenino	periodista
6	@user007	femenino	politico
7	@user008	masculino	politico
8	@user009	femenino	periodista
9	@user010	femenino	politico
10	@user011	femenino	politico
11	@user012	femenino	politico
12	@user013	femenino	politico
13	@user014	femenino	politico
14	@user015	masculino	politico
15	@user016	femenino	politico
16	@user017	femenino	politico
17	@user018	masculino	politico
18	@user019	masculino	politico
19	@user020	masculino	politico

Fig. 7. Sample of prediction results

3   Results

Once the application of the stylometric characteristics, the use of frequent words, training, and prediction, was performed, it was evaluated by means of the metrics Accuracy, Balanced Accuracy, Precision, Recall, f1. In Fig. 8, the matrix with the values in which each algorithm was correct in the classification is observed.

```
para genero
                     accuracy balanced_accuracy precision recall     f1
RandomForest           0.6300            0.5357    0.6625 0.8548 0.7419
MLP                    0.5900            0.4917    0.6327 0.8667 0.7243
Logistic regression    0.5700            0.4518    0.6100 0.8786 0.7156
GBT                    0.5500            0.4792    0.6251 0.7167 0.6600
Decision tree          0.5100            0.4643    0.6137 0.6119 0.6042
para profesion
                     accuracy balanced_accuracy precision recall     f1
MLP                    0.8400            0.7369    0.8504 0.9571 0.8969
Logistic regression    0.8300            0.7202    0.8446 0.9571 0.8924
Decision tree          0.8400            0.8009    0.8849 0.9018 0.8876
GBT                    0.8200            0.7426    0.8590 0.9018 0.8770
RandomForest           0.7800            0.6643    0.8053 0.9286 0.8595
```

Fig. 8. Results by applying evaluation metrics

The best score for gender is obtained with the Random Forest method with f1 of 0.7419, surpassing the rest of the classifiers. For profession, the MLP Classifier method stands out with 0.8969.

With the Cross Validation technique implemented in the five ML classification methods, the following results were obtained. The f1 metric was chosen to observe that, for gender, the Random Forest method obtained 0.7419, followed by the MLP Classifier with 0.7243, in third place Logistic Regression with 0.7156, in fourth place Gradient Boosting with 0.6600 and in last place Decision Tree with 0.6042, giving as best result the training with Random Forest, Fig. 9.

Similarly, the methods for profession were evaluated, obtaining the first place to Multi-Layer Perceptron Classifier with an f1 of 0.8969, followed by Logistic Regression with 0.8924, in third place, Decision Tree with 0.8876, in fourth place Gradient Boosting with 0.8770 and finally Random Forest with 0.8595, as shown in Fig. 10.

4   Discussion

The selected classifiers met the expectations of the project. For the determination of gender, Random Forest was the classifier that gave the best results, while for the determination of profession, MLP gave the best results. The Logistic Regression classifier also gave good results for both labels. It can also be seen that for the profession label, all classifiers show good results. It should be noted that there are other supervised learning methods that could be applied to the same case study and give better results than those obtained, for example Naive Bayes, Support Vector Machine (SVM), K-Neighbors, among others.

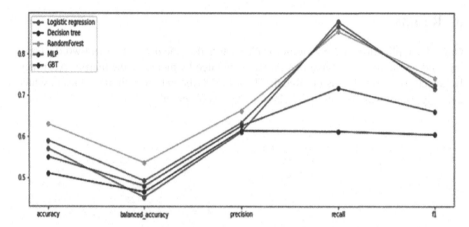

Fig. 9. F1 score for gender determination

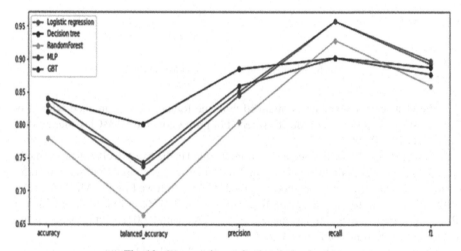

Fig. 10. F1 score for profession determination

On the other hand, there are other techniques to measure the performance of machine learning models, e.g., simple validation, bootstrap, confusion matrices, however, the cross-validation technique proved to be effective by measuring the performance of the whole dataset for training and evaluation, instead of a part.

Also, the size of the dataset could be important for the learning of the models, surely with a larger dataset better result can be obtained.

Stylometric features were important for attributing a style type of the texts according to the domain analyzed, in our case gender and profession. The use of phraseological type features and frequently used words of the Spanish language made good results were obtained, it would be interesting to continue experimenting with different types of stylometric features.

5 Conclusions

An investigation was carried out based on tweets published by users in Ecuador to determine their gender and profession, extracting stylometric characteristics based on frequently used words in the Spanish language, being a reference in this type of research in the country.

It is possible to determine the type of writing of a text by extracting stylometric characteristics and the use of machine learning methods, being an important task in the identification of the author of a text.

Random Forest, with an f1 of 0.7419, was the best classifier for the prediction of the genre label and MLP, with f1 of 0.8969, the best for the profession label. In both cases, very close performance values were obtained with the use of the following three classifier models.

The prediction results demonstrate the feasibility of using classifier models for the task of authorship attribution of short texts. The most important contribution is the generality of machine learning models that can be applied to any language.

The stylometric characteristics of the frequently used words of the Spanish language listed in CREA, together with the phraseological characteristics, turned out to be determinant in the style of an author and the analysis according to the research domain, being important for an adequate training of the classifiers and obtaining a good prediction.

It would be interesting to determine what influence the number of frequently used words has and to perform experiments with various numbers; there could be a threshold above which they no longer have an important influence on training and prediction.

Likewise, the lemma or type of word used could have more weight depending on whether it is a verb, noun, adjective, etc.

We hope to work in the future with the definition of new stylometric features that will substantially improve the classification results, use standard datasets such as those provided by PAN-CLEF in their campaigns to compare our work with other implemented ones, also test other classification methods and new techniques such as Transformers models.

References

1. Juola, P.: Authorship attribution. Foundations and Trends®in Information Retrieval 1, 233–334 (2007). https://doi.org/10.1561/1500000005
2. Lutoslawski, W.: Principes de stylométrie appliqués à la chronologie des œuvres de Platon. Rev Etud Grec 11, 61–81 (1898). https://doi.org/10.3406/reg.1898.5847
3. Springer, J.F.: A mechanical solution of a literary problem. Sci Am 128, 100 (1923). https://doi.org/10.1038/scientificamerican0223-100
4. Zipf, G.K.: Selected Studies of the Principle of Relative Frequency in Language. Harvard University Press (1932)
5. Raschka, S., Kaufman, B.: Machine learning and AI-based approaches for bioactive ligand discovery and GPCR-ligand recognition. (2020). https://doi.org/10.1016/j.ymeth.2020.06.016
6. O'Rourke, J.J., Morton, A.Q., McLeman, J.: Paul, the man and the Myth: a study in the authorship of greek prose. J. Biblic. Lit. 86, 110 (1967). https://doi.org/10.2307/3263256

7. Mosteller, F., Wallace, D.L.: Inference in an authorship problem. J Am Stat Assoc **58**, 275–309 (1963)

8. McCulloch, W.S., Pitts, W.: A logical calculus of the ideas immanent in nervous activity. The bulletin of mathematical biophysics **5**(4), 115–133 (1943). https://doi.org/10.1007/BF0247 8259

9. Saygin, A.P., Cicekli, I., Akman, V.: Turing test: 50 years later. Minds and Machines **10**(4), 463–518 (2000). https://doi.org/10.1023/A:1011288000451

10. Rámirez, D.H.: El Machine Learning a Través de Los Tiempos, y Los Aportes a La Humanidad Denniye Hinestroza Ramírez **17** (2018)

11. Cox, D.R.: The regression analysis of binary sequences. J. Royal Statis. Soc. Series B (Methodological) **20**, 215–232 (1958). https://doi.org/10.1111/j.2517-6161.1958.tb00292.x

12. Morgan, J.N., Sonquist, J.A.: Problems in the analysis of survey data, and a proposal. J Am Stat Assoc **58**, 415–434 (1963). https://doi.org/10.1080/01621459.1963.10500855

13. Minsky, M., Papert, S.: Perceptrons, Introduction, pp. 1–20 and p. 73. Cambridge, MA: MIT Press (1988). (1969) (figure 5.1). In: Neurocomputing, vol 1. The MIT Press, pp 157–170

14. Breiman, L.: Arcing classifier (with discussion and a rejoinder by the author). The Annals of Statistics 26 (1998). https://doi.org/10.1214/aos/1024691079

15. Breiman, L.: Random Forests. **45**, 5–32 (2001)

16. Navarro, P.P.: Estilometría con fines geolingüísticos aplicada al corpus {COSER}. Revista de Humanidades Digitales **6**, 22–42 (2021). https://doi.org/10.5944/rhd.vol.6.2021.30870

17. Savoy, J.: Is Starnone really the author behind Ferrante? Digital Scholarship in the Humanities **33**, 902–918 (2018). https://doi.org/10.1093/llc/fqy016

18. Álvaro, C., Germán Vega, G.L.: Estilometría aplicada al Teatro del Siglo de Oro | ETSO (2022)

19. Maitra, P., Ghosh, S., Das, D.: Authorship verification-an approach based on random forest (2016). arXiv preprint arXiv:160708885

20. Akhtyamova, L., Cardiff, J., Ignatov, A.: Twitter author profiling using word embeddings and logistic regression. In: CLEF (Working Notes) (2017)

21. Staykovski, T.: Stacked Bots and Gender Prediction from Twitter Feeds

22. GitHub - jpotts18/stylometry: A Stylometry Library for Python

23. scikit-learn: machine learning in Python — scikit-learn 1.1.2 documentation

24. 3.1. Cross-validation: evaluating estimator performance — scikit-learn 1.1.2 documentation

Identification of Tropical Dry Forest Transformation from Soundscapes Using Supervised Learning

Andrés E. Castro-Ospina[1]([⊠]) [ID], Susana Rodríguez-Buritica[2] [ID],
Nestor Rendon[3] [ID], Maria C. Velandia-García[1] [ID], Claudia Isaza[3] [ID],
and Juan D. Martínez-Vargas[4] [ID]

[1] Instituto Tecnológico Metropolitano, Medellín, Colombia
{andrescastro2705,mariavelandia2095}@correo.itm.edu.co
[2] Alexander Von Humboldt Institute, Bogotá, Colombia
drodriguez@humboldt.org.co
[3] SISTEMIC, Engineering Faculty, Universidad de Antioquia-UdeA,
calle 67 No. 53 - 108, Medellín, Colombia
{nestor.rendon,victoria.isaza}@udea.edu.co
[4] Universidad EAFIT, Medellín, Colombia
jdmartinev@eafit.edu.co

Abstract. Biodiversity loss in tropical ecosystems is advancing due to factors such as human pressure and climate change, and determining their ecological transformation level can help to monitor climate change trends. Soundscapes can indicate the health of an ecosystem; therefore, passive acoustic monitoring is interesting because of its non-invasive nature, low cost, and allows recording over long periods. However, soundscapes generate a large amount of data that must be analyzed using automatic techniques such as machine learning to reduce manual labor. This process is generally based on acoustic indices, which present limitations such as sensitivity to background noise or biased results to the study sites under evaluation. Therefore, in this document, we propose training supervised models to identify landscape transformation from studied site soundscape at three stages: low, medium, and high. These models are trained on data collected in 24 tropical sites in the Colombian Caribbean region from 2015 to 2017. To achieve this, we extracted high-level features from a VGGish architecture from each recording to assess the performance of features obtained from the raw time series with neural networks. Furthermore, we compared the features from VGGish with 60 acoustic indices as features to train Random Forest, Neural Network, and XGBoost classifiers. F1-score for test data accomplishes a performance of 90% with the XGBoost classifier on the acoustic indices set, and the neural network achieves 95% for the VGGish feature set. Through supervised models, it is possible to identify the level of transformation of an ecosystem from its soundscape.

Keywords: Landscape transformation · passive acoustic monitoring · soundscape · supervised learning

© The Author(s), under exclusive license to Springer Nature Switzerland AG 2023
F. R. Narváez et al. (Eds.): SmartTech-IC 2022, CCIS 1705, pp. 173–184, 2023.
https://doi.org/10.1007/978-3-031-32213-6_13

1   Introduction

In recent decades, climate change, human expansion, and massive land use have led to a deterioration in the world's biodiversity, mainly reflected in habitat fragmentation and loss [12]. It is essential to generate strategies that promote the conservation and restoration of ecosystems based on their monitoring and evaluation. Traditional methods for ecological monitoring are limited because they depend on the expertise of whoever performs them; they are costly, invasive, and labor-intensive, both for acquisition and subsequent analysis [7]. Among the possible solutions to these problems, passive acoustic monitoring (PAM) stands out, which is non-invasive and allows continuous data acquisition without disturbing the natural environment of the habitats. PAM seeks to relate the soundscape to the processes occurring within ecosystems since sound is abundant in animal environments and can be highly informative, allowing the opportune transfer of information without the need for visual contact between transmitter and receiver [20]. Furthermore, the soundscape can account for the health and dynamics of an ecosystem, reflecting its structure and functioning [19].

PAM has generated an area known as soundscape ecology, which has rapidly grown in recent years. Due to the large amount of data it generates, it is necessary to automate their processing since changes in ecosystems can be evidenced by changes in the patterns of their soundscapes. Machine learning techniques are a valuable tool for analyzing large amounts of data and identifying patterns and modifications of these patterns. With the current machine learning techniques, it is possible to automatically analyze large amounts of sounds and make conservation-relevant decisions such as abundance estimation, individual species identification, and ecosystem health assessment [21]. The use of acoustic indices generated from audio signals or representations in other domains is widespread. It seeks to explain the characteristics or behaviors of the different components of the soundscape [3,15]. Some researchers have used some of these acoustic features to answer ecological questions. For example, Ferroudj et al. used decision trees for rainfall identification in ecoacoustic signals [4], Do Nascimento et al. showed that it is possible to predict habitat type from acoustic indices [2], and Rendón et al. proposed a beta index to quantify acoustic heterogeneity related to landscape transformation [13].

On the other hand, some studies have shown relationships between acoustic complexity, measured by acoustic indices, and some landscape components. A work showed that acoustic diversity is related to patch size [10]. Another component that has been evaluated is acoustic heterogeneity between geographical points of recording based on three GMM models, one for each period of the day (morning, day, and night). They were trained on acoustic indices to establish a general pattern for low, medium, and high transformation levels [13]. As a result, the Acoustic Heterogeneity Index (AHI) index was proposed. However, it has also been shown that acoustic indices can be limited because they are sensitive to background noises such as rain or wind and anthropogenic sounds [1,14]. Additionally, they can give results biased to the study regions and present unpredictable behaviors when used in new environments [17]. Furthermore, some studies have reported contradictory patterns using the same indices [6]. These factors have led to the need for more consensus on which indexes are the most efficient, leading to the idea that consistency in data acquisition should be pursued.

In this work, we aimed to train supervised learning models to automatically identify the gradient of transformation levels based on the soundscapes acquired by passive acoustic monitoring. Transformation is the capability for an ecosystem to become another [5], and its evaluation could directly impact tropical dry forest conservation efforts, being a fast and easy way to evaluate conservation devotions. Random forest, Neural Network, and Extreme Gradient Boosting (XGBoost) classifiers are trained on two feature sets to identify transformation: acoustic indices and VGGish high-level features [9]. Low, medium and high levels of ecosystem transformation are identified with high reliability. The highest accuracy achieved was 90% for XGBoost for the acoustic indices set and 95% for Neural Network on the VGGish features. These high-level features are calculated entirely from the raw recorded information.

2   Materials and Methods

2.1   Site of Study

The study sites are areas with tropical dry forest ecosystems. They are located in the Caribbean region of Colombia in the departments of La Guajira and Bolivar, specifically in the basins of the Arroyo and Cañas rivers. Recordings locations are depicted in Fig. 1, and it is worth noting that similar recording points were used for some of the 24 recorders in different years. These locations have high endemism levels, high precipitation changes, an altitude between 0 and 1000 m above sea level, and dry periods of between 3 and 6 months.

2.2   Recordings

The acoustic recordings were provided by the Alexander Von Humboldt Institute (IAVH) and were acquired between December 2015 and March 2017. SM2 and SM3 recorders (wildlife acoustics) were programmed to record 5 min every 10 min for five continuous days and stop recording for five days. These records were acquired as part of the Global Environment Facility (GEF) project, designed to characterize the biodiversity of tropical dry forest remnants in Colombia [8].

IAVH labeled the sample sites soundscapes according to the gradient of ecological transformation level (high, medium, low). Each transformation level was given through the proportions of Retained/Lost/New forest patches of subwatersheds changes in 20 years. With this approximation, forest age was defined by grouping patches into three groups: Retained were forests older than 22 years, Lost were forests younger than four years, and New were forests between 22 and 4 years. Each category was given using baseline geographic information (hydrology, digital elevation models, topographic attributes, roads, urban and rural centers, Corine Land Cover vegetation maps, among others). Then a low level of

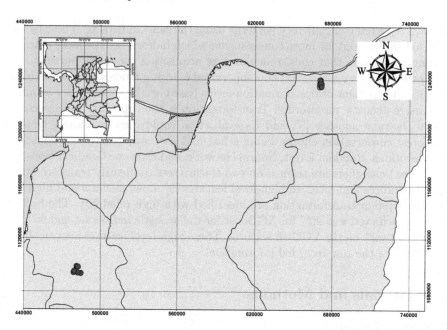

Fig. 1. Geographical location of passive acoustic monitoring devices in the Caribbean region of Colombia. ● 2015, ● 2016 and ● 2017.

transformation corresponds to areas with a higher proportion of Retained/New forests and a lower proportion of lost forests. High transformation level refers to sites with high forest loss and medium transformation in the remaining sites.

2.3   Feature Extraction and Classification Approaches

Figure 2 shows the flow of the experimental setup. On the one hand, 60 acoustic indices were extracted from each recording recorded at the 24 locations. Table 1 and Table 2 provide each of the 16 temporal and 44 spectral indices considered. These were computed with the Python package scikit-maad [22]. On the other hand, a widely used deep audio embedding model, namely the VGGish model, is used as a feature extractor. This model was trained on Youtube-8M data and is composed of multiple convolutions and max-pooling layers using ReLU activation functions, followed by three fully connected layers of dimensions 4096, 4096, and 128, respectively. Therefore, a 128-dimensional vector is computed for every segment of 0.96 s. Since the total duration for each recording is 5 min, a total of 312 vectors are estimated. These are averaged, leading to a single 128-dimensional feature vector for every recording. Finally, the corresponding label of the study site is assigned to the computed feature sets (acoustic index or VGGish).

80% of each feature set is used as the training set, while the remaining 20% as the test set. From the training set, it is extracted 20% as the validation set to validate the performance and tune the hyperparameters of the classifiers. After this split, supervised models are trained, namely a Random Forest, a Neural Network, and XGBoost classifier. Finally, results for each model are reported on test data.

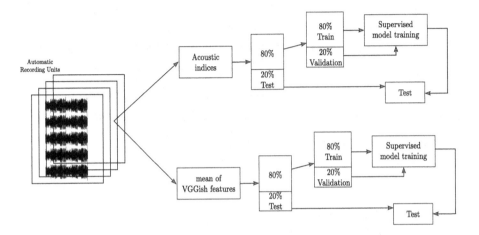

Fig. 2. Proposed experimental setup.

Random Forest. As a first step, a random forest classifier is fitted with the training set. Maximum depth and number of trees hyperparameters were tuned by assessing the performance on the validation test. Values between 5 and 30 were evaluated for maximum depth, and for the number of trees, values between 80 and 150. Finally, 20 was set as the maximum depth value, and the number of trees was established at 100. This classifier is selected because of its status as an embedded feature selector. The Python scikit-learn module was used to train this classifier.

Neural Network. A fully connected network is implemented and trained on the training set. The network comprises an input layer of 60 neurons for the acoustic indices and 128 for the VGGish features. Values between 10 and 50 were evaluated for the number of hidden units, and 16, 32, 64, and 128 as batch size. The best results were achieved with a hidden layer of 10 neurons with ReLU as an activation function and batches of size 64. The output layer has a size of three since that is the number of classes to identify. The network was trained by minimizing cross-entropy loss as the loss function with an Adam optimizer set with a learning rate of 0.005 and trained along 50 epochs. These hyperparameter values were chosen by assessing the performance of the neural network on the

Table 1. Temporal acoustic indices extracted from each recording

Temporal Acoustic Index	Description
ZCR	Zero Crossing Rate
MEANt, VARt, SKEWt, KURTt	First four statistical moments of an audio signal
LEQt	Equivalent Continuous Sound level
BGNt	Estimation of the background energy computed in the time domain
SNRt	Signal-to-noise ratio computed in the time domain
MED	Median of the envelope of an audio signal
Ht	Entropy of the envelope of an audio signal
ACTtFraction, ACTtCount, ACTtMean	Acoustic activity index in the temporal domain
EVNtFraction, EVNtMean, EVNtCount	Acoustic event index from an audio signal

validation set. The PyTorch library was used to implement and train this neural network classifier [11].

XGBoost. Finally, an XGBoost classifier was trained on both feature sets. Maximum depth and the number of estimators hyperparameters were tuned by assessing the performance on the validation test achieving a value of 20 for maximum depth and 100 for the number of estimators. This classifier was trained using the XGBoost library for Python.

2.4   Performance Measures

Accuracy, recall, and F1-score were used to evaluate the trained classifiers' performance. These measures are based on the elements that can be defined in a confusion matrix, which are:

- *True Positive (TP)*: number of correct predictions made by the supervised model for the target class
- *False Positive (FP)*: number of data belonging to the non-target class but classified as of the target class
- *False Negative (FN)*: number of data belonging to the target class but classified as of the non-target class
- *True Negative (TN)*: number of correct predictions made by the supervised model for the non-target class.

Table 2. Spectral acoustic indices extracted from each recording

Spectral Acoustic Index	Description
MEANf, VARf, SKEWf, KURTf	First four statistical moments of an amplitude spectrogram
NBPEAKS	Number of frequency peaks on a mean spectrum
LEQf	Equivalent Continuous Sound level from a power spectrogram
ENRf, BGNf, SNRf	signal-to-noise ratio of audio from its spectrogram
Hf	Spectral entropy of a power spectrogram density
EAS, ECU, ECV, EPS, EPS_KURT, EPS_SKEW	Different entropies based on the average spectrum, its variance, and its maxima
ACI	Acoustic Complexity Index from a spectrogram
NDSI, rBA, AnthroEnergy, BioEnergy	Normalized Difference Soundscape Index from a power spectrogram
BI	Bioacoustics Index from a spectrogram
ROU	roughness of spectrogram
ADI	Acoustic Diversity Index from a spectrogram
AEI	Acoustic Evenness Index from a spectrogram
LFC, MFC, HFC	Proportion of the spectrogram above a threshold for low, medium, and a high-frequency band
ACTspFract, ACTspCount, ACTspMean	Acoustic activity on a spectrogram
EVNspFract, EVNspMean, EVNspCount	Acoustic events from a spectrogram
TFSD	Time-frequency derivation index from a spectrogram
H_Havrda, H_Renyi, H_pairedShannon, H_gamma, H_GiniSimpson	Entropy of an audio signal using multiple methods
RAOQ	Rao's quadratic entropy on a power spectrum
AGI	Acoustic Gradient Index from a raw spectrogram
ROItotal, ROIcover	acoustic activity index based on the regions of interest detected on a spectrogram

Precision. Quantifies the proportion of data classified in the target class that belongs to it, expressed as Eq. (1):

$$Precision = \frac{TP}{TP + FP} \tag{1}$$

Recall. Calculates the proportion of data belonging to the target class that is correctly classified and is expressed as Eq. (2):

$$Recall = \frac{TP}{TP + FN} \tag{2}$$

F1-Score. F1-score is used to combine the precision and recall measures into a single value by computing their harmonic mean, expressed as Eq. (3):

$$Recall = 2 \frac{Precision \cdot Recall}{Precision + Recall} \tag{3}$$

3   Results

Achieved results are summarized in Table 3 and Table 4, reporting precision, recall, and F1-score for each trained supervised model. The former shows results on the acoustic indices features, while the latter on the VGGish features. Moreover, on Fig. 3 and Fig. 4 are presented the confusion matrices for the trained supervised models for acoustic indices and VGGish high-level features, respectively.

From the results of the classifiers on the acoustic indices feature set shown in Table 3, it can be seen how XGBoost achieves an accuracy of 0.9, higher than Random Forest and Neural Network classifiers. Accordingly, it achieves higher precision and recall measures.

For VGGish features results, as shown in Table 4, the highest accuracy results are achieved by the Neural Network classifier, namely 0.95. However, the classifier with higher precision for the low transformation label is XGBoost. Fewer false positives and false negatives occur when using VGGish features compared to acoustic indices for the three classifiers used, which can be seen in the confusion matrices in Fig. 3 and Fig. 4.

The 60 acoustic indices required an average computation time of 26.41 ± 6.5 seconds per recording, whereas the high-level VGGish features took an average computation time of 16.24 ± 3.87 seconds per recording.

It is worth noting that all three trained classifiers performed better when using VGGish features than acoustic index features. This is consistent with results on x-vectors over i-vectors on automatic sound tasks [18] and with the work presented by Sethi et al. [17], where a common feature space is computed through a VGGish model and is used to predict biodiversity and habitat quality metrics with a random forest classifier, achieving more accurate predictions than those based on acoustic indices. The same feature space served as input for

Table 3. Achieved results of supervised classification of acoustic indices

| | Classifier | | | | | | | | |
| | Random Forest | | | Neural Network | | | XGboost | | |
	precision	recall	F1-score	precision	recall	F1-score	precision	recall	F1-score
Low	0.86	0.83	0.85	0.88	0.86	0.87	0.9	0.88	0.89
Medium	0.89	0.91	0.9	0.91	0.93	0.92	0.92	0.94	0.93
High	0.83	0.82	0.83	0.87	0.86	0.87	0.88	0.86	0.87
Accuracy			0.87			0.89			0.9
macro avg	0.86	0.86	0.86	0.89	0.88	0.89	0.9	0.89	0.9
weighted avg	0.87	0.87	0.87	0.89	0.89	0.89	0.9	0.9	0.9

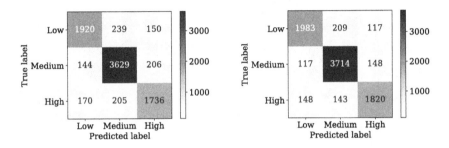

(a) Confusion matrix for Random forest classifier.   (b) Confusion matrix for Neural Network classifier.

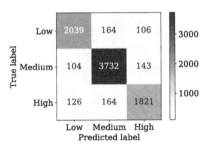

(c) Confusion matrix for XGBoost classifier.

Fig. 3. Confusion matrices for trained classifiers on test data for acoustic indices

subsequent supervised (classification) and unsupervised (outlier identification) learning tasks, demonstrating that automatic soundscape analysis enables fast and scalable ecological monitoring. In another similar work, birds were differentiated from anurans using CNN architectures, correctly identifying 34 of 39 species [16]. This work takes advantage of acoustic features inferred by a CNN, which subsequently served as indicative of species occurrence.

Table 4. Achieved results of supervised classification of VGGish high-level features

| | Classifier | | | | | | | | |
| | Random Forest | | | Neural Network | | | XGboost | | |
	precision	recall	F1-score	precision	recall	F1-score	precision	recall	F1-score
Low	0.93	0.88	0.9	0.93	0.95	0.94	0.95	0.92	0.93
Medium	0.92	0.95	0.94	0.97	0.96	0.96	0.94	0.96	0.95
High	0.89	0.89	0.89	0.94	0.94	0.94	0.91	0.92	0.92
Accuracy			0.92			0.95			0.94
macro avg	0.91	0.91	0.91	0.94	0.95	0.95	0.94	0.93	0.93
weighted avg	0.92	0.92	0.92	0.95	0.95	0.95	0.94	0.94	0.94

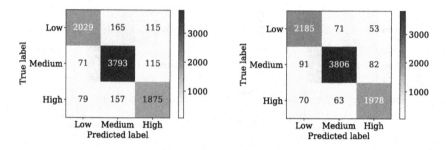

(a) Confusion matrix for Random forest classifier. (b) Confusion matrix for Neural Network classifier.

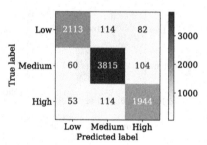

(c) Confusion matrix for XGBoost classifier.

Fig. 4. Confusion matrices for trained classifiers on test data for VGGish features.

4   Conclusions

This paper compared different supervised models to classify tropical dry forest transformation from its soundscapes. Acoustic indices and high-level features extracted from a deep audio embedding model are used as feature sets. The results show that the training and use of supervised models allow identifying with high reliability the transformation levels of an ecosystem from its soundscape, namely low, medium and high. It should be noted that deep audio embedding allows obtaining higher accuracy results for the three trained classifiers: Random

Forest, Neural Network, and XGBoost, achieving an accuracy of 92%, 95%, and 94%, respectively. Using acoustic indices has proven to achieve results biased to the study sites. At the same time, the embedded spaces are fully calculated from the recorded information, achieving superior results when used for the purpose presented in this paper.

Time dynamics should be included in these supervised approaches for future work, either by periods or the time of day. Furthermore, a method must be established to provide ecological interpretability to the features estimated with the VGGish model since they are related to the spectrograms estimated from the soundscapes. Finally, the data used in this work should be tested in an unsupervised setting, with the advantage of not needing labeled data.

Acknowledgments. This work was supported by Universidad de Antioquia, Instituto Tecnológico Metropolitano de Medellín, Alexander von Humboldt Institute for Research on Biological Resources and Colombian National Fund for Science, Technology and Innovation, Francisco Jose de Caldas - MINCIENCIAS (Colombia). [Program No. 111585269779].

References

1. Browning, E., Gibb, R., Glover-Kapfer, P., Jones, K.E.: Passive acoustic monitoring in ecology and conservation. WWF Conserv. Technol. Ser. **1**(2), 75 (2017). https://www.wwf.org.uk/conservationtechnology/documents/Acousticmonitoring-WWF-guidelines.pdf

2. Do Nascimento, L.A., Campos-Cerqueira, M., Beard, K.H.: Acoustic metrics predict habitat type and vegetation structure in the Amazon. Ecol. Ind. **117**(May), 106679 (2020). https://doi.org/10.1016/j.ecolind.2020.106679

3. Doser, J.W., Finley, A.O., Kasten, E.P., Gage, S.H.: Assessing soundscape disturbance through hierarchical models and acoustic indices: a case study on a shelterwood logged northern Michigan forest. Ecol. Ind. **113**, 106244 (2020). https://doi.org/10.1016/j.ecolind.2020.106244

4. Ferroudj, M.: Detection of rain in acoustic recordings of the environment using machine learning techniques **8862**(March), 104–116 (2015)

5. Folke, C., Carpenter, S.R., Walker, B., Scheffer, M., Chapin, T., Rockström, J.: Resilience thinking: integrating resilience, adaptability and transformability. Ecol. Soc. **15**(4), 9 (2010)

6. Fuller, S., Axel, A.C., Tucker, D., Gage, S.H.: Connecting soundscape to landscape: which acoustic index best describes landscape configuration? Ecol. Ind. **58**, 207–215 (2015). https://doi.org/10.1016/j.ecolind.2015.05.057

7. Gibb, R., Browning, E., Glover-Kapfer, P., Jones, K.E.: Emerging opportunities and challenges for passive acoustics in ecological assessment and monitoring. Meth. Ecol. Evol. **10**(2), 169–185 (2019). https://doi.org/10.1111/2041-210X.13101

8. Hernández, A., González, R., Villegas, F., Martínez, S.: Bosque seco tropical. Monitoreo Comunitario de la Biodiversidad. cuenca río Cañas (2019)

9. Hershey, S., et al.: CNN architectures for large-scale audio classification. In: 2017 IEEE International Conference on Acoustics, Speech and Signal Processing (ICASSP), pp. 131–135. IEEE (2017)

10. Müller, S., et al.: Ecoacoustics of small forest patches in agricultural landscapes: acoustic diversity and bird richness increase with patch size. Biodiversity **21**(1), 48–60 (2020). https://doi.org/10.1080/14888386.2020.1733086
11. Paszke, A., et al.: Pytorch: an imperative style, high-performance deep learning library. In: Advances in Neural Information Processing Systems, vol. 32 (2019)
12. Pörtner, H., et al.: IPBES-IPCC co-sponsored workshop report on biodiversity and climate change (2021)
13. Rendon, N., Rodríguez-Buritica, S., Sánchez-Giraldo, C., Daza, J.M., Isaza, C.: Automatic acoustic heterogeneity identification in transformed landscapes from Colombian tropical dry forests. Ecolo. Ind. **140**, 109017 (2022)
14. Ross, S.R., Friedman, N.R., Yoshimura, M., Yoshida, T., Donohue, I., Economo, E.P.: Utility of acoustic indices for ecological monitoring in complex sonic environments. Ecol. Ind. **121**(October), 107114 (2021). https://doi.org/10.1016/j.ecolind.2020.107114
15. Sánchez-Giraldo, C., Correa Ayram, C., Daza, J.M.: Environmental sound as a mirror of landscape ecological integrity in monitoring programs. Perspect. Ecol. Conserv. **19**(3), 319–328 (2021). https://doi.org/10.1016/j.pecon.2021.04.003
16. Sethi, S.S., et al.: Soundscapes predict species occurrence in tropical forests. Oikos **2022**, e08525 (2021)
17. Sethi, S.S., et al.: Characterizing soundscapes across diverse ecosystems using a universal acoustic feature set. Proc. Nat. Acad. Sci. **117**(29), 17049–17055 (2020)
18. Snyder, D., Garcia-Romero, D., Sell, G., Povey, D., Khudanpur, S.: X-vectors: Robust DNN embeddings for speaker recognition. In: 2018 IEEE International Conference On Acoustics, Speech and Signal Processing (ICASSP), pp. 5329–5333. IEEE (2018)
19. Stowell, D., Sueur, J.: Ecoacoustics: acoustic sensing for biodiversity monitoring at scale (2020)
20. Sugai, L.S.M., Silva, T.S.F., Ribeiro, J.W., Llusia, D.: Terrestrial passive acoustic monitoring: review and perspectives. BioScience **69**(1), 5–11 (2019). https://doi.org/10.1093/biosci/biy147
21. Tolkova, I.: Feature representations for conservation bioacoustics: review and discussion. Harvard University (2019)
22. Ulloa, J.S., Haupert, S., Latorre, J.F., Aubin, T., Sueur, J.: Scikit-maad: an open-source and modular toolbox for quantitative soundscape analysis in python. Meth. Ecol. Evol. **12**, 2334–2340 (2021)

Atmospheric Dispersion Prediction for Toxic Gas Clouds by Using Machine Learning Approaches

Maria Ines Valle Rada$^{(\boxtimes)}$, Bethsy Guerrero Granados, Christian G. Quintero M, César Viloria-Núñez, Jairo Cardona-Peña, and Miguel Ángel Jimeno Paba

Universidad del Norte, KM5 Vía Puerto, Barranquilla, Atlántico, Colombia
`{Mivalle,bethsyg,christianq,caviloria,jacardona,`
`majimeno}@uninorte.edu.co`

Abstract. The to the frequent industrial accidents of chemical origin present today, some tools can predict atmospheric dispersion considering meteorological and chemical factors and the incident scenario. However, they have limitations, such as not being scalable and not allowing integrations with other software, e.g., ALOHA (Areal Locations of Hazardous Atmospheres). This work seeks to develop an intelligent system to predict atmospheric dispersion in common chemicals in industries. The variables involved in the process are studied and characterized, and the tool is designed and implemented using machine learning techniques and validated through different case studies. After characterizing the parameters, the following step is creating the database to develop the automatic learning tool. Furthermore, the results obtained by applying the techniques such as Random Forest (RF), K-Nearest Neighbors (KNN), and Multi-Layer Perceptron (MLP) were compared to evaluate them as suitable alternatives for atmospheric dispersion prediction, the objective is to obtain a predictive tool as accurately as possible without using ALOHA software. The results shows that the KNN technique obtained the best performance in the RMSE measurement in the three scenarios evaluated: Chlorine spill, Gasoline spill and Benzene Leak.

Keywords: Atmospheric dispersion · Machine learning · Random forest · Multilayer perceptron · Support vector machines · Aloha

1 Introduction

Due to the massive growth of industries in recent decades, sudden accidents are becoming more frequent. In these accidents, the released chemicals harmfully affect the environment and people around it [1]. Knowing the atmospheric dispersion of the released chemical is crucial to measuring the accident impact and taking the necessary preventive actions.

There are several cases of industrial accidents in the world. For instance, the technological accident described in [24] where more than 40 tons of methyl isocyanate gas

© The Author(s), under exclusive license to Springer Nature Switzerland AG 2023
F. R. Narváez et al. (Eds.): SmartTech-IC 2022, CCIS 1705, pp. 185–198, 2023.
https://doi.org/10.1007/978-3-031-32213-6_14

in Bohpal, leaked from a pesticide plant, killing at least 3800, many injured and premature death for many thousands more. At national level, in Colombia, the spill of nitric acid on a highway due to the collision of two dump trucks, the leak of sulfuric acid on streets, two emergencies due to chlorine emanations on the route, and the fire of two isopropyl alcohol tanks in a company, all of them in Barranquilla city [2]. In order to attend to this type of emergency, laws, groups, and guidelines as PNUMA (United Nations Environment Program), also as APELL a worldwide program, established in 1986 by UNEP in partnership with the US EPA, CEFIC andthe internationalchemical industry (right after the 1984 Bhopal accident). APELL is now implement in more than 30 countries, providing several guidance materials and promoted a series of awareness raising workshops and pilot demonstration projects [25].

At local level, APELL Barranquilla process were created. APELL supervises the prevention, preparation, and response to risk situations in the industries belonging to this group. In 2017, companies that adhered to the APELL process in Barranquilla carried out a study of risk scenarios. The study showed a methodological guide to identify the main risk scenarios in companies and evaluate the consequences to determine the emergency plan. In this sense, ALOHA is a software package used to plan for and respond to chemical emergencies; It helps to determine threat zones [3]. The software receives information about an actual or potential chemical release and then generates estimations about the threat zones as shown in Fig. 1. ALOHA can model toxic gas clouds, flammable gas clouds, boiling liquid expanding vapor explosions, jet fires, swimming pool fires, and vapor cloud explosions. Hazard area estimation is displayed on a grid in ALOHA and can also plot on maps in MARPLOT, Esri's ArcMap, Google Earth, and Google Maps [4].

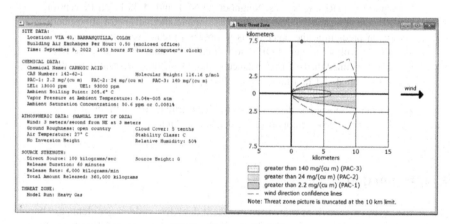

Fig. 1. Aloha results [4]

Nevertheless, ALOHA has some limitations. Although it is free software, ALOHA cannot be integrated with other platforms to perform automatic data entry and extract simulation results. Also, the list of optional chemicals to simulate cannot be updated.

Nationwide, many companies use ALOHA software to simulate atmospheric dispersion in chemical accidents and predict atmospheric dispersion in each chemical. Using the latest generation tools to strengthen this process in industries is evident. The use of machine learning tools emerges as an alternative to improve and optimize this process thanks to its efficiency and high capacity for data analysis, which would not require the formulas used by the ALOHA software to simulate each of the scenarios.

The modeling of the atmospheric dispersion of certain substances is important for the preservation of the environment and the nearby population [5–7]. It is relevant to have a system to assess the consequences and environmental impact on air quality, nevertheless, it is also crucial to make an adequate and rapid prediction. It is appropriate to have more than one tool in case there are different types of substance release events [8], or otherwise, to have one that is functional for all the scenarios that may occur.

Nowadays, machine learning techniques are an alternative that offers advantages to be able to make all kinds of predictions. In chemistry, toxicity prediction can benefit from machine learning thanks to the wide variety of computational techniques on offer [9].

2 Related Work

In recent years, Colombia has proposed machine learning tools to deal with social, environmental, and health problems. For example, to make predictions related to covid-19 [10], predict trends in homicides and robberies in the country [11], or the generation of urban waste in the city of Bogotá [12]. Nevertheless, there are no works related to predicting atmospheric dispersion at the national level.

Therefore, it is relevant to investigate whether there are already machine learning solutions for atmospheric dispersion prediction and the progress made in this field. There are some machine learning solutions for predicting toxic dispersions. For instance, an approach to build a toxic dispersion database using PHAST simulations (paid software to risk analysis) included 30,022 toxic release scenarios of 19 chemicals. A quantitative consequence prediction model to efficiently and accurately predict dispersal distances downwind was created based on this database. The developed model had favorable results that demonstrated the power of deep learning in analyzing the consequences of toxic dispersion [13]. Likewise, there are other articles in which the developed models try to predict the behavior of certain chemical substances using other machine learning techniques.

Reference [14] presents an approach of an ecological risk assessment for a river. The study revealed the potential of machine learning models for predicting the reproductive toxicity effects of chemical endocrine disruptors, which cause many ecological problems. The results showed that the SVM model is more accurate than the correlation model.

Another study applied back propagation (BP) and support vector regression (SVR) models to predict atmospheric dispersion. The challenge with these models is determining the input variables. Therefore, two inputs are selected: the original monitoring parameters and integrated Gaussian parameters. The results indicate that the integrated Gaussian parameters present better results in machine learning models [15].

As it is known, predicting the limits of atmospheric dispersion is relevant to taking the necessary actions. It is significant to know the atmospheric dispersion over time. In [16], a study was conducted to predict atmospheric dispersion using a neural network.

The factors to consider are the variables that define the atmospheric dispersion, the time, and the design of the facilities since those change constantly [16].

Another solution is to use model combinations to refine the results. For example, reference [17] presents a prediction algorithm with SVM combined with the traditional Gaussian model. The results show that the model adequately predicts atmospheric dispersion.

On the other hand, an approach implemented the five more popular machine learning techniques for air pollution prediction where the Multilayer Perceptron (MLP) showed the best performance [18].

Reference [19] shows the results obtained from an investigation to predict air pollution. The study conducted experiments with two specific contaminants. The several compared models determined that the best one is the autoregressive nonlinear neural network.

Reference [20] also attempts to predict air pollution. The authors propose a multi-point deep learning model based on convolutional long short-term memory. The results show that the proposed model is superior to other more common ones.

This research aims to check if it is feasible to develop a solution based on machine learning for atmospheric dispersion prediction of different types of chemical products in different risk scenarios. The objective is to obtain the impact distances from atmospheric dispersion. With a tool that will predict the impact zone of a chemical accident, preventive actions can be taken, such as preparing and alerting the nearby community and protecting the environment.

This work aims to develop an intelligent system for predicting atmospheric dispersion in common chemicals in industries. For this, research and characterization of variables involved in atmospheric dispersion are conducted. Then, an intelligent system to predict gas dispersion is designed and implemented. Finally, the validation of the developed system through different case studies is carried out.

3   Scenarios

To define the industrial accident to be evaluated, a group of experts reported on the most common in the case study industrial zone (city of Barranquilla, Colombia). The experts determined the scenarios of a chlorine spill, a gasoline spill, and a benzene leak as potential accidents in the area. Therefore, those are the scenarios chosen for their study in this article.

Table 1 shows the required meteorological variables for the simulation of the scenarios for each chemical. In addition, Table 1 shows the range of variation for each variable. These ranges are determined by the software options and the geographical area in which the accident is evaluated.

Table 2 shows the variables that describe the scenario of each chemical. Unlike the meteorological variables, which are the same for the three scenarios, the variables in Table 2 are different depending on the scenario to be simulated, since different aspects must be considered for each one.

Table 1. Characterization of Inputs Meteorological Variables

Variable	Range or Options
Building	Enclosed office building, Single storied building, Double storied building
Building surroundings	Unsheltered surroundings, Sheltered surroundings
Location	Vía 40
Wind speed (m/s)	3, 4, 5, 6
Wind direction	NE, NNE, ENE, ESE
Measurement height (m)	3
Ground roughness	Urban or forest, Open country
Cloud cover (Scale)	0, 3, 5, 7, 10
Air temperature (°C)	Between 18 and 35
Humidity (%)	Between 77 and 87

Table 2. Characterization of input variables for each chemical

Chemical	Variable	Range or Options
Chlorine	Source	Instantaneous or continue
	Amount pollutant entering the atmosphere	Instantaneous source: 1ton, 68kg. Continue source: 1ton/min, 68kg/min
	Source height (m)	Length of the tank
Gasoline	Source	Instantaneous or continue
	Amount pollutant entering the atmosphere (Kg)	Between 10 and 300
	Source height (m)	Between 0 and 100
	Store	Liquid
	Initial Puddle Temperature	Ambient temperature
Benzene	Tank type	Vertical
	Length (m)	Between 20 and 60
	Diameter (m)	Between 9 and 27
	Chemical state	Liquid
	Temperature within tank (°C)	Ambient temperature
	Liquid volume (%)	Between 0 and 100
	Type of tank failure	BLEVE
	Percentage of mass in the fireball (%)	Between 0 and 100

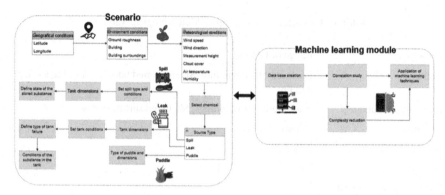

Fig. 2. Methodology's block diagram

4 Methodology

The methodology implemented can be seen in Fig. 2, which consists of two (2) modules, the first one that summarizes the characterization of the scenario to be evaluated (Scenario section) and the second (2) that represents the Machine Learning module (Machine Learning Module section) that receives as input the defined scenario and whose implemented methodology is explained below.

After defining the scenarios and their parameters, a Python code is developed to generate the cases to be simulated in ALOHA to register the outputs and save the information in a CSV file.

Studying the correlation between the inputs and outputs of the system to validate the information is very important. In the case of finding a high correlation between two or more inputs, only one of them is used to reduce the complexity of the data set. The correlation study is also needed to determine which inputs are most influential and essential for the resulting outputs. The simulator is trained with the synthetic data from the scenarios modeled in the ALOHA software.

Subsequently, different machine learning techniques to determine which one is the most suitable for the experiment are implemented. The algorithms selected for the implementation of machine learning techniques are the Random Forest model (RF), K-Nearest Neighbors (KNN), and Multi-Layer Perceptron (MLP). These techniques are selected in the review in the state of the art since they have been applied to similar problems and the results obtained have been satisfactory.

The decision tree is a graph like structure in the form of a tree which shows possible consequences based on the inputs given. RF is a collection of such multiple decision trees. The result is based on the decision of the majority of trees [18]. For the implementation of this model in Python, the RandomForestRegressor library of sklearn is used. The algorithm is configured with 100 trees in the forest, with a minimum of 1 sample required to split an internal node and the maximum number of features Random Forest can test on a single tree is 1. The decision tree is a graph-like structure in the form of a tree that shows possible consequences based on the inputs given. RF is a collection of multiple decision trees. The result is based on the decision of the majority of trees [18]. The RandomForestRegressor library of sklearn is used to implement this model in Python.

The algorithm is configured with 100 trees in the forest, with a minimum of 1 sample required to split an internal node, and the maximum number of features Random Forest can test on a single tree is 1.

In KNN, the relation of a query to a neighboring sample is measured by a similarity metric, such as Euclidean distance. This process starts with mapping the training dataset onto a one-dimensional distance space based on the calculated similarities and then labeling the query by the most dominant or mean of the labels of the k nearest neighbors [21]. The KNeighborsRegressor library of sklearn three (3) neighbors is used.

The MLP consists of multiple layers of neurons that interact using weighted connections. After a lowermost input layer, there is usually any number of intermediate or hidden layers followed by an output layer at the top. Weights measure the degree of correlation between the activity levels of neurons that they connect [22, 23]. The MLPRegressor library of sklearn is used to implement this model in Python. The configured hyperparameters are one (1) layer, three (3) neurons, the rectified linear unit activation function, and how to solve an optimizer in the quasi-Newton family of methods. Finally, the results are compared with the actual data through a specific evaluation metric.

5   Testing and Results

A database with 200 chlorine spills, 200 gasoline spills, and 200 benzene leak cases is created. The input variables for chlorine are 16 and three (3) output variables. So on, for gasoline spills with a total of 21 input variables and three (3) output variables. Finally, in benzene leak case with 20 input and three (3) output variables. Having account for all the possible values for each input variable, the different combinations between them are made. To obtain the outputs and complete the database each case is simulated in ALOHA. The results generated by ALOHA are three different distances identified by the colors yellow, orange, and red These distances represent the gas dispersion zones, and the colors allude to the toxicity levels.

Once the database is completed, a correlation study between the variables is carried out. The study is necessary to evaluate if variables depend on each other. If this happens, the complexity level of the system could be reduced.

Pearson's correlation is implemented in the input and output variables of the three scenarios. Figures 3, 4, and 5 show the results for each scenario. Most of the variables show a low correlation with each other. In some cases, there are high levels of correlation. For example, there is a high correlation between the source type (continuous and instantaneous) and the duration of the spill in the cases of chlorine spills and gasoline spills. That happens because the duration of the spill depends on the type of source. In this case, the type of source could be eliminated since this information can be known with the value of the duration. In addition, the type of source also plays an important role in defining the amount of contaminant that is spilled. Therefore, there is no reduction in complexity between these two variables.

Based on the results, it is determined that most of the variables are independent of each other. Therefore, it is not possible to reduce the variables for the proposed algorithms. These results confirms that a correct processing of the data is carried out.

160 of the cases from the database are used to train the machine learning models. The remaining 40 cases are used for validation (to compare them with the predictions

of each model). Each machine learning model is run 10 times to have 40 random cases in each iteration so 400 predictions are then obtained for each model.

	Wind speed	Cloud cover	Air themperature	Humidity	Duration (For)	Source height	Amount pollutant	Double storied	Enclosed office	Single office	Urban or forest	Open country	Continue	Instantaneous	Sheltered	Unsheltered	Red distance	Orange distance	Yellow distance
Wind speed	1	-0,02	-0,02	0,06	-0,12	-0,01	0,03	-0,04	0,02	0,02	-0,06	0,06	-0,1	0,1	-0,06	0,05	0,05	-0,12	-0,11
Cloud cover	-0,02	1	0,05	-0,01	-0,02	-0,05	-0,03	-0,01	0,05	-0,04	0,04	-0,04	0,08	-0,08	0,04	-0,1	0,07	0,04	0,01
Air themperature	-0,02	0,05	1	0,09	-0,05	-0,08	0,06	0,04	0,03	-0,08	0	0	-0,03	0,03	0,08	-0,12	0,14	0	-0,03
Humidity	0,06	-0,01	0,09	1	-0,08	-0,03	-0,1	0	-0,03	0,02	-0,11	0,11	-0,06	0,06	0,03	0	-0,02	-0,08	-0,1
Duration (For)	-0,12	-0,02	-0,05	-0,08	1	0,04	-0,52	-0,09	-0,03	0,12	0,01	-0,01	0,81	-0,81	0,03	-0,02	-0,09	0,18	0,28
Source height	-0,01	-0,05	-0,08	-0,03	0,04	1	-0,03	-0,05	0,14	-0,08	0,05	-0,05	0,02	-0,02	-0,02	-0,1	-0,14	0	0,02
Amount pollutant en	0,03	-0,03	0,06	-0,1	-0,52	-0,03	1	-0,01	0,04	-0,03	0,03	-0,03	-0,61	0,61	-0,04	0,01	-0,05	-0,01	-0,03
Double storied	-0,04	-0,01	0,04	0	-0,09	-0,05	-0,01	1	-0,51	-0,54	0,04	-0,04	-0,13	0,13	0,22	0,26	0,03	-0,14	-0,14
Enclosed office	0,02	0,05	0,03	-0,03	-0,03	0,14	0,04	-0,51	1	-0,44	-0,03	0,03	-0,06	0,06	-0,46	-0,49	0,03	-0,06	-0,05
Single office	0,02	-0,04	-0,08	0,02	0,12	-0,08	-0,03	-0,54	-0,44	1	-0,02	0,02	0,2	-0,2	0,23	0,21	-0,07	0,2	0,19
Urban or forest	-0,06	0,04	0	-0,11	0,01	0,05	0,03	0,04	-0,03	-0,02	1		-0,03	0,03	0,04	0	-0,02	-0,12	-0,13
Open country	0,06	-0,04	0	0,11	-0,01	-0,05	-0,03	-0,04	0,03	0,02		1	0,03	-0,03	-0,04	0	0,02	0,12	0,13
Continue	-0,1	0,08	-0,03	-0,06	0,81	0,02	-0,61	-0,13	-0,06	0,2	-0,03	0,03	1	-1	0,04	0,01	-0,1	0,48	0,52
Instantaneous	0,1	-0,08	0,03	0,06	-0,81	-0,02	0,61	0,13	0,06	-0,2	0,03	-0,03	-1	1	-0,04	-0,01	0,1	-0,48	-0,52
Sheltered	-0,06	0,04	0,08	0,03	0,03	-0,02	-0,04	0,22	-0,46	0,23	0,04	-0,04	0,04	-0,04	1	-0,54	0,05	0,09	0,07
Unsheltered	0,05	-0,1	-0,12	0	-0,02	-0,1	0,01	0,26	-0,49	0,21	0	0	0,01	-0,01	-0,54	1	-0,08	-0,02	-0,01
Red distance	0,05	0,07	0,14	-0,02	-0,09	-0,14	-0,05	0,03	0,03	-0,07	-0,02	0,02	-0,1	0,1	0,05	-0,08	1	-0,07	-0,08
Orange distance	-0,12	0,04	0	-0,08	0,18	0	-0,01	-0,14	-0,06	0,2	-0,12	0,12	0,48	-0,48	0,09	-0,02	-0,07	1	0,98
Yellow distance	-0,11	0,01	-0,03	-0,1	0,28	0,02	-0,03	-0,14	-0,05	0,19	-0,13	0,13	0,52	-0,52	0,07	-0,01	-0,08	0,98	1

Fig. 3. Correlation study in chlorine scenario.

	Wind speed	Cloud cover	Air themperature	Humidity	Amount pollutant	Duration	SourceHeight	Stored Themperature	Direction ENE	Direction ESE	Direction NE	Direction NNE	Urban or forest	Open country	Continue	Instantaneous	Double storied	Enclosed office	Single office	Sheltered	Unsheltered	Red distance	Orange distance	Yellow distance
Wind speed		-0,09	-0,02	-0,07	0,09	-0,06	0,03	-0,02	0,04	0,01	-0,11	0,07	0	0	0	0	0,01	0,05	-0,06	0,03	-0,07	-0,02	0,06	0,08
Cloud cover	-0,09		-0,07	0,05	0,06	-0,04	-0,1	-0,07	-0,14	0	0,01	0,15	-0,07	0,04	-0,04	-0,03	0	0,03	0	0	0,03	-0,04	-0,05	
Air themperature	-0,02	-0,07		0,07	-0,02	-0,01	-0,03		0,04	-0,07	0,07	-0,06	0,04	-0,04	-0,01	0,01	-0,03	-0,02	0,05	-0,06	0,08	-0,04	-0,05	-0,06
Humidity	-0,07	0,05	0,07		0,07	0,06	-0,03	0,07	-0,01	0,08	0,03	-0,11	0,05	-0,05	0,08	-0,08	0,04	-0,03	-0,01	0	0,03	0,03	0,09	0,08
Amount pollutant	0,09	0,06	-0,02	0,07		-0,62	-0,04	-0,06	-0,03	-0,1	0,1	0,02	-0,02		0,73	0,73	0,11	-0,18	0,07	0,04	0,13	-0,16	-0,34	-0,39
Duration	-0,06	-0,04	-0,01	0,06	-0,62		0,06	-0,01	-0,1	0,06	0,09	-0,05	-0,02	0,02	0,77	-0,77	-0,13	0,21	-0,07	-0,04	-0,16	0,01	0,38	0,47
SourceHeight	0,03	-0,1	-0,03	-0,03	-0,04	0,06		-0,03	0,05	0,14	-0,06	-0,13	0,01	-0,01	0,04	-0,04	0,02	0,03	-0,05	-0,04	0,02	0,02	0	0
Stored Themperature	-0,02	-0,07		0,07	-0,02	-0,01	-0,03		0,04	-0,07	0,07	-0,06	0,04	-0,04	-0,01	0,01	-0,03	-0,02	0,05	-0,06	0,08	-0,04	-0,05	-0,06
Direction ENE	0,04	-0,14	0,04	-0,01	0,04	-0,1	0,05	0,04		-0,31	-0,43	-0,33	-0,05	0,05	-0,08	0,08	0,01	-0,04	0,03	-0,03	0,07	-0,07	-0,09	-0,09
Direction ESE	0,01	0	-0,07	0,08	-0,03	0,06	0,14	0,07	-0,31		-0,32	0,25	0,07	-0,07	0,01	-0,01	-0,05	0,1	-0,04	-0,08	-0,01	-0,06	-0,04	-0,04
Direction NE	-0,11	0,01	0,07	0,03	-0,1	0,09	-0,06	0,07	-0,43	-0,32		-0,35	0,01	-0,01	0,13	-0,13	0,04	-0,07	0,03	0,11	-0,04	0,13	0,2	0,19
Direction NNE	0,07	0,15	-0,06	-0,11	0,1	-0,05	-0,13	-0,06	-0,33	-0,25	-0,35		-0,02	0,02	-0,07	0,07	-0,01	0,03	-0,02	-0,01	-0,02	-0,02	-0,08	-0,08
Urban or forest	0	0,04	0,05	0,02	-0,02	0,06	0,04	-0,06	-0,05	0,07	0,01	-0,02		-1	-0,01	0,01	-0,07	0,03	0,1	0,01	0,02	-0,14	-0,05	-0,03
Open country	0	0,07	-0,04	-0,05	0,02	0,02	-0,01	-0,04	0,05	0,07	-0,01	0,02	-1		0,01	-0,01	0,07	0,03	-0,1	-0,01	-0,02	0,14	0,05	0,03
Continue	0	-0,04	-0,01	0,08	0,73	0,77	-0,04	0,07	-0,08	0,01	0,13	-0,07	-0,01	0,01		-1	-0,16	0,17	-0,01	-0,06	-0,11	0,5	0,72	0,77
Instantaneous	0	0,04	0,01	-0,08	0,73	-0,77	-0,04	0,01	0,08	-0,01	-0,13	0,07	0,01	-0,01	-1		0,16	-0,17	0,01	0,06	0,11	-0,5	-0,72	-0,77
Double storied	0,01	-0,03	-0,03	0,04	0,11	-0,13	0,02	-0,03	0,01	-0,05	0,04	-0,01	-0,07	0,07	-0,16	0,16		-0,51	-0,51	0,27	0,24	-0,03	-0,12	-0,15
Enclosed office	0,05	0	-0,02	-0,03	-0,18	0,21	0,03	-0,02	-0,04	0,1	-0,07	0,03	0,03	0,03	0,17	-0,17	-0,51		-0,47	-0,48	-0,5	0,05	0,12	0,14
Single office	-0,06	0,03	0,05	-0,01	0,07	-0,07	-0,05	0,05	0,03	-0,04	0,03	-0,02	0,1	-0,1	-0,01	0,01	-0,51	-0,47		0,21	0,26	-0,02	0,01	0,01
Sheltered	0,03	0	-0,06	0	0,04	-0,04	-0,04	-0,06	0,03	-0,08	0,11	-0,01	0,01	-0,01	-0,06	0,06	0,27	-0,48	0,21		-0,51	-0,01	0,01	0,01
Unsheltered	-0,07	0	0,08	0,03	0,13	-0,16	0,02	0,08	0,07	-0,01	-0,04	-0,02	0,02	-0,02	-0,11	0,11	0,24	-0,5	0,26	-0,51		-0,04	-0,12	-0,14
Red distance	-0,02	0,03	-0,04	0,03	-0,16	0,01	0,02	-0,04	-0,07	-0,06	0,13	-0,02	-0,14	0,14	0,5	-0,5	-0,03	0,05	-0,02	-0,01	-0,04		0,78	0,7
Orange distance	0,06	-0,04	-0,05	0,09	-0,34	0,38	0	-0,05	-0,09	-0,04	0,2	-0,08	-0,05	0,05	0,72	-0,72	-0,12	0,12	0,01	0,01	-0,12	0,78		0,99
Yellow distance	0,08	-0,05	-0,06	0,08	-0,39	0,47	0	-0,06	-0,09	-0,04	0,19	-0,08	-0,03	0,03	0,77	-0,77	-0,15	0,14	0,01	0,01	-0,14	0,7	0,99	

Fig. 4. Correlation study in gasoline scenario.

To compare the results of the models, the Root Mean Square Error (RMSE) is used as an evaluation metric, also used by the authors in [13] and [18]. The RMSE is a common metric for comparing different predictive models because it is a suitable measure of how

	Wind speed	Cloud cover	Air themperature	Humidity	Diameter	Lenght	Temperature in tank	Liquid Volume	Percentage Mass Fireball	Direction ENE	Direction ESE	Direction NE	Direction NNE	Urban or forest	Open country	Double storied	Enclosed office	Single office	Sheltered	Unsheltered	Red distance	Orange distance	Yellow distance
Wind speed	1	0,02	-0,03	-0,11	-0,01	-0,07	-0,05	0,11	-0,01	-0,14	0,2	0	-0,06	0,01	-0,01	0,04	-0,02	-0,02	0,13	-0,11	0,04	0,04	0,03
Cloud cover	0,02	1	-0,04	0,19	-0,01	-0,04	-0,07	-0,06	-0,09	-0,11	0,05	0,12	-0,05	-0,09	0,09	-0,05	-0,06	0,11	-0,01	0,07	-0,1	-0,1	-0,09
Air themperature	-0,03	-0,04	1	0,08	0,06	0	0,96	0,07	0,07	-0,04	0,02	0,03	0	0,02	-0,02	0,07	-0,18	0,11	0,1	0,07	0,02	0,03	0,02
Humidity	-0,11	0,19	0,08	1	-0,05	0	0,09	-0,14	-0,02	0,08	-0,18	-0,02	0,12	0,04	-0,04	-0,03	0,07	-0,04	-0,03	-0,04	-0,1	-0,1	-0,1
Diameter	-0,01	-0,01	0,06	-0,05	1	0,06	0,08	-0,03	0,03	-0,05	-0,05	-0,01	0,11	0,03	-0,03	-0,06	-0,15	0,21	0,07	0,08	0,48	0,49	0,49
Lenght	-0,07	-0,04	0	0	0,06	1	0,05	-0,04	-0,02	0,14	-0,06	-0,03	-0,06	-0,02	0,02	0,04	-0,04	0	-0,01	0,05	0,43	0,42	0,43
Temperature within	-0,05	-0,07	0,96	0,09	0,08	0,05	1	0,07	0,05	-0,03	0	0,07	-0,03	0,04	-0,04	0,07	-0,2	0,13	0,11	0,09	0,05	0,05	0,04
Liquid Volume	0,11	-0,06	0,07	-0,14	-0,03	-0,04	0,07	1	0,05	-0,07	-0,08	0,05	0,11	0,04	-0,04	0,12	-0,15	0,02	0	0,14	0,47	0,48	0,47
Percentage Mass in F	-0,01	-0,09	0,07	-0,02	0,03	-0,02	0,05	0,05	1	0,02	0,07	-0,05	-0,04	0,1	-0,1	0	-0,01	0,01	-0,11	0,12	0,52	0,52	0,52
Direction ENE	-0,14	-0,11	-0,04	0,08	-0,05	0,14	-0,03	-0,07	0,02	1	-0,38	-0,35	-0,37	-0,04	0,04	0,02	0,02	-0,04	-0,11	0,09	0	-0,01	0
Direction ESE	0,2	0,05	0,02	-0,18	-0,05	-0,06	0	-0,08	0,07	-0,38	1	-0,29	-0,31	-0,01	0,01	0,13	-0,03	-0,1	0,07	-0,04	-0,04	-0,04	-0,04
Direction NE	0	0,12	0,03	-0,02	-0,01	-0,03	0,07	0,05	-0,05	-0,35	-0,29	1	-0,29	-0,04	0,04	-0,08	-0,11	0,19	0,13	-0,02	-0,03	-0,02	-0,03
Direction NNE	-0,06	-0,05	0	0,12	0,11	-0,06	-0,03	0,11	-0,04	-0,37	-0,31	-0,29	1	0,1	-0,1	-0,07	0,11	-0,04	-0,08	-0,04	0,06	0,06	0,06
Urban or forest	0,01	-0,09	0,02	0,04	0,03	-0,02	0,04	0,04	0,1	-0,04	-0,01	-0,04	0,1	1	-1	0,07	0	-0,06	0,01	-0,01	0,03	0,04	0,03
Open country	-0,01	0,09	-0,02	-0,04	-0,03	0,02	-0,04	-0,04	-0,1	0,04	0,01	0,04	-0,1	-1	1	-0,07	0	0,06	-0,01	0,01	-0,03	-0,04	-0,03
Double storied	0,04	-0,05	0,07	-0,03	0,06	0,04	0,07	0,12	0	0,02	0,13	-0,08	-0,07	0,07	-0,07	1	-0,48	-0,51	0,34	0,14	0,04	0,05	0,05
Enclosed office	-0,02	-0,06	-0,18	0,07	-0,15	-0,04	-0,2	-0,15	-0,01	0,02	-0,03	-0,11	0,11	0	0	-0,48	1	-0,51	-0,49	-0,5	-0,13	-0,14	-0,13
Single office	-0,02	0,11	0,11	-0,04	0,21	0	0,13	0,02	0,01	-0,04	-0,1	0,19	-0,04	-0,06	0,06	-0,51	-0,51	1	0,14	0,36	0,1	0,09	0,09
Sheltered	0,13	-0,01	0,1	-0,03	0,07	-0,01	0,11	0	-0,11	-0,11	0,07	0,13	-0,08	0,01	-0,01	0,34	-0,49	0,14	1	-0,51	-0,05	-0,05	-0,05
Unsheltered	-0,11	0,07	0,07	-0,04	0,08	0,05	0,09	0,14	0,12	0,09	-0,04	-0,02	-0,04	-0,01	0,01	0,14	-0,5	0,36	-0,51	1	0,18	0,18	0,18
Red distance	0,04	-0,1	0,02	-0,1	0,48	0,43	0,05	0,47	0,52	0	-0,04	-0,03	0,06	0,03	-0,03	0,04	-0,13	0,1	-0,05	0,18	1	1	1
Orange distance	0,04	-0,1	0,03	-0,1	0,49	0,42	0,05	0,48	0,52	-0,01	-0,04	-0,02	0,06	0,04	-0,04	0,05	-0,14	0,09	-0,05	0,18	1	1	1
Yellow distance	0,03	-0,09	0,02	-0,1	0,49	0,43	0,04	0,47	0,52	0	-0,04	-0,03	0,06	0,03	-0,03	0,05	-0,13	0,09	-0,05	0,18	1	1	1

Fig. 5. Correlation study in benzene scenario.

well a model predicts the response. Table 3 shows the RMSE in each scenario for the three models developed. The lower the RMSE value, the better the model.

According to Table 3, the KNN model is the most suitable for predicting atmospheric dispersion. In each of the scenarios, the KNN model is the one that shows the best results for the three different distances. Additionally, Table 4 shows the accuracy of the machine learning models in predicting the yellow distance, the orange distance, and the red distance. In the case of chlorine, the best model according to this metric is the KNN, confirming the conclusions obtained with the RMSE. In contrast, in the case of a gasoline spill, the accuracy is very similar for the KNN model and the MLP model. However, considering the results when comparing the RMSE, the KNN model is still the best candidate to predict the danger distance in a gasoline spill. For the case of a benzene leak, the three models have a similar accuracy in predicting the yellow and orange distances. On the other hand, for the red distance, the RF and MLP models are less accurate. For this reason, the KNN model turns out to be the most suitable for this scenario.

Table 3. RMSE Results

Scenario	Model	Yellow	Orange	Red
Chlorine spill	RF	4.52	5.07	712.03
	KNN	0.55	0.86	12.23
	MLP	39.3	47.93	119.75
Gasoline spill	RF	10.83	7.22	3.79
	KNN	2.36	2.04	0.87
	MLP	59.11	45.32	108.13
Benzene leak	RF	70.11	180.75	203.42
	KNN	0.33	0.23	0.14
	MLP	87.65	126.12	176.51

Table 4. Accuracy results

Scenario	Model	Yellow	Orange	Red
Chlorine spill	RF	93.08	93.37	20.84
	KNN	90.37	91.45	84.66
	MLP	83.59	80.5	73.77
Gasoline spill	RF	89.62	85.89	69.46
	KNN	85.13	83.06	88.09
	MLP	87.66	80.38	67.97
Benzene leak	RF	88.18	86.82	34.91
	KNN	83.68	80.38	80.94
	MLP	82.65	81.06	72.85

On the other hand, Figs. 6, 7 and 8 present a box-and-whisker plot for the chlorine, gasoline and benzene scenarios, respectively. This diagram is helpful to compare the total of the actual results (those predicted by ALOHA) with the results predicted with the proposed KNN model. Box-and-whisker plots are a visual presentation of data characteristics such as spread and symmetry.

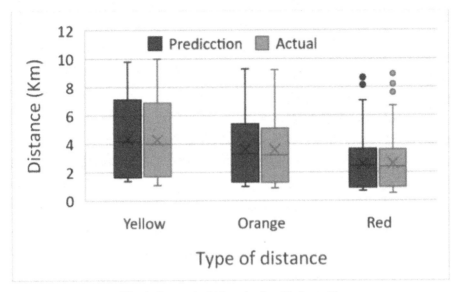

Fig. 6. Box and whisker plot for chlorine spill.

In Figs. 6, 7, 8 it can be seen that for each type of distance evaluated, the behavior of the predictions made is very similar to the behavior of the training data. In Figs. 5 and 6, outliers in the ALOHA's predictions for the red distance, and our system also predicts them adequately.

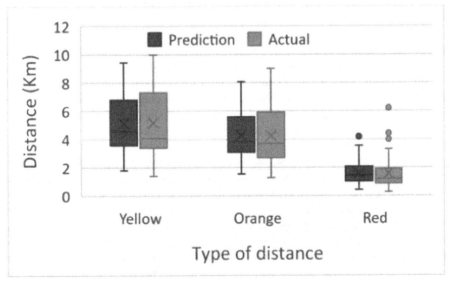

Fig. 7. Box and whisker plot for gasoline spill.

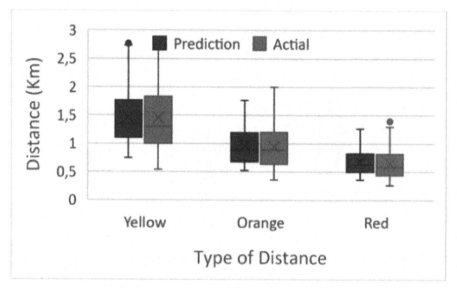

Fig. 8. Box and whisker plot for benzene leak.

6   Conclusions

The research determined that the application of machine learning techniques fits the requirements of this assessment.

The main chemicals and scenarios are identified in the development of the system, considering the most common accidents in the industry (e.g., tank leakage, fire, or exploitation). Likewise, the characterization of the variables is a crucial part of each process, atmospheric variables (wind speed, air temperature, location, altitude) and accident scenario variables (tank type, volume, chemical state, bottom of leak). With the characterized variables, the design of experiments to fill the database was carried out.

Subsequently, the database created has information about simulations in ALOHA for the chemicals (chlorine, gasoline, and benzene) in changing scenarios. With this information and the implementation of a simulator developed in Python, the different machine learning techniques are trained and tested. The simulator plots the correlation of the selected database and graphics the machine learning techniques results for each case of the risk areas (red, yellow, and orange), contrasting the algorithm's prediction vs. the actual data from the database. The results are satisfactory; The KNN technique obtained the best performance in the RMSE measurement in all the scenarios evaluated.

In conclusion, the research fully complied with the objectives set allowing in the future work, the replication of the procedure implemented for other chemicals and scenarios. With the purpose of analyze which is the machine learning technique that shows the best performance according to the selected chemical to determinate if there is a technique that in general encompasses the trend for all chemicals. In future work, the distances obtained with the predictive model will be used to make atmospheric scatter plots.

References

1. Xie, Y., Kuang, J., Wang, Z.: Atmospheric dispersion model based on GIS and Gauss algorithm. In: Proceedings of the 29th Chinese Control Conference, pp. 5022–5027 (2010)
2. APELL: PREVENCIÓN Y ATENCIÓN DE LAS EMERGENCIAS QUÍMICAS: El Tiempo, [En línea]. Disponible en: https://www.eltiempo.com/archivo/documento/MAM-573542
3. Consuegra, J.M.: Guía para la gestión de los riesgos tecnológicos para las empresas adherentes al proceso APELL del D.E.I.P Barranquilla. Prospectiva **15**(2), 96–106 (Julio 2017)
4. United States Environmental Protection Agency: CAMEO (Computer-Aided Management of Emergency Operations). [Online]. Available in: https://www.epa.gov/cameo. Consulted in: 7 May 2022
5. Leung, W.H., Ma, W.M., Chan, P.K.Y.: Nuclear accident consequence assessment in Hong Kong using JRODOS. J. Environm. Radioactiv. **183**, 27–36 (March 2018). https://doi.org/10.1016/j.jenvrad.2017.12.002
6. Beckett, F.M., et al.: Atmospheric dispersion modelling at the London VAAC: a review of developments since the 2010 eyjafjallajökull volcano ash cloud. Atmosphere **11**(4), 352 (2020). https://doi.org/10.3390/atmos11040352
7. Abdul-Wahab, S., Al-Rawas, G., Ali, S., Fadlallah, S., Al-Dhamri, H.: Atmospheric dispersion modeling of CO2 emissions from a cement plant's sources. Clean Technol. Environ. Policy **19**(6), 1621–1638 (2017). https://doi.org/10.1007/s10098-017-1352-y
8. Bradley, M.M.: NARAC: an emergency response resource for predicting the atmospheric dispersion and assessing the consequences of airborne radionuclides. J. Environ. Radioactiv. **96**(1–3), pp. 116–121 (Jul 2007). https://doi.org/10.1016/j.jenvrad.2007.01.020
9. Wu, Y., Wang, G.: Machine learning based toxicity prediction: from chemical structural description to transcriptome analysis. Int. J. Mol. Sci. **19**(8), 2358 (2018). https://doi.org/10.3390/ijms19082358
10. Espinosa, O., et al.: Vulnerability interactive geographic viewer against COVID-19 at the block level in Colombia: analytical tool based on machine learning techniques. Regional Science Policy & Practice (Sep. 2021). Accessed: 18 May 2022. [Online]. Available: https://doi.org/10.1111/rsp3.12469
11. Ordoñez-Eraso, H.A., Pardo-Calvache, C.J., Cobos-Lozada, C.A.: Detection of Homicide Trends in Colombia Using Machine Learning. Rev. Fac. Ing. **29**(54), e11740 (2019). Oct.
12. Solano Meza, J.K., Orjuela Yepes, D., Rodrigo-Ilarri, J., Cassiraga, E.: Predictive analysis of urban waste generation for the city of Bogotá, Colombia, through the implementation of decision trees-based machine learning, support vector machines and artificial neural networks. vol. 5, no. 11. Heliyon (Nov. 2019). Art. no. e02810. Accessed: 18 May 2022. [Online]. Available: https://doi.org/10.1016/j.heliyon.2019.e02810
13. Jiao, Z., Ji, C., Sun, Y., Hong, Y., Wang, Q.: Process safety and environmental protection, 2021–08, Vol. 152, p. 352–360
14. Fan, J., et al.: Prediction of chemical reproductive toxicity to aquatic species using a machine learning model: An application in an ecological risk assessment of the Yangtze River, China. Science of The Total Environment **796**, 148901 (Nov. 2021). Accessed: 18 May 2022. [Online]. Available: https://doi.org/10.1016/j.scitotenv.2021.148901
15. Wang, R., et al.: Comparison of machine learning models for hazardous gas dispersion prediction in field cases. Int. J. Environm. Res. Pub. Heal. **15**(7), 1450 (Jul. 2018). Accessed: 18 May 2022. [Online]. Available: https://doi.org/10.3390/ijerph15071450
16. Song, D., Lee, K., Phark, C., Jung, S.: Spatiotemporal and layout-adaptive prediction of leak gas dispersion by encoding-prediction neural network. Process Safety and Environmental Protection **151**, 365–372 (Jul. 2021). Accessed: 18 May 2022. [Online]. Available: https://doi.org/10.1016/j.psep.2021.05.021

17. Ma, D., Zhang, Z.: Contaminant dispersion prediction and source estimation with integrated Gaussian-machine learning network model for point source emission in atmosphere. J. Hazardous Materials **311**, pp. 237–245 (Jul. 2016). Accessed: 18 May 2022. [Online]. Available: https://doi.org/10.1016/j.jhazmat.2016.03.022

18. Simu, S., et al.: Air pollution prediction using machine learning. IEEE Bombay Section Signature Conference (IBSSC) **2020**, 231–236 (2020). https://doi.org/10.1109/IBSSC51096.2020.9332184

19. Delavar, M., et al.: A novel method for improving air pollution prediction based on machine learning approaches: a case study applied to the capital city of Tehran. ISPRS Int. J. Geo-Information **8**(2), 99 (Feb. 2019). Accessed: 19 May 2022. [Online]. Available: https://doi.org/10.3390/ijgi8020099

20. Mokhtari, I., Bechkit, W., Rivano, H., Yaici, M.R.: Uncertainty-aware deep learning architectures for highly dynamic air quality prediction. IEEE Access **9**, 14765–14778 (2021). https://doi.org/10.1109/ACCESS.2021.3052429

21. Erturul, M. F., Taluk, M.E.: Una versión novedosa de k vecino más cercano. Appl. Computación blanda **55**(núm. C), p. 480490 (junio de 2017). [en línea] Disponible: https://doi.org/10.1016/j.asoc.2017.02.020

22. Pal, S.K., Mitra, S.: Multilayer perceptron fuzzy sets classifiaction (1992)

23. Caballero, L., Jojoa, M., Percybrooks, W.: Optimized neural networks in industrial data analysis. SN Applied Sciences **2**(2) (2020)

24. Broughton, E.: The bhopal disaster and its aftermath: a review. Environmental Health **4**(1) (2005)

25. Suikkanen, J.: APELL Programme and Success Stories. UNEP-DTIE, Presentation material on the APELL Programme and Success Stories (June 2014). [Online]. Available: https://www.unep.org/resources/report/overview-apell-programme

Facial Recognition System with Liveness Detection Integrated into Odoo for Attendance Registration in a Software Laboratory

Oscar M. Cumbicus-Pineda[1]([✉]) [ID], Dayanna M. Alvarado-Castillo[1] [ID],
and Lisset A. Neyra-Romero[2] [ID]

[1] Carrera de Ingeniería en Sistemas/Computación, Universidad Nacional de Loja,
Ciudadela Universitaria, Loja, Ecuador
{oscar.cumbicus,dayanna.alvarado}@unl.edu.ec
[2] Dirección General de Tecnologías de la Información y Transformación Digital,
Universidad Técnica Particular de Loja, San Cayetano Alto, Loja, Ecuador
laneyra@utpl.edu.ec

Abstract. Facial recognition is currently adaptable to any context where the identification of individuals is required and has succeeded in replacing traditional form-filling authentication methods. Moreover, due to the current Covid-19 health crisis, face recognition turns out to be one of the main technologies useful for authentication without requiring the manipulation of community instruments. This paper presents the development of a facial recognition system with liveness detection integrated into Odoo ERP for the registration of attendance to a software laboratory, providing an alternative attendance registration that does not require the manipulation of community use instruments, shortening registration times and facilitating the creation of reports of laboratory use. The Design Thinking framework and its five phases, empathy, definition, ideation, prototyping, and testing, were used for the development of the project. The final face recognition system with liveness detection was developed using face-recognition and three-dimensional neural networks (3D-CNN). The system averages 95% prediction accuracy, requires an average of 9.2 s per person for registration and facilitates timely reporting of lab usage.

Keywords: Liveness detection · Face recognition · Odoo ERP · Design thinking · 3D CNN

1 Introduction

The two most important universal rights and factors in life are privacy and security [8]. Facial recognition is one of the most popular technologies in security today, this technology has currently been coupled to multiple global procedures, such as authentication in web/mobile applications [10], unlocking vehicles [20], access to rooms [15], smart education applications [11], registration of attendance in public and private institutions [2,3], among others [7,12], managing to replace traditional methods of authentication and translating as a technology that contributes positively [5].

In Ecuador few institutions have decided to apply facial recognition technology; despite its apogee, this technology is still an infrequent topic that has not reached a good development in our country, however, users should use and implement this type of technology that allows them to perform tasks in an agile, fast, simple, automated way and that in addition to being convenient in the face of the health crisis, it provides the opportunity to be competitive with the constant evolution of technologies [4].

For face recognition authentication to be categorized as a robust authentication method, it is essential to distinguish between a genuine live face and an attempt to spoof the system with a presentation attack [1]. Automatic detection of presentation attacks such as the one proposed by [14], and in particular, liveness detection models such as [19], have become a necessary component of any authentication system that relies on facial biometric technology in which the human does not monitor the authentication [13].

Liveness detection technology in biometrics is the ability of a system to detect whether a fingerprint or face (or other biometric data) is real (from a live person present at the point of capture) or fake (from a fake artifact or lifeless body parts such as photographs or videos) [18].

The objective of this research was to develop a facial recognition system with liveness detection integrated into Odoo ERP [9] for the registration of attendance in a software laboratory, as an alternative to manipulate instruments of community use, reduce registration times and allow the technical staff to create reports of laboratory use.

This work was developed taking as a guide the Design Thinking framework [16], which according to Tim Brown, CEO of IDEO is: "A human-centered approach to innovation that uses the designer's tools to integrate the needs of people, the possibilities of technology and the requirements for business success"[1]; the execution of each of its phases allowed the fulfillment of this project.

2 Methodology

One of the first steps for the project's execution is the architecture's design (Fig. 1). Within the presentation layer, there is the user interface which is accessed through a web browser Chrome, Opera, Firefox, etc., available on a computer, and in turn, there is a webcam that will act as a capture point for face detection, all this interface communicates directly with the web server that provides OpenERP, The same that interacts with the Odoo framework belonging to the business logic layer, here is the model, the view, the controller and the ORM that the business logic requires, the model is in constant communication with the model of facial recognition with liveness detection. The ORM (object-relational mapping) communicates directly with the PostgreSQL relational database.

---

[1] designthinking.ideo.com.

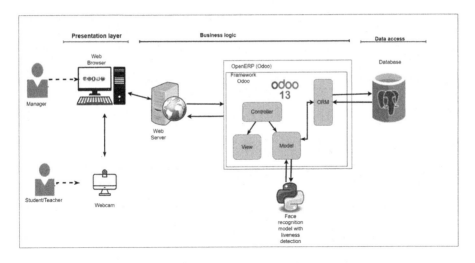

Fig. 1. Facial recognition system architecture

We used Design Thinking and its 5 phases to develop the work [6] (Fig. 2). In the empathy phase, information was collected on the current attendance registration process in the software laboratory, through interviews and surveys with the technician in charge, as well as with teachers and student users of the laboratory. Based on the information obtained, the diagramming of the current process according to the BPMN 2.0 notation was carried out with the tool, which is shown in Fig. 3.

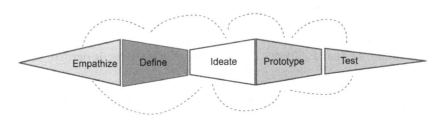

Fig. 2. Phases of the Design Thinking framework. The dotted lines on the figure refer to the fact that the phases of the framework can be addressed in a different order than presented here.

In the second phase, known in this framework as definition, the revelations or insights were identified. These insights were obtained from the analysis of the surveys and interviews, and are as follows:

– It is considered that if the attendance registration process continues to be carried out in the same way as it was done before the pandemic, the return to face-to-face practices could be an infectious focus on Coronavirus issues.

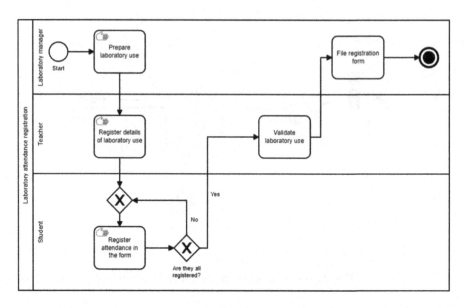

Fig. 3. The current attendance registration process in the software laboratory. Three actors are identified: the person in charge, the teacher, and the student. The process starts when the person in charge prepares the use of the laboratory, then the teacher registers the details of the use of the laboratory, the student registers his attendance in the form, they return to the teacher who validates the use of the laboratory and he hands it over to the person in charge who files the registration form.

- An alternative for attendance recording that does not require the manipulation of community-use instruments is desired.
- An alternative is desired where attendance recording does not consume an extended period.
- An alternative that facilitates reporting of laboratory use is desired.

The two challenges were also posed in this phase, using the How could we? technique. This technique focuses on turning disclosures into questions and results in the following challenges:

- How could we develop an alternative for attendance registration in the software lab using facial recognition?
- How could we develop liveness detection in facial recognition for attendance registration in the software lab?

To resolve the third phase, the brainstorming technique (Fig. 4) was applied to compile each of the possible solutions to the proposed challenges.

For the face recognition challenge, 4 techniques were proposed: Eigen-Face[2], Fisher-Face[3], Local Binary Pattern Histogram (LBPH)[4], and Face-Recognition[5]. For the second challenge, which was liveness detection (Fig. 4b), two techniques were considered: active focusing and passive focusing.

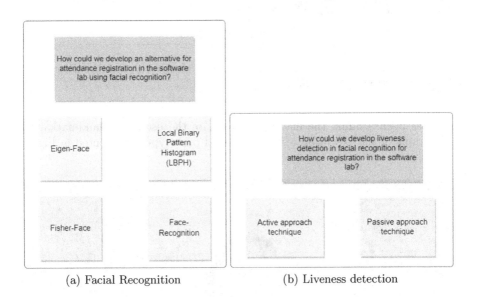

(a) Facial Recognition   (b) Liveness detection

Fig. 4. Brainstorming technique for the development of facial recognition and liveness detection method.

In the prototyping phase, prototypes were created for each of the ideas raised in the previous phase. For face recognition, prototypes were first developed with EigenFace, FisherFace, and LBPHFace, which are pre-trained methods with convolutional neural networks for feature extraction, these features are represented in the form of unique codes (Fig. 5).

A face recognition prototype was also made with Face-Recognition, an open source library developed in Python language that in turn implements dlib, the simplest face recognition library in the world that includes a pre-trained convolutional neural network, which allows detecting faces and facial features with an effectiveness of 99.38%.

In the case of prototyping for liveness detection, two prototypes were made, in the first one a method was executed to be able to recognize when the eyes have gone from open, closed, and again open state, that is, to recognize when

---

[2] https://docs.opencv.org/4.x/dd/d7c/classcv_1_1face_1_1EigenFaceRecognizer.html.

[3] https://docs.opencv.org/4.x/d2/de9/classcv_1_1face_1_1FisherFaceRecognizer.html.

[4] https://docs.opencv.org/4.x/df/d25/classcv_1_1face_1_1LBPHFaceRecognizer.html.

[5] https://pypi.org/project/face-recognition/.

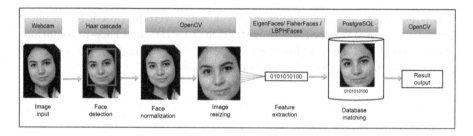

Fig. 5. Technologies applied in the face recognition phases with the EigenFaces, FisherFaces and LBPHFaces models.

there has been a blink, the method is based on the use of eye landmarks [17]. An example of the execution of the developed prototype is presented in Fig. 6.

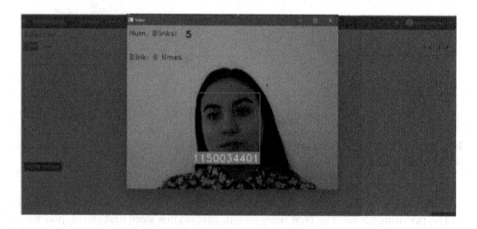

Fig. 6. Execution of the blink counter model

In the second prototype designed for liveness detection, a 3D convolutional network was used. Unlike 2D convolutional networks, this type of network measures the depth of the face presented at the point of capture. Since a photograph is a 2D coplanar image, it has no depth, likewise in video reproduction, it is not possible to measure its depth since the depth would be of the device that reproduces the video and not of the face presented in it. What was intended with this experiment is that in case a person in real-time is presented in front of the capture point, the depth of the face can be measured and the liveness detection will be approved.

Finally, in the testing phase, we evaluated the prototypes designed for both face recognition (Table 1) and liveness detection, with the result that the prototypes chosen were Face-Recognition and 3D convolutional neural networks, the latter being chosen because the prototype of the blink counter (Fig. 6) with the presentation of a video shows a false positive, which is why it is not taken as a solution.

Table 1. Comparison of experimentation with facial recognition models.

	Eigen-Face	Fisher-Face	LBPH-Face	Face-Recognition
The number of photographs per individual for the database	300	300	300	1
Training time	7	7	2	0
Need establishing a comparison threshold	Need	Need	Need	No need
Face detection model included	No included	No included	No included	Included
Recognition accuracy	Medium	Low	Medium	High

3   Results

3.1   Face Recognition with the Pre-trained Model Face-Recognition

For the evaluation of the model, the participation of 40 users of the software laboratory was requested. A total of 80 experiments were carried out, 40 corresponded to people registered (Fig. 7) in the system and the remaining ones with unregistered people.

After 80 experiments, the confusion matrix was constructed (Table 2), obtaining, as a result, a precision of the model concerning the positive values of 0.90, which corresponds to 90%, concerning the recognition sensitivity concerning the negative values, 1.00 was obtained, which corresponds to 100%, in total the harmonic mean between the positive and negative values is 0.94, which corresponds to 94%, finally the accuracy of the model, in general, is 95%. The results are detailed in Table 3.

3.2   Development of the Liveness Detection Model

In this experiment, a 3D convolutional network (Fig. 8) was used to develop the liveness detection model. Once the face has been recognized, the life detection begins by first taking as input the sequence of frames present in the frame, resizing it and changing it to grayscale, then detecting the height, width, and depth of the incoming image. These calculations are compared with the values

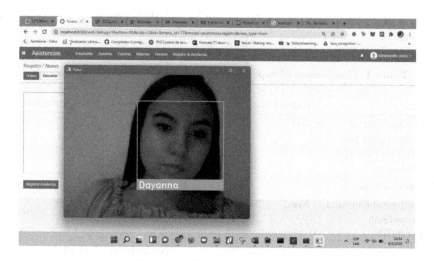

Fig. 7. Face recognition with Face-recognition framework

Table 2. Facial recognition confusion matrix

	Prediction	
Actual	VP	FN
	40	0
	FP	VN
	4	36

Table 3. Facial recognition model evaluation results

Metrics	Value
Accuracy	0.90
Sensitivity	1.00
Harmonic mean	0.94
Precision	0.95

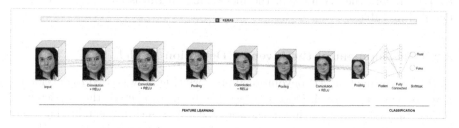

Fig. 8. 3D convolutional neural network architecture for liveness detection.

obtained in the liveness detection model with 3D convolutional neural networks, and a prediction is made, if the prediction is greater than 85%, the input is defined as an image of a user in real-time. The experimentation verified that the system is not vulnerable to both photo and video presentation attacks.

In the Fig. 9, a user's face was presented in front of the capture point in real-time, and it is observed that the life detector worked correctly, the result is as expected since the life of the input image was checked, the attendance was registered and the statement "Registered" was issued.

Fig. 9. Liveness detection with CNN 3D (user in real-time).

For the Fig. 10 experiment, the model also works correctly, it detected that it is not a person's face in real-time, therefore, although the face was recognized, the attendance was not recorded and the message "FAKE FACE" was issued, referring to it being a presentation attack.

Fig. 10. Liveness detection with CNN 3D (video playback).

To evaluate the liveness detection model, a total of 80 experiments were carried out, among which 40 times people in real-time and 40 times photographs or video reproductions were presented in front of the capture point, with which it was possible to construct the confusion matrix (Table 4), 97% was obtained as a result of the accuracy of the model in terms of the positive values, also according to the negative values a sensitivity of the model of 93% was obtained, the total harmonic mean between the positive values concerning the negative ones is 95%, finally, the global accuracy of the model constructed is 0. 95 which corresponds to 95% (Table 5).

Table 4. Confusion matrix of liveness detection.

	Prediction	
Actual	VP	FN
	37	3
	FP	VN
	1	39

Table 5. Results of the liveness detection model evaluation.

Metrics	Value
Accuracy	0.97
Sensitivity	0.93
Harmonic mean	0.50
Precision	0.95

3.3 Odoo Integration with Facial Recognition and Liveness Detection Module

Odoo ERP version 13 and the programming language Python version 3.7 were used, in addition, for the coding of the module the PyCharm programming IDE was used, which allowed editing, debugging the code, and configuring the execution of the Odoo service, to control the system versions the GitHub platform was used.

The default modules that are part of the ERP are located in the path /Odoo13.0/server/odoo/addons/, likewise, within this directory is stored the module for the attendance record that was developed for this work, it has been named attendances (Fig. 11), the system is structured as follows:

init.py: File containing the reference of the models and controllers.
manifest.py: File of utmost importance as it contains the necessary configurations for the module and decides which files to run and when.
controllers: The directory stores Python files that establish certain business logic, in this case, it has not been necessary to use it since the functions have been defined in the files of the model's directory.

Fig. 11. Structure of the attendance registration system.

When a new module is created in Odoo, there is the possibility of inheriting a default template called "base", which are defined the login methods, the methods to create, modify, list, and delete objects, so it was not necessary for the coding of these functionalities, it was necessary to create the module objects with their attributes and the coding of the respective views.

Figure 12 presents some attendance records within the administration system created in Odoo.

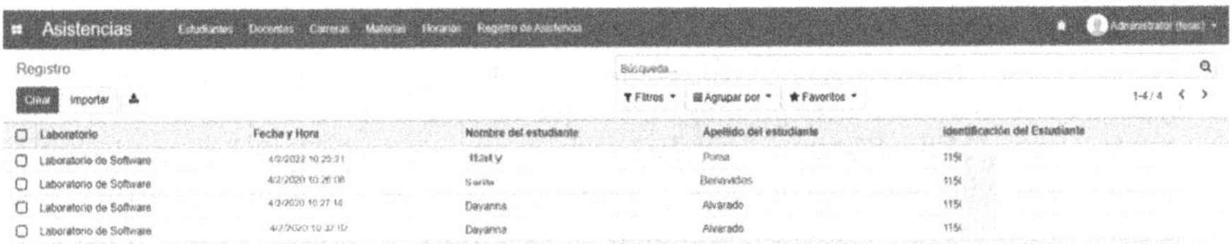

	Laboratorio	Fecha y Hora	Nombre del estudiante	Apellido del estudiante	Identificación del Estudiante
☐	Laboratorio de Software	4/2/2022 10:25:21	Itzel y	Poma	115i
☐	Laboratorio de Software	4/2/2020 10:25:06	Stanlie	Benavides	115i
☐	Laboratorio de Software	4/3/2020 10:27:18	Dayanna	Alvarado	115i
☐	Laboratorio de Software	4/3/2020 10:27:10	Dayanna	Alvarado	115i

Fig. 12. The attendance registration module was created in Odoo, where you can list all attendance records.

4   Discussion

In the present work it has been possible to create a module for facial recognition and liveness detection, developed using Face-Recognition and 3D Convolutional Networks, this module has been successfully integrated into Odoo ERP version 13.

The tests executed in a real environment, with the participation of volunteer students who make use of the software laboratories, allowed us to corroborate the good performance of the developed system, which has a global accuracy of 95%, both for face recognition and liveness detection.

In the tests performed, it was corroborated that even though the photos stored in the database were captured in a different scenario from the one in which the facial recognition was performed and that they contained different luminosity and gestures, Face-recognition yielded good results, besides having the advantage that it only requires one image per user in the database, its computational cost is low.

The use of 3D convolutional neural networks gives security to the system against any attempt of impersonation using photos or videos of the students. Finally, the system takes an average of 9.2 s to register and its web module facilitates the creation of lab usage reports.

5 Conclusions

The pre-trained classifier called Face-Recognition enabled face detection and recognition using a considerably small database with only one photo per user. Three-dimensional convolutional neural networks allowed the development of the liveness detection model with a passive approach since they determine the depth of the image.

The tests performed on the system allowed the construction of confusion matrices to determine the accuracy of the system, obtaining an overall accuracy of 95%, thus considering the system to be functional and safe.

References

1. Dang, A.T.: Facial Recognition: Types of Attacks and Anti-Spoofing Techniques. Towards Data Science (2020). https://towardsdatascience.com/facial-recognition-types-of-attacks-and-anti-spoofing-techniques-9d732080f91e
2. Ayala Goyes, M.S.: Sistema biométrico de reconocimiento facial para el control de asistencia del personal docente y administrativo de la uniandes tulcán. Ph.D. thesis, Universidad Regional Autónoma de los Andes "Uniandes" (2018). https://dspace.uniandes.edu.ec/handle/123456789/8694
3. Bastidas Gavilanes, J.R.: Registro De Asistencia De Alumnos Por Medio De Reconocimiento Facial Utilizando Visión Artificial. Ph.D. thesis, Universidad Técnica de Ambato (2019). https://repositorio.uta.edu.ec/jspui/handle/123456789/29179
4. Camacho, M.: El reconocimiento facial se posiciona como la mejor tecnología para el fichaje en las empresas (2021). https://www.rrhhdigital.com/editorial/147879/El-reconocimiento-facial-se-posiciona-como-la-mejor-tecnologia-para-el-fichaje-en-las-empresas
5. Catalán, R.C.: Pandemia incrementa uso de aplicaciones de identificación sin contacto - Pontificia Universidad Católica de Chile (2021). https://www.uc.cl/noticias/pandemia-incrementa-uso-de-aplicaciones-de-identificacion-sin-contacto/

6. Diderich, C., et al.: Design Thinking for Strategy. Springer, Heidelberg (2020)
7. Electronic IDentification. Casos de uso 2021 del servicio de autenticación biométrica facial SmileID (2021). https://www.electronicid.eu/es/blog/post/autenticacion-biometrica-facial-smileid/es
8. Fegade, V., et al.: Residential security system based on facial recognition. In: 2022 6th International Conference on Trends in Electronics and Informatics (ICOEI), pp. 01–09 (2022). https://doi.org/10.1109/ICOEI53556.2022.9776940
9. Ganesh, A., et al.: OpenERP/Odoo - an open source concept to ERP solution. In: 2016 IEEE 6th International Conference on Advanced Computing (IACC), pp. 112–116 (2016). https://doi.org/10.1109/IACC.2016.30
10. Girmay, S., Samsom, F., Khattak, A.M.: AI based login system using facial recognition. In: 2021 5th Cyber Security in Networking Conference (CSNet), pp. 107–109 (2021). https://doi.org/10.1109/CSNet52717.2021.9614281
11. Guo, Y., et al.: Facial expressions recognition with multi-region divided attention networks for smart education cloud applications. Neurocomputing **493**, 119–128 (2022). https://www.scopus.com
12. Hik Vision. Reconocimiento facial para control de acceso. - Telefonia total (2020). https://telefoniatotal.com/seguridad/reconocimiento-facial-rapido-y-preciso-para-control-de-acceso/
13. IDR&D. El importante papel de la detección de vida en la autenticación biométrica facial, p. 14 (2020). https://www.idrnd.ai/wp-content/uploads/2020/09/IDRD-Facial-Liveness-Whitepaper-Spanish.pdf
14. Kumar, S., et al.: Face spoofing, age, gender and facial expression recognition using advance neural network architecture-based biometric system. Sensors (Basel, Switzerland) **22**(14) (2022). https://doi.org/10.3390/s22145160. https://www.scopus.com/inward/record.uri?eid=2-s2.0-85135131549&doi=10.3390%2fs22145160&partnerID=40&md5=4f4e4f8162748eb140e7a3233b9f2eb9. Cited by: 0; All Open Access, Gold Open Access, Green Open Access
15. Priyakanth, R., et al.: IoT based smart door unlock and intruder alert system. In: 2021 2nd International Conference on Smart Electronics and Communication (ICOSEC), pp. 6–11 (2021). https://doi.org/10.1109/ICOSEC51865.2021.9591822
16. Rowe, P.G.: Design Thinking. MIT Press, Cambridge (1991)
17. Soukupova, T., Jan, C.: Real-Time Eye Blink Detection using Facial Landmarks (2016). https://vision.fe.uni-lj.si/cvww2016/proceedings/papers/05.pdf
18. Thales. Liveness in biometrics: spoofing attacks and detection (2020). https://www.thalesgroup.com/en/markets/digital-identity-and-security/government/inspired/liveness-detection
19. Tolendiyev, G., Al-Absi, M.A., Lim, H., Lee, B.-G.: Adaptive margin based liveness detection for face recognition. In: Singh, M., Kang, D.-K., Lee, J.-H., Tiwary, U.S., Singh, D., Chung, W.-Y. (eds.) IHCI 2020. LNCS, vol. 12616, pp. 267–277. Springer, Cham (2021). https://doi.org/10.1007/978-3-030-68452-5_28 ISBN 978-3-030-68452-5
20. Wang, Z., et al.: Design and implementation of vehicle unlocking system based on face recognition. In: 2019 34rd Youth Academic Annual Conference of Chinese Association of Automation (YAC), pp. 121–126 (2019). https://doi.org/10.1109/YAC.2019.8787608

Classification of Epileptic Seizures Based on CNN and Guided Back-Propagation for Interpretation Analysis

Yomin Jaramillo-Munera[1]([✉]), Lina M. Sepulveda-Cano[2],
Andrés E. Castro-Ospina[1], Leonardo Duque-Muñoz[1],
and Juan D. Martinez-Vargas[2]

[1] Instituto Tecnológico Metropolitano, Medellín, Colombia
`yominjaramillo2283@correo.itm.edu.co`
[2] University EAFIT, Medellín, Colombia

Abstract. Epilepsy is a brain disorder that affects nearly 50 millions people around the world. However, despite its high prevalence, the diagnosis of epilepsy is complex and usually guided by the medical team's expertise using several neuroimaging techniques such as the Electroencefiphalogram (EEG). In this sense, several studies aim to automatically detect epilepsy events to improve the diagnosis or predict epilepsy crises from EEG recordings to overtake a preventive action. Most recent studies using deep learning approaches to detect Epilepsy Seizures (ES) achieve outstanding classification results but lack interpretability. This work proposes a methodology for classifying ES from EEG signals using intra-subject models in 10 patients from Siena Scalp EEG Database using Time Frequency Representations. In this approach a standard Convolutional Neural Network (CNN) structure is used and several parameters of CNN are optimized using bayesian optimization. Additionally, we used a combination of GradCam and Guided Backpropagation as a strategy to interpret the performance of trained models. The classification results suggest that the intra-subject approach is effective when few data are available. Most of the analyzed subjects got an accuracy that outperform the standard architecture by using optuna tuning. Additionally, the computation of gradients using GradCam-BP show an increased mean gradient for some patients finding the relevant channel in the ES condition.

Keywords: Epileptic Seizure · CNN · Guided Backpropagation · Classification · EEG

1 Introduction

Epilepsy is a non-transmissible chronic neurological disease that affects people of any age and causes an irregular discharge of neurons, leading to transient brain dysfunction [27]. In general, any clinical manifestation of abnormal electrical

F. R. Narváez et al. (Eds.): SmartTech-IC 2022, CCIS 1705, pp. 212–226, 2023.
https://doi.org/10.1007/978-3-031-32213-6_16

behavior in cortical neurons is called Epileptic Seizure (ES) or Epileptic Event. Considering that approximately 50 million people worldwide have epilepsy, it is considered in the neuroscience field one of the most relevant subject of study [26].

The diagnosis of this disease is a long and expensive process that includes the work of various specialists. This process has many problems because it is often time-consuming, the specialist perform the visual analysis of the EEG, and could have questionable accuracy considering the person's subjectivity and other factors such as fatigue. All these factors could compromise the success of the treatment [14,16,18]. One of the characteristics of EEG tests for the diagnosis of epilepsy is that they are performed over comprehensive-time ranges, thus obtaining EEG recordings of long duration, waiting for the spontaneous generation of ES [9,18,21]. With the analysis of the EEG recordings and the electrode locating system, it is possible to locate the origin of the ES. Subsequently, the specialist could use this information for planning different treatment strategies like surgery.

Many researchers have used Machine Learning techniques to improve ES detection, looking for a suitable model generalization and trying to make the first steps to their clinical application [5,20,28]. Most of the work has addressed a supervised approach and uses widely known data for this type of study; one of the best-used datasets for epilepsy detection and prediction algorithms is the University of Bonn dataset [4] which has 500 single-channel segments, which are divided into five groups of 100 segments, obtaining results of even 100% of accuracy [1]. In addition, many feature selection strategies have been implemented to improve the algorithms' performance; the latest techniques reported in the literature are based on Wavelet transforms, and entropy features [11,15,17,25].

On the other hand, the Deep Learning (DL) methodologies are gaining popularity and obtaining significant results [1,2,11]. The problem with this kind of methodology is that using a DL approach makes it is challenging to analyze eventual treatment. These algorithms are complex to interpret, and it is commonly tricky to conclude something about the classification process.

This paper aims to present a methodology that allows for detecting ES in different patients while brings interpretability to the results. This is reached with the intra-patient classification strategy allows to handle few data. Additionally, the application of Grad_Cam-Guided Backpropagation (Grad_Cam-GB) is presented as interpretation alternative of the classification results, here, the analysis of mean gradient in Guided Backpropagation is made by identifying the most relevant channels of EEG on classifier decision. The methodology allows to find those EEG channels that are close to the focal point by using Grad_Cam-GB from a Convolutional Neural Network (CNN).

2   Methodology

2.1   Data-Base

In this study, we used ten out of the fourteen epilepsy patients in the database created by the Unit of Neurology and Neurophysiology of the University of Siena. We discarded the patients with only one record for analysis because we considered those few data could negatively affect the training and testing process. Additionally, patient PN10 was excluded due to differences in the electrode distribution. This dataset is freely available at Physionet under the name "Siena Scalp EEG Database" [6]. Data are held in 14 folders containing EEG recordings in European Data Format (EDF) and additional information such as EGG layout, recording starting and finishing times, and seizure starting and finishing times. More information about the data is detailed in [7].

In this study, subjects were monitored with a video-EEG (sampling rate 512 Hz), with electrodes arranged based on the international 10–20 system. In that sense, 29 channels were taken in acquisition process as shown in Fig. 1.

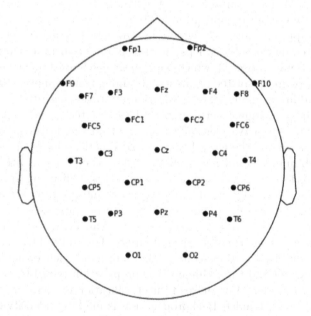

Fig. 1. Description of channel distribution in acquisition process based on 10–20 standard. Figure built using MNE package 1.2.1 version

The data were acquired employing EB Neuro and Natus Quantum LTM amplifiers and reusable silver/gold cup electrodes. Patients were asked to stay in bed as much as possible, either asleep or awake. For most subjects, several recordings were taken having at least one ES labeled. Moreover, we used ES episodes of each subject to train classification algorithms using an intra-subject approach; namely, we trained a classifier for each subject. The dataset includes 37 ES episodes we used to develop supervised learning algorithms. A deeper description of the dataset used in this work is shown in Table 1.

Table 1. Description of the data set, adapted from [7]

Patient_id	number_records	number_seizures	rec_time_minutes
PN00	5	5	198
PN03	2	2	752
PN05	3	3	359
PN06	5	5	722
PN09	3	3	410
PN12	3	4	246
PN13	3	3	519
PN14	4	4	1408
PN16	2	2	303
PN17	2	2	308

2.2 Pre-processing and Feature Extraction

Figure 2 describes the five pre-processing steps applied to each recording used in the study. First, we applied a bandpass filter with cut-off frequencies of 1 30 Hz following suggestions of [1,7,23]. For that, the method *Filter* of *mne.io.Raw* [13] was used. The method uses a FIR filter with a filter length automatically set and a hamming window.

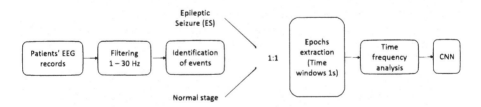

Fig. 2. Pre-processing stage applied to EEG recordings

Then, we performed an event identification process following specifications in the database, where we extracted seizure (ES) and non-seizure (NS) segments of each filtered recording. We took ictal and non-ictal segments of each recording. Figure 3 shows examples of the two different types of events defined in this work (ES, NS) taken from a single recording of patient PN00.

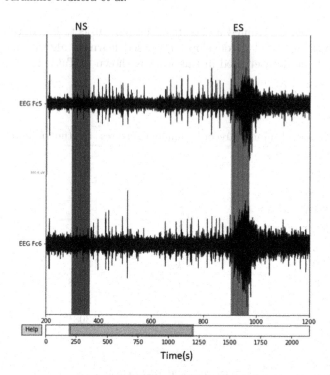

Fig. 3. Event identification (No seizure NS, and Epileptic seizure ES) in the first recording of patient PN00 (channels Fc5 - Fc6)

The ESs on each patient were marked as the positive class with id = 1,
whereas NSs events were defined as the negative class (id = 0). We defined a 1:1
ratio between samples belonging to both classes to avoid overfitting the classifier.
We took the NSs from sections without indicating epileptic activity; i.e., we used
data taken 5 min after the recording, avoiding overlapping with ES segments. It
is important to mention that we consider only one record of each patient for the
composition of his respective test-data set; then, the training algorithm was fed
with the segmentation of all the records but one.

Once ES and NS events were identified, we took short epochs (equal-length
spans of data) of each event, allowing for increasing the number of samples of
each class. Specifically, we defined epochs as one-second-long segments without
overlap. As a result, we obtain a set of epochs of each event that we will further
use for feature selection and classification.

The characterization of the epochs was performed by computing Time Frequency Representations (TFR's). A domain transformation is made in order to
manage several spectrograms (1 per epoch). The TFR's are the inputs of the classification model. Taking into count that a time-frequency transformation using
multitapers was applied. The multitapers method makes use of Discrete Pro-
late Spheroidal Sequences (DPSSs) and is designed for signals without time and

phase locking. The method calculates an average of several estimates of TFR's in defined band spectra, for this, epochs are operated with several DPSS's in order to highlight the most relevant aspects of each one. After that, a domain transformation using FFT is applied; finally, the average of TFR's is computed. This procedure is shown in Fig. 4.

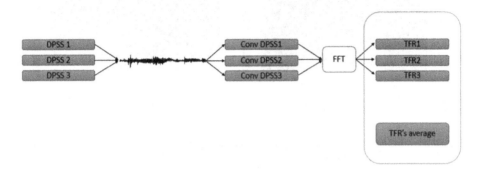

Fig. 4. Description of TFR's estimation for epochs

For the estimation of TFR's we used the package specialized in EEG signal processing and analysis: MNE [13]. Specifically, we used the method: $mne.time\_frequency.tfr\_array\_multitaper()$

This method allows the calculation of the TFR's without changing the data structure obtained during the pre-processing $[epochs, channels, time]$. The TFR's are used to train and test the classifier. In that sense, three tapers (Default value), were used over the extracted epochs. Here, the study frequencies were defined based on the band-pass filter (1–30 Hz), and we defined the number of cycles for each frequency bin f as $n_{cycles} = f/2$. From this process, it is possible to obtain arrays of shape $[n_{epochs}, 29, 29, 513]$, where dimension 2 and 3 represents the channels, frequency bands and time dimension. Figure 5 shows the Time-Frequency Representations (TFR's) of two epochs, NS and ES, respectively. Both samples are taken from patient "PN00" in channel Fp1.

2.3   Neural Network Design

A CNN was designed to extract features from the TFR of each epoch and classify it into one of the analyzed classes, namely ES or NS. The basic CNN architecture comprised two convolutional and three fully-connected layers. A pooling layer followed the first convolutional layer was used to reduce the feature map size. As explained before, we trained a CNN for each patient. A better description of the basic network architecture is presented in Fig. 6. Models were implemented in Pytorch [19].

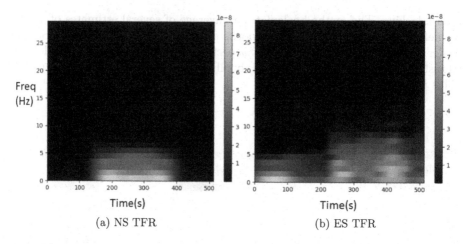

(a) NS TFR   (b) ES TFR

Fig. 5. Example of Time-Frequency Representations (TFRs) of two epochs, taken from patient "PN00" on channel Fp1

Moreover, we applied a Bayesian optimization process using Optuna [3] to tune some of the network hyperparameters: kernel size and the number of neurons in the fully connected layers. On the other hand, some hyperparameters (output channels in the convolutional layer, learning rate and momentum) were set as fixed values to avoid an ample searching space. As a result, we defined a search space for each hyperparameter to tune (see Table 2) and set it to 20 times that each experiment is repeated. The Bayesian optimization process was set to maximize the F1 score of the validation set when training the neural network.

Table 2. Definition of search space for each variable

Parameter	Oputuna tuning			Standard Architure
	Min	Max	Value	Value
Learning Rate	*	*	0.001	0.001
Momentum	*	*	0.5	0.5
C1	*	*	32	32
C2	*	*	64	64
Optimizer	*	*	Adam	Adam
K1	3	10	*	3
K2	3	10	*	3
Hidden Size 1	64	512	*	128
Hidden Size 2	32	128	*	64

For the training process, we took N-1 recordings from each subject to extract train and validation epochs and 100 samples were defined for training. Such

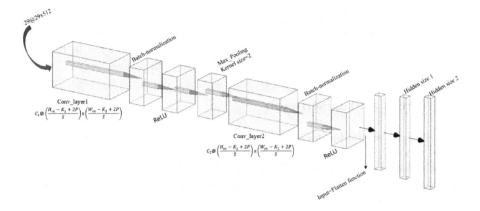

Fig. 6. CNN architecture description

epochs were used to find the best hyperparameter configuration with Optuna. Once this process was done, train and validation epochs were used to train the final model. Finally, the epochs belonging to the remaining recording were used to test the performance of the trained model. Table 3 shows the number of epochs for each subset in train, validation and test subsets.

Table 3. Epochs extracted from patient's recordings for classification task

Patient	Epochs		
	Train	Val	Test
PN00	412	104	134
PN03	177	45	266
PN05	104	26	78
PN06	380	96	88
PN09	196	50	128
PN12	363	91	126
PN13	180	46	302
PN14	128	32	166
PN16	196	50	214
PN17	112	28	166

2.4 Interpretability Analysis

Once the final model for each patient was obtained by tuning the hyperparameters with Optuna, we proceeded to carry out the interpretability analysis using Grad_Cam-Guided Backpropagation (Grad_Cam-GB) [12]. In brief, Grad_Cam-GB returns an array of gradients of size $[n_{channels}, n_{frequencies}, n_{times}]$ when we feed it with the TFR of each channel of an EEG epoch. In this array, the higher the gradient in a specific point, the more representative such point for the analyzed class. In this case, we aimed to find the more representative channels and frequency bins regarding the ES, therefore, we averaged gradients in the time axis and all the epochs of the test set belonging to such a class.

3   Results and Discussion

Table 4 shows results for each subject in the test set both with hyperparameter tuning using Optuna and with the fixed architecture described in Table 2. It can be noticed that the lower the number of ES episodes for the subject, the lower the classification algorithm's performance, regardless of the number of epochs. For example, subjects 3 and 16 achieved F1 scores lower than 80%. Nevertheless, for eight out of ten subjects, the sensibility (capability of the classifier to detect ES epochs) overcome 90%, which can be enough to detect an epilepsy crisis. Patient $PN09$ achieves the worst accuracy rate, He is highly sensible to ES detection, but has a low level of specificity, and this affects F1-Score. For an appropriate clinical application these cases should be minimized because involve a high rate of False Positives. On the other hand, the lower values for sensibility ($PN06$ and $PN13$) are very close to 90% and present high accuracy and F1-Score rates, that indicates a better algorithm adaptation for the differentiation process. Moreover, from Table 4, we can observe that the bayesian optimization-based hyperparameter tuning, in most cases, improves the performance of the basic CNN architecture.

Table 4. Performance of the models trained for each patient

ID	Optuna Tuning				Standard Architure			
	SENS	SPEC	F1-SCORE	ACC	SENS	SPEC	F1-SCORE	ACC
PN00	0.92	0.98	0.95	95.50%	0.94	0.67	0.83	80.50%
PN03	0.96	0.55	0.8	76%	0.93	0.23	0.69	58.20%
PN05	0.9	1	0.95	94.80%	0.85	1	0.92	92.30%
PN06	0.86	0.9	0.88	88.63%	0.84	1	0.91	92.04%
PN09	1	0.39	0.77	69.53%	0.98	0.19	0.7	59%
PN12	0.97	0.94	0.95	95.23%	0.97	0.82	0.9	90%
PN13	0.87	0.99	0.93	93%	0.9	0.99	0.95	95.03%
PN14	0.97	0.65	0.84	81.32%	0.75	0.85	0.79	80.12%
PN16	0.94	0.67	0.83	80.84%	0.98	0.5	0.79	74.29%
PN17	0.94	0.89	0.92	91.56%	0.91	0.93	0.92	92.16%

Results presented in Table 4 show that intra-subject approach is able to handle with the inter-variability across patients, and the optimization of a CNN architecture could boost the performance. However, it is important to diversify the characterization process in future works. An example is [24], where the authors proved several features for this data set obtaining good level of class discrimination. However in that paper the author did not consider the inter-variability across patients, since they merged all the epochs for training and testing, the above could affect their performance due to the maximum F1-Score obtained was 0.90 for KNN classifier. Additionally, it is worth mentioning that several strategies could be applied to the model to improve its performance. One could be to define a more extensive hyperparameter search space, or restructure the network by adding more layers. It is important to note that recent work suggests prior feature extraction on this data set, such as Mel Frequency Cepstrum Coefficients (MFCCs), as they contain predictive biomarkers related to epileptic seizures [8]. Those prior feature extraction stages, combined with a more robust network, could improve the model performance significantly.

Furthermore, we applied Grad_Cam-Guided Back Propagation Algorithm (Grad_Cam-GB) to infer the most relevant channels and frequency bins regarding the ES class. To this end, we used the implementation available in [12]. Table 5 presents the localization and lateralization labels for each patient whereas Fig. 7 shows obtained relevance maps for patients highlighted in Table 5.

Table 5. Performance of the models trained for each patient adapted from [7], IAS: focal onset impaired awareness; WIAS: focal onset without impaired awareness; T: temporal; R: right; L: left

Patient Id	Seizure	Localization	Lateralization
PN00	**IAS**	**T**	**R**
PN03	**IAS**	**T**	**R**
PN05	IAS	T	L
PN06	IAS	T	L
PN09	IAS	T	L
PN12	IAS	T	L
PN13	**IAS**	**T**	**L**
PN14	WIAS	T	L
PN16	**IAS**	**T**	**L**
PN17	IAS	T	R

Figure 7 shows four heat maps in which the frequency bands and channels of the 10–20 standard EEG are related. In this figure, it is possible to observe the influence of each channel and frequency bins in the classification of ES events from the mean of the gradients along epochs using Grad_Cam-GB. It is possible to identify focal epilepsy when the mean gradient estimation is bigger in the electrodes associated to that foci (see Fig. 1). The same case is presented in right hemisphere, however it is possible obtaining some exceptions as the case of PN03. Based on Fig. 7, the results suggest that for the range of frequencies taken, there are not a set of frequency bins that had special relevance in the classifier

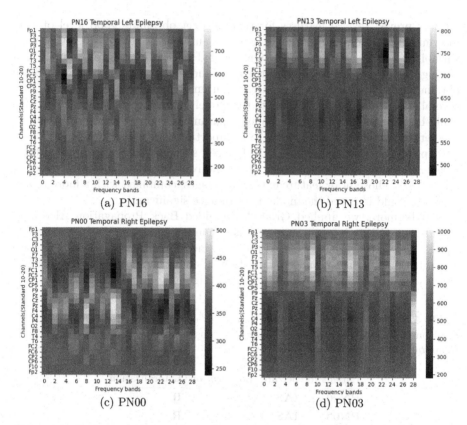

Fig. 7. Obtained heat-maps using Grad_Cam-GB for several patients (a-b) Shows relevant channels in PN16 and PN13 which are consistent with patient diagnostic, (c-d) Shows them for PN00 and PN03 where the first is consistent with diagnostic but PN03 is not

decision, however, in general, it seems that the lowest frequencies below 5 and the highest frequencies above 25 contribute the least to the average gradient. In [10] the authors identified the relevance of some frequency bins with a bigger window size, the increased size could help to improve data representation.

The problem of Deep Learning models interpretability for epilepsy in EEG has been addressed by some authors in the literature, for example, Grad_Cam-GB is introduced in [22] as a valuable method for classification compression. The article explains how the Grad_Cam-GB algorithm works and how it can be used to obtain generic results equivalent to the use of deconvolutions. In [10], is addressed the interpretation of CNN models in epilepsy detection problems, in this case the authors got over the patient inter-variability applying a methodology that did not take an intra-patient approach. That is due to a their data-base is bigger (568 patients). In cases where data are more limited the intra-patient approach is a good method for handling the patient inter-variability [7]. The authors in [10] implemented 3 possible models of CNN which changed the applied kernels in its first layer kernel size, obtaining highlighted results ($F1 - score = 0.873$). It is important to mention that all of the proposed CNN models have a more complex architecture than the presented in Fig. 6, since they used six convolutional and 2 Fully connected layers. Due to the implemented optimization method for our models, the training process for an overly complex architecture is not practical in time cost terms. However it is important to consider that although few data for training intra-patients models the results got are over 80% for most of the patients.

For their models, the authors also used images as inputs of their CNN architectures, they used a method of interpretation based on gradient descent which allow inferring if a frequency component is associated to ictal or interictal class. Although this paper also makes use of images as input of CNN, which are also considering the frequency bands on EEG, the interpreting analysis implemented is looking for identify the most relevant channels in the class differentiation. The prior described approach was thought for diagnostic applications where an idea of epileptic focus localities is given.

Finally, in order to compare the gradient behavior in each hemisphere Table 6 shows the sum of the gradients in the temporal left and right one. In Fig. 7a ($PN16$), it is possible to identify that the gradients around the left hemisphere involving $T_3 - T_5$ are larger than gradients if the right one ($T_4 - T_6$). In the same sense, it is possible to observe that in Fig. 5b ($PN13$), the general gradient trend is also higher in the left hemisphere. Those differences can be observed in a more subtle way in Table 6.

Table 6. Mean of the gradients in the temporal channels of each hemisphere

Patient	Temporal Left	Temporal Right
PN00	**379**	**386**
PN03	**751**	**577**
PN05	247	252
PN06	265	255
PN09	254	254
PN12	259	244
PN13	**644**	**626**
PN14	381	381
PN16	**524**	**506**
PN17	393	374

Although, in general, the methodology performs well as expected in majority of patients, there are some patients in whom it does not so clear, for example, in the patient $PN00$. Although the gradients are more prominent in the right hemisphere (which is consistent with the database tag), this is challenging to identify if we would only had the heat map in Fig. 7c.

4   Conclusions

This paper presents an end-to-end methodology to classify ES from NS epochs using time-frequency features and a CNN classifier. Moreover, a Bayesian optimization framework was used to tune in the CNN hyperparameters. Finally, an interpretability analysis was carried out for the best model to identify the most relevant channels and frequency bins regarding the ES class. Here, an intra-subject model approach for handling with inter-variability is presented. The paper uses Grad_Cam-Guided Backpropagation which returns an array of gradients. The higher the gradient, the more representative the analyzed class. Here we look for the most relevant channels and frequency bins to obtain the heat maps representing the channels' influence in the classification. The improvement of this technique could eventually consolidate a diagnostic tool since this procedure provides information on epileptic foci. However, it is important to carry out further studies with other databases and a larger volume of labeled data.

It is worth noting that by using Optuna tunning, the classification results were improved compared to the standard architecture on average 5.1%. Although, this increment is more notable in the patients with fewer ES events. In future work, we propose first performing feature extraction with MFCCS, broadening the hyperparameter search space, and trying with other architectures. These results can be used in future studies to find alternative methods for monitoring and diagnosing ES using less costly and noninvasive equipment.

Acknowledgments. This work is supported by Instituto Tecnológico Metropolitano project: "Metodología para evaluación cuantitativa de Imágenes de Resonancia Magnética estructural en sujetos con epilepsia no lesional P20214". YJM is financed by Minciencias, Convocatoria 891 de 2020 "Vocaciones y Formación en CTeI para la reactivación económica en el marco de la postpandemia 2020".

References

1. Abdelhameed, A.M., Bayoumi, M.: Semi-supervised EEG signals classification system for epileptic seizure detection. IEEE Signal Process. Lett. **26**(12), 1922–1926 (2019). https://doi.org/10.1109/LSP.2019.2953870
2. Acharya, U.R., Oh, S.L., Hagiwara, Y., Tan, J.H., Adeli, H.: Deep convolutional neural network for the automated detection and diagnosis of seizure using EEG signals. Comput. Biol. Med. **100**, 270–278 (2018). https://doi.org/10.1016/j.compbiomed.2017.09.017
3. Akiba, T., Sano, S., Yanase, T., Ohta, T., Koyama, M.: Optuna: a next-generation hyperparameter optimization framework. In: Proceedings of the 25rd ACM SIGKDD International Conference on Knowledge Discovery and Data Mining (2019)
4. Andrzejak, R.G., Lehnertz, K., Mormann, F., Rieke, C., David, P., Elger, C.E.: Indications of nonlinear deterministic and finite-dimensional structures in time series of brain electrical activity: dependence on recording region and brain state. Phys. Rev. E Stat. Phys. Plasmas Fluids Relat Interdiscip. Topics **64**(6), 8 (2001). https://doi.org/10.1103/PhysRevE.64.061907

5. Chakrabarti, S., Swetapadma, A., Pattnaik, P.K.: A review on epileptic seizure detection and prediction using soft computing techniques. Stud. Fuzziness Soft Comput. **374**, 37–51 (2019). https://doi.org/10.1007/978-3-030-03131-2

6. Detti, P.: Siena Scalp EEG Database (version 1.0.0) (2020). https://doi.org/10.13026/5d4a-j060. https://physionet.org/content/siena-scalp-eeg/1.0.0/

7. Detti, P., Vatti, G., de Lara, G.Z.M.: EEG synchronization analysis for seizure prediction: a study on data of noninvasive recordings. Processes **8**(7), 1–15 (2020). https://doi.org/10.3390/pr8070846

8. Dissanayake, T., Fernando, T., Denman, S.: Independent epileptic seizure prediction using scalp EEG signals. IEEE J. Biomed. Health Inform. **26**(2), 527–538 (2022)

9. Florez, D.S.M.: Electroencefalograma en epilepsia (2017). https://colegiomedico.org.sv/videos/2017/09/14/2017-09-09-jornada-de-actualizacion-en-epilepsia/

10. Gabeff, V., et al.: Interpreting deep learning models for epileptic seizure detection on EEG signals. Artif. Intell. Med. **117**, 102084 (2021)

11. Gao, X., Yan, X., Gao, P., Gao, X., Zhang, S.: Automatic detection of epileptic seizure based on approximate entropy, recurrence quantification analysis and convolutional neural networks. Artif. Intell. Med. **102** (2020). https://doi.org/10.1016/j.artmed.2019.101711

12. Gildenblat, J.: Pytorch library for cam methods (2021). https://github.com/jacobgil/pytorch-grad-cam

13. Gramfort, A., et al.: MEG and EEG data analysis with MNE-Python. Front. Neurosci. **7**(267), 1–13 (2013). https://doi.org/10.3389/fnins.2013.00267

14. Hassan, A.R., Subasi, A.: Automatic identification of epileptic seizures from EEG signals using linear programming boosting. Comput. Methods Programs Biomed. **136**, 65–77 (2016). https://doi.org/10.1016/j.cmpb.2016.08.013

15. Khan, K.A., Shanir, P.P., Khan, Y.U., Farooq, O.: A hybrid local binary pattern and wavelets based approach for EEG classification for diagnosing epilepsy. Expert Syst. Appl. **140**, 112895 (2020). https://doi.org/10.1016/j.eswa.2019.112895

16. Li, M., Chen, W., Zhang, T.: FuzzyEn-based features in FrFT-WPT domain for epileptic seizure detection. Neural Comput. Appl. **31**(12), 9335–9348 (2019). https://doi.org/10.1007/s00521-018-3621-z

17. Liu, Y., Li, Y.: A multi-view unified feature learning network for EEG epileptic seizure detection. In: Series on Computional Intelligence, Xiamen, China, pp. 2608–2612. IEE (2019)

18. Orosco, L., Laciar, E.: Review: a survey of performance and techniques for automatic epilepsy detection. J. Med. Biol. Eng. **33**(6), 526–537 (2013). https://doi.org/10.5405/jmbe.1463

19. Paszke, A., et al.: Pytorch: an imperative style, high-performance deep learning library. In: Wallach, H., Larochelle, H., Beygelzimer, A., d' Alché-Buc, F., Fox, E., Garnett, R. (eds.) Advances in Neural Information Processing Systems, vol. 32, pp. 8024–8035. Curran Associates, Inc. (2019). https://papers.neurips.cc/paper/9015-pytorch-an-imperative-style-high-performance-deep-learning-library.pdf

20. Poorani, S., Balasubramanie, P.: Seizure detection based on EEG signals using asymmetrical back propagation neural network method. Circuits Syst. Signal Process. **40**(9), 4614–4632 (2021). https://doi.org/10.1007/s00034-021-01686-w

21. Rasheed, K., et al.: Machine Learning for Predicting Epileptic Seizures Using EEG Signals: A Review (2020). https://arxiv.org/abs/2002.01925

22. Rathod, P., Naik, S.: Review on epilepsy detection with explainable artificial intelligence. In: International Conference on Emerging Trends in Engineering

and Technology, ICETET 2022 (2022). https://doi.org/10.1109/ICETET-SIP-2254415.2022.9791595

23. Sahani, M., Rout, S.K., Dash, P.K.: FPGA implementation of epileptic seizure detection using semisupervised reduced deep convolutional neural network. Appl. Soft Comput. **110**, 107639 (2021). https://doi.org/10.1016/j.asoc.2021.107639

24. Sánchez-Hernández, S.E., Salido-Ruiz, R.A., Torres-Ramos, S., Román-Godínez, I.: Evaluation of Feature Selection Methods for Classification of Epileptic Seizure EEG Signals. Sensors **22**(8) (2022). https://doi.org/10.3390/s22083066

25. Wang, Y., Li, Z., Feng, L., Bai, H., Wang, C.: Hardware design of multiclass SVM classification for epilepsy and epileptic seizure detection. IET Circuits Devices Syst. **12**(1), 108–115 (2018). https://doi.org/10.1049/iet-cds.2017.0216

26. World Health Organization: Epilepsy. Technical report, World Health Organization (2016)

27. Zhang, Z., Li, X., Geng, F., Huang, K.: A semi-supervised few-shot learning model for epileptic seizure detection. In: Proceedings of the Annual International Conference of the IEEE Engineering in Medicine and Biology Society, EMBS, pp. 600–603 (2021). https://doi.org/10.1109/EMBC46164.2021.9630363

28. Zhao, X., Lhatoo, S.D.: Seizure detection: do current devices work? And when can they be useful? Curr. Neurol. Neurosci. Rep. **18**(7) (2018). https://doi.org/10.1007/s11910-018-0849-z

An Approach to the Presumptive Detection of Road Incidents in Cuenca, Ecuador Using the Data from the Social Media Twitter and Spanish Natural Language Processing

Pablo E. Loja-Morocho, Robbyn T. Reyes-Duchitanga,
and Gabriel A. León-Paredes[✉] [ID]

Grupo de Investigación en Cloud Computing, Smart Cities & High Performance
Computing, Universidad Politécnica Salesiana, Cuenca, Ecuador
{plojam,rreyesd}@est.ups.edu.ec, gleon@ups.edu.ec

Abstract. The road situation in Ecuador, specifically in the city of Cuenca and its surroundings, can vary according to various aspects related mainly to the weather, or traffic incidents caused due to reckless actions by drivers. Therefore, many times these problems can cause some drivers to be forced to delay their trip or look for alternative routes to reach their destination, others can plan their departure according to the related news they find when browsing social media, which can be somewhat time-consuming and even unlikely to find. For this reason, in this paper, a mobile application is presented whose primary function is to collect publications from social media Twitter from different Twitter accounts that are related to road incidents and to classify them using Natural Language Processing (NLP) and Machine Learning (ML) models such as BERT. Then, we present an approximate location of the presumptive incident on an interactive map which allows each of these tweets to be displayed with a personalized icon that can indicate different types of road incidents and, at the same time, the details of the event that occurred. Two main experiments were carried out to find (a) the model accuracy, where a value of 80% was obtained as a result, which is considered a positive result for road incident classification, and (b) the execution of acceptance tests, where a questionnaire based on the ISO 9126 standard was presented to a group of bikers belonging to the city of Cuenca, obtaining as a result that for most users the application is new (85.8%), efficient (85.7%) and easy to use (64.3%). This research makes it possible to present news of road incidents in a centralized manner, which makes it easier for drivers to stay informed and thus avoid annoying interruptions in their circulation.

Keywords: BERT Model · Data Extraction · Machine Learning · Natural Language Processing · Twitter · Social Media Processing

Supported by the Universidad Politécnica Salesiana.

1 Introduction

The road situation in Ecuador, specifically in the city of Cuenca and its surroundings, can vary according to different aspects related mainly to the weather
or traffic incidents caused due to reckless actions by drivers [4,5]. Therefore,
many times these problems can cause some drivers to be forced to delay their
trip or look for alternative routes to reach their destination, others can plan their
departure according to the related news they find when browsing social media,
which can be somewhat time-consuming and even unlikely to find. In addition,
it is important to indicate that according to the *Agencia Nacional de Tránsito*
(ANT) of Ecuador [2], a total of 498 cases of traffic accidents are recorded from
January to May 2022, as well as an average of 1,280 accidents per year at the
level of the province of Azuay in the same year. Also, according to the *Servicio Nacional de Gestión de Riesgos y Emergencias* of Ecuador [1], a total of
56 dangerous events were recorded, specifically 41 landslides and 15 floods from
January to June 2022. All these road incidents become difficult to identify at
specific times for mobility users, even more so if they happen simultaneously in
different areas.

Thus, based on the problems raised above, this research proposes the creation of a mobile application that facilitates the analysis of Twitter social media
information related to road incidents or road closures that can complicate mobility in the city. Thereby, Natural Language Processing (NLP) and unsupervised
Machine Learning (ML) models have been used to help us infer the following
classes, traffic accidents, road emergencies, traffic, landslides, overflows rivers, or
'general' roads closed due to external causes such as human mobilizations or cultural events. This proposal has been implemented in three main stages related
to, the collection and preprocessing of tweets, data classification and analysis
using the BERT model [3], and the final integration in the mobile application.
In addition, locations are shown, if possible, approximately the place where the
road incident occurred. Moreover, it will also allow users to have the ability to
link their Twitter accounts, so that they can be active participants in spreading
information. Finally, the mobile application has the ability to display the results
quickly and organized its details and drawbacks. Hence, all related information
is centralized and available.

Consequently, our proposal seeks to be useful for all the users of mobility
in the city of Cuenca and its surroundings, even for travelers who wish to go
sightseeing and avoid setbacks during their mobilization around the city, taking
into account that many times the various road users seek the most optimal and
fastest areas or routes to reach their destination.

The rest of the paper has been organized as follows. Section 2 introduces some
related works. In Sect. 3, the mobile application built to solve this problem is
presented. Section 4 describes the experiments carried out with this mobile application on information retrieval and discusses the results of these experiments.
Finally, Sect. 5 summarizes the conclusions drawn from this work.

2   Related Works

This section presents some previous works that have tried to analyze social media data in order to obtain a presumptive road incident. To start with, [9] seeks to analyze posts on Twitter social media using NLP techniques together with the BERT model in order to obtain the details regarding occurrences, locations, and nature of traffic incidents that occur in the city of New York. The authors have classified these incidents into accidents, construction zones, and temporary closures.

So they detail four phases of development focusing, first, on the collection of data from Twitter, the tweets will be taken from accounts related to traffic management agencies and certain recurring users, their idea is to obtain three groups of data which are: related tweets, unrelated tweets that mention words related to road incidents, and unrelated tweets that do not mention words about road incidents. These related words are: "incident, delay, construction, crash, lanes, road", among others. Next, they present their evaluation metrics, according to a confusion matrix they verify that the BERT model classifier generates adequate results according to their approach and compare them with other models such as Naive Bayes (NB) and Support Vector Machines (SVM). The BERT model applied is the "BERT-For-Question-Answering", which is based on Q-A for data extraction. The authors have focused mainly on three questions: "What", to identify the type of accident, "When", to identify the time in which the road incident occurred, and "Where", which helps to identify the location of the event.

Another related work is [6], which proposes to analyze news from the social media, Twitter, in order to detect traffic incidents in Indonesia, using Convolutional Neural Networks (CNN) classification techniques and BERT pre-trained model, specifically IndoBert model, in this way they managed to tag the information into incidents, nature, traffic intensity, among others. The authors have defined several phases, starting with the data collection for which they use two libraries, Tweepy and TWINT, as keywords for the search for traffic-focused tweets they have used: "lalu lintas macet" (traffic jam), "lalu lintas padat" (another way of traffic jam), "kecelakaan lalu lintas" (traffic accident), "perbaikan jalan" (road maintenance), "penutupan jalan" (road closure), "jalan banjir" (flooded road), and "jalan hujan" (rainy road). With these data extracted, they proceed to manually label them as different events: "Insiden" (incident), referring to events about traffic accidents, social mobilizations, and road maintenance, among others; "Alam" (nature), referring to events caused by nature such as rains, floods, landslides, or others; "Intesitas Lalu Lintas" (traffic intensity), referring to all news that talks about heavy traffic such as traffic jams or traffic intensity; and "Lainnya" (other), referring to tweets that do not represent any of the previous events. Then, processing of the data is proposed, hence, they first clean the corpus of the text, trying to maintain the greatest similarity to the original text, words are normalized, and the text is tokenized, moreover with the help of the trained algorithm, In-doBERT, extracts the features of the data and then compares the results with other algorithms such as ELMo ForManyLangs, and Word2vec embedding. Finally, for each of these model, the authors present experimental architectures with the use of CNN, resulting in BERT-CNN, ELMo-CNN, and Word2vec-CNN that differ in their parameters and weights when applying them in the classification. According to their details and variations, they offer results based on a confusion matrix that validates the values obtained according to each label and the original values.

In [8], it has been presented a study on accidents that occur in the city of Bogotá, Colombia. The authors specified four phases that go from data collection, data classification using SVM to build a doc2vec model, detection of entities to extract locations and time of the event, and obtaining geographic coordinates according to a geocoder. The data collection phase refers to the tweets extraction with the help of the Twitter API, using two specific resources that are the Search API and the Stream API. The authors define some considerations for the search of tweets and they filter according to the geographical area, language, keywords, and publication dates. Then proceed to manually label these tweets in three categories: related to traffic accidents, not related, and don't know. Subsequently, the collected data is passed to the classification phase, where it is first cleaned and normalized to continue with the extraction of characteristics with the doc2vec technique, however other models such as TF-FDI and BERT are used with the Support Vector Machine algorithm to build an ML model. Next, they proceed to obtain the entities of location and time in which the incident occurred, likewise, the data is processed to eliminate redundancies and other specials character. With the use of the Spacy library, these entities were detected using the pre-trained model "es_core_news_lg". In the last phase, they proceed to obtain the geolocation data of the chosen tweets, for which they have (a) eliminated tweets that do not offer enough information to detect exact location entities; (b) normalized certain addresses with the help of the Libpostal library, which standardizes addresses that are generally abbreviated or lacking in detail; and, (c) removed tweets that offered similar location information. Finally, to obtain geolocation data they used the Batch_geocode library. As results obtained from the training, their model was rated 96.8% with respect to other similar studies proposed, likewise for the extraction of location and time tags, obtaining 91.97%, results generated from 26,362 filtered tweets.

Thus, it is important to mention at this point that our proposal differs from other authors starting that this paper has focused on the city of Cuenca, and to our knowledge, no studies have been conducted in this city. Additionally, regarding the implementation of the classification model of tweets where we use the Spanish Pre-Trained BERT Model and Evaluation Data [3], and for the detection of entities like the locations of the events where the presumptive road incident occurred, we used a list of keywords that refers to roads, avenues, sectors, or neighborhoods in the city of Cuenca. Moreover, several authors propose the analysis and study of traffic accidents or events related to vehicular traffic, we work with all possible incidents or activities that generate a road closure so that these are useful to road users. Finally, and most importantly, we propose a mobile application that centralizes all this information collected. In the following table, we present a comparison of data collection, data processing, classification model, entity detection, and geographic coordinates collection between the works reviewed and our proposal (Table 1).

Table 1. Comparison of data collection, data processing, classification model, entity detection, and geographic coordinates collection between the works reviewed and our proposal

	Wan et al. 2020	Neruda and Winarko 2021	Suat-Rojas et al. 2022	Our work
Data Collection	Twitter from accounts related to traffic management agencies and recurring users	Twitter according to related keywords	Twitter filtering by language, keywords, and publication dates	Twitter according to keywords, related local news, and collaborating users
Data Processing	n/a	Manually tagged	Normalization, and special characters removal	Normalization, and stopwords, special characters, emojis, and links removal
Classification	BERT For Question Answering	In-doBERT, BERT-CNN, ELMo-CNN, and Word2vec-CNN	doc2vec technique with TF-IDF and BERT models	Recognai/ bert-base-spanish model
Entity Detection	Yes	n/a	Yes	Yes
Geographic coordinates collection	Google Geocoder API	n/a	Batch_geocode library	Google Geocode API

3   The Presumptive Detection of Road Incidents Application in Cuenca - Ecuador

In this section, we present the three established stages and the mobile application workflow as shown in Fig. 1, as well as detail each stage with the appropriate specifications to understand the implemented techniques and their functionality.

3.1   Stage 1. Twitter Data Collection

The first stage consists of the development of a model that allows collecting data from publications on Twitter social media and in this way, in the next stage, carrying out the classification process. In order, to construct this model and ensure that it is functional, the logic is separated into two important aspects.

The first aspect involves obtaining the Twitter accounts that are of interest for the data classification stage. For this, a connection is made between the database of the application and the official API offered by Twitter, which allows obtaining the IDs of each of these accounts. As an important part of this process, it is taken into consideration that there are default accounts that belong to different newscasts of the city of Cuenca and accounts that are added after a user has been registered to the application. Therefore, the number of accounts to be taken into consideration for data collection will be in constant change. Thus,

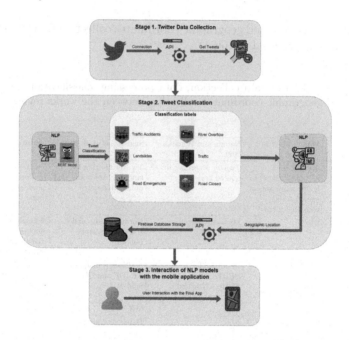

Fig. 1. Stages followed for the implementation of the Presumptive Detection of Road Incidents Application in Cuenca - Ecuador.

in order to solve this condition, multiprocessing programming is applied, which allows periodic queries to be made to the database in a process to check whether or not there is a change in the interest accounts, while the second process is responsible for executing the second aspect of this stage which will be explained below.

The second aspect involves deciding what tweet data is considered useful to classify it, to do this we use the official API of Twitter to receive information about the different interactions that are made in the social media environment. Then, a filter is applied where the IDs of the previously obtained accounts are used to be able to limit the collection of data only to the users that are of interest. Once this filter is done, it is necessary to ignore some interactions, for example, the likes, responses to tweets, and retweets. Allowing only to obtain the tweets posted only by the users, which are relevant to the development of the application.

Once this model has been made and applied, it is possible to obtain all the important interactions carried out by each of the Twitter accounts to which it has been decided to listen. In this way, all these data will be evaluated in the next stage to determine whether or not they belong to news related to road incidents.

3.2   Stage 2. Tweet Classification

After the Twitter data collection has been completed, up next the second stage is described, which is responsible for classifying and saving the data that is considered useful for the mobile application. The first process that is done in this stage is to clean the tweet data, in this process, it is essential to leave the text of the "news" tweet as clean as possible so that the classification model obtains the best possible results in terms of accuracy, that is why the elimination of emojis, stopwords, links, and additional spaces from poor writing is taken into account.

Then, the data is analyzed through natural language processing where it is possible to determine whether or not they allude to a road incident. Due to the previous research on different classification models, the Spanish Pre-Trained BERT Model and Evaluation Data [3] is used, which can work with text in Spanish. The application of this model allows not only to classify the data and determine if it is a road incident or not but also allows to determine different categories of incidents to which it belongs, these being: traffic accidents, landslides, road emergencies, river overflow, traffic, and road closed; allowing to give greater detail to the "news" tweets that will be presented in the final application.

Next, all the tweet data that have been classified in any of the categories described before are analyzed again using another model of natural language processing, in order to find keywords and entities that appear within the text and thus be able to determine which parts of the text refer to the location where the presumptive road incident occurred. Once this information is obtained, a geolocation API is applied, which allows for obtaining longitude and latitude coordinates for presenting the "news" tweets on an interactive map in the mobile application.

Finally, all the "news" tweets that have been classified with some type of road incident will be sent to the database, where the detail of the news, the classification inferred, the date of when the publication occurred, and the user who posted it is saved.

3.3   Stage 3. Integration of NLP Models with the Mobile Application

The last stage consists of the development of a mobile application that allows viewing the "news" tweets that have been obtained and classified in the previous stages. For this, the development of a session management module is presented as a first point, which includes a login, registration, and password reset form for users who want to use the application and have access to its functionalities. This is due that the user can optionally include their Twitter account, which will be saved in the database and will be part of the accounts of interest for the Twitter data collection stage.

Also, the mobile application has several screens for users who have logged in, the first of these is the home screen which has the implementation of a Google plugin, which allows the inclusion of a map where all the "news" tweets that have been analyzed will be presented. Additionally, these tweets are presented by means of personalized icons according to the type of road incident with which it was determined, as can be seen in Fig. 2(a) and, when interacting with these icons, the full version of the "news" tweet and its author is presented as shown in Fig. 2(b). The last functionality that this screen presents is the listing in detail of other "news" tweets, which means tweets that have been classified, but for which the location of the event has not been obtained.

Furthermore, the "news" tweets screen is another of the functionalities to which a user has access, in this section, all the tweets that have been classified and saved as a presumptive road incident over the last two days are shown with the feature that these are not shown through the interactive map, but rather, they are presented according to their category based on the road incident, providing a more orderly way of viewing the "news" tweets for the user. Although road incidents have a variable resolution time, these can be standardized according to their type, for example, a landslide would take longer to resolve than a traffic accident between two vehicles. So, it would be prudent to have different time ranges for display different types of road incidents within our application. However, due to the number of accounts chosen to filter and the delimitation

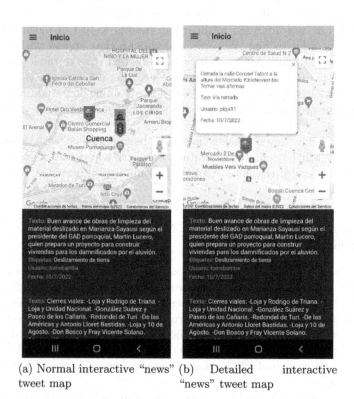

(a) Normal interactive "news" tweet map

(b) Detailed interactive "news" tweet map

Fig. 2. Screens of the mobile application where the interactive map is shown together with the classification of some "news" tweets.

of carrying out this project only for the city of Cuenca, the number of road incidents that occurred in the city were not enough, this leads to the decision to show all the tweet "news" that occurred of the last 2 days in order to better expose the result obtained from the classification of road incidents.

Finally, another of the screens that the user can access presents the information of the Twitter account with which it is linked in the system, allowing its modification in order to ensure that a user registers its real Twitter account and thus, can help the purpose of the application by tweeting about road incidents which will be collected and processed as described in the previous stages.

4   Results

Next, in this section, we present some results obtained when experimenting with the mobile application and all its functionalities. These results are presented separately in the following accuracy and user acceptance testing.

4.1   Accuracy Testing

In order to obtain the accuracy of NLP models integrated with the application, a script was developed that, with the use of the concepts related to the confusion matrix, facilitates the evaluation of the models used. From this matrix, we can obtain different metrics such as Accuracy, Precision, Sensitivity, Specificity, and F1 Score. Therefore, specifically, we utilize the accuracy metric, which returns the ratio of predictions that the model correctly classified, using the following equation,

$$Accuracy = \frac{\# \ correct \ classifications}{\# \ all \ classifications} = \frac{TP + TN}{TP + TN + FP + FN} \tag{1}$$

where TP equals True Positive, TN equals True Negative, FP equals False Positive, and FN equals False Negative.

Hence, we proceed to humanely classify some "news" tweets collected from the different accounts of interest and compared them to the classification obtained with the BERT model. With the use of the sklearn [7] metrics library and its *precision_score* function, which requires working with the true values and predicted values in the classification. Thus, we used 50 "news" tweets in total, in Table 2, 10 of these 50 tweets are presented as an example of the labeling. Also, it should be noted that in the table, we have codified the label as 1: traffic accident, 2: landslide, 3: river overflow, 4: road closed, and 5: traffic - road emergency. According to this experiment, it was found an accuracy of 80% for the proposed models. In certain cases, the results varied depending on the redaction of the tweet.

Table 2. Some examples of the comparison for the "news" tweets classification using human knowledge and BERT model

"News" Tweets	Human Clasification	BERT Clasification
#ATENCIÓN — Se reporta un deslizamiento de tierra en el km 50 de la vía #Calacalí - #Nanegalito. Al momento, este tramo se encuentra cerrado al paso vehicular	2	2
Desde el #ECU911 se coordinó la atención con @Bomberos_Cuenca, @AzuayIess y @emov_ep. Se brinda apoyo visual a través de #VideovigilanciaECU911	0	0
Reportan la caída de un puente peatonal en el sector Capulispamba, vía #Cuenca - #Azogues. Un tráiler habría chocado en la estructura. Paso vehicular restringido	5	3
#Cuenca: El río Machángara se desborda en el sector Ochoa León. Vídeo: @_REDInformativa	3	3
Cierres viales por manifestaciones en #Cuenca: Eloy Alfaro y Guapondelig. De Las Américas y Del Chofer. Loja y 12 De Abril. Paucarbamba y Miguel Cordero. Ordóñez Lasso y De Las Américas	4	4
@aquezada918 @tomebamba @elmercurioec @NuevoTiempoCue @WRadioec @complicefm @radialvision @RadioCiudad1017 @antenaunofm @teleramaec @EcosCanar Buenos días Ana, según el reporte de tránsito más reciente al momento la vía Cuenca-Girón-Pasaje se encuentra cerrada en Tarqui. Saludos	4	4
#ECU911Reporta— siniestro de tránsito en sector Monjas Huayco (El Cabo), Paute. Los recursos de @BomberosPaute y @CTEcuador atienden la emergencia	1	1
#ECU911Reporta Se registra deslizamiento en el sector de Granadillas, la vía Gualaquiza - Sigsig se encuentra cerrada. Se coordinó la atención mediante @Riesgos_Ec con @ObrasPublicasEc y @GADMGualaquiza. Ruta alterna: Gualaquiza - Plan de Milagro - Gualaceo	2	4
16h37 - El río Machángara se desborda en el sector del condominio Buenaventura, junto a la avenida del Migrante, al norte de Cuenca	3	3
Actualización: 18 ríos desbordados y 1.295 metros de vías afectadas por las lluvias. Zamora Chinchipe, Azuay y Tungurahua son las tres provincias más afectadas de un total de 13. Existen más de 5 hectáreas de cultivos afectados	5	3

4.2   User Acceptance Testing

Another experiment presented in this paper is the evaluation of the acceptance of the proposed application. Thus, a survey was established with questions related to the ISO 9126 standard according to its six basic characteristics, which are: functionality, reliability, usability, efficiency, maintainability, and portability. We have evaluated four of these six characteristics. Based on these premises, six questions were proposed with a five-point scale, indicating that 1 represents *Totally Disagree*, and 5 *Totally Agree*. Table 3, presents the questions and ISO 9126 characteristics with which they are related.

Table 3. Questions used in the survey for the user acceptance test with its corresponding characteristic of the ISO 9126 standard

Question	Characteristic	Sub-Characteristic
1. Does the application show the expected results according to the needs for which it was created?	Functionality	Accuracy
2. Does the application fulfill the tasks that were specified in the description?	Functionality	Adequacy
3. Is the application easy to use?	Usability	Ease to learn
4. Do you consider that the help of an expert is necessary to use the application?	Usability	Comprehensibility
5. Does the application display news and locations quickly?	Efficiency	Behavior in relation to time
6. Does the application present new functionalities compared to other similar applications?	Portability	Replacement Capability

To show the functionality of our application, due to COVID-19, a video was recorded where all the functionalities that can be executed on the mobile application are presented. Also, the survey was developed on the Google Forms platform, where we indicated the background and the main objective of the application before the user begin the survey. As we mentioned before, our research was focused on being useful for all drivers belonging to the city of Cuenca and its surroundings. Therefore, a group of motorcyclists called *MotOsados*[1] was considered as the sample users that will test the functionality and evaluate its acceptance.

The results obtained by each user are presented in Table 4, where we add their values and get the percentage of independent satisfaction, the final values are represented in three satisfaction groups: Low Satisfaction (0–15), Medium Satisfaction (16–25), and High Satisfaction (25–30).

---

[1] https://www.instagram.com/motosados/.

Table 4. Results obtained by applying the survey of user acceptance to a group of 14 motorcycles in the city of Cuenca

Users	Q1	Q2	Q3	Q4	Q5	Q6	Total	Ratio of Satisfaction
User 1	5	5	5	4	5	5	29	0.97
User 2	5	5	5	3	4	4	26	0.87
User 3	3	4	3	1	4	4	19	0.63
User 4	5	5	5	3	5	5	28	0.93
User 5	5	4	4	4	5	3	25	0.83
User 6	5	4	3	3	4	5	24	0.80
User 7	5	5	4	1	4	4	23	0.77
User 8	4	5	5	3	5	5	27	0.90
User 9	3	3	1	5	3	3	18	0.60
User 10	4	5	4	3	5	5	26	0.87
User 11	4	4	5	3	4	4	24	0.80
User 12	4	4	5	3	4	4	24	0.80
User 13	1	5	1	4	4	4	19	0.63
User 14	4	4	3	2	3	5	21	0.70

As shown in the previous table, a total of fourteen users were evaluated, where the results present that a total of six users consider the application highly satisfactory, eight users consider the application moderately satisfactory, and zero users consider the application low satisfactory.

Likewise, we have evaluated in a general way the total percentages of acceptance per question, comparing its approval rating with its counterpart, as shown in Fig. 3. For this, we have considered the answers to options 4 (Somewhat Agree), and 5 (Totally Agree) as values that indicate approval, and for options 1 (Totally Disagree), and 2 (Disagree) we have considered as values that indicate denial. The answer for option 3 (Neutral) is not considered for this evaluation. Also, in the 4th question, these results are taken to the contrary. According to these, it is specified that Low Satisfaction is in the range of 0–60%, and High Satisfaction is in the range of 60% to 100%.

The results observed in the previous Figure show that most of the questions were evaluated with a high percentage (greater than 60%), where only the 4th question is required to control the details of the options and functionalities that the application has in order to facilitate its use and interaction with the user. However, it is understood that despite this the help of experts who indicate how to use the application is not completely necessary.

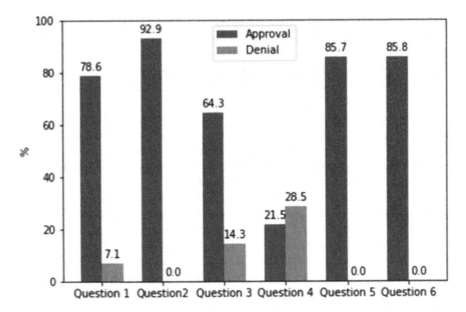

Fig. 3. Results in percentages of the user acceptance per question, comparing its approval rating with its counterpart.

5   Conclusions

The application presented in this paper has been based on the research of detailed fundamentals for Natural Language Processing and Text Classification obtained from the unstructured information of social media, in this particular case Twitter. Our paper aims to identify presumptive road incidents and present them in an interactive map of a mobile application.

For the development of the model regarding the preprocessing of the data, we considered an important point the collection of a corpus of tweets. Thus, we have extracted selected tweets, for example, by ignoring or eliminating the tweet responses, and filtering according to selected accounts of interest. Also, we have cleaned the tweet text by avoiding useless words, links, or mentions that are not relevant to the text classification. At this point, we can conclude that this stage is of vital importance to the objective of our proposal because from this arises the correct selection and presentation of the "news" tweets and the extraction of useful data, which can infer road incidents in the city of Cuenca. Finally, we have integrated these tasks as the back-end module in our mobile application in order to store the preprocessed data according to the needs of the project.

Furthermore, regarding the front-end of the application, it turns out to be the most crucial visual point to be accepted by the users, as we have presented a user acceptance of 92.9% in question #2, which was related to the application functionality and adequacy. Therefore, the design for the presentation is essential, for example by including the customization of images or objects, as is the case of the pointers to indicate the locations on the map, which according to each label of the classification shows a unique related design. Indeed, it is necessary to have a high acceptance by the users for which the mobile application was developed. So, the acceptance evaluation proposed was based on a questionnaire related to the sub-characteristics and characteristics of the ISO 9126 standard. We have focused on the sub-characteristics, such as (a) accuracy and adequacy, (b) ease of learning and comprehensibility, (c) behavior over time, and (d) replaceability, which correspond to functionality, usability, efficiency, and portability characteristic. This evaluation has made it clear that the application has good user acceptance but it is necessary to consider certain points regarding how easy it is to identify the functionalities that it presents.

In conclusion, the mobile application fulfills the proposed objectives efficiently and adequately by presenting a functional and visually pleasing product for the user. It shows the "news" tweets related to traffic incidents and, in the case of extracting the necessary information, points out the approximate locations with customized icons that facilitate its understanding. Also, with the possibility of integrating the user's personal Twitter account so, the user can participate in the dissemination of related information and feel more active with the continuous use of the application.

References

1. Época lluviosa 2021–2022 a nivel nacional (2022). https://www.gestionderiesgos.gob.ec/epoca-lluviosa-a-nivel-nacional-desde-el-01-de-octubre-del-2021/
2. Visor de siniestralidad nacional (2022). https://www.ant.gob.ec/?page_id=2670
3. Cañete, J., Chaperon, G., Fuentes, R., Ho, J.H., Kang, H., Pérez, J.: Spanish pre-trained bert model and evaluation data. In: PML4DC at ICLR 2020 (2020)
4. León-Paredes, G.A., et al.: Virtual reality and data analysis based platform for urban mobility awareness as a tool for road education. In: 2020 IEEE ANDESCON, pp. 1–6 (2020). https://doi.org/10.1109/ANDESCON50619.2020.9272084
5. Leon-Paredes, G.A., Bravo-Quezada, O.G., Sacoto-Cabrera, E.J., Calle-Siavichay, W.F., Jimenez-Gonzalez, L.L., Aguirre-Benalcazar, J.: Virtual reality platform for sustainable road education among users of urban mobility in Cuenca, Ecuador. Int. J. Adv. Comput. Sci. Appl. 13(6) (2022). https://doi.org/10.14569/IJACSA.2022.01306106, https://dx.doi.org/10.14569/IJACSA.2022.01306106
6. Neruda, G.A., Winarko, E.: Traffic event detection from twitter using a combination of CNN and Bert. In: 2021 International Conference on Advanced Computer Science and Information Systems (ICACSIS), pp. 1–7. IEEE (2021)
7. Pedregosa, F., et al.: Scikit-learn: machine learning in python. J. Mach. Learn. Res. 12, 2825–2830 (2011)
8. Suat-Rojas, N., Gutierrez-Osorio, C., Pedraza, C.: Extraction and analysis of social networks data to detect traffic accidents. Information 13(1), 26 (2022)
9. Wan, X., Ghazzai, H., Massoud, Y.: Leveraging personal navigation assistant systems using automated social media traffic reporting. In: 2020 IEEE Technology & Engineering Management Conference (TEMSCON), pp. 1–6. IEEE (2020)

Financial Credit Risk Measurement Using a Binary Classification Model

Oscar Chiluiza[1], Cathy Guevara-Vega[2($\boxtimes$)] ⓘ, Antonio Quiña-Mera[2] ⓘ, Pablo Landeta-López[2] ⓘ, and Javier Montaluisa[1]

[1] Universidad de las Fuerzas Armadas ESPE, Quijano y Ordoñez Street, Latacunga, Ecuador
`{owchiluiza,fjmontaluisa}@espe.edu.ec`
[2] eCIER Research Group, Universidad Técnica del Norte, 17 de Julio Avenue, Ibarra, Ecuador
`{cguevara,aquina,palandeta}@utn.edu.ec`

Abstract. Currently, financial institutions have several problems in the analysis of information to grant a credit or a loan, causing losses that involve collection expenses, notifications, legal processes, among others. Thanks to the digital transformation and technological progress, Artificial Intelligence and especially Machine Learning can be used to analyze customer data and predict non-compliance with the payment of their obligations to institutions. The objective of this work is to apply CRISP-DM (Cross Industry Standard Process for Data Mining) methodology and the Random Forest (XGBoost), Logistic Regression and Neural Networks of supervised learning models, to implement a predictive model that allows evaluating credit risk. With the result of the application of the predictive model, it is concluded that the use of Machine Learning tools helps to optimize the evaluation of credit risk in financial entities. Once CRISP-DM methodology was used for the analysis, development, and evaluation of the models, it was concluded that the most efficient model is the Random Forest. Based on this experience, future work could implement this type of model in other areas such as: fraud detection, customer segmentation or a recommendation engine that can suggest financial products and services based on customer needs and behaviors.

Keywords: Predictive model · CRISP-DM · Random Forest · Logistic Regression · Neuronal Networks

1 Introduction

The risks are the possibility of occurrence of adverse events that can modify the normal progress of the established functions, which can generate delays in achieving the established objectives and losses in the financial entities [1]. In Ecuador a problem has been evidenced. SEPS (Superintendencia de Economía Popular y Solidaria) [2] as a control and regularization entity for the Savings and Credit Cooperatives of Ecuador, has not established regulations that allow the use of models for credit management, this has even caused some cooperatives to close due to the increase in late payments in their credit portfolios and the lack of liquidity. On the other hand, we have noticed that there is a limitation of technological tools that help control risk in financial entities; therefore, these

F. R. Narváez et al. (Eds.): SmartTech-IC 2022, CCIS 1705, pp. 241–254, 2023.
https://doi.org/10.1007/978-3-031-32213-6_18

entities have been forced to invest more resources to find their own alternatives to mitigate credit risk. Considering this problem, we decided to apply Design Science Research (DSR) approach [3] as the research methodology for this study. The following research question is proposed: *How to assess credit risk in Savings and Credit Cooperatives by applying a prediction model.*

In addition to this, we propose the following hypothesis:

H_0: If a predictive model is developed, then the credit risk will be evaluated, optimizing the granting of credits in the financial institution.

This work aims to answer the research question with the creation of a predictive model for the evaluation of the credit risk of Savings and Credit Cooperatives using Machine Learning models and prediction techniques and the CRISP-DM methodology (Cross Industry Standard Process for Data Mining) [4] which contains six phases: business understanding, data understanding, data preparation, modeling, evaluation, and deployment. We decide to use CRISP-DM because it is a popular methodology for Data Mining projects [4, 5]. The purpose of the predictive model is to identify the most important aspects that characterize credit clients, and with an evaluation using Machine Learning techniques, determine the ideal predictive model that helps establish the client's credit status accurately and with a percentage of minimal error. The investigation was carried out in a Savings and Credit Cooperative of Ecuador, whose credit risk management process is carried out through credit rating, but it has been shown that this process is not sufficient to assess whether a loan can be granted to a client. For all this, there is a need to use technological tools and specifically prediction models for credit risk to better evaluate their clients.

The rest of the document is structured as follows: Sect. 2) Research design based on DSR, which shows the theoretical foundation, design, and construction of the artifact (predictive model). Section 3) Results of the evaluation of the designed artifact. Section 4) Discussion of the results with related works. Section 5) Conclusions of the study and future work.

2 Research Design

We have designed the research based on the guidelines of the Design Science Research approach [3], see Table 1.

2.1 Population and Sample

Total data is the sum of all clients with a credit history within the institution, giving a total of 68,164 records stored in its production and historical database and made up of 27 variables. For data protection due to banking secrecy, the names and personal identifications were hidden.

One of the most important points is the process of cleaning and eliminating unnecessary, inconsistent, redundant, or erroneous information in the extraction of data from the variables, it is observed that there is information with null values, which may be due to

Table 1. Research design methodology.

Activity	Components	Paper section
Problem diagnosis	Problem; Objective Population and sample	Introduction Research design
Theoretical foundation	Machine Learning Supervised learning Logistic Regression Model Random Forest Model Neuronal Network Model Confusion Matrix CRISP-DM	Research design
Artefact design: predictive model development	Based on CRISP-DM	Predictive model development
Artifact evaluation	Evaluation of the models with the classification algorithms	Results

failures in the filling in the client file, in addition there are inconsistencies or omissions in filling out the information.

2.2 Theoretical Foundation

A practical approach to Machine Learning with tools and techniques for Java implementations is discussed in the work of Witten et al. [6].

The survey conducted by Sebastiani, discusses the main approaches to text categorization that fall within the machine learning paradigm. The dominant approach to this problem is based on machine learning techniques: a general inductive process automatically builds a classifier by learning, from a set of preclassified documents, the characteristics of the categories [7]. There is an article about classification and regression trees, it gives an introduction to the subject by reviewing some widely available algorithms and comparing their capabilities, strengths, and weakness in two examples [8].

An important book as a guide to logistic regression modeling for health science and other applications is presented in [9]. It provides an easily accessible introduction to the logistic regression (LR) model and highlights the power of this model by examining the relationship between a dichotomous outcome and a set of covariables.

Random forests are an effective tool in prediction. Because of the Law of Large Numbers, they do not overfit. Injecting the right kind of randomness makes them accurate classifiers and regressors. Furthermore, the framework in terms of strength of the individual predictors and their correlations gives insight into the ability of the random forest to predict. Using out-of-bag estimation makes concrete the otherwise theoretical values of strength and correlation. This es analyzed in the work of Breiman [10], it is a necessary article to understand Random Forests basics.

University of Washington researchers propose a novel sparsity-aware algorithm for sparse data and weighted quantile sketch for approximate tree learning. More importantly, we provide insights on cache access patterns, data compression and sharding to build a scalable tree boosting system. By combining these insights, XGBoost scales beyond billions of examples using far fewer resources than existing systems [11].

A review of deep supervised learning, unsupervised learning, reinforcement learning & evolutionary computation, and indirect search for short programs encoding deep and large networks is presented in [12], to assign credit to those who contributed to the state of the art about Deep Learning (DL). Finally, we must mention the work of Tharwat [13], who introduces a detailed overview of the classification assessment measures with the aim of providing the basics of these measures and to show how it works to serve as a comprehensive source for researchers who are interested in this field. This overview starts by highlighting the definition of the confusion matrix in binary and multi-class classification problems. Many classification measures are also explained in detail, and the influence of balanced and imbalanced data on each metric is presented.

3 Predictive Model Development

We use the CRIPS-DM.v3 (Cross-Industry Standard Process for Data Mining) methodology [4] to develop the predictive model, from business analysis to implementation and presentation of results.

Phase 1: Business Understanding

Determine Business Goals. According to the business situation of the financial entity, there is a database of current and even historical credits. However, there are no studies of customer behavior that can provide conclusions and patterns that make predictions about future customers who may or may not receive credit.

The Savings and Credit Cooperative is a financial entity of segment 2, which seeks to integrate itself into this new Data Mining technology, which projects an analysis of historical and current data that the institution has stored, with this process the institution seeks to improve the following objectives: i) Improve the evaluation of a client to know if he is suitable or not for a loan. ii) Streamline the credit rating and delivery process. Iii) Minimize the probability of non-compliance in credit payments.

From a business perspective, predicting that a new customer is trustworthy can reduce the rate of arrears of loans, this is considered a success criterion, another measure of success is the increase in the percentage of agility when granting a loan.

Evaluate the Initial Situation. The Savings and Credit Cooperative is a de facto company dedicated to productive microcredits. It currently has more than 40,000 members, mostly: merchants, farmers, artisans, public and private employees, carriers; its capital is made up of the contributions of all the members and savings of its depositors, who have been contributing based on the trust generated during all these years of work, the Savings and Credit Cooperative has 12 Agencies and its Head Office in the city of Latacunga.

For this project, the databases that store current and historical information of all the credits granted and whose statuses are canceled, active, reclassified, and expired are required. Due to banking secrecy, the presentation of data such as personal identification, names and surnames is restricted.

The existing risks that must be considered for this work are the following:

- The development time of the project, once the proposal was accepted by the General Management, all the credit information of the financial entity was downloaded and saved in another SQL Server 2016 database engine.
- Additional or outstanding costs: we will work with the initial data, so no additional costs are required by the entity or the researcher.
- The quality of data: the process of granting credit starts from the update of the account, that is, the member updates the data such as personal information, home, spouse, work, and financial status. With this, it can be considered that the data quality is good.

Set Data Mining Goals. The objectives set for the development of the project are the following: i) Generate patterns that help the evaluation of a client to verify if he is suitable or not for a loan. ii) Generate patterns that help with the problem of increased arrears and low profitability.

The data mining criterion was to predict with the variables or data already trained, if a partner is subject to credit or not with a percentage of 90% success and effectiveness.

Regarding the techniques for data extraction, the SQL programming language was used to generate the scripts that allow the information consulted and extracted. Classification tasks were used to generate predictive models, and the modeling techniques were Random Forest, Logistic Regression and Neural Networks.

Phase 2: Understanding the Data

Collect Initial Data. For the development of this project, the following data was collected: customer information, type of credit, amount, payment frequency, economic activity, etc., these data are stored in tables related to the credit granting process, also for reasons legal and banking secrecy identification data, names and surnames were omitted. Because the objective of the project is to make predictions, the client was classified good and bad according to the last credit rating they obtained at the time of canceling Due to the large number of records that are necessary for the development of the project, it was decided to develop SQL statements that help generate all the information based on the data investigated in conjunction with the financial institution.

Describe Data. According to the analysis, the variables with which to work for the development of the model are disclosed. Each of them is detailed, classified into 27 input variables, and one output variable, which are described in [14].

Explore Data. With the variables obtained, a search was made to the database, to identify all the information that can be obtained and will be necessary for the realization of this research project, a statistic of each variable to be processed was made.

Verify Data Quality. To data quality verification, ISO/IEC 25012 standard - "Data Quality Model" [15] will be used, which specifies a general quality model for those data that are defined in a structured format within a computer system; through a matrix the good and bad data will be valued.

Characteristics that will be consider to data verification matrix: i) Accessibility (AC): Specifies the degree to which data can be accessed in a specific context. ii) Accordance (CO): Verifies that the corresponding data complies with current standards, conventions, or regulations. iii) Confidentiality (CF) (associated with information security): ensures that data is only accessed and interpreted by specific authorized users. iv) Efficiency (EF): Analyzes the degree to which data can be processed and provided with expected performance levels. v) Precision (PR): The data requires exact values or with discernment in a specific context. vi) Traceability (TZ): Analyzes whether the data provides a record of the events that modify it. vii) Understandability (CP): The data is expressed using appropriate languages, symbols and units and can be read and inter-preted by any type of user.

Phase 3: Data Preparation

Select Data. Data is made up of the sum of all clients with a credit history within the institution, giving a total of 68164 records stored in its production and historical database and made up of 27 variables.

Clean Data. An important process is cleaning and eliminating unnecessary, inconsistent, redundant, or erroneous information in the extraction of variable data. It is detected that there is information with null values, which may exist due to failures at the time of filling out the client file, in addition there are inconsistencies or omissions in filling out the information.

Build Data. A count of ranges was carried out where the minimum and maximum are specified, which will help transform the categorical data to numbers, facilitating the training of the algorithm and improving the interpretation of data.

Integrate Data. Only the data stored in the Core from the Informix database engine was used, so integration with other sources was not necessary.

Format Data. Once the categorization is done, as a result processed data with numerical values that reflect the value of each record are obtained. Data is available at: [14]. This type of processing is part of a data normalization. The order of the variables does not affect the development of the project, so it is not necessary to change, the normalization of variables is a great help when generating a model.

Phase 4: Modeling

Select Modeling Techniques. The selected models focused on predictive models aimed at solving problems in banking areas such as predictions of arrears, predictions of non-payment. The selected techniques are the following: Decision Trees (Random Forest), Neural Networks and Logistic Regression.

The three techniques are supported by Python as a tool to be used for model generation and evaluation to find the most accurate model.

Design Model Tests. Before the construction of the models for the research work, a test plan was considered, to determine the procedures to validate the quality and accuracy of each model. Two stages were contemplated for the design of the test plan. The first stage consisted in divide the data in training data that covers 70% and test data that covers 30%. The second stage was the validation of the models for which the Confusion

Matrix Evaluation Technique was used. The metrics to evaluate the models are listed: Accuracy, Error rate, Sensitivity, Specificity, Precision, and Negative predictive value. The selection of the metrics was based on the review of several research papers [16–18].

Build the Models. Random Forest: For the construction of the model, XGBoost tool was used, (Extreme Gradient Boosting) [11], the following parameters were defined: A bi-nary classification was used as the main objective of the model, a maximum depth of 150, a minimum observation weight of 25, a subsample of 0.85, the column per tree sample of 0.8, a minimum loss reduction needed of 5, job number 16, a learning rate of 0.025, and a speed of 1305. Additionally, the scale_pos_weight parameter was used to adjust the behavior of the algorithm with unbalanced classification problems. In Lo-gistic Regression and Neural Network, the class_weight = "balanced" was used to bal-ance the data in training.

For this model, its construction was in accordance with the definition of the initial parameters: import of the libraries, connection to the database, division of the data in training and testing. The most important variable for this model was the type of client, that is, if a member is new or has already had credits in the financial institution before (recurring).

Logistic regression: For the construction of the model, the parameters that are defined by default were used. It was based on the default parameters since they meet the objective of the project, which is to verify if a member is subject to credit or not, for this model the most important variable is age.

Neural network: For the creation of the neural network with scikit-learn, the sklearn.neural_network.MLPClassifier class was used for classification, the following parameters were defined: the number of hidden neurons (10, 10, 10), maximum number of iterations (500), regularization parameter (0.0001), Adam-based solution optimizer for large volumes of data, random number for the weights (21) and a tolerance of 0.000000001.

Evaluate Models. For the verification of the Confusion Matrix, confusion_matrix was imported from the sklearn library, and it was used together with the real data and those that have been previously predicted.

The results of the evaluation are displayed in the Results section.

Phase 5: Evaluation
For the development of this research work, three Machine Learning classification models were applied: Random Forest, Logistic Regression and Neural Networks.

The results of the evaluation are displayed in the Results section.

Phase 6: Implementation or Deployment

Schedule Deployment. To implement the model within the financial institution, four phases were created, which helped employees to use Machine Learning for credit risk assessment:

Phase 1: After creating the model and reviewing which is the best option to achieve the business objectives, it is necessary to export the model, that is, serialize the trained model to be able to use it in a Web API.

Phase2: A web API is developed with Flask [15], which helps to create web applications with Python. Through this application, collaborators will be able to enter from any web browser and will be able to make the prediction of the client after entering some data.

Phase3: In this phase, a training in the use of the web API is carried out for the collaborators who work in credits and operations area, being these the ones in charge of generating the credit requests and the respective approvals.

Phase4: As a last phase, interviews or work meetings will be held with those responsible for the operational processes to see the results obtained when classifying the partner through the model and the web API that was carried out using Machine Learning.

Plan Monitoring and Maintenance. Monitoring and maintaining the implementation of the model is one of the important steps to carry out a good prediction of the client. It should be considered that there is a data update program that the financial entity carries out from time to time and with the refinement of the parameters, the model classification process can be improved. Also, each month there is cancellation of credits or pre-cancellations, these historical data are updated in the institution's database.

As a monitoring and maintenance plan, the following processes can be followed: i) Selection and extraction of data updated every six months, that is, a data mining process. ii) Generation of the model with the new data, without forgetting that 70% is needed for training and 30% for testing. iii) Exporting the model using the serialize and update process in the Web API. iv) Have a model update log and save a version for each model.

4 Results

4.1 Evaluation of the Models

For the verification of the Confusion Matrix, in the Python programming language, confusion_matrix is imported from the sklearn library, and it is used together with the real data and those that have been previously predicted.

Table 2 represents a comparison of the data with the metrics of our models, resulting in a general model with a very good accuracy percentage of 90%.

Decision Tree Model (Random Forest). The error matrix generally indicates that the degree of classification is quite good with 90% accuracy and an error or misclassification rate of 10%.

The model also indicates that it classifies positive cases with a probability of 99.6% and negative cases with a probability of 6%.

Also, if the classifier detects that a customer is good, it is with a 91% probability. And if he says he isn't, then the customer is bad with a probability of 58%.

Logistic Regression Model. The error matrix generally indicates that the degree of classification is quite good with 90% accuracy and an error or misclassification rate of 10%.

The model also indicates that it classifies positive cases with a probability of 99% and negative cases with a probability of 0.3%.

Table 2. Comparative table of the models

Model/Metric	Accuracy	Error Rate	Sensitivity	Specificity	Precision	Negative Prediction
Random Forest (ML1)	0.90	0.10	0.99	0.06	0.91	0.58
Logistic regression (ML2)	0.90	0.10	0.99	0.003	0.90	0.33
Neural network (ML3)	0.90	0.10	0.99	0.06	0.91	0.53

Also, if the classifier detects that a customer is good, it is with a 90% probability. And if he says he isn't, then the customer is bad with a probability of 33%.

Neural Network Model. The error matrix generally indicates that the degree of classification is quite good with 90% accuracy and an error or misclassification rate of 10%.

The model also indicates that it classifies positive cases with a probability of 99% and negative cases with a probability of 6%.

Also, if the classifier detects that a customer is good, it is with a 91% probability. And if he says he's not, then the customer is bad with a probability of 53%.

Now, the data of the models applied to the business objectives and the Data Mining objectives are analyzed.

Business Objectives:

a) Improve the evaluation of a client to know if he is suitable or not for a loan: if the comparison table is observed, the ML1 and ML3 model predicts with an accuracy of 91% if a client is good, but only the ML1 model predicts that a client is bad with 58%.
b) Streamline the credit qualification and delivery process: the three models meet this objective since when entering the data of the variables and executing the model there is a very short time in which the model solves and gives a good or bad result.
c) Minimize the probability of default in credit payments: both the ML1 and ML3 models give this probability, but ML1 has the 58% higher of the two models.

Data Mining Objectives:

a) Generate patterns that help the evaluation of a client to verify if he is suitable or not for a loan. The ML1 and ML2 models show a summary of the Important Variables of each model indicating which pattern is the most outstanding at the time of generating a model and with this verify if a client is suitable or not.

The pattern shows the client's behavior regarding direct obligations to the institution. To determine what these patterns are, the classification of variables by their importance was generated. This indicates that a classification of clients can be made using these variables through an interview or survey to generate a pre-selection of the ideal clients to deliver a loan. In addition, with the selection of variables, a model can be generated, thus improving the effectiveness of the algorithm.

b) Generate patterns that help with the problem of increased delinquency and low profitability: the ML1 and ML2 models show a summary of the Important Variables of each model, indicating which pattern is the most prominent when generating a model and with this verify the delinquency and low profitability.

Approved models

When reviewing the objectives of both the business and Data Mining, it is noted that the three most important factors in choosing the best model are Accuracy, Precision and Negative Prediction. Summarizing these metrics, the first two represent the percentage of success and quality of the model at the time of making the true predictions, while the third metric indicates the percentage of negative prediction, that is, the percentage of non-compliance in the payment of the credit.

It is concluded that the Random Forest model applying XGBoost with an accuracy of 90%, a precision of 91% and a negative prediction of 58%, is the accepted model for implementation.

4.2 Results Validation

The results of the models evaluated with the extracted data are presented below:

Random Forest. The first model is developed with XGBoost, one of the modules of the Scikit-learn library. The data of the confusion matrix are shown in the following graph:

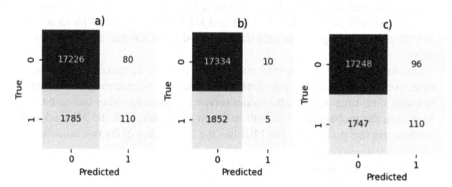

Fig. 1. a) Random Forest Confusion Matrix, b) Logistic Regression confusion matrix and c) Confusion matrix Neural Networks

Figure 1(a) indicates that there are 17,336 records that were classified correctly and that 1,865 were erroneously classified. In addition, the following can be detailed:

17,226 clients who are classified as subject to credit.
110 clients who were correctly classified as not subject to credit.
80 clients that were erroneously classified as not subject to credit.
1785 clients who were erroneously classified as subject to credit.

Logistic Regression. The second model developed with Logistic Regression in the same way a module of the Scikit-learn library, Fig. 1 (b) shows the data of the confusion matrix.

Figure 1(b) indicates that there are 17,339 records that were classified correctly and that 1,862 were erroneously classified. In addition, the following can be detailed:

17,334 clients who are classified as subject to credit.
5 clients who were correctly classified as not subject to credit.
10 clients who were wrongly classified as not subject to credit.
1,852 clients who were erroneously classified as subject to credit.

Neural Networks. The third model is developed with the MLPClassifier module of the Scikit-learn library, Fig. 1 (c) shows the confusion matrix data.

Figure 1(c) indicates that there are 17,358 records that were classified correctly and that 1,843 were erroneously classified. In addition, the following can be detailed:

17,248 clients who are classified as subject to credit.
110 clients who were correctly classified as not subject to credit.
96 clients who were erroneously classified as not subject to credit.
1747 clients who were erroneously classified as subject to credit.

5   Discussion

In the study by Li and Wang [19], they present the development of credit risk measurement models based on data mining, they do it in the same context of our research; however, they do not provide or do not have an appropriate deployment plan for the normal user or customer. This finding motivated the realization of this work to help the credit analyst by entering data, verify whether the client is subject to credit.

In another study found by Kruppa, Schwarz, Arminger y Ziegler [20], propose a framework to estimate credit risks for consumer loans, using Machine Learning. They refer to logistic regression as the main model construction technique, which is related to our research work. However, this technique has its limitations, being the easiest to use and its configuration is based on data by default. Faced with these difficulties, we present our contribution with the analysis and evaluation of the models with various machine learning techniques, Random Forest being the most effective.

The work proposed by Song and Wu [21] uses data mining to determine the risk of excessive financialization. They used the genetic algorithm (GA), neural network and principal component analysis (PCA) data collection and processing methods. The results suggest that the data mining technology based on back propagation neural network

(BPNN) can optimize the input variables and effectively extract the hidden information from the data.

Another study about financial risk prevention with data mining is proposed by Gao [22], who analyzed 21 companies with high trust. The results show that the financial risk evaluation index system of four dimensions of solvency, operation ability, profitability, growth ability and cash flow ability can affect the financial risk of enterprises. Compared with the traditional data mining algorithm, the algorithm of financial risk index evaluation model constructed in this study has the best performance.

Greek researchers Lappas and Yannacopoulos [23], affirm that in addition to the automatic processing of credit ratings, the opinion of experts is required. They propose a combination strategy of integrating soft computing methods with expert knowledge. The ability of interpretation of the predictive power of each feature in the credit dataset is strengthened by the engagement of experts in the credit scoring process. Testing instances on standard credit dataset were established to verify the effectiveness of the proposed methodology.

Among the limitations presented by our research work, it is considered that the development of the model is tailor-made for the financial institution. It would be advisable to take this model to another context, to evaluate and instantiate the performance of said model. In addition, the analysis of credits according to the manuals, policies and regulations of each financial entity is considered another limitation. This means that the variables for the model would not be the same and it would be necessary to reengineer the ideal variables for the construction of the model.

6 Conclusions and Future Work

Once the CRISP-DM methodology was used for the analysis, development and evaluation of the models as mentioned in phase 5 of said methodology, it was concluded that the most efficient model is the Random Forest.

In addition, to verify if the problem was solved and the solvency of the hypothesis, a web application was made, in which the data of the variables is entered and with the processing of the trained model it results in whether the client is good (the person is subject to credit) or bad (the person is not subject to credit) and with this analysis verify if the credit granting process was optimized.

Hypothesis H0 raised with 95% is accepted, in the development of the research work. It is verified that the use of binary classification techniques is an effective method for the evaluation of credit risk in the Savings and Credit Cooperative. The choice of the CRISP-DM methodology helped to generate objectives that meet the needs of the business line and focus on solving the hypothesis. It is clarified that the customer data used in the model to test the hypothesis were real and correspond to a financial institution in Ecuador.

For the elaboration of the models, an investigation of the Machine Learning techniques was carried out, which are within the predictive analysis and that focus on credit risk, with this analysis three classification-type models were used: Random Forest, Logistic Regression and Neural Networks.

With the development and evaluation of these Machine Learning models, it was confirmed that the Random Forest model using the XGBoost module is the most accurate to predict whether a client is subject to credit.

Through the evaluation of the models, performance patterns of a client were generated, based on the extraction of the important variables, this helped the operations personnel to carry out a brief validation of the partner in the field.

With the application of Machine Learning for the generation of the most effective model and the development of a Web API (data entry through a form and prediction process through the serialized model), the credit delivery process was improved, and the customer service and attention improved. Customer by 40% more, in reference to the manual process. As future work, it is proposed to apply empirical strategies to evaluate the proposed model. In addition, develop a predictive model for the collection area, to predict customer behavior when deciding to pre-cancel an investment. Finally, it is proposed to carry out an analysis with Machine Learning in the compliance area, verifying if there is or will be money laundering through the behavior of the transactions carried out by the client. Supplementary material for this research study is available at: [14].

References

1. Duffie, D., Singleton, K.: Credit risk: Pricing, Measurement, and Management. Princeton University Press (2012)
2. Superintendencia de Economía Popular y Solidaria: Inicio – Superintendencia de Economía Popular y Solidaria. https://www.seps.gob.ec/ (2022). Accessed 21 Mar 2022
3. Hevner, A.R., March, S.T., Park, J., Ram, S.: Design science in IS research. Manag. Inf. Syst. **28**(1), 75–105 (2004)
4. Chapman, P., et al.: CRISP-DM 1.0: Step-by-step data mining guide (2000)
5. Moro, S., Laureano, R.M.S., Cortez, P.: Using data mining for bank direct marketing: an application of the CRISP-DM methodology. In: ESM 2011 – 2011 European Simulation Modelling Conference Modelling Simulation 2011, no. Figure 1, pp. 117–121 (2011)
6. Witten, I., Frank, E., Hall, M., Pal, C.: Data Mining: Practical Machine Learning Tools and Techniques (2016)
7. Sebastiani, F.: Machine learning in automated text categorization. ACM Comput. Surv. **34**(1), 1–47 (2002). https://doi.org/10.1145/505282.505283
8. Wei-Yin, L.: Classification and regression trees. Wiley Interdiscip. Rev. Data Min. Knowl. Discov. **1**(1), 14–23 (2011). https://doi.org/10.1002/widm.8
9. Hosmer, D.W., Lemeshow, S., Sturdivant, R.X.: Applied Logistic Regression, 3rd edn. Wiley (2013)
10. Breiman, L.: Random Forests. Mach. Learn. **45**, 5–32 (2001). https://doi.org/10.1023/A:1010933404324
11. Chen, T., Guestrin, C.: XGBoost: a scalable tree boosting system. In: Proceedings of the ACM SIGKDD International Conference on Knowledge Discovery and Data Mining, vol. 13, pp. 785–794 (2016). https://doi.org/10.1145/2939672.2939785
12. Schmidhuber, J.: Deep learning in neural networks: an overview. Neural Netw. **61**, 85–117 (2015). https://doi.org/10.1016/j.neunet.2014.09.003
13. Tharwat, A.: Classification assessment methods. Appl. Comput. Informatics **17**(1), 168–192 (2018). https://doi.org/10.1016/j.aci.2018.08.003

14. Chiluiza, O., Guevara-Vega, C., Quiña-Mera, A., Landeta-López, P., Montaluisa, J.: Supplementary material: financial credit risk measurement using a binary classification model. Zenodo (2022).https://doi.org/10.5281/zenodo.7274756

15. Iso25000.com: ISO/IEC 25012. https://iso25000.com/index.php/en/iso-25000-standards/iso-25012 (2021). Accessed 26 Mar 2022

16. Buckland, M., Gey, F.: The relationship between Recall and Precision. J. Am. Soc. Inf. Sci. **45**(1), 12–19 (1994). https://doi.org/10.1002/(SICI)1097-4571(199401)45:1%3c12::AID-ASI2%3e3.0.CO;2-L

17. Visa, S., Ramsay, B., Ralescu, A., Van Der Knaap, E.: Confusion matrix-based feature selection. In: CEUR Workshop Proceedings, vol. 710, pp. 120–127 (2011)

18. Marom, N.D., Rokach, L., Shmilovici, A.: Using the confusion matrix for improving ensemble classifiers. In: 2010 IEEE 26th Convention Electrical Electronics Engineers in Israel IEEEI, pp. 555–559 (2010).https://doi.org/10.1109/EEEI.2010.5662159

19. Li, W., Wang, S.: Research on assessment method for credit risk in commercial banks of china based on data mining. Appl. Mech. Mater. **303–306**, 1361–1364 (2013). https://doi.org/10.4028/www.scientific.net/AMM.303-306.1361

20. Kruppa, J., Schwarz, A., Arminger, G., Ziegler, A.: Consumer credit risk: Individual probability estimates using machine learning. Expert Syst. Appl. **40**(13), 5125–5131 (2013). https://doi.org/10.1016/j.eswa.2013.03.019

21. Song, Y., Wu, R.: The impact of financial enterprises' excessive financialization risk assessment for risk control based on data mining and machine learning. Comput. Econ. **60**, 1245–1267 (2021). https://doi.org/10.1007/s10614-021-10135-4

22. Gao, B.: The use of machine learning combined with data mining technology in financial risk prevention. Comput. Econ. **59**, 1385–1405 (2021). https://doi.org/10.1007/s10614-021-10101-0

23. Lappas, P.Z., Yannacopoulos, A.N.: A machine learning approach combining expert knowledge with genetic algorithms in feature selection for credit risk assessment. Appl. Soft Comput. **107**, 107391 (2021). https://doi.org/10.1016/j.asoc.2021.107391

FPGA-Based Four-Band Multispectral Camera Prototype for Precision Agriculture Applications

Julian Uribe-Rios[(✉)] , David Marquez-Viloria , Luis Castano-Londono ,
and Maria C. Torres-Madronero

Instituto Tecnológico Metropolitano, Medellín 50034, Colombia
julianuribe209085@correo.itm.edu.co,
{davidmarquez,luiscastano,mariatorres}@itm.edu.co

Abstract. Precision agriculture can use multispectral systems to acquire data over large crops. These data contain information on the spectral properties of the plants and the soil which can be used to calculate vegetation indices. These are algebraic combinations between several spectral bands and are useful to know the state of the crops. However, multispectral systems need to acquire and process a large amount of data due to the number of spectral bands and spatial resolution, for this reason the processing time can be high if the multispectral system has only one processor. In this work, we describe a prototype of a four-band multispectral system based on a Field-programmable gate array (FPGA) and calculate the normalized difference vegetation index (NDVI). The heterogeneneus architecture based on FPGA controls the simultaneous acquisition of the four spectral bands and the hardware acceleration for the band registration. We use a heterogeneous architecture combining FPGA and ARM (Advanced RISC Machines) that achieves to accelerate almost 5 times the image registration algorithm by taking advantage of the parallel operations capacity of FPGAs.

Keywords: Multispectral Camera · FPGA · Precision Agriculture · Image Registration · Remote Sensing · Normalized Differential Vegetation Index

1 Introduction

Remote sensing is responsible for acquiring information about an object from a distance, using sensors onboard different platforms such as satellites, aircraft, unmanned aerial vehicles (UAV) [20]. Remote sensing data provide timely, non-destructive, instantaneous and accurate estimates of the Earth's surface in different areas [8]. Remote sensing systems used for agriculture can be classified according to platform used and the type of sensor. The sensors used for remote sensing differ according to spatial, spectral, radiometric, and temporal resolution. Spatial resolution relates the size of the pixel to the area on the ground,

F. R. Narváez et al. (Eds.): SmartTech-IC 2022, CCIS 1705, pp. 255–269, 2023.
https://doi.org/10.1007/978-3-031-32213-6_19

and spectral resolution is a function of the number of spectral bands and their bandwidth along the electromagnetic spectrum [18].

Multispectral imaging systems use tens of discrete spectral bands, making these systems suitable for real-time applications [9]. Multispectral sensors are widely used over UAVs facilitating their use for crop monitoring. In addition, these also alleviate the repetitive and exhausting routines of manual acquisition of data. Multispectral imagery provides a better spatial resolution which allows a deeper and more accurate data analysis [11].

In the literature, there are different architectures of multispectral cameras for applications in agricultural crops. One is the filter wheel camera, where a motor turns a wheel containing different optical filters in front of the lens or sensor to capture images in different spectral ranges sequentially by turning the wheel. In this design, the cost is reduced by using a single image sensor, but the acquisition is slow due to having a mechanical element that also requires maintenance or replacement. A multispectral camera with a filter wheel is developed in [11], The authors used the low-cost solution onboard a UAV to calculate vegetation indices in a palm plantation. The systems used CMOS (complementary metal oxide semiconductor) sensor, a stepper motor that drives the rotating wheel, an Arduino Nano to control the motor, and an Odroid XU4 as a processing system. The authors of [6] designed a multispectral camera system based on a Field-programmable gate array (FPGA), where they use a single camera and several optical filters for the spectral bands. Instead of a wheel, this design uses a vertical and horizontal displacement system to perform the exchange of filters using two stepper motors. An FPGA EP2C35F672 controls motors and the communication with the camera. In this design, changing the filters is a time-consuming and labor-intensive task, which makes the system inefficient. In [2], show the design of a multispectral imaging system using a linear array sensor Tsl1401cl and a varifocal lens coupled to a bandpass filter wheel. The system allows the acquisition of raw spectral data for seven spectral bands using the Atmega32a microcontroller for image acquisition.

In the second type of architecture, beam splitters are used to carry the incident light to the different sensors of the system and capture the same scene in two or more spectral bands. This architecture alleviates the problem of image registration that occurs when several sensors are used. Still, this architecture is expensive due to the optical components that it handles, in addition to the loss of light intensity that can occur by using beam splitters. In the article [9], a three-band multispectral camera system is developed, where two images in the visible spectrum and one Near InfraRed (NIR) image are acquired simultaneously. The system design incorporates three monochromatic sensors, three optical filters, and an optical system that is composed of a front lens, a cold mirror, and a beam splitter. The design has the facility to interchange the filters, making it flexible enough to be used for a variety of applications. In [10], a portable multispectral camera also with 3 bands is presented, here they used a beam-splitter prism array, an XC3S500E FPGA module for system control, and three filters that can be easily changed for the selection of specific spectral bands for an application in the 400 to 1000 nm nm region.

In a third architecture, a sensor array is used where there is an image sensor, a lens, and a certain optical bandpass filter for each spectral band. This camera design captures simultaneously several bands, but an image registration algorithm is required to match the pixels between the different spectral bands. The article [5] presents a multispectral system that collects data in the visible spectrum (blue, green, and red) and near-infrared. The first prototype uses the Tiva^{TM}C Series LaunchPad evaluation kit from Texas Instruments, which is responsible for sending the capture order to the cameras, acquiring the image data, and transmitting them to the storage module. The low transfer speed of the cameras and the storage system led to changing the controller for another that offered greater speed and versatility by obtaining a time of 90 s to acquire and store the images. For this reason, the Raspberry Pi model B was selected to replace the previous development board, obtaining a time of 5 s. In [7], the authors developed a modular two-channel multispectral imaging system where a NIR and a Short-wave infrared (SWIR) image are acquired, and unlike other works they do not acquire in the visible spectrum. The system has as central computing unit the Nvidia Jetson TX2 integrated system module and the system is lightweight and compact for use in a UAV. The work in [21] introduced a multispectral camera using three CMOS KAC-9628 sensors, and a heterogeneous FPGA-based architecture (NIOS-II provided by Altera) as control unit. The collected information is stored as BMP files on a Compact Flash card. In [15], a 6-band multispectral imaging system is presented including the Jetson TK1 embedded system. The monochromatic cameras are mounted on a UAV with other electronic modules such as GPS and autopilot system for geolocated image acquisition. However, the image resolution limits the altitude at which the UAV can fly. In the research of [3,4] an economical and open source solution is given to build multispectral camera for vegetation monitoring in the visible and near-infrared spectrum, they use one Raspberry Pi board to drive each sensor. The authors of [12] develop a system for precision agriculture tasks composed of two modified low-cost Mobius cameras which are equipped with an aptina AR0330 CMOS sensor. In this work they use multispectral images to calculate 8 vegetation indices. In the article [17], two Mobius cameras are also used due to their low cost and light weight, and a Rapsberry Pi is used to control the triggering of the cameras and with the acquired images calculate the normalized difference vegetation index (NDVI).

This paper presents a system to capture four spectral bands using a heterogeneous FPGA-based architecture to reduce the processing load on the central processing unit (CPU), achieving an acceleration in the system by taking advantage of the parallel processing of the FPGA and its low power consumption. This work presents the first stage of what is expected to be an eight-spectral band prototype. The implementation speeds up the processing of the image registration algorithm on the FPGA compared to the implementation on the Advanced RISC Machines (ARM). The NDVI is calculated and the spectral signature obtained is presented to evaluate the performance of the system. The remainder of the paper is organized as follows. Section 2 describes the development of the prototype, starting with the hardware part and ending with the software description. Section 3 explains how the image registration was performed to align the images captured in the different spectral bands, then Sect. 4 shows the results obtained in the image registration and in the calculation of the NDVI. Finally, Sect. 5 presents the conclusions and future work.

2   Multispectral Camera Development

The design of a camera prototype seeks to reduce the cost to make it more affordable, increasing the interest of different sectors in remote sensing technologies. In addition, we aim to design a system with parts easily replaced, especially the optical filters, so that the system can be updated for different applications. Our system uses an array of monochromatic sensors with one sensor for each spectral band to be acquired, allowing a simultaneous capture as opposed to the sequential capture performed in multispectral cameras with a filter wheel. Optical elements such as beam splitters are not used in the design since these increase the cost. This sensor array design has the disadvantage that it requires an algorithm for the image registration of all spectral bands, since each sensor has a different field of view of the scene. The following sections describe a four-band spectral camera's hardware and software development.

2.1   Hardware Development

The system consists of four monochromatic sensors, four optical bandpass filters installed in front of the lens of each sensor, a USB 3.0 hub, and a heterogeneous FPGA-based architecture (Ultra96-V2) [1]. The FPGA performed the image acquisition and control of all processes. Figure 1 shows the diagram of the implemented system.

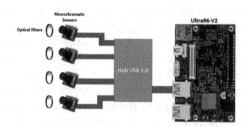

Fig. 1. Diagram of the implemented system.

Monochrome Sensor OV2311. In this design, we used the OmniVision OV2311 monochromatic sensor of the See3CAM 20CUG camera [19]. This sensor was selected due to its near-infrared quantum efficiency, as shown in Fig. 2. In addition, the sensor captures up to 60 frames per second (fps) of high-quality images. Table 1 summarizes the technical specifications.

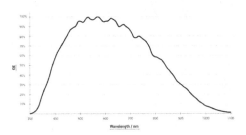

Fig. 2. Quantum efficiency of the OV2311 sensor [19].

Table 1. Specifications of the camera module and monochrome sensor.

See3CAM_20CUG camera	
Model	See3CAM_20CUG
Interface	USB 3.1
Weight	21.5 g
Operating voltage	5V ± 5%
Operating temperature	−30 °C to 85 °C
OV2311 sensor	
Model	OV2311 OmniVision
Optical format	1/2.9"
Pixel size	$3\,\mu m \times 3\,\mu m$
Resolution	2 MP
Shutter type	Global shutter
Output format	Monochromatic (Y8 and Y16)

Ultra96-V2. The prototype requires some processing unit to control the OV2311 sensors and to perform the data preprocessing. We selected an FPGA-based heterogeneous architecture for our system for two main reasons. On the one hand, FPGA allows us to perform multiple operations in parallel; thus, we can use the FPGA to acquire and preprocess the images. This feature is desirable for real-time applications. On the other hand, FPGAs have high performance per watt, with lower consumption for applications such as systems used in unmanned aerial vehicles. The FPGA-based heterogeneous architecture selected was the Ultra96-V2 because it has an excellent performance-to-price ratio. It also has a Xilinx Zynq UltraScale+ MPSoC ZU3EG A484 chip equipped with an ARM Cortex-A53 Quad Core and has all the necessary input and output interfaces. Table 2 shows some of its features.

Table 2. Ultra96 specifications.

Ultra96 V2
Xilinx Zynq UltraScale+ MPSoC ZU3EG A484
Memory LPDDR4 2GB RAM
16 GB microSD
Wi-Fi 802.11b/g/n
Bluetooth
One USB 3.0 type Micro-B upstream port
Two USB 3.0 ports and one USB 2.0 downstream
Mini DisplayPort

Bandpass Filters. Four bandpass filters were placed in front of the lens of each sensor to allow radiation to pass only at the specific wavelength and reject the rest. Figure 3 shows the narrow bandwidth for the used filters, each with a bandwidth of 10 nm. The design camera allows the easy change of filters to adapt the system according to the application. We use blue, green, red, and near-infrared filters from manufacturer Edmund Optics [14]. Table 3 summarizes the details for these filters.

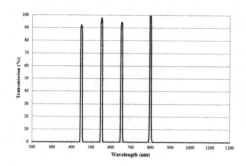

Fig. 3. Curves of the optical filters used [14].

Table 3. Characteristics of the filters implemented in the multispectral camera.

	Central wavelength (nm)	Bandwidth (nm)	Minimum transmission (%)
Blue	450 ± 2	10 ± 2	≥ 85
Green	550 ± 2	10 ± 2	≥ 85
Red	650 ± 2	10 ± 2	≥ 85
NIR	800 ± 2	10 ± 2	≥ 85

Mechanical Assembly. The mechanical structure of the multispectral camera that integrates the optical filters with the image sensors was designed with Inventor software. Figure 4 shows the developed two-piece design. The piece on the left side is used to locate the optical filter in the center of it. The second piece includes the sensor with its respective lens. Both pieces are joined so that the optical filter is just in front of the lens, and it is easy to interchange with another optical filter.

Fig. 4. 3D model for the location of the optical filters.

2.2 Software Development

The software developed for the control of the prototype is implemented in the Ultra96-V2 using the PYNQ operating system [16], an open-source Xilinx project based on Ubuntu that allows working with Python and all its libraries. For image acquisition, the connection between the monochrome cameras and the Ultra96-V2 was made using USB 3.0. Since the Ultra96-V2 has only two USB 3.0 downstream ports, a four-port USB hub was used to connect the four monochrome cameras and the output of the USB hub to one of the USB ports of the Ultra96-V2. The cameras are compatible with the Linux UVC driver, so OpenCV [13] was used to acquire the images on the ARM, acquiring 720×1280 images.

Conversion of Acquired Data to Reflectance Values. To calculate the NDVI, the data captured with each of the sensors were converted to reflectance values. For this purpose, two reference patterns were used, one white and one black, since knowing the reflectance response in these patterns, the other values can be calculated using Eq. 1.

$$Reflectance = \frac{Image - Black\_reference}{White\_reference - Black\_reference} \quad (1)$$

Fig. 5. Reference patterns to find the reflectance.

To find the patterns' black and white reference values, the areas where the patterns are located were selected in the image as shown in Fig. 5 and the average of the pixels in these regions was calculated. This procedure was performed with each of the four spectral bands captured. Knowing the reference values, the equation was applied to all the pixels of the image and for each spectral band, obtaining as a result a data cube where the width and height contain the spatial information and the third dimension contains the spectral information. The values in this data cube are between zero and one, where zero represents low reflectance and one represents high reflectance.

Web Application. A web application was designed to control the prototype of the multispectral camera allowing from a cell phone to capture images, calibrate the system and calculate the NDVI. To make this possible, the cell phone shares a Wi-Fi network to which the Ultra96 is connected and accesses the application with the IP address assigned to it. For the development of the web application that runs on the Ultra96's processing system (PS), the Flask framework available in Python was used and HTML was used for the structure of the web page. Figure 6 shows the diagram of the application where first the image sensors are initialized and the resolution of the images to be captured is established. When everything is configured, the application waits for a request from the user to take a capture or calculate the vegetation index and save the result in memory. There is also the option to calibrate the system, which consists of modifying the exposure time of the sensors to avoid obtaining opaque or very saturated images.

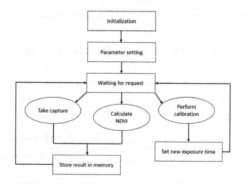

Fig. 6. Web application diagram.

3   Image Registration

As mentioned above, in this multispectral camera design, where there is an array of sensors, an image registration algorithm is required to match the pixels between all the captured spectral bands because there is a distance between the optical centers of the sensors and therefore, they do not have the same field of view. Homography matrices were used to perform translation, rotation and scaling operations on the acquired images to perform this correction. A reference sensor was chosen so that the images acquired with the other sensors are aligned to the images acquired with the reference sensor. To find these homography matrices, feature extraction was performed using Scale-Invariant feature transform (SIFT), and the corresponding features were found between each sensor and the reference sensor, as illustrated in Fig. 7. The three homography matrices were found with the findHomography function of OpenCV with these corresponding features.

Fig. 7. Corresponding characteristics between the image captured with the reference sensor and the image acquired with the sensor.

After obtaining the homography matrices, each image to be registered is traversed pixel by pixel, multiplying the indices of its position by its corresponding homography matrix, which are of size 3×3. This multiplication gives, as a result, the homogeneous coordinates of the transformed point. To know the position of each pixel in the target image, the obtained X and Y components are divided by the Z component, as shown in Eqs. 2 and 3:

$$p3 = \begin{bmatrix} x' \\ y' \\ z' \end{bmatrix} = \mathbf{M} \begin{bmatrix} x \\ y \\ 1 \end{bmatrix} \tag{2}$$

$$p2 = \begin{bmatrix} x'' \\ y'' \end{bmatrix} = \begin{bmatrix} \frac{x'}{z'} \\ \frac{y'}{z'} \end{bmatrix} \tag{3}$$

where x, y are the positions of the pixels in the unregistered image, M is the homography matrix found for that image, x', y', z' are the homogeneous coordinates of the transformed point and x", y" is the final position in the target image. As the positions of the pixels in the transformed target image are calculated, their values are assigned to the resulting image. As the positions of the pixels in the transformed target image are calculated, their values are assigned to the resulting image as shown in Fig. 8.

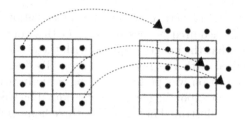

Fig. 8. Assignment of the pixels in their new location.

This procedure can be performed with an OpenCV function called WarpPerspective. However, the average execution time to register a single image with this function on the ARM is 38.3 ms. For this reason, we implemented the image registration part on the FPGA, looking for better execution times. The Xilinx library xfOpenCV contains about 60 FPGA optimized kernels, including the WarpPerspective function. Although with this kernel, the average execution time on the FPGA was reduced to 22.8 ms when registering an image, a kernel was created using Vivado HLS to take advantage of the parallelization capability that FPGAs have, in order to simultaneously register the images of the three sensors with respect to the reference sensor. The images are sent from the ARM to the FPGA using the direct memory access (DMA) to transfer the data stored in RAM to the kernel created in the FPGA. Three of the four high-speed buses present in the Ultra96 that communicate the ARM with the FPGA were used. The DATAFLOW parallelization directive was used in the kernel so that the three images are received, processed and sent back to the ARM simultaneously. A diagram of the architecture created is shown in Fig. 9.

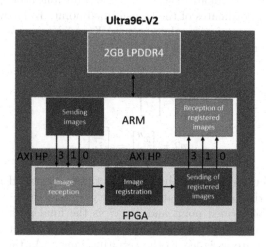

Fig. 9. Block diagram of the FPGA-based heterogeneous architecture to perform image registration.

4   Results and Discussion

4.1   Image Registration

Figure 10 shows the result of the transformations performed in the image registration process where it is possible to observe the displacement performed in each one of them to adjust to the image acquired with the reference sensor. In the upper left corner is an image captured with the reference sensor to which no transformation is performed; this sensor has the filter corresponding to the wavelength of 450 nm. In the upper right corner is an image captured using the filter for the 550 nm wavelength, and in the lower part from left to right are images captured with the 650 nm and 800 nm filters, respectively.

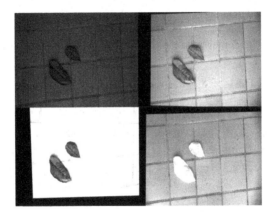

Fig. 10. Image transformations performed.

Figure 11 shows the result of forming a multispectral image without image registration, there it can be seen that there is a displacement between the different spectral bands that causes the leaves present not to coincide. Figure 12 shows the results applying the image registration algorithm, for the visualization of these images the bands in the blue, green and red spectrum were used.

Fig. 11. Multispectral imaging without image registration.

Fig. 12. Multispectral imaging with image registration.

Table 4 shows the amount of logical resources used in the kernel created to perform the image registration in the FPGA. A high consumption of BRAM_18K is evident due to the fact that the pixels of the three images that arrive at the kernel to perform the registration must be temporarily stored.

Table 4. Logic resources used in the FPGA.

Resources	BRAM-18K	DSP48E	FF	LUT
Total	336	183	30935	55841
Available	432	360	141120	70560
Use (%)	77	50	21	79

The execution times of the image registration are presented in Fig. 13, where it is observed that when the image registration is executed in the ARM the images are processed sequentially and each one of them takes approximately 38.3 ms, while in the FPGA the 3 images are processed in parallel and the average time for all of them is 23.4 ms achieving an acceleration of almost five times.

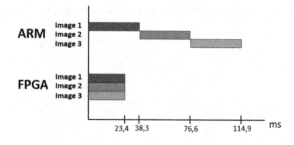

Fig. 13. Image registration runtimes on the ARM and the FPGA.

4.2   NDVI Vegetation Index

The normalized difference vegetation index uses the near infrared and red infrared bands as shown in Eq. 4 to provide information on the health status of plants by obtaining the difference between these two bands.

$$NDVI = \frac{NIR - Red}{NIR + Red} \qquad (4)$$

The result of applying this equation gives as a result values in a range between -1 and 1, for the visualization the data were normalized between 0 and 1. Figure 14 shows the result of the NDVI calculation for the image presented in Fig. 5, to capture this image the camera was placed on a tripod at a height of approximately one meter and twenty centimeters pointing towards the ground where there were two leaves to verify the result of this index. As can be seen, the areas where there is vegetation correspond to values close to 1 while the rest of the image is represented by the blue color with values close to 0.

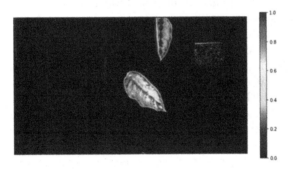

Fig. 14. Result obtained in the calculation of the NDVI.

Each type of material responds to radiation in a different way. Some wavelengths are absorbed and others are reflected at different rates. This is known as spectral signature and allows the classification of different materials. With the reflectance values of the four bands used, the spectral signature was found in the top sheet shown in Fig. 14. For this, a pixel was randomly selected within the sheet and its reflectance values were plotted for each spectral band, obtaining a value of 0.0535 for the blue band, 0.2910 for the green band, 0.0945 for the red band and 0.7782 for the near infrared band. The graph in Fig. 15 shows that the spectral signature obtained corresponds to the characterization of healthy vegetation, where low values are obtained in the visible spectrum with a small peak in the green band due to chlorophyll, and a high reflectance value in the near infrared band.

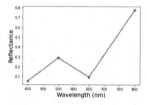

Fig. 15. Spectral signature result.

5 Conclusions

In this work we present a prototype of a multispectral camera using a heterogeneous FPGA-based architecture for precision agriculture applications. We present a prototype to capture four spectral bands in blue, green, red and near infrared wavelengths, together with an algorithm to implement image registration and perform NDVI calculation.

Among the features sought in the prototype, it is to have a design that facilitates the exchange of optical filters to adapt the system to different applications, in addition to achieving good processing times and low power consumption. For this reason we use a heterogeneous FPGA-based architecture to achieve an acceleration in the algorithms using High-level synthesis (HLS) design methodologies.

The execution times obtained in the image registration comparing the results between ARM and FPGA in the Ultra96 showed that a hardware acceleration close to 5 times was achieved in the image registration algorithm and its ability to perform concurrent operations to meet the computational demand required by multispectral systems was exploited.

As future work, it is proposed to implement an 8-band multispectral system and to calculate and analyze more vegetation indices.

Acknowledgments. This work was financed with resources from the *Patrimonio autónomo fondo nacional de financiamiento para ciencia, tecnología e innovación Francisco José de Caldas* through RC 80740-475-2020, supported by the Ministerio de Ciencias, Tecnología e innovación - Minciencias, Instituto Tecnológico Metropolitano - ITM, Corporación Colombiana de Investigación Agropecuaria - AGROSAVIA, and BLACKSQUARE S.A.S.

References

1. Boards: Ultra96. https://www.96boards.org/product/ultra96/. Accessed 10 Aug 2022
2. Akkoyun, F.: Inexpensive multispectral imaging device. Instrum. Sci. Technol. **50**, 1–17 (2022)
3. Barreiros, J., Magne, N.: Open source multispectral camera array for vegetation analysis. In: 2015 CHILEAN Conference on Electrical, Electronics Engineering, Information and Communication Technologies (CHILECON), pp. 879–884. IEEE (2015)

4. Doering, D., et al.: MDE-based development of a multispectral camera for precision agriculture. IFAC-PapersOnLine **49**(30), 24–29 (2016)
5. Galindo, A.K.T., Rivera, A.F.G., López, A.F.J.: Development of a multispectral system for precision agriculture applications using embedded devices. Sistemas Telemática **13**(33), 27–44 (2015)
6. Geng, Y., Zhao, H., Yang, F., Yan, L.: Filter changer's system design on airborne multi-spectral camera based on FPGA. In: 2010 Second IITA International Conference on Geoscience and Remote Sensing, vol. 2, pp. 108–111. IEEE (2010)
7. Jenal, A., Bareth, G., Bolten, A., Kneer, C., Weber, I., Bongartz, J.: Development of a VNIR/SWIR multispectral imaging system for vegetation monitoring with unmanned aerial vehicles. Sensors **19**(24), 5507 (2019)
8. Kasampalis, D.A., Alexandridis, T.K., Deva, C., Challinor, A., Moshou, D., Zalidis, G.: Contribution of remote sensing on crop models: a review. J. Imaging **4**(4), 52 (2018)
9. Kise, M., Park, B., Heitschmidt, G.W., Lawrence, K.C., Windham, W.R.: Multispectral imaging system with interchangeable filter design. Comput. Electron. Agric. **72**(2), 61–68 (2010)
10. Lee, H., Park, S.H., Noh, S.H., Lim, J., Kim, M.S.: Development of a portable 3CCD camera system for multispectral imaging of biological samples. Sensors **14**(11), 20262–20273 (2014)
11. Morales, A., et al.: A multispectral camera development: from the prototype assembly until its use in a UAV system. Sensors **20**(21), 6129 (2020)
12. de Oca, A.M., Flores, G.: The AgriQ: a low-cost unmanned aerial system for precision agriculture. Expert Syst. Appl. **182**, 115163 (2021)
13. OpenCV. https://opencv.org/. Accessed 03 Aug 2022
14. Edmund Optics. https://www.edmundoptics.com/c/bandpass-filters/617/. Accessed 23 Oct 2022
15. Paredes, J.A., González, J., Saito, C., Flores, A.: Multispectral imaging system with UAV integration capabilities for crop analysis. In: 2017 First IEEE International Symposium of Geoscience and Remote Sensing (GRSS-CHILE), pp. 1–4. IEEE (2017)
16. PYNQ: PYNQ: Python Productivity. https://www.pynq.io/. Accessed 25 July 2022
17. Rajapu, A., Madisetty, S.A., Thokala, S., Mahendra, P.R., Raju, V.V.R., Reddy, C.S.V.: Cost-effective multispectral imaging system for precision agriculture. In: 2022 IEEE 2nd International Conference on Sustainable Energy and Future Electric Transportation (SeFeT), pp. 1–8. IEEE (2022)
18. Sishodia, R.P., Ray, R.L., Singh, S.K.: Applications of remote sensing in precision agriculture: a review. Remote Sens. **12**(19), 3136 (2020)
19. e-con Systems. https://www.e-consystems.com/industrial-cameras/ov2311-monochrome-global-shutter-camera.asp. Accessed 23 Oct 2022
20. Weiss, M., Jacob, F., Duveiller, G.: Remote sensing for agricultural applications: a meta-review. Remote Sens. Environ. **236**, 111402 (2020)
21. Ze, Z., Minzan, L., Xin, L.: The development of a hand-held multi-spectral camera based on FPGA. In: 2010 World Automation Congress, pp. 469–475. IEEE (2010)

Small-Scale Precision Agriculture: A Case Study Applied to a Seed Germination Chamber

Roberto S. Velazquez-Gonzalez[1] , Julio C. Sosa[1(✉)] ,
and Elsa Ventura-Zapata[2]

[1] Instituto Politécnico Nacional CICATA-Qro, Cerro Blanco 141,
Colinas del Cimatario, 76090 Querétaro, Qro., Mexico
rvelazquezg1900@alumno.ipn.mx, jcsosa@ipn.mx
[2] Centro de Desarrollo de Productos Bióticos, Instituto Politécnico Nacional,
Calle Ceprobi No. 8, 62739 San Isidro, Morelos, Mexico
eventura@ipn.mx

Abstract. Precision agriculture is one of the most relevant paradigms in recent years, as it represents the integration of information technologies with traditional agriculture. However, a decentralized approach to food production is necessary, taking advantage of limited spaces in urban areas such as rooftops, patios, gardens, etc. The application of precision agriculture on a small and medium scale will be vital in this regard, since much of the technology that is currently integrated is oriented to massive production. In this document, an example of precision agriculture for small-scale production is shown by developing a low-cost germination chamber based on a Raspberry Pi control card, as well as the use of a Fuzzy Logic for the control of environmental variables. Methodology V was implemented, there adopting as control parameters the temperature and relative humidity of the substrate within the germination chamber. Tomato seeds were used to evaluate plant development during the first 30 days of life by comparing yield between plants developed in the germination chamber and plants developed under natural environmental conditions. The control system based on Fuzzy Logic proved to be efficient in maintaining temperature and soil moisture within the desired ranges, with an error of $\pm 1.5\,^{\circ}$C and $\pm 5\%$ respectively; this resulted in obtaining a quality plant compared to control plants.

Keywords: precision agriculture · controlled environment · fuzzy logic · germination chamber

1 Introduction

By 2050, the world's population will exceed 9 billion inhabitants [1], where one of the most important challenges will be to meet the global demand for food.

This work was supported by Instituto Politécnico Nacional, trhough grants SIP-20220086 and SIP-20220086.

For this reason, scientists from all over the world are joining efforts on issues such as precision agriculture (PA), which includes information technologies, data analysis techniques, intelligent algorithms and remote sensing systems, among others, for the optimization of food production processes to allow for the saving of resources such as water and fertilizers [10,14]. PA is a reorganization approach towards sustainable agriculture, where technology plays an essential role in saving inputs and increasing efficiency [17].

One of the most significant stages in intensive food production is the seedling generation stage, in which hundreds and even thousands of seeds have to be germinated to begin the development of plants that will later be transplanted into a definitive planting system [3]. In hydroponic crops, for example, a fundamental aspect for the transplant stage is to obtain seedlings with a healthy root system, a good size and number of leaves, in addition to the fact that the plant must be free of fungi or pathogens that may affect the crop. To ensure success in the production of seedlings, many factors are decisive, such as the quality of the seed, the type of substrate, the frequency of irrigation, among others. Environmental factors also play an important role in the proper development of plants, with light, environment temperature and the amount of nutrients being the most crucial [2].

However, in order to meet the global demand, a paradigm shift in food production is necessary; decentralization will play an important role, since currently food is produced in areas far from the point of consumption, increasing the cost, decreasing the life of the shelf and above all, generating an important carbon footprint due to factors such as transport [15].

Existing technologies for food production focus mainly on large-scale systems, leaving aside small and medium-scale production ecosystems, this mainly due to the costs of such technologies, making unfeasible their implementation in urban environments for purposes of either small business or self-consumption.

This document proposes the application of an example of precision agriculture through the design and implementation of a germination chamber for seedling production, with a focus on small-scale production, since much of the technology currently being developed has an application to industrialized production, which makes it difficult for small farmers to benefit from technological advances.

We use a Raspberry Pi card as a processing element, as well as Fuzzy Logic for the control of variables such as temperature and moisture (humidity). To evaluate the yield of the germination chamber, the development of tomato seeds (*Solanum lycopersicum*) in a natural environment and within the germination chamber was compared, showing the seedlings a larger size and contribution of biomass when developed within the germination chamber. The data was recorded on the open source platform `MyCodo`. This work contemplates a local control and a monitoring of variables, in order to facilitate their possible application in places where internet access is limited.

This document is structured as follows: in Sect. 2 we review previous work related to the control of germination systems; then, in Sect. 3, we present the methodology and materials used. In Sect. 4 we show the development of our work. In Sect. 5 we present the results of the control system, as well as the qualitative and quantitative metrics in seed germination. Section 6 presents a discussion of the relevance of the results in context with other works. Section 7 concludes with a summary of the work done.

2   Literature Review

Automated systems for seed germination have been shown to promote seedlings, for example, in tomato plants, with larger diameter stems, a greater number of leaves and a healthy root system have been observed, compared to the development of seedlings in uncontrolled systems [8].

Some works related to the automation of germination chambers are those presented in [13], who worked mainly on the correct humidification and circulation of air inside the chamber, testing with 9 different species of seeds and evaluating the total percentage of germinated seeds, as well as the length of the roots and the plant itself.

Differently, [16] proposes a prototype germination chamber for the study of plant growth under both favorable and unfavorable conditions, since it is possible to modify the development environment by manipulating artificial light and ambient temperature, where this system has a wireless communication interface for remote monitoring; however, there is no mention of the metrics used to evaluate germination chamber performance and yield. With regard to the control of variables within germination chambers, techniques based on PID controllers are the most popular, although algorithms based on Fuzzy Logic have also been implemented, this due to the easy implementation and efficiency, maintaining errors below 5% with respect to a desired value [4,7].

Otherwise, [9] proposes the study of the effect of seed exposure in the germination stage to different magnitudes of magnetic fields, demonstrating that frequencies 10 Hz favored an increase of up to 20% in total germination rates with respect to control plants. This shows that it is possible to include other variables in the germination stage that can favor the development of plants. Of the works mentioned above, only [15] and [16] mention the equipment used in the construction of germination chambers, weighting the Arduino platform as a signal processing element.

On the other hand, the studies found related to the automation of germination chambers only show partial results in the monitoring of crop development, limiting the majority to reporting the percentage of germination. The works found in the literature have an experimental application approach, that is, their possible scaling is not contemplated either on a small, medium, or large scale.

3   Methodology and Materials

We use the V methodology for the design and construction of the germination chamber. The stages of this methodology are shown in Fig. 1.

- **Requirements analysis**. At this point, technical aspects under which the chamber must operate under normal conditions are studied. In consultation with a horticultural specialist, the general system requirements are shown in Table 1.
- **Global design**. It is the general design proposal for the germination chamber. For this point, a closed chamber with transparent material was proposed to take advantage of daylight. Also, a heating and ventilation system was integrated for temperature regulation, as well as an irrigation system to maintain the relative humidity of the substrate at the desired value. A control strategy based on Fuzzy Logic for temperature regulation was proposed. The overall design at the prototype level is shown in Fig. 2.
- **Design in detail**. At this point, the design was considered separately for each of the components of the overall design. The subsystems that make up the germination chamber are 3: Mechanical structure, temperature control system and humidity control in substrate.
- **Implementation**. Here, both the overall design and the detailed designs come to life as they materialize.
- **Local testing**. The control systems for temperature and humidity were tested separately, there corroborating the correct operation.
- **Global tests**. Temperature and soil moisture control systems were integrated for seed germination, but still in a semi-controlled environment, this to verify that sensors, actuators and control algorithms had a correct performance.
- **Operational testing**. Tests were carried out in a real environment, incorporating the seeds and taking samples of the development of the seedlings over a period of 30 days.

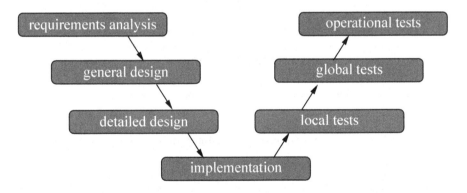

Fig. 1. V Methodology.

Once the prototype is assembled, the sensors and actuators are connected to the Raspberry board, in which the control algorithms for temperature and humidity on the substrate were programmed. To evaluate the influence of the controlled environment in the germination chamber on the number of germinated

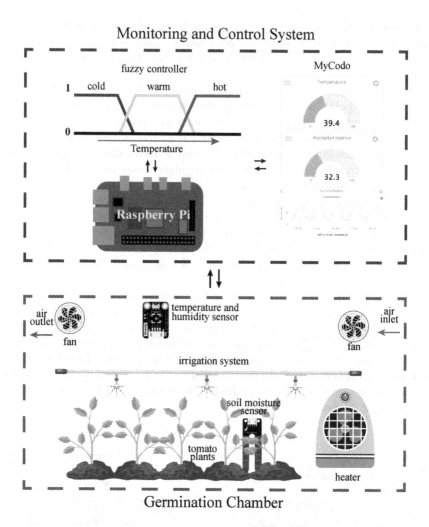

Fig. 2. General design of the monitoring and control system of the germination chamber.

Table 1. General requirements of the germination chamber.

Parameter	Technical description
Total seeds	200
Plants to germinate	Tomato seeds (*Solanum lycopersicum*)
Dimensions (length, width, height)	1.5 m × 0.7 m × 0.5 m
Average temperature	27 °C
Moisture in substrate for seeds	≥ 90%
Expected germination	≥ 60%

seeds and their growth quality during the first 30 days, both qualitative and quantitative metrics were used. There are several methods of analysis in seed germination. We use two metrics to evaluate germination according to [6]. The first of these is the total percentage of seeds (TPS), defined in Eq. 1. The second metric we used was the average germination time (AGT) which is a measure of the average time in which seed germination occurred (Eq. 2). To assess seedling growth, measurements of average height and stem diameter were made over a 30-day period. The materials used for germination chamber automation are shown in Table 2.

$$TPS(\%) = \frac{g}{n} \cdot 100\% \tag{1}$$

where TPS is the percentage of germinated seeds, g is the number of germinated seeds, and n represents the total number of seeds.

$$AGT = \frac{\sum_{i=1}^{n} n_i t_i}{\sum_{i=1}^{n} n_i} \tag{2}$$

where AGT is the average germination time (days), t_i is the number of days after sowing, and n_i is the number of seeds germinated on day i.

Table 2. Materials for the implementation of the germination chamber.

Element	Model	Quantity
Temperature and temperature sensor	SHT10	2
Humidity sensor in substrate	SEN0193 DFROBOT	4
Submersible pump 250 gal/h	P6004	1
Control card	Raspberry Pi 4	1
Analog-to-digital converter	ADS1115	1
Fans 12 VDC	YM2412PMS1	8
H Bridge	L298	4
Dimmer PWM 1400 W	JTDB-V2	1
Heater 1200 W	FH04	1
Light sensor	TSL2561	1

4   Development

The implementation of the germination chamber is shown in Fig. 3. To maintain the moisture value in the substrate that houses the seeds, an On-Off control with hysteresis was used, which is governed by Eq. 3. The operating principle for humidity control is based on an activation threshold for the irrigation pump, when the moisture of the substrate is below this threshold, the irrigation pump is activated to supply water to the seeds inside the germination chamber. Figure 4

shows a graph of irrigation pump operation for a lower threshold of 30% soil
moisture and an upper threshold of 80% soil moisture (example values).

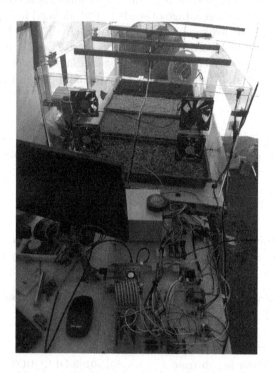

Fig. 3. Physical implementation of the germination chamber.

$$u(t) = \begin{cases} 1 & \text{if soil moisture} \leq \text{threshold 1} \\ 0 & \text{if soil moisture} > \text{threshold 2} \end{cases} \tag{3}$$

For temperature control, a control algorithm based on Fuzzy Logic was used.
Two input variables were defined for the algorithm, the first is error, which is
defined as the difference between the desired value and the actual temperature
reading, and the second is the relative humidity in the environment. 5 membership functions were defined for the error: LN (large negative), N (negative),
Z (zero), P (positive) and LP (large positive) and 3 membership functions for
relative humidity: Low, Normal and High. On the other hand, the control action
was defined with 5 membership functions: MC (much cooling), C (cool), O (turn
off), H (heat) and MH (much heating). The control laws are shown in Table 3.
The definition of the input, output variables and the resulting control curve are
shown in Fig. 5.

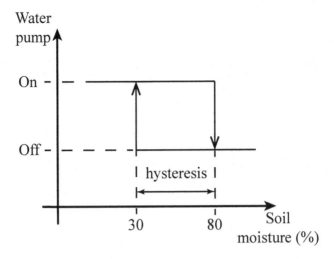

Fig. 4. On-Off control with hysteresis for the substrate irrigation system.

Table 3. Rules for the Fuzzy temperature controller.

No	Rule
1	If (error is LN) and (Humidity is High) then (Control is MC)
2	If (error is N) and (Humidity is Normal) then (Control is C)
3	If (error is Z) and (Humidity is Normal) then (Control is O)
4	If (error is P) and (Humidity is Normal) then (Control is H)
5	If (error is LP) and (Humidity is Low) then (Control is MH)

To evaluate the yield of the germination chamber, 4 trays were placed inside the chamber and 50 seeds for each tray. Also, seeds were germinated in trays outside the chamber, these samples worked as control elements. For monitoring and data logging, the open source platform Mycodo [5] was used, which is compatible with the Raspbian operating system of the Raspberry Pi card. Using a digital vernier, every 3 days 20 samples per tray were manually measured both in the germination chamber and at the control samples, to observe the influence of the controlled environment on the development of the tomato plants. The properties observed in the crops were: average plant size (mm) and average stem diameter (mm).

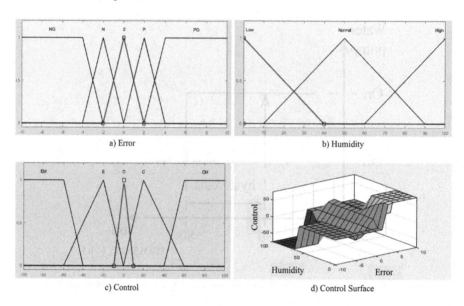

a) Error   b) Humidity

c) Control   d) Control Surface

Fig. 5. Membership functions for input variables Error (a), relative air humidity (b), for the output variable (c), and control surface (d).

5 Results

5.1 Control System

In Fig. 6 the control profile for temperature is measured; note that for a period of approximately 3 days the environment or ambient temperature (outside the chamber) and the regulated temperature inside the germination chamber were recorded. The control system allowed the average temperature inside the chamber to be maintained at $27\,°C \pm 1.5\,°C$.

On the other hand, the humidity in the substrate was recorded in the same way for a period of approximately 3 days. During this registration period, different values were experimented for the lower thresholds, there varying between 90% and 95%. The upper threshold was set at 100%, this to keep the seeds hydrated. The results are shown in Fig. 7.

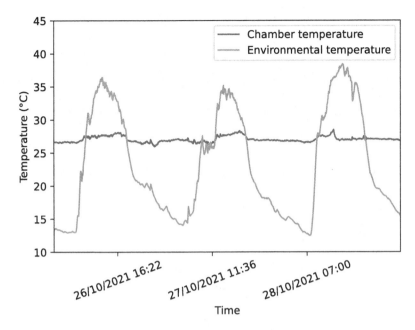

Fig. 6. Profile of the variable temperature in the germination chamber and environment temperature (outside the chamber).

5.2 Development of Seedlings

A better germination rate was observed in the germination chamber compared to seedlings developed under uncontrolled conditions. The results are shown in Table 4.

Table 4. Percentage of germinated seeds (TPS) and average germination time (AGT) under controlled and uncontrolled conditions.

Environment	TPS (%)	AGT (days)
Controlled	61	9
Uncontrolled	38	12

Regarding the development of plants, a higher yield was recorded for those plants under controlled conditions (CC); in the case of the average height, indeed, the yield was 200% compared to the development of seeds in uncontrolled conditions (UC). Figure 8 shows the development of seedlings at average height and stem diameter after 30 days. Figure 9 shows the development of the plants under controlled and uncontrolled conditions.

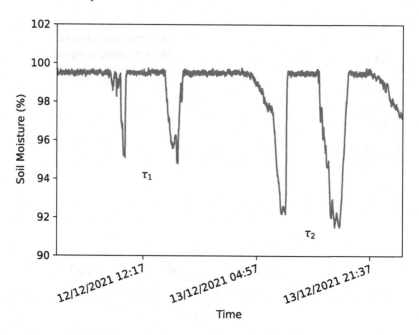

Fig. 7. Relative humidity profile in the substrate of germination trays. τ_1 and τ_2 represent different threshold for water pump activation.

6   Discussion

Some works related to the automation of germination chambers focus only on technological aspects; nonetheless, we believe that it is important to show the interaction with the biological system, since it is in this manner that improvements can be evaluated and facilitate their application in real environments. For example, the work presented by [4], emphasizes the monitoring and control of a germination chamber using an IoT approach; however, it is only mentioned that basil seeds were used, but not what was the yield in germination and the quality of the crops. Another work with an IoT focus was presented by [7], which shows a germination chamber embedded in a floating root system. In this work, the interaction of automation with crops is not presented either, delimiting the work only to the technological part.

Different from the work presented by [12], where the automation of a small greenhouse for tomato production is shown, we did not implement an artificial light system, which affects energy savings, in addition to evaluating the metrics presented in Sect. 5.

In the manuscript presented by [11], the necessary and urgent transition from controlled environments for agriculture focused on vertical farming and urban agriculture is emphasized. We believe that precision agriculture should also be accessible to small producers in rural areas; therefore, it is essential to analyze the level of automation according to the reality of the place where it is applied.

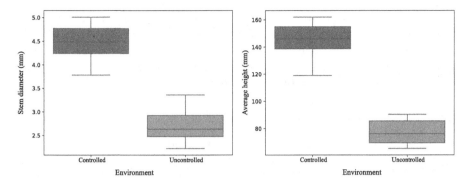

Fig. 8. Average height and stem diameter of plants grown inside the germination chamber (controlled environment) and outside the germination chamber (uncontrolled environment) after 30 days.

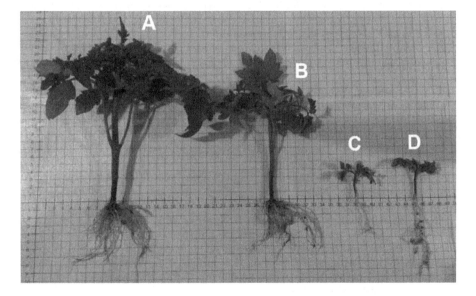

Fig. 9. Development of tomato plants. (a, b) in the germination chamber. (c, d) under uncontrolled conditions.

7 Conclusion

The technological advance in the development of new and better devices for the sensing and control of variables, favors the introduction of technology in small and medium-scale food production systems, allowing small producers to increase their productivity and therefore compete in an increasingly globalized world. We know that the situation in the coming years in terms of food demand can become difficult if we continue to think of agriculture as an activity whose responsibility is only of the large producers; therefore, the implementation of automated systems is of vital importance to contribute to cleaner production, a sustainable one, and with a view to decentralization. This work is an example of how sensing and control elements can be integrated to make processes related to agriculture more efficient, and that, in addition, this technology can be accessible to small producers and even for self-consumption purposes.

References

1. Bahar, N.H., et al.: Meeting the food security challenge for nine billion people in 2050: what impact on forests? Glob. Environ. Chang. **62**, 102056 (2020). https://doi.org/10.1016/j.gloenvcha.2020.102056. https://www.sciencedirect.com/science/article/pii/S095937801930929X
2. Belmehdi, O., El Harsal, A., Benmoussi, M., Laghmouchi, Y., Skali Senhaji, N., Abrini, J.: Effect of light, temperature, salt stress and pH on seed germination of medicinal plant Origanum elongatum (Bonnet) Emb. & Maire. Biocatalysis Agric. Biotechnol. **16**, 126–131 (2018). https://doi.org/10.1016/j.bcab.2018.07.032. https://www.sciencedirect.com/science/article/pii/S1878818118304018
3. Carrera-Castaño, G., Calleja-Cabrera, J., Pernas, M., Gómez, L., Oñate-Sánchez, L.: An updated overview on the regulation of seed germination. Plants **9**(6) (2020). https://doi.org/10.3390/plants9060703. https://www.mdpi.com/2223-7747/9/6/703
4. Franco-Ramírez, J.D., Ramírez-delReal, T.A., Gárate-García, A., Ruíz, M.A., Villanueva-Vásquez, D.: MOSyG: monitoring system for germination chamber using fuzzy control based on Cloudino-IoT and FIWARE. In: 2019 IEEE International Autumn Meeting on Power, Electronics and Computing (ROPEC), pp. 1–6 (2019). https://doi.org/10.1109/ROPEC48299.2019.9057127. https://ieeexplore.ieee.org/document/9057127
5. Gabriel, K.: Mycodo environmental regulation system (2018). https://doi.org/10.5281/zenodo.824199. https://kizniche.github.io/Mycodo/. Accessed 10 May 2022
6. Gonzalez-Zertuche, L., Orozco-Segovia, A.: Methods for seed germination data analysis. an example: Manfreda brachystachya. Bot. Sci. (58), 15–30 (1996). https://doi.org/10.17129/botsci.1484. https://www.botanicalsciences.com.mx/index.php/botanicalSciences/article/view/1484
7. Marinelli, M., Acosta, N., Toloza, J.M., Kornuta, C.: Fuzzy control of a germination chamber. J. Comput. Sci. Technol. **17**(01), 74–78 (2017). https://sedici.unlp.edu.ar/handle/10915/59991
8. Nafees, K., Kumar, M., Bose, B.: Effect of different temperatures on germination and seedling growth of primed seeds of tomato. Russ. J. Plant Physiol. **66**(5), 778–784 (2019). https://doi.org/10.1134/S1021443719050169
9. Namba, K., Sasao, A., Shibusawa, S.: Effect of magnetic field on germination and plant growth, vol. 15, pp. 143–148 (1995). https://doi.org/10.17660/ActaHortic.1995.399.15. https://doi.org/10.17660/ActaHortic.1995.399.15
10. Shafi, U., Mumtaz, R., García-Nieto, J., Hassan, S.A., Zaidi, S.A.R., Iqbal, N.: Precision agriculture techniques and practices: from considerations to applications. Sensors **19**(17) (2019). https://doi.org/10.3390/s19173796. https://www.mdpi.com/1424-8220/19/17/3796
11. Shamshiri, R., et al.: Advances in greenhouse automation and controlled environment agriculture: a transition to plant factories and urban agriculture. Agric. Biol. Eng. **1**(11), 1–22 (2018). https://doi.org/10.25165/j.ijabe.20181101.3210. https://ijabe.org/index.php/ijabe/article/view/3210

12. Siddiqui, M.F., ur Rehman Khan, A., Kanwal, N., Mehdi, H., Noor, A., Khan, M.A.: Automation and monitoring of greenhouse. In: 2017 International Conference on Information and Communication Technologies (ICICT), pp. 197–201 (2017). https://doi.org/10.1109/ICICT.2017.8320190. https://ieeexplore.ieee.org/document/8320190

13. Springer, S.L., Tharel, L.M.: Growth chamber modification to emulate a seed germination chamber. Agron. J. **84**, 1070–1073 (2021). https://doi.org/10.2134/agronj1992.00021962008400060031x. https://acsess.onlinelibrary.wiley.com/doi/pdf/10.2134/agronj1992.00021962008400060031x

14. Srinivasan, A.: Handbook of Precision Agriculture. Principles and Applications, 1 edn. CRC Press (2006). https://doi.org/10.1201/9781482277968. https://www.taylorfrancis.com/books/edit10.1201/9781482277968/handbook-precision-agriculture-ancha-srinivasan

15. Tsuchiya, K., et al.: Decentralization & local food: Japan's regional ecological footprints indicate localized sustainability strategies. J. Clean. Prod. **292** (2021). https://doi.org/10.1016/j.jclepro.2021.126043. https://www.sciencedirect.com/science/article/pii/S0959652621002638

16. Wójcicki, P.: Design and build of a plant growth chamber. In: ICERI 2019 Proceedings, pp. 11640–11644. 12th Annual International Conference of Education, Research and Innovation, IATED (11–13 November 2019) (2019). https://doi.org/10.21125/iceri.2019.2913. https://dx.doi.org/10.21125/iceri.2019.2913

17. Zhang, N., Wang, M., Wang, N.: Precision agriculture-a worldwide overview. Comput. Electron. Agric. **36**(2), 113–132 (2002). https://doi.org/10.1016/S0168-1699(02)00096-0

Diagnosis and Degree of Evolution in a Keratoconus-Type Corneal Ectasia from Image Processing

Diego Otuna-Hernández[1] , Leslie Espinoza-Castro[1] , Paula Yánez-Contreras[1] ,
Fernando Villalba-Meneses[1] , Carolina Cadena-Morejón[2] , César Guevara[3,4] ,
Jonathan Cruz-Varela[1] , Andrés Tirado-Espín[2] ,
and Diego Almeida-Galárraga[1,5,6(✉)]

[1] School of Biological Sciences and Engineering, Universidad Yachay Tech,
San Miguel de Urcuquí, Urcuqui 100119, Ecuador
dalmeida@yachaytech.edu.ec
[2] Department of Human Development, Universidad Yachay Tech,
San Miguel de Urcuquí, Urcuqui 100119, Ecuador
[3] Centro de Mecatrónica y Sistemas Interactivos - MIST, Universidad Indoamérica, Quito,
Ecuador
[4] Instituto de Ciencias Matemáticas, ICMAT-CSIC, 28049 Madrid, Spain
[5] Universidad de Otavalo, Av. De los Sarances y Av. Los Pendoneros, Otavalo, Ecuador
[6] Facultad de Ingeniería - Sistemas de Información, Pontificia Universidad Católica del
Ecuador, Quito, Ecuador

Abstract. Keratoconus is a degenerative ocular pathology characterized by the
thinning of the cornea, thus affecting many people around the world since this
corneal ectasia causes a deformation of the corneal curvature that leads to astigma-
tism and, in more severe cases, to blindness. Treating physicians use non-invasive
instruments, such is the case of Pentacam®, which takes images of the cornea,
both the topography and the profile of the cornea, which allows them to diagnose,
evaluate and treat this disease; this is known as morphological characterization of
the cornea. On the other hand, Berlin/Ambrosio analysis helps in the identification and subsequent diagnosis since this analysis uses a mathematical model of
linear progression, which identifies the different curves with the severity of the
disease. Therefore, the aim of this study is to use the images provided by Penta-
cam®, Berlin/Ambrosio analysis, and vision parameters in a convolutional neural
network to evaluate if this disparity could be used to help with the diagnosis of
keratoconus and, consequently, generate a more precise and optimal method in
the diagnosis of keratoconus. As a result, the processing and comparison of the
images and the parameters allowed a 10% increase in the results of specificity and
sensitivity of the mean and severe stages when combining tools (corneal profile
and vision parameters) in the CNN reaching ranges of 90 to 95%. Furthermore, it
is important to highlight that in the early-stage study, its improvement was around
20% in specificity, sensitivity, and accuracy.

Keywords: Ectasia Corneal · Keratoconus · Image processing · Edge-Sobel
filter · Berlin/Ambrosio

© The Author(s), under exclusive license to Springer Nature Switzerland AG 2023
F. R. Narváez et al. (Eds.): SmartTech-IC 2022, CCIS 1705, pp. 284–297, 2023.
https://doi.org/10.1007/978-3-031-32213-6_21

1   Introduction

Cornea is a structure of the eye that allows and controls the passage of light from the outside to the inside of the eye and protects the iris and lens, as well as other ocular structures [1]. Cornea shares this protective function with the eyelid, eye socket, tears, and sclera. The morphological characterization of the cornea is essential in clinical practice because it is very important to be able to understand the changes in the cornea that affect the visual quality of patients [1, 2]. Keratoconus is a degenerative ocular pathology that arises from a constant thinning of the thickness of the cornea in the central and paracentral areas of the cornea, thus creating a cone-shaped cornea with a thinner appearance and with little resistance, which produces a distortion of images and progressively reduces vision [2, 3].

This disease affects more and more people around the world, especially in places with high exposure to ultraviolet rays, as is the case in Ecuador [4]. Also, in some cases, corneal involvement is so severe that a corneal transplant is necessary due to severe opacity. This illness has been the subject of several studies due to the level of damage it can cause to the human eye, which is why several methods have been developed to characterize this sickness [5]. Some methods try to be as invasive as possible, trying not to use anesthesia or have contact with the cornea for the comprehensive characterization of the corneal topography [5]. This ailment can be acquired by family inheritance or in sporadic cases. However, in Ecuador, this pathology has developed more frequently due to the geographical area in which the country is exposed to ultraviolet radiation. According to the National Institute of Meteorology and Hydrology (INAMHI), the city of Quito, specifically, the inter-Andean region, has an ultraviolet radiation index between 7 and 13, respectively, between high and extremely high in the exposure category. The malady begins after puberty or late adolescence, at approximately ten years of age, and progresses until age 25 in men and women. Patients older than 40 years are not excluded [6].

This study will show the processing of images of corneal profiles of a model with keratoconus and a non-pathological eye. Once the images are collected, you will filter them with Matlab® to focus on the region of interest. In addition, Berlin/Ambrosio mathematical method and its vision parameters (pachymetry, diopter, and ART) are used to identify and differentiate critical levels of keratoconus. With this, the aim is to simulate the behavior and deformation of the corneas by applying the same conditions to all the models and comparing them with a model of a healthy cornea [7, 8].

2   Related Work

Recently, the study of the evolution in a keratoconus-type corneal ectasia has been carried out through the analysis of topographic maps of the cornea, but the use of tools such as convolutional neural networks with the study of specific parameters for their differentiation has become increasingly such as indices of asymmetry, regularity of the corneal surface [9, 10], anterior/posterior pachymetry, elevation maps [11], and average keratometry, among others. All these studies have used various neural network models capable of identifying patterns according to their principle, giving results of sensitivity and specificity greater than 90%, as indicated in Table 4. However, the analysis of corneal physiology indices does not achieve a subclinical diagnosis of keratoconus [12], which limits the follow-up of this disease in its early stages. Nevertheless, the processing of the maps of the angles of the affected eye has given results with greater precision, as well as reliability [11], and is a great candidate for the study and/or monitoring of the evolution of keratoconus in its early stages. Based on this, this project focuses on processing the corneal profile, Berlin/Ambrosio curve, and vision parameters to obtain a more precise and accurate diagnosis in the early stages of the evolution of keratoconus.

3 Methodology

To make the diagnosis and degree of evolution in a keratoconus-type corneal ectasia, the following is needed: (i) Process the images in normal, initial, mean, and severe conditions of the ectasia, (A) Image filtering (B) Berlin/Ambrosio mathematical analysis, (C) Detection and degree of evolution in a keratoconus-type corneal ectasia through an algorithm (Fig. 1).

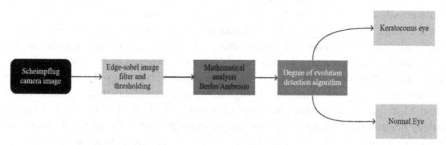

Fig. 1. Flowchart proposal in the diagnosis and degree of evolution in a Keratoconus-type corneal ectasia.

3.1 Scheimpflug Camera Images

Scheimpflug camera images were obtained with Oculus Pentacam®, which is a tool for diagnosing pathologies such as cataracts, and glaucoma, including keratoconus. Pentacam® has indicated very good repeatability in its keratometry and posterior keratometry measurements compared to other cameras [12], as it evaluates the cornea and the anterior segment from the anterior surface of the cornea to the posterior surface of the lens; this measurement makes from 12 to 50 individual captures, and a total of 25,000 points [13] are evaluated.

For this project, we have a database of eighteen patients, of which eleven have keratoconus in both eyes, two patients have it in the right eye, one patient has it in the left, and five patients are in normal conditions, that is, say, no not having the disease. The analysis is performed with a total of 950 images. Furthermore, three patients with a clinical diagnosis of keratoconus and one with normal conditions will be used.

3.2 Edge-Sobel Image Filter and Thresholding

In the images obtained from the patients, an edge detection line can be verified, which helps a lot to visualize the state of the cornea and increases the confidence in the measurements. However, the area of interest must have a higher resolution at its edges without increasing noise. For this reason, Sobel filter is used to detect edges due to their strong intensity contrast and to differentiate keratoconus corneas from corneas with altered transparency.

Edge detection process that gives Sobel filter significantly reduces the amount of data and filters the necessary information, preserving the important structural properties of an image; that is, it eliminates the greatest amount of noise and highlights and locates the edges [14]. On the other hand, the images obtained by Pentacam® have a low noise level, so applying a filter will eliminate the noise, and the resolution of the corneal edges will be clearer cut.

3.3 Mathematical Analysis Berlin/Ambrosio

Berlin/Ambrosio curves are used to reliably detect corneal ectasias from the first levels, such as preclinical keratoconus, to phases in which the disease is advanced. These curves represent the data of the heights of the anterior surface in combination with an analysis of the evolution of the thickness of the cornea [15]. For this, the analysis of the thickness evolution employs concentric rings that start from the thinnest point and extend to the cornea's periphery. Through polynomial regression of the curves, the equations that determine the Berlin/Ambrosio curves will be obtained [16].

- General Equation for Berlin/Ambrosio curves [15].
  Equation 1. Berlin-Ambrosio curve

$$G = a0 + a1d1 + a2d2 + a3d3 + a4d4 \qquad (1)$$

where:

G: It is the corneal thickness of the human eye.
a0, a1, a2, a3, a4: They are the coefficients of the polynomial.
d = vertical corneal diameter.

3.4 Affectation Degree Classification Algorithm

Based on the literature, because other vision parameters are affected as keratoconus progresses, several investigations have proposed using more than two parameters for the development of algorithms and predictive models, such as corneal profile images, pachymetry, diopter, aberrometry, corneal topography, among others [17–20] in order to corroborate and ensure greater precision in the diagnosis of keratoconus.

This work focused on determining parameters such as diopter, pachymetry, and ART; and the appropriate ranges thereof to define the proper classification of detection levels. With the above and the entry of the corneal profiles, the aim is to combine parameters with improving the sensitivity and specificity in the detection and diagnosis of keratoconus in its various stages. That is why the implementation of these parameters in a convolutional neural network is ideal because this type of network allows the recognition and classification of images; that is, it will recognize the specific changes in the morphology and the angle of inclination of the cornea as keratoconus progresses; and through a conditional function of the vision parameters, it allows us to differentiate each of these ranges into four categories according to the degree of keratoconus involvement (Normal, Initial, Mean and Severe) from minor to major respectively.

4 Results

4.1 Variation in Berlin/Ambrosio Curves

In the results of the corneal curvature, described by the Berlin/Ambrosio analysis and with the help of mathematical modeling of linear progression, the following parameters were obtained for their subsequent classification in the diagnostic algorithm of the keratoconus severity level. For this study, we base ourselves on three fundamental parameters for the diagnosis. The first parameter is the diopter, which expresses the refractive power of a lens and is equivalent to its reciprocal or inverse value. However, these diopters do not have units of measurement since they are obtained from simulated keratometry by Pentacam® [21]. The second parameter is pachymetry; to use this value, we must differentiate the distance from the PT to the diameter on the Y axis [22]. Finally, the third parameter to be used is Ambrosio Relational Thickness (ART); it is calculated for average and maximum progression indices (ART-Ave and ART-Max); the ART metrics represent the best metrics for detecting eyes at risk of ectasia [23]. All these values are represented in Table 1 below:

Table 1. Corneal topography parameters are given by Berlin/Ambrosio analysis.

Corneal Topography	Parameters		
	Diopter	*Pachymetry (μm)*	*Ambrosio Relational Thickness (ART)*
Normal	≤47.2	≤490	≥400
Initial	47.3–48	500–699	399–350
Moderate	48.1–48.7	700–999	349–301
Severe	≥48.8	≥1000	<300

Moreover, once the parameters have been identified, we proceed to use the mathematical modeling of polynomial regression to obtain Berlin/Ambrosio curves, this analysis is carried out with the help of Eq. (1). As a result, the four figures differ from each other by their level of curvature. As shown in Table 2 below:

Table 2. Berlin/Ambrosio curves analysis.

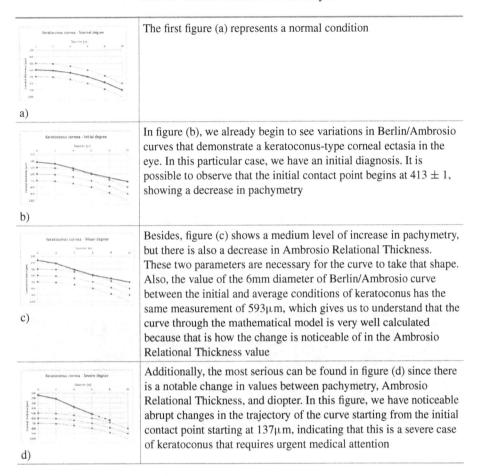

a)	The first figure (a) represents a normal condition
b)	In figure (b), we already begin to see variations in Berlin/Ambrosio curves that demonstrate a keratoconus-type corneal ectasia in the eye. In this particular case, we have an initial diagnosis. It is possible to observe that the initial contact point begins at 413 ± 1, showing a decrease in pachymetry
c)	Besides, figure (c) shows a medium level of increase in pachymetry, but there is also a decrease in Ambrosio Relational Thickness. These two parameters are necessary for the curve to take that shape. Also, the value of the 6mm diameter of Berlin/Ambrosio curve between the initial and average conditions of keratoconus has the same measurement of 593μm, which gives us to understand that the curve through the mathematical model is very well calculated because that is how the change is noticeable of in the Ambrosio Relational Thickness value
d)	Additionally, the most serious can be found in figure (d) since there is a notable change in values between pachymetry, Ambrosio Relational Thickness, and diopter. In this figure, we have noticeable abrupt changes in the trajectory of the curve starting from the initial contact point starting at 137μm, indicating that this is a severe case of keratoconus that requires urgent medical attention

4.2 Parameters and Processing Image

In this work, after having determined the ranges of the diopter, pachymetry, and ART parameters using Berlin/Ambrosio analysis Table 1, diagnostic factors were considered in the analysis of the cases. With this, an algorithm was developed where each of these parameters was classified. Each time the patient's data is entered, a response on the level of keratoconus is generated based on the contrast of the data, as detailed in (Fig. 2).

On the other hand, the processed images were of the corneal profiles because they allow the analysis of corneal thickness and volume. These profiles verify edge detection lines on the profiles which increases confidence in the measurements. Additionally, indices generated from profile measurements can identify mild to moderate keratoconus [11]. Therefore, to obtain greater contrast at the edges of the cornea, the corneal profiles were processed using the filter, favoring the differentiation between the profiles of the normal and initial stages of the database used (Fig. 3).

290 D. Otuna-Hernández et al.

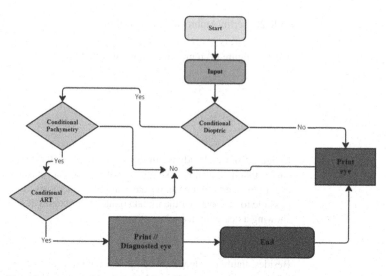

Fig. 2. Flowchart proposal in the algorithm of the affectation grade of keratoconus-type corneal ectasia, considering. Conditions in pachymetry, diopter, and increased with decreased Ambrosio relational thickness ART.

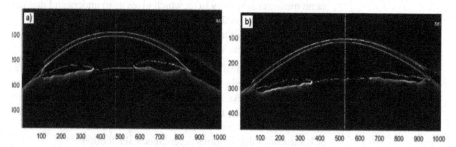

Fig. 3. Image processing by Sobel filter to increase the contrast of the edges. a) Corneal profile with Sobel filter of an eye in a normal state. b) Corneal profile with Sobel filter of an eye in an initial state.

4.3 Affectation Classification Algorithm

Mahmoud et al. state that using only frontal and lateral images of the eye it is possible to detect keratoconus without the need to subject patients to lengthy analysis processes [24]. Still, this study will not be able to detect or differentiate early-stage keratoconus.

On the other hand, Lavril et al. created a tool based on a learning algorithm that automatically detects keratoconus disease based on corneal topographies that analyzes corneal curvature to detect cones [25]. Even so, its accuracy in diagnosis was limited due to the lack of information to determine the level of disease progression, the state of the cornea, and the patient's visual condition. Therefore, these studies do not assess the posterior cornea and thickness profile and thus miss early ecstatic changes.

For this reason, with the established parameters and the processed corneal profiles, a convolutional neural network was performed where the corneal profile under study is

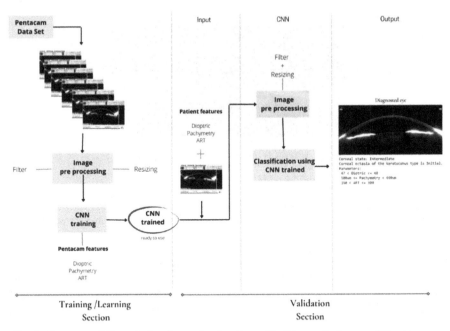

Fig. 4. Structure of Convolutional neural network used in Diagnostic Image of Keratoconus.

entered with its respective diopter, pachymetry, and ART indices so that these data are classified according to their level of illness. This algorithm will compare the input image with the trained database (Fig. 4). Once the image has been compared, it will be placed in a group with greater compatibility, and each entered data will be located according to the range belonging to the established parameters. Finally, the result will be the image with a legend printed with the patient's conditions (Fig. 5). This algorithm provides a diagnosis with greater specificity by comparing images and verifying the established parameters.

4.4   Performance Evaluation of CNN

To analyze the performance of the CNN [29–38], the CNN was first evaluated solely by entering the corneal profiles (CP) and seeing its degree of detection according to the established stages. In this process, it was possible to appreciate the difficulty in differentiating the profiles between "normal/initial" and "initial/severe." The "mean" and "severe" stages managed to have between 80 to 90% sensitivity and specificity. On the other hand, the normal and initial stage reflects values of 60% sensitivity and 80% specificity.

As for the second stage, the CNN was evaluated with the entry of the CP, and the vision parameters (VP), where it was obtained that: There was a greater differentiation between the CP of the "normal/initial" stage, decreasing its false negatives and false positives, resulting in an almost 20% increase in sensitivity and specificity in these two stages. As for the "medium" and "severe" stages, their false negatives and positives decreased

Diagnosted eye

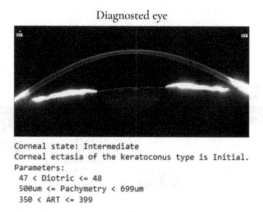

```
Corneal state: Intermediate
Corneal ectasia of the keratoconus type is Initial.
Parameters:
   47 < Diotric <= 48
   500um <= Pachymetry < 699um
   350 < ART <= 399
```

Fig. 5. Diagnosis of keratoconus suspicion in an initial state and its parameters validation.

with weakened patients, achieving an increase of almost 15% in their diagnoses and differentiations, achieving 92–95% sensitivity and specificity. Finally, the "initial" stage, despite a significant improvement (80% sensitivity and 93% specificity), is the stage with the greatest confusion between normal and medium CP. Data performance is indicated in Table 3.

Table 3. Keratoconus probability prediction of CNN CP evaluation and CP + VP evaluation.

Corneal Topography	Sensitivity		Specificity		Accuracy	
	CP (%)	*CP + VP (%)*	*CP (%)*	*CP + VP (%)*	*CP (%)*	*CP + VP (%)*
Normal	67,56	83,3	82,41	92,59	78,12	90,09
Initial	62,5	80,64	85,22	93,75	78,12	89,28
Mean	80,64	92,59	90,36	96,15	87,71	95,23
Severe	86,2	92,59	94,93	98,68	92,59	97,08

5 Discussion

Employing Berlin/Ambrosio curves is effective and safe because it is used to detect corneal ectasias such as keratoconus from the earliest stages. These curves represent the data of the heights of the anterior surface in combination with an analysis of the evolution of the thickness of the cornea. For this, analysis of the evolution of the thickness is using concentric rings that start from the thinnest point and extend to the periphery of the cornea.

According to [23], Ambrosio Relative Thickness (ART) can be used to measure corneal thickness because this parameter is useful in diagnosing subclinical keratoconus.

As stated by [22], the existence of a group of patients with pachymetry that exceeds 500 μm reflects the diagnosis in the initial stages of the disease. Diopter is another very important parameter to use for the diagnosis of keratoconus.

As claimed by [21], if the value of the apical zone is less than 47.2 diopters, the presence of keratoconus could be ruled out, values between 47.3 to 48.00 diopters can be initial, and values ranging from 48.1 to 48.7 diopters, the diagnosis can be average. Still, if it exceeds 48.8 diopters, there is a high probability of having keratoconus, which can even be severe. Therefore, using Berlin/Ambrosio curves in diagnosing the level of keratoconus is reliable because it expresses exact values in pachymetry, diopter, and Ambrosio Relative Thickness.

On the other hand, the combination of tools for studying the state of the cornea against keratoconus has become necessary to establish relationships between the affected indices after facing the disease [26]. Thus, the study of the cornea using Scheimpflug cameras generates results with high repeatability and concordance, providing Berlin/Ambrosio curves, the corneal profile, and the topographic map of the cornea with the potential to improve the detection of mild ecstatic corneas without the need for previous experience in the interpretation of images of the cornea [12, 27], however, the diagnosis is based on the interpretations of the doctors, which decreases the specificity and does not provide a clear detail of the progress of the disease in stages initials.

Therefore, determining the parameters to start analysis and relate their interaction with each other as the ectasia progresses is essential to verify and specify a diagnosis of the same node; improving the contrast of the edges of the cornea with the Sobel filter notably increases confidence in measurements, being able to more accurately differentiate corneas with initial stage from corneas in normal state. In this case, eyes with keratoconus have been found to have thinner corneas with less corneal volume and a sharp increase in parameters from the thinnest point towards the periphery, high diopter levels, and ART values less than 300 um [11, 18, 20]. Therefore, developing a tool that classifies a database and can identify the corneal profile that is entered provides greater sensitivity and specificity to the result, even more so in the analysis of early stages, as indicated in Table 4. Likewise, the values of diopter, pachymetry and ART entered optimize the analysis time to locate the values within the established ranges of each parameter and increase the precision, such were the cases of the "mean" and "severe" stages, whose results were highly significant and satisfactory. However, the implementation of much larger databases is very necessary to be able to establish the results of the predictions with greater reliability. In addition, the results obtained from the "initial" stage compromise the detection and evaluation of subclinical cases.

Table 4. Related work for the keratoconus detection by deep learning.

Author	Technique	Parameters	Results	Ref.
Accardo (2002)	CNN with bilateral indices	Corneal maps to characterize some index	Sensitivity of 94.1% and specificity of 97.6% have been reached	[9]

(*continued*)

Table 4. (*continued*)

Author	Technique	Parameters	Results	Ref.
Lavric (2019)	CNN	Corneal topography	KeratoDetect algorithm obtains an accuracy of 99.33% on the data test set	[12]
Kuo (2020)	VGG16 model InceptionV3 model ResNet152 model	Average keratometry Cylinder Surface regularity index Surface asymmetric index	The sensitivity and specificity of all CNN models were over 0.90	[10]
Chen (2021)	CNN VGG16 model	Corneal topography Axial map Anterior/posterior elevation map Pachymetry map	A CNN model detected keratoconus with an accuracy of 0.9785 on the testing set, considering all four maps concatenated	[11]
Ours (2022)	CNN	Corneal profile Diopter Pachymetry ART	Normal: Sen. of 83.3% and Spec. of 92.59% Initial: Sen. of 80.64% and Spec. of 93.75% Medium: Sen. of 92.59% and Spec. of 96.15% Severe: Sen. of 92.59% and Spec. of 98.68%	-

6　Conclusion

Berlin-Ambrosio characteristic curves were obtained by linear regression because, in all the documents read on the subject, there is not enough information to determine or indicate values taken as a reference to obtain the curves. The abnormal corneal thickness is found in Table 1, presented in the results section. These values indicate a high variation in the thickness of the cornea between the central part and the periphery, which results in a diagnosis of the level of progression of Keratoconus.

Mathematical models obtained through the equations of a linear progression of each stage of Keratoconus not only offer information on the degree of affectation of this disease but also specify the location of the cone and allow knowing the corneal thickness in that location, thus describing the cornea in case a cornea transplant is needed in the future.

Keratoconus is a disease that has no cure because the level of deterioration or the affected area is not exactly known. However, knowing the minimal features or identifying a variety of keratoconus conditions provides early diagnosis and treatment. So far, it has been determined that the progression of the illness is closely related to the thinning of the cornea, presenting less volume and a sudden increase in topographic parameters such as diopter, pachymetry, and ART. In conclusion, the keratoconus diagnostic algorithm can identify.

Images entered with Sobel filtering and classifying them according to their level of involvement with greater effectiveness. Their sensitivity was enhanced by the effective combination and interpretation of topographic indices and patterns.

Continuing with the subsequent analysis of Keratoconus is recommended to obtain complete software that allows for establishing the appropriate treatment.

Although the corneal profile allows the evaluation of the posterior cornea and the thickness profile, the combination and interpretation of the topographic indices and patterns gives greater sensitivity to the algorithm and allows the analysis of early ecstatic changes, elevation, pressures, asymmetric conditions, and stocks of cones as easily as the corneal topography allows. Therefore, for future work, it is recommended to implement the analysis of the corneal topography within the algorithm to analyze it together with the topographic parameters and the corneal profile to obtain a much more specific result free of interpretations, which may also be able to strengthen the subclinical diagnosis of said disease and thus avoid its evolution from early stages.

If Keratoconus is detected in a patient, it is recommended to monitor the evolution of said ectasia (every six months) to establish whether surgical intervention is necessary. When Keratoconus has been detected, it is not progressive but maintains its stage (Frustrated Keratoconus).

References

1. Collar, C.V., González-Méijome, J.M.: El queratocono y su tratamiento. Órgano Oficial del Colegio Nacional de Ópticos-Optometristas de España, Gaceta óptica, pp. 16–22 (2009)
2. Marrero Rodríguez, E., Sánchez Vega, O., Barrera Garcél, B.R., Díaz Ramírez, S., Somoza Mograbe, J.Á.: Caracterización de pacientes con queratocono. Medisan **15**, 1698–1704 (2011)
3. Cavas Martínez, F.: Modelado geométrico personalizado de la córnea humana y su aplicación a la detección de ectasias corneales (2018). https://doi.org/10.31428/10317/6797
4. Vanegas, S.M.B.: Una revisión del queratocono. Cienc. tecnol. para salud vis. ocular **7**, 95–106 (2009)
5. Cavas-Martínez, F., et al.: Modelado geométrico personalizado de córnea humana in vivo y su uso para el diagnóstico de ectasia corneal. Más uno. **9**, e110249 (2014). https://doi.org/10.1371/journal.pone.0110249
6. René Moreno, N., Miguel Srur, A., Carlos Nieme, B.: Cirugía refractiva: indicaciones, técnicas y resultados. Rev. médica Clín. Las Condes. **21**, 901–910 (2010). https://doi.org/10.1016/s0716-8640(10)70614-3
7. Jain, R., Grewal, S.P.S.: Pentacam: principio y aplicaciones clínicas. J. Curr. Práctica de glaucoma **3**, 20–32 (2009). https://doi.org/10.5005/jp-journals-10008-1012
8. Motlagh, M.N., et al.: Tomografía corneal Pentacam® para la detección de candidatos a cirugía refractiva: una revisión de la literatura, parte I. Med. Hipótesis Descubrimiento. innovador Oftalmol. **8**, 177–203 (2019)
9. Accardo, P.A., Pensiero, S.: Sistema basado en redes neuronales para la detección temprana del queratocono a partir de la topografía corneal. J. Biomédica. Informar. **35**, 151–159 (2002). https://doi.org/10.1016/s1532-0464(02)00513-0
10. Kuo, B.-I., et al.: Detección de queratocono basada en el enfoque de aprendizaje profundo de la topografía corneal. Traducir Vis. ciencia Tecnología **9**, 53 (2020). https://doi.org/10.1167/tvst.9.2.53

11. Chen, X., et al.: Detección de cambios en el queratocono mediante el aprendizaje profundo de mapas codificados por colores. BMJ Open Oftalmol. **6**, e000824 (2021). https://doi.org/ 10.1136/bmjophth-2021-000824

12. Mahmoud, H.A.H., Mengash, H.A.: Automated keratoconus detection by 3D corneal images reconstruction. Sensors **21**, 2326 (2021). https://doi.org/10.3390/s21072326

13. Ambrósio, R., Alonso, R.S., Luz, A., Coca Velarde, L.G.: Perfil espacial del grosor corneal y distribución del volumen corneal: índices tomográficos para detectar el queratocono. J. Catarata refractaria. Cirugía **32**, 1851–1859 (2006). https://doi.org/10.1016/j.jcrs.2006. 06.025

14. Shetty, R., et al.: Repetibilidad y acuerdo de tres sistemas de imágenes basados en Scheimpflug para medir los parámetros del segmento anterior en el queratocono. Invertir. Oftalmol. Vis. ciencia **55**, 5263 (2014). https://doi.org/10.1167/iovs.14-15055

15. Kanopoulos, N., Vasanthavada, N., Baker, R.L.: Diseño de un filtro de detección de bordes de imagen utilizando el operador Sobel. IEEE J. Circuitos de estado sólido. **23**, 358–367 (1988). https://doi.org/10.1109/4.996

16. Bamdad, S., Sedaghat, M.R., Yasemi, M., Vahedi, A.: Sensibilidad y especificidad de la visualización de ectasia mejorada de Belin Ambrosio en el diagnóstico temprano del queratocono. J. Oftalmol. **2020**, 1–5 (2020). https://doi.org/10.1155/2020/7625659

17. Belin, M.W., Meyer, J.J., Duncan, J.K., Gelman, R., Borgstrom, M.: Assessing progression of keratoconus and cross-linking efficacy: the Belin ABCD progression display. Int. J. Keratoconus Ectatic Corneal Dis. **6**, 1–10 (2017). https://doi.org/10.5005/jp-journals-10025- 1135

18. Sánchez Villacis, L.S., Álvarez Mena, P.R., Benavides Bautista, P.A., Sánchez Sola, H.R., Zambrano Jordán, D.R.: El queratocono, su diagnóstico y manejo. Una revisión bibliográfica. Enfermería Investiga: Investigación, Vinculación, Docencia y Gestión **3**, 1–8 (2018). https:// doi.org/10.29033/ei.v3sup1.2018.01

19. Martínez-Abad, A.: Piñero, DP: Nuevas perspectivas sobre la detección y progresión del queratocono. J. Catarata refractaria. Cirugía **43**, 1213–1227 (2017). https://doi.org/10.1016/ j.jcrs.2017.07.021

20. Avitabile, T., et al.: Estadificación del queratocono: Comparación de un método ultrabiomicroscópico asistido por computadora con análisis videoqueratográfico. Córnea **23**, 655–660 (2004). https://doi.org/10.1097/01.ico.0000127486.78424.6e

21. Belin, M., Khachikian, S.: Detección de queratocono/ectasia con Oculus Pentacam: Belin/Ambrósio Enhanced Ectasia Display (2008)

22. Ortega Pacific, E.: Diferencias entre queratoconos con ectasias de diámetro grande y pequeño. Cienc. Tecnol. Para Salud Vis. Ocular **5**, 19–26 (2007). https://doi.org/10.19052/sv.1511

23. Rojas-Álvarez, E.: Queratocono en edad pediátrica: características clínico-refractivas y evolución. Centro de Especialidades Médicas Fundación Donum, Cuenca, Ecuador, 2015-2018. Revista Mexicana de Oftalmología **93**, 221–232 (2019). https://doi.org/10.24875/RMO.M19 000082

24. Reyes, N., Arias-Díaz, A., Ortega-Díaz, L., Cuevas-Ruiz, J.: Corneal topography by placido discs for the detection of keratoconus in pediatric patients **86**, 204–212 (2012)

25. Consejo, A., Solarski, J., Karnowski, K., Rozema, J.J., Wojtkowski, M., Iskander, D.R.: Detección de queratocono basada en una sola imagen de Scheimpflug. Traducir Vis. ciencia Tecnología **9**, 36 (2020). https://doi.org/10.1167/tvst.9.7.36

26. Lavric, A., Valentin, P.: Keratodetect: keratoconus detection algorithm using convolutional neural networks. Computat. Intell. Neurosci. **2019**, 1–9 (2019). https://doi.org/10.1155/2019/ 8162567

27. Imbornoni, L., McGhee, C., Belin, M.: Evolución del queratocono: del diagnóstico a la terapéutica. Klin. Monbl. Augenheilkd. **235**, 680–688 (2018). https://doi.org/10.1055/s-0044- 100617

28. Mas Tur, V., MacGregor, C., Jayaswal, R., O'Bart, D., Maycock, N.: Una revisión del quera-tocono: diagnóstico, fisiopatología y genética. Sobrev. Oftalmol. **62**, 770783 (2017). https://doi.org/10.1016/j.survophthal.2017.06.009

29. Aguiar-Salazar, E., Villalba-Meneses, F., Tirado-Espín, A., Amaguaña-Marmol, D., Almeida-Galárraga, D.: Rapid detection of cardiac pathologies by neural networks using ecg signals (1d) and secg images (3d). Computation **10**(7), 112 (2022)

30. Caicho, J., et al.: Diabetic retinopathy: Detection and classification using alexnet, googlenet and resnet50 convolutional neural networks. In: Narváez, F.R., Proaño, J., Morillo, P., Vallejo, D., Montoya, D.G., Díaz, G.M. (eds.) Smart Technologies, Systems and Applications: Second International Conference, SmartTech-IC 2021, Quito, Ecuador, December 1–3, 2021, Revised Selected Papers, pp. 259–271. Springer International Publishing, Cham (2022). https://doi.org/10.1007/978-3-030-99170-8_19

31. Gualsaquí, M.G., et al.: Convolutional neural network for imagine movement classification for neurorehabilitation of upper extremities using low-frequency eeg signals for spinal cord injury. In: Narváez, F.R., Proaño, J., Morillo, P., Vallejo, D., González Montoya, D., Díaz, G.M. (eds.) SmartTech-IC 2021. CCIS, vol. 1532, pp. 272–287. Springer, Cham (2022). https://doi.org/10.1007/978-3-030-99170-8_20

32. Herrera-Romero, B., Almeida-Galárraga, D., Salum, G.M., Villalba-Meneses, F., Gudiño-Gomezjurado, M.E.: GUSignal: an informatics tool to analyze glucuronidase gene expression in arabidopsis thaliana roots. IEEE/ACM Trans. Comput. Biol. Bioinform. **20**(2), 1073–1080 (2023). https://doi.org/10.1109/TCBB.2022.3190427

33. Matamoros-Alcivar, E., et al.: Implementation of MPC and PID Control algorithms to the artificial pancreas for diabetes mellitus type 1. In: 2021 IEEE International Conference on Machine Learning and Applied Network Technologies (ICMLANT), Soyapango, El Salvador, pp. 1–6 (2021). https://doi.org/10.1109/ICMLANT53170.2021.9690529.

34. Niles, D.N., et al.: Covid-19 pulmonary lesion classification using cnn software in chest x-ray with quadrant scoring severity parameters. In: Narváez, F.R., Proaño, J., Morillo, P., Vallejo, D., Montoya, D.G., Díaz, G.M. (eds.) Smart Technologies, Systems and Applications: Second International Conference, SmartTech-IC 2021, Quito, Ecuador, December 1–3, 2021, Revised Selected Papers, pp. 370–382. Springer International Publishing, Cham (2022). https://doi.org/10.1007/978-3-030-99170-8_27

35. Suquilanda-Pesántez, J.D., et al.: Prediction of parkinson's disease severity based on gait signals using a neural network and the fast fourier transform. In: Botto-Tobar, M., Cruz, H., Cadena, A.D. (eds.) CIT 2020. AISC, vol. 1326, pp. 3–18. Springer, Cham (2021). https://doi.org/10.1007/978-3-030-68080-0_1

36. Suquilanda-Pesántez, J.D., Salazar, E.D.A., Almeida-Galárraga, D., Salum, G., Villalba-Meneses, F., Gomezjurado, M.E.G.: Nifthool: an informatics program for identification of nifh proteins using deep neural networks. F1000Research **11**, 164 (2022). https://doi.org/10.12688/f1000research.107925.1

37. Tene-Hurtado, D., et al.: Brain tumor segmentation based on 2d u-net using mri multi-modalities brain images. In: Narváez, F.R., Proaño, J., Morillo, P., Vallejo, D., Montoya, D.G., Díaz, G.M. (eds.) SmartTech-IC 2021. CCIS, vol. 1532, pp. 345–359. Springer, Cham (2022). https://doi.org/10.1007/978-3-030-99170-8_25

38. Yanchatuña, O.P., et al.: Skin lesion detection and classification using convolutional neural network for deep feature extraction and support vector machine. Int. J. Adv. Sci., Eng. Inform. Technol. **11**(3), 1260 (2021). https://doi.org/10.18517/ijaseit.11.3.13679

Finite Element Analysis of Uncovered Coplanar Interdigital Electrodes for Capacitive Sensor Applications

Bremnen Véliz$^{(\boxtimes)}$ ⓘ, Renato Dueñas ⓘ, Orlando Barcia ⓘ,
and Lenin E. Cevallos Robalino ⓘ

NANOTECH Research Group, Electronic Engineering Department, Universidad Politécnica Salesiana, Guayaquil, Ecuador
bveliz@ups.edu.ec

Abstract. In this paper, COMSOL simulations are used to analyze the capacitance of uncovered coplanar interdigital capacitors of two configurations varying the dimensions, but with constant finger electrode spacing and active area: one of 8 mm × 4 mm, and the second with 4 mm × 8 mm. The expression of a finite-layer conformal mapping model has been modified to consider the finger electrode thickness which is in very good agreement with the simulations. The results indicated that the capacitance for the two configurations is insignificantly different, so either can be used in a sensing application. It has been verified the designs with the highest capacitances are those that have a smaller electrode width, higher thickness of the dielectric substrate, and higher thickness of the electrode, but a capacitance saturation exits when the ratio of substrate thickness and electrode width is approximately 2.5 or the substrate thickness is half of the periodicity ratio. Electrostatic simulations showed a higher concentration of 2D electrical potential in the active area when electrode width decreases, reason why the capacitance is increased. The finding found should be taken into account by designers to fabricate capacitive sensors and micro-supercapacitors based on interdigital electrodes.

Keywords: Interdigital electrodes · Capacitance · Finger thickness

1 Introduction

Since the invention of the first capacitor called the Leyden bottle, a wide variety of capacitor technologies have emerged that are indispensable to running any electronic device around us [1]. For instance, capacitors are used for the design of a variety of industrial sensors. The simplest form of a capacitor is composed of two parallel metal plates of section A, separated by a distance d in which there is an insulator or dielectric material with permittivity ε.

The application of a voltage generates the accumulation of charges on the capacitor plates and the constant of proportionality C is the capacitance that is measured in farads

F. R. Narváez et al. (Eds.): SmartTech-IC 2022, CCIS 1705, pp. 298–312, 2023.
https://doi.org/10.1007/978-3-031-32213-6_22

(F). The capacitance value depends on the dimensions and permittivity of the dielectric located between the plates. The expression for a capacitor is [2]:

$$C = \varepsilon \frac{A}{d} \qquad (1)$$

A more complex form is the coplanar interdigital electrodes capacitor called IDEs, which has proven to be easy to manufacture and low costs. In this geometry, the electrodes have fingers' shape placed on a substrate and an active dielectric material that is laid on the fingers. The electric field moves up, down and between the fingers, which when passing through the material produces the polarization of its molecules, and therefore its dielectric properties can be measured [3]. It has been found in a wide variety of applications such as sensors, for example IDEs include their use in clustered elements for microwave integrated circuits, optical and surface acoustic wave devices, tunable devices, and thin-film acoustic electronic transducers and dielectric studies on thin films [4]. Many capacitive Biosensors are based on IDEs for measuring specific proteins or biomolecular substances [5] because IDEs provide a non-invasive detection technique.

An example of a cross-section view of an interdigital capacitor is shown in Fig. 1, where the electrode fingers are arranged at d distance on a plane of the insulating substrate. The electric field lines interact between electrode fingers of oppositive voltage.

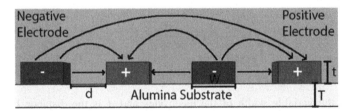

Fig. 1. An example of a cross-section view of an interdigital capacitor.

Interdigital electrodes are becoming so popular that electrodes of gold [6], silver, and platinum with substrates such as FR4, alumina, and glass can commercially be founded. For instance, FR4 is a composite of fiberglass-reinforced epoxy resin [7] and alumina which is an aluminum oxide compound that is strongly influenced by its purity and man-ufacturing process [8]. These electrodes are arranged in different finger spacings, widths, lengths, and thickness, but there is no clear statement of which geometric configuration of a coplanar rectangular area is more efficient to obtain more capacitance per unit area. Knowing exactly how to size the electrodes is important to optimize the arrangement of a sensor, and secondly to distinguish how much capacitance the naked interdigital electrodes provide on their own. For instance, having a high capacitance before elec-trodes are coated with any electrolyte is advantage if the goal is the capacitance in micro-supercapacitors [9–11].

Then, the present paper seeks to find the structure with the greatest capacitance and therefore the highest density of integration. An analysis of various designs is carried out, varying the width and length of the electrodes, the thickness of the substrate and the thickness of the electrodes, but keeping other variables constant such as the distance between the electrodes and the active working area. The results are obtained in COMSOL and MATLAB.

2 Theory

2.1 The Model of Interdigital Electrodes Capacitors

A. Quershi and C. Tsouti have defined the capacitance of an interdigital sensor by means of the following equation [5].

$$C = N\varepsilon\frac{Lt}{d} \tag{2}$$

where N is the number of electrodes, ε is the permittivity of the length of the interdigital electrodes, t is the thickness of the interdigital electrodes, and d is the distance between the electrodes [12]. However, this capacitance calculation is not entirely reliable, and in our view omits the important detail of the metallization ratio that we will see below.

In the case of the metallization ratio η, it determines the ratio between the width and distance between the electrodes. And the periodicity of electrodes λ, that determines a length that is repeated along the capacitor area. The metallization and periodicity ratio equations are:

$$\eta = \frac{W}{W+d} \tag{3}$$

$$\lambda = 2(W+d) \tag{4}$$

where W is the variable width of the electrodes and d is the distance between the electrodes.

In 1970 Alley proposed a model to calculate the capacitance of an interdigital capacitor which has been restructured over the years [4, 13, 14]. This equation is based on a mapping model, which considers the thickness of the dielectric material T by means of the parameter r that relates the dielectric thickness T with the periodicity of electrodes λ. Below is the equation to find the capacitance of a coplanar interdigital capacitor:

$$C_T = (N-3)\frac{C_I}{2} + 2\frac{C_I C_E}{C_I + C_E} \tag{5}$$

where C_T represents the total capacitance of the sensor and it is an increasing function of the metallization ratio η and the parameter r. N is the number of interdigital fingers presents on the sensor (the sum of all both positive and negative electrodes). C_I is the capacitance between the electrodes inside the sensor, while C_E is the capacitance at the edges of the sensor. In addition to this, it is necessary to determine each of these capacitances in order to get the total capacitance.

$$C_E = \varepsilon_0\varepsilon_r L\frac{K(k_E)}{K(k'_E)} \tag{6}$$

$$C_I = \varepsilon_0 \varepsilon_r L \frac{K(k_I)}{K(k_I')} \tag{7}$$

where $K(k)$ is the first class complete elliptic integral of module k and its complementary module k'. L is the length of the electrodes, ε_0 is the permittivity of vacuum and ε_r is the relative permittivity of the substrate [4].

2.2 The Model of Interdigital Electrodes Capacitors Considering the Electrode Thickness

Furthermore, Eq. 5 was modified, so that the thickness of the electrodes can be incorporated into the analysis of the results by combining Eq. 1. Then Eq. 8 shows that the Total capacitance is:

$$C_T = (N - 3)\left(\frac{C_I}{2} + Cp\right) + 2\left(\frac{C_I C_E}{C_I + C_E} + Cp\right) \tag{8}$$

where Cp is the parallel plate capacitance of a pair of electrodes considering the thickness of the electrodes t and the distance d in between them, described by the Eq. 9 shown below:

$$C_p = \varepsilon_0 \varepsilon_{r2} L \frac{t}{d} \tag{9}$$

where ε_0 is the vacuum permittivity, ε_{r2} is the relative permittivity of the air which is 1 and L is the length of the electrodes.

To implement the Eq. 8, it is important to apply different functions such as the complete elliptic integral of first kind and Jacobi theta functions in MATLAB [15] which are summarized in [4].

3 Methodology

The design and simulation were carried out with COMSOL Multiphysics software. An evaluation is executed by means of the parametric sweep tool that allows a sweep of all the parameters entered to solve possible variations of the system [16]. The proposed geometries are two configurations with different dimensions. On one hand, an 8 mm × 4 mm vertical rectangle was taken as a work area, and on the other hand, a 4 mm × 8 mm horizontal rectangle, being height (a) by base (b), the dimensions of the active area. Both configurations can be seen in Fig. 2. In Fig. 3 is observed the detail of the variables for the rest of the interdigital capacitor dimensions.

In the simulations, gold and alumina were stablished as the materials of the electrodes and substrate respectively. Table 1 shows the dimensions proposed for the design of the electrodes with vertical and horizontal rectangular configurations. Variables a and b refer to the sides of the geometry for the entire interdigital device. It has been developed 10 forms of geometries in two dimensions, five with vertical configuration and five with horizontal configuration. This means, two different lengths of electrodes with 3800 um

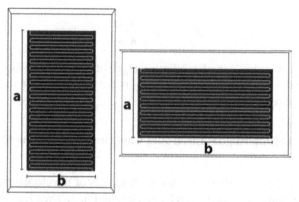

Fig. 2. Vertical and horizontal rectangular configuration, where *a* represents the height and *b* represents the base.

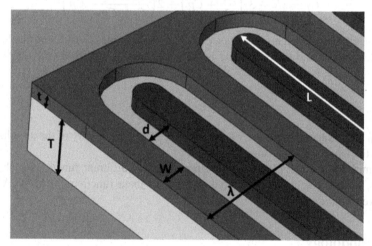

Fig. 3. All the variables that are part of the coplanar capacitor analysis. The length of the electrodes *L*, width of the electrodes *W*, distance between electrodes *d*, thickness of electrodes *t*, thickness of dielectric substrate *T* and periodicity of electrodes λ.

for vertical way and 7800 um for horizontal way. 100 um is the gap that avoids the front touch of the blue finger with the red portion, and the remaining measure is 100 um. Also, the distance between electrodes is set at 100 um, while the width of the electrodes varies from 100 um to 800 um. In the electrode number section, we have + and − as the number of positive and negative electrodes respectively that can be obtained for each of the electrode values keeping constant the active area. In addition, the electrodes' thickness is constant and is set at 50 um in the first data analysis. Finally, we have the ratios of metallization η and periodicity of electrodes λ for each parameter, these were defined in Eqs. 3 and 4.

Table 1. Proposed parameters for the rectangular geometry of the interdigital sensors.

Sample	Electrode Width	Area (mm)		Electrodes Number (N)		Metallization Ratio	Electrodes Periodicity	Distance
	W	a	b	+	-	η	λ	d
1	100um	8	4	20	20	0.5	400um	100um
2	200um	8	4	14	13	0.67	600um	100um
3	400um	8	4	8	8	0.8	1000um	100um
4	600um	8	4	6	5.5	0.86	1400um	100um
5	800um	8	4	5	4	0.89	1800um	100um
6	100um	4	8	10	10	0.5	400um	100um
7	200um	4	8	7	6.5	0.67	600um	100um
8	400um	4	8	4	4	0.8	1000um	100um
9	600um	4	8	3	2.83	0.86	1400um	100um
10	800um	4	8	2.5	2	0.89	1800um	100um

Regarding to the first dataset, five different thicknesses of the substrate sheet shown in Table 2 will be analyzed. This alumina substrate has a relative permittivity of $\varepsilon_r = 9.8$ much greater than the air relative permittivity which is 1.

Table 2. Group of samples for different thicknesses of the substrate.

Sample	Substrate Thickness (T)
1	50um
2	100um
3	150um
4	200um
5	250um

And finally, in the second dataset, four different electrode thicknesses will be analyzed to know if there are important changes if this parameter is modified. It can review the Table 3.

Table 3. Group of samples for the different electrode thicknesses

Sample	Electrode Thickness (t)
1	25um
2	50um
3	100um
4	200um

4 Results

4.1 Simulations of the Samples with a Variable Electrode Width and Substrate Thickness

Figure 4 shows the results of the 2D electrical potential plots for the 10 configurations of Table 1 at a substrate thickness $T = 200$ um, where the fingers increase in width for both 8 mm × 4 mm and 4 mm × 8 mm configurations. The blue color means the negative electrical potential, while red is the positive potential. We can conclude that, by increasing the width of the electrodes, the 2D potential in the substrate around electrodes increases, that is, the potential diffuses more outside the active area.

Fig. 4. Geometric designs for the 10 proposed configurations shown in Table 1, the electrodes are arranged vertically in the first row and horizontally in the second row, with columns showing the W = [100 200 400 600 800] um and all of this over an active area of 32 mm^2.

Figure 5 shows a diagram of the lateral view of the electrical potential for the substrate thicknesses of Table 2. The potential is intense between the electrodes, but it is also more concentrated in the depth of the substrate when the thickness is increased, which means that the substrate contributes with a capacitance.

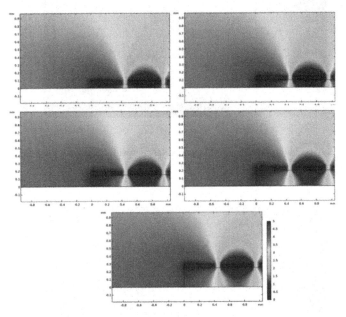

Fig. 5. Thickness from 50 to 250 um of the alumina substrate for your reference.

When performing the electrostatics physics stationary study, COMSOL calculates Maxwell's Capacitance using the Volume Maximum tool. Figures 6 and 7 show the 2D surface plots with the capacitance surf graphs of the 8 mm × 4 mm and 4 mm × 8 mm configurations respectively, where the highest values are painted in red and the lowest in blue. It is observed that the capacitance depends on two variables, dielectric thickness (T) and electrodes width (W). The capacitance is greater when the electrode width is smaller and when dielectric thickness is greater. Obviously, when the electrode width is reduced, the electrical potential is concentrated more in the active area as seen in Fig. 4 and then the capacitance increases. In addition, both surface charts are quite similar, which means that the capacitance behavior does not change significantly for the two configurations.

The capacitance results based on the two variables for each configuration are also shown in Fig. 8 and 9. As there are five electrode widths (100, 200, 400, 600, 800) and five substrate thicknesses (50, 100, 150, 200, 250), the total combinations are 25 results for each configuration. It can be verified that the generated function with a saw form is the result of the ratio of electrode width W and substrate thickness T. It can be seen in the first five data of the configuration 8 mm × 4 mm with the same electrode width $W = 100$ um, the capacitance increases if the substrate thickness increases, so the maximum value is 8.42 pF when $T = 250$ um, which means the ratio $T/W = 250/100$. For that same configuration the minimum capacitance is 1.61 pF when $W = 800$ um and $T = 50$ um, that is, for the widest electrodes and the thinnest substrate thickness. For the

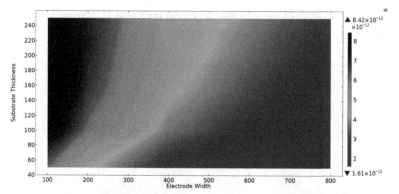

Fig. 6. Table surface with the Maxwell's capacitance results, configuration 8 mm × 4 mm. Relation between Substrate thickness and Electrode width.

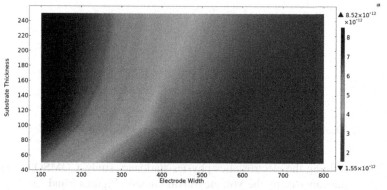

Fig. 7. Table surface with the Maxwell's capacitance results, configuration 4 mm × 8 mm. Relation between Substrate thickness and Electrode width.

4 mm × 8 mm configuration shown in Fig. 9, the maximum and minimum capacitance are 8.52 pF and 1.55 pF respectively for the same electrode width and dielectric thickness values as in the other configuration. Moreover, begins a capacitance saturation when $T = 200$ um and $W = 100$ um, this is $T = \lambda/2$ (samples #4 and sample #29).

Table 4 presents the results obtained by means of the Eq. 8 computed in MATLAB, the simulation in COMSOL and the error percentage between these two. Note that the electrode thickness is maintained at 50 um for all tests. With fifty results, it can be observed that there are 2 results with less than 29% error, 9 results with less than 19% error and 39 results with less than 10%. In this way it is ratified that the results obtained in COMSOL are like those calculated with the model of the Eq. 8.

4.2 Simulations of the Samples with a Variable Electrode Width and Electrode Thickness

These tests were carried out now, keeping the dielectric substrate at a constant value $T = 200$ um and the electrodes thickness at a variable value $t = [2550100200]$ um

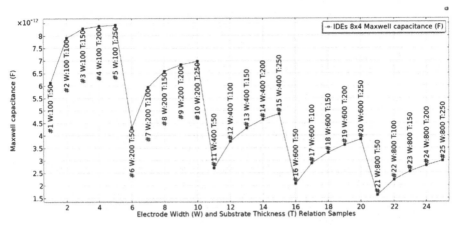

Fig. 8. The 25 capacitance results of the combinations with the variables electrode width (W) and substrate thickness (T). Configuration 8 mm × 4 mm. In the domain you can see the samples starting from $W = 100$ um, $T = 50$ um until the final sample $W = 800$ um, $T = 250$ um.

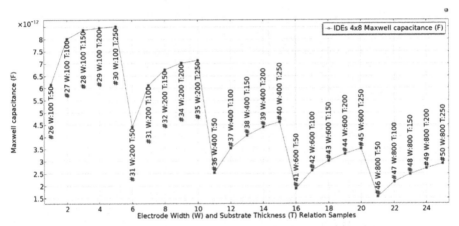

Fig. 9. The 25 capacitance results of the combinations with the variables electrode width (W) and substrate thickness (T). Configuration 4 mm × 8 mm. In the domain you can see the samples starting from $W = 100$ um, $T = 50$ um until the final sample $W = 800$ um, $T = 250$ um.

for a better understanding of the behavior of the interdigital capacitor and make a new comparison of results between COMSOL and MATLAB.

The Maxwell's capacitance results in Figs. 10 and 11 show the behavior of the electrode width ratio respect to the electrodes thickness in both configurations. The capacitance also decreases as W increases because metallization ratio decreases which agrees with study reported by [4]. Furthermore, the capacitance increases as t increases due to that the area of the parallel plate capacitor (Eq. 9) increases. Finally, a capacitance saturation is no observed when $t = \lambda/2$ (samples #4 and #24).

Table 4. Error margin between theoretical and simulated values for the relation W and T.

#	a x b	t	N	W	T	MATLAB	COMSOL	Error
1	4x8	50	20	100	50	5,7763E-12	6,1481E-12	6,05%
2	4x8	50	20	100	100	7,8229E-12	8,0164E-12	2,41%
3	4x8	50	20	100	150	8,1855E-12	8,3783E-12	2,30%
4	4x8	50	20	100	200	8,1846E-12	8,4592E-12	3,25%
5	4x8	50	20	100	250	8,1497E-12	8,5173E-12	4,32%
6	4x8	50	14	200	50	3,9370E-12	4,4121E-12	10,77%
7	4x8	50	14	200	100	5,8860E-12	6,1150E-12	3,74%
8	4x8	50	14	200	150	6,6703E-12	6,7491E-12	1,17%
9	4x8	50	14	200	200	6,9171E-12	7,0204E-12	1,47%
10	4x8	50	14	200	250	6,9702E-12	7,1293E-12	2,23%
11	4x8	50	8	400	50	2,2329E-12	2,5370E-12	11,98%
12	4x8	50	8	400	100	3,4415E-12	3,5387E-12	2,75%
13	4x8	50	8	400	150	4,1354E-12	4,0575E-12	1,92%
14	4x8	50	8	400	200	4,5386E-12	4,3962E-12	3,24%
15	4x8	50	8	400	250	4,7634E-12	4,6159E-12	3,20%
16	4x8	50	5,8	600	50	1,5406E-12	1,8879E-12	18,40%
17	4x8	50	5,8	600	100	2,3837E-12	2,6208E-12	9,05%
18	4x8	50	5,8	600	150	2,8955E-12	3,0149E-12	3,96%
19	4x8	50	5,8	600	200	3,2374E-12	3,3017E-12	1,95%
20	4x8	50	5,8	600	250	3,4718E-12	3,5183E-12	1,32%
21	4x8	50	4,5	800	50	1,1095E-12	1,5528E-12	28,55%
22	4x8	50	4,5	800	100	1,7185E-12	2,1553E-12	20,27%
23	4x8	50	4,5	800	150	2,0952E-12	2,4718E-12	15,24%
24	4x8	50	4,5	800	200	2,3567E-12	2,7114E-12	13,08%
25	4x8	50	4,5	800	250	2,5496E-12	2,9015E-12	12,13%
1	8x4	50	40	100	50	5,9363E-12	6,1168E-12	2,95%
2	8x4	50	40	100	100	8,0138E-12	7,9111E-12	1,30%
3	8x4	50	40	100	150	8,3552E-12	8,2834E-12	0,87%
4	8x4	50	40	100	200	8,3350E-12	8,3802E-12	0,54%
5	8x4	50	40	100	250	8,2883E-12	8,4241E-12	1,61%
6	8x4	50	27	200	50	4,1098E-12	4,3263E-12	5,00%
7	8x4	50	27	200	100	6,1365E-12	5,9361E-12	3,38%
8	8x4	50	27	200	150	6,9286E-12	6,5731E-12	5,41%
9	8x4	50	27	200	200	7,1589E-12	6,8325E-12	4,78%
10	8x4	50	27	200	250	7,1932E-12	6,9760E-12	3,11%
11	8x4	50	16	400	50	2,4130E-12	2,6964E-12	10,51%
12	8x4	50	16	400	100	3,7196E-12	3,7639E-12	1,18%
13	8x4	50	16	400	150	4,4581E-12	4,3019E-12	3,63%
14	8x4	50	16	400	200	4,8764E-12	4,6472E-12	4,93%
15	8x4	50	16	400	250	5,0991E-12	4,8663E-12	4,78%
16	8x4	50	12	600	50	1,6976E-12	2,0703E-12	18,00%
17	8x4	50	12	600	100	2,6288E-12	2,8790E-12	8,69%
18	8x4	50	12	600	150	3,1851E-12	3,3061E-12	3,66%
19	8x4	50	12	600	200	3,5511E-12	3,6114E-12	1,67%
20	8x4	50	12	600	250	3,7965E-12	3,8368E-12	1,05%
21	8x4	50	9	800	50	1,2945E-12	1,6067E-12	19,43%
22	8x4	50	9	800	100	2,0082E-12	2,2182E-12	9,47%
23	8x4	50	9	800	150	2,4403E-12	2,5487E-12	4,25%
24	8x4	50	9	800	200	2,7362E-12	2,7915E-12	1,98%
25	8x4	50	9	800	250	2,9511E-12	2,9798E-12	0,96%

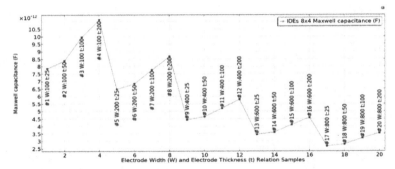

Fig. 10. The 20 capacitance results of the combinations with the variables electrode width (W) and electrode thickness (t). Configuration 8 mm × 4 mm. In the domain you can see the samples starting from $W = 100$ um, $t = 25$ um until the final sample $W = 800$ um, $t = 200$ um.

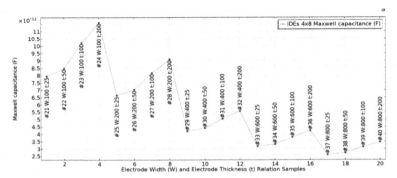

Fig. 11. The 20 capacitance results of the combinations with the variables electrode width (W) and electrode thickness (t). Configuration 4 mm × 8 mm. In the domain you can see the samples starting from $W = 100$ um, $t = 25$ um until the final sample $W = 800$ um, $t = 200$ um.

Table 5 presents the new results obtained by means of the Eq. 8 computed in MAT-LAB, the simulation in COMSOL and the error percentage between these two. Note that the dielectric thickness is constant at 200 um for all tests. With the forty results, there are 2 samples with less than 21% error, 8 samples with a range of 10% to 14% error and 30 samples with less than 10% error. In this way, the simulations are again corroborated with the new equation.

Table 5. Error margin between theoretical and simulated values for the relation W and t.

#	a x b	t	N	W	T	MATLAB	COMSOL	Error
1	4x8	25	20	100	200	7.8481E-12	7.9392E-12	1.15%
2	4x8	50	20	100	200	8.1846E-12	8.4592E-12	3.25%
3	4x8	100	20	100	200	8.8575E-12	1.0212E-11	13.26%
4	4x8	200	20	100	200	1.0203E-11	1.1584E-11	11.92%
5	4x8	25	13.5	200	200	6.6958E-12	6.6350E-12	0.92%
6	4x8	50	13.5	200	200	6.9171E-12	7.0204E-12	1.47%
7	4x8	100	13.5	200	200	7.3599E-12	8.1529E-12	9.73%
8	4x8	200	13.5	200	200	8.2453E-12	9.0806E-12	9.20%
9	4x8	25	8	400	200	4.4147E-12	4.1877E-12	5.42%
10	4x8	50	8	400	200	4.5386E-12	4.3962E-12	3.24%
11	4x8	100	8	400	200	4.7865E-12	5.0326E-12	4.89%
12	4x8	200	8	400	200	5.2824E-12	5.5563E-12	4.93%
13	4x8	25	5.83	600	200	3.1518E-12	3.1555E-12	0.12%
14	4x8	50	5.83	600	200	3.2374E-12	3.3017E-12	1.95%
15	4x8	100	5.83	600	200	3.4084E-12	3.7776E-12	9.77%
16	4x8	200	5.83	600	200	3.7506E-12	4.2256E-12	11.24%
17	4x8	25	4.5	800	200	2.2947E-12	2.5940E-12	11.54%
18	4x8	50	4.5	800	200	2.3567E-12	2.7114E-12	13.08%
19	4x8	100	4.5	800	200	2.4807E-12	3.1180E-12	20.44%
20	4x8	200	4.5	800	200	2.7286E-12	3.4449E-12	20.79%
1	8x4	25	40	100	200	7.9896E-12	7.8455E-12	1.84%
2	8x4	50	40	100	200	8.3350E-12	8.3802E-12	0.54%
3	8x4	100	40	100	200	9.0256E-12	9.9573E-12	9.36%
4	8x4	200	40	100	200	1.0407E-11	1.1106E-11	6.30%
5	8x4	25	27	200	200	6.9287E-12	6.4761E-12	6.99%
6	8x4	50	27	200	200	7.1589E-12	6.8325E-12	4.78%
7	8x4	100	27	200	200	7.6194E-12	7.7510E-12	1.70%
8	8x4	200	27	200	200	8.5402E-12	8.6691E-12	1.49%
9	8x4	25	16	400	200	4.7435E-12	4.4306E-12	7.06%
10	8x4	50	16	400	200	4.8764E-12	4.6471E-12	4.93%
11	8x4	100	16	400	200	5.1420E-12	5.2038E-12	1.19%
12	8x4	200	16	400	200	5.6732E-12	5.7971E-12	2.14%
13	8x4	25	11.5	600	200	3.4581E-12	3.4528E-12	0.15%
14	8x4	50	11.5	600	200	3.5511E-12	3.6114E-12	1.67%
15	8x4	100	11.5	600	200	3.7370E-12	4.1116E-12	9.11%
16	8x4	200	11.5	600	200	4.1089E-12	4.5809E-12	10.30%
17	8x4	25	9	800	200	2.6654E-12	2.6665E-12	0.04%
18	8x4	50	9	800	200	2.7362E-12	2.7915E-12	1.98%
19	8x4	100	9	800	200	2.8779E-12	3.2108E-12	10.37%
20	8x4	200	9	800	200	3.1612E-12	3.5438E-12	10.80%

5 Conclusion

The COMSOL simulation of two configurations of digital electrodes arranged vertically (8 mm × 4 mm) and horizontally (4 mm × 8 mm) has been carried out, the active area and the distance between electrodes has been kept constant, the results have been validated with a model based on mapping to which we have added the capacitance that considers the thickness of electrodes.

It can be concluded that the parameters of electrode width and dielectric thickness have affected the capacity of the device in the same way in both configurations. It was shown that the greater the thickness of the dielectric substrate and the smaller the width of the electrodes, the simulated Maxwell capacitance is greater.

In addition, we note that the capacitance is saturated after constantly increasing the dielectric thickness with the samples observed until its ratio of substrate thickness was approximately 2.5 or when it is proximately half of the periodicity, that is there comes a time when, the greater the dielectric thickness, the increase in capacity is insignificant. Otherwise, what happens with electrode width is that the capacitance increases as the width decreases.

The value of greater capacity in both configurations was found with an electrode width of 100 um and a substrate thickness of 250 um, being 8.52 pF (for 4 × 8) and 8.42 pF (for 8 × 4) for the horizontal and vertical configuration respectively, that it cannot be concluded that only one configuration is more efficient than another. It was found that if we left the distance (d) constant and varied the electrode width (W), this indisputably increases the number of interdigital electrodes (N) which is directly proportional to the capacity.

We recommend further testing with parameters of wider distance between electrodes and substrate thickness, to highlight more significant differences that can differentiate with greater potential which of the two configurations is better.

With regard to the electrode thickness, a new formula was incorporated that allows to extract the capacitance considering different thicknesses of electrodes and in both configurations, it was found that with an electrode width of 100 u, and an electrodes thickness of 200 um the highest capacitance of 11.58 pF (for 4 × 8) and 11.11 pF (for 8 × 4) is obtained. If the substrate thickness is kept constant and the electrode thickness is increased, it can be concluded that the capacitance increases.

References

1. Ho, J., Jow, T.R., Boggs, S.: Historical Introduction to Capacitor Technology. IEEE Electr. Insul. Mag. **26**, 20–25 (2010)
2. Abdul Rahman, M.S., Mukhopadhyay, S.C., Yu, P.-L.: Novel Sensors for Food Inspection: Modelling, Fabrication and Experimentation. Springer International Publishing, Cham (2014)
3. Tsouti, V., Boutopoulos, C., Zergioti, I., Chatzandroulis, S.: Capacitive microsystems for biological sensing. Biosens. Bioelectron. **27**(1), 1–11 (2011). https://doi.org/10.1016/j.bios.2011.05.047
4. Igreja, R., Dias, C.J.: Analytical evaluation of the interdigital electrodes capacitance for a multi-layered structure. Sens. Actuators A **112**(2–3), 291–301 (2004). https://doi.org/10.1016/j.sna.2004.01.040

5. Mazlan, N.S., et al.: Interdigitated electrodes as impedance and capacitance biosensors. In: AIP Conference Proceedings, vol. 1885, p. 020276 (2017)
6. Mackay, S., Hermansen, P., Wishart, D., Chen, J.: Simulations of interdigitated electrode interactions with gold nanoparticles for impedance-based biosensing applications. Sensors **15**, 22192–22208 (2015)
7. National Electrical Manufacturers Association, "NEMA". https://www.nema.org (2021)
8. Alumina Systems GmbH: Alumina systems. https://alumina.systems (2019)
9. Chen, Y., et al.: In-situ selective surface engineering of graphene micro-supercapacitor chips. Nano Res. **15**(2), 1492–1499 (2021). https://doi.org/10.1007/s12274-021-3693-4
10. Mata, M.C., Orpella, A., Domínguez-Pumar, M., Bermejo, S.: Space-charge limited ionic conductivity enhancement in gel polymer electrolyte capacitors by embedding nanoparticles. Electrochimica Acta **393**, 138952 (2021). https://doi.org/10.1016/j.electacta.2021.138952
11. Ludeña-Choez, J., et al.: Capacitance sensitivity study of interdigital capacitive sensor based on graphene for monitoring Nitrates concentrations. Comput. Electron. Agric. **202**, 107361 (2022). https://doi.org/10.1016/j.compag.2022.107361
12. den Otter, M.W.: Aproximate expressions for the capacitance and electrostatic potential of interdigitated electrodes. Sens. Actuators, A **96**, 140–144 (2002)
13. Claudel, J., Alves de Araujo, A. L., Kourtiche, D., Nadi, M., Bourjilat, A.: Optimization of Interdigitated Sensor Characteristics. In: Mukhopadhyay, S.C., George, B., Roy, J.K., Islam, T. (eds.) Interdigital Sensors. SSMI, vol. 36, pp. 91–122. Springer, Cham (2021). https://doi.org/10.1007/978-3-030-62684-6_5
14. Gevorgian, S.S., Martinsson, T., Linner, P.L.J., Kollberg, E.L.: CAD models for multilayered substrate interdigital capacitors. IEEE Trans. Microwave Theory Tech. **44**(6), 896–904 (1996). https://doi.org/10.1109/22.506449
15. Batista, M.: Elfun18 – A collection of MATLAB functions for the computation of elliptic integrals and Jacobian elliptic functions of real arguments. SoftwareX **10**, 100245 (2019). https://doi.org/10.1016/j.softx.2019.100245
16. COMSOL INC.: COMSOL. https://www.comsol.com (2021)

Smart Trends and Applications

Algorithm for Medical Diagnostic Support Using Machine and Deep Learning for Depressive Disorder Based on Electroencephalogram Readings

Lady L. González[1], Giovana F. Vaca[1], Marilyn E. Figueroa[1],
Adriana E. Estrella[1], Evelyn G. González[1], Carolina Cadena-Morejón[2],
Diego A. Almeida-Galárraga[1], Andres Tirado-Espín[2,3],
Jonathan Cruz-Varela[1], and Fernando Villalba-Meneses[1(✉)]

[1] Escuela de Ciencias Biológicas e Ingeniería, Universidad Yachay Tech, Hacienda
San José s/n, San Miguel de Urcuquí 100119, Ecuador
gvillalba@yachaytech.edu.ec
[2] Escuela de Ciencias Matemáticas y Computacionales, Universidad Yachay Tech,
Hacienda San José s/n, San Miguel de Urcuquí 100119, Ecuador
[3] Universidad Complutense de Madrid, 28040 Madrid, CP, Spain

Abstract. Depression is one of the most common mental disorders affecting 121 million people worldwide. Depression is more than a low mood and those who suffer from it can experience a lack of interest in daily activities, lack of concentration, low energy, feelings of worthlessness and in the worst cases, it can lead to suicide. For this reason, correct detection of the disorder is essential to reduce the number of cases of misdiagnosed people. In addition to psychological analysis, EEG signals are also one of the tools that help in the detection of mental disorders, such as depressive disorder. Therefore, the purpose of this study is to develop an algorithm for the detection of depressive disorder based on the classification of EEG signals. For this purpose, machine learning was used with the Welch method and four different classifiers, which are: LDA, LR, KNN and RFC. Also was used neural network that combines (IC-RNN) and (C-DRNN). Despite working with few data from only 26 depressed patients and 29 healthy patients, it could be obtained an accuracy of 57%.

Keywords: Depressive disorder · Medical diagnostic support · Welch method · EEG signal · Classifiers

1 Introduction

1.1 Depressive Disorder

Depressive disorder is a mental disorder with characteristic but nonspecific symptoms and signs of sufficient intensity and duration to interfere with the daily functioning and quality of life of the affected person [20, 31]. This disorder is the leading cause of disability and contributes greatly to the overall burden of disease. It affects both men and women, although it is important to mention that women are the most affected [46]. Also, it is important to mention that worldwide an estimated 5% of adults suffer from depression, and 5.7% of adults over 60 years of age, making it a common mental disorder [23, 46].

Depression is a serious health problem, especially when it is recurrent, and if its intensity is moderate to severe [35]. Moreover, it not only causes suffering to those who suffer from depression, it also interferes with work, school and family activities. One of the main problems that arise in this disease is that people suffering from depression are often not correctly diagnosed, therefore, they do not receive adequate treatment [2]. Likewise, people who do not suffer from depression are misdiagnosed and treated with antidepressants, which can lead to increased anxiety, gastric discomfort or problems in sexual functioning. Consequently, it is important that a proper diagnosis is made to avoid relapses in the disease, or in the worst case, suicide [1, 36]. For this reason, it has been proposed to develop machine learning and deep learning techniques, which will allow us to classify EEG signals to obtain a more accurate diagnosis and at the same time serve as a diagnostic tool.

People may have mild, moderate or severe depressive episodes. Symptoms in these episodes are feelings of sadness, emptiness, loss of concentration and/or interest, low self-esteem, feelings of guilt, sleep problems, low energy, and thoughts of death or suicide. This usually lasts for at least 2 weeks. The different typologies of mood disorders are described in Table 1 [46].

Table 1. Different typologies of mood disorders

Typologies	Description
Single-episode Depressive Disorder	The person experiences a first and only one episode
Recurrent Depressive Disorder	The person has already had at least two depressive episodes
Bipolar Disorder	Depressive episodes alternate with periods of maniac episodes, with symptoms such as euphoria or irritability, increased activity or energy, racing thoughts, and impulsive and reckless behavior

1.2 Electroencephalogram (EEG) for Detection of Depressive Disorder

EEG signals are signals produced in electroencephalograms, where the electrical activity of the brain is recorded [42], and obtained with the use of electrodes placed on the scalp of the patient. These signals are useful, and have helped neurophysiologists to identify pathologies and abnormalities in the patient's EEG data [17, 24]. The altered brain function caused by depressive disorder can be observed in the signals produced in an electroencephalogram, as mentioned by [27]. Many studies have used EEG signal to understand the complex mechanisms behind the disorder of depression and find biomarkers, which are characteristics that can be precisely evaluated in order to identify or diagnose this disorder. The most relevant biomarkers presented in the literature are alpha asymmetry and brain laterality, evoked potential, signal features, functional connectivity, and bands power [11]. It is possible to use linear and nonlinear methods to identify these biomarkers and classify between healthy patients (without depressive disorder) and patients with the disorder. In addition, there are studies using machine learning for the diagnosis and treatment of depressive disorder [48].

[37] Indicates that although the human brain reaches adult size around 12 years of age, there are a number of structural changes that occur in adolescence and young adulthood that may be important in interpreting maturational changes in EEG activity. Surface EEG amplitudes are markedly reduced and are between 10 and 100 µV in children and between 10 and 50 µV in adults. Theta rhythm is common in children under 15 years of age and in sleepy adults. The morphology of theta activity of the child under 15 years of age is irregular. However, at any age, in the wake-sleep transition, it adopts a rhythmic and high-voltage character, greater than 100 µV. The frequency of the alpha rhythm is between 8 and 13 Hz in the normal adult and remains very constant, varying ±1 Hz for years. In childhood, a progressive increase in the frequency of the basic rhythm of the posterior regions is observed: 4 Hz at 4 months of life, 6 Hz at 12 months, 8 Hz at 3 years, 10 Hz at 10 years. Finally, the delta rhythm is a slow rhythm whose activity is between 0.5 and 3.5 Hz in frequency. It is the main activity in the first two years of life. In contrast, delta waves are not seen in the EEG of normal adults, both in the awake and relaxed states. This study has been developed with a database of adolescents and adults, so we cannot generalize the results to all age ranges. Since there are physiological differences in the brain of a child and an adolescent or adult who have already reached brain maturity, and these differences lead to different EEGs [25].

Diagnosing a potential patient with depression is a complex task of looking at the EEG as well as their clinical history [30]. A principal component analysis (PCA) and linear discriminant analysis (LDA) classifier determine whether depression is present or not and provide a valuable tool for the diagnosis made by the specialist. Singular value decomposition (SVD) is a multivariate data analysis technique that can help reduce EEG data sets. In the paper [17], mentions that, fundamental statistical features are extracted from EEG signals by means of PCA-SVD, singular values, which were used to define a pattern of a patient. Dimension reduction with PCA improves LDA performance. The EEG classification result is promising and an alternate application is an automatic diagnostic system [47]. The LDA technique shows that with a good characterization of the EEG signal obtains results with an efficiency of 80%.

The use of EEG is uncommon for the detection of depression, despite the fact that it gives more accurate results [3]. Therefore, the present work proposes the creation of an algorithm capable of reading and filtering EEG signals according to defined parameters, using machine learning to detect depressive disorder in adolescents and adults. In this way, our algorithm would help to avoid misdiagnosis and thus be able to provide adequate and timely treatment, avoiding the aggravation of the disease or the mistreatment of those who do not suffer from it [43]. However, it will still be necessary for the treating physician to identify the type of depressive disorder (e.g., single-episode depressive disorder, recurrent depressive disorder, or bipolar disorder) in order to appropriately medicate the patient. In the future, it is hoped to add portable and accurate software and/or hardware capable of taking EEG signals and, along with the software, providing diagnosis. This will result in a more efficient biomedical device [18].

1.3   State of the Art

In the literature consulted, we find several authors who have dared to use the Welch Method, both for the processing of EEG signals and for the detection of psychiatric illnesses [13]. The Welch Method is an improved periodogram method, it is an estimator of the power spectrum [50]. "Welch method is one of the most popular method of analysis of frequency EEG content". [7] For example, [28] who use the Welch method to find the PSD log (it allows image editing through the use of layers), and later use parameter classification tools such as Adaptive Neuro-Fuzzy Inference System (ANFIS) and Neural Network Pattern Recognition Tool (nprtool), and finally, obtain a depression level diagnosis with a maximum accuracy of 88.32%. On the other hand, we have [27], and [29] who used the Welch Method to calculate the power spectrum of the bands. [27] additionally use multiple cluster functions (MCFS) and classifiers such as Support Vector Machine (SVM), Logistic Regression (LR), Naïve-Bayesian (NB) and Decision Tree (DT), obtaining a maximum accuracy of 88.33%.

In another way, [29] uses Fast Fourier Transform (FFT) to calculate the magnitudes of the bands, and implementing ANN achieves the classification of healthy or depressed people, obtaining a maximum accuracy of 84.00%. But [40] went a little further, using the Welch Method not only to calculate the power spectrum, but also to "splitting the time series signal into (possibly overlap) epochs, computing a modified periodogram of each epoch, and then averaging the power spectrum density estimates". However, he does not show results in terms of the accuracy of his method. Likewise, [49] combines the Welch Method for calculating a power spectral density estimate with a Hamming window (with 50% overlap), managing to apply a combination of machine learning and EEG for the detection of major depressive disorder and anxiety disorder post-traumatic stress. In this case, the authors do not show the accuracy of their methods.

In addition to the literature used to compare the different methods used, we have consulted [11,22,32,48] and their review papers, which have been very useful to have clear concepts and a general idea of the different methods used, and their percentage of accuracy. Based on all this information, we have opted for the Welch Method power band classification combining it with four types of classifiers; LDA, LR, KNN and Random Forest Classifier (RFC). This way we will be able to compare how these classifiers interact with the precision of the final result. In addition, we seek to obtain the same or better results compared to the authors consulted.

2   Materials

Among the materials used in this analysis, there is the database pre-existing, belonging to the MODMA platform (which presents a multimodal open dataset for the analysis of mental disorders) [8]. MODMA ensures that its patients were carefully diagnosed and selected by professional psychiatrists in hospitals. This database has potential recordings related to 3-channel resting events, 26 subjects with major depressive disorder and 29 healthy control subjects, in an age range: 16–56 years [8,41]. For data processing we use Google colaboratory, which is a data analysis and machine learning tool [6]. In addition, for each channel, the Welch method was used to calculate the maximum, the middle, and the center of the spectrum, and to extract the Delta, Theta, Alpha, and Beta power bands and for the training of the neural network, this combines: Inception Convolutional Gated Recurrent Neural Network (IC-RNN), and Convolutional Densely Connected Gated Recurrent Neural Network (C-DRNN) [5].

3   Methods

As mentioned above, the authors of numerous papers consulted have shown that the use of machine learning gives positive results in the detection of depressive disorder. For our goal of achieving a computer-aided diagnosis, we have selected to work with machine and deep learning, which has proven to be efficient for handling high-level feature data.

3.1   Machine Learning Techniques

Feature Extraction

– EEG band power

For the management of eeg signals we use MNE-Python, which allows us to explore, visualize, and analyze human neurophysiological data such as MEG, EEG, sEEG, ECoG, NIRS, and more [15]. In order to extract the features of the signals, the data was converted into an mne type object, considering that the position of the electrodes is according to the standard 10/20 law. Also, each band of each channel of selected data (in this case Fp1, Fpz, and Fp2). The dataset used consists of a 60-second recording, however, 20 s were chosen for signal processing. Furthermore, the signal has a sampled frequency 250 Hz so we worked with a size of 5000 samples for each subject [44].

Then, all EEG signals were highpass filtered with 0.5 Hz cutoff frequency, and lowpass filtered 70 Hz cutoff frequency. The samples were divided into segments with a possible overlapping. The Welch method was applied to calculate power spectrum of EEG bands. For this, the EEG signals are filtered with bandpass butterworth filter to extract four common frequency bands, Delta (0.5–4 Hz), Theta (4–8 Hz), Alpha (8–13 Hz) and Beta (13–30 Hz). The frequencies of each band were considered according to [41], in this paper there are information about data collection. Figure 1 summarizes the procedure to follow for signal classification.

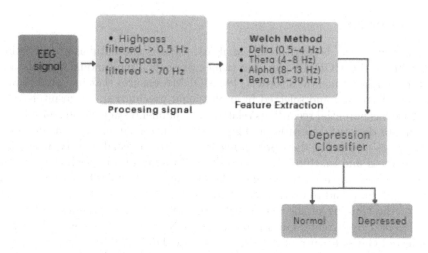

Fig. 1. Block diagram of the machine learning classification with Welch method

3.2 Classification

For the classification of the signals, four types of techniques were used. This in order to find the classifier that would give us a better result. Among them:

– **Linear discriminant analysis (LDA)**
One of the techniques used for data classification is LDA, also known as Fisher's linear discriminant. This method was used to categorize the classes [45]. The LDA function for two classes (c1, c2) is defined as:

$$g(x) = w^t(x) + w_0 \tag{1}$$

where the LDA function uses the following parameters: the characteristics of the input vector (x), the weight (w), and the threshold value(wo) [4].

– **Logistic regression (LR)**
The second technique used in the training is LR. This technique is a powerful technique for classification that fits the training data to a logistic function and the logistic function is a continuous function between 0 and 1 [26]. This is defined as:

$$\pi(x) = \frac{1}{1 + e^{\beta_0 + \beta_1 x_1 + \beta_2 x_2 + \cdots + \beta_n x_n}} \tag{2}$$

This is a binary classification that has x as the input feature vector to the logistic function and β as the parameter vector. The output is the probability of classifying the input data into positive or negative classes [8].

– **K-nearest neighbors classifier (KNN)**
The third technique used is the KNN classifier, which is one of the simple classifications that uses labeled data sets to help predict results. Such data sets are designed to "monitor" or train algorithms to accurately predict outcomes or classify the data [34]. Thus, the labeled inputs and outputs allowed the

model to learn over time while improving its accuracy. This is because the K-NN algorithm uses the feature similarity between the new data points and the points in the training set to predict the values of the new data points [41].

– **Random Forest Classifier (RFC)**
  The fourth method is the RFC which is based on a supervised learning algorithm that can be used for regression and classification problems [9]. Its function in this case was to create decision trees based on a random selection of data samples. In this way, predictions of each tree were obtained. And then he was able to select the best viable solution through votes to predict the disease [10].

3.3 Deep Learning Techniques

Another method that was used for signal classification is a neural network that combines: IC-RNN, and C-DRNN. This combination is called ChronoNet [38], the network is structured by stacking several 1D convolution layers followed by deep gated recursive unit (GRU) layers, which in turn convolution layer uses exponentially varying length filters and the stacked GRU layers are densely connected in a feedback manner (see the Fig. 2).

Unlike the technique used in the Sect. 3.1, in which feature extraction is performed before entering the classifier, the ChronoNet network allows us to extract features as the signal passes through it. Since the multiple filters in the Conv1D layers allow to extract and combine the features from different time scales, therefore a previous extraction of features from the EEG signals is not necessary.

4   Results

4.1 Result of Classification Based on Each Power EEG Bands

For this first part, a classification of the signals was performed using each of the EEG bands separately with 6-fold cross-validation. Table 2 shows the means accuracy obtained by classifying the EEG signals using each band with each previously detailed classifiers. In addition, in this table, we can see the highest accuracy obtained. In this case 56.75%, for the Alpha band using the LDA classifier.

The results obtained can be seen more clearly in Fig. 3, in this we can see that there is greater accuracy for the Alpha band.

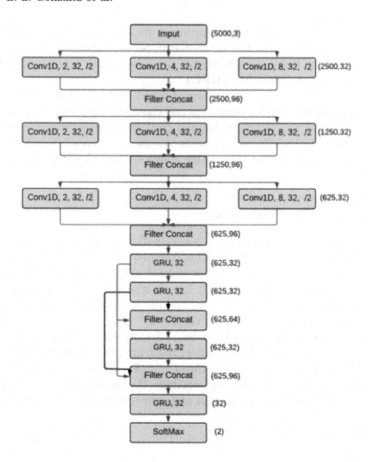

Fig. 2. Block diagram of the Deep Recurrent Neural Network

4.2 Results of Classification Based on Combining Power EEG Bands

For this section, all EEG bands combined were used. In Table 3 you can see the mean accuracy results of 6-fold cross-validation for each classifier. Using this combination, the highest precision is achieved using the classified LDA, which is clearly seen in Fig. 4.

If we compare the results obtained with those of Sect. 4.1, we can see that from the four classifiers used, the LDA presents better results and the LR with a minimal difference. While the RFC and KNN are the ones that present the lowest results. However, the accuracy of the LDA and LR classifiers decreases when using the combination of the EEG bands. This tendency can be seen in Fig. 5.

Table 2. Results of classification accuracy for power EEG bands.

EEG bands	Classifier			
	LDA (%)	LR (%)	KNN (%)	RFC (%)
Delta	54.66	54.45	49.96	49.80
Theta	51.81	52.50	49.48	48.97
Alpha	56.75	52.78	50.88	50.82
Beta	53.19	50.46	48.98	49.20

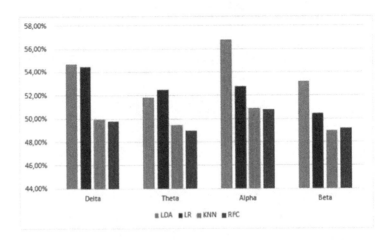

Fig. 3. Comparison of classifier's accuracy by power bands.

4.3 Results of Deep Recurrent Neural Network ChronoNet

For neuronal network training, the same dataset described above is used. Like the section, the data was converted into an mne type object, and a duration of 20 s was used with a sampled frequency 250 Hz. As the three channels (Fp1, Fpz, Fp2) were used, the input of our network is (5000,3). Likewise, a learning rate of 0.01 was used for the SGD optimizer, and a batch size of 56. The network was trained for 100 epochs. The precision obtained by carrying out 5 repetitions of this experiment is 57%.

5   Discussion

Based on the results obtained, it was noted that there is better precision when the Alpha band is used, and in this investigation, the highest precision was achieved using this band. These results are consistent with other researches. In [19], an accuracy of 73.3% was obtained for this band, in which a frequency range between 8–13Hz was used for the frequency band. Furthermore, their research found a statistically significant difference in the Alpha band between the right

324   L. L. González et al.

Table 3. Results of classifiers accuracy with all EEG bands.

EEG bands	Classifier			
	LDA (%)	LR (%)	KNN (%)	RFC (%)
All bands (Delta, theta, alpha, beta)	54.55	54.08	50.40	51.11

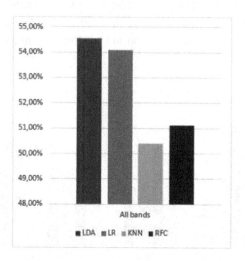

Fig. 4. Accuracy of classifiers for combined power bands.

and left hemispheres of the brain, between normal and depressed people [16]. This is a component that can be taken into account for future research. In addition, a similar result was observed in [14], in this research the highest accuracy was obtained for the alpha and beta bands, using the signals from both cerebral hemispheres. The Alpha band frequency is the same as that used in the previously mentioned work. Similarly, in [12] a significant difference was found for the Alpha band in patients with depression since the difference between the inter-hemispheric power in patients with depression was observed to be larger. Even in an investigation carried out by [21] with a biological psychological approach, it was found that the power of the alpha wave is increased in people with major depressive disorder.

However, there are investigations in which different results have been obtained. For example [40], in this paper the band that presented the highest accuracy is beta, with a frequency of 13–30 Hz. While in [39], the highest precision was obtained in the gamma band with a result of 91.38%, with a frequency between 30–50 Hz. For the present study this band was not taken into account, since the bands that are most commonly used to extract power bands using the Welch method are Delta, Theta, Alpha and Beta [33]. But in a future study, this band could be added to see what results are obtained.

On the other hand, in this work the combination of all the bands was also used. The results we obtained in accuracy were a little lower compared to using

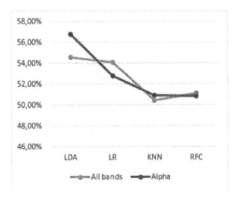

Fig. 5. Comparison of the accuracy between the power of the alpha band and the combination of all the bands.

the bands separately. Since with the alpha band using the LDA classifier, the highest accuracy obtained was 56.75%, while the highest accuracy using all the bands was 54.55%, it was using the same LDA classifier. This result differs from those obtained in the literature, since in other investigations it has been observed that there is an increase in precision when all the bands are used. For example, in [19] using all the bands, it get 90% accuracy compared to 73.3% using only the alpha band. In addition, in this study the classifier that gave the best result is LR. The same thing happened in [39], in this work the accuracy rose to 92% from the 91.38% obtained for the Gamma band, using an E-KNN classifier.

On the other hand, for the implemented neural network, a 57% accuracy was obtained. Although this technique gave us the highest precision in this study, the difference with the results obtained from machine learning is not significant. It was expected that with this technique higher results would be obtained, but the expected result was not. For example, in [12] machine learning and deep learning techniques are contrasted, and the best result was obtained with the convolutional neural network.

The relevance of this algorithm is that it aims to contribute to a better prediction of depressive disorder using EEG signals. In this way, reduce the number of people misdiagnosed with depression, by confusing these with other conditions. For this reason, it can be used as a basis for future jobs or other people who want to follow this line of mental disorders. Nevertheless, given the precision achieved in this study, it would be interesting to apply new techniques that allow us to achieve better precision. In addition, to try with other databases that could be obtained to check if the quality of the chosen data was ideal.

Among the limitations that we found during the development of this work was the poor accessibility to data of EEG signals from patients with depressive disorders, therefore our results were lower compared to related works, this we consider a problem, since despite the fact that depression is currently a problem that is growing, free access data is very few.

6 Conclusions

The Welch method turns out to be a useful technique to extract the power spectral density. In this case, it allowed us to extract the Delta (0.5–4 Hz), Theta (4–8 Hz), Alpha (8–13 Hz), and Beta (13–30 Hz) bands from the EEG signals. Which were used to make a classification with four different types of classifiers (LDA, LR, KNN and RFC). In this case, a better precision was obtained with the LDA classifier, both for classifying bands separately and when combining them, obtaining an accuracy of 56.75% when using the Alpha band, and 54.55% when combining them all. On another hand, for the implemented neural network, a 57% accuracy was obtained, it is the highest precision in this study but the difference with the results obtained from machine learning is not significant.

During the development of our algorithm, different tests were performed with different classifiers and different parameters based on different papers. Even so, it is important to emphasize that not in all the papers the best classifier was the LDA, since this depends on the vector used. In which we could notice that the LDA classifier gave us better results. This also depends on whether the bands are combined or not, since the frequency in this case is relevant for network training.

For future works, an alliance could be made with clinics that can provide more current and specific data. In addition, it would also be possible to work with more specific parameters, such as age, consumption of psychotropic substances, work, social or economic status. Thus, this information could emphasize the prevalence of depressive disorder in a more specific group of people.

References

1. Aalbers, G., McNally, R.J., Heeren, A., De Wit, S., Fried, E.I.: Social media and depression symptoms: a network perspective. J. Exp. Psychol. Gen. **148**(8), 1454 (2019)
2. Aguiar-Salazar, E., Villalba-Meneses, F., Tirado-Espín, A., Amaguaña-Marmol, D., Almeida-Galárraga, D.: Rapid detection of cardiac pathologies by neural networks using ECG signals (1D) and SECG images (3D). Computation **10**(7), 112 (2022)
3. Akbari, H., Sadiq, M.T., Payan, M., Esmaili, S.S., Baghri, H., Bagheri, H.: Depression detection based on geometrical features extracted from SODP shape of EEG signals and binary PSO. Traitement du Signal **38**(1) (2021)
4. Balakrishnama, S., Ganapathiraju, A.: Linear discriminant analysis-a brief tutorial. Inst. Signal Inf. Process. **18**(1998), 1–8 (1998)
5. Barbé, K., Pintelon, R., Schoukens, J.: Welch method revisited: nonparametric power spectrum estimation via circular overlap. IEEE Trans. Signal Process. **58**(2), 553–565 (2009)
6. Branding, M.: Google colaboratory colab - guía completa español. Marketing branding (2020)
7. Budunova, K., Kravchenko, V., Churikov, D.: Application of the family of Kravchenko-Rvachev atomic weight functions (windows) in welch method EEG power spectral density estimation, pp. 500–506 (2019)

8. Cai, H., et al.: Modma dataset: a multi-modal open dataset for mental-disorder analysis. arXiv preprint arXiv:2002.09283 (2020)
9. Caicho, J., et al.: Diabetic retinopathy: detection and classification using alexnet, googlenet and resnet50 convolutional neural networks, pp. 259–271 (2022)
10. Chaudhary, A., Kolhe, S., Kamal, R.: An improved random forest classifier for multi-class classification. Inf. Process. Agric. 3(4), 215–222 (2016)
11. De Aguiar Neto, F.S., Rosa, J.L.G.: Depression biomarkers using non-invasive EEG: a review. Neurosci. Biobehav. Rev. 105, 83–93 (2019)
12. Duan, L., et al.: Machine learning approaches for MDD detection and emotion decoding using EEG signals. Front. Hum. Neurosci. 14, 284 (2020)
13. Ergin, T., Ozdemir, M.A., Akan, A.: Emotion recognition with multi-channel EEG signals using visual stimulus, pp. 1–4 (2019)
14. Forouzandeh, N., Saeedi, M., Maghooli, K.: Depression diagnosis based on KNN algorithm and EEG signals. Int. J. Smart Electr. Engi. 10(01), 17–22 (2021)
15. Gramfort, A., et al.: MEG and EEG data analysis with MNE-Python. Front. Neurosci. 7(267), 1–13 (2013). https://doi.org/10.3389/fnins.2013.00267
16. Gualsaquí, M.G., et al.: Convolutional neural network for imagine movement classification for neurorehabilitation of upper extremities using low-frequency EEG signals for spinal cord injury, pp. 272–287 (2022)
17. Guevara, G.L.: Classification of egg signals for diagnosing depression. Departamento de Psiquiatria y Salud Mental, Facultad de Medicina Universidad Nacional Autonoma de Mexico (2016)
18. Herrera-Romero, B., Almeida-Galárraga, D., Salum, G.M., Villalba-Meneses, F., Gudiño-Gomezjurado, M.: Gusignal: an informatics tool to analyze glucuronidase gene expression in arabidopsis thaliana roots. IEEE/ACM Trans. Comput. Biol. Bioinform. 20(2), 1073–1080 (2022)
19. Hosseinifard, B., Moradi, M.H., Rostami, R.: Classifying depression patients and normal subjects using machine learning techniques and nonlinear features from eeg signal. Comput. Methods Programs Biomed. 109(3), 339–345 (2013)
20. Hu, R.: Diagnostic and statistical manual of mental disorders: DSM-IV. In: Encyclopedia of the Neurological Sciences, vol. 25, no. 2, pp. 4–8 (2003)
21. Kemp, A., et al.: Disorder specificity despite comorbidity: resting EEG alpha asymmetry in major depressive disorder and post-traumatic stress disorder. Biol. Psychol. 85(2), 350–354 (2010)
22. Khosla, A., Khandnor, P., Chand, T.: Automated diagnosis of depression from EEG signals using traditional and deep learning approaches: a comparative analysis. Biocybern. Biomed. Eng. 42(1), 108–142 (2021)
23. Köhler-Forsberg, O., et al.: Association between c-reactive protein (CRP) with depression symptom severity and specific depressive symptoms in major depression. Brain Behav. Immun. 62, 344–350 (2017)
24. Lakshmi, M.R., Prasad, T., Prakash, D.V.C.: Survey on EEG signal processing methods. Int. J. Adv. Res. Comput. Sci. Softw. Eng. 4(1) (2014)
25. Lu, L.H., et al.: Relationships between brain activation and brain structure in normally developing children. Cereb. Cortex 19(11), 2595–2604 (2009)
26. Maalouf, M.: Logistic regression in data analysis: an overview. Int. J. Data Anal. Tech. Strat. 3(3), 281–299 (2011)
27. Mahato, S., Paul, S.: Classification of depression patients and normal subjects based on electroencephalogram (EEG) signal using alpha power and theta asymmetry. J. Med. Syst. 44(1), 1–8 (2020)
28. Mallikarjun, H., Suresh, H.: Depression level prediction using EEG signal processing, pp. 928–933 (2014)

29. Mantri, S., Patil, D., Agrawal, P., Wadhai, V.: Non invasive EEG signal processing framework for real time depression analysis, pp. 518–521 (2015)
30. Matamoros-Alcivar, E., et al.: Implementation of MPC and PID control algorithms to the artificial pancreas for diabetes mellitus type 1, pp. 1–6 (2021)
31. Mingote Adán, J.C., Gálvez Herrer, M., Pino Cuadrado, P.d., Gutiérrez García, M.: El paciente que padece un trastorno depresivo en el trabajo. Medicina y seguridad del trabajo 55(214), 41–63 (2009)
32. Mumtaz, W., Xia, L., Ali, S.S.A., Yasin, M.A.M., Hussain, M., Malik, A.S.: Electroencephalogram (EEG)-based computer-aided technique to diagnose major depressive disorder (MDD). Biomed. Signal Process. Control 31, 108–115 (2017)
33. Niles, D.N., et al.: COVID-19 pulmonary lesion classification using CNN software in chest X-ray with quadrant scoring severity parameters, pp. 370–382 (2022)
34. Peterson, L.E.: K-nearest neighbor. Scholarpedia 4(2), 1883 (2009)
35. Piscoya Tenorio, J.L., Heredia Rioja, W.V.: Niveles de ansiedad y depresión en estudiantes de medicina de universidades de lambayeque-2018 (2018)
36. Rice, F., et al.: Adolescent and adult differences in major depression symptom profiles. J. Affect. Disord. 243, 175–181 (2019)
37. Rodríguez Martínez, E.I.: Indicadores de maduración cerebral y su relación con la memoria de trabajo (2014)
38. Roy, S., Kiral-Kornek, I., Harrer, S.: Chrononet: a deep recurrent neural network for abnormal EEG identification, pp. 47–56 (2019)
39. Saeedi, M., Saeedi, A., Maghsoudi, A.: Major depressive disorder assessment via enhanced k-nearest neighbor method and EEG signals. Phys. Eng. Sci. Med. 43(3), 1007–1018 (2020)
40. Shen, J., Zhao, S., Yao, Y., Wang, Y., Feng, L.: A novel depression detection method based on pervasive EEG and EEG splitting criterion, pp. 1879–1886 (2017)
41. Shi, Q., Liu, A., Chen, R., Shen, J., Zhao, Q., Hu, B.: Depression detection using resting state three-channel EEG signal. arXiv preprint arXiv:2002.09175 (2020)
42. Supriya, S., Siuly, S., Wang, H., Zhang, Y.: Automated epilepsy detection techniques from electroencephalogram signals: a review study. Health Inf. Sci. Syst. 8(1), 1–15 (2020)
43. Suquilanda-Pesántez, J., et al.: Prediction of Parkinson's disease severity based on gait signals using a neural network and the fast fourier transform, pp. 3–18 (2020)
44. Suquilanda-Pesántez, J.D., Salazar, E.D.A., Almeida-Galárraga, D., Salum, G., Villalba-Meneses, F., Gomezjurado, M.E.G.: NIFtHool: an informatics program for identification of NifH proteins using deep neural networks. F1000Research 11 (2022)
45. Tene-Hurtado, D., et al.: Brain tumor segmentation based on 2D U-net using MRI multi-modalities brain images, pp. 345–359 (2022)
46. WHO: Depression. World Health Organization (2021)
47. Yanchatuña, O., et al.: Skin lesion detection and classification using convolutional neural network for deep feature extraction and support vector machine (2021)
48. Yasin, S., Hussain, S.A., Aslan, S., Raza, I., Muzammel, M., Othmani, A.: EEG based major depressive disorder and bipolar disorder detection using neural networks: a review. Comput. Methods Programs Biomed. 202, 106007 (2021)
49. Zandvakili, A., Philip, N.S., Jones, S.R., Tyrka, A.R., Greenberg, B.D., Carpenter, L.L.: Use of machine learning in predicting clinical response to transcranial magnetic stimulation in comorbid posttraumatic stress disorder and major depression: a resting state electroencephalography study. J. Affect. Disord. 252, 47–54 (2019)
50. Zhao, L., He, Y.: Power spectrum estimation of the welch method based on imagery EEG, vol. 278, pp. 1260–1264 (2013)

Effects of a Robotic Lower-Limb Orthosis on Gait Based on the Analysis of sEMG Signals and Kinematic Data: Preliminary Results

J. Souza-Lima[1], A. C. Villa-Parra[2]([✉]), L. Vargas-Valencia[1], D. Delisle-Rodriguez[3], and T. Freire-Bastos[1]

[1] Robotic and Assistive Technology Lab, Universidade Federal do Espirito Santo, Vitoria, Brazil
[2] Biomedical Engineering Research Group GIIB, Universidad Politécnica Salesiana, Cuenca, Ecuador
avilla@ups.edu.ec
[3] Santos Dumont Institute, Macaiba, Brazil

Abstract. Devices such as robotic orthosis and exoskeletons oriented to assist mobility are required to support rehabilitation treatments and to improve quality of life of disability population. In order to evaluate these devices, kinematic data and myoelectric activity are used, thus, robust protocols and analysis can demonstrate the impact of this technology. The aim of this work is to study the effects on surface electromyography (sEMG) and inertial signals for healthy subjects and chronic stroke survivors when using a robotic lower-limb orthosis (ALLOR). Kinematics effects evaluated on hip flexion-extension angles show that they present high bilateral reproducibility for both groups of four healthy subjects and one post-stroke patient, achieving a strong concordance correlation ($\rho c > 0.80$). Furthermore, a strong concordance correlation ($\rho c > 0.80$) of knee. Flexion/extension angles was achieved at one side for five healthy subjects and one post-stroke patient. On the other hand, effects evaluated on myoelectric activity through sEMG show that, for a post-stroke patient, a significant increase ($p < 0.05$) was obtained for activation over the Erector Spinae muscle at L4 level and Semitendinosus muscle at the left side. For the other post-stroke patient, a significant decrease ($p < 0.05$) was noticed for activation over the Erector Spinae muscle at L4 level and Rectus femoris muscle. This research also presents results related to the satisfaction level regarding the use of ALLOR through the Quebec User Evaluation of Satisfaction with Assistive Technology (QUEST 2.0). From the outcomes of this research, we believe our results may be used to improve protocols for post-stroke rehabilitation.

Keywords: robotic lower limb orthosis · stroke · electromyography · kinematic · gait assistance

Supported by organization CAPES.

F. R. Narváez et al. (Eds.): SmartTech-IC 2022, CCIS 1705, pp. 329–341, 2023.
https://doi.org/10.1007/978-3-031-32213-6_24

1 Background

Chronic diseases, such as stroke, can greatly affect a normal gait, increasing the risk of falls [1]. As a result, many post-stroke patients use gait support devices, such as crutches, canes, and walkers [2]. Studies have shown promising results employing lower-limb orthoses to assist these patients during walking, as such devices reduce energy expenditure, allow early rehabilitation, promoting physical exercise, and may improve mobility and independence in non-ambulatory people, enhancing gait parameters as speed, step length and balance associated with gait stability [1,3–6].

Previous research has concluded that post-stroke patients undergoing gait training with robotic devices in combination with physical rehabilitation increased the chance of walking independently, in addition to get higher gait speed, provide higher duration and more repetitious walking practice, and have more participation in the therapy than conventional training [7,8]. The evaluation of the effect of the rehabilitation treatment include standardized questionnaires and instrumental gait analysis, in order to collect data [9].

In fact, robotic rehabilitation provides an intervention that is complementary to conventional gait therapies. For instance, when using robotic lower-limb orthoses and exoskeletons, these act in parallel to the human body, aiding spatial movement between segments and offering different modalities to control and execute physical exercises [11–14].

However, further studies are needed to elucidate the more suitable devices and training protocols to achieve favourable outcomes [1,8,10]. As an example, people affected by stroke normally use mal-adaptive and non-effective compensatory strategies, which are caused by specific adaption of the paresis on the affected side, for support, balance, and progression phases of gait purposes [21]. In this case, a robotic exoskeleton can allow the user to get greater independence to perform functional and work activities [4,6,14].

Rehabilitation protocols can include monitoring muscle activity using surface electromyography (sEMG) in order to evaluate the usability of the rehabilitation technology with a non-invasive technique. This approach can provide information to avoid injury and optimize rehabilitation therapies [15,16] and also to propose rehabilitation devices with controllers based on motion intention from sEMG [17, 18]. Thus, the quantitative evaluation of these devices is fundamental to estimate their biomechanical effectiveness, allowing the development and validation of this novel technology.

In addition, it is important to also evaluate its usability, which includes relevant points, such as ease of use, comfort, and safety [19,20].

The aim of this work is to study the effects on sEMG and inertial signals for healthy subjects and chronic stroke survivors when using a robotic lower-limb orthosis. The work also provides a comprehensive description of these effects, considering our findings. Inertial and sEMG signals were used to compare the user's performance for both non-assisted and orthoses-assisted gait conditions. Sagittal, frontal, and transverse plane kinematics, as well as muscle activations over trunk and lower limbs, were analysed for both gait conditions. In this regard, we hypothesized that the use of an exoskeleton will (1) change joint angular motion during gait, and (2) reduce muscle activation time and amplitude.

2   Materials and Methods

2.1   Subjects

Thirteen subjects were enrolled in this study: eleven healthy subjects (U1-U11), aged between 22 to 38 years (8 males and 3 females) without motor dysfunction; and two post-stroke patients (P1 and P2) with left hemispheric paresis, aged 53 and 58 years old (1 male and 1 female), and presenting a clinical history of injury from 9 months to 21 months, assisted by the Physical Rehabilitation Center of Espirito Santo - CREFES/Brazil. Patients with significant balance and cognitive alteration were excluded of this study, based on their score in the Berg Balance Scale [22] and Mini Mental State Exam - MMSE [23].

This study was approved by the Ethics Committee of UFES/Brazil (CAAE: 64801316.5.0000.5542) and all volunteers read and signed the Consent Form.

2.2   Robotic Lower-Limb Orthosis ALLOR

In this research, the robotic lower-limb orthosis ALLOR (termed Advanced Lower Limb Orthosis for Rehabilitation - ALLOR), built at the Centre for Assistive Technology at UFES/Brazil, was used here, which is shown in Fig. 1. ALLOR consists of an active knee joint with one degree of freedom, designed to be used on the left leg. During walking, ALLOR can be used without any support device, however, depending on the user's clinical condition, an additional device, such as walker, cane, parallel bar, or crutch is required to provide a safe gait for users.

In this study, a conventional four-wheels walker was used to provide stability and safety to the users when wearing this robotic lower-limb orthosis. ALLOR has a DC Motor, Harmonic Drive, PC 104, an instrumented insole, a potentiometer, a Hall effect sensor, a torque sensor, and a backpack used to allow support, alignment and weight redistribution over the user's body (see Fig. 1(a)).

For gait assistance, the control strategy used in ALLOR is based on admittance control [24]. Thereby, when the support gait phase is identified, the orthosis gradually provides a suitable support for knee joint, preventing the user's fall.

2.3   Signal Acquisition

The sEMG signals from trunk and lower-limbs muscles were collected using the data acquisition equipment BrainNET BNT36 (from EMSA/Brazil). Ten sEMG channels were used, with a frequency range 10 Hz to 100 Hz, sampled 600 Hz. These signals were bilaterally collected on the Erector Spinae (ES) (at levels T7, T12 and L4), Rectus Femoris (RF) and Semitendinosus (S) muscles (see Fig. 1(b) and (c)).

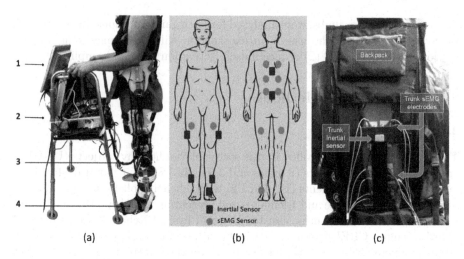

Fig. 1. (a) Setup 1. Monitor, 2. walker, 3. ALLOR, 4. instrumented insole; (b) electrodes and sensor locations; (c) backpack adaptation and sensors locations.

A motion capture system (Tech MCS v 3.0, from Technaid/Spain) composed of seven inertial sensors was used to acquire inertial information from the user. Data from body segment orientation was collected at the spine and lower limbs in a quaternion format, using the Tech MCS Studio software, sampled 50 Hz (see Fig. 1(b)and (c)).

2.4 Protocol

The healthy and post-stroke subjects used the walker as body weight support during the trials, which were evaluated in two different situations, at self-selected velocity for: (a) non-assisted walking, where all of them walked 10 m using the walker; (b) assisted walking, where they walked 10 m, using the active orthosis ALLOR attached on their left leg.

Additionally, to evaluate the ALLOR regarding satisfaction related to the use of this Assistive Technology, the QUEST 2.0 instrument was used [25].

2.5 Data Processing and Analysis

The sEMG signals were pre-processed by a bandpass filter zero-phase shift forward/backward (Butterworth, 2nd order), 20 Hz to 100 Hz. Then, the envelope of the sEMG signals corresponding to each filtered sEMG channel was computed, first rectifying the signals, and after smoothing these rectified signals by applying the root-mean square (RMS) over sliding windows of 100 ms, over-lapped at the sampling rate. Afterwards, these enveloped signals were segmented, considering each gait cycle determined by the angular velocity obtained from the inertial sensor placed on the users' left foot.

The gait cycle normalization (percentage of gait cycle) into the time domain was done with the initial contact events detected by the inertial sensors, which are synchronized with the equipment for signal acquisition. Statistical analysis was performed using the Wilcoxon non-parametric test, considering a significance level of $p < 0.05$, and comparing the mean amplitude of the muscle activation peaks during the normal non-assisted gait, and the gait with ALLOR.

The kinematic parameters of the hip, knee and ankle joints were estimated using a sensor-to-body calibration procedure as well as a joint angle estimation method (sagittal plane) previously presented in [26].

Frontal and transverse planes for trunk evaluation was also used. Mean joint angles were calculated for each healthy participant using thirty gait cycles. For the post-stroke patients, twelve gait cycles were used. The first walking trial, in both groups, was considered an adaptation trial and was not considered in the analysis.

According to a previous study [25], the inertial sensors used in this work (model Tech IMUs v 3.0 from Technaid, Spain) presented on the sagittal plane a RMSE approximately $<2°$, with an excellent reliability in terms of Concordance Correlation Coefficient (CCC), with $\rho c > 0.98$.

On frontal and transversal planes, RMSE was approximately $<15°$, with a poor reliability ($\rho c < 0.40$). However, in this work, these planes were assessed only for the trunk, and the range of motion was between $±10°$. In this interval, RMSE was $<5°$ ($\rho c > 0.69$).

On the other hand, the term Mediolateral Rotation (ML) was used here referring to movements on the sagittal plane, anteroposterior rotation (AP) to the frontal plane, and proximal distal rotation (PD) to the transverse plane. The joint angles were also normalized as a percentage of the gait cycle. It is worth commenting that the ρc value used here evaluates the reproducibility of angular variation between the conditions studied, being considered moderate to high for $\rho c > 0.80$ [25].

3 Results

3.1 Myoelectric Activity

All healthy subjects decreased bilaterally their activation (see Fig. 2(a) and (b)) during the assisted gait, which was significant at bilateral Erector Spinae on level T12 and Semitendinosus. For the right side at Erector Spinae on level L4, and left side Erector Spinae on level T7 and Rectus Femoris.

In contrast, the post-stroke patient P1 (see Fig. 2(c) and (d)) increased bilaterally his activation over the Erector Spinae at T7 and L4 levels ($p < 0.01$). Furthermore, a significant muscle activation increase ($p < 0.01$) was also achieved on the Semitendinosus and Rectus Femoris muscles. As a highlight, patient P1 activated less the right Erector Spinae at T12 level, presenting non-myoelectric activity over the left Rectus Femoris.

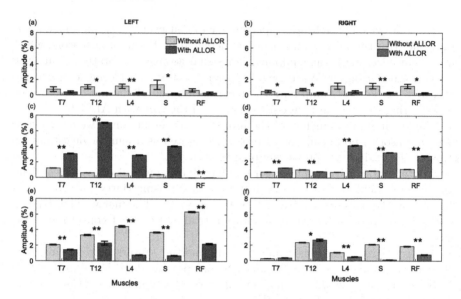

Fig. 2. Comparison of myoelectric activation of Erector spinae at T7, T12 and L4 levels, Semitendinosus (S), and Rectus Femoris (RF) between non-assisted (light) and ALLOR-assisted gait (dark). Green vertical bars represent right side; blue bars represent left side. (a) Right side of healthy users; (b) Left hemisphere of healthy users; (c) Right side of patient 1; (d) Left side of patient 1; (e) Right side of patient 2; (d) Left side of patient 2. $*$ $p < 0.05$ $**$ $p < 0.01$. (Color figure online)

On the other hand, the post-stroke patient P2 (see Fig. 2(e) and (f)) decreased $(p < 0.01)$ her muscle activation at the left side and increased her muscle activation at right T7 and T12 levels, being considered significant $(p < 0.05)$ at T7.

3.2 Kinematic Analysis

Low reproducibility was obtained on mediolateral (ML, flexion-extension), proximal-distal (PD, rotation) and antero-posterior (AP, lateral balance) rotation axes for trunk movements when comparing non-assisted and ALLOR-assisted walking conditions for both healthy subjects and post-stroke patients P1 and P2, as shown in Fig. 3 and Fig. 4(a–c) $(\rho c < 0.62)$.

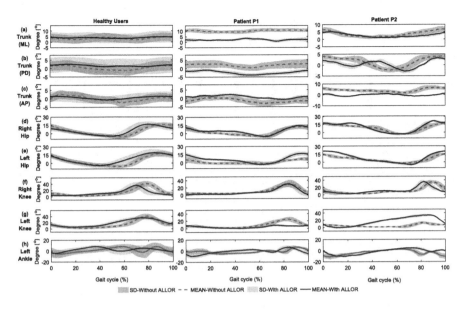

Fig. 3. Non-assisted and ALLOR-assisted walking results for both healthy subjects and post-stroke patients

Notice that healthy subjects restricted to neutral aligned erect posture during trunk flexion-extension at assisted walking. Patient P1, when performing assisted walking, reduced his trunk flexion angles ($8.20° \pm 0.97$), and increased his anteroposterior rotation ($2.17° \pm 0.54$) towards the left. On the other hand, Patient P2 increased her anteroposterior rotation towards the right ($4.35° \pm 1.65$) and corrected her neutral aligned erect posture during proximal-distal rotation ($1.05° \pm 1.97$), as shown in Fig. 3.

Furthermore, a moderate to high reproducibility of hip flexion-extension movements was obtained on both body sides when heathy subjects U5, U6, U7 and U10 executed non-assisted and assisted gait (ρc between 0.83 and 0.96). Also, notice that a moderate reproducibility of hip flexion-extension was obtained for Patient P2 ($\rho c > 0.80$).

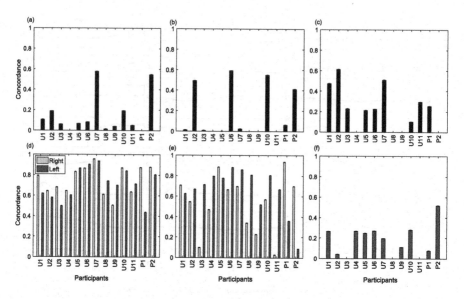

Fig. 4. Concordance Correlation Coefficient (pc) of healthy users (U1-U11) and post-stroke patients (P1, P2) in the comparison between non-assisted and ALLOR-assisted gait. (a) Trunk mediolateral translation, (b) Trunk proximo-distal translation, (c) Trunk antero-posterior translation, (d) Hip Flexion, (e) Knee Flexion, (f) Ankle Plantar flexion and Dorsiflexion. Green vertical bars represent right side; blue bars represent left side. (Color figure online)

Patient P1 presented high reproducibility only for hip flexion-extension, corresponding to the right side, increasing his range of motion (11.33° ± 3.85) over the left side during hip flexion-extension for the assisted condition ($\rho c > 0.87$). Moreover, a moderate to high reproducibility of knee flexion-extension movements was achieved for the right side of healthy subject U5, and for the left side of subjects U6, U7, U8, U10, as shown in Figs. 2 and 3(e) (ρc between 0.80 and 0.89).

It is worth noting that the mean stance phase time decreased on left leg for all healthy subjects using ALLOR, increasing consequently the mean swing phase time over their right leg. In addition, a high reproducibility ($\rho c > 0.93$) of the right knee flexion-extension was obtained for Patient P1 for both gait conditions, but he reduced the left knee flexion-extension range of motion (about 14.90° ± 5.58) during the swing phase. Patient P2 presented a low reproducibility ($\rho c < 0.70$), performing knee flexion-extension for both body sides, achieving the highest left knee flexion-extension range of motion (about 22.88° ± 5.50) and the lowest stance phase time for the right leg using ALLOR. Low reproducibility ($\rho c < 0.55$) was obtained for all participants when comparing ankle dorsi-plantar flexion movements for both gait conditions.

3.3   Technology Satisfaction

The Quebec User Evaluation of Satisfaction with Assistive Technology (QUEST 2.0) test was used to analyze the post-stroke patient's satisfaction walking with ALLOR, considering scores from 0 to 5. As a result, our robotic system achieved score of 3.50 ± 0.50 for dimension, 3.50 ± 0.50 for weight, 5.00 ± 0.00 for adjustments, 5.00 ± 0.00 for safety, 5.00 ± 0.00 for durability, 5.00 ± 0.00 for facility, 4.50 ± 0.50 for comfort, and 3.50 ± 0.50 for efficacy.

4   Discussion and Conclusions

This research had as main objective to evaluate the effects of using a robotic knee orthosis on sEMG and kinematics for healthy subjects and chronic stroke survivors during gait. A comprehensive description of these effects was carried out, considering our findings. Dynamic balance during gait involves a complex sensorimotor integration, and it is influenced by age, kind of pathology, unstable surfaces, and other factors [27]. In addition trunk and lower limb motor control seem to be the best predictors of gait recovery [5].

To maintain the balance during these interference, compensatory strategies can be adopted, which help in the accomplishment of the daily tasks and execution of exercises in the short term. However, for post-stroke patients, these conditions can lead to musculoskeletal injuries, pain, and reduction of the joint mobility as well as risk of falls [28].

Among the changes in the trunk movements, it is possible to emphasize that ten out of eleven healthy subjects presented reduction at the angular variation in flexion of this segment, and three out of them presented reduced trunk rotation values. The reduction of trunk movements was also found in another work [27], which was justified by the postural stability provided by the exoskeleton. In addition to this variation, three out of these subjects presented trunk flexor pattern throughout the walk using the exoskeleton, and two maintained a left rotation pattern.

Only three subjects had important angular changes in the lateralization movements, all of them with reduction of the angular variation during the use of the orthosis. In addition, we observed in our study a variability on hip and knee angle patterns, even in the left knee, where the exoskeleton was directly controlled. The increase of knee flexion in the swing phase on the impaired leg was also reported by [29] for a population of chronic stroke survivors.

For four healthy subjects, a standardization of the ankle movement was observed in the initial contact, which usually occurs with the foot in a slight ankle dorsi-plantar flexion, in a neutral position or in a small dorsiflexion, that can be observed in Fig. 2. A previous study [30], conducted with a motion support equipment during walking, showed an ankle pattern like the found here, with such movement being intensified by the resistance imposed by the equipment. Then, this suggests, for our findings, that there is a resistance of ALLOR to the subjects during gait.

The subjects adopted different gait strategies, and a significant difference was found in the comparison of the sEMG peaks for all healthy users, except subjects U8 and U11 (Fig. 4). This differs from the study of [31], in which a significant difference was detected only in the RF and medial gastrocnemius muscles, presenting an established pattern in gait with their robotic device acting on the hip in 30 elderly subjects evaluated.

The patient P1 presented a statistically significant difference at all muscle activation analysis ($p < 0.05$) in the comparative analysis between the two walking modalities, consistent with the presence of large angular variation previously discussed (Fig. 4). There was no pattern in the variation of muscle activation peak in this subject at the highest trunk levels (T7 and T12), but it was possible to notice an increase in the muscular activation of the ES at the L4 level, bilaterally. In relation to the lower limbs, there was an increase in the level of muscle activation of STs and right RF, but without variation in the peak of left RF muscle activation, which presented a very low muscle contraction (probably as a sequel of hemiparesis to the left). In addition, there was an anticipation of muscle activation peak with ALLOR, which is consistent with the kinematic analysis that shows a shorter support time on the left lower limb. The increase of the muscular activation of the lower limbs, also found in [32], was justified by these authors by the limitation of movements of the hip abduction and rotation, causing the subject to exercise greater muscular activity in Rectus Femoris and Gastrocnemius, avoiding the contact of the foot with the ground during the balance phase of this limb.

Regarding the patient P2 (Fig. 4), our study did not detect a significant difference ($p > 0.05$) in the comparative analysis between the free and ALLOR gait, evidencing a better adaptation to the walker. As shown by the kinematic analysis of the trunk, this subject obtained a reduction in muscle contraction and consequent trunk movement, which is a probable variation resulting from the body stability with the use of ALLOR [27].

In relation to QUEST, the items related to size, weight and efficacy of ALLOR were identified with lower scores, whereas the items of evaluation of adjustments, safety, durability, ease, and comfort presented mean values higher than 4.50. As ALLOR is a prototype, it was expected to obtain low value in the analysis of comfort, which, positively, presented a good score. The comfort is directly related to the user's interaction with the device [19,20], in this case evidencing a good adaptation to the imposed controller as a gait aid. The patients, especially, related optimistic comments about rehabilitation therapy supported by technology, which agrees with other experiences of exoskeleton-based physiotherapy [8]. For improvements in size and weight, structural adjustments are required, such as the use of other materials in the composition of the orthosis.

For more conclusive statements, specially regarding efficacy, there is a need for long-term assessments and a greater number of volunteers are needed in our study. This to include consider a sample of healthy, older adults for comparison and evaluate acute responses during gait with the active orthosis and the walker.

It is worth commenting that this is a preliminary study with a relatively small sample of impaired participants. The reduced number of participants that underwent this research as well as the variability of the parameters is a limitation to be highlighted, and by now, it is not possible to conclude a muscular or kinematic response pattern of the patients. However, the previous results obtained are important for the improvement of our robotic lower limb orthosis (total weight and hip support mechanism) and for the creation of specific experimental protocols for stroke and other neurological dysfunctions, required in research studies related to rehabilitation [4].

This study highlights the changes in muscle activation and kinematics patterns when healthy and post-stroke individuals adapt themselves to assistance of a robotic knee exoskeleton. The use of an exoskeleton change joint angular motion measured during gait and reduce muscle activation time and amplitude.

With the increasing understanding about how this population adapts to robotic lower limb orthosis, this research has contributed to show the importance of a study to make a correct choice of exoskeleton based on its characteristics and tasks it is exposed to.

References

1. Winstein, C.J., et al.: Guidelines for Adult Stroke Rehabilitation and Recovery. American Health Association and American Stroke Association Guide-line (9) (2016)
2. Polese, J.C., et al.: The effects of walking sticks on gait kinematics and kinetics with chronic stroke survivors. Clin. Biomech. **27**, 131–137 (2012)
3. Tyson, S.F., et al.: A systematic review and meta-analysis of the effect of an ankle-foot orthosis on gait biomechanics after stroke. Clin. Rehabil. **27**(10), 879–891 (2013)
4. Rodríguez-Fernández, A., Lobo-Prat, J., Font-Llagunes, J.M.: Systematic review on wearable lower-limb exoskeletons for gait training in neuromuscular impairments. J. Neuroeng. Rehabil. **18**(1), 1–21 (2021)
5. Selves, C., Stoquart, G., Lejeune, T.: Gait rehabilitation after stroke: review of the evidence of predictors, clinical outcomes and timing for interventions. Acta Neurol. Belg. **120**(4), 783–790 (2020)
6. Cifuentes, C.A., Múnera, M.: Interfacing Humans and Robots for Gait Assistance and Rehabilitation. Springer, Cham (2022). https://doi.org/10.1007/978-3-030-79630-3
7. Mehrholz, J., et al.: Electromechanical-assisted training for walking after stroke. Cochrane Database Syst. Rev. (7) (2013)
8. Louie, D.R., et al.: Patients' and therapists' experience and perception of exoskeleton-based physiotherapy during subacute stroke rehabilitation: a qualitative analysis. Disabil. Rehabil. 1–9 (2021)
9. Bevilacqua, R., et al.: Rehabilitation of older people with Parkinson's disease: an innovative protocol for RCT study to evaluate the potential of robotic-based technologies. BMC Neurol. **20**(1), 1–8 (2020)
10. Tamburella, F., et al.: Influences of the biofeedback content on robotic post-stroke gait rehabilitation: electromyographic vs joint torque biofeedback. J. Neuroeng. Rehabil. **16**(1), 1–17 (2019)

11. Pons, J.L.: Wearable Robots: Biomechatronic Exoskeletons. Chichester, UK (2008)
12. Kozlowski, A.J., et al.: Time and effort required by persons with spinal cord injury to learn to use a powered exoskeleton for assisted walking. Top. Spinal Cord Inj. Rehabil. **21**(2), 110–121 (2015)
13. Villa-Parra, A.C., Lima, J., Delisle-Rodriguez, D., Vargas-Valencia, L., Frizera-Neto, A., Bastos, T.: Assessment of an assistive control approach applied in an active knee orthosis plus walker for post-stroke gait rehabilitation. Sensors **20**(9), 2452 (2020)
14. Koch, M.A., Font-Llagunes, J.M.: Lower-limb exosuits for rehabilitation or assistance of human movement: a systematic review. Appl. Sci. **11**(18), 8743 (2021)
15. Barsotti, A., Khalaf, K., Gan, D.: Muscle fatigue evaluation with EMG and acceleration data: a case study. In: 2020 42nd Annual International Conference of the IEEE Engineering in Medicine & Biology Society (EMBC), pp. 3138–3141. IEEE (2020)
16. Rodríguez-Tapia, B., Soto, I., Martínez, D.M., Arballo, N.C.: Myoelectric interfaces and related applications: current state of EMG signal processing-a systematic review. IEEE Access **8**, 7792–7805 (2020)
17. Villa-Parra, A.C., Delisle-Rodriguez, D., Botelho, T., Mayor, J.J.V., Delis, A.L., Carelli, R., et al.: Control of a robotic knee exoskeleton for assistance and rehabilitation based on motion intention from sEMG. Res. Biomed. Eng. **34**, 198–210 (2018)
18. Kyeong, S., Feng, J., Ryu, J.K., Park, J.J., Lee, K.H., Kim, J.: Surface electromyography characteristics for motion intention recognition and implementation issues in lower-limb exoskeletons. Int. J. Control Autom. Syst. **20**(3), 1018–1028 (2022)
19. Hobbs, B., Artemiadis, P.: A review of robot-assisted lower-limb stroke therapy: unexplored paths and future directions in gait rehabilitation. Front. Neurorobot. **14**, 19 (2020)
20. McDonald, C., Fingleton, C., Murphy, S., Lennon, O.: Stroke survivor perceptions of using an exoskeleton during acute gait rehabilitation. Sci. Rep. **12**(1), 1–9 (2022)
21. Beyaert, C., et al.: Gait post-stroke: pathophysiology and rehabilitation strategies. Neurophysiol. Clin. **45**(4–5), 335–355 (2015)
22. Maeda, N., et al.: Predicting the probability for fall incidence in stroke patients using the Berg Balance Scale. J. Int. Med. Res. **37**(3), 697–704 (2009)
23. Brucki, S.M.D.: Sugestões para o uso do mini-exame do estado mental no Brasil. Arq. Neuropsiquiatr. **61**(3B), 777–781 (2003)
24. Villa-Parra, A.C., et al.: Knee impedance modulation to control an active orthosis using insole sensors. Sensors **17**(12), 2751 (2017)
25. Carvalho, K.E.C.D., et al.: Tradução e validação do Quebec user evaluation of satisfaction with assistive technology (QUEST 2.0) para o idioma por-tuguês do Brasil. Revista Brasileira de Reumatologia **54**(4), 260–267 (2014)
26. Vargas-Valencia, L.S., et al.: An IMU-to-body alignment method applied to human gait analysis. Sensors **16**(12), 2090 (2016)
27. Martino, G., et al.: Neuromuscular adjustments of gait associated with unstable conditions. J. Neurophysiol. **114**(5), 2867–2882 (2015)
28. Aprile, I., et al.: Efficacy of robotic-assisted gait training in chronic stroke patients: preliminary results of an Italian bi-center study. NeuroRehabilitation **41**(4), 775–782 (2017)
29. Bonnyaud, C., et al.: Effects of gait training using a robotic constraint (Lokomat(R)) on gait kinematics and kinetics in chronic stroke patients. J. Rehabil. Med. **46**(2), 132–138 (2014)

30. Mun, K.R., et al.: Biomechanical effects of body weight support with a novel robotic walker for over-ground gait rehabilitation. Med. Biol. Eng. Comput. **55**(2), 315–326 (2017)
31. Lee, H.J., et al.: A wearable hip assist robot can improve gait function and cardiopulmonary metabolic efficiency in elderly adults. IEEE Trans. Neural Syst. Rehabil. Eng. **25**(9), 1549–1557 (2017)
32. Hidler, J.M., Wall, A.E.: Alterations in muscle activation patterns during robotic-assisted walking. Clin. Biomech. **20**(2), 184–193 (2005)

Design and Evaluation of a Prototype of Dual Channel Electrical Stimulator: Application in the Assessment of Current Perception Thresholds to Multiple Stimuli

D. A. Molina-Vidal[1]([⊠]) [iD], P. Cevallos Larrea[2], L. Guambaña Calle[2], D. Liquori[1],
and C. J. Tierra-Criollo[1] [iD]

[1] Biomedical Engineering Program, Alberto Luiz Coimbra Institute for Graduate Studies and
Research in Engineering (Coppe), Federal University of Rio de Janeiro, Rio de Janeiro, Brazil
dmolinav@peb.ufrj.br
[2] Universidad Politécnica Salesiana, Biomedical Engineering Research Group - GIIB, Cuenca,
Ecuador

Abstract. The Current Perception Threshold (CPT) to sinusoidal electrical current stimulus can assess different types of peripheral nervous fibers, 1 Hz can stimulate thin and 3 kHz thick fibers. The behavior of CPT to multiple simultaneous sinusoidal electrical stimuli remains unexplored. This work aims to present a two-channel Electrical Stimulator (ES) design and evaluation to investigate the CPT at multiple stimuli. The ES includes a user interface in LabVIEW (to configure and control the stimulation) and an Electronic Circuit for two independent current sources with arbitrary waveforms. The prototype underwent a functional test with sinusoidal waveforms and showed a Total Harmonic Distortion of less than 1% and a non-linearity factor of less than 1.6%. The output current with a square waveform on loads from 100 Ω to 100 kΩ was constant. The crosstalk between the channels showed values less than 0.1% for sinusoidal frequencies of 1 Hz (channel 1) and 3 kHz (channel 2). Eight healthy subjects participated of the preliminary experiment, which consisted of obtaining the CPT for median nerve to 1 Hz, 3 kHz, and both stimuli simultaneously. The mean CPT to 1 Hz and 3 kHz showed similar values to the literature, 154 $\pm$ 17 μA, and 1011 $\pm$ 37 μA, respectively. The results with simultaneous stimuli showed a more significant interference of 3 kHz above 1 Hz CPT than 1 Hz above 3 kHz CPT. The results suggest that the system could generate controlled and repeatable stimuli in two independent channels and can be used to investigate the peripheral nerve fibers in scenarios of multiple electrical stimuli.

Keywords: Sinusoidal electrical stimulation · Current Perception Threshold · Dual-channel electrical stimulator

---

The original version of this chapter was revised: The author name tagging are corrected in the citation. The correction to this chapter is available at https://doi.org/10.1007/978-3-031-32213-6_38

1 Introduction

The somatosensory system captures, transduces, and identifies somatic sensations such as pain, temperature, and pressure [1, 2]. Sensations are transduced by axons passing through a vast network of peripheral nerves to the central nervous system [2]. The peripheral nerve fibers are selectively affected by diseases such as *Diabetes Mellitus* [3], Parkinson's [4] and Hansen´s disease [5] that result in neuropathies such as diabetic peripheral neuropathy [6, 7], neuropathic pain [8], carpal tunnel syndrome [9] among others.

The application of electrical current on a nerve (transcutaneous electrostimulation – TES) is an important technique used to support the diagnosis and therapy of the somatosensory system [10]. In diagnosis, the TES can be used to identify the Current Perception Threshold (CPT), which supports the assessment of disturbances in sensory fibers such as, for example, abnormalities in myelinization or changes in the velocity of conduction [8, 11]. Particularly, the sinusoidal electrical stimulus is recommended for the selective assessment of the functional state of nervous fibers using typical frequencies of 2000, 250, and 5 Hz to evaluate types of peripheral fibers as large myelinated (Aβ), medium-size myelinated (Aδ) and unmyelinated (C), respectively [7]. Some studies have investigated the relation of stimulating different fiber types with specific sensations [11].

The use of multiple transcutaneous electrical stimulations has also been investigated in medical applications. Some studies have proposed a multiple stimulation strategy as therapy, for example, to restore or improve motor functions in subjects affected by nervous system diseases [12–14]. In diagnosis, the study of using multiple TES is more limited, particularly when using sinusoidal electrical stimulation. We found a study that evaluated the impact of varying parameters and the number of electrical stimuli on perception thresholds [15].

The study of scenarios involving the simultaneous application of current sinusoidal stimuli requires an adequate multichannel electrical stimulator with a wide configuration possibility. Most of the systems in the market have predefined stimulation patterns and limit the configuration of protocols to be used. There are some single-channel current stimulators used in research as the Neurometer [7, 8], which provides only stimulation frequencies of 2000, 250, and 5 Hz, or Neuroestim [11, 16] which covers stimulus frequencies from 1 to 5000 Hz, both having automatic detection of CPT. Other stimulators in the literature present multiple electrical stimulus features [17, 18], but there was not found any evidence of using it in the study of perception thresholds (CPTs) by sinusoidal stimulation.

This paper presents the design and evaluation of a prototype of a dual-channel electrical stimulator projected for the research field, which can generate arbitrary current stimulus. The performance parameters of the prototype are obtained to be compared with similar devices in the literature. In addition, the prototype is evaluated in a preliminary experimental test to obtain the Current Perception Thresholds (CPT) on healthy subjects for sinusoidal current stimulation to a single stimulus and also in the condition of adding an interfering current stimulus at a different frequency.

2   Materials and Methods

2.1   Design

The Electric Stimulator (ES) was designed having two components; a User Interface – UI (software) to configure and control the stimulation process and an Electronic Circuit – EC (hardware) that generate controlled current stimuli in two independent channels. A general diagram of the device is shown in Fig. 1.

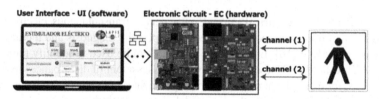

Fig. 1. General structure of the Electric Stimulator – ES.

Hardware

The hardware structure is composed of four main units: power, control, actuator, sensors, and protections, as shown in Fig. 2. In the power unit, the main voltage source is a 110 VAC/12 VDC medical grade voltage regulator (using an input jack connector) providing input/output isolation compatible with two Means of Patient Protection (2xMOPP), according to IEC60601-1, and EMI/EMC compliance according to IEC60601-1-2 and IEC61000-4-2/3 and IEC61000-3-2/3. In addition, it was added a selector to enable a USB mini-B connector to use a battery as a voltage source in scenarios that require low levels of electromagnetic interference, as in electrophysiological tests (e.g., in somatosensory evoked potential).

The Control Unit (CU) is based on the 32 bits ARM Cortex-M4 STM32F407 working at 168 MHz [19]. A voltage regulator reduces the input voltage to 3.3 VDC, which is the operating voltage of the CU. The microcontroller establishes communication with the computer through the MAC Ethernet 10/100 peripheral. The CU incorporates an SD-card module controlled by a Serial Peripheral Interface (SPI), which allocates digital stimuli. The SD card enables the use of long-duration stimulus. Stimulus generation used two independent 12-bit Digital-to-Analog Converters (DAC) embedded in the microcontroller, both operating with the Direct Memory Access (DMA) module to transfer the stimulus to the DAC. The analog outputs have a voltage range from 0 to 3.3 V and frequency varying from 1 Hz to 3 kHz. The data rate for stimulus generation can reach up to 64 kHz. Each DAC output signal is conditioned by a 5-order lowpass elliptical filter with a cut-off frequency of 5.3 kHz. In addition, a digitally-configurable selector can disable the filter when generating square or rectangular waveforms. The CU also incorporates other features such as i) generation of digital signals synchronously with stimuli for use in evoked potential tests, ii) digital inputs to monitor subject activity on threshold detections, and iii) digital signals to control the sensors and protection unit.

The Actuator Unit (AC) transforms low-voltage signals from the CU to high-voltage and low-current signals to be applied to the subject. A first conditioning circuit converts

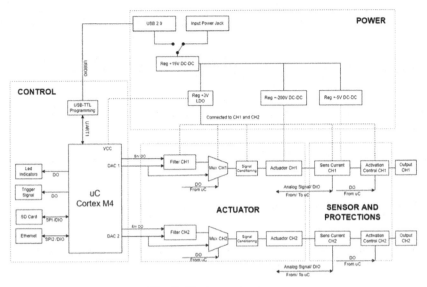

Fig. 2. Hardware structure.

the analog levels from the output of the CU to a range between ± 5 V; such a circuit takes voltage from a DC/DC converter that also acts as isolation between CU and CA. The conditioned signals pass through a constant current amplifier circuit based on the *Bootstrapping* technique [20, 21]. The amplifier uses a set of cascaded transistors that step up the voltage to positive and negative high-voltage rails. The high voltage levels were obtained from a pair of DC/DC converters having a maximum voltage of ± 200 V. These DC/DC converters are compatible with 1xMOPP according to IEC/EN60950-1 (3 kV$_{DC}$ isolating characteristics).

The Protection and Sensor Unit (PSU) is an additional electronic block for patient protection and stimulus monitoring. The circuit incorporates a set of solid-state relays that enable/disable the connection of the stimulus to the subject, an r-sunt sensor with an amplification circuit, and a logical circuit. Two relays are controlled directly from the microcontroller (i.e., CU) and react according to the status of the stimulation defined by the user or if the monitored signal of the sensor exceeds a threshold established in the software. In addition, the sensor's signal also enters the logical circuit without the influence of the microcontroller, which activates a third relay that disconnects the subject when the current exceeds a maximum threshold established by hardware.

Software

The design of the User Interface (UI) was based on a model created with the System Modelling method [22] and using the software Visual Paradigm. Figure 3 presents the model of Use Cases, which guides the development of the software. The application of the UI was finally implemented in the software LabVIEW.

In resume, the software comprises three blocks: i) stimulus configuration, ii) stimulation control, and iii) communication with hardware. The stimulus configuration corresponds to the block of software that enables the user the selection and configuration

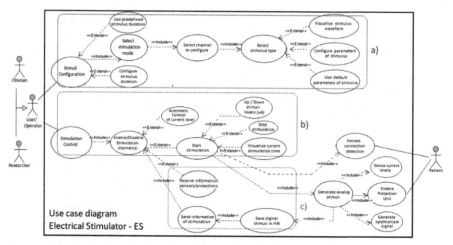

Fig. 3. Use case diagram exhibiting three blocks of software. a) stimulus configuration, b) stimulation control, c) communication with hardware.

of predefined stimulus types (sine, square, triangular, sawtooth, pulse train) or arbitrary stimulus loaded from a file, having controls to establish frequency, amplitude, and duration. The stimulation control is the block of software that enables the user to set between four stimulation modes: continuous, per a predefined number of cycles, increasing amplitude ramp, and automatic threshold detection. Also, this block allows the operator to power on/off the stimulation channels and establishes the state of the stimulation (play, stop). The block of communication with hardware is an internal block of software implemented as a Dynamic Link Library developed in C++, having methods that will be called by the LabVIEW application to manage the ethernet communication with the hardware. An example of the UI is shown in Fig. 4.

2.2 Functional Tests

The functional tests aimed to characterize the operational parameters of the ES and obtain performance indicators by means of three trials. All tests were developed using resistive loads connected to each of the outputs of the ES, and a digital oscilloscope (Tektronix MSO2024B) was used to measure voltage and current.

The first test aimed to obtain the linearity and Total Harmonic Distortion (THD) of the output of each channel separately to a sinusoidal stimulus with frequencies varying on values of 1, 5, 250, 2000, and 3000 Hz and amplitudes varying at 13 different points of the full scale of the DAC (0–4096 levels) output. The second test evaluates the ability of the stimulator to maintain a constant current for loads varying in values of 100, 1000, and 10000 ohms when applying a rectangular waveform stimulus of 1 kHz. Simulations of the current amplifier were developed to compare with measured signals. The third test consisted of measuring the crosstalk effect between channels. This condition was evaluated by measuring the change in THD for a stimulus in channel 1 at 20% of the full scale when a second stimulus is simultaneously applied at channel 2 at 90% of the full scale.

Fig. 4. User interface presenting controls for stimulation and configuration.

2.3 Experimental Protocol

Eight healthy subjects (3M, 5F) age between 18 and 35 years participated in the validation of the ES. The experiments were developed at the Signals and Images Processing Laboratory in the Biomedical Engineering Program (COPPE/UFRJ/Brazil). Experimental procedures were approved by the ethical committee with the number CAAE: 58744222.2.100.15257. All participants were assigned a consent term before participating in experiments.

The experimental protocol applied to each subject consisted of the following steps. First, to obtain the CPT for a single stimulus at the frequencies of 1 Hz and 3 kHz. The order of the frequencies for testing was randomized. Second, to obtain the CPT of a stimulus by adding another interference stimulus: i) the CPT at 3 kHz simultaneously applying 1 Hz interference stimuli at a fixed level, and ii) the CPT at 1 Hz simultaneously applying 3 kHz interference stimuli at a fixed level. The levels of the interfering stimulus were set at 0.8, 1.0, and 1.2 times the CPT obtained under single stimulus conditions.

The protocol to estimate a CPT was similar to such used in [23]. In resume, first, the magnitude of the stimulus was increased to obtain the level of the first somatosensory perception of the subject. The half and the fourth part of this level were used as "initial stimulation amplitude (Ai)" and "increment (INCi)," respectively. Then, starting at Ai were presented with intercalated sets of stimulation and no-stimulation, each lasting four seconds. At each new set, the amplitude of the stimulus increases by INCi. When the subject reports the perception of the stimulus, the INCi is halved, and the last amplitude decreases by INCi. This loop continues until the issue detects the stimulus five times, and so the last amplitude of the stimulus is considered the CPT.

The electrodes used in the experiment were the Silver Spike Point configuration (SSP) and the Planar Concentric Ring configuration (PCR) (Fig. 5) [11]. The SSP consists of a conical silver spike point cathode (11.3 mm diameter) and a gold disc electrode anode (10 mm diameter). The PCR consists of a 9 to 7 mm diameter ring anode and a 4 mm diameter central disc cathode.

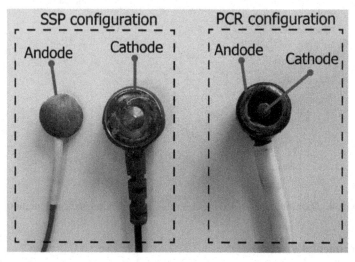

Fig. 5. Electrodes configurations: Silver Spike Point configuration (SSP) and the Planar Concentric Ring configuration (PCR).

The stimulus of 1 Hz was applied using SSP configuration while the stimulus at 3 kHz used PCR configuration, which follows the reports of studies indicating such electrode types as efficient for stimulating thin and thick fibers, respectively [11]. All sinusoidal stimuli were applied to the median nerve of the right hand. Before placing the electrode, the stimulation region was cleaned with alcohol at 70%, and the conductive gel was used on the electrodes to improve conductivity. The terminals of the SSP electrode were separated apart by 2.5 cm. The SSP electrodes were placed on the anterior region of the wrist to stimulate the median nerve. The PCR electrodes were placed on the anterior region of the right forearm, approximately halfway along the length of the forearm. Figure 6 demo Electrodes were fixed with adhesive. The experiment lasted from 45 to 60 min for each volunteer.

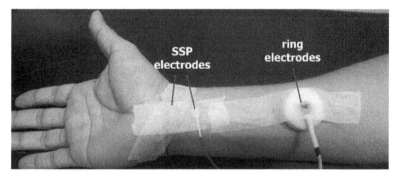

Fig. 6. Location of the electrodes for electrical stimulation.

3   Results

The Fig. 7 shows a representation of the hardware of the ES marking the different units of the System.

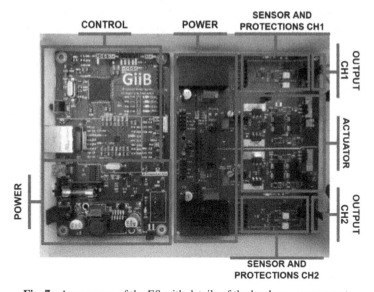

Fig. 7. Appearance of the ES with details of the hardware component.

3.1   Functional Evaluation

The Fig. 8 shows the generation of three different current stimuli varying in waveform (pulse train, sawtooth, custom), frequency (5, 250 and 3000 Hz), and magnitude (10, 50 and 90% of the full scale). All measures were taken from a resistive load of 10 kΩ.

The Fig. 9 summarizes the output current levels obtained for sinusoidal stimuli of frequencies 1 and 3000 Hz applied on a resistive load of 10 kΩ. The figure also shows

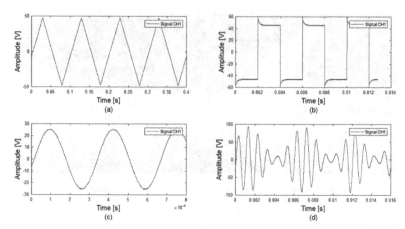

Fig. 8. Stimuli generated with the ES. (a) Triangular, 10 Hz, 50% FS. (b) Square, 250 Hz, 50% FS, (c) Sinusoidal, 3 kHz, 25% FS, (d) Arbitrary.

a curve for linear regression of the individual values. The non-linearity was obtained following the formula: error$_{max}$/FS. The THD for the different frequencies is shown in Table 1. All stimuli used to calculate the THD were obtained at an output of 90% of the full scale. In general, the TDH was lower than 1% for all conditions.

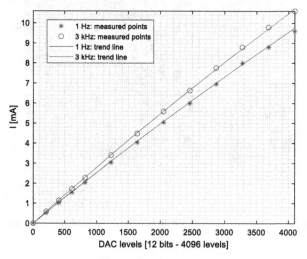

Fig. 9. Linearity curves.

The non-linearities at frequencies of 1 and 3000 Hz are 1.64% and 1.50% respectively.

The Fig. 10 summarizes the waveform of the output current generated for a rectangular stimulus. In the Fig. 10 a, it is shown the how the voltage level increases as increasing the resistive load from 100 to 10 kΩ to maintain a constant current. Figure 10 b, shows

Table 1. THD analysis

Frequency (Hz)	1	5	250	2000	3000
THD (%)	0.49	0.49	0.57	0.33	0.34

the current waveform where it is possible to observe the near-to-constant current levels of the output. The simulations of the Actuator Unit presented in Fig. 10 c y d show similar behavior to those observed in experimental measures (show the simulation of the constant current amplifier circuit based on the *Bootstrapping* with fixed input and different loads at its output).

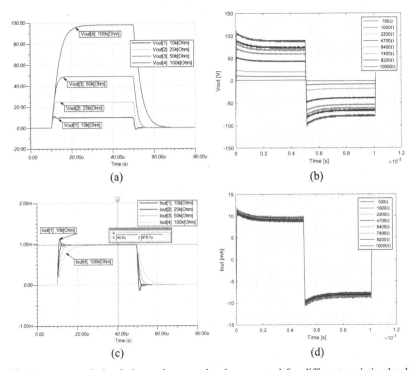

Fig. 10. Measures and simulations of current levels generated for different resistive loads. (**a**) Simulated voltage output, (**b**) Measured volage output, (**c**) Simulated current output, (**d**) Measured current output.

When channel 1 was 20% full scale at 1 Hz, and channel 2 was 90% full scale at 3 kHz, the TDH was 0.44%.

3.2 Experimental Evaluation

In the single stimulus condition, the mean CPTs obtained were 154 μA (±17 μA) and 1011 μA (± 37 μA) for stimuli of 1 Hz and 3 kHz, respectively (Fig. 11). The sensations (cognitive responses) reported with the 1 Hz stimuli were mainly sting and needlesful, but also existed reports of sensations of heat and itching (all related to thin fibers). For the 3 kHz stimuli, the subjects reported mainly the sensations of vibration, tingling, and contraction (all related to thick fibers).

In the multiple stimulus conditions, the results varied depending on which were the control and interfering stimuli (Fig. 11). The CPT at 1 Hz stimulus was not affected when adding the interfering 3 kHz at 0.8 or 1.0 CPT, but it showed a trend to increase when the interfering 3 kHz was 1.2 CPT (Fig. 11.A). The standard deviation of the CPT of 1 Hz showed to increase as increased the level of the interfering 3 kHz. When the interfering of 3 kHz was 0.8 CPT, the main sensations reported were pricks and needles (all related to thin fibers), but when the interfering of 3 kHz increased to 1.2 CPT, most participants reported difficulties identifying sensations or the specific electrode stimulating.

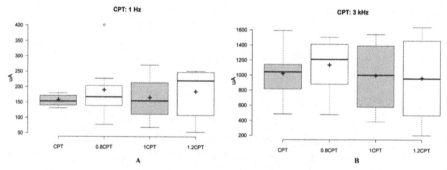

Fig. 11. (**A**) CPT 1 Hz (Interfering 3 kHz with fixed magnitude at a factor of 0.8, 1 and 1.2 of its single CPT), (**B**) CPT 3 kHz (Interfering 1 Hz with fixed magnitude at a factor of 0.8, 1 and 1.2 of its single CPT). Averages are represented by crosses.

The 3 kHz CP was not affected when adding the 1 Hz interference. However, the standard deviation of the 3 kHz CPT showed a trend to increase as increased the level of the interference of 1 Hz. Moreover, the sensations reported were tingling, pressure, vibration, and contraction (all related to thick fibers).

4   Discussion and Conclusions

The Electrical Stimulator (ES) can be powered with a medical-grade power supply that has insulation or with batteries for scenarios that require minimizing interference from electromagnetic interference, such as electrophysiological studies.

Functional tests of the ES prototype indicate that it can generate sine, square, triangular, sawtooth, pulse train waves, or an arbitrary stimulus from a file. The maximum frequency the Control Unit (CU) can reproduce is 64 kHz. The frequencies of the signals are limited by the conditioning filter placed at the output of the DAC, however, the literature mentions frequencies up to 3000 Hz, so the ES can be used for applications that require electrical stimulation.

The THD analysis indicates that the values are less than 1% for loads from 100 to 100 kΩ, unlike the Neuroestim that presents THD less than 1.5% for loads from 100 to 10 kΩ [24]. These values were also verified with the simulation. The maximum current capacity for generating the ES is 10.6 mA.

The trend lines for frequencies of 1, 5, and 250 Hz have no significant difference. For frequencies of 2000 and 3000 Hz, there was a difference, and the coefficients were found to have a trend line. The non-linearity value was calculated, giving 1.64% for 1 Hz and 1.50% for 3000 Hz. The crosstalk between channels showed less than 0.1%, representing low crosstalk.

Eight healthy subjects participated in the stage of experimental evaluation. The mean CPT values 154 μA (±17 μA) and 1011 μA (±37 μA) for stimuli of 1 Hz and 3 kHz, respectively, found in this study, are in agreement with the literature [11]. The cognitive responses for this test were consistent with [11].

The apparent increase in the 1 Hz CPT when interfered with 3 kHz stimulus at 1.2 CPT, the difficulty in identifying sensations, and the difficulty in identifying the local stimulus suggest the blockade of thin fibers by thick fibers. A possible physiological mechanism that can explicate these results is the Gate Theory of Pain [25]. On the other hand, the 3 kHz stimulus at 0.8 CPT has no influence on the 1 Hz CPT but shows a greater standard deviation. Moreover, sensations reported were related to thin fibers. This fact suggests that thin fibers were not blocked by thick fibers.

The preliminary results suggest that 3 kHz CPT was minor affected due to 1 Hz stimulus interference. That is, the thin fibers have little influence over the thick fibers.

The statistical inference is not feasible due to the small number of samples. Therefore, a larger sample is needed to confirm the results.

The results of functional tests and experimental tests suggest that the system can be used to investigate peripheral nerve fibers and somatosensory perceptions in multiple electrical stimulus scenarios.

Acknowledgements. The authors wish to thank the CAPES, FINEP, CNPq, and GIIB for their financial support.

References

1. Purves, D., Augustine, G.J., Fitzpatrick, D., Hall, W.C., Lamantia, A.-S., Mcnamara, J.O., White, L.E.: Neurociências (2010)
2. Bear, M.F., Connorsm Barry W., Paradiso, M.A.: Neurociências: Desvendando o Sistema Nervoso (2017)
3. Jahantigh Akbari, N., Hosseinifar, M., Sadat Naimi, S., Mikaili, S., Rahbar, S.: The efficacy of physiotherapy interventions in mitigating the symptoms and complications of diabetic peripheral neuropathy: a systematic review. J. Diabetes Metab Disord. **19**(2), 1995–2004 (2020). https://doi.org/10.1007/s40200-020-00652-8
4. Abdulbaki, A., Kaufmann, J., Galazky, I., Buentjen, L., Voges, J.: Neuromodulation of the subthalamic nucleus in Parkinson's disease: the effect of fiber tract stimulation on tremor control. Acta Neurochir. **163**(1), 185–195 (2020). https://doi.org/10.1007/s00701-020-044 95-3

5. da Fernanda Silva Santos, R.: Avaliação da excitabilidade elétrica neuromuscular em Pacientes com hanseníase (2018)

6. So, W.Z., et al.: Diabetic corneal neuropathy as a surrogate marker for diabetic peripheral neuropathy. Neural Regen Res. **7**, 2172–2178 (2022)

7. Lv, S.-L., et al.: Assessment of Peripheral Neuropathy Using Measurement of the Current Perception Threshold with the Neurometer® in patients with type 1 diabetes mellitus. Diabetes Res. Clin, Pract. **109**(1), 130–134 (2015). https://doi.org/10.1016/j.diabres.2015.04.018

8. Chen, Y., et al.: Quantitative and fiber-selective evaluation of pain and sensory dysfunction in patients with Parkinson's disease. Parkinsonism Relat. Disord. **21**, 361–365 (2015). https://doi.org/10.1016/j.parkreldis.2015.01.008

9. de Araújo Júnior, J.O., et al.: A eletroterapia no tratamento da síndrome do túneldo carpo: uma revisão integrativa de literature. Varia Scientia – Ciências da Saúde **8**, 91–109 (2022)

10. Daroff, R.B., Aminoff, M.J.: Encyclopedia of the Neurological Sciences. Academic press (2014)

11. Junqueira De Souza, B.: Avaliação da percepção por corrente senoidal: uma nova perspectiva para neuropatias. Thesis, Federal University of Rio de Janeiro, COPPE, Rio de Janeiro, Brazil (2016)

12. Malešević, N.M., et al.: A multi-pad electrode based functional electrical stimulation system for restoration of grasp. J. NeuroEng. Rehabili. **9**(1), 66 (2012). https://doi.org/10.1186/1743-0003-9-66

13. Qu, H., et al.: Development of network-based multichannel neuromuscular electrical stimulation system for stroke rehabilitation. J. Rehabil. Res. Dev. **53**, 263–278 (2016). https://doi.org/10.1682/JRRD.2014.10.0227

14. Lim, J., et al.: Patient-specific functional electrical stimulation strategy based on muscle synergy and walking posture analysis for gait rehabilitation of stroke patients. J. Int. Med. Res. **49**(5), 030006052110167 (2021). https://doi.org/10.1177/03000605211016782

15. Geng, B., Yoshida, K., Jensen, W.: Impacts of selected stimulation patterns on the perception threshold in electrocutaneous stimulation. J Neuroeng Rehabil. **8**, 9 (2011). https://doi.org/10.1186/1743-0003-8-9

16. Passos Volpi, L.: Efeitos dos estímulos elétricos senoidais na resposta induzida cerebral: estudo da seletividade das fibras sensitivas. Thesis, Federal University of Rio de Janeiro, COPPE, Rio de Janeiro, Brazil (2017)

17. Sevastyanov, V.V.: A device for multichannel electrical stimulation of the human neuromuscular system. Biomed. Eng. **54**(4), 244–247 (2020). https://doi.org/10.1007/s10527-020-10013-7

18. de Paula, W.A., de Almeida, L.V., Fachin-Martins, E., Zanetti, R., Martins, H.R.: Somatosensory electrical stimulator for assessment of current perception threshold at different frequencies. In: Proceedings of the 5th World Congress on Electrical Engineering and Computer Systems and Science. Avestia Publishing (2019)

19. STMicroelectronics: STM32F405xx STM32F407xx. (2020)

20. Cornman, J., Akhtar, A., Bretl, T.: A portable, arbitrary waveform, multichannel constant current electrotactile stimulator. In: International IEEE/EMBS Conference on Neural Engineering, NER, pp. 300–303. IEEE Computer Society (2017)

21. Gift, S.J.G., Maundy, B.: Electronic Circuit Design and Application. Springer International Publishing, Cham (2022). https://doi.org/10.1007/978-3-030-79375-3

22. Delligatti, L., Steiner, R., Soley, R.: SysML Distilled (2014)

23. Martins, H.R., Zanetti, R., dos Santos, C.C., Manzano, G.M., Tierra-Criollo, C.J.: Current perception threshold and reaction time in the assessment of sensory peripheral nerve fibers through sinusoidal electrical stimulation at different frequencies. Revista Brasileira de Engenharia Biomedica. **29**, 278–285 (2013). https://doi.org/10.4322/rbeb.2013.028

24. Martins, H.R.: Sistema para avaliação de fibras nervosas periféricas utilizando corrente elétrica senoidal: estudo de caso em hanseníase. Thesis, Universidade Federal de Minas Gerais, UFMG (2013)

25. Ropero Peláez, F.J., Taniguchi, S.: The gate theory of pain revisited: Modeling different pain conditions with a parsimonious neurocomputational model. Neural Plast. **2016**, 4131395 (2016). https://doi.org/10.1155/2016/4131395

System for Postural Stability Assessment Based on an Inertial Sensors Network

Jorge E. Inlago⬭, Byron R. Zapata⬭, and Fabián R. Narváez$^{(\boxtimes)}$⬭

GIB&B Research Group, Department of Biomedicine,
Universidad Politécnica Salesiana, Quito, Ecuador
fnarvaeze@ups.edu.ec

Abstract. This paper presents a system for quantitative analyzing the postural stability and balance of elderly people. For doing that, a computational biomechanics model is developed, for which body segment information from lower limps are captured by using an inertial sensors network. For this, an alignment and calibration strategy based on quaternion theory is implemented, which constructs a reference coordinate system aligned and calibrated to each body segments for obtaining the joint movements from elderly in static state. Once biomechanics model is calibrated, the body centre of mass is estimated by approximating the origin of the sensor from the distal to proximal body segments, which allows the segmentation of each anatomical region of the body. Finally, the complete body centre of mass from biomechanics model is obtained for postural balance analysis. The proposed system was evaluated with volunteers using 3 different stability tests, the data obtained in each stability test were analyzed with box plots and a K-means classifier, establishing indices of postural stability and showing alterations during the testing phase. The results demonstrate some difficult levels to maintain postural balance during these stability test, where postural balance on one foot proved to be a great challenge for elderly people, with displacements of their centre of mass of around 30 cm. The contribution of this work is to analyze the deterioration of stability in elderly people based on the centre of mass (COM), which in the future could be used as a study alternative for specialized walking centers.

Keywords: Inertial sensors · COM · Postural stabilometry

1 Introduction

Postural stability (PS) is the ability of individuals to maintain their center of mass over the base of support, maintaining an upright posture and avoiding swaying during any activity [1]. The vestibular, visual and somatosensory systems are responsible for maintaining balance. The older adult population presents a higher rate of instability due to the changes that the human body undergoes and the problems inherent to aging, the diseases that weaken the PS in older adults are

© The Author(s), under exclusive license to Springer Nature Switzerland AG 2023
F. R. Narváez et al. (Eds.): SmartTech-IC 2022, CCIS 1705, pp. 356–369, 2023.
https://doi.org/10.1007/978-3-031-32213-6_26

chronic diseases such as cancer, neuropsychological factors and the aging of the motor systems contribute to the degradation of the PS [2,3].

For years the common way of assessing Parkinson Disease (PD) by a specialist, where a series of tests involving standing and eye closure are performed, testing the patients' ability to remain in a state of purposeful standing [4,5]. These conventional techniques are applied to people suffering from chronic diseases such as Parkinson's, osteoarthritis, among others, with good empirical results [4,6]. The need to assess these anomalies quantitatively employs several methods, the most commonly used at the clinical level are force platforms that determine the limits of static stability, but limits the study to finding spatial parameters [7].

Another method of motion analysis is based on cameras and light markers, this method is used for dynamic analysis associated with the study of temporo-spatial parameters linked to the dynamics of human gait. This technique uses cameras and markers to capture the movements performed [8]. The main problem is the need for a specialized environment with good lighting and high-speed cameras which makes postural control analysis very costly and resource intensive for a complete and reliable study [19].

Currently, proposals and research have been developed for motion capture based on inertial measurement units (IMUs), which have demonstrated clinical use suitable for non-specialized environments [9]. This novel technology uses gyroscopes, accelerometers and magnetometers to estimate orientation, position and direction in a global coordinate system.

In addition, these devices have an imperceptible weight and are non-invasive, allowing them to capture movements without alterations. These characteristics are very appealing to the scientific community, which carries out multiple studies related to gait, postural control, activity detection and centre of mass estimation, using from one to a network of sensors located in different anatomical regions of the body [10,11]. The number and location of sensors is an extensive area of research showing different results from optimal to excellent. Insufficient use of sensors coupled with location and orientation can lead to errors in the different types of studies required [12,13].

2   Methodology

For the methodological development, a biomechanical model based on the lower body is proposed, which is composed of a network of 7 Xsens Awinda inertial sensors that are structured in a rigid body model. For the acquisition of data, the calibration and alignment methodology based on quaternions is used, with which a global reference system is obtained. This new reference system allows obtaining the information of the segmentation of the lower extremities, with which the displacement of the COM is calculated and analyzed.

2.1 Experimental Protocol

For this study, 4 persons, 2 men and 2 women, were involved in the study. A 25-year-old young adult with a height of 1.75 m and a body mass of 65 kg as a control person. A 55-year-old adult with a height of 1.50 m and a body mass of 50 kg as an adult. Two older adults aged 75 and 83 years with a height of 1.50 m and a body mass of 60 kg; it should be noted that none of the subjects had chronic diseases and only one of the older adults had vertigo at the time of testing, thus providing a margin of separation from the other data. All participants voluntarily gave informed consent and received counselling for the different types of tests.

To gather information on the centre of mass (COM), the subjects performed tests that are normally performed when assessing postural stability; the tests lasted about one minute and consisted of standing with eyes closed, eyes open and maintaining balance on one foot with eyes open; several studies use similar tests in the diagnosis of balance in a static state [21,22]. These static stability tests present different ranges of movement according to the postures adopted by the subject.

2.2 Calibration and Alignment IMUs

IMUs (Inertial Measurement Units) are devices used to estimation parameters in static or dynamic states such as rotational speed, acceleration or three-dimensional positioning. For this study, inertial sensors of the brand name XSENS MTw Awinda Wireless 3DOF Motion Tracker, which guarantee data sampling up to 1000 Hz, latency of 30 ms, accelerometer $\pm 160\,\frac{m}{a^2}$, gyroscope $\pm 1200\,\frac{deg}{s}$ and a magnetometer $\pm 1.5 Gauss$ [14].

The International Society of Biomechanics (ISB) proposes a general reporting standard for joint kinematics based on the joint coordinate system, which details the movement of lower limb segments [15], it is also necessary to define the reference frames of the local centre of mass of the segments in order to describe the position and orientation with respect to the global frame [16]. For the inertial sensor network to be implemented it is necessary to know the locations and orientations on the body, following the ISB recommendations we propose a biomechanical model at each origin of the segment as shown in Fig. 1.

Once the reference frames are defined, we implement a biomechanical model of 7 inertial sensors, a sensor-body calibration and alignment method based on [17,18] is applied. First the rotation is corrected to calibrate the sensor frame to a new general body frame, again the rotation is corrected to align each sensor frame with the body frames. The goal is to define a common coordinate system for all devices with the same orientation for each body segment so that the x-axis faces up, the y-axis points to the left, and the z-axis faces forward.

The calibration and alignment process is based on operations with quaternions, the quaternions p and q can be represented as $p = p_0 + \hat{i}p_1 + \hat{j}p_2 + \hat{k}p_3$ y $q = q_0 + \hat{i}q_1 + \hat{j}q_2 + \hat{k}q_3$. Applying relations between the components of the quaternion are used to establish their angles with respect to their principal axes.

Fig. 1. Global reference frame and local centre-of-mass reference frame of the segment [16].

A new sensor coordinate system is then established and this is represented as the following zero-set calibration problem:

$$q_0' = r_{\hat{j}90} \otimes q_0 \tag{1}$$

$$p_0 = c_{0q'}^* \otimes r_{\hat{i}180} \otimes q_0' \tag{2}$$

where q_0 is the quaternion component due to the initial orientation of the sensor in the pelvis q_0' corresponds to the orientation with respect to the vertical plane $c_{0q'}^*$ component defined in the rotation sequence a^3, b^2, c^1 this component describes the rotation with respect to the magnetic field vector, p_0 which defines the correction factor with respect to the vertical axis around the y-axis and r_{j90}. Once the new general frame is established in the pelvis, it is necessary to align each inertial sensor with its body segment, having that:

$$q_n' = p_0 \otimes q_0^* \otimes q_n^* \tag{3}$$

where q_n' represents the corrected quaternion of any n-IMU at time $t = 0$. Thus $p_0 \otimes q_0^*$ defines the enhanced rotation of the pelvis sensor frame. The body frames are then aligned with the principal axis of the body segments using the corrected quaternion q_n' defining a common body frame.

$$p_n = q_n'^* \otimes r_{y180} \otimes b_{c_{q_n}^*} \otimes c_{q_n'}^* \tag{4}$$

where p_n defines the corrected position for each IMU. Since the anatomical frame was aligned, these quaternions are used to estimate some body segment rotations with respect to our rigid body model.

$$R_n = p_0^* \otimes q_0^* \otimes q_n \otimes p_n \tag{5}$$

where R_n is the rotation of any IMU in time $t \neq 0$. Basically the joint rotation is estimated by combining two rotations of continuous body segments by:

$$CR = R_{n-1} \otimes R_n \tag{6}$$

2.3   Centre of Mass (COM)

The main problem of inertial sensors compared to optoelectronic systems is to identify the anatomical regions of the human body; in the literature there are several methods that allow the recognition of these body regions, for this research we use a method that allows mathematically approximate the body segments showing excellent results in the estimation of the centre of mass.

The objective of this method is to align the distal origin of each sensor to the proximal segment of each anatomical region of the human body, which allows the segmentation of the joints. In [20] details that, for COM estimation we use rotation-translation matrices between two segments pelvis-thigh (pl, th), thigh-calf (th, sh), calf-heel (sh, hft), heel-forefoot (hft, fft) having that:

$$T = \begin{bmatrix} R & O \\ 0\ 0\ 0 & 1 \end{bmatrix} \tag{7}$$

where R, is the inhomogeneous rotation matrix between the I-th body segment and the I-th sensor such that the quaternion is $s = 1$, otherwise $s = ||q||^2$ and is represented in Eq. 8 as the rotation for each segment.

$$R_{pl,fft} = \begin{bmatrix} 1 - 2s(q_j^2 + q_k^2) & 2s(q_i q_j - q_k q_r) & 2S(q_i q_k + q_j q_r) \\ 2S(q_i q_j + q_k q_r) & 1 - 2S(q_i^2 + q_k^2) & 2s(q_j q_k - q_i q_r) \\ 2s(q_i q_k - q_j q_r) & 2s(q_j q_k + q_i q_r) & 1 - 2s(q_i^2 + q_j^2) \end{bmatrix} \tag{8}$$

From Eq. 8, O is the origin of each body segment and each origin is fixed according to the anthropometry of the patient, considering the following measurements: pelvic width (W_{pl}), pelvic height (h_{pl}), thigh length (l_{th}), calf length (l_{sh}), ankle height (h_{hft}) and forefoot length (l_{fft}), which in matrix form are shown below on the right-hand side:

$$O_{pl,rth} = \begin{bmatrix} 0 & \frac{W_{pl}}{2} & 0 \end{bmatrix}^T \tag{9}$$

$$O_{rth,rsh} = \begin{bmatrix} -(h_{rpl} + l_{rth}) & 0 & 0 \end{bmatrix}^T \tag{10}$$

$$O_{rsh,rhft} = \begin{bmatrix} -l_{rsh} & 0 & 0 \end{bmatrix}^T \tag{11}$$

$$O_{rhtf,rfft} = \begin{bmatrix} -h_{rft} & 0 & l_{rft} \end{bmatrix}^T \tag{12}$$

After obtaining the rotation-translation matrices for each segment from the pelvis to the right forefoot, the matrix of all body segments is obtained. In order to estimate the position of the centre of mass of the right leg, the transpose of the rotation matrix was multiplied by the origin of each segment from the pelvis to the right forefoot, in the same way for the left leg.

$$COM_r = -(R_{pl,rfft})^T O_{pl,rfft} \tag{13}$$

Equation 13 is used to obtain the value of the centre of mass of the right segment, the data is obtained by means of the biomechanical model consisting of 7 inertial sensors distributed in the lower limbs.

3   Results and Discussions

In order to assess balance, patients were subjected to a series of postural tests to determine the displacement of the COM in the different activities; the centre of mass of each subject was analysed for both the left and right leg, obtaining data from the lower extremities.

In the first test, subjects had to maintain an upright posture, standing with eyes open and facing forward; the second postural test is similar to the previous one, subjects had to maintain an upright posture, standing with eyes closed; finally, the third test subjects had to maintain an upright posture leaning on one foot only.

The results obtained during the static stability tests reveal the motor control of the subjects and their limitations to perform certain activities. Table 1 presents the results of the study in the estimation of the right center of mass, where Subject 1 represents the 25 year old person, Subject 2 the 55 year old person, Subject 3 the 75 year old person and Subject 4 the 83 year old person.

Table 1. Right COM average data

Patients	Test 1			Test 2			Test 3		
Axes	X	Y	Z	X	Y	Z	X	Y	Z
Subject 1	118.9	17.8	25.3	118.9	17.0	26.0	118.0	15.0	22.5
Subject 2	100.1	17.3	22.0	100.3	17.0	22.0	100.5	23.5	25.0
Subject 3	99.9	17.8	22.0	97.5	18.0	21.0	92.5	20.0	40.0
Subject 4	106.1	18.1	24.25	106.0	18.0	25.0	103.0	30.0	20.0

Table 2 presents the results of the study in the estimation of the left center of mass.

Table 2. Left COM average data

Patients	Test 1			Test 2			Test 3		
Axes	X	Y	Z	X	Y	Z	X	Y	Z
Subject 1	118.9	18.0	25.0	118.9	17.8	26.0	118.0	22.0	27.0
Subject 2	99.5	18.5	23.0	100.5	17.0	21.0	95.0	20.0	30.0
Subject 3	106.1	17.7	24	106.0	18.0	25.0	105.5	20.0	22.5
Subject 4	99.9	16.8	22.5	99.8	16.3	22.0	170.5	35.0	40.0

The data are shown for each subject in the different tests carried out. The first young adult subject presented excellent results in all the tests, maintaining high levels of stability with minimal displacements in his centre of mass.

In the third activity, the subject presented a slight difficulty in maintaining a stable posture during the established time, with a displacement in his right COM from 3 cm to 6.5 cm and in the left COM from 3 cm to 9 cm compared to test 1.

The older adults in test 1 and 2 presented a slight displacement in their COM of between 1 cm to 2 cm, having good results maintaining the posture with good stability; the subjects during test 3, presented problems to culminate with this activity, the displacements of their COM go from 3 cm to 20 cm having very low indexes of stability.

In the following figures, we analyse the different COM displacements presented by the patients when maintaining balance. However, the results will depend on the postures required, but these will differ because the subject will adopt a different posture due to his or her abilities, which is the subject of studies. In addition, some postures will be influenced by respiratory movements and body sway in the upright posture, and these changes will be reflected in the change of posture. In Fig. 2(a), we observe the displacement of the COM of the young adult subject, which maintains good stability with minimal oscillations during the entire test phase of less than 1 cm. As shown in Fig. 2(b), these slight oscillations do not affect balance, maintaining good postural stability.

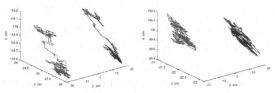

(a) Centre of mass subject   (b) Centre of mass subject
1 - test 1   2 - test 1

Fig. 2. Centre of mass test 1

In Fig. 3(a), we have the displacement of the COM of the older adult presenting slight oscillations, these slight oscillations are almost imperceptible to the human eye, by collecting this information from the data it will help in the diagnosis of diseases, In Fig. 3(b) we have the next older adult subject who also shows slight oscillations when maintaining the posture, a little higher compared to the previous subject. The stability indices are within the parameters without affecting balance.

In the second test our first subject maintains good results by holding steady during this activity, with minimal COM shifts of less than 1 cm as shown in Fig. 4(a). In comparison to test 1 of the same subject, we note the minimal variations that occur when closing the eyes. For the second subject in this test we see a slight displacement in the COM of up to 1 cm as shown in Fig. 4(b). We see that when we close our eyes we start to generate more oscillations than when we have our eyes open, it is worth mentioning that these results do not compromise our balance.

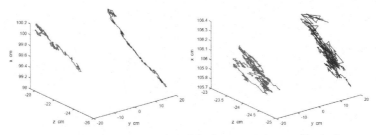

(a) Centre of mass subject 3 - test (b) Centre of mass subject 4 - test
1   1

Fig. 3. Centre of mass test 1 (b)

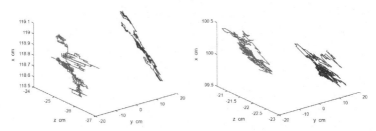

(a) Centre of mass subject 1 - test (b) Centre of mass subject 2 - test
2   2

Fig. 4. Centre of mass test 2 (a)

For the third subject we witnessed slight displacements of his COM around 1.5 cm as shown in Fig. 5(a). These slight oscillations do not represent any problem in maintaining balance, demonstrating good stability during the test phase. In this test the fourth subject presents about 1.5 cm and 2.5 cm in the displacement of his COM as shown in Fig. 5(b). Although the subject presents higher oscillations compared to the other subjects, he does not represent any risk in maintaining his balance, negating any risk of falling.

In the third test, due to the fact that our body reduces the base of support, it presents greater ranges in the displacement of the COM. The first subject presents displacement of his COM around 2 cm to 10 cm as shown in Fig. 6(a). This oscillatory range is stable, which allows us to maintain the posture during the activity without losing balance. For the second subject we see how the supported leg keeps the COM stable, while the unsupported leg presents a greater oscillation between 30 cm as shown in Fig. 6(b). This disparity between data assumes that the subject was unable to maintain the posture by leaning on the ground to avoid falling, this activity was highly complex for the patients, maintaining very low stability indices.

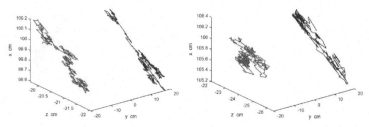

(a) Centre of mass subject 3 - test(b) Centre of mass subject 4 - test
2   2

Fig. 5. Centre of mass test 2 (b)

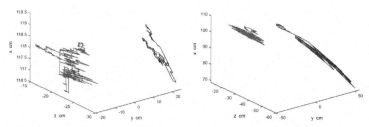

(a) Centre of mass subject 1 - test(b) Centre of mass subject 2 - test
3   3

Fig. 6. Centre of mass test 3 (a)

For the third patient this activity represented a challenge having low stability, the oscillatory ranges were around 20 cm to 40 cm as shown in Fig. 7(a). This high perturbation of 40 cm is shown in the graph because the subject took a step to avoid a fall, having a high range in the displacement of the COM. Finally, the third subject presents high perturbations in this activity around 12 cm to 40 cm. The subject during the test took a step to avoid a fall and therefore high oscillatory ranges are maintained in the COM displacement. This type of test helps to identify the welfare of the vestibular and motor systems to maintain a stable posture without losing balance.

To define the oscillatory parameters between the tests we used box plots to identify the outliers present. The results of the first test can be seen in Fig. 8, the analysed data show that all attributes are within the established ranges without the presence of outliers; the assessment of this test allows inferring that the COM parameters are stable and that the patients have the ability to maintain equilibrium without any limitations.

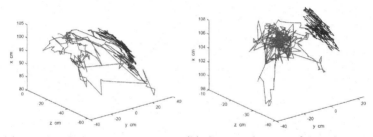

(a) Centre of mass subject 3 - test 3 (b) Centre of mass subject 4 - test 3

Fig. 7. Centre of mass test 3 (a)

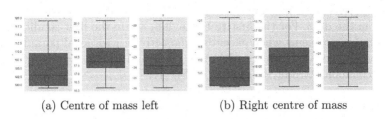

(a) Centre of mass left   (b) Right centre of mass

Fig. 8. COM displacement stability results with eyes open

In the second test, the data present slight outliers or outliers within the parameters considered normal as shown in Fig. 9. The y $axis$ presents these disturbances in stability with outliers between 1 to 2 cm corresponding to the displacement of the centre of mass of the human body. The data are related to the activity described, as the subjects witnessed a slight difficulty in completing this activity.

Finally, the third test showed great difficulty in completing the activity within the established time. The box plots show the large number of outliers, indicating little or no stability. The subjects witnessed large oscillations along the $axis$ y, z with instability ranges between 10 to 30 cm as shown in Fig. 10. In this case the displacement of the COM is very chaotic and the subject was prone to falls.

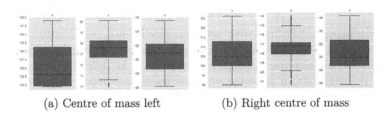

(a) Centre of mass left   (b) Right centre of mass

Fig. 9. Stability results for COM displacement with eyes closed.

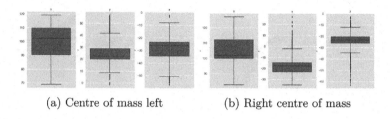

(a) Centre of mass left   (b) Right centre of mass

Fig. 10. Stability results of unipodal COM displacement

For the data analysis we use K-means which is one of the most used cluster-ing algorithms in artificial intelligence to separate or categorise a group of data, this unsupervised learning algorithm helps us to delimit patterns and find irreg-ularities in the data. For the first test, the data are in the best conditions since there were no problems when executing the activity with ideal parameters, the data in x, y, z do not converge with each other and were categorised according to their common attributes, resulting in Fig. 11.

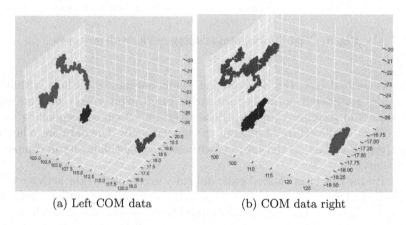

(a) Left COM data   (b) COM data right

Fig. 11. The results show ideal data when standing with eyes open, the information collected shows the divergence of the data from each other, ruling out any stability anomalies.

Implementing algorithms with artificial intelligence, which streamlines the categorisation of K-means data, greatly helps to identify irregularities in a data set; in the second test the patients presented a slight difficulty in maintaining balance, the information collected shows convergence between data exhibiting outliers in the oscillations of postural stability, as shown in Fig. 12.

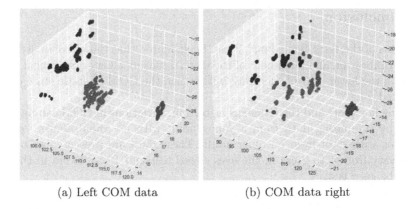

(a) Left COM data   (b) COM data right

Fig. 12. The results when standing with eyes closed show a slight convergence of data, which is greater in front of the left COM(a), as the support on the right leg was greater.

The results during the tests demonstrate the difficulty of carrying out an activity, in the third test the patients failed to complete the task making it difficult to maintain their posture. This test reveals that the patients are unable to maintain their balance which generates large peaks between the data, by analysing the data, we can observe the almost total convergence between the data which points to irregularities. Figure 13 shows these attributes as outliers, showing great instability during the activity.

The results obtained from the COM allow to study and analyze the existence of the deterioration in balance with the advancement of the years, which in this article has been tested under the realization of daily and non-daily activities that are easy for a young person. These results will contribute to the development of future research that will help in the study and early detection of conditions that affect balance.

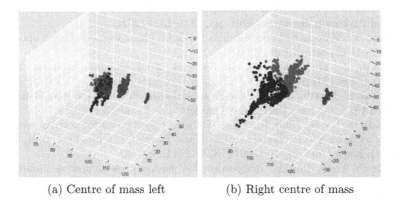

(a) Centre of mass left   (b) Right centre of mass

Fig. 13. The results show convergence of data, with outliers in postural stability being the most difficult test.

4 Conclusion

By means of the tests carried out, it can be validated that the use of quaternions for the calibration and alignment of the inertial sensors allows obtaining a model based on the lower part of the body, with which the COM in static state can be estimated.

Using box plots and the K-means algorithm, variations in COM can be determined by comparing data from a young adult with no somatosensory system problems with data from an older adult. These data are presented as outliers which vary from 1 to 2 cm in the eyes closed test and 10 to 40 cm in the one-footed balance test.

By means of the results of tests 2 and 3, it is possible to verify a displacement of the COM of the older people compared to the young person, this allows us to demonstrate that with the passage of time, it is more difficult for older adults to maintain the balance of the center of mass in normal situations.

References

1. Petrocci, K.E., Cárdenas Sandoval, R.P.: La medición del control postural con estabilometría- una revisión documental. Rev. Colomb. Rehabil. **10**(1), 16 (2017). https://doi.org/10.30788/revcolreh.v10.n1.2011.73
2. Aftanas, L.I., Bazanova, O.M., Novozhilova, N.V.: Posture-motor and a putative marker of psychomotor retardation and depressive rumination in patients with major depressive disorder. **12**, 1–9 (2018). https://doi.org/10.3389/fnhum.2018.00108
3. Lacour, M.: Envejecimiento del control postural y del equilibrio. EMC - Podol. **18**(1), 1–9 (2016). https://doi.org/10.1016/s1762-827x(15)76065-7
4. Nagymate, G., Kiss, R.M.: Balancing strategy differences in bilateral knee osteoarthritis patients, pp. 154–157 (2017)
5. Safi, K., et al.: Human static postures analysis using empirical mode decomposition, pp. 3765–3768 (2016)
6. Gimenez, F.V., Ripka, W.L., Maldaner, M., Stadnik, A.M.W.: Stabilometric analysis of Parkinson disease patients, pp. 1341–1344 (2021)
7. Bellini, B.: Sensores de presión utilizados en las plataformas de fuerza aplicadas al estudio de la posturografía (2009)
8. Richards, J.: The Comprehensive Textbook of Clinical Biomechanics, 2nd edn. Preston, UK (2018)
9. Cuadros, S.: Estudio de viabilidad de sensores inerciales (IMUs) para el análisis de Timed Up & Go test. Universitat Politécnica de Catalunya (2020)
10. Atallah, L., Lo, B., King, R., Yang, G.: Sensor positioning for activity recognition using wearable accelerometers. IEEE Trans. Biomed. Circuits Syst. **5**(4), 320–329 (2011). https://doi.org/10.1109/TBCAS.2011.2160540
11. McGrath, T., Stirling, L.: Body-worn IMU human skeletal pose estimation using a factor graph-based optimization framework. Sensors (Switzerland) **20**(23), 1–29 (2020). https://doi.org/10.3390/s20236887
12. Méndez, R.M., Huertas, M.R.: Uso de sensores inerciales en la medición y evaluación de movimiento humano para aplicaciones en la salud. Researchgate, no. July, p. 21 (2016)

13. Castellanos, J., Montealegre, L., Martínez, D., Gallo, J., Almanza, O.: Uso de sensores inerciales en fisioterapia: Una aproximación a procesos de evaluación del movimiento humano (2020)
14. Xsens. MTw Awinda User Manual MTw, no. May (2021)
15. Wu, G., et al.: ISB recommendation on definitions of joint coordinate system of various joints for the reporting of human joint motion-part I: ankle, hip, and spine. Int. Soci. Biomech. **35**, 543–548 (2002)
16. Wu, G., Cavanagh, P.R.: ISB recommendations in the reporting for standardization of kinematic data. **28**(10), 1257–1261 (1995)
17. Narváez, F., Árbito, F., Proaño, R.: A quaternion-based method to IMU-to-body alignment for gait analysis. In: Duffy, V.G. (ed.) DHM 2018. LNCS, vol. 10917, pp. 217–231. Springer, Cham (2018). https://doi.org/10.1007/978-3-319-91397-1_19
18. Narváez, F., Arbito, F., Luna, C., Merchán, C., Cuenca, M.C., Díaz, G.M.: Kushkalla: a web-based platform to improve functional movement rehabilitation. In: Valencia-García, R., Lagos-Ortiz, K., Alcaraz-Mármol, G., Del Cioppo, J., Vera-Lucio, N., Bucaram-Leverone, M. (eds.) CITI 2017. CCIS, vol. 749, pp. 194–208. Springer, Cham (2017). https://doi.org/10.1007/978-3-319-67283-0_15
19. Narváez, F., Marín-Castrillón, D.M., Cuenca, Ma., Latta, M.: Development and implementation of technologies for physical telerehabilitation in Latin America: a systematic review of literature, programs and projects. TecnoLógicas **20**, 155–176 (2017)
20. Germanotta, M., Mileti, I., Conforti, I., Aprile, I., Palermo, E.: Estimation of human center of mass position through the inertial sensors-based methods in postural tasks: an accuracy evaluation. Eval. Sens. **21**(601), 2021 (2021)
21. Balaguer García, R.: Valoración De Un Método De Posturografía Estática Con Pruebas Dinámicas Para Evaluar Funcionalmente Pacientes Vestibulares En Edad Laboral Y Su Relación Con El Índice De Discapacidad, p. 146 (2012). https://www.uv.es/mediodont
22. Barbosa, F.A., Del Pozo Cruz, J., Del Pozo Cruz, B.: Entrenamiento vibratorio en personas institucionalizadas mayores de 80 años para la mejora del equilibrio estático. Retos **29**, 38–41 (2016)

Perspectives on Climate Change Until 2030

R. Llugsi[(✉)]

National Polytechnic School, Quito, Ecuador
ricardo.llugsi@epn.edu.ec

Abstract. The study of climate change has become a priority due to the sudden changes that occur with increasing frequency and affects the different activities worldwide. In recent studies, parameters such as the Temperature anomaly show an increase that indicates a warming never seen before. In this work, we present a methodology based on the use of filtering to improve the Neural Network's forecast. Four meteorological parameters are analyzed: Anomaly Temperature, CO_2 Concentration, CO_2 Emissions and Solar Irradiance. The methodology allows a drastic error reduction specially for the CO_2 Concentration, where the MSE, RMSE and MAE values are decreased in a 99.63%, 93.9% and 95.46% respectively. From the predictions obtained up 2030 a tendency to the oscillation for the Solar irradiance is observed and an increase for the Temperature anomaly, the concentration of CO_2 and the amount of CO_2 emitted to the atmosphere around 1.5 °C, 430 PPM and 35000 Millions of Metric Tons respectively is predicted.

Keywords: CO_2 · Temperature Anomaly · Solar Irradiance · Neural Networks

1 Introduction

In recent years, climate change and its effects have become more noticeable and its impact has manifested itself even more around the planet. The most obvious manifestations of climate change can include extreme weather events such as storms, floods and forest fires. Several authors have sought to implement metrics for the analysis of climate change through the analysis of certain weather parameters such as the temperature anomaly [1], solar radiation [2], the global annual average of Carbon Dioxide (CO_2) present in the atmosphere [3] and the amount of tons of Carbon Dioxide emitted into the atmosphere [4]. In [5] we realize that the global distribution of seasonal mean temperature anomalies shifts towards higher temperatures, the range of anomalies also increases. This implies that an adequate knowledge of the trend of the temperature anomaly is essential to determine the extent of climate change on the planet [6]. Despite the

---

Supported by the National Polytechnic School.

fact that there is a clear relationship between the Temperature Anomaly and the CO_2 concentration [3], it cannot simply be concluded that the amount of CO_2 that is emitted annually into the atmosphere is the main cause of climate change. It is also necessary to take into account the amount of CO_2 that is already present in the atmosphere. We can confirm that looking the information from the first half of 2020. When despite the fact that there was a decrease of 8.8% in global CO_2 emissions (due to the restrictions taken worldwide by the Covid 19 pandemic) compared to the emissions in the same period in 2019 [7], there was no decrease in the concentration of CO_2 present in the atmosphere. Finally, we analyse the rate of energy coming from the Sun (solar irradiance) to determine to what extent the change in irradiation affects, for instance, the cloud formation processes. We do this analysis bearing in mind that the Sun is the main source of energy for the planet and that even a slight change in its output energy can make a big difference in the climatic conditions of the planet [2]. The scientific community around the world already knows the above. However, this is where a point of debate originates. The question that arises is what could be the best forecast methodology that allows obtaining the future trend of the parameters described above.

At this point, it is necessary to emphasize that the conservation and proper use of the information should have priority when carrying out this task. Why conservation? In some cases, the use of filters is carried out to reduce the variation on Time scales to smooth the historical anomaly curve [8,9]. With this process is clear that traditional processes omits important information for no malicious purpose but for a statistical methodology. However, to what extent the restriction of frequencies of a filter affects the obtaining of an adequate trend of a parameter in the future is important. In [8] it is mentioned that the Climate-related oscillation data at decimal year time t can be compared with the tidal oscillations as captured by cosine relationships. The same author even mentions that we can obtain a good mathematical approximation of tidal oscillation (for a period of 60 years) from the sum of two components of the cosine form, that is, only two frequencies. So, what happens if the filtering modifies the future trend of a certain parameter related to climate change? Taking into account the relevance of the parameters described above, and the importance of generate a good forecast based on the use of all the frequency components in a dataset to generate proper alternatives for resilience to climate change. In this work, we introduce an alternative to improve forecasting of weather trends, based on a novel approach that uses a Savitzky-Golay filter stage.

We present the methodology based on two axes of analysis: 1) the use of Filtering and the Fourier Transform to work with the data not only in the Time Domain but also in the Frequency Domain, retrieving a secondary group of frequency components (vestigial components) eliminated during the filtering stage. 2) The use of Neural Networks to obtain the forecast of the data at the output of the filter as well as the vestigial components and combining them to obtain a more reliable trend. We organize the remainder of the paper as follows. First, we present in Sect. 2 the methodology applied to obtain the Temperature Anomaly from year 300 to 2020 to illustrate the global warming. Section 2.1

addresses the theory that supports how we can exploit the frequency components to improve the parameter forecast using the filtering process. Section 3 is devoted to provide the basis of the experimentation and the analysis of results. Sections 4 concludes the paper.

2 Methodology

As mentioned at the beginning, the objective of this work is to obtain a better trend of the forecast of meteorological variables based on the use of filtering. To accomplish with this aim, first, we transfer the data series from Time to Frequency domain by using the Fourier transform. We obtain the components that characterize the series before and after filtering. In this way the eliminated frequency components by the filter, which constitute the vestigial variation of the parameter trend, are recovered and then returned to the Time domain. Once we have carried out this task, we use a Neural Network to make a prediction of this vestigial component. In a similar way, the smoothed data (namely after the filtering stage) in Time is also entered in a Neural Network to obtain its prediction. Once we finish the above, we transfer the result of the smoothed and the vestigial data predictions to the Frequency domain. Here, we add together both and the outcome is transferred back to the Time domain to obtain in this way the proposed corrected trend. To start the discussion, we describe first the theoretical basis that supports the present work, secondly, we verify the methodology described above is used and its effectiveness, and thirdly, we obtain a trend of the expected weather parameter up to the year 2030.

2.1 Processing in the Frequency Domain

Fourier Transform. In order to transfer the information from Time to Frequency Domain, it is necessary to utilize the Fourier Transform. The Discrete Fourier Transform (DFT) makes it possible to implement the Fourier transform considering as inputs sequences of data of finite duration, that is to say discretized. At present, the DFT allows to implement a wide variety of methodologies and techniques for Digital Signals and Images Processing. However, it is necessary to clarify that its practical application is given by the implementation of the Fast Fourier Transform (FFT) and the Goertzel algorithm [10].

A signal $X_p(t)$ can be considered periodic if it holds that $X_p(t) = X_p(t+T)$, for all t and a part of T. The part of T mentioned above is named T_0 and it is the smallest value of T for which the signal $X_p(t)$ is periodic. The Fourier series allow to carry out the analysis of periodic signals basically because it states that any periodic function can be expressed as the sum of a series of harmonic sinusoids. The Fourier Series can be represented in a trigonometric form or in a complex exponential form. In this case the constitutive component is the complex exponent $Ae^{j(2\pi ft+\varphi)}$, with A as the amplitude of the signal and considering the linear frequency f in (Hz) and φ as the phase of the angle at t = 0 (in radians or degrees).

Similar to periodic signals, we can represent non-periodic signals in the frequency domain. But, since in this case there is a continuous spectrum of the signal the frequency components must be analyzed in a range that goes from $-\infty$ to ∞ $x(t) = \int_{-\infty}^{\infty} X(f)e^{j2\pi ft}dt$ [11]. Thanks to an adequate distribution of complex exponents, in a continuous range of frequencies, this equation becomes a good approximation of the signal x(t), which is why is called the synthesis ratio or Inverse Fourier Transform. Now, with the purpose of analyzing the equivalent of the transform considering discretization, it is initially necessary to consider that the equivalent in frequency of X(t) can be obtained with $X(f) = \int_{\infty}^{-\infty} x(t)e^{-j2\pi ft}dt$. If $f(t)$ is the continuous signal which is the source of the data and its discretized equivalent can be written as $f[0], f[1], f[2], \ldots, f[k], \ldots, f[N-1]$, then each sample $f[k]$ can be considered as an impulse having area $f[k]$. Then, since the integral exist only at the sample points, the equivalent of the Fourier Transform can be written as $F(j\omega) = \sum_{k=0}^{N-1} f[k]e^{-j\omega kT}$. Now, and since there are only a finite number of input points, the DFT treats the samples as if it were periodic, thus, the DFT equation for the fundamental frequency and its harmonics can be generalized as $F[n] = \sum_{k=0}^{N-1} f[k]e^{-j\frac{2\pi}{N}nk}$.

In a similar way the discretized equivalent of the Inverse transform can be described as $f[k] = \frac{1}{N}\sum_{n=0}^{N-1} F[n]e^{+j\frac{2\pi}{N}nk}$. The DFT computing is a process that involves the decomposition of a series of data into components of different frequencies. In practice, this operation is difficult to perform due to the complexity represented by the number of operations that should be performed. To solve this problem and be able to implement the discrete transform process in hardware, use is made of the Fast Fourier Transform (FFT) [10]. An FFT quickly calculates such transformations by factoring the DFT matrix into a product of scarce factors that mostly have a value of zero. The FFT is nowadays one of the fastest DFT algorithm for computing the exact DFT which need to take time at least proportional to its output size.

Filtering Process. Filtering is a type of processing that involves the elimination of frequency components (or even frequency bands) and therefore of certain characteristics contained in a signal. In a general way, filters can be classified by its Frequency Response $H(t)$ and by its type of implementation (analog or digital). Additionally, in signal processing, filters can be classified as nonlinear, linear and by its response to the impulse (Infinite Impulse Response (IIR) or Finite Impulse Response (FIR)) [12]. However, there are filtering methodologies that do not focus exclusively on work in the Frequency domain, but rather make use of the convolutional process in order to smooth short-term fluctuations in a Time Series and highlight long-term trends or cycles. In this work, we have adopted the Savitzky-Golay filter in order to obtain a secondary group (vestigial) of frequency components that will be used to improve the forecast from a Neural Network. The Savitzky-Golay operation is based on the convolution process over successive subsets of adjacent data points with a low-degree polynomial using the method of least squares [13].

The Savitzky-Golay filter is implemented based on a polynomial estimator $\tilde{p}[n] = \sum_{k=0}^{\lfloor \frac{N}{2} \rfloor} \tilde{a}_{2k} n^{2k}$, of degree N and coefficients $\tilde{a}$, that fits the data by the difference of the least squares error that is, applying $\sum_{n=-M}^{M} \left(\sum_{k=0}^{N} a_k n^k - x[n] \right)$ [14].

Because its impulse response can span a range $-M \leq n \leq M$, it allows more degrees of freedom to carry out the estimation. In [14] it is mentioned that the half drop of the filter (half power point) is determined by the order N and by its length M, thus, the longer M is, the shorter the cutoff frequency. The higher the order of the polynomial N, the higher the cutoff frequency, and thus the smaller the number of points M. Namely, to obtain an adequate approximation of the samples entered into the filter, it is necessary to choose the best compensation between the size of the window frame, the order of the derivative and the polynomial coefficients. Considering the above, it is possible to obtain better results than when working with standard FIR filters due to a better interpolation adjustment, which results in a better conservation of high frequency signals, very useful, for example when talking about noise removal. Consequently, the result at the output of the filter becomes an approximation whose function is similar to the input data, but which tends to preserve the characteristics of the initial distribution, that is, maintaining its relative maxima and minima, which normally disappear with other averaging techniques.

2.2   Neural Networks

Once we have explained the theory related to the filtering stage it is necessary to talk about the forecast of the weather parameters. The use of Neural Networks to forecast data has become quite popular during recent years and its efficacy has been extensively tested. Many models have been proposed till the date but in this work 4 models (LSTM, Stacked LSTM, Dense and ARIMA [15,16]) whose effectiveness to obtain a reliable weather forecast has been extensively verified by the author, are presented. We have inspected and validated the prediction obtained from the models by error metrics values and the Correlation Coefficient between the real and forecasted data in the test set. We detail these models below.

LSTM Neural Networks. A Recurrent Neural Network (RNN) is a generalization of the Feed-Forward network that makes use of memory stages and that was used in its beginnings for the treatment of Time Series. An RNN uses the same function for every input of data whereas the output of the current input depends on the past one computed. Consequently, its performance deteriorates rapidly as the length of the input stream increases [17,18]. Conversely, an LSTM network is a type of RNN which information is updated or removed through the use of special structures called gates. These structures are grouped into memory stages called "cells", which can better store information and thus effectively handle long time dependencies. Today, this type of network is used to forecast environmental parameters such as wind speed [19] or others such as temperature or dew point [20].

Stacked LSTM Neural Networks. Model stacking involves the use of 2 or more Neural Networks connected one after the other, that is, using the outputs of one model as inputs of another. The advantage of this configuration is that the representation of the Time Series becomes more complex at the output of each model allowing describing in greater depth the existing relationships within the Time Series that has been entered in the structure. As in the previous case, LSTM Stacking has been widely used in recent years and has been shown to be very suitable for obtaining meteorological predictions based on historical records [21]. For example, in [22] it is mentioned that the meteorological data collected from 9 stations installed in the airports of 9 cities were used to make a 12-hour forecast using a multilayer model with LSTM. In this case, the error per hour was in the range between $0.01\,°C$ to $3\,°C$.

Dense Network. In its most basic concept, it can be said that the dense layer neuron performs a matrix-vector multiplication between the matrix A_{MxN} of the input data and the column vector of the dense layer X_N, by which can be said that as a rule the row vector must have as many columns as the column vector [23]. Nowadays this type of network is utilized to implement classification models or to implement the final processing layer of forecasting models.

ARIMA Network. The Auto Regressive Integrated Moving Average (ARIMA) model is one of the most widely used approaches to forecasting Time Series nowadays. Its operation is based on the representation of a random process, in which the variable of interest depends on its past observations and at the same time uses an indicator that combines the variable values over a certain period, and divides them by the number of data collected to generate a trend. This happens because ARIMA allows the handling of autoregressive components (AR), that is, in the representation of the random process and moving average components (MA) for the generation of the combination of the variable values, so that the most recent changes in the Time Series can be easily modeled [21] to determine its trend [24,25]. For stationary Time Series, the ARIMA (p, d, q) model can be written in terms of past temperature data, residuals, and prediction errors [26] as follows:

$$x_t = \sum_{i=1}^{p} \varphi_i x_{t-i} - \sum_{j=1}^{q} \theta_j a_{t-j} + a_t \tag{1}$$

where:

x: Temperature time series data.
a_t: Random white noise Time Series.
φ_i: Auto regressive parameters.
θ_j: Moving average parameters.
p: Order of auto regressive model.
q: Order of moving average model.
d: Degree of differencing.

If the Time Series is non-stationary differencing is performed to transform the series into a stationary model. First order differencing can be expressed as $y_t = x_{t-i} - x_t$. If y_t is not stationary, when d = 1 then, it is needed to difference using d-1 times until it becomes stationary.

Nowadays, this Neural Network model has been already used for weather forecast. For instance, in [27] it is mentioned that a 30 -year record of air temperature and precipitation in the cities of Jokioinen, Dikopshof, Lleida and Lublin was utilized to implement a weather forecasted through an ARIMA model. In this case, it can be seen that the error per hour falls in the range of between approximately 3.02 °C and 4.5 °C.

Walk Forward Validation. The Walk Forward technique consist in a shifting moving window [28] utilized to carry out the validation and prediction process. The methodology carry out the optimization on a subset of the training set that changes its size every iteration during the validation [29].

$$TW = \sum_{i}^{n} tWL_i \tag{2}$$

where:

TW: Testing Window.
tWL_i Window length for test per iteration.

This is an interesting alternative to deeply exploit the classic approach of dividing the available data in training, validation and testing sets [30]. Additionally, it can be said that this technique is a really valuable tool to work with environmental information since usually it tends to be non-stationary (trend + pseudo cycle) and its order should be preserved.

3   Experimentation

Initially a graphical comparison between Temperature anomaly, CO_2 Concentration, CO_2 Emissions and Solar irradiation is presented. Then, the information retrieved during the filtering is presented separately to analyze its relationship. And finally, the forecasts are obtained and combined in the Frequency Domain to carry out the respective validations. For more information on experimentation, the reader can go to the respective GitHub files at the following link https://github.com/Llugsi/SmartTechIC2022.

3.1   Data Set Selection

The data series of Surface Temperature product version 4 (GISTEMP v4) from the Goddard Institute for Space Studies of the NASA from the period 1880 to 2020 [31] is used to represent the Temperature Anomaly. On the other hand, the Mauna Loa CO_2 records are utilized to analyze the CO_2 concentration (PPM) in the atmosphere [3]. This dataset is product of the work of Dr. Pieter Tans, NOAA/GML (gml.noaa.gov/ccgg/trends/) and Dr. Ralph Keeling, from the Scripps Institution of Oceanography (scrippsco2.ucsd.edu/), and is courtesy of the Global Monitoring Laboratory of the Earth System Research Laboratories from NOAA https://gml.noaa.gov/ccgg/trends/data.html. The amount of CO2 emissions (in millions of metric tons) has been obtained courtesy of the International Energy Agency (IEA, Paris) through the Global Energy Review 2021, https://www.iea.org/reports/global-energy-review-2021/co2-emissions. And finally, the records utilized to model the Total Solar Irradiance (W/m^2) are courtesy of the Max Planck Institute for Solar System Research, Germany through the SATIRE-T2 model, http://www2.mps.mpg.de/projects/sun-climate/data.html.

The proposed forecasts are done using the data from 1880 to 2010 to predict the data from the period 2010 to 2020. We have done the above because of two reasons. Firstly, these data set series have not been previously filtered so they represent the ideal scenario to be able to demonstrate the methodology proposed in this work. Secondly, in reason of the COVID-19 pandemic both economic and environmental behaviour have been substantially modified and analysis based on the prediction for the second decade of the 21st century becomes mandatory. In Figs. 1 and 2, the four data series mentioned above are presented separately in order to avoid confusion because of overlapping of graphs when carrying out graphical analyses specially with the solar information.

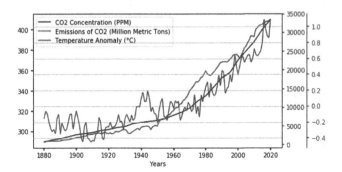

Fig. 1. Concentration and emission of CO_2 and Temperature Anomaly.

3.2   Data Set Analysis

In Fig. 1 it can be seen that apparently the concentration of CO_2, the emission of CO_2 and the temperature anomaly are directly related. However, it is necessary to consider that the Fig. 2 does not clearly show a relationship between solar irradiance and the other weather parameters. However, when carrying out the filtering process, and inspecting the information retrieved in the Frequency

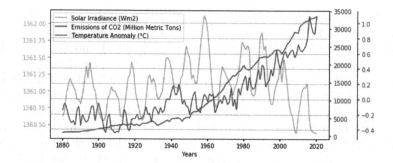

Fig. 2. CO_2 Concentration, Temperature Anomaly and Total Solar Irradiance.

Domain, it can be seen that the data set of CO_2 Emissions, temperature anomaly and solar irradiance, are now the values that can be related in a better way, see Fig. 3.

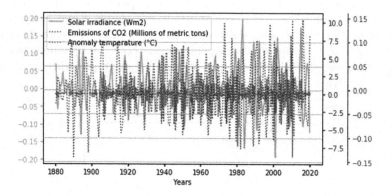

Fig. 3. CO_2 Concentration, Temperature Anomaly and Total Solar Irradiance.

The information shown in Fig. 3, has been obtained from the use of a Savitzky-Golay filter configured with a window size of 71 and a polynomial order 3, except for the treatment of the series of CO_2 emissions, where a window of size 11 has been used. The size of the window has been selected to contrast the impact of filtering information from the data series without incurring the risk of biasing the information too much and to carry out an adequate forecast of the Vestigial component.

To carry out the predictions using the four models described in Sect. 3, the following configuration was adopted: A distribution of 90 % and 10%, for the Training and Validation/Test sets. The number of neurons for the LSTM model was 300 while for the LSTM stacked model a structure of 75, 150 neurons was selected. The above models were trained with dropout percentage of 30 %. On the other hand, the Dense model uses 100 neurons. Finally the ARIMA model

Table 1. Comparison between real and forecasted data for Temperature Anomaly

Model	Error Metrics			Correlation (r)
	MSE	*RMSE*	*MAE*	
LSTM	0.043	0.208	0.177	0.681
Stacked LSTM	0.043	0.209	0.178	0.696
Dense	0.030	0.174	0.147	0.724
ARIMA	0.026	0.163	0.126	0.596
Filter Correction	0.008	0.091	0.068	0.805

used for each one of the parameters was configured in the following way, a 2nd order Auto-Regressive model with a non-seasonal differencing equal to 1 and a 3rd order Moving Average model for the Temperature Anomaly. Then, to implement the adjusted forecast based on the use of the Vestigial component retrieved from the filtering stage and the smoothed series at the output of the filter the ARIMA model has been selected. This decision was made bearing in mind that thanks to its auto-regressive processing, the ARIMA model produces forecasts based on previous values in the original Time Series, while due to the Calculation of Moving Average at the same time determines the errors made by predictions in each of the components (vestigial and smoothed). That is, with this strategy it is sought to efficiently adjust the forecast of each component based on the sudden changes that occur in the original Time Series. In this stage a different configuration for the ARIMA model was structured for each one of the four parameters studied in this work. Excluding the ARIMA network all the models were trained using 150 epochs, a batch size of 5 and the Adam optimizer. Once the predictions of the Vestigial Component and the Smoothed Component are obtained, the two are then transferred to the Frequency domain. Here the spectrum of both signals is summed and transferred back to the Time domain.

Now, to contrast the forecasts obtained from the first Neural Networks and the methodology proposed in this work, the error metrics and the correlation coefficients obtained between the predicted value and the real value of the series is presented. In order to be clear in the presentation of results, the analysis is presented in two parts, the first, that includes a punctual forecast comparison between the four models and the Filtered correction proposal for the Temperature Anomaly parameter (see Table 1). And the second, that implies a general analysis of the four parameters in comparison with the ARIMA model (see Table 2), that was the Neural Network that presented the lowest error metrics among the four models reviewed in this work.

The data set comparison described for the first part shows that from all the four models, the ARIMA network obtained the lowest error metrics with MSE, RMSE and MAE values of $0.026\,°C, 0.163\,°C$ and $0.126\,°C$ respectively. Additionally, it can be said that from this analysis the forecasted data sets that is con-

Table 2. Comparison between real and forecasted data for all parameters

Dataset Forecasted	Error Metrics			(r)
	MSE	RMSE	MAE	
Anomaly	0.026	0.163	0.126	0.596
Corrected Anomaly	0.008	0.091	0.068	0.805
Concentration	21.087	4.592	4.192	0.996
Corrected Concentration	0.078	0.280	0.190	0.999
Emissions	753057	867.7	767.4	0.960
Corrected Emissions	1852390	1361	1105	0.938
Irradiance	0.379	0.615	0.571	0.772
Corrected Irradiance	0.130	0.361	0.315	0.771

siderably best correlated with the real data is the one obtained from the Dense model, reaching a correlation coefficient of 0.724. Nevertheless, when the Filtered correction is used, all error metrics are reduced (MSE, RMSE and MAE values of $0.008\,°C$, $0.091\,°C$ and $0.068\,°C$ respectively) and correlation is increased (0.805). On the other hand, from the second part of the experimentation it can be concluded that with the exception of the CO2 emission, in all cases the corrected forecast based on filtering allows a reduction in the error metrics. The best improvement occurs for the CO_2 Concentration where the MSE, RMSE and MAE values are reduced to $0.078\,°C$, $0.28\,°C$ and $0.19\,°C$ respectively. Nonetheless, it is important to say that in this case the correlation improvement does not look so promising except for the temperature anomaly where the improving reach a 35%.

3.3   Forecasted Trend

Once the methodology proposed has been experimentally proven, the same procedure is applied but now considering a period of time between 2020 and 2030. In Fig. 4, the total Temperature Anomaly using the Goddard data set.

In this case the Temperature Anomaly trend equation can be described as:

$$2.343e^{-8}x^4 - 1.822e^{-4}x^3 + 0.5314x^2 - 688.7x + 3.347e^5 \qquad (3)$$

In Fig. 5, the CO_2 Concentration in the atmosphere and its respective trend equation are presented.

In this case the CO_2 Concentration trend equation can be described as:

$$-5.181e^{-7}x^4 + 4.115e^{-3}x^3 - 12.24x^2 - 1.617e^4x - 8e^6 \qquad (4)$$

In Fig. 6, the quantity of CO_2 Emissions in the atmosphere and its respective trend equation are presented.

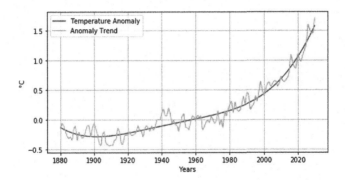

Fig. 4. Temperature Anomaly forecasted and trend.

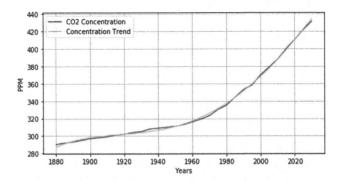

Fig. 5. CO_2 Concentration forecasted and trend.

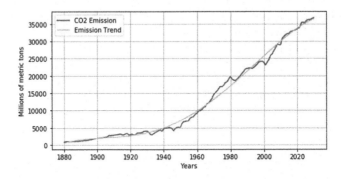

Fig. 6. CO_2 Emission forecasted and trend.

In this case the CO_2 Emissions trend equation can be described as:

$$-2.772\mathrm{e}^{-4}x^4 + 2.161x^3 - 6317x^2 + 8.201\mathrm{e}^6 x + 3.991\mathrm{e}^9 \tag{5}$$

In Fig. 7, the Solar Irradiance and its respective trend equation are presented.

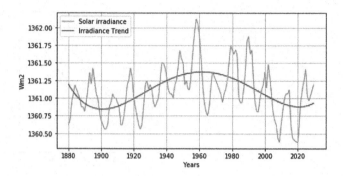

Fig. 7. Solar Irradiance forecasted and trend.

In this case the Solar Irradiance trend equation can be described as:

$$3.951\mathrm{e}^{-8}x^4 - 3.1\mathrm{e}^{-4}x^3 + 0.9116x^2 - 1191x + 5.848\mathrm{e}^5 \tag{6}$$

4 Conclusions

The methodology proposed in this work allows a drastic error metric reduction for the CO_2 Concentration, where the MSE, RMSE and MAE values are decreased in a 99.63%, 93.9% and 95.46% respectively (in comparison with the best forecast obtained from the four models proposed to compare the proposed methodology). The limitation of the proposed methodology is related to the correlation between the forecasted data and the real values. It can be said that the improvement was not really significant except for the case of Temperature anomaly were the improvement reach a 35%. The trend equation obtained for the four meteorological variables presented in this work has been successfully modeled using a polynomial function of 4th grade. Speaking of the prediction until 2030, it can be said that, with the exception of Solar irradiation, whose forecast shows a tendency to oscillate, the Temperature anomaly, the concentration of CO_2 and the amount of CO_2 emitted to the atmosphere, increase by more than 1.5 °C, 430 PPM and 35000 Millions of Metric Tons respectively.

Disclosure Statement. No potential conflict of interest was reported by the author.

References

1. Dessler, A.: Introduction to Modern Climate Change, 3rd edn. Cambridge University Press (2021). ISBN 978-1108793872
2. Bhargawa, A., Singh, A.K.: Solar irradiance, climatic indicators and climate change - an empirical analysis. Adv. Space Res. **64**(1), 271–277 (2019). https://doi.org/10.1016/j.asr.2019.03.018

3. Etheridge, D., Steele, P., Langenfelds, R., Francey, R., Barnola, J., Morgan, V.: Natural and anthropogenic changes in atmospheric CO_2 over the last 1000 years from air in Antarctic ice and firn. J. Geophys. Res. **101**, 4115–4128 (1996). https://doi.org/10.1029/95JD03410

4. Ağbulut, Ü., Ceylan, İ, Gürel, A., Ergün, A.: The history of greenhouse gas emissions and relation with the nuclear energy policy for Turkey. Int. J. Ambient Energy **42**, 1447–1455 (2019). https://doi.org/10.1080/01430750.2018.1563818

5. Bárcena-Martín, E., Molina, J., Hueso, P., Ruiz-Sinoga, J.: A class of indices and a graphical tool to monitor temperature anomalies. Air Soil Water Res. **13**, 1–11 (2020). https://doi.org/10.1177/1178622120938384

6. Clark, J., Feldstein, S.: What drives the North Atlantic oscillation's temperature anomaly pattern? Part I: the growth and decay of the surface air temperature anomalies. J. Atmos. Sci. **77**(1), 185–198 (2021). https://doi.org/10.1175/JAS-D-19-0027.1

7. Liu, Z., Ciais, P., Deng, Z., et al.: Near-real-time monitoring of global CO_2 emissions reveals the effects of the COVID-19 pandemic. Nat. Commun. **11**, 1–12 (2020). https://doi.org/10.1038/s41467-020-18922-7

8. Treloar, N.: Deconstructing global temperature anomalies: an hypothesis. Climate **5**(4) (2017). https://doi.org/10.3390/cli5040083

9. Qian, G., et al.: A novel statistical decomposition of the historical change in global mean surface temperature. Environ. Res. Lett. **16**(5) (2021). https://doi.org/10.1088/1748-9326/abea34

10. Zhong, L., Lichun, L., Huiqi, L.: Application research on sparse fast Fourier transform algorithm in white Gaussian noise. In: Advances in Information and Communication Technology: Proceedings of 7th International Congress of Information and Communication Technology, vol. 107, pp. 802–807. Elsevier (2017). https://doi.org/10.1016/j.procs.2017.03.176

11. Tianshuang, Q., Ying, G.: 5. discrete Fourier transform and fast Fourier transform. In: Signal Processing and Data Analysis, pp. 135–183. De Gruyter, Boston (2018). https://doi.org/10.1515/9783110465082-005

12. Gaydecki, P.: Foundations of Digital Signal Processing: Theory, Algorithms and Hardware Design. Institution of Electrical Engineers, EngineeringPro Collection, vol. 15, no. 15 (2004)

13. Luo, J., Ying, K., Bai, J.: Savitzky-Golay smoothing and differentiation filter for even number data. Signal Process. **85**, 1429–1434 (2005). https://doi.org/10.1016/j.sigpro.2005.02.002

14. Jardim, R., Morgado-Dias, F.: Savitzky-Golay filtering as image noise reduction with sharp color reset. Microprocess. Microsyst. **74**, 1–9 (2020). https://doi.org/10.1016/j.micpro.2020.103006

15. Llugsi, R., Fontaine, A., Lupera, P., El Yacoubi, S.: Comparison between Adam, AdaMax and AdamW optimizers to implement a Weather Forecast based on Neural Networks for the Andean city of Quito. In: ETCM. IEEE (2021). https://doi.org/10.1109/ETCM53643.2021.9590681

16. Llugsi, R., Fontaine, A., Lupera, P., El Yacoubi, S.: A novel approach for detecting error measurements in a network of automatic weather stations. Int. J. Parallel Emergent Distrib. Syst. (2022). https://doi.org/10.1080/17445760.2021.2022672

17. Oliver, J.: Comparing classic time series models and the LSTM recurrent neural network: an application to S P 500 stocks. Financ. Markets Valuation (2021). https://hal.archives-ouvertes.fr/hal-03149342

18. Mateus, B., Mendes, M., Farinha, J., Assis, R., Cardoso, A.: Comparing LSTM and GRU models to predict the condition of a pulp paper press. Energies (2021). https://doi.org/10.3390/en14216958

19. Elsaraiti, M., Merabet, A.: Application of long-short-term- memory recurrent neural networks to forecast wind speed. Appl. Sci. (2021). https://doi.org/10.3390/app11052387

20. Karevan, Z., Suykens, J.: Transductive LSTM for time-series prediction: an application to weather forecasting. Neural Netw. (2020). https://doi.org/10.1016/j.neunet.2019.12.030

21. Kreuzer, D., Munz, M., Schlüter, S.: Short-term temperature forecasts using a convolutional neural network - an application to different weather stations in Germany. Mach. Learn. Appl. 2(15) (2020). https://doi.org/10.1016/j.mlwa.2020.100007

22. Zaytar, M., El Amrani, C.: Sequence to sequence weather forecasting with long short-term memory recurrent neural networks. Int. J. Comput. Appl. 143(11), 7–11 (2016). https://doi.org/10.5120/ijca2016910497

23. Josephine, V., Nirmala, A., Alluri, V.: Impact of hidden dense layers in convolutional neural network to enhance performance of classification model. In: Conference Series: Materials Science and Engineering, vol. 1131, no. 1, pp. 1–9. IOP Publishing (2021). https://doi.org/10.1088/1757-899x/1131/1/012007

24. Dimri, T., Ahmad, S., Sharif, M.: Time series analysis of climate variables using seasonal ARIMA approach. J. Earth Syst. Sci. 129(1), 1–16 (2020). https://doi.org/10.1007/s12040-020-01408-x

25. Alsharif, M., Younes, M., Kim, J.: Time series ARIMA model for prediction of daily and monthly average global solar radiation: the case study of Seoul, South Korea. Symmetry (2019). https://doi.org/10.3390/sym11020240

26. Zhou, K., Wang, W., Hu, T., Wu, C.: Comparison of time series forecasting based on statistical ARIMA model and LSTM with attention mechanism. In: Journal of Physics: Conference Series, vol. 1631 (2020). https://doi.org/10.1088/1742-6596/1631/1/012141

27. Murat, M., Malinowska, I., Gos, M., Krzyszczak, J.: Forecasting daily meteorological time series using ARIMA and regression models. Int. Agrophys. 32, 253–264 (2018). https://doi.org/10.1515/intag-2017-0007

28. Ładyżyński, P., Żbikowski, K., Grzegorzewski, P.: Stock trading with random forests, trend detection tests and force index volume indicators. In: Rutkowski, L., Korytkowski, M., Scherer, R., Tadeusiewicz, R., Zadeh, L.A., Zurada, J.M. (eds.) ICAISC 2013. LNCS (LNAI), vol. 7895, pp. 441–452. Springer, Heidelberg (2013). https://doi.org/10.1007/978-3-642-38610-7_41

29. Falessi, D., Huang, J., Narayana, L., Thai, J.F., Turhan, B.: On the need of preserving order of data when validating within-project defect classifiers. Empirical Softw. Eng. 25, 4805–4830 (2020). https://doi.org/10.1007/s10664-020-09868-x

30. Hyndman, R., Athanasopoulos, G.: Forecasting: Principles and Practice. OTexts, Melbourne, Australia (2018). https://otexts.com/fpp2/

31. Lenssen, N., et al.: Improvements in the GISTEMP uncertainty model. J. Geophys. Res. Atmos. 124(12), 6307–6326 (2019). https://doi.org/10.1029/2018JD029522

Virtual Power Plants as a Management Strategy to Improve Resilience in Electrical Distribution Networks

Alejandro Arias[✉], Willmar Suarez, Edwin Rivas, and Darin Mosquera

Universidad ECCI, Bogotá, Colombia
lincarias@yahoo.com, lariasb@ecci.edu.co

Abstract. In this article, the dispatch of energy in a distribution network that includes virtual power plants (VPP) is proposed as a strategy that improves the resilience of the Electric System in the face of a disruptive event linked to a natural phenomenon or technical failures such as blackouts that involve an interruption in the service of users for hours or even days. A case study was developed in a test network made up of distribution companies, conventional users and users with distributed energy resources (DER). The management of the DER is carried out through the VPP focusing on meeting the demand for the critical loads of the network during a disruptive event. As a test scenario, an IEEE-34 node network was selected in which an energy dispatch is carried out during one day, supported by distribution companies that regularly supply the distribution network and VPP when disruptive event has occurred. The mathematical modeling of the problem was carried out by posing an optimization problem, considering the objective functions of the distribution companies, VPP and their respective restrictions such as the maximum level of energy that they can supply and the coverage of Critic Loads (CL) required demand. For the solution quadratic criteria was used. The results show the viability of covering the energy demands of critical loads, optimally, when a disruptive event occurs, using virtual power plants.

Keywords: Energy Dispatch · Density Probabilistic function · Distributed Energy Resources · Distributed Generation · Virtual Power Plant · Resilience

1 Introduction

A disruptive event causes the system to go out of its stable state to an interrupted state, being these of a random type or of a deliberate type. Electric grids can be susceptible to random or deliberate contingencies in their infrastructure, with effects that can spread, causing economic losses and interruption of service. Random interruptions can be due to natural disasters and/or contingencies of the operation (symmetric or asymmetric failures), while deliberate interruptions are due to actions carried out by a disruptor agent that aims to maximize the damage produced to the network (cyber-attacks or malicious attacks).

Resilience for an energy system is interpreted in this paper as the series of measures and methods that characterize the behavior of the infrastructure in the network after a

© The Author(s), under exclusive license to Springer Nature Switzerland AG 2023
F. R. Narváez et al. (Eds.): SmartTech-IC 2022, CCIS 1705, pp. 385–399, 2023.
https://doi.org/10.1007/978-3-031-32213-6_28

disruptive event, giving the possibility of creating methodologies that lead to the energy system having the capacity fast restoration.

This document does not contemplate the improvement of resilience due to cyberattacks, however, it is stated that the network operator knows that the attacker's resources are limited and ignores his attack plan, so it requires from the point of view of the theory of games a vulnerability analysis of the system that allows identifying the elements that when destroyed generate the greatest load shedding and that therefore will be part of the disruptor agent's attack plan [1]. Therefore, it is necessary for the system operator (SO) to identify the elements of the network to which they must allocate a greater number of resources in order to maximize the resilience of the network. Development trends indicate risk management is emerging at last to become a science, as well as an art and a practice [2].

Faced with a disruptive event, authors such as [3] propose the introduction of auxiliary type services, using different types of production and consumption devices in the local network, in order to make the total system more reliable at the distribution level; [4] describe a Methodology for Assessing the Resilience of Networked Infrastructure; [5] use a heuristic approach based on cooperative optimization of the particle swarm, to optimize the provision of residential energy services; [6] present two topological models and several strategies based on topologies to improve the loss of resilience in a power system; [7] present a predictive control model for the optimal operation of microgrid managed in a coordinated manner to supply electricity reliably with renewables; [8] present an effectiveness study to strengthen strategies in energy distribution systems vulnerable to extreme failures; [9] propose a load restoration optimization model to coordinate the reconfiguration of the topology with distributed generators; [10] provides a conceptual framework for improving resilience and restoration of critical loads; [11] propose an advanced feeder restoration approach to improve the resilience systems using DER to restoring critical loads in power distribution system; The review of references shows a close correlation between the management of DER in a centralized and distributed manner in order to improve resilience in electrical systems [12] propose the participation of distributed energy resources of consumers in the electricity system and markets in the Spanish State; [13] present the development of a biased random key evolution (BRKGA) genetic algorithm for an optimal configuration in distribution networks using renewables; [14] use the Monte Carlo method to evaluate the resilience and impact of critical loads in distribution networks; [15] present a methodology based on the analysis of emerging threats for the evaluation of energy security in terms of resilience of the energy system.

One perspective for the integration of DER not only in the face of emerging events but also in situations of normal operation of the network, is the inclusion of Virtual Power Plants (VPP) in the management process of a distribution network, and particularly in the energy dispatch [16]. The VPP can participate in short-term power markets during peak hours due to the inclusion of DG that provides power to the grid. DG energy can be stored outside of peak hours [17]. VPP allows the group's users to participate as agents in the negotiation of the energy dispatch, which stimulates the integration of the DER in the process of diversification of the energy matrix.

Resilience in the electricity grid is complex due to a wide variety of threats that affect the system including digitization, cybersecurity, technological changes in the electricity system and extreme climate change events. The latter have affected the operation of multiple energy systems (MES) making there are case studies which focus on evaluating the resilience of the (MES) using the Monte-Carlo method, showing that the performance has a large variation with respect to the region and the month of study [18].

To control and manage resilience in the electrical system, in many cases virtual power plants (VPP) are implemented, which are involved in the energy distribution, commercialization and management processes, allowing to relate different sources of renewable energy with the residential, commercial and industrial electrical system [19]. Some studies relate VPP to different DER, managing the energy demanded and supplied, controlling fluctuations through response to demand (DR) and electric vehicles (EV), with the aim of minimizing the required cost and improving the restoration of the load [20].

Some automation technologies, including VPP, enable faster restoration and shutdown of loads efficiently to the power system, providing better visibility into system fluctuations and disturbances, including Advanced Metering Infrastructure (AMI) which allows in real time to provide information on all the events that have occurred and to know the affected areas, improving the resilience of the system. [21] These VPP can be controlled by a distributed or centralized strategy. In the first case, communication has some advantages with DER and VPP because they use the 61850 protocol and their greatest advantage is interoperability, in the second case, the Centralized communication has more complications since it must transfer all the information from the DER [22].

The review of the scientific literature on resilience highlights strategies aimed at reducing demand losses when an interruption occurs, taking as a reference for the quantification of the components of the system with less resilience and therefore with greater vulnerability to an event that generates losses in energy supply [23]. A correct evaluation of the capacity to restore the network after the occurrence of an event that causes an abrupt cut in the energy supply is the starting point to better identify the actions to be taken to control this situation, authors such as [24] suggest the measurement of three fundamental factors in resilience of the supply chain network: criticality, complexity and density of the failures presented. From another new perspective, resilience metrics based on the concept of reliability and maintainability combined with the system modeling approach are analyzed [25].

The methodology used in this paper is based on the dispatch of energy in a distribution network with the inclusion of energy DER through VPP. VPP are quickly emerging as a viable means of integrating energy resources, which are formed through generation from DER that involves both alternative generation sources supported by renewable resources (solar, wind and other) and non-renewable (microturbines, fuel cells, Diesel generators among others), in such a way that the characteristics of a traditional generator are exhibited in terms of predictability and robustness to be able to meet the needs of critical loads in the network in the event of a disruptive event and managing them when they cannot be supplied completely [26].

This article considers the changing profile of network users from passive consumers to energy providers or prosumers [27, 28]. VPP manages two resources: distributed generation sources and demand response resources that provide firmness to the energy supply in the face of possible decreases in DG energy due to their stochasticity. VPP management is done using cloud computing.

A relevant point of the present work is to propose the management of the critical loads of the electrical network managing the resource of response to the demand from the VPP in order that the available DG reach to supply the greater amount of energy demand possible than requires the critical loads, reliably, after the occurrence of the disruptive event. The work is organized as follows: Firstly, the introduction of DER and their possibility of use to increase the resilience of electrical networks through virtual power plants. Section 2 presents the proposed scheme for energy dispatch using VPP; Sect. 3 shows the proposed scenario to test the network in the case of a disruptive event; in Sect. 4 the analysis of the test results is performed. Finally, the conclusions of the work carried out are shown.

2 Methodology

In the Initial phase of the methodology, a coordination scheme for energy dispatch including VPP is described in the event of a deliberate disruptive event in the network. In the same way, the operation of the dispatch coordination scheme is proposed in a preliminary way. In a second phase, the design of the sequence diagram is shown, where the interactions between the different actors of the Network Management System are illustrated: Network Operator; Management System Application Manager in the Cloud Computing space; the participating VPPs and the users with the DER resources belonging to each VPP.

As a third phase, a test scenario corresponding to an IEEE network of 34 nodes is selected, which performs the characterization of loads for a distribution network at the voltage level of 11.4 kV. For each VPP, its stochastic energy profile is shown due to the randomness of alternative energy sources based on renewable resources such as solar photovoltaic and wind energy.

In a fourth phase, the cost functions are evaluated for each VPP that is able to participate in energy dispatch in the hours after the occurrence of the disruptive event. In the objective functions of each VPP, the random nature of the amount of energy that the VPPs can deliver was taken into account, through probability density functions.

Finally, the results of the energy dispatch are shown, comparing the amount of energy required and that dispatched by the VPPs to the critical loads of the network.

3 The Proposed Scheme for Coordinating Energy Dispatch Using VPP in the Case of a Disruptive Event in the Network

Figure 1 below shows the way in which the energy dispatch is structured based on the VPP in case it is required that the energy supply to the loads of an Electric System be carried out both jointly with the distribution companies and in a manner Independent. As can be seen, there is a cloud computing space where requests for energy supply for the network will be received. In the cloud computing space, the administration of VPP is carried out that gather resources from users and that at the time of the occurrence of a disruptive event can be made available for the coordination of an energy dispatch in an atypical emergency situation where the main objective is to allow the system's resilience to increase. This resilience is supported above all by guaranteeing the supply for critical type loads of the System such as hospitals, health centers, food storage, risk management and coordination facilities such as the police and the army. These loads are referred to as CL (Critic Load) [29].

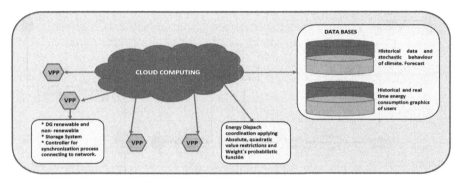

Fig. 1. Structure of the system to carry out energy dispatch using VPP

The way the system operates is supported according to the following stages:

1. The request from the network operator is received in relation to the energy demanded for the next day because the disruptive event has occurred and the usual Generation sources do not present the service. The requirement made by the DNO is primarily intended to supply critical loads. **2**. Said request reaches the management applications created in the Cloud Computing space: there, a search of the VPP registered and available at the moment is carried out initially. **3**. From the Cloud Computing management application, a request message is sent to the different VPP available. **4**. Each VPP performs a verification of the available resources: capacity of the storage systems, firm generation capacity of renewable sources, stochastic evaluation of the non-renewable energy resource using the respective weight function. Figure 2 shows how the VPP establishes the sum of its resources: Stored energy, energy from non-renewable sources, and energy from renewable sources adjusted with the help of the weight function. **5**. Once the VPP has evaluated the available energy capacities, it sends messages to the users possessing the energy resources available for the preparation of the activation processes of the DC-AC investment devices and the controllers for the synchronization of the sources in the time to connect to the electrical network. **6**. Once confirmation is given by the users' automated systems, the VPP announces to the Cloud computing management application the available power levels for each hour. **7**. The cloud computing management application performs the evaluation of the energy dispatch by applying the quadratic value restriction to know what the participation of each VPP will be during the different hours of the day. **8**. From cloud computing, the respective information is sent to the network operator. **9**. When dispatch turns out to be an optimization problem with an infeasible solution to supply critical loads, DNO will proceed with the help of VPP to manage Demand Response resources for critical loads.

Figure 2 shows the sequence diagram that describes the coordinated operation for the energy dispatch of VPP, considering the stable and random behavior of their energy resources.

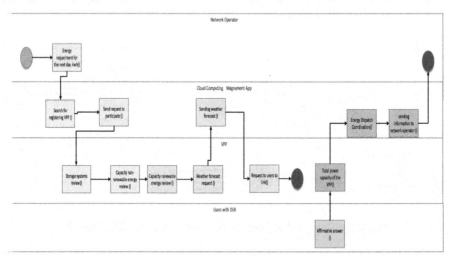

Fig. 2. Sequence diagram for the operation of energy dispatch from VPP

4 Test Scenario: Scenario with Disruptive Event: Energy Dispatch in the Network Under Atypical Operating Conditions When No Conventional Distribution Company is Operating

As a test scenario, an IEEE-34 node network was proposed (Fig. 3). The proposed network shows the points indicated as G1, G2 and G3 that correspond to places where that day the energy supply to the network by three conventional distribution companies with ideally unlimited capacities to supply the demand of the entire network are shown. Points such as VPP1, VPP2 and VPP3 are indicated in the same network, which correspond to VPP where DER from various users have been grouped and which at the time of contingency come into operation to provide a sufficient supply to the System loads while its re-establishment is achieved.

Tables 1 shows characteristics of the tested network and the power levels of the loads.

For this scenario, it has been proposed that a cloud application carry out the assessment of the consumption needs of the critical loads present in the different areas of the network, and the availability of VPP that the DER can manage for emergency supply to said loads during the disruptive event. The energy dispatch to the critical loads is made from the VPP available in the network. In this scenario, it is observed that the test electrical network has suffered a collapse that has implied that the companies in charge

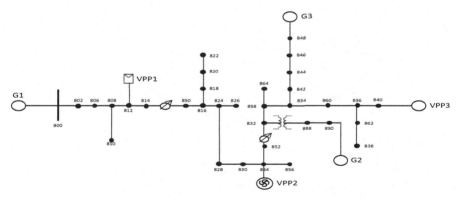

Fig. 3. IEEE-34 network used as test scenario

Table 1. Power parameters for the loads of the IEEE-34 network used

User-node	Power		User-node	Power	
	Active (kW)	Reactive (kVAr)		Active (kW)	Reactive (kVAr)
816	5	2,5	824	24,5	12
842	5	2,5	806	27,5	14,5
864	5	2,5	802	27,5	14,5
856	5	2,5	846	34	17
854	5	2,5	840	47	31
828	5,5	2,5	830	48,5	21,5
832	7,5	3,5	836	61	31,5
810	8	4	822	67,5	35
808	8	4	848	71,5	53,5
862	14	7	820	84,5	43,5
838	14	7	834	89	45
818	17	8,5	860	174	106
826	20	10	844	432	329
858	24,5	12,5	890	450	225

of the supply cease supply. The network has been sectioned off and some critical loads of the System such as hospitals, health centers, food supply centers, disaster management points have been deprived of power. In Fig. 4, these loads are identified as CL (Critic Loads). The three nodes that are indicated as VPP appear as an orientation for readers and denote the center of the zone of influence that each VPP will have. It should be taken into account that the different elements that make up a VPP do not have to be linked in physical form as happens in a microgrid, but can be dispersed and virtually linked, which is a great advantage for management.

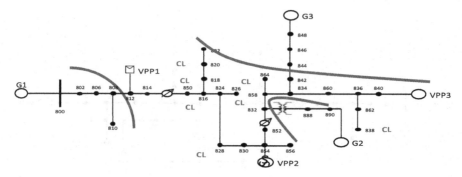

Fig. 4. Electrical network after disruptive event.

For the supply, it has been proposed that the VPP enter the energy delivery capacity of which turns out to be the sum of the potentialities of the distributed energy resources of the users as shown in Fig. 5. As can be seen, the VPP has an energy capacity from its storage systems, then it adds the energy that in real time can be provided by non-renewable Distributed Generation sources and renewable Generation sources. It should be noted that in a particular way the Energy Generation profile from renewables has been applied a probabilistic density function that finally determines the closest likely profile that will be had for each hour of the day that is needed.

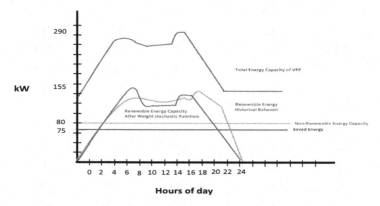

Fig. 5. Total Energy capacity of VPP.

However, it must be considered that due to the stochasticity of renewable energy resources, the energy capacity of each VPP is not constant but varies hours throughout the day. To illustrate this particularity of the VPP in Figs. 6, the supply capacity profiles of the three VPP taken into consideration are shown as an example to organize an emergency energy supply that can supply the CL for some hour while the system is running resets. Generation profiles for each VPP in each hour of the day once the probabilistic weight's function has been applied with the help of a density probabilistic function as a Markov chain [30–32] for modeling VPP based on solar is in [33]; and the wind in [34]. For the probability density functions of each VPP, the average deviation of the previous month was considered with respect to the historical average of the last 30 years (1989–2019) that were provided by the district secretary of the environment of Bogota for each hour [35].

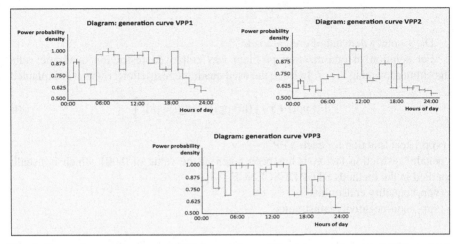

Fig. 6. Generation profiles for each VPP in each hour of the day once the probabilistic weight's function has been applied with the help of density probabilistic function.

To carry out the energy dispatch using the VPP for the supply of the critical loads, cost functions were considered with dynamic restrictions in each hour linked to the generation profile that is varying hour by hour, contrary to the energy delivery capacities of the distributors that is practically invariant in time.

Equation 1 shows the Objective function used to define the cost of the energy supplied by the VPP and which corresponds to the energy not served in relation to its acquisition costs.

$$F(VPP_1) = \left[\mu * P_{vpp1} + \int * P_{vpp1}^2 \right] * fdp1 \ [USD/kWh] \tag{1}$$

where:

μ Scorresponds to the cost associated with the control devices for the connection of the Distributed Generation elements to the existing electrical network.

$\int$ it corresponds to the cost associated with the energy not served by the usual energy suppliers.

The objective functions for the VPP and their dynamic type restrictions are shown for each hour that critical loads demand supply. As can be seen, the objective functions of the VPP do not have a fixed component since they will only be related to the power, supply to the loads every hour. In Eqs. 2–5.

$$F(VPP_1) = \left[1, 5P_{vpp1} + 0.5P_{vpp1}^2 \right] * fdp1 \quad [USD/kWh] \tag{2}$$

$$F(VPP_2) = \left[1, 7P_{vpp2} + 0.21P_{vpp2}^2 \right] * fdp2 \quad [USD/kWh] \tag{3}$$

$$F(VPP_3) = \left[1, 9P_{vpp3} + 0.17P_{vpp3}^2\right] * fdp3 \quad [USD/kWh] \quad (4)$$

s.to.

$$\sum_{h=1}^{24} \sum_{i=1}^{n} VPP_i \geq D_{hCL} \ h = 1, 2, 3 \ldots ..24 \quad (5)$$

D_{hCL} hourly demand of critical loads.

For solution of optimization problem was employed restriction quadratic value algorithm showed in Fig. 7. In Eq. 6 the used quadratic restriction criterion is explained.

$$F(vppi) + r * \left[(h(vppi)^2 + (g(vppi)^2\right] \quad (6)$$

f (vpp_i) cost function for each VPP

r penalty restriction factor. It has been taken at the value of 0.001 which is usually handled in the methods STEP DESCENCE [33].

h (vpp_i) equality constraints

g (vpp_i) non-negativity constraints

It is important to note that D_{hCL} it corresponds to critical loads demand. In event that resources of VPP are not able to supply the required demand, a gradual decrease of the power of the critical loads is made through resources of Demand Response (DR). The proposal is a gradual decrease of 10% from the original value. From the methodological point of view, once the original value of demanded energy has been reduced, it is evaluated whether the dispatch of the VPP is sufficient to supply the demand required by the critical loads.

Note: In Fig. 7, $L = \sum_{h=1}^{24} D_{hCL}$ corresponds to sum of Total Critic Load demand each hour

S is the sum of delivered energy VPP each hour.

The VPP are made up of DG elements whose synchronization at the time of connecting to the network considers the IEEE 1547 protocol.

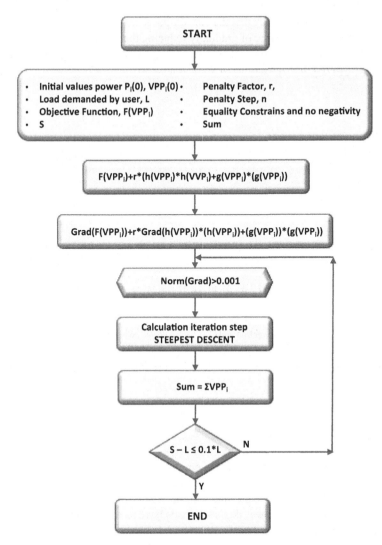

Fig. 7. Quadratic value restriction algorithm for dispatch using VPP

5 Results Obtained

Critical loads are associated with demand response mechanisms that allow managing their energy consumption. To carry out this management, it is proposed that a priori control systems be installed in critical loads that can reduce consumption in critical loads. Demand response control systems allow, for example, to reduce the consumption of lights, lower the speed of elevator motors, water pumps and other elements associated with critical loads.

As an example, in Fig. 8 showed how the energy demand of the critical loads is responded to once a demand response mechanism coordinated by the VPP or by each user is established in such a way that the consumption of these loads is reduced by 20%. The DR mechanism is in charge of gradually reducing the energy demand of the critical load in different ways, by turning off some loads, reducing the consumption of others, or making staggered disconnections of some loads [36].

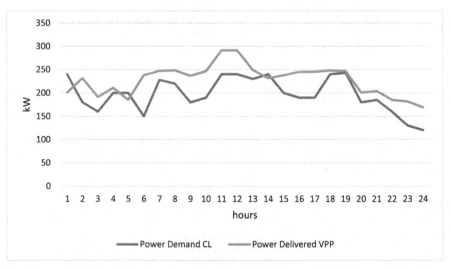

Fig. 8. Energy dispatch for critical loads from VPP, applying demand response management on critical loads.

6 Conclusions

The energy dispatch strategy with VPP in emergency situations such as the occurrence of a disruptive event, allow the temporary supply of critical loads that, although they are not fully supplied in an instant, they can be able to do so when activating control systems of the manageable power that such loads have as a mechanism associated with the demand response resource.

The inclusion of the stochasticity of the sources from the inclusion of probability density functions allows a closer approach to the real behavior that can occur of VPP in scenarios that require a rapid response, as is the case of the attention of abstention of loads in the event of emergencies in the network, which undoubtedly increases the resilience of the entire energy system.

The inclusion of DER management through VPP in close coordination with Applications in the cloud computing space allows a rapid response to the energy demand of critical loads. This management results in an improvement of the resilient behavior of the network, allowing to minimize the response times for the restoration of the network. Similarly, the management of the DER with VPP allows it to be used in normal work scenarios of the network to, for example, correct peaks in demand.

In an electrical energy system, the restoration mechanisms that characterize the behavior of the infrastructure in the network after a disruptive event give the possibility of creating methodologies that allow the energy system to be restored and become resilient due to the ability to anticipate, absorb, respond to and recover from adversity as quickly as possible. In that sense, when a disruptive event occurs where energy dispatch is affected, there must be a mechanism that allows the user not to be affected and temporary supply resources such as VPP are used.

References

1. Agudelo, L., López, J.M., Muñoz, N.: Análisis de vulnerabilidad de sistemas de potencia mediante programación binivel. Inf. Tecnol. **25**(3), 103–114 (2014). https://doi.org/10.4067/S0718-07642014000300013
2. Luoisot, J.P.: Risk and/or resilience management. Risk Gov. Control Finan. Mark. Inst. **5**(2), 84–91 (2015)
3. Warmer, C.J., Hommelberg, M.P.F., Kok, J.K., Kamphuis, I.G.: Local DER driven grid support by coordinated operation of devices. In 2008 IEEE Power and Energy Society General Meeting - Conversion and Delivery of Electrical Energy in the 21st Century, pp. 1–5. IEEE (2008). https://doi.org/10.1109/PES.2008.4596644
4. Reed, D.A., Kapur, K.C., Christie, R.D.: Methodology for assessing the resilience of networked infrastructure. IEEE Syst. J. **3**(2), 174–180 (2008)
5. Pedrasa, M.A.A., Spooner, T.D., MacGill, I.F.: A novel energy service model and optimal scheduling algorithm for residential distributed energy resources. Electr. Power Syst. Res. **81**(12), 2155–2163 (2011). https://doi.org/10.1016/j.epsr.2011.06.013
6. Ouyang, M., Zhao, L.: Do topological models contribute to decision making on post-disaster electric power system restoration? Chaos **24**(4) (2014). https://doi.org/10.1063/1.4898731
7. Bordons, C., García, F., Valverde, L.: Gestión Óptima de la Energía en Microrredes con Generación Renovable. Revista Iberoamericana de Automática e Informática Industrial **12**, 117–132 (2015). https://doi.org/10.1016/j.riai.2015.03.001
8. Salman, A.M., Li, Y., Stewart, M.G.: Evaluating system reliability and targeted hardening strategies of power distribution systems subjected to hurricanes. Reliab. Eng. Syst. Saf. **144**, 319–333 (2015). https://doi.org/10.1016/j.ress.2015.07.028
9. Ding, T., Lin, Y., Bie, Z., Chen, C.: A resilient microgrid formation strategy for load restoration considering master-slave distributed generators and topology reconfiguration. Appl. Energy **199**, 205–216 (2017). https://doi.org/10.1016/j.apenergy.2017.05.012
10. Panteli, M., Mancarella, P.: Modeling and evaluating the resilience of critical electrical power infrastructure to extreme weather events resilience of electric power systems to earthquakes and tsunamis view project DIMMER view project. IEEE Syst. J. **11**(3), 1733–1742 (2017). https://doi.org/10.1109/JSYST.2015.2389272
11. Dubey, A., Poudel, S.: A robust approach to restoring critical loads in a resilient power distribution system. In: IEEE Power and Energy Society General Meeting, 2018-Janua, pp. 1–5 (2017). https://doi.org/10.1109/PESGM.2017.8274597
12. Pep, S., Carrasco, A.: Agregación de Recursos Energéticos Distribuidos (DER) Obstáculos y recomendaciones para un desarrollo íntegro del mercado Barcelona, diciembre de 2017 (2017)
13. Cavalheiro, E.M.B., Vergílio, A.H.B., Lyra, C.: Optimal configuration of power distribution networks with variable renewable energy resources. Comput. Oper. Res. **96**, 272–280 (2018). https://doi.org/10.1016/j.cor.2017.09.021
14. Luo, D., et al.: Evaluation method of distribution network resilience focusing on critical loads. IEEE Access **6**, 61633–61639 (2018). https://doi.org/10.1109/ACCESS.2018.2872941

15. Martišauskas, L., Augutis, J., Krikštolaitis, R.: Methodology for energy security assessment considering energy system resilience to disruptions. Energ. Strat. Rev. **22**(July), 106–118 (2018). https://doi.org/10.1016/j.esr.2018.08.007

16. Ramirez, A., Chica, A., Arias, L.A.: Mr inteligente sustentable de biogas para zona no interconectada. I Congr. Int. Tecnol. Limpias (2013)

17. Karabiber, A., Keles, C., Kaygusuz, A., Alagoz, B.B.: An approach for the integration of renewable distributed generation in hybrid DC/AC microgrids. Renew. Energy **52**, 251–259 (2013). https://doi.org/10.1016/j.renene.2012.10.041

18. Hollande, E.: Resilience engineering: a new understanding of safety. J. Ergon. Soc. Korea **35**(3), 185–191 (2016). https://doi.org/10.5143/jesk.2016.35.3.185, (Ld (Universidad Autónoma De Occidente), Landau. 1937, Calidad de la energía eléctrica, Zhurnal Eksp. i Teor. Fiz. (1937)

19. Bao, M., Ding, Y., Sang, M., Li, D., Shao, C., Yan, J.: Yan J; Modeling and evaluating nodal resilience of multi-energy systems under windstorms. Appl. Energy **270**, 115136 (2020). https://doi.org/10.1016/j.apenergy.2020.115136

20. Ramos, D.S., Huayllas, T.E.D.C., Filho, M.M., Tolmasquim, M.T.: New commercial arrangements and business models in electricity distribution systems: the case of Brazil. Renew. Sustain. Energy Rev. **117**, 109468 (2020). https://doi.org/10.1016/j.rser.2019.109468

21. Sheidaei, F., Ahmarinejad, A.: Multi-stage stochastic framework for energy management of virtual power plants considering electric vehicles and demand response programs. Int. J. Electr. Power Energy Syst. **120**, 106047 (2020). https://doi.org/10.1016/j.ijepes.2020.106047

22. Nosratabadi, S.M., Hooshmand, R.A., Gholipour, E.: A comprehensive review on microgrid and virtual power plant concepts employed for distributed energy resources scheduling in power systems. Renew. Sustain. Energy Rev. **2016**(67), 341–363 (2017). https://doi.org/10.1016/j.rser.2016.09.025

23. Van Summeren, L.F.M., Wieczorek, A.J., Bombaerts, G.J.T., Verbong, G.P.J.: Community energy meets smart grids: reviewing goals, structure, and roles in virtual power plants in Ireland, Belgium and the Netherlands. Energy Res. Soc. Sci. **2019**, 63 (2020). https://doi.org/10.1016/j.erss.2019.101415

24. Royapoor, M., Pazhoohesh, M., Davison, P.J., Patsios, C., Walker, S.: Building as a virtual power plant, magnitude and persistence of deferrable loads and human comfort implications. Energy Build. **213**, 109794 (2020). https://doi.org/10.1016/j.enbuild.2020.109794

25. Lin, Y., Bie, Z.: Study on the resilience of the integrated energy system. Energy Procedia **2016**(103), 171–176 (2016). https://doi.org/10.1016/j.egypro.2016.11.268

26. Zhong, W., Murad, M.A.A., Liu, M., Milano, F.: Impact of virtual power plants on power system short-term transient response. Electr. Power Syst. Res. **189**, 106609 (2020). https://doi.org/10.1016/j.epsr.2020.106609

27. Wei, C., et al.: A bi-level scheduling model for virtual power plants with aggregated thermostatically controlled loads and renewable energy. Appl. Energy **2016**(224), 659–670 (2018). https://doi.org/10.1016/j.apenergy.2018.05.032

28. Navid, A., Lim, G.J., Cho, J., Bora, S.: A quantitative approach for assessment and improvement of network resilience. Reliab. Eng. Syst. Saf. **200**, 106977 (2020). https://doi.org/10.1016/j.ress.2020.106977

29. Falasca, M., Zobel, C.W., Cook, D.: A decision support framework to assess supply chain resilience. In: 5th International ISCRAM Conference, Washington, pp. 596–605 (2008)

30. Rioshar, Y., Chuan, G., Faisal, K.: A simple yet robust resilience assessment metrics. Reliab. Eng. Syst. Saf. **197**, 106810 (2020). https://doi.org/10.1016/j.ress.2020.106810

31. Palizban, O., Kauhaniemi, K., Guerrero, J.M.: Microgrids in active network management - Part I: hierarchical control, energy storage, virtual power plants, and market participation. Renew. Sustain. Energy Rev. **36**, 428–439 (2014). https://doi.org/10.1016/j.rser.2014.01.016

32. Basso, T., DeBlasio, R.: IEEE Smart Grid Series of Standards IEEE 2030 (Interoperability) and IEEE 1547 (Interconnection) Status, Grid-Interop, vol. 2030, no. September, pp. 5–8 (2011)

33. Prete, C.L., Hobbs, B.F.: A cooperative game theoretic analysis of incentives for microgrids in regulated electricity markets. Appl. Energy **169**, 524–541 (2016). https://doi.org/10.1016/j.apenergy.2016.01.099

34. Robu, V., Chalkiadakis, G., Kota, R., Rogers, A., Jennings, N.R.: Rewarding cooperative virtual power plant formation using scoring rules. Energy **117**, 19–28 (2016). https://doi.org/10.1016/j.energy.2016.10.077

35. Sowa, T., et al.: Method for the operation planning of virtual power plants considering forecasting errors of distributed energy resources. Electr. Eng. **98**(4), 347–354 (2016). https://doi.org/10.1007/s00202-016-0419-9

36. Ghavidel, S., Li, L., Aghaei, J., Yu, T., Zhu J.: A review on the virtual power plant: components and operation systems. In: IEEE International Conference on Power System Technology (POWERCON) (2016). https://doi.org/10.1109/powercon.2016.7754037

Design of an Integrated System for the Measurement and Monitoring of Electrical Parameters Under ISO 50001: A Case Study

Washington Garcia-Quilachamin[1](✉) ⓘ, Kelvin Atiencia-Fuentes[1] ⓘ,
Jenniffer Ante-Moreno[1] ⓘ, Jorge Herrera-Tapia[1] ⓘ, Francisco Ulloa-Herrera[2] ⓘ,
and Marjorie Coronel-Suárez[3] ⓘ

[1] Universidad Laica Eloy Alfaro de Manabí, Cdla. Universitaria, 130802 Manta, Ecuador
profegarcia501@gmail.com, jorge.herrera@uleam.edu.ec
[2] Università della Calabria, 87036 Rende, Italy
llhfnc94c19z605i@studenti.unical.it
[3] Universidad Estatal Península de Santa Elena, 240350 La Libertad, Ecuador
mcoronel@upse.edu.ec

Abstract. Using energy management system tools in universities opens the possibility of efficiently managing electrical consumption through a real-time electrical parameter monitoring system to develop the analysis of consumption patterns, subsequently applying methods concerning energetic efficiency. The study's objective was to implement an integrated connection system of the S7–1200 PLC and Raspberry Pi with SENTRON PAC-3200 energy meters for real-time monitoring of electrical parameters. The Modbus TCP/IP protocol collects the data, and the S7 communication selects the parameters to upload to the cloud through Node-Red programming. Finally, a web application was designed and developed to visualize the electrical parameters of the energy meters installed at the University in real-time, which are under the ISO 50001 standard.

Keywords: Communication · Energy management · Measurement · Electrical parameters

1 Introduction

An Energy Management System (EMS) comprises a group of policies and objectives that enable organizations to manage energy consumption efficiently [1]. These arguments translate into energy cost savings by applying methods and tools to collect, analyze, review and predict energy data without affecting the performance or activity performed [2, 3]. In addition, the ISO 50001 standard with the EMS has the main objective of establishing minimum and specific requirements that ensure continuous improvement of the energy performance of the organization that works following [4, 5].

The development of society and the economy causes an increasing energy demand in universities and varies according to the equipment and activities performed according

F. R. Narváez et al. (Eds.): SmartTech-IC 2022, CCIS 1705, pp. 400–413, 2023.
https://doi.org/10.1007/978-3-031-32213-6_29

to the university careers [6, 7]. In addition, the Intergovernmental Panel on Climate Change states that universities represent a large part of worldwide energy consumption [8]. Therefore, the absence of an energy management system in universities leads to increased energy consumption and economic expenditures [9, 10].

In Ecuador, the energy consumption of the Universidad Laica Eloy Alfaro de Manabí (ULEAM) in 2021 was 3,836,324 kWh, according to the electric service billing of CNEL EP [11]. However, ULEAM installed fourteen SENTRON PAC-3200 energy meters in different faculties, which allow obtaining more than fifty magnitudes measured from maximum and minimum values of the different electrical parameters of each meter [12], to examine energy consumption through the project according to [13] based on ISO 50001.

ULEAM's supplies are compatible with integrating technological equipment that supports communication and remote monitoring of electrical values [14]. In this way, an EMS tool called an electrical parameter monitoring system is implemented, thus collecting historical data, cloud storage, and real-time display of electrical parameters obtained from energy meters. Allowing the development of energy analysis, generation of consumption patterns, and subsequently defining methods for energy efficiency [15, 16].

This research aims to implement an integrated system using a PLC S7–1200 and a Raspberry PI 3 to connect and monitor the electrical parameters of the SENTRON PAC-3200 m. In addition, collect and store the data obtained from the energy meters in the cloud and be visualized through the design and development of a web application that allows real-time monitoring of electrical parameters linked to energy efficiency.

The paper is organized as follows: Sect. 2 presents the materials and communication protocols used to collect data from the energy meters and then upload it to the cloud. Section 3 describes the programming and design of the web application for the visualization of the electrical parameters in real-time, as well as a comparison with the power manager software to verify the collected data. Finally, Sect. 4 contains the conclusions of the research and references.

2 Methodology

2.1 Hardware Design

The integrated communication system has a control panel composed of the necessary elements for its operation (see Fig. 1).

2.2 Structure of the Network

The devices can send and receive data between them, thanks to merging IP addresses in the same network. The VLAN network is integrated by fourteen energy meters (E.M.), the PLC, and the Raspberry Pi, as shown in Table 1.

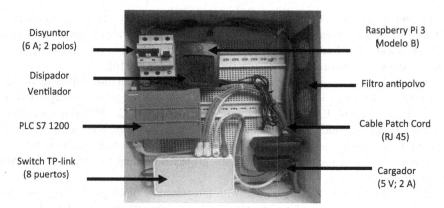

Fig. 1. Inside view of the control panel with its respective elements.

Table 1. Monitoring system equipment - IP address.

N°	Equipment	IP address	N°	Equipment	IP address
1	Gateway	10.253.100.1	10	E.M. - Eng. Industrial	10.253.100.10
2	E.M. - Medicine	10.253.100.2	11	E.M. - C. Education	10.253.100.11
3	E.M. - Informatic 1	10.253.100.3	12	E.M. – Communication	10.253.100.12
4	E.M. - Informatic 2	10.253.100.4	13	E.M. - Architecture	10.253.100.13
5	E.M. - A. Business	10.253.100.5	14	E.M. - Odontology	10.253.100.14
6	E.M. - M. Naval	10.253.100.6	15	E.M. - Agricultural	10.253.100.15
7	E.M. - Engineering 1	10.253.100.7	16	Raspberry Pi 3	10.253.100.20
8	E.M. - Engineering 2	10.253.100.8	17	PLC S7 1200	10.253.100.21
9	E.M. - Engineering 3	10.253.100.9			

2.3   Overall Design and Communication of the Monitoring System

The development of the monitoring system consists of three blocks, as shown in the diagram in Fig. 2. The first block collects the electrical data from the SENTRON PAC3200 meters using the PLC S7–1200 through the Modbus TCP/IP protocol. The second block uses a Raspberry Pi 3 card via S7 protocol. Furthermore, the most relevant parameters are selected for data storage in the cloud with MySQL via Node-Red. Finally, block 3 establishes the communication between the Raspberry Pi and the Internet by creating databases in MySQL where the selected electrical parameters are hosted. Then the web application is developed to allow real-time monitoring of electrical parameters.

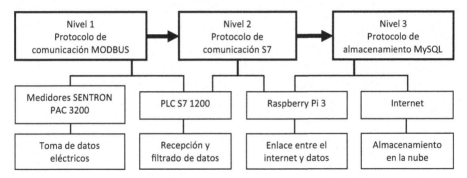

Fig. 2. Operation and communication block diagram.

2.4 Modbus Communication Protocol

El The S7 1200 PLC obtains data through the Modbus TCP/IP protocol, which allows communication with SENTRON PAC 3200 m using a master-slave network relationship [17], as shown in Fig. 3.

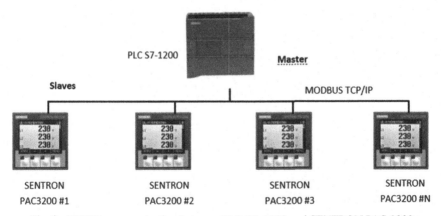

Fig. 3. TCP/IP communication between PLC S7–1200 and SENTRON PAC-3200

2.5 Electrical Data Acquisition with PLC S7–1200

The collection process was performed by programming in TIA Portal with two data blocks in the PLC S7-1200. Block one, called "Station Counter," is defined according to the number of meters (14) and is responsible for counting the position of each meter in a time of 2 Hz. Block 2, called "Modbus reading of stations," reads the values collected by the counter after passing through each station (see Fig. 4).

Figure 5 shows the programming performed to extract the values from the SENTRON PAC-3200 m, in this case, from the meter of the Faculty of Architecture. The process is replicated for the other faculties.

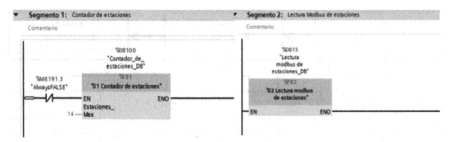

Fig. 4. TIA's block program in meter and station reading portal.

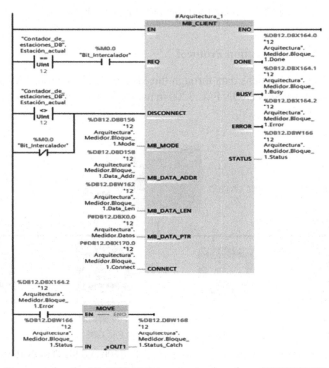

Fig. 5. Programming the S7–1200 PLC to extract values from SENTRON PAC-3200.

Each electrical parameter collected was stored in a database (DB) in the TIA portal program, see Fig. 6, and has a unique record required by the Network-node when extracting data from the PLC to be displayed in the web application.

The data collected from the S7-1200 PLC to the web application is performed every fifteen minutes following the IEC 61000-4-30 standard that defines the measurement procedures based on the quality of the electrical supply.

Electrical Parameters. Thirty-eight electrical data are collected through the TIA Portal. However, the data that allow energy efficiency is displayed in the web application, the data are Current (L1; L2; L3), energy consumed, total power factor, Total power (Active; Apparent; Reactive), Voltage (L1-L2; L2-L3; L3-L1).

01 Medicina											
	Nombre		Offset	Valor de ...	Valor de obse..	Remanen...	Accesible d...	Escrib...	Visible en ..	Valor de a..	Comentario
	▼ Datos		0.0			▣	☑	☑	☑	▢	
	Datos[1]		0.0	0.0	127.7588	▣	☑	☑	☑	▢	TENSIÓN L1 N
	Datos[2]		4.0	0.0	128.9841	▣	☑	☑	☑	▢	TENSIÓN L2 N
	Datos[3]		8.0	0.0	127.4447	▣	☑	☑	☑	▢	TENSIÓN L3 N
	Datos[4]		12.0	0.0	223.35	▣	☑	☑	☑	▢	TENSIÓN L1 L2
	Datos[5]		16.0	0.0	222.0768	▣	☑	☑	☑	▢	TENSIÓN L2 L3
	Datos[6]		20.0	0.0	220.0061	▣	☑	☑	☑	▢	TENSIÓN L1 L3
	Datos[7]		24.0	0.0	24.99496	▣	☑	☑	☑	▢	CORRIENTE L1
	Datos[8]		28.0	0.0	40.27695	▣	☑	☑	☑	▢	CORRIENTE L2
	Datos[9]		32.0	0.0	1.270514	▣	☑	☑	☑	▢	CORRIENTE L3
	Datos[10]		36.0	0.0	3193.25	▣	☑	☑	☑	▢	POTENCIA APARENTE L1
	Datos[11]		40.0	0.0	5194.897	▣	☑	☑	☑	▢	POTENCIA APARENTE L2
	Datos[12]		44.0	0.0	161.9028	▣	☑	☑	☑	▢	POTENCIA APARENTE L3
	Datos[13]		48.0	0.0	2933.887	▣	☑	☑	☑	▢	POTENCIA ACTIVA L1
	Datos[14]		52.0	0.0	5119.942	▣	☑	☑	☑	▢	POTENCIA ACTIVA L2
	Datos[15]		56.0	0.0	143.0494	▣	☑	☑	☑	▢	POTENCIA ACTIVA L3
	Datos[16]		60.0	0.0	-1182.204	▣	☑	☑	☑	▢	POTENCIA REACTIVA L1
	Datos[17]		64.0	0.0	678.1608	▣	☑	☑	☑	▢	POTENCIA REACTIVA L2
	Datos[18]		68.0	0.0	70.31399	▣	☑	☑	☑	▢	POTENCIA REACTIVA L3
	Datos[19]		72.0	0.0	0.9183143	▣	☑	☑	☑	▢	FACTOR DE POTENCIA L1
	Datos[20]		76.0	0.0	0.985615	▣	☑	☑	☑	▢	FACTOR DE POTENCIA L2
	Datos[21]		80.0	0.0	0.8832906	▣	☑	☑	☑	▢	FACTOR DE POTENCIA L3
	Datos[22]		84.0	0.0	0.0	▣	☑	☑	☑	▢	THDR TENSIÓN L1
	Datos[23]		88.0	0.0	0.0	▣	☑	☑	☑	▢	THDR TENSIÓN L2
	Datos[24]		92.0	0.0	0.0	▣	☑	☑	☑	▢	THDR TENSIÓN L3
	Datos[25]		96.0	0.0	14.20955	▣	☑	☑	☑	▢	THDR CORRIENTE L1
	Datos[26]		100.0	0.0	12.74215	▣	☑	☑	☑	▢	THDR CORRIENTE L2
	Datos[27]		104.0	0.0	18.39735	▣	☑	☑	☑	▢	THDR CORRIENTE L3
	Datos[28]		108.0	0.0	60.0036	▣	☑	☑	☑	▢	FRECUENCIA
	Datos[29]		112.0	0.0	128.2846	▣	☑	☑	☑	▢	TENSIÓN MEDIA VLN
	Datos[30]		116.0	0.0	222.1936	▣	☑	☑	☑	▢	TENSIÓN MEDIA VLL

Fig. 6. SENTRON PAC-3200-m electrical data storage block.

2.6 Communication Protocol S7

The "node-red-contrib-s7" function allows connection using the Ethernet S7 protocol. The tool mentioned above has default settings that can be configured as inputs and outputs, the IP address of the PLC, communication class, and names of the variables to be used with their respective register and cycle time. In our case, it was configured with the following parameters (see Fig. 7).

Data Acquisition Algorithm on Raspberry Pi 3. The first node, called "Inject," writes to the database. It will also emit a TRUE signal every fifteen minutes to the "Data Storage Table" nodes, thus storing the data for downloading in the history report. Additionally, the "Data Display Table" writes the data to the main page and stores it temporarily for display. The table is updated with each TRUE of the Node Inject. Figure 8 presents this process and how it is the network node programmed.

Node-Network Programming on Raspberry Pi 3. The S7–1200 PLC communication and storage variables were placed according to the programming done in the TIA Portal, creating an equivalent of variables in the programming of the S7 node. Figure 9 shows the programming nodes of the eleven selected electrical parameters.

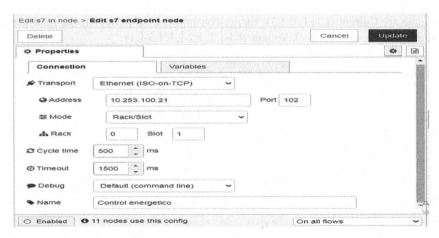

Fig. 7. Node s7 communication setup

Fig. 8. Data collection nodes.

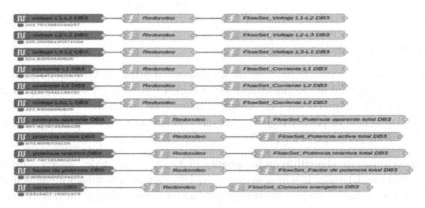

Fig. 9. Data storage programming

2.7 Hosting Implementation

To carry out tests, a database was hired from a server called Hostinger, in which the information will be stored and distributed through the client-server model to the web application (Fig. 10).

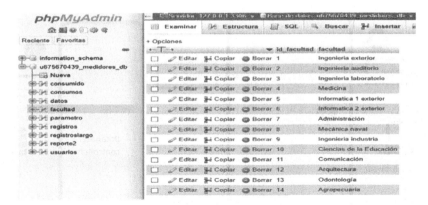

Fig. 10. Hosting – database

2.8   Web Application Development Methodology

The methodology "Phases for the development of projects and web applications" [18] is used. It provides the course to be carried out and to be more accessible. In Fig. 11, the phases used for the development of the web application are presented.

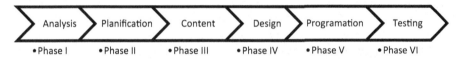

Fig. 11. Phases for the development of web projects and applications

Phase I Analysis. Considering that the web application has two types of users, public and administrator, the users' needs are examined to define the objective of the planning and development of the web application. In addition, the necessary aspects for correctly monitoring the electrical parameters are fulfilled. The web application aims to provide the university community with the electrical parameters of each of the faculties that integrate a SENTRON PAC3200 energy meter in real-time and allow exporting information through Excel-type reports.

Phase II Planification. The programming languages implemented in the development of the web application are Html, PHP, Java script, and CSS, based on the authors [19, 20].

Phase III Content. It determines the contents, functions, and interactions in the graphical interface that will fulfill each element of the web application. The above-mentioned is developed with the communication and exchange of information stored in a web server using the MySQL database [21].

Figure 12 shows the architecture of how a query is made in the web application. In action (1), the user makes a request to the web browser. In (2) (3), the request reaches

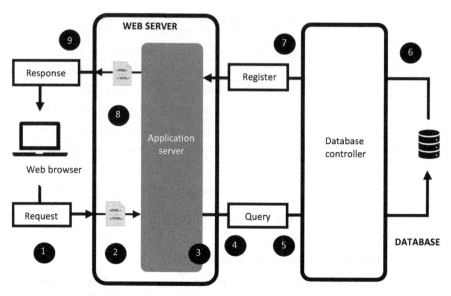

Fig. 12. General web application architecture diagram

the web server through a script page developed with PHP language. In (4) (5), the PHP page accesses the database and extracts the records in HTML code from the page. In (6), (7) (8), the data is delivered to the PHP interpreter to build the page in browser-readable code. Finally, in (9), the web server transfers the constructed page to the user's browser for display in HTML.

Phase IV Design Based on ISO 50001. Considering the ISO 50001 standards, the design of the web application was established regarding an energy baseline, which considers periods for data collection appropriate to the use and consumption of energy in the ULEAM. Regarding the energy performance indicators, sequence diagrams were structured indicating the processes each element performs manually and the flow of information they manage on the main page of the web application, as shown in Fig. 13.

3 Results

3.1 Web Application Graphical Interface

Phase V Programming. It was developed with the languages mentioned in phase three. Figure 14 shows the code for communicating electrical data with the web application and the database using PHP.

Implementation. The aesthetic part of the web application was developed by programming the codes. Figure 15 shows the central part of the web application with the eleven selected electrical parameters.

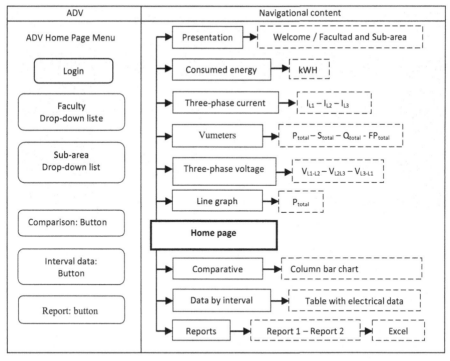

Fig. 13. ADV home page module based on ISO 50001

```php
<?php
 $servidor= "212.1.208.151";
 $usuario= "u675670439_medidores"; $password = "d1B/e0xdszC";
 $nombreBD= "u675670439_medidores_db";
    $conexion   =   mysqli_connect($servidor,   $usuario,   $password,
$nombreBD);
      if ($conexion->connect_error) {
         die("la conexión ha fallado: " . $conexion->connect_error);
      }   //echo "Conexión exitosa...";
?>
```

Fig. 14. PHP database connection

3.2   Analysis of Results

The comparison option allows choosing an electrical parameter and the date to compare the data of all the faculties with the SENTRON PAC-3200 (see Fig. 16).

The Reports tab allows the administrator user to download two types of reports in Excel format by entering a username and password. Report 1 includes all eleven electrical parameters. However, only one faculty is selected. Report 2 includes all the faculties

Fig. 15. Display of electrical parameters.

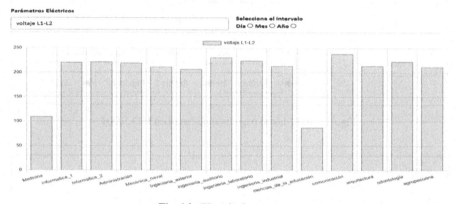

Fig. 16. Electrical parameters

that integrate the SENTRON PAC-3200. Nonetheless, only one electrical parameter is selected.

The results were analyzed to verify the accuracy of the data acquired from the SEN-TRON PAC-3200 m. Therefore, a comparison of the data obtained in the web application was performed with the electrical parameters of the SENTRON power manager software, which is used to acquire, visualize, monitor, evaluate and archive energy data from any Modbus-enabled metering device [22]. Table 2 presents two powers with their data obtained online and through the reports.

The values of the electrical parameters coincide with the values of the Power manager, see Table 2. Therefore, the real-time web application allows for collecting the electrical data correctly and reliably for their respective monitoring concerning the ISO 50001 standard.

Table 2. Comparison of electrical parameters for June 13, 2022, at 01:45 am

Faculty	Business Administration		Informatics outdoors 1	
Electrical Parameters	Web application	Power manager	Web application	Power manager
Voltage $_{L1\text{-}L2}$	217,64 V	217,29 V	218,46 V	218,43 V
Voltage $_{L2\text{-}L3}$	213,26 V	213,82 V	213,24 V	213,98 V
Voltage $_{L3\text{-}L1}$	215,07 V	215,18 V	215,75 V	215,73 V
Current $_{L1}$	4,56 A	4,58 A	0,71 A	0,71 A
Current $_{L2}$	10,37 A	10,38 A	3,71 A	3,70 A
Current $_{L3}$	12,72 A	12,70 A	0,48 A	0,48 A
P $_{Total}$	2983,41 W	2,98 kW	494,86 W	0,49 kW
S $_{Total}$	3427,53 VA	3,42 kVA	610,51 VA	0,61 kVA
Q $_{Total}$	998,01 var	0,99 kvar	−158,46 var	−0,15 kvar
FP $_{Total}$	0.87	—	0,8	—
Energy consumed	132887,98 kWh	132888,35 kWh	93644,78 kWh	93644,80 kWh

4 Conclusions

A historical database was established in MySQL with information from the Node-RED program located on the Raspberry Pi card, which is responsible for collecting the electrical measurements collected from the SENTRON PAC-3200 m through the PLC S7-1200 for their respective visualization.

The web application has hierarchical access that allows, according to the type of user, to perform different actions in the application, such as administrator and public, only the administrator can download information through a username and password and Excel Xlsx reports.

Comparisons were made of the electrical values through the reports exported by the SENTRON power manager software and the web application to verify that the information collected from the SENTRON PAC-3200 m is correct.

The development of this project will allow basing the studies towards reliable and feasible energy efficiency at ULEAM. Also, the information obtained from the electrical data allows for handling the respective energy management indicators according to the ISO 50001 standard and determining the factors that affect the electricity consumption generated in a Higher Education Institution.

References

1. Chumo, E.A.M., Vélez, N.R.B., Mera, G.E.P.: Eficiencia Energética en Función del Desarrollo del Plan Maestro de Electrificación (PME) en Ecuador. Rev. Investig. en Energía, Medio Ambient. y Tecnol. RIEMAT **3**(2), 1 (2018). ISSN 2588–0721

2. Imran, S., Akhand, M.A.H., Shuvo, M.I.R., Siddique, N., Adeli, H.: Optimization of university course scheduling problem using particle swarm optimization with selective search. Expert Syst. Appl. **127**, 9–24 (2019)
3. Sánchez-Cano, J.E., García-Quilachamin, W.X., Pérez-Véliz, J., Herrera-Tapia, J., Fuentes, K.A.: Review of methods to reduce energy consumption in a smart city based on IoT and 5G technology. Int. J. online Biomed. Eng. **17**(8), 4–21 (2021)
4. De Laire, M., Fiallos, Y., Aguilera, Á.: Beneficios de los sistemas de gestión de energía basados en ISO 50001 y casos de éxito, p. 429 (2017)
5. de la Rue du Can, S., Pudleiner, D., Pielli, K.: Energy efficiency as a means to expand energy access: a Uganda roadmap. Energy Policy **120**(January), 354–364 (2018)
6. Ge, J., Wu, J., Chen, S., Wu, J.: Energy efficiency optimization strategies for university research buildings with hot summer and cold winter climate of China based on the adaptive thermal comfort. J. Build. Eng. **18**, 321–330 (2018)
7. Mohammadalizadehkorde, M., Weaver, R.: Quantifying potential savings from sustainable energy projects at a large public university: an energy efficiency assessment for texas state university. Sustain. Energy Technol. Assessments **37**, 100570 (2020)
8. Sun, Y., Luo, X., Liu, X.: Optimization of a university timetable considering building energy efficiency: An approach based on the building controls virtual test bed platform using a genetic algorithm. J. Build. Eng. **35**, 102095 (2021)
9. Guan, J., Nord, N., Chen, S.: Energy planning of university campus building complex: Energy usage and coincidental analysis of individual buildings with a case study. Energy Build. **124**, 99–111 (2016)
10. Kim, D.W., Jung, J.W., Seok, H.T., Yang, J.H.: Survey and Analysis of Energy Consumption in University Campuses (2019)
11. Ep, C.N.E.L.: Tipo Consumo : Factor Potencia. Inf. Electr. **2**, 4–5 (2022)
12. PCE-Iberica. Medidor energía Siemens Sentron PAC3200, pp. 542–544 (2014)
13. Rodriguez, O., Alemán, G., Lara, V.: caracterización del consumo de energía eléctrica en la universidad laica eloy alfaro de Manabí. Int. Congr., 16 (2018)
14. Sancán, C.: Diseño y construcción de un sistema de alarmas mediante el uso de equipos PLC y microprocesadores Open Source en medidores de energía de la Facultad de Ingeniería. Repos. Inst. ULEAM (2020)
15. Fichera, A., Volpe, R., Cutore, E.: Energy performance measurement, monitoring and control for buildings of public organizations: Standardized practises compliant with the ISO 50001 and ISO 50006. Dev. Built Environ. **4**, 100024 (2020)
16. Liu, Q., Ren, J.: Research on the building energy efficiency design strategy of Chinese universities based on green performance analysis. Energy Build. **224**, 110242 (2020)
17. Yuksel, H., Altunay, Ö.: Host-to-host TCP / IP connection over serial ports using visible light communication. Phys. Commun. **43**, 101222 (2020)
18. Rodrigo, R.Q.B., Leonardo, C.Z.W.: Análisis, Diseño E Implementación De Un Sitio Web Para La Escuela De Informática Aplicada A La Educación De La Universidad Nacional De Chimborazo Utilizando Software Libre. Universidad Nacional De Chimborazo (2014)
19. Savidis, A., Stephanidis, C.: Automated user interface engineering with a pattern reflecting programming language. Autom. Softw. Eng. **13**(2), 303–339 (2006)
20. Eda, R., Do, H.: An efficient regression testing approach for PHP Web applications using test selection and reusable constraints. Softw. Qual. J. **27**(4), 1383–1417 (2019). https://doi.org/10.1007/s11219-019-09449-2
21. Singh, S.P., Nayyar, A., Kumar, R., Sharma, A.: Fog computing: from architecture to edge computing and big data processing. J. Supercomput. **75**(4), 2070–2105 (2018). https://doi.org/10.1007/s11227-018-2701-2

22. Del Valle, Á.J.Z., Bravo, V.M.A.: Adquisición Digital de Datos Aplicado a un Módulo de Pruebas Feedback para el Monitoreo de Parámetros Eléctricos en Máquinas en Corriente Alterna. Univ. politécnica Sales, pp. 1–56 (2020)

Aerodynamic Analysis Based on Materials and Shapes of Different Types of Wind Turbine Blades for Wind Energy Production Using Fast and MATLAB Simulink

Luis Daniel Jara Chacon[ID], José Javier Cali Sisalima[ID],
and Edy Leonardo Ayala Cruz[✉][ID]

Universidad Politécnica Salesiana, Cuenca Campus, Mechatronics Engineering,
Quito, Ecuador
eayala@ups.edu.ec

Abstract. In this work, it is analyzed the aerodynamic response of some wind turbine blades in terms of the Power Coefficient (Cp). The aim of this experiment is test aerodynamic models of different blades and also measure how these aspects affect the power generation of a Doubly Fed Induction Generator (DFIG). In order to determine the efficiency, the Cp of the entire system has been measured. This study is based on the evaluation of different structural blade materials and airfoils. In order to establish the mathematical models, the experiments have been performed using MATLAB-Simulink and the Fatigue, Aerodynamics, Structures and Turbulence program of the National Renewable Energy Laboratory (FAST). Moreover, the model has been subjected to variable wind conditions and perturbations. The type of wind turbines have been limited to a three-bladed horizontal axis with DFIG generator. The size of the blades are 33.25 m long. The blades models are: WindPact 1.5 MW v1.3, SNL100-00 and pseudoSERI8. In addition, the tested materials are: aluminum 2014T6, Ochroma pyramidale wood also known as balsa wood and composite materials. As a result of the analysis, it could be determined that within the tested samples, the most efficient performance in terms of aerodynamic is the pseudoSERI8 made with composite materials. It is important to emphasize that it also presented a similar performance with the Aluminum 2014T6 generating an output power of approximately 0.6 MW allowing the wind turbine to respond efficiently.

Keywords: Aerodynamic analysis · Wind energy production · Blade shapes and materials · FAST NREL and MatLab Simulink Software · Doubly-Fed Induction Generator (DFIG)

1 Introduction

The basic element of a wind turbine is the rotor, which consists of several blades. These blades are responsible for converting the wind energy into mechanical

F. R. Narváez et al. (Eds.): SmartTech-IC 2022, CCIS 1705, pp. 414–424, 2023.
https://doi.org/10.1007/978-3-031-32213-6_30

energy and by means of a generator converts it into electrical energy. But to perform this energy conversion, the blades must have certain specifications and characteristics [1], since wind turbines are large, dynamically flexible and complex structures that must operate in highly turbulent and unpredictable environmental conditions [2].

Wind energy is captured through the rotation of the blades of the wind turbine, historically the blades have been built with wood, but due to the humidity and the high cost of processing, modern materials such as carbon fiber reinforced plastic or fiberglass have been chosen for the construction of steel and aluminum, which nowadays are replacing the traditional wood [3].

The efficiency of a wind turbine is intrinsically linked to factors such as the wind turbine design, the type of airfoil used in the creation of the blades, the rotor diameter, the propeller height, the wind characteristics in the areas to be installed [4].

At present, Blade designs are available that offer low aerodynamic performance. The values between 30% and 45% for high-power wind turbines are the consequence of the geometric simplifications carried out when manufacturing the blades and the lack of deep aerodynamic studies to design them [5]. It is also important to take into account the material of the blades of the wind turbines. Materials that satisfy complex design restrictions, which are capable of providing good resistance to static and aerodynamic load [6].

The objective of this research has been to perform an aerodynamic analysis based on materials and shapes of different types of wind turbine blades for wind energy production through the interconnection of FAST aerodynamic models and generator models of the MatLab Simulink library. In order to achieve the objective, a quantitative approach research with exploratory, descriptive, correlational and explanatory scope has been carried out.

2   Materials and Methods

2.1   Selection of the Aerodynamic Variables to Be Studied

Variable wind speeds are used for 100 s: 7 m/s (time 0–49 s) and 8 m/s (50 s–100 s). The second variable is the blade tip ratio (TSR) which is the ratio between the linear velocity at the blade tip and the absolute wind speed [7]. The third variable is the final useful power which is the product between the speed multiplier output and the generator efficiency [8]. The fourth variable is the Cp, which is the ratio between the power at the rotor shaft and the available wind power [8]. The fifth variable is generator speed: for the study, it is expressed in RPM [9]. It's important to mention that the blade variables will be discussed in more detail in Sect. 2.3.

2.2   Coupling of FAST and MatLab Simulink

To carry out the coupling between FAST and MatLab it is necessary to refer to the National Renewable Energy Laboratory article Simulation for Wind Turbine Generators-With FAST and MATLAB-Simulink Modules [9]. It's necessary to reproduce the application case of Appendix B: Integrating FAST with a Type 3 Wind Turbine Generator Model of the mentioned article. Once FAST and Simulink are coupled, it is necessary to verify its correct operation. Once the operation is verified, we proceeded to make the necessary modifications to be adapted to our case study. First, in the Simulink program, the variables to be studied are specified by means of fcn blocks. The variables are a function of the FAST file [9]. The variables are: wind-TotWindV, Cp-HSShftCp, Tip Speed Ratio (TSR)-TipSpdRat, Generator Speed-HSShftV [10]. The output power is obtained from the DFIG generator. The adaptations in FAST-Simulink are shown in Fig. 1. Second, it is important to declare the same variable in the .fst file of the FAST programs (TotWindV, HSShftCp, TipSpdRat, HSShftV) [10].

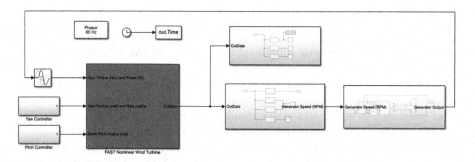

Fig. 1. Modification made for adaptation to the case study between FAST and MatLab Simulink

2.3   Obtaining the Blades to Be Tested

The design of wind turbine blades has changed over the years. This has resulted in much more attention being paid to blade design and analysis. It has become necessary to use finite element structural models in much greater detail in order to verify the final design. NuMAD is a software tool that provides an intuitive interface to define the external geometry of the blade [11]. Numerical Manufacturing And Design, version 2.0 (NuMAD) [11] is the software tool used to obtain the wind turbine blades. This tool allows to simplify the 3-D finite element modeling. This program manages all the information of the blades such as the database of aerodynamic profiles and the materials to be used in the creation of blades.

Three blades models are used for the aerodynamic analysis: the SNL100-00 model, the pseudoSERI8 model and the WindPact 15 MW v1.3 model. Three different materials are also used for the propellers. The materials are aluminum 2014T6, balsa wood and fiber composites. It is important to mention that the three blade models are adapted to a size of 33.25 m.

WindPact 15 MW v1.3 Model: The WindPact 15 MW v1.3 model has a length of 33.25 m and has been designed for turbines with a capacity to produce 1.5 MW. The blade has been designed with the following airfoils (circular, S818, S825, S826) [12]. And distributed as shown in Table 1.

Table 1. Table with airfoil distribution for WindPact 1.5 MW v1.3 blade construction.

Station	Airfoil	Location (m)	Chord (m)
1	circular	0.000	1.89
2	circular	0.7	1.89
3	Interp-001600	1.6	1.94
4	Interp-002500	2.5	2.0704
5	Interp-003400	3.4	2.2482
6	Interp-004300	4.3	2.4418
7	Interp-005200	5.2	2.61
8	Interp-006100	6.1	2.7496
9	S818	7	2.8
10	Interp-005200	5.2	2.61
11	Interp-010500	10.5	2.63
12	Interp-012250	12.25	2.47
13	Interp-014000	14	2.3072
14	S825 24	15.75	2.1583
15	Interp-017500	17.5	2.03
16	Interp-019250	19.25	1.9017
17	Interp-021000	21	1.77
18	Interp-022750	22.75	1.64
19	S825	24.5	1.5168
20	Interp-026250	26.255	1.3884
21	Interp-028000	28	1.2601
22	Interp-029750	29.75	1.1317
23	Interp-031500	31.5	1.0034
24	S826	33.25	0.875

The material properties have also been modified for analysis. Three different samples have been obtained. In the first sample the blade is made entirely of 2014T6 aluminum. For the second sample the blade is also designed entirely in Balsa. For the third sample it has been designed combining several elements

(A260 Uniaxial fabrici, CDB340 Triaxial fabric, Spar Cap Mixture, Random Mat, Balsa, Gel Coat, Fill Epoxy) [13]. The shape of the blade together with the materials can be seen in Fig. 2.

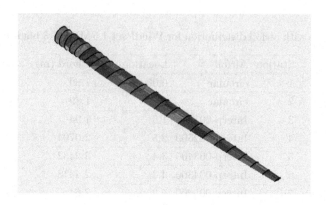

Fig. 2. WindPact 1.5 MW v1.3 blade shape for FAST-MATLAB analysis

SNL100-00 Model: The size of the SNL100-00 model had to be modified because in the previous study it had a length of 100 m [14], and for the analysis of this study it is being done with a length of 33.25 m, Fig. 3. The airfoils used for the design of the SNL100-00 model are detailed in Table 2. Also, as in the previous design, the same materials, Balsa wood, aluminum 2014T6 and composite, have been used.

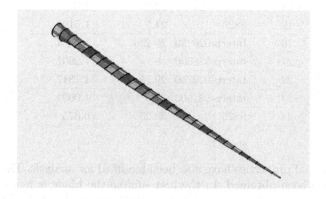

Fig. 3. SNL100-00 blade shape for FAST-MATLAB analysis

Table 2. Table with airfoil distribution for SNL100-00 blade construction.

Station	Airfoil	Location (m)	Chord (m)
1	Interp-000000	0.000	1.496
2	Interp-003448	1.147	1.5
3	Interp-006896	2.293	1.506
4	Interp-010344	3.44	1.512
5	Interp-013793	4.586	1.52
6	Interp-017241	5.733	1.529
7	Interp-020689	1.54	8.324
8	Interp-024137	8.026	1.557
9	Interp-027586	9.172	1.573
10	Interp-031034	10.319	1.576
11	Interp-034482	11.466	1.551
12	Interp-037931	12.612	1.506
13	Interp-041379	13.759	1.447
14	Interp-44827	14.905	1.357
15	Interp-048275	16.052	1.278
16	Interp-051724	17.198	1.2
17	Interp-055172	18.345	1.124
18	Interp-058620	19.491	1.05
19	Interp-062068	20.638	0.976
20	Interp-065517	21.784	0.903
21	Interp-068965	22.931	0.83
22	Interp-072413	24.078	0.757
23	Interp-075862	25.224	0.684
24	Interp-079310	26.371	0.61
25	Interp-082758	27.517	0.536
26	Interp-086026	28.664	0.462
27	Interp-089655	29.81	0.388
28	Interp-093103	30.957	0.314
29	Interp-096551	32.103	0.24
30	Interp-010000	31.5	0.166

PseudoSERI8 Model: The procedure is similar to the previous ones for obtaining the blade design. The pseudoSERI8 model initially has a length of 7.95 m [15]. The size of the other blades, which are 33.25 m, has to be adapted to the model for the purposes of the study. The design is based on the following airfoils (circular, S807, S808, S805AS807, S805A, S806A), for more details refer to Table 3. The selection of materials is the same. Three blades will be obtained with the materials already described: Aluminum 2014T6, Balsa and composite Fig. 4.

Table 3. Table with airfoil distribution for pseudoSERI8 blade construction.

Station	Airfoil	Location (m)	Chord (m)
1	circular	0.000	1.757
2	circular	1.917	1.971
3	S808	6.393	4.69
4	S807	9.44	4.581
5	S805AS807	17.09	3.834
6	S805A	24.745	2.79
7	S806A	31.542	1.695
8	S806A	33.25	1.384

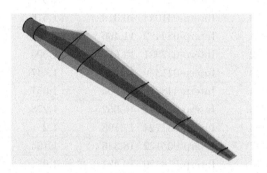

Fig. 4. pseudoSERI8 blade shape for FAST-MATLAB analysis

2.4   Software Simulation

Once the different wind turbine blade models have been completed, we proceed to the simulation. For this, it is necessary to initialize the program created in MatLab Simulink, which together with FAST will perform an aerodynamic analysis. Nine different tests (due to the 3 different blade models and 3 different materials) need to be performed to obtain data and make a comparison of the efficiency of the different wind turbine blades. The tests are performed to help predict the behavior of the system.

3   Results

3.1   Results of the Analysis of Blades with the Use of Aluminum 2014T6

The left part of Fig. 5 shows the results after simulating the Cp (ratio between the power at the rotor shaft and the available wind power). The right part of the same figure shows the results of the tip speed coefficient (ratio between the linear velocity at the blade tip and the absolute wind speed). This figure compares the three blade models according to the material used in the blades. For this part, the 2014T6 aluminum is analyzed. Figure 6 shows the generator speed expressed in (rpm). Data located on the left side of the image. The output power generated by the wind system is shown on the right side.

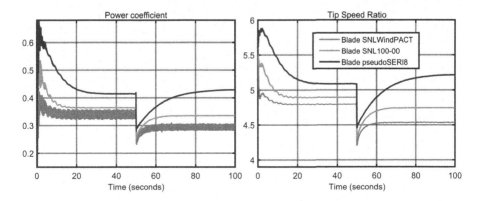

Fig. 5. Cp and TSR

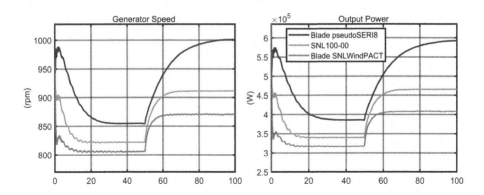

Fig. 6. Generator Speed and Output Power

3.2 Results of the Analysis of Blades with the Use of Balsa Wood

The left part of Fig. 7 shows the results after simulating the Cp (ratio between the power at the rotor shaft and the available wind power). The right part of the same figure shows the results of the tip speed coefficient (ratio between the linear velocity at the blade tip and the absolute wind speed). This figure compares the three blade models according to the material used in the blades. For this part, the Balsa wood is analyzed. Figure 8 shows the generator speed expressed in (rpm). Data located on the left side of the image. The output power generated by the wind system is shown on the right side.

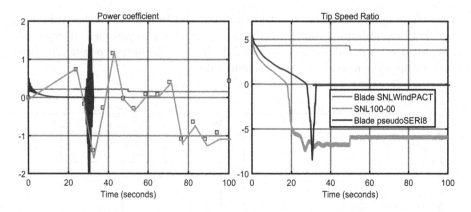

Fig. 7. Cp and TSR

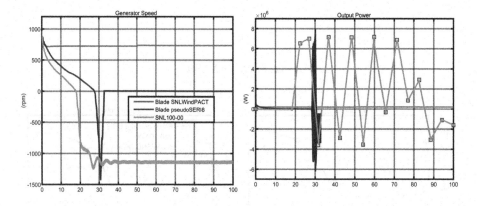

Fig. 8. Generator Speed and Output Power

3.3   Results of the Analysis of Blades with the Use of Composite Material

The left part of Fig. 9 shows the results after simulating the Cp (ratio between the power at the rotor shaft and the available wind power). The right part of the same figure shows the results of the tip speed coefficient (ratio between the linear velocity at the blade tip and the absolute wind speed). This figure compares the three blade models according to the material used in the blades. For this part, the composite material is analyzed.

Figure 10 shows the generator speed expressed in (rpm). Data located on the left side of the image. The power output generated by the wind system is shown on the right side.

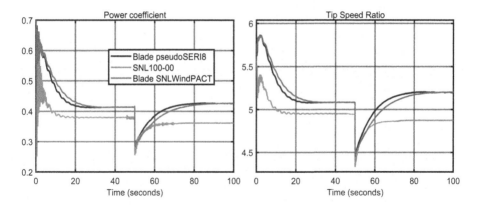

Fig. 9. Cp and TSR for aluminum 2014T6

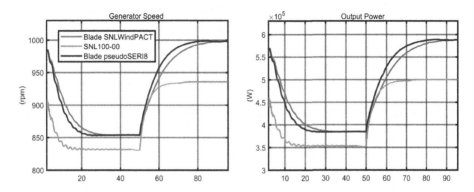

Fig. 10. Generator Speed and Output Power for aluminum 2014T6

4   Conclusions

In this work, the aerodynamics based on materials and shapes of different types of wind turbine blades for wind energy production are analyzed by means of FAST and Matlab Simulink. The result of the analysis indicated that the pseudoSERI8 blade with composite material presented the best aerodynamic performance of the three propellers taken as samples, allowing to obtain a useful power of approximately 0.6 MW. The Cp is 0.42 and the TSR is 5.25. It is also important to highlight that, when analyzing the same turbid model, but this time with Aluminum 2014T6, a power output similar to 0.48 MW is generated. On the other hand, the lowest performance model presented is the SNL100-00 with a power output of 0.02 MW and even presented a series of disturbances where the other models remained stable.

The aerodynamic analysis is subject to certain limitations, as it is applied to wind turbines of 1.5 MW of power and the dimensions of the blades are 33.25 m.

The work has a research utility and in the future new simulations could be carried out with methodologies compatible with the materials and propeller shapes used, making possible the analysis and comparison of aerodynamic results. It is also recommended to use different types of generated and new propeller models for future research.

References

1. Caratoña, A.: Análisis del Comportamiento Aerodinámico de Perfiles empleados en Aerogeneradores de Baja Potencia, 2nd edn (2009)
2. Wilson, D.G., Berg, D.E., Zayas, J.R., Lobitz, D.W.: Optimized active aerodynamic blade control for load alleviation on large wind turbines. SAND2008-4202C **2**(5), 99–110 (2008)
3. Babu, K.S., Raju, N.S., Reddy, M.S., Rao, D.N.: The material selection for typical wind turbine blades using a MADM approach & analysis of blades. **2**(5), 99–110 (2006)
4. Ganiele, M.J., et al.: Perfiles de Microaerogeneradores HAWT a Bajo Número de REYNOLDS. Journal **2**(5), 99–110 (2016)
5. Caballero, J., Resendiz, C., Gómez, A.: Análisis de cargas aerodinámicas sobre el perfil estático de la hélice de una turbina eólica. Revista de Ingeniería Mecánica **2**(5), 59 (2017)
6. Rocha, J.: Diseño y análisis de un álabe utilizando materiales compuestos para un aerogenerador de baja potencia, 2nd edn. Universidad Autónoma de Baja California, Mexicali (2019)
7. Villarubia, M.: Ingeniería de la Energía Eólica, 2nd edn. MARCOMBO, S.A., España (2012)
8. Hansen, M.: Aerodynamics of Wind Turbines, 2nd edn. EARTHSCAN, S.A., London (2008)
9. Singh, M., Muljadi, E., Jonkman, J., Gevorgian, V.: Simulation for Wind Turbine Generators-With FAST and MATLAB-Simulink Modules, 1st edn. NREL, UUEE (2008)
10. Jonkman, J.M., Buhl, M.L.: FAST Usets Guide, 1st edn. NREL, UUEE (2005)
11. Berg, J.C., Resor, B.R.: Numerical manufacturing and design tool (NuMAD v2.0) for wind turbine blades: user's guide. Journal **2**(5), 24–32 (2012)
12. Resor, B., Bushnell, T.: A 1.5 MW NuMAD blade model. Sandia Natl. Laboratories **2**(5), 10 (2016)
13. Resor, B., Bushnell, T.: WindPACT turbine design scaling studies technical area 1-composite blades for 80- to 120-meter rotor. Sandia Natl. Laboratories **2**(5), 8 (2021)
14. Griffith, D., Ashwill, T.: The Sandia 100-meter all-glass baseline wind turbine blade: SNL100-00r. Sandia Natl. Laboratories **2**(5), 19–26 (2011)
15. Griffith, D., Ashwill, T.: Numerical manufacturing and design tool (NuMAD v2.0) for wind turbine blades: user's guide. Sandia Natl. Laboratories **2**(5), 30 (2012)

Numerical Comparison Using CFD of R134a and R600a Condensation in Helical and Spiral Exchangers

Fernando Toapanta-Ramos[✉] [iD], Tito Hidalgo, Jefferson Parra, and William Quitiaquez[iD]

Universidad Politécnica Salesiana, Quito, Ecuador
ltoapanta@ups.edu.ec
https://www.ups.edu.ec/

Abstract. The objective of this research document is to analyze numerically through the ANSYS software using the CFD (Computational Fluid Dynamics) tool, to determine the behavior of refrigerants R134a and R600a in the condensation process that is generated in the helical and spiral exchangers. For the investigation, fluid mechanics parameters were adjusted as thermal, for this the work equations were obtained through different texts and investigations and initial parameters were established for the work fluids and characteristics of the pipe. In addition, in the specific analysis of condensation, the Fluent tool of the ANSYS software was used, defining the mesh and applying the Euler volume fraction model. It is evident that the best results obtained in the simulations correspond to cases E and M with ambient temperatures of 20 °C and 17 °C at an inlet velocity of 1.2 m/s with geometry of the helical-type exchanger for refrigerants. R134a and R600a, respectively. Where outlet temperatures of 296.025 K and 295.622 K are obtained, in addition to visualizing that in all the study cases the condensation phenomenon occurs and the temperature at the outlet of the coil register values like those obtained numerically.

Keywords: ANSYS · condenser · CFD · refrigerant · R134a · R600a · spiral · helical

1 Introduction

In history to the present, water is known as the pioneer coolant, in addition, the historical and elemental use of ice, is identified as a refrigeration unit, in addition the ton of refrigeration is described as the amount of heat that is used to melt ice in 24 h. In refrigeration great advances were achieved, in the year 1600, a combination of ice with salt was found, it generated temperatures with greater reduction than ice without mixing [1].

In 1930, by Thomas Midgley Jr., he created the beginning of the fluorocarbon called freon 12, with which a step is taken to a new stage of refrigeration [2]. Years later, the

F. R. Narváez et al. (Eds.): SmartTech-IC 2022, CCIS 1705, pp. 425–438, 2023.
https://doi.org/10.1007/978-3-031-32213-6_31

family of freons, also known as CFCs (chlorofluorocarbons), with special qualities, was developed [1].

In the early 1980s, NASA carried out scientific studies, through satellites, a decrease in the thickness of the ozone layer in Antarctica was found, this is validated with later studies that show the damage of stratospheric ozone caused by the use of halogenated compounds [3].

The refrigerants that have been used frequently are those designated HFCs (hydrofluorocarbons), made from hydrocarbons that have replaced hydrogen particles with fluorine ones [4]. Isobutane or commercially known as R600a appears as an alternative, to supply CFCs, HCFCs (hydrochlorofluorocarbons) and HFCs in air conditioning and refrigeration use, having characteristics of safe operation, durability and reduction of environmental inconveniences such as the decrease in ozone layer and global warming [5].

Akhavan et al. [6] carries out a study regarding the hydrocarbon refrigerant, Isobutane (R600a), which contains within its advantages appropriate thermodynamic characteristics, high energy efficiency, insignificant ozone depletion and potential global warming. Court et al. [7] comment that the use of more efficient and friendly refrigerants for the environment is currently promoted, so certain manufacturers provide compressors that are more compatible with this refrigerant, specifically refrigerants with mixtures of R600a and HC, present a better performance in the Carnot cycle, compared to R134a.

Cai et al. [8] performs a numerical study about the condensation flow and heat transfer properties of refrigerants for hydrocarbons in a spiral tube, for which they make a computational model of a spiral tube from the consideration of computational efficiency., as results, the heat transfer ratio and the pressure drop due to friction increase with the increase in mass flow.

Ahmed et al. [9] carry out a thermodynamic analysis of the performance of R600 and R600a compared to R134a, with said analysis they conclude that the energy efficiency of Isobutane is 50% greater than that of R134a, in addition the analyzes discover that the yields of Butane and Isobutane as refrigerants are similar to those of HFC R134a.

Kumar et al. [10] investigate a CFD (Computational Fluid Dynamics) analysis of a heat exchanger applied in spiral and helical tubes, where they mention that the helical tube heat exchanger is commonly used in industrial applications, this is due to its structure. Compact, increasing heat transfer area, larger heat transfer extent, have narrow residence time distributions, and a compact structure.

Jiawen et al. [11] carry out a numerical investigation, taking into account the peculiarities of heat transfer in the condensation of the mixed refrigerant with hydrocarbons such as CFC, HCFC and HFC in a helical tube. Tube diameter and mass flow are found to play a significant role in the condensation heat transfer coefficient.

The objective in writing is to numerically investigate the condensation process in helical and spiral type heat exchangers, to identify how refrigerants R600a and R134a behave when they are circulating inside a spiral or helical heat exchanger under the condensation process.

2 Materials and Methods

The parameters of the copper pipe for the coil through which R134a and R600a refrigerant will circulate inside, the fluid that transits in the periphery of the exchanger is water, is supported by the research of Barbosa and Sigwalt [12]. These characteristics are displayed in Table 1.

Table 1. Coil geometry characteristics [13].

Characteristics	Details
Internal diameter (Di)	8,001 mm
External diameter (Do)	9,525 mm
Thickness (e)	1.524 mm
Thermal conductivity (k)	386 W/m·K
Coil area (A)	$5,027 \times 10^{-5}$ m^2

Figure 1 shows schematically how the heat exchangers are designed: a) helical and b) spiral.

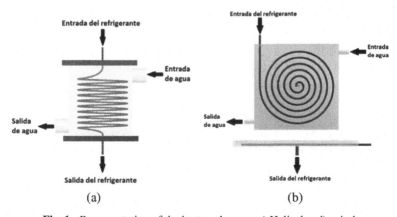

(a)   (b)

Fig. 1. Representation of the heat exchanger: a) Helical and) spiral.

To carry out the condensation phenomenon, it is required that R134a and R600a have a higher temperature compared to water. Consequently, the working fluid is treated as a pure gas in a superheated state at the entrance of the condenser and at the exit of the condenser it is treated as a compressed liquid, due to the discharge generated by the compressor [14]. Table 2 and Table 3 show the characteristics of R134a and R600a, respectively.

To obtain results that resemble reality through CFD, it is necessary that there is an adequate meshing, the same that is done in a product called ANSYS Workbench, where

Table 2. Parameters for R134a refrigerant input [15].

Properties of R134a	Characteristics
Inlet pressure (PRi)	0,89 MPa
Inlet temperature (TRi)	63,3 °C
Outlet temperature (TRo)	28,9 °C
Specific volume at 63,3 °C (v)	0,04407 m³/kg
Density at 63,3 °C (ρv)	37,15 kg/m³
Viscosity at 63,3 °C (μ)	9,149 × 10–6 kg/m·s
Specific heat capacity at 63,3 °C (Cp)	1,025 kJ/kg·K
Thermal conductivity at 63,3 °C (k)	0,01743 W/m·K

Table 3. Parameters for R600a refrigerant input [15].

Properties of R600a	Characteristics
Inlet pressure (PRi)	0,46 MPa
Inlet temperature (TRi)	56, 2 °C
Outlet temperature (TRo)	28, 2 °C
Specific volume at 56,2 °C (v)	0,09291 m³/kg
Density at 56,2 °C (ρv)	10,76 kg/m³
Viscosity at 56,2 °C (μ)	8,555 × 10–6 kg/m·s
Specific heat capacity at 56,2 °C (Cp)	1,931 kJ/kg·K
Thermal conductivity at 56,2 °C (k)	0,02046 W/m·K

the quality of the meshing is highlighted, for this reason it is required that the refinement of the mesh is indicated, said refinement depends on the computational capacity and precision of the computer [16].

Figure 2 shows the specific and proper meshing for each coil, which are: Helical with R134a (a), helical with R600a (b), spiral with R134a (c) and spiral with R600a (d).

In order to obtain the correct results for the asymmetry of the mesh in the development of the heat transfer of flows carried out in ANSYS, the Skewness parameter must be less than 0.95 and its average must be between 0–0.25 [17].

Figure 3 indicates the quality of the condenser mesh for each geometry, which are: (a) Helical with R134a with a mesh average of 0.19363, (b) Helical with R600a with 0.17773, for the spiral with R134a is 0.1834 and the spiral with R600a has 0.2491.

The following equations are used for CFD models, where the equation of continuity, conservation of momentum and energy intervene.

$$\frac{\partial \rho}{\partial t} + \nabla \cdot \left(\rho \overline{V} \right) = S_n \tag{1}$$

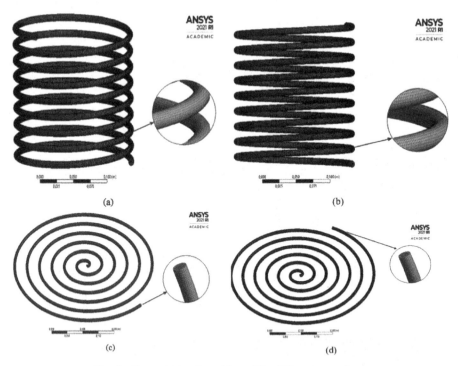

Fig. 2. Computational meshing of the different capacitors.

$$\frac{\partial}{\partial t}(\rho \overline{V}) + \nabla \cdot (\rho \overline{VV}) = -\nabla P + \nabla \left\{ \mu \left[\left(\nabla \overline{V} + \nabla \overline{V}^T \right) - \frac{2}{3} \nabla \cdot \overline{V} I \right] \right\} + \rho \overline{g} + \overline{F} \quad (2)$$

$$\frac{\partial}{\partial t}(\rho E) + \nabla \cdot \left[\overline{V}(\rho E + P) \right] = -\nabla \cdot \left(\sum_j h_j J_j \right) + S_b \quad (3)$$

The phase change model presents three equations that are related to a single pressure and velocity, also temperatures and entropies. Therefore, modeling phase change and thermal relaxation limit, the following equilibrium conditions are present in Eqs. (4), (5) and (6) respectively [18].

$$\frac{\partial}{\partial t}(\alpha_q \rho_q) + \nabla \cdot (\alpha_q \rho_q \overline{v}_q) = \sum_{p=1}^{n} (\dot{m}_{pq} - \dot{m}_{qp}) + S_q \quad (4)$$

$$\frac{\partial}{\partial t}(\alpha_q \rho_q h_q) + \nabla \cdot (\alpha_q \rho_q \overline{u}_q h_q) = \alpha_q \frac{\partial p_q}{\partial t} + \overline{\overline{\tau}}_q : \nabla \overline{u}_q - \nabla \cdot \overline{q}_q + S_q \dots$$
$$\dots + \sum_{p=l}^{n} (Q_{pq} + \dot{m}_{pq} h_{pq} - \dot{m}_{qp} h_{qp}) \quad (5)$$

$$\frac{\partial}{\partial t}(\alpha_q \rho_q \overline{v}_q) + \nabla \cdot (\alpha_q \rho_q \overline{v}_q \overline{v}_q) = -\alpha_q \nabla P + \nabla \cdot \overline{\overline{\tau}}_q + \alpha_q \rho_q \overline{g} \dots$$
$$\dots + \sum_{p=l}^{n} \left[K_{pq}(\overline{v}_p - \overline{v}_q) + \dot{m}_{pq} \overline{v}_{pq} - \dot{m}_{qp} \overline{v}_{qp} \right] + \dots \quad (6)$$
$$\left(\overline{F}_q + \overline{F}_{uftq} + \overline{F}_{u^2q} + \overline{F}_{ruq} + \overline{F}_{uq} \right)$$

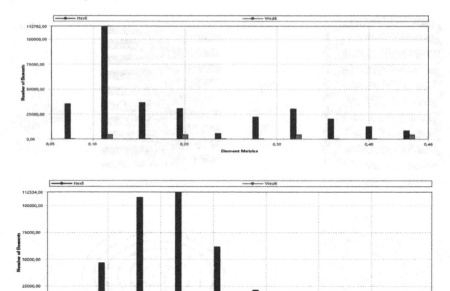

Fig. 3. Convergence of the mesh of each condenser.

Equation (7) represents the Lee model, the same one that is part of the ANSYS software and is defined as multiphase, it is used as a suitable method in the condensation and evaporation processes, it will assume a negative sign for the transfer that occurs in condensation and a positive sign in evaporation [19, 20].

$$\frac{\partial}{\partial t} \cdot \rho_v \cdot \alpha_v + \rho_v \cdot \alpha_v \cdot \vec{V} = \dot{m}_{vl} - \dot{m}_{lv} \tag{7}$$

The k-ε RNG model is presented that handles a complementary variable ε in order to mainly improve the precision of the time flows in a more agile way [21], as indicated in Eqs. (8) and (9).

$$\frac{\partial(\rho k)}{\partial t} + \frac{\partial(\rho k u_i)}{\partial x_i} = \frac{\partial}{\partial x_j}\left[\left(\mu + \frac{\mu_t}{\sigma_k}\right)\frac{\partial k}{\partial x_j}\right] + G_k + G_b - \rho\varepsilon - Y_M + S_k \tag{8}$$

$$\frac{\partial(\rho\varepsilon)}{\partial t} + \frac{\partial(\rho\varepsilon u_i)}{\partial x_i} = \frac{\partial}{\partial x_j}\left[\left(\mu + \frac{\mu_t}{\sigma_k}\right)\frac{\partial\varepsilon}{\partial x_j}\right] + C_{l\varepsilon}\frac{\varepsilon}{k}(G_k + C_3 G_b) - C_{2k}\rho\frac{\varepsilon^2}{k} + S_\epsilon \tag{9}$$

3   Results

When performing the forced convection simulation, the objective is to reduce the inlet temperature of each refrigerant and to produce a phase change in order for the condensation process to occur. Table 4 reflects the conditions proposed for the helical and spiral type condenser with their respective working fluid.

Table 4. Previous data from the simulations.

Simulation	Ambient temperature	Refrigerant type	Coil material	Refrigerant inlet rate	Condenser type
A	20 °C	R134a	Copper	1,5 m/s	Helical
B	20 °C	R600a	Copper	1,5 m/s	Helical
C	20 °C	R134a	Copper	1,5 m/s	Spiral
D	20 °C	R600a	Copper	1,5 m/s	Spiral

The simulations can be seen in Fig. 4. Which are the results of the parameters shown in Table 4 as initial conditions, where the phase change with respect to volume two is evidenced, which corresponds to the phenomenon that occurs in the liquid phase of each refrigerant in the condenser, both helical and spiral, demonstrating that the condensation process occurs in each condenser.

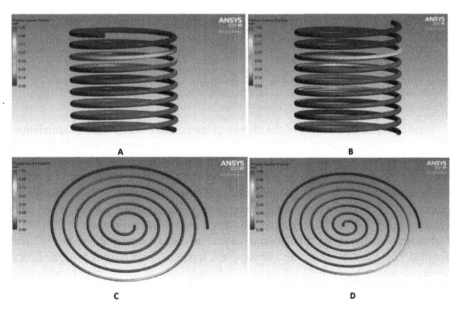

Fig. 4. Change of phase with the initial conditions in the condensers of spiral and helical type. (a) Helical R134a, (b) Helical R600a, (c) Spiral R134a and (d) Spiral R600a.

The planes referring to cases A, B, C and D are observed, where the decrease in temperature is displayed along the length of the coil, both helical and spiral, with the parameters and conditions established in Table 4 until the temperature reaches a stabilization.

For the variables that intervene in the simulation such as ambient temperature, input speed is detailed in Table 5. It should be emphasized that it is taken into account in order to find an alternative in obtaining results for comparison with the simulations and previous data obtained analytically.

Table 5. Variation of spiral and helical type condensers with R134a and R600a.

Simulation	Ambient temperature	Refrigerant type	Coil material	Refrigerant inlet rate	Condenser type
E	20 °C	R134a	Copper	1,2 m/s	Helical
F	17 °C	R134a	Copper	1,5 m/s	Helical
G	17 °C	R134a	Copper	1,2 m/s	Helical
H	20 °C	R134a	Copper	1,2 m/s	Spiral
I	17 °C	R134a	Copper	1,5 m/s	Spiral
J	17 °C	R134a	Copper	1,2 m/s	Spiral
K	20 °C	R600a	Copper	1,2 m/s	Helical
L	17 °C	R600a	Copper	1,5 m/s	Helical
M	17 °C	R600a	Copper	1,2 m/s	Helical
N	20 °C	R600a	Copper	1,2 m/s	Spiral
O	17 °C	R600a	Copper	1,5 m/s	Spiral
P	17 °C	R600a	Copper	1,2 m/s	Spiral

Figure 5 shows the results of the change in temperature and volume of simulations E, F and G that are compared with simulation A, which corresponds to the helical-type condenser with refrigerant R134a. On the other hand, different coolant outlet temperatures are recorded, it should be noted that there is no notable difference in terms of final temperature where results are obtained that in the simulation of case A presents a temperature of 296.45 at the outlet of the coil. K. In the simulation of case E an outlet temperature of 296.025 K is recorded. In case F an outlet temperature of 296.395 K is obtained. Finally, in the simulation of case G an outlet temperature of 296.387 K is recorded These results show that a lower outlet temperature is obtained for the helical condenser with working fluid R134a in case E with ambient temperature conditions of 17 °C and a refrigerant inlet speed of 1.2 m/s.

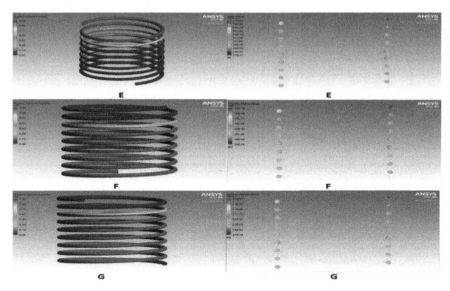

Fig. 5. Simulations of the variants of the helical condenser with R134a.

Figure 6 shows the results of the simulations of the variants of cases H, I and J. Which will be compared with case C that corresponds to the spiral type condenser with refrigerant R134a; where the phase change and the temperature change suffered by the refrigerant in the process are shown, respectively, which is evidenced in the values of phase two of the refrigerant where at the entrance the liquid phase registers a quality of 0 and at the output a quality of 1 which shows that I know that it produces condensation in the working fluid. In addition, different coolant outlet temperatures are shown in the different simulation cases, with outlet temperature results of 297.72 K, 297.245 K, 297.615 K and 297.255 K for cases C, H, I and J, respectively. Clearly, which shows that there is a lower outlet temperature for the spiral condenser with working fluid R134a in case H with the conditions of ambient temperature of 20 °C and an inlet speed of 1.2 m/s.

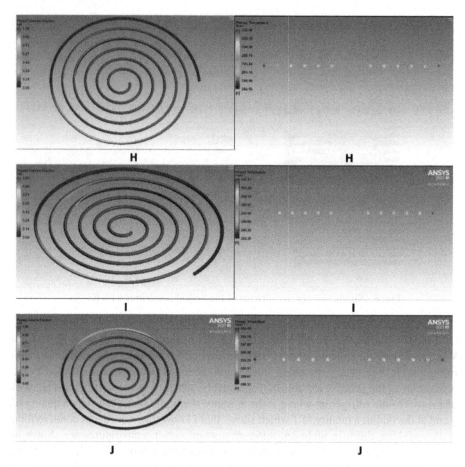

Fig. 6. Simulations of the variants of the spiral condenser with R134a.

It can be seen in Fig. 7 the values obtained in the simulations of the variants for the helical condenser with R600a refrigerant; which are given in cases K, L and M, these simulations will be compared with case B which corresponds to the variant with initial conditions, these results reflect the phase change and the temperature change suffered by the coolant in the process respectively. It is observed that all cases comply with the condensation process because the values of phase two of the refrigerant show that at the entrance the liquid phase registers a quality of 0 and at the exit a quality of 1. Also, they are verified different coolant outlet temperatures in the different simulation cases, there are results of outlet temperatures of 296.276 K, 295.971 K, 295.647 K and 295.622 K for cases B, K, L and M respectively, which shows that there is a lower outlet temperature occurs in case M with the initial conditions for the simulation being 17 °C ambient temperature and an inlet speed of 1.2 m/s.

Figure 8 describes the graphs of the results of the simulations of the variants for the spiral type of condenser with refrigerant R600a, which are given in the cases N,

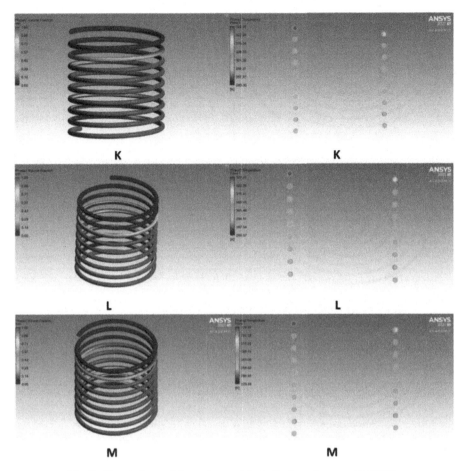

Fig. 7. Simulations of the variants of the helical condenser with R600a.

O and P, these will be compared with the corresponding case D. to the variant with initial conditions of the model. The results show the phase change and the temperature change that is generated in the working fluid in the process, respectively. It is verified that all the simulation cases comply with the condensation process, since the values of phase two of the refrigerant indicate that at the entrance the liquid phase registers a quality of 0 and at the exit a quality of 1, which shows that there is condensation in the process. On the other hand, different coolant outlet temperatures are displayed in the different simulation cases, results are recorded with outlet temperature values of 296.236 K, 296.182 K, 295.830 K and 296.002 K for cases D, N, O and P respectively, which shows that a lower outlet temperature is obtained in case O with the variants of ambient temperature at 17 °C and at an inlet speed of 1.5 m/s.

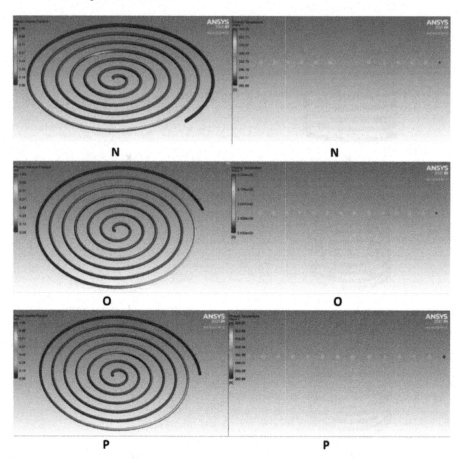

Fig. 8. Simulations of the variants of the spiral condenser with R600a.

4 Conclusions

After carrying out the numerical investigation of two types of exchangers with two different refrigerants, the following conclusions were determined, described below:

- The condenser was sized, obtaining an energy balance where a total heat transfer of −0.5936 kW was obtained for the R134a refrigerant and −0.3107 [kJ/s] for the R600a refrigerant. With these heat transfer values and with the dimension parameters mentioned in chapter 3. It is evident for R134a and R600a a time of 23.31 min and 44.60 min, respectively, to generate heat transfer.
- For the simulations, the ANSYS software was used, where a numerical analysis was obtained. The Euler model was applied with a bubble diameter of 0.01 mm, the Lee method was used for the condensation process in both condensers. The k-epsilon turbulence method was chosen with its realizable variable, relaxation values were

used to obtain an adequate simulation process and a number of 520 interactions was estimated, with which a change of state was obtained in all cases. of simulation.

– The software corroborated the results of the temperatures obtained at the outlet of the condenser with refrigerant R134a, this being an average value of

– 296.3 K. Which gives an estimated error of 2% with respect to the value of the outlet temperature calculated theoretically, on the other hand, the simulations carried out for the R600a refrigerant record an average temperature value of 295.73 K giving a estimated error of 1.8% with respect to the values obtained numerically and analytically.

– The simulations demonstrated the efficiency that exists in all the cases, due to the fact that in all the simulations carried out the condensation phenomenon occurred and the desired outlet temperatures were obtained. However, the helical-type exchanger model with R600a working fluid with initial ambient temperature conditions at 17 °C and a refrigerant inlet velocity of 1.2 m/s, which corresponds to case M of the simulations, record a coolant outlet temperature at 295,622 K, this in comparison with the other variants and exchanger models is the lowest outlet temperature recorded in all study cases.

Acknowledgements. The authors of this research thank the mechanical engineering career of the Salesian Polytechnic University, the Research Group on Renewable Energies and Mechanical Implementation of SMEs GIERIMP, Industrial Production Research Group (GIPI) and the Branch ASHRAE UPS-QUITO.

References

1. Renedo, C.: Refrigerantes. In: Termodin. Y Refrig., pp. 136–163 (2003)
2. Hernandez, M.N.: Cero GradosCelsius. cero gradoscelsius, vol. 42, pp. 28–29 (2015)
3. Plazas, J.P.: Universidad Politécnica de Catalunya Facultad de Náutica de Barcelona Proyecto Final de Carrera LOS REFRIGERANTES Y EL MEDIO AMBIENTE Autor : Juan Pablo Plazas Monroy Tutor : Ignacio Echevarrieta Sazatornil, pp. 1–139 (2012)
4. Cabello, R.: de bajo GWP, no. May (2016)
5. Messineo, A.: R744-R717 Cascade refrigeration system: performance evaluation compared with a HFC two-stage system. Energy Procedia **14**, 56–65 (2012). https://doi.org/10.1016/j.egypro.2011.12.896
6. Akhavan-behabadi, M.A.L.I., Torabian, A., Nasr, M.: Effect of multi-wall carbon nanotubes on flow condensation heat transfer of R-600a/Oil Mixture, no. March, pp. 16–20 (2016)
7. Corte, E., Flores, C., Jara, N., Isaza, C.: Sistemas de refrigeración doméstica - estado del arte de las mejoras en la eficiencia energética. Rev. la Fac. Ciencias Químicas la Univ. Cuenca Ecuador **9**(March 2015), 19–40 (2014)
8. Cai, W., et al.: Numerical study on condensation flow and heat transfer characteristics of hydrocarbon refrigerants in a spiral tube. Elsevier Inc. (2020)
9. Ahamed, J.U., Saidur, R., Masjuki, H.H.: Thermodynamic performance analysis OF R-600 And R-600A as refrigerant. Eng. e-Trans. **5**(1), 11–18 (2010)
10. Reddy, K.V.K., Kumar, B.S.P., Gugulothu, R., Anuja, K., Rao, P.V.: CFD analysis of a helically coiled tube in tube heat exchanger. Mater. Today Proc. **4**(2), 2341–2349 (2017). https://doi.org/10.1016/j.matpr.2017.02.083

11. u, J., Jiang, Y., Cai, W., Li, F.: Numerical investigation on flow condensation of zeotropic hydrocarbon mixtures in a helically coiled tube. Appl. Thermal Eng. **134**, 322–332 (2018). https://doi.org/10.1016/j.applthermaleng.2018.02.006
12. Barbosa, J.R., Sigwalt, R.A.: Air-side heat transfer and pressure drop in spiral wire-on-tube condensers. Int. J. Refrig. **35**(4), 939–951 (2012). https://doi.org/10.1016/j.ijrefrig.2012.02.010
13. Productos Nacobre. Manual Técnico Nacobre, p. 121 (2010)
14. Toapanta-Ramos, F., Nieto-Londoño, P.D.C., Quitiaquez, W., Toapanta, J.K.,: Ansys CFD analysis of the thermal behavior of coolant 134a in a condenser within a refrigeration cycle. Int. J. Eng. Trends Technol. **63**(2), 85–90 (2018). https://doi.org/10.14445/22315381/IJETT-V63P215
15. Gracia, A.O.: Evaluación experimental del Isobutano (R600a) como substituto del R134a en instalaciones de compresión simple de vapor que utilizan compresores herméticos (2015)
16. ANSYS - Análisis Estructural - Simulación Computacional - ESSS. https://www.esss.co/es/ansys-simulacion-computacional/analisis-estructural/. Accessed 13 May 2021
17. Gautam, K.: Skew bridge analysis using "ANSYS." Int. J. Eng. Res. **9**(06), 870–875 (2020). https://doi.org/10.17577/IJERTV9IS060664
18. Zhang, J.: A simple and effective five-equation two-phase numerical model for liquid-vapor phase transition in cavitating flows. Int. J. Multiph. Flow **132**, 103417 (2020). https://doi.org/10.1016/j.ijmultiphaseflow.2020.103417
19. Vinuesa, L.F.D.: Análisis y desarrollo de la simulación termo-hidráulica de flujo multifase en CFD con ANSYS Fluent ® (2017)
20. Blanco, D.: Análisis Termohidráulico del Proceso de Condensación por Contacto Directo de un Flujo de Vapor Inyectado en Agua con ANSYS Fluent, p. 72 (2016)
21. Ramos, L.F.T., Andrade, C., Álvarez, E.D., Zaldumbide, S.L., Quitiaquez, W.: Análisis térmico de un disipador de calor con tubos de calor para procesadores de alto rendimiento. Enfoque UTE **10**(2), 39–51 (2019). https://doi.org/10.29019/enfoque.v10n2.469

CIEMS: A Review Towards a Collaborative Industrial Emergency Management Information System

Miguel Jimeno[1]([✉])(iD), Nicolas Buitrago[1], Hector Camacho[1], César Viloria[2], and Jairo Cardona[2](iD)

[1] Systems Engineering Department, Universidad del Norte, Barranquilla, Colombia
{majimeno,nicolasbuitrago,trujilloh}@uninorte.edu.co
[2] Electrical Engineering Department, Universidad del Norte, Barranquilla, Colombia
{caviloria,jacardona}@uninorte.edu.co

Abstract. Technological accidents are vital in terms of safety and health at work, along with social and environmental conditions. It is essential to emphasize the need for security in processes within industries to avoid loss of human lives, environmental pollution, and economic losses. Existing emergency management systems do not consider how conglomerates of companies improve emergency handling. Thus, following a qualitative approach, this paper extensively reviews the existing academic and commercial solutions as input for a features-based design of a new system. The system covers all the management needs of technological accidents found in the review. The system infrastructure uses cloud services and peripheral devices to obtain real-time information on meteorological variables. As a result, it provides a comprehensive review of the current tools and proposals and a novel solution for an adapted emergency management system.

Keywords: Emergency management system · Cloud computing · Internet of Things

1 Introduction

Technological accidents have emphasized the need for process safety within industries. One of the main concerns in industrial areas is managing these potential accidents, similarly mitigating the effects of accidents that occur [1]. The sudden release of hazardous chemicals triggers alarms in emergency management systems used by the private or public sector. Other entities typically interested in such accidents are chemical accident emergency rescue centers, firefighters, and dangerous chemicals production industries, as long as any other entity in charge of transportation or storage. They generate a maneuverable emergency rescue plan in the shortest time according to the geographical location and the

---

Supported by Ministry of Science, Colombia.

F. R. Narváez et al. (Eds.): SmartTech-IC 2022, CCIS 1705, pp. 439–452, 2023.
https://doi.org/10.1007/978-3-031-32213-6_32

specific situation of the accident [2]. Unmanaged accidents produce many significant damages to the environment [3]. Existing management systems deploy a rapid response process according to the analysis of accident situations, where accidents occur, and means to instruct the scene personnel to carry out the initial accident emergency work promptly [4]. Depending on the type of industry, the incident management process should also be used in the emergency decision system for hazardous chemical leakage accidents. This system focuses on specific accident emergencies, such as hazardous chemical leaks, and provides an effective emergency decision scheme for areas with production, transportation, storage, and use of dangerous chemicals [5]. Chemical spills affect human health and the safety of the ecological environment, threatening the development of the economy and society [6]. Therefore, developing contingency plans for chemical hazards involves collecting data on accident characteristics, environmental scenarios, and human and material resource requirements to cope with the emergency [1].

A crucial aspect of emergency management is to have the necessary information for decision-making [1]. The situation might become even more challenging when companies around the accidents are not properly and promptly informed about the situation. Even though public entities should be in charge of informing the community and the industry around the location, information might not arrive at the expected time or even arrive complete. The management process thus should be benefited from a sense of community inside the groups of companies around the accident's location.

For this reason, this paper starts with a comprehensive review of academic and commercial solutions. It then proposes a new emergency management information system that combines traditional management systems for knowledge manipulation, risk reduction, and management of technological emergencies with an impact on communities. The structure of the paper is as follows: it first presents a review of existing systems from the literature, and it devises the proposed system with its architectural components and services. From there, the paper ends with the main conclusions. The contributions of this work are the following:

- A comprehensive, up-to-date comparison of existing emergency management systems
- The first management system to handle the collaborative treatment of industrial emergencies
- The modular architecture of the proposed system.

2   Methodology

This work uses a qualitative methodology, and it is essential to highlight that the final objective is not to assess the proposed design quantitatively. Such an approach would need a complete implementation and evaluation with real users and might be the subject of future work. The proposed methodology focuses on highlighting the most common features from the literature and proposing new ones currently not implemented, which should be necessary for any system of this type. Thus, the steps are the following:

- A systematic literature review of existing academic and commercial solutions
- A feature-based analysis of existing solutions to establish which features are common and which features might be missing
- An iterative process for the system design using the results from the previous analysis step
- The design of the modular architecture of the proposed system

Then, the background work in the following section looks at the features of studied academic and commercial solutions, followed by the system design proposed, given the results of the upcoming section.

3 Background Work

3.1 Academic Proposals

The topic of emergency management systems has drawn the attention of researchers from different perspectives. Given the type of application, multiple disciplines intersect in the resulting systems. Some research areas include information systems design, cloud architectures for systems deployment, novel emergency management strategies at industrial levels, and technological tools to add new efficient features for the solutions, such as the Internet of Things (IoT) to add sensing and acting capabilities. For example, the work proposed in [24] highlighted the importance of designing an efficient cloud-based architecture for deploying emergency management systems, given the elastic potential for analyzing historical data from previous events. On the other side, other works have highlighted the importance of collaboration with the community, as the work in [23] states. The authors depicted a distributed system that enables the community and supporting agents to collaborate, coordinate, and communicate.

For IoT, there are several proposals to add features for those systems using IoT architectures to increase not only emergency detection but also response. One example is the work from [22], where the authors depicted an IoT-based EMS using sensors and video capabilities to monitor emergency environments.

3.2 Comparison of Existing Information Systems

Web and mobile applications allow people to have a wide range of possibilities, improving communication between different groups or individuals. Applications allow mutual and uninterrupted communication involving groups of individuals who identify with the exact needs, problems, and threats [15]. In the case of companies, it is beneficial to have a web application or mobile application when managing risks to provide communication between those involved and the continuous construction of the risk management system.

Different web and mobile applications on the market facilitate risk, emergency, and mutual aid management. D4H Incident Management is a real-time incident management platform that enables the coordination of an effective response to various situations [7]. With the platform's help, industrial facilities and public safety teams can work together by sharing real-time information, communicating objectives, and collaborating on a resolution through forms, tasks, and status dashboards. D4H Incident Management has a built-in interactive geographic information system. Using part of Esri's geospatial cloud, the platform uses ArcGIS base layers with satellite imagery, street maps, geocoding, grouped visualizations, annotations, and image overlays [7]. D4H enables the management of mutual aid through the platform, considering that technological emergencies caused by industrial processes can seriously affect the environment and neighboring communities.

The assistance of emergency services is essential during technological accidents, significantly when these emergencies exceed the response capabilities of the industry. On the platform, mutual aid can be managed in the presence of an emergency that requires it, or a formal permanent agreement [9]. The operation with companies and emergency services is possible thanks to the effective response system, standardization of procedures, resource management, and knowledge bases.

Konexus is a critical event, and emergency notification management platform [10]. The platform can be used through a web browser and on IOS or Android devices, facilitating access from any device to safety procedures, guidelines for risk management, and historical knowledge bases. The application seeks to ensure a real-time response to critical events. In this way, it alerts the team and coordinates its disaster recovery in an emergency through the management of alerts employing accurate and fast communication of critical events. Konexus enables companies, governments, or emergency systems to securely send alerts through mobile applications, text messages, emails, or voice calls. In addition, it facilitates the visualization and classification of incidents through highly advanced ESRI mapping functions [10]. As a result, it is possible to visualize and manage incidents in real-time and manage the sending of alerts by using integrated maps on the platform.

RAPID-N is a scientific web application designed for rapid risk assessment and facilitates the location of accidents caused by Natural Hazards Triggering Technological Disasters (Natech) [11]. In addition, it seeks to help industry and government prepare by seeking event response plans, considering existing safety measures, site characteristics, and expected release scenarios depending on the natural disaster. The RAPID-N methodology evaluates the interrelationship of natural and technological hazards in industrial plants to create natural disaster scenarios, using an embedded geographic information system for quick and easy application [12]. Using the natural hazard scenario as input, it estimates the extent and probability of damage to industrial process equipment and models the consequences of likely Natech events (e.g., fire, explosion, chemical release) that the estimated damage may trigger b12. RAPID-N aims to facilitate risk assessment and mapping and improve event information sharing by providing a collaborative and open-access environment. The results are presented as summary reports and interactive risk maps used for emergency planning purposes or a quick assessment of the consequences after actual Natech events [13].

The Veoci emergency management application is an emergency management software that provides response plan mapping, workflows, task management, dashboard visualization, and operational tools necessary for industrial emergency management [14]. The application aims to facilitate the management of disaster recovery processes and the management of mitigations in response plans during emergency management. The solution provided by Veoci also has an integrated interactive geographic information system. This GIS mapping helps to geospatially represent the data stored in the application, helping to make better decisions and take more decisive action during daily operations, emergencies, or critical events [14]. Visually filtering the information through a map in Veoci allows observing real-time changes in the data stored in the application about the situation. Veoci can be accessed through web browsers and iOS and Android devices (Table 1).

Table 1. Comparison of existing information systems

	DH4 Incident Management	Konexus	RAPID-N	Veoci
Available platforms	Web, Android and iOS	Web, Android and iOS	Web	Web, Android and iOS
Integrated GIS	Yes	Yes	Yes	Yes
Notification management	No	No	No	Yes
Integration via API	Yes	Yes	No	No
Mutual aid management	Yes	No	No	Yes

[a]System information comparison.

3.3   Mobile Applications for Emergency Management

"Yo reporto" is a web application that aims to prevent and alert different levels of risk. The end-user application is for all people in the Colombian national territory, allowing them through an interactive web/Mobile to notify in case of witnessing a natural phenomenon. The web page has two main options: one that generates a geographic report, and the second produces a consolidated report. The geographic report lists events reported by users. Furthermore, the geographic data also provides information such as location, person reporting, date, and the event in question. On the other hand, the consolidated report option allows grouping tables and graphs on the country's risks.

The European project "Risk assessment developed the application for occupational dermal exposure to chemicals." This app is available in a web browser, iPhone, and Android devices and aims to assess the risk of exposure to chemical agents. It uses the Safety Data Sheet (SDS) and the exposure in the work environment to provide the risk estimation. These data generate a risk estimation and a series of control measures. According to the website of the national institute for safety and health at work of the Spanish government [17], the application has the following functionalities:

- Qualitatively assesses the degree of danger a product or chemical substance can cause through the dermal route.
- Qualitatively assesses the degree of exposure to a product or chemical substance during the performance of a specific task.
- To estimate the level of risk due to dermal exposure to a product or chemical substance and to obtain proposals for improvement.
- Manage the risk by dermal exposure. The user can introduce additional control measures to reassess the risk and determine the degree of effectiveness of the measures considered.

Hazmat Flic is a mobile tool available on iPhone and Android devices. This application's objective is to manage accidents involving oil spills in pipelines and rail cars. The application seeks to guide users through incidents, identify how the agency meets accident requirements, and generate a document as the basis for the action plan. It also provides the user with strategic information for risk management, including the execution and use of the risk-based response methodology [18].

The Wireless Information System for Emergency Responders (WISER) is a free application developed for Windows, iPhone, and Android, which aims to provide users to respond to hazardous materials incidents. The app is targeted at first responders and hazardous materials units. It provides the user with accurate information about hazardous substances, available emergency resources, and environmental conditions to save lives and minimize the impact on the environment [19].

From the review of different web and mobile applications used for risk management and management of technological emergencies, and the management of mutual aid, we obtain a series of characteristics that are vitally important to take into account:

- The interface allows the user to obtain real-time information quickly.
- Indicate the specific location in case of a risk.
- Have a document view that enables the user to deal with a situation that requires risk control, while others use a set of variables to generate the document that serves as the basis for the action plan.
- Have multiple profiles that provide the user with solutions that adapt better to the user's needs.

Finally, the implementation of the previously mentioned features would result in a complete application in terms of risk management, with the capacity to provide accurate and specific solutions that vary depending on the risk to be dealt with and the role of the person managing the risk (Table 2).

Table 2. Mobile applications for emergency management

	Yo reporto	Risk due to dermal exposure	Hazmat Flic	WISER
Available platforms	Web, Android and iOS	Web, Android and iOS	Android and iOS	Web, Android and iOS
Type of target risk	Natural Hazard	Exposure to chemical agents	Oil spills	Hazardous Materials Incidents
Risk prevention documentation	No	Yes	Yes	Yes
Multiple roles	No	No	No	Yes
Information according to different risks	No	Yes	No	Yes

[a]System information comparison.

4   Architecture of the Collaborative Management System

To achieve the objective of the desired information system, it is important to establish a set of goals. The goals are the following:

- The designed system must implement an internationally recognized standard for industrial management
- The designed system must follow a collaborative approach so that multiple companies can create a supportive environment to attend to emergencies as a system
- The system needs a portable and reusable design that can be escalated as the user base changes.

4.1   Description

This section then shows how these goals were achieved. This paper considers the philosophy of the Awareness and Emergency Preparedness Program at the Local Level (APELL) as the core of the system design to reduce technological risks. APELL is a program developed by the United Nations Environment Programme (UNEP) in conjunction with governments and industries to minimize the occurrence of the harmful effects caused by technological accidents and environmental emergencies. The system is aimed at strengthening mutual assistance between companies in a dynamic and agile manner, strengthening the collaborative response group for emergency care, and providing the government with updated information on significant accident risks, major accident risk maps, risk maps of these accidents, and standard operating procedures, for the attention of each one of them.

It is necessary to have the following structured information to accomplish the desired goals:

- The dangerous chemical substances are stored, processed, and transported through the different routes of the city.
- Information on the resources available to deal with emergencies.
- Risk management plans.
- Contingency and emergency plan.
- Support group information.
- Information from the specialized directories of personnel with competence in spills, fires, explosions, investigators, welders, spills in aquatic systems, equipment suppliers, and contacts in each company.

Once the system has the required information, the ALOHA software will be used to calculate and model the impact areas of the different prioritized substances and scenarios for both the industrial corridors and the transport routes of chemical substances in the city. Each of these risk maps and impact areas will be uploaded to the system for further analysis, where they will be used during emergencies as a reference along with the related standard operating procedures for each case.

During an emergency, companies may need other resources that they do not have at the moment. For this reason, the system offers a module for mutual help between companies in a dynamic and agile way to share technical resources and trained personnel for managing resources or the determined emergency. The loan of the resources will have a clause accepted at the time of the request for the resources, which indicates the maximum number of days that the user will have to be able to return the used items in optimal conditions. A substitute item must be returned if the borrowed item is for single-use (Fig. 1).

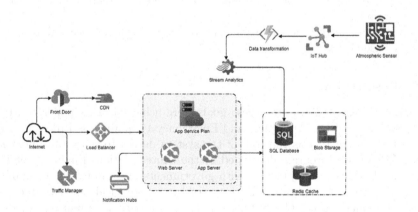

Fig. 1. Architecture of the Solution

4.2   Architecture

The proposed infrastructure uses the services offered by Microsoft Azure as a cloud provider. It is leveraging the App Service Platform as a Service (PaaS) service in Azure to serve both the web server and the application server. App Service is a fully managed platform for building and deploying apps in the cloud, so it does not require support to manage the servers or compute resources used to run the instantiated apps [20].

The managed virtual machines that host the web server and the application server are provided through the App Service Plan. Plan App Service has the Per-App Scaling alternative to efficiently scale the number of applications running per plan, automatically assigning computational resources to the instantiated applications. This way, the architecture will allow the application to grow as required.

The proposed architecture consists of the following components:

- An application server to deploy the set of services that will be used through the API.
- A web server serves requests from the Internet from the clients of the information system.
- A repository of objects for storage of files such as standard operating procedures, reports, regulations
- A DNS server for routing requests to servers
- A database to store the data for which persistence needs to be guaranteed
- Caching system to speed up queries to data layers and latency performance
- A messaging server for messages to users in case of emergencies
- Load balancer to distribute the requests between the different instances of the applications within the App Service Plan.
- A Cloud Content Delivery Network (CDN) service
- A platform for IoT devices to wirelessly publish, distribute and manage updates
- A serverless function that allows the transformation of the data that will be processed and stored in the database so that the information can be used to perform emergency simulations that vary according to weather conditions

Azure App Service provides a web hosting service where the application designed in Ruby on Rails runs on Linux. The application is served using Passenger as the application server. Passenger allows users to run and manage aspects such as the reliability, scalability, and security of the application [21]. Likewise, Azure App Service provides web hosting where Nginx runs as a web server to provide the front-end's static files and as a reverse proxy for the application server.

4.3   Services

The system has twelve main components that will communicate with each other as required, covering all risk management needs. The services provided by the system consist of the following (Figs. 2 and 3):

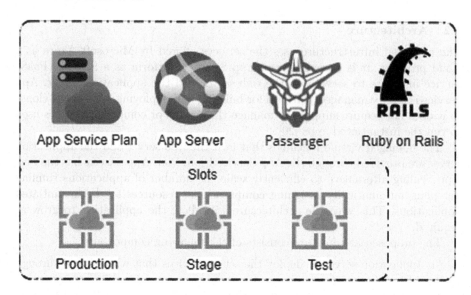

Fig. 2. Application server

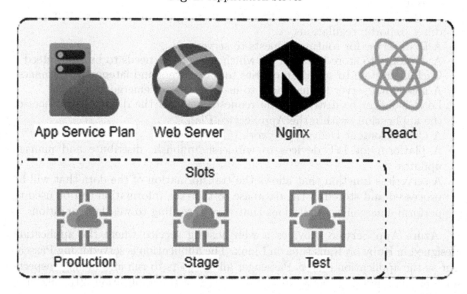

Fig. 3. Detail of the running services

The user administration service stores the basic information of who operates the application, apart from serving to establish a means of contact with the person. The administration service handles companies' information to connect them to the users. Communication between both services within the system is required since a user belongs to a company (Fig. 4).

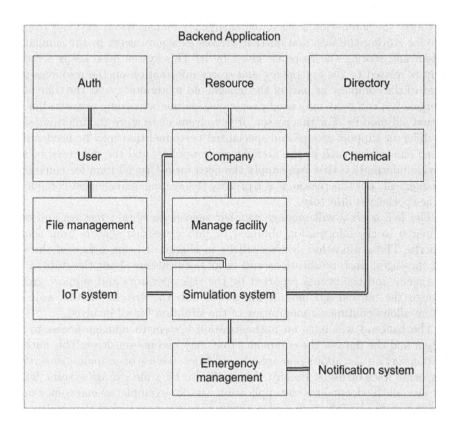

Fig. 4. Detailed interaction of services in the Web server

Service for the administration of information related to the headquarters of each of the companies entered into the system. The information stored for each of the company's facilities includes the location to make estimates and analyze risk scenarios during an emergency. Hazardous chemicals and their respective safety data sheets must be stored within the system's records. The resource management system service manages the information related to the resources entered. The information is stored as the user who entered the resource, the total amount, and the units available to lend. This difference between the units is mainly because the company has a specific inventory to manage emergencies. The resources made available by the companies to attend to emergencies are also managed within this system as part of the emergency management module for mutual aid.

The simulation service will model the emergencies using parameters such as chemical information, transport or storage conditions, weather conditions, and the location of the emergency. With this information, the system will use a trained model to generate a risk map that facilitates analysis and decision-making during the emergency in the main areas affected by the spill or accident.

Unlike the simulation service, the emergency management service is responsible for storing the information that arrives as a parameter to the simulation system and storing the response given by it. This system also keeps a record of users related to the emergency and stores information on the resources provided to the company as part of the mutual aid methodology. At the time of an emergency, a company may need people outside the help group organized in the mutual aid module. For this reason, it is convenient to store the information of the different support groups and specialized personnel that may be needed during an emergency, such as the firefighters, the police, and the red cross, or also provide information that can supply the need for a Crucial item for emergency management. For this reason, it is a priority to have the management component of the specialized directory.

The IoT service will manage weather sensors to obtain metrics and data compared to the information obtained by public weather sensors from nearby airports. The notification system will be in charge of being informed through text messages, push notifications and email notifications about the state of the emergency and the events reported by the risk operators and support groups through the mutual aid module integrated into the system. In this way, the system allows continuous monitoring of the situation for all involved.

The backend will have an authentication system to manage access to the system and the data of the companies that may become sensitive. This authentication service also allows managers to condition the use of endpoints or services to specific roles or users. Finally, there will also be a file storage system, which will save all the documents the application uses-for example, an emergency management manual or the technical data sheets of the companies' chemicals.

5   Conclusions and Future Works

We achieved a thorough review of commercial and academic solutions for energy management systems that expect to raise the bar of requirements design by adding technological-advance features. The literature shows more promising new features from the academic perspective, focused primarily on the use of IoT. Commercial solutions, however, have not yet included innovating approaches to existing problems. We demonstrated through this review the necessity of newly-designed systems.

The previously designed goals were achieved by designing a new emergency management system that enables collaboration between the companies closely located within a region. This collaboration creates synergies between the participating companies, which in case of emergencies, could help them to solve issues that otherwise would be harder to handle each by themselves. Implementing the APELL process and the system's core design enables these synergies, visible through functionalities such as the resource sharing process explained above.

It is important to remember that the purpose of this work was to propose an architectural design of the information system, based on the results of the literature review. In future work, we expect to implement a complete version of the design system and test it with a group of companies located in the Caribbean region of Colombia. A key component to test would be the resource-sharing process.

References

1. Aparicio, L.V., Tonelli, S.M.: Technological risk planning as part of environmental management. Latin Am. Appl. Res. **36**(4), 295–300 (2006)
2. Yanju, H., Yanling, H., Yiwei, H.: Study of the data exchanging safely and quickly for sudden leakage of dangerous chemicals emergency decision system based on VPN. Int. Forum Inf. Technol. Appl. **2010**, 52–54 (2010). https://doi.org/10.1109/IFITA.2010.54
3. Ness, A.: Lessons learned from recent process safety incidents. Am. Inst. Chem. Eng. Prog. **111**(3), 23–29 (2015)
4. Qibo, Z., Lili, M., Hua, D.: Construction of emergency disposal decision system based on PDA. In: 2010 International Conference on E-Business and E-Government, pp. 1516–1519 (2010). https://doi.org/10.1109/ICEE.2010.385
5. Yanju, H., Yanling, H., Yiwei, H.: Development of the emergency decision system for dangerous chemicals burst leaking accident. In: 2010 International Forum on Information Technology and Applications, pp. 49–51 (2010). https://doi.org/10.1109/IFITA.2010.50
6. Chen, W., Yue, L.: Design and realization of emergency space database for chemical accident based on GIS. In: 2008 4th International Conference on Wireless Communications, Networking and Mobile Computing, pp. 1–4 (2008). https://doi.org/10.1109/WiCom.2008.2697
7. Incident Management Software. D4H Technologies. https://d4h.com/incident-management. Accessed 27 Jan 2022
8. API Quick Start Guide - D4H Knowledge Base. Support.d4h.org. https://support.d4h.org/shared-services/api/api-quick-start-guide. Accessed 27 Jan 2022
9. Industrial Incidents: Does Your Facility Have a Mutual Aid Agreement?. Bravo Zulu by D4H. https://d4h.com/blog/20141022-industrial-incidents-does-your-facility-have-a-mutual-aid-agreement. Accessed 27 Jan 2022
10. Konexus — The easiest to use Emergency Notification Platform. Konexus.com. https://www.konexus.com/. Accessed 27 Jan 2022
11. F. team. Rapid natural-hazard triggered technological accidents (Natech) risk analysis and mapping. EU Science Hub - European Commission (2015). https://ec.europa.eu/jrc/en/scientific-tool/rapid-natural-hazard-triggered-technological-accidents-natech-risk-analysis-and-mapping. Accessed 27 Jan 2022
12. Girgin, S.: RAPID-N. Rapidn.jrc.ec.europa.eu. https://rapidn.jrc.ec.europa.eu/. Accessed 27 Jan 2022
13. Girgin, S., Krausmann, E.: RAPID-N: Rapid natech risk assessment and mapping framework. J. Loss Prev. Process Ind. **26**(6), 949–960 (2013). https://doi.org/10.1016/j.jlp.2013.10.004
14. Veoci - Virtual Emergency Operations Center Software. Veoci.com. https://veoci.com/. Accessed 27 Jan 2022
15. Acevedo, P., Abad, E.: Mejoramiento en la comunicación e integración de los estudiantes en la comunidad universitaria mediante un sitio de red social. Universidad Autónoma de Ciudad Juárez (2010)

16. Yo reporto. Portal.gestiondelriesgo.gov.co. https://portal.gestiondelriesgo.gov.co/Paginas/Slide_home/Yo-reporto.aspx. Accessed 27 Jan 2022
17. Herramientas Prevención Riesgos Laborales - INSST. Herramientasprl.insst.es. https://herramientasprl.insst.es/seguridad/riesgo-por-exposicion-dermica/contenido/205. Accessed 27 Jan 2022
18. Hazmat Flic (NFPA) — REDCIATOX. Redciatox.org. https://www.redciatox.org/hazmat-flic-nfpa. Accessed 27 Jan 2022
19. WISER Home. Wiser.nlm.nih.gov. https://wiser.nlm.nih.gov/. Accessed 27 Jan 2022
20. Overview - Azure App Service. Docs.microsoft.com (2022). https://docs.microsoft.com/en-us/azure/app-service/overview. Accessed 01 June 2022
21. Passenger - Enterprise grade web app server for Ruby, Node.js, Python. Phusion Passenger (2022). https://www.phusionpassenger.com/features. Accessed 01 Jun 2022
22. Ji, Z., Anwen, Q.: The application of internet of things(IOT) in emergency management system in China. In: IEEE International Conference on Technologies for Homeland Security (HST) 2010, pp. 139–142 (2010). https://doi.org/10.1109/THS.2010.5655073
23. Dorasamy, M., Raman, M., Kaliannan, M.: Integrated community emergency management and awareness system: a knowledge management system for disaster support. Technol. Forecast. Soc. Change **121**, 139–167 (2017). https://doi.org/10.1016/j.techfore.2017.03.017
24. Qiu, M., Ming, Z., Wang, J., Yang, L.T., Xiang, Y.: Enabling cloud computing in emergency management systems. IEEE Cloud Comput. **1**(4), 60–67 (2014). https://doi.org/10.1109/MCC.2014.71

PID and Model Predictive Control (MPC) Strategies Design for a Virtual Distributed Solar Collector Field

Kevin Muyón$^{(\boxtimes)}$ ⓘ, Lenin Chimbana ⓘ, Jacqueline Llanos ⓘ,
and Diego Ortiz-Villalba ⓘ

Universidad de Las Fuerzas Armadas ESPE, Sangolqui, Ecuador
{kpmuyon,lichimbana,jdllanos1,ddortiz5}@espe.edu.ec

Abstract. Distributed solar collector fields are an interesting case in the area of control since apart from presenting several disturbances, their main source of energy is solar irradiation that cannot be manipulated, depends on daily and seasonal variations causing the solar resource is not always available. This makes it necessary to research control techniques that can optimize the use of the existing solar resource. Therefore, in this research, a model predictive control strategy MPC is designed for a virtual distributed solar collector field where the control objective is to maintain the output temperature of a fluid at the desired value. In addition, a PID control strategy with a Feedforward block is also implemented that it's used to compare the results obtained with the MPC to determine which controller has better performance, which one allows a longer operation time, optimizing the use of the available solar irradiation and which one responds better to disturbances. All this is through an immersive virtual environment where the user can interact with all the instrumentation of the virtual distributed solar collector field and can visualize the evolution of the variables and modify the state of the virtual plant by manipulating the disturbances as well as the parameters of the PID and MPC controllers designed. Finally, the results show a better performance of the plant when implementing the MPC control strategy and the advantages of implementing a virtual environment interactive with the user.

Keywords: Model Predictive Control · Solar Collector Field · Virtual Industrial Process

1 Introduction

The electricity demand has grown over the years due to social and economic development and the improvement of people's living conditions. In this context, the predominant energy source since 1850 has been fossil fuels which has led to a rapid increase in carbon dioxide emissions [1]. It is for this reason and due to the 1973 oil crisis that renewable energies received a strong impulse and new ways of obtaining energy through solar irradiation began to be developed, one of these technologies is the distributed solar collector fields such as the ACUREX field located in Almeria, Spain [2].

F. R. Narváez et al. (Eds.): SmartTech-IC 2022, CCIS 1705, pp. 453–467, 2023.
https://doi.org/10.1007/978-3-031-32213-6_33

Distributed solar collector field plants have non-linear dynamics, are affected by various disturbances such as ambient temperature, inlet temperature and depend on solar irradiance which cannot be manipulated and is not always available making it necessary to take full advantage of the solar resource [3].

It is because of all these characteristics that the distributed solar collector field is a very interesting system in the area of implementing control techniques that can cope with changes in solar irradiation, existing disturbances while optimizing the plant operation time, maximizing the solar resource and fulfilling the safety conditions of the plant.

Since having real industrial processes for experimental tests represents a high investment of money, it is necessary to look for methodologies such as the virtualization of industrial processes where control techniques can be implemented at the same time that the real behavior of the process can be simulated, such as those that have been developed in [4] where a virtual laboratory of a combined cycle thermal power plant is implemented, virtual laboratory of multivariable level and temperature processes in [5], design and implementation of a predictive control model for a pressure control plant in [6], model predictive control strategy for a combined-cycle power-plant boiler in [7], advanced control algorithms for a horizontal three-phase separator in a hardware in the loop simulation environment in [8], which allow us to implement traditional controllers and advanced controllers in order to implement the best controller for the process. However, virtual laboratories have not been developed in the renewable energy sector that base their operation on solar irradiation such as a distributed solar collector field.

This is why, in this research, a virtual environment of a distributed solar collector field based on the ACUREX field is designed, in which a model predictive control MPC strategy can be tested with a PID control strategy to validate the MPC controller.

The main contributions of this paper are *i)* An immersive environment that allows the user to interact with the virtual distributed solar collector field, *ii)* The design of a PID control strategy for the implementation in the virtual distributed solar collector field *iii)* The design of model predictive control MPC for the implementation in the virtual distributed solar collector field.

For the development of this research the next methodology is followed where Sect. 2 shows the description of the plant and the mathematical model, then Sect. 3 shows the steps to implement the virtualization, and finally, Sect. 4 shows the design of the control algorithms.

2 Description and Mathematical Model of the Virtual Distributed Solar Collector Field

This section describes the operation of the virtual distributed solar collector field and the mathematical model implemented for the virtual plant.

2.1 Description of the Virtual Distributed Solar Collector Field

The distributed solar collector field uses solar irradiation as an energy source to heat a fluid that circulates through the solar collectors, this hot fluid can be used at a later stage for electric power generation or water desalination [9], the fluid outlet temperature also depends of other factors such as the fluid inlet temperature and the ambient temperature.

As can be seen (see Fig. 1), the virtual distributed solar collector field implemented in this research has two storage tanks that store the hot fluid and the cold fluid respectively, it has solar tracking to ensure that solar radiation is reflected on the reflecting mirrors of the solar collectors and is received by the tube that transports the fluid, thus heating the cold fluid that enters the solar collector field to a maximum temperature of 300 [°C], the temperature control is performed by manipulating the flow rate of the fluid that circulates through the solar collectors. The fluid used is Santotherm 55 oil, which is a thermal oil that allows working with temperatures higher than 300 [°C].

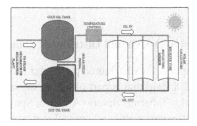

Fig. 1. Elements of the virtual distributed solar collector field.

To better understand the operation of the virtual distributed solar collector field implemented in this paper, the piping and instrumentation diagram P&ID (see Fig. 2) shows the instrumentation and components of the entire plant.

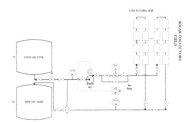

Fig. 2. P&ID diagram of the virtual distributed solar collector field.

At the beginning and end of the day when solar irradiation is below 400 [W/m^2] the plant is not operating as this is the minimum temperature for start-up, so the plant is in sleep mode, once the plant is in operation it can be in 2 different modes which are recirculation mode and tank mode [10].

The objective of control loop 01 is to maintain the oil outlet temperature at the end of the collector's loop at the desired level, the control loop 01 consists of a temperature indicator transmitter (TIT-1) that sends the temperature value of the outlet oil to the temperature indicator controller (TIC), this is responsible for sending the control signal to the hydraulic pump (M1), the hydraulic pump (M1) is used to modify the amount of oil flow that circulates through the solar collector field by decreasing the oil flow to heat the fluid or increasing the oil flow to cool the fluid, the oil flow varies from 0.002 to 0.012 [m³/s] where the lower limit is used so that the oil outlet temperature does not exceed 305 [°C] because if it exceeds 305 °C the oil could decompose [11].

Additionally, loop 01 consists of a second temperature indicator transmitter (TIT-2) and a flow indicator transmitter (FIT) which are used for the operator to visualize the oil inlet temperature and oil flow respectively. The plant is also equipped with a cold oil tank (T1) which is used to store the oil that will be heated in the solar collector field, once the oil is heated it is stored in the hot oil tank (T2), there is also a 3-way valve (V1) that is responsible for recirculating the oil flow inside the collector loop which is initially at a very low temperature and finally, there is a valve (V2) that allows the circulation of the fluid inside the cold oil tank to the collector field.

2.2 Mathematical Model of the Virtual Distributed Solar Collector Field

The model used for this paper is the distributed parameter model displayed in [9] which corresponds to the ACUREX field that is part of one of the installations of the Almeria Solar Platform located in the Tabernas desert (Almeria, Spain) and has been used as a test laboratory for different experiments and control structures, in addition to detailing each loop of parabolic collectors that constitute the plant.

The distributed parameter model adequately shows the dynamics of the distributed solar collector field since it simulates well the temperature distribution by applying the conservation of energy in a length dl over a time interval dt along the collector loop, modeling separately the oil fluid and the metal tube as shown in Eq. 1 and Eq. 2.

$$A_m \rho_m C_m \frac{dT_m(t,l)}{dt} = \eta GI(t) - D_m \pi H_l(T_m(t,l) - T_{amb}(t,l)) - D_f \pi H_t(T_m(t,l) - T_f(t,l)) \quad (1)$$

$$A_f \rho_f C_f \frac{dT_f(t,l)}{dt} + \rho_f c_f q(t) \frac{dT_f(t,l)}{dl} = D_f \pi H_t(T_m(t,l) - T_f(t,l)) \quad (2)$$

In Eqs. 1 and 2 the subindices m refer to the metal tube while f refer to the oil fluid. Where A is the transversal section [m²], ρ the density [kg/m³], C the thermal capacity [J/kg °C], T the temperature °C, η the collector efficiency, G the aperture of the collector [m], I the solar irradiation [W/m²], T_{amb} the ambient temperature [°C], D the external diameter [m], H_l the global coefficient of thermal losses [W/m² °C], H_t the heat transfer coefficient metal-oil [W/m² °C], q the oil flow [m³/s], t the time [s], l the length [m], a more detailed description of the parameters used in the model can be found in [12].

As can be seen (see Fig. 3), the inputs for the virtual plant are the oil inlet temperature T_{in}, the ambient temperature T_{amb}, the irradiance I, the oil flow q, and the output parameter is the oil outlet temperature T_f at the end of the collector loop.

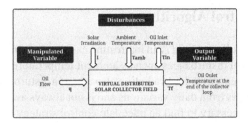

Fig. 3. Variables of the virtual distributed solar collector field.

3 Virtualization Methodology

Nowadays, technological progress has allowed the implementation of virtual laboratories in the area of medicine, education, and particularly in industry, which makes it easier to understand and become familiar with the industry through virtual environments that emulate a real process, as shown in [13].

This is why a virtualization methodology (see Fig. 4) is applied to design a virtual environment that resembles a real distributed solar collector field, where it is possible to visualize all the instrumentation of the plant, the evolution of the variables, and manipulate the behavior of the plant.

The environment is designed in the UNITY 3D graphic engine. The methodology consists of 5 layers: *i)* Layer 1. In this layer we start with the virtualization of the solar collector field through the 3D design of the elements that conform to the P&ID diagram through a CAD software, *ii)* Layer 2. Layer that allows the export of the graphic models developed in layer 1 to a format compatible with the Unity 3D graphic engine, as well as modifying characteristics of the 3D models such as reference axes, rotation axes, colors, textures, etc. *iii)* Layer 3. This layer allows to design of the virtual environment in Unity using the 3D models designed in the previous layers, adding animations and response curves, making the environment immersive and intuitive. *iv)* Layer 4. In this research the shared memory method is implemented to allow bilateral communication, this is through the use of a dynamic link library DLL that generates a shared memory in the RAM for the exchange of the process variables data between the 3D environment in Unity and the mathematical software Matlab, such as solar irradiance, ambient temperature, oil inlet temperature, set point, oil outlet temperature, oil flow. The method of shared memories is used because it is an easy technique to apply, with short delays and low computational cost as shown in [14] *v)* Layer 5. In this layer are the mathematical model and the designed controllers of the virtual plant that are implemented in the Matlab software.

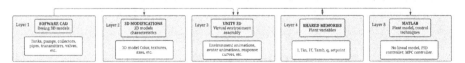

Fig. 4. Virtualization methodology of the virtual distributed solar collector field.

4 Design of Control Algorithms

The distributed solar collector field is an interesting case study in the area of control since it is affected by several disturbances such as ambient temperature, inlet oil temperature and its main source of energy solar irradiation also acts as a disturbance since it cannot be manipulated and suffers from daily variations and is not always available. All the aspects mentioned make it necessary to find an adequate control strategy that can cope with the changes in solar irradiation as well as increase the plant operation time by optimizing the use of the available solar resource, all this while complying with the plant safety conditions such as the maximum temperature of the oil.

For this reason, in this section, it is designed an MPC control and additionally a PID control with a feedforward block that will be used to analyze the performance of the MPC, where the control objective is to maintain the oil outlet temperature at the desired level.

4.1 PID Control Strategy Design

Although the output of this process is affected by several disturbances, the solar irradiance, and the oil inlet temperature are the ones that most affect the process, causing the control action, oil flow, by itself to be insufficient to bring the response of the plant to a steady state since the oil outlet temperature would have a similar trend to the solar irradiance profile and the oil inlet temperature, therefore, the system response is more affected by the disturbances than by the control action, making the system identification process and the PID control design more difficult.

Since these disturbances are measurable, a Feedforward block is implemented, which takes this information and attenuates the changes produced by the disturbances, making the necessary corrections to the control action. The feedforward block used is shown in Eq. 3. Where u represents the output of the PID control, this equation has been developed experimentally in [15] and widely implemented in experiments carried out in the ACUREX field.

$$q = \frac{0.7869I - 0.485(u - 151.5) - 80.7}{u - T_{in}} \tag{3}$$

The PID control is implemented in series with the Feedforward block (see Fig. 5) which acts as part of the plant mitigating the effect of disturbances to facilitate the control PID tuning.

The control strategy is defined by Eq. 4. Where u is the control action, K_p is the proportional gain, T_i is the integral time gain, and T_d is the derivative time gain. To obtain the control gains, the Lambda tuning method was used [16].

$$u(t) = K_p\left(e(t) + \frac{1}{T_i}\int_0^t e(t)dt + \frac{1}{T_d}\frac{d}{dt}e(t)\right) \tag{4}$$

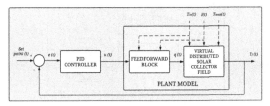

Fig. 5. PID control strategy with a feedforward block implemented in the virtual distributed solar collector field.

4.2 Model Predictive Control MPC Strategy Design

A model predictive control MPC consists of a prediction model, cost function, and constraints, the particularity of this controller is that it uses a prediction model that allows to know the future behavior of the controlled variable using a prediction horizon N_w and a control horizon N_c[17]. The MPC includes a cost function which has as its first objective to minimize the oil outlet temperature errors and has as its second objective to smooth the abrupt variations of the control action as detailed in Eq. 5.

$$J(k) = \sum_{\substack{u \\ i=N_w}}^{N_p} \delta(k) \left[\hat{T}_f(k+i|k) - T_{fd}(k+i|k) \right]^2 + \sum_{i=0}^{N_c-1} \lambda(k)[\Delta u(k+i-1)]^2 \quad (5)$$

where the first term $\left[\hat{T}_f(k+i|k) - T_{fd}(k+i|k) \right]^2$ is the squared error between the desired value and the predicted value of the oil outlet temperature, $\delta(k)$ is the weight for the first control objective, the objective function also includes the squared variation of the control action $[\Delta u(k+i-1)]^2$, where $\lambda(k)$ represents the weight of the second control objective, additionally N_p represents the total number of samples of the prediction horizon.

The optimization problem considers oil flow operation constraints as in Eq. 6.

$$q_{min} \leq q \leq q_{max} \quad (6)$$

where the values of the constraints are $q_{min} = 0.0002[\text{m}^3/\text{s}]$ and $q_{max} = 0.0012[\text{m}^3/\text{s}]$, these limits help to keep the temperature below 305 [°C]. Finally, (see Fig. 6) shows the MPC strategy implemented in the virtual distributed solar collector field.

5 Results

This section describes the results obtained in the development of the virtual environment, as well as in the design of the PID and MPC control strategies, analyzing the virtual environment designed, the interactivity and immersivity, also the response of each controller, which one reacts better to disturbances, which one allows longer operation time and which one satisfies the security conditions of the virtual distributed solar collector field.

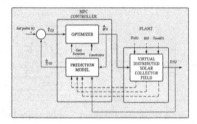

Fig. 6. Model predictive control MPC strategy implemented in the virtual distributed solar collector field.

5.1 Analysis of the Virtual Distributed Solar Collector Field Implemented

Once the virtualization strategy of Sect. 3 has been implemented, the results of the virtualized solar collector field environment are shown (see Fig. 7) which resembles a real distributed solar collector field plant.

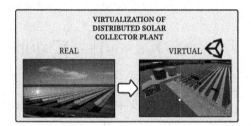

Fig. 7. Virtual distributed solar collector field compared to a real solar collector field.

For the visualization and control of the virtual distributed solar collector field there is a control room (see Fig. 8), where there are several screens that allow to visualize the status of the virtual plant showing if the plant is in sleep mode, recirculation mode or tank mode as well as alerts on the outlet temperature and solar irradiation, it also shows the evolution of the variables of interest such as: solar irradiation, ambient temperature, oil inlet temperature, oil outlet temperature, oil flow, as well as sliders and interactive buttons where the user can manipulate the set point value, the value of the oil inlet temperature, add the presence of clouds in the solar irradiance and be able to select between PID control and MPC as well as being able to modify the tuning constants of both controllers.

The virtual plant also has animations (see Fig. 9a) such as filling the storage tanks, solar tracking of the solar collectors, changing solar irradiance, and avatar control, allowing the user to understand the operation of a field of distributed solar collectors while moving through the virtual environment.

Finally, to ensure interactivity between the user and the solar collector field, each component that compounds the virtual plant has an interactive element that is activated when the user approaches it, displaying important information for the operator (see Fig. 9b).

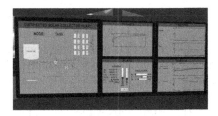

Fig. 8. Control room of the virtual distributed solar collector field.

Fig. 9. a) Animations inside the virtual distributed solar collector field, b) Interactivity between the user and the components of the virtual distributed solar collector field.

The environment was tested with different students where they were able to design the PID and MPC controllers by manipulating the tuning constants, visualize through the graphs the evolution of the variables that affect the virtual plant, and interact with the instruments of the virtual plant by identifying the type of instrument and its function.

5.2 Analysis of the Control Strategies Implemented in the Virtual Distributed Solar Collector Field

To validate the design of the MPC implemented in the virtual distributed solar collector field, the results obtained are compared with the PID control designed for this purpose, 3 scenarios are analyzed *i)* Day with high solar irradiation, *ii)* Day with medium solar irradiation, *iii)* Day with medium solar irradiation, but with the presence of clouds and variation in the oil inlet temperature. The response of the virtual plant is shown from 8:00 to 18:30.

The solar irradiation and ambient temperature profiles for these scenarios correspond to the Almeria solar platform in December for scenario *i)* and in June for scenario *ii)*. These profiles are obtained through the European Commission Photovoltaic Geographical Information System [18], for scenario *iii)* the data of scenario *ii)* is taken by adding the presence of clouds in the solar irradiation and varying the value of the oil inlet temperature.

The following control parameters are used for the PID control, $K_p = 0.03$, $T_i = 70.55$, $T_d = 2.86$. For the MPC the design parameters are, the value of the weight for the oil outlet temperature error is $\delta = 10000$, the weight for the control action is $\lambda = 1$, for the prediction horizon we have $N_w = 10$, and for the control horizon $N_c = 5$.

Scenario i) Day with High Solar Irradiation. The disturbances of the virtual distributed solar collector field are shown in (see Fig. 10) where a) is the solar irradiance *I* b) is the ambient temperature T_{amb} c) is the oil inlet temperature T_{in}. It is observed in (Fig. 11a) that the highest solar irradiation is from 9:06 to 16:18 where the solar irradiation is higher than 1000 [W/m²], the lowest solar irradiation is from 8:00 to 9:06 and also from 16:18 to 18:30 in which the solar irradiation remains below 1000 [W/m²], the ambient temperature in (Fig. 10b) starts with a value of 7.35 [°C] at 8:00 and ends with a value of 13.4 °C at 18:30. For the oil inlet temperature in (Fig. 10c) a constant temperature of 100 [°C] is given throughout the simulation.

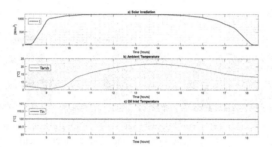

Fig. 10. Scenario i): a) Solar irradiation, b) Ambient temperature, c) Oil inlet temperature.

The response of the implemented controllers is shown (see Fig. 11) where (Fig. 11a) corresponds to the response of the controlled variable the oil outlet temperature, where the oil temperature set point (red), the response of the PID control (blue), the response of the MPC (green). (Fig. 11b) and (Fig. 11c) correspond to the responses of the control action oil flow for the PID control and MPC respectively.

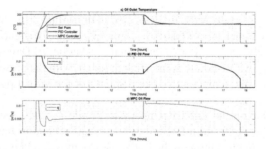

Fig. 11. Scenario i): a) Oil outlet temperature, b) PID control oil flow, c) MPC oil flow.

The virtual plant will be in operation (see Fig. 11) from 8:37 to 17:45 since during this period the solar irradiation is higher than 400 [W/m²]. For the oil outlet temperature, there is a set point of 300 [°C] from 8:00 to 13:25, the set point changes to 200 [°C] at 13:25 until the end of the simulation.

Looking at the response of the controllers (see Fig. 11a), the PID control with a set point of 300 [°C] has an overshoot of 0% and a settling time of 1 h and 24 min, the steady state error is 6.66×10^{-4} which is within the 1% tolerance. On the other hand, the MPC for a set point of 300 [°C] has an overshoot of 1.17%, a settling time of 33 min, the steady state error is 1.66×10^{-4} which is within the 1% tolerance.

Looking at the response of the control action (see Fig. 11b and Fig. 11c), at the beginning of the operation with a set point of 300 [°C] both the PID control and the MPC send 100% of the flow, by the time the set point changes to 200 [°C] the PID control sends 40% of the flow while the MPC sends 100% of the flow. It can be said that both the PID control and the MPC have a slow response being the PID control a smoother response compared to the response of the MPC which is a little more aggressive.

Scenario Ii) Day with Medium Solar Irradiation. The disturbances of the virtual distributed solar collector field are shown in (see Fig. 12) where a) is the solar irradiance I b) is the ambient temperature T_{amb} c) is the oil inlet temperature T_{in}. It is observed in (Fig. 12a) that the highest solar irradiation is from 11:00 to 15:19 where the solar irradiation is higher than 700 [W/m²], and it can be seen that the lowest solar irradiation is from 8:00 to 11:00 and also from 15:19 to 18:30 in which the solar irradiation remains below 700 [W/m²], the ambient temperature in (Fig. 12b) starts with a value of 2.59 [°C] at 8:00 and ends with a value of 6.69 [°C] at 18:30. For the oil inlet temperature in (Fig. 12c) a constant temperature of 100 [°C] is given throughout the simulation.

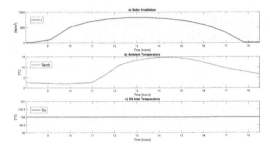

Fig. 12. Scenario ii): a) Solar irradiation, b) Ambient temperature, c) Oil inlet temperature.

The response of the implemented controllers is shown (see Fig. 13) where (Fig. 13a) corresponds to the response of the controlled variable the oil outlet temperature, where the oil temperature set point (red), the response of the PID control (blue), the response of the MPC (green). (Fig. 13b) and (Fig. 13c) correspond to the responses of the control action oil flow for the PID control and MPC respectively.

The virtual plant will be in operation (see Fig. 13) from 9:45 to 16:46 since during this period the solar irradiation is higher than 400 [W/m²]. For the oil outlet temperature, there is a set point of 300 [°C] from 8:00 to 13:25, the set point changes to 200 [°C] at 13:25 until the end of the simulation.

Looking at the response of the controllers (see Fig. 13a), the PID control with a set point of 300 [°C] has an overshoot of 4% and a settling time of 2 h and 21 min, the steady state error is 2.33×10^{-3} which is within the 1% tolerance. On the other hand, the MPC for a set point of 300 [°C] has an overshoot of 0.3%, a settling time of 1 h, the steady state error is 1×10^{-3} which is within the 1% tolerance.

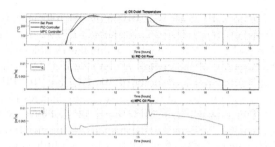

Fig. 13. Scenario ii): a) Oil outlet temperature, b) PID control oil flow, c) MPC oil flow.

Looking at the response of the control action (see Fig. 13b and Fig. 13c), at the beginning of the operation with a set point of 300 [°C] both the PID control and the MPC send 100% of the flow, by the time the set point changes to 200 [°C] the PID control sends 40% of the flow while the MPC sends 100% of the flow. It can be said that both the PID control and the MPC have a slow response being the PID control a smoother response compared to the response of the MPC which is a little more aggressive.

Scenario iii) Day with Medium Solar Irradiation, the Presence of Clouds, and Variation in the Oil Inlet Temperature. The disturbances are shown in (see Fig. 14). It is observed in (Fig. 14a) that there is the presence of clouds from 12:00 to 12:37 which causes the solar irradiation to have a value of 630 [W/m²] during that period. The oil inlet temperature in (Fig. 14c) where a value of 130 [°C] is given from 8:00 to 13:43 and then changes to 90 [°C] from 13:43 to 18:30. For the ambient temperature in (Fig. 14b) no changes were made because its impact on the oil outlet temperature is insignificant compared to the solar irradiation and inlet oil temperature.

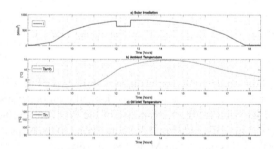

Fig. 14. Scenario iii): a) Solar irradiation, b) Ambient temperature, c) Oil inlet temperature.

The response of the implemented controllers is shown (see Fig. 15) where (Fig. 15a) corresponds to the response of the controlled variable the oil outlet temperature, where the oil temperature set point (red), the response of the PID control (blue), the response of the MPC (green). (Fig. 15b) and (Fig. 15c) correspond to the responses of the control action oil flow for the PID control and MPC respectively.

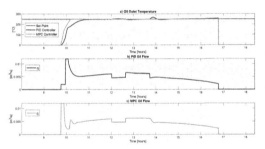

Fig. 15. Scenario iii): a) Oil outlet temperature, b) PID control oil flow, c) MPC control oil flow.

The virtual plant will be in operation (see Fig. 15) from 9:45 to 16:46 since during this period the solar irradiation is higher than 400 [W/m^2]. For the oil outlet temperature, a set point of 250 [°C] is used for the whole simulation.

Looking at the response of the controllers (see Fig. 15a), the PID control when there is the presence of clouds in the solar irradiation from 12:00 to 12:37 causes an oscillation in the oil outlet temperature with an overshoot of 1.45% and takes 1 h to resettle for 1% tolerance, when the oil inlet temperature changes to 90 [°C] at 13:43 it causes an oscillation in the oil outlet temperature with an overshoot of 7% and takes 43 min to resettle for 1% tolerance. For the MPC when there is the presence of clouds in the solar irradiation from 12:00 to 12:37 it causes a small oscillation in the oil outlet temperature with an overshoot of 0.48%, when the oil inlet temperature changes to 90 [°C] at 13:43 it causes an oscillation in the oil outlet temperature with an overshoot of 0.68%, for the 2 disturbances in the MPC the temperature value is still within the tolerance of 1%.

Looking at the response of the control action (see Fig. 15b and Fig. 15c), during the presence of clouds and the variation in the value of oil inlet temperature, the response of the control action for the MPC is smoother compared to the response of the control action for the PID control which is more aggressive causing greater oscillations.

6 Conclusions

In this research, a model predictive control MPC strategy and a PID control strategy for a virtual distributed solar collector field are designed and compared.

The implemented virtual environment presents a high realism, it is interactive and immersive. The virtual plant allows the interaction with the components that conform the plant, the visualization of the evolution and state of the variables of interest, as well as allowing the operator to insert disturbances and manipulate the tuning constants of the MPC and PID controllers.

The distributed solar collector field requires efficient controls due to solar irradiation which is its main disturbance and source of energy. It is observed that the MPC has a better performance in the scenarios of high and medium irradiation and in the presence of clouds, presenting an average overshoot of 0.65%, an average settling time of 46 min that is less compared to the PID control that has an average overshoot of 3.1% and an average settling time of 1 h and 22 min. Demonstrating that the MPC, due to its shorter settling time, better optimizes the use of solar irradiation available throughout the day. In addition, because it has a low overshoot, it does not exceed the maximum safe temperature of 305 [°C], which the PID control does at certain points of operation. The MPC performs better than the PID control when faced with sudden changes in the oil inlet temperature and the solar irradiation caused by the presence of clouds.

References

1. Intergovernmental panel on climate change. Climate Change 2022: Mitigation of Climate Change (2022)
2. Alsharkawi, A., Rossiter, J.A.: Modelling analysis of a solar thermal power plant. In: 2017 6th International Conference on Clean Electrical Power (ICCEP) (2017). https://doi.org/10.1109/iccep.2017.8004766
3. Arévalo, A.T.B.: Diseño de estrategias de control difuso robusto ante incertidumbre paramétrica para plantas de colectores solares. Universidad de Chile (2016). https://reposi torio.uchile.cl/handle/2250/140821
4. Burgasi, D., Orrala, T., Llanos, J., Ortiz-Villalba, D., Arcos-Aviles, D., Ponce, C.: Fuzzy and PID controllers performance analysis for a combined-cycle thermal power plant. In: Botto Tobar, M., Cruz, H., Díaz Cadena, A. (eds.) CIT 2020. LNEE, vol. 762, pp. 78–93. Springer, Cham (2021). https://doi.org/10.1007/978-3-030-72208-1_7
5. Feijoo, J.D., Chanchay, D.J., Llanos, J., Ortiz-Villalba, D.: Advanced controllers for level and temperature process applied to virtual festo MPS® PA workstation. In: 2021 IEEE International Conference on Automation/XXIV Congress of the Chilean Association of Automatic Control (ICA-ACCA) (2021). https://doi.org/10.1109/icaacca51523.2021.9465269
6. Llanos-Proano, J., Pilatasig, M., Curay, D., Vaca, A.: Design and implementation of a model predictive control for a pressure control plant. In: 2016 IEEE International Conference on Automatica (ICA-ACCA) (2016). https://doi.org/10.1109/ica-acca.2016.7778490
7. Orrala, T., Burgasi, D., Llanos, J., Ortiz-Villalba, D.: Model predictive control strategy for a combined-cycle power-plant boiler. In: 2021 IEEE International Conference on Automation/XXIV Congress of the Chilean Association of Automatic Control (ICA-ACCA) (2021). https://doi.org/10.1109/icaacca51523.2021.9465302
8. Aimacaña, L., Gahui, O., Llanos, J., Ortiz, D.: Advanced control algorithms for a horizontal three-phase separator in a hardware in the loop simulation environment. In: CIT (2022)
9. Camacho, F., Berenguel, M., Rubio, F.R.: Advanced control of solar plants. Adv. Ind. Control (1997). https://doi.org/10.1007/978-1-4471-0981-5
10. Yebra, L.J., Berenguel, M., Bonilla, J., Roca, L., Dormido, S., Zarza, E.: Object-oriented modelling and simulation of ACUREX solar thermal power plant. Math. Comput. Model. Dyn. Syst. **16**(3), 211–224 (2010). https://doi.org/10.1080/13873954.2010.507420
11. Camacho, E.F., Rubio, F.R., Berenguel, M., Valenzuela, L.: A survey on control schemes for distributed solar collector fields. Part I: modeling and basic control approaches. Sol. Energy **81**(10), 1240–1251 (2007). https://doi.org/10.1016/j.solener.2007.01.002
12. Contreras, R.C.: Análisis, modelado y control de un campo de colectores solares distribuidos con un sistema de seguimiento de un eje. Universidad de Sevilla, España (1985)
13. Andaluz, V.H., Castillo-Carrión, D., Miranda, R.J., Alulema, J.C.: Virtual reality applied to industrial processes. In: De Paolis, L.T., Bourdot, P., Mongelli, A. (eds.) AVR 2017. LNCS, vol. 10324, pp. 59–74. Springer, Cham (2017). https://doi.org/10.1007/978-3-319-60922-5_5
14. Ortiz, J.S., Palacios-Navarro, G., Andaluz, V.H., Guevara, B.S.: Virtual reality-based framework to simulate control algorithms for robotic assistance and rehabilitation tasks through a standing wheelchair. Sensors **21**(15), 5083 (2021). https://doi.org/10.3390/s21155083

15. Camacho, E.F., Rubio, F.R., Hughes, F.M.: Self-tuning control of a solar power plant with a distributed collector field. IEEE Control Syst. **12**(2), 72–78 (1992). https://doi.org/10.1109/37.126858

16. Pruna, E., Sasig, E.R., Mullo, S.: PI and PID controller tuning tool based on the lambda method. In: 2017 CHILEAN Conference on Electrical, Electronics Engineering, Information and Communication Technologies (CHILECON) (2017). https://doi.org/10.1109/chilecon.2017.8229616

17. Kouvaritakis, B., Cannon, M.: Model predictive control. In: Advanced Textbooks in Control and Signal Processing (2016). https://doi.org/10.1007/978-3-319-24853-0

18. JRC Photovoltaic Geographical Information System (PVGIS) - European Commission. https://re.jrc.ec.europa.eu/pvg_tools/es/

Speed Controller by Neural Networks Trained by Invasive Weeds for a DC Motor

Ricardo Timbiano Romero[ID], Aldenice Rosales Sanguano[ID],
and William Montalvo[✉] [ID]

Universidad Politécnica Salesiana, UPS, 170146 Quito, Ecuador
{rtimbiano,arosaless}@est.ups.edu.ec, wmontalvo@ups.edu.ec

Abstract. Throughout history, the implementation of intelligent machines capable of performing activities that help humans has been a complicated task, then the need to seek new sources of inspiration to solve effective control solutions arises, giving rise to the emergence of bio-inspired algorithms which adopt phenomena present in nature. In this research, speed control by Artificial Neural Networks (ANN) or Neuro controller (NC) is developed for its application on an industrial machine such as a DC motor. For the training of the ANN, a novel and almost unexploited algorithm such as the Invasive Weed Optimization (IWO) is used, as a useful tool when training a neuro-controller for complex systems. The neuro controller has superior characteristics to a conventional controller, and if parameterized correctly it does not require a large computational effort. The MatLab/Simulink ANN toolbox is used to develop the basic structure of the ANN and a Control Plant Trainer (CPT) with a DC motor is used as a test plant. An ARDUINO board is used as an acquisition and control board. To validate the performance, the Wilcoxon test is used to compare the Time Weighted Error Integral (TWEI) of an NC trained by Back-propagation with the one trained by IWO and a conventional Proportional Integral and Derivative (PID) controller. The results obtained are good and interesting from the point of view of industrial automatic control.

Keywords: Bioinspired · Invasive Weed Optimization (IWO) · Neurocontroller (NC) · Artificial Neural Networks (ANN)

1 Introduction

Nowadays, the application of Artificial Neural Networks (ANN) is found in several control processes, because they allow the identification of pattern recognition from different process data, resulting in a robust and efficient control [1, 2].

Neural Networks are artificial and simplified models of the brain that can emulate human characteristics. Therefore, controllers are born due to the need to control complex and nonlinear processes, which is why Artificial Intelligence (AI) is being used in industry, for example, in fault detection, quality control, and identification of cracks in machinery [3, 4].

F. R. Narváez et al. (Eds.): SmartTech-IC 2022, CCIS 1705, pp. 468–479, 2023.
https://doi.org/10.1007/978-3-031-32213-6_34

The flagship ANN training algorithm is Backpropagation, which tends to have problems such as local minima. Faced with this, it is proposed to use a bio-inspired optimization algorithm such as Invasive Weed Invasion (IWO), which performs a sweep of all possible solutions and thus achieves an optimization with accurate values [4].

The metaheuristic weed algorithm is inspired by the growth process of weeds in nature as they naturally grow in excess and this severe growth is a serious threat to useful plants. It is a new and powerful optimization method that finds the global optimum of a mathematical function by mimicking the compatibility and randomness of weed colonies; it was presented by Mehrabian and Lucas in 2006 and can be used as a basic design for effective optimization approaches [5, 6, 7].

An application of the Neuro controller (NC) can be evidenced in the work of Bustiza, Yapuchura and Villarroel, where an NC is shown for a process (DC motor) that was identified by the curve fitting technique by linear interpolation, in which a NIDAQ USB-6008 data acquisition card was used, the adjustment of the neuro controller was performed by the Back-propagation algorithm, by finalizing in the control signal it was possible to minimize the over impulses and error [8].

As could be seen in the research, the NC show several improvements in the control of various processes, the training of these is done by various methods but there is little information on tuning by the IWO algorithm, which is why, this study is intended to optimize the speed control of a DC motor, through an NC trained by the bioheuristic algorithm IWO, the results obtained by experimental tests, both for a PID, an NC tuned with BackPropagation and an NC tuned by IWO will be verified [9].

2 Methodology

2.1 Data Acquisition

For the data acquisition of the system, the Arduino Mega board with an ATMEGA 2560 processor was chosen, with which the data of the DC motor speed in revolutions per minute (RPM) was obtained by reading the incremental encoder that the plant has. Four thousand samples were taken with a sampling time of 1 ms. The data were normalized using a Kalman filter. Figure 1 shows the input and output signals of the system [10].

For the acquisition of the transfer function, the Matlab identification toolbox was used, where 90% of the 4000 samples were taken and the remaining 10% of the samples were used to corroborate the model, resulting in a transfer function in continuous time Eq. (1) and later being transformed into discrete time Eq. (2).

The verification criterion was the simulation of the model at an input voltage (0.41 V), in such a way that it approximates the real system function, having a response of 276 (RPM), as shown in Fig. 2

The transfer function representing this system has the mathematical expression of Eq. (1):

$$G(s) = \frac{683.1}{0.1121s + 1} \tag{1}$$

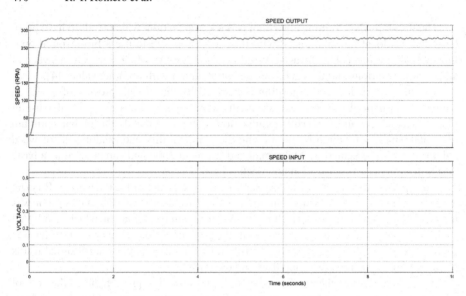

Fig. 1. Plant response for data acquisition.

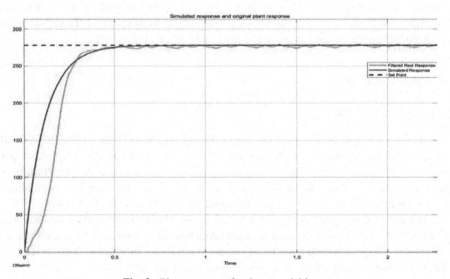

Fig. 2. Plant response for data acquisition.

The Z transform of the transfer function in Eq. (1) was calculated with the Matlab®
command "c2d", which is shown in Eq. (2):

$$G(z) = \frac{6.065}{z - 0.9911} \tag{2}$$

2.2   Control Topology

The structure is shown in Fig. 3, which is implemented in the Matlab-Simulink software, through a serial communication bus (USB). The Arduino Mega communicates via the internal integrated circuit protocol (I2C) with a conditioning card DAC-MCP4725, which is responsible for supplying alternating voltage to the DC motor of the plant [11].

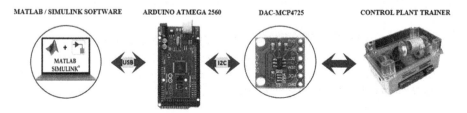

Fig. 3.   Operating structure for the control system.

2.3   Tuning by MatLab PID Tuner

The tuning was performed using the PID Tuner tool, which allows finding the proportional, integral and derivative gain values of a PID controller. To achieve the desired behavior and comply with the design characteristics within the Matlab software [12], the transfer function obtained in Eq. (2) is used.

Then the tuning of the controller is performed, resulting in the response in Fig. 4.

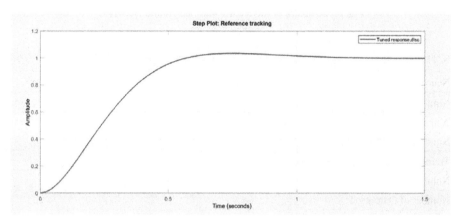

Fig. 4.   PID-Tuner step signal response.

With this toolbox, the gain values shown in Table 1 were obtained.

Table 1. PID gain values with PID Tuner.

Gain	Values
Kp	6.1230296
Ki	0.0011558
Kd	8.1087315

2.4 Neuro Controller Development

For the development of the Neurocontroller, it was based on the control structure presented in [13] as an ANN trained online, which presented a decrease in the error in the steady state, in such a way that it was a starting point for the investigation.

25 experimental tests were carried out with different types of neural networks, this amount was sufficient to determine that a feedforwardnet type network, as shown in Fig. 5, is viable due to its ability to adapt to any finite input mapping problem and output, with the characteristics for the ANN in Table 2.

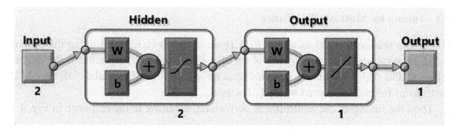

Fig. 5. Structure of the feedforward net Neural Network.

Table 2. Neuro controller Structure.

Neuro controller
Number of neurons: 3
Activation Function: Sigmoide-Linear
Number of hidden layers: 2
Training function: Levenber-Marquardt
Number of entries: 2
Number of Outputs: 1

The training was performed by Levenberg-Marquardt back-propagation, in which two input vectors corresponding to the steady-state error and set point were taken. Another vector corresponding to the PID output was considered, so that the training will be given as the current input error and the desired output, as shown in Fig. 6, resulting in Fig. 7 [14].

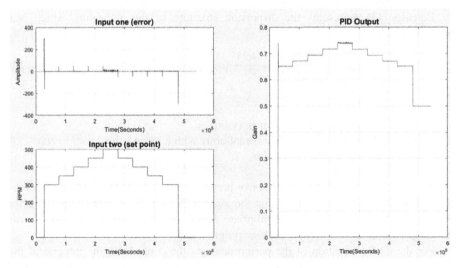

Fig. 6. Inputs and outputs for NC training.

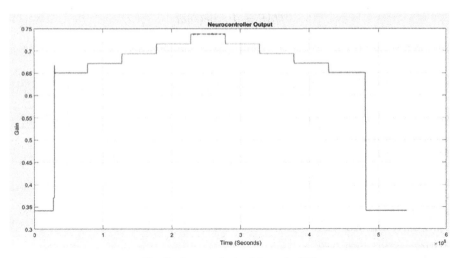

Fig. 7. Output obtained from the NC.

2.5 Tuning by IWO Algorithm

The tuning is based on finding the appropriate weight of the neural network, for which the positions of the weeds with greater aptitude are added to the weight to be optimized, having a response for each interaction and obtaining a weight that adapts according to the learning cases [15].

Equation (3) represents the dispersion structure of the algorithm, which was postulated in [6].

$$\sigma_{iter} = \frac{(iter_{max} - iter)^n}{(iter_{max})^n}(\sigma_{initial} - \sigma_{final}) + \sigma_{final} \tag{3}$$

where:

– $iter_{max}$:is the maximum number of interactions.
– σ_{iter} : is the distribution of the plants randomly with a mean value equal to zero.
– n : is the nonlinear modulation index.

As a cost function of the NC, the error presented between the desired output minus the obtained output was used, so that the algorithm focused on decreasing the error and therefore showing the most appropriate weight to the desired output, which was developed in Matlab-inspired in the base program shown in [6].

For the final evaluation of the performance of the controllers, the integral of the absolute error over time (ITAE) was used. Equation (4) shows its mathematical structure [16].

$$ITAE = \int_0^\infty t|e(t)|dt \tag{4}$$

The IWO has been configured with the parameters shown in Table 3:

Table 3. IWO algorithm parameters.

Optimization for invasive weeds
Number of iterations: 25
Minimum population size: 5
Maximum population size: 20
Maximum number of seeds: 14
$\sigma_{initial}$: 0.5
σ_{final}: 0.00001
Minimum search limit: -2.90
Maximum search limit: 0.90

3 Results

3.1 Discrete-Time Plant Responses for Speed Control of a DC Motor

Figure 8 shows the control plant for a DC motor, which was used to collect the dataset of the real plant. The data was used to train the Neuro controller and to perform the optimization by IWO.

Figure 9 shows the response of the PID, NC and NC-IWO to a set point of 0.65 V (V), where it is shown that the rise time for the NC has decreased, as well as its overshoot and settling time, compared to the PID control.

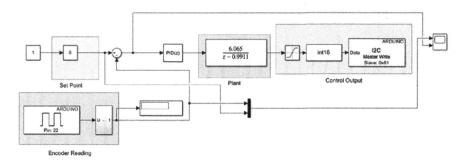

Fig. 8. Plant schematic in Simulink.

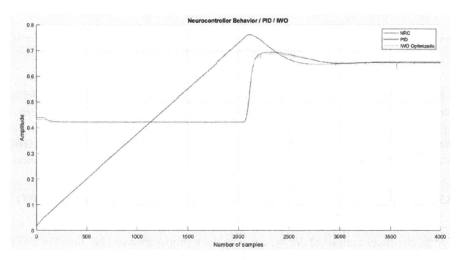

Fig. 9. Responses obtained from controllers.

3.2 Statistical Results Using the Wilcoxon Test for PID and Back-Propagation Tuned Controllers

The Wilcoxon statistical test allows the analysis and comparison of two related samples within a population, in this case of the PID controller and the NC, having an assertiveness of 95%. To determine the performance of the controls, a function that measures the performance index of the controllers was established as the Integral of the Absolute error weighted in time (ITAE).

Taking 30 samples of the ITAE of the PID control and the NC, two hypotheses were determined.

- Null Hypothesis (Ho): The ITAE of the PID is equal to the ITAE of the NC tuned by Back-propagation, for the speed control of a DC motor.
- Alternate Hypothesis (Ha): The ITAE of the PID is greater than the ITAE of the NC tuned by Backpropagation, for the speed control of a DC motor.

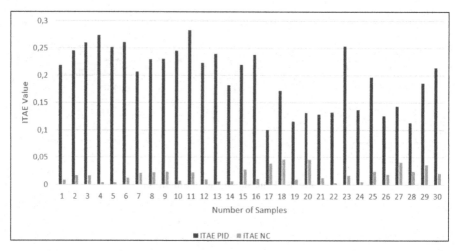

Fig. 10. ITAE of PID and NC.

For the Wilcoxon test, it is established that $Z_a = 1.96$ for a confidence level of 95%, obtaining the difference of the samples obtained, the sum is calculated and represented by the variable T = 468, the decision value is represented by Z, where Z = 4.84. After the statistical analysis and taking into account that $Z > Z_a$, , the Alternate hypothesis (Ha) is accepted. Figure 10 shows the different ITAE performance indexes of the controllers.

3.3   Statistical Results Using the Wilcoxon Test for Back-Propagation and IWO Tuned Controllers

For the statistical analysis of the NC tuned by Back-propagation and NC tuned by IWO, 30 samples were taken from the ITAE and two hypotheses were defined:

- Null Hypothesis (Ho): The ITAE of the NC tuned by Back-propagation is greater than the ITAE of the NC tuned by IWO, for the speed control of a DC motor.
- Alternate Hypothesis (Ha): The ITAE of the NC tuned by Back-propagation is equal to the ITAE of the NC tuned by IWO, for the speed control of a DC motor.

After performing the difference and sum of the two performance index variables, a value of T = 440 was obtained, and the decision variable symbolized by Z has a value of Z = −4.17, after performing the corresponding calculations and statistical analysis and taking into account that $Z < Z_a$, the null hypothesis is accepted. Figure 11 shows the different ITAE performance indexes of the controllers.

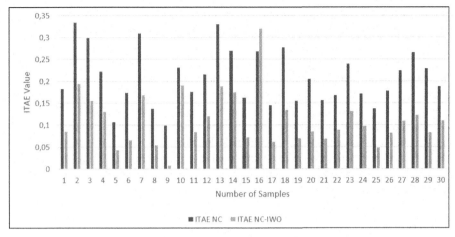

Fig. 11. ITAE of NC and NC-IWO.

4 Discussion

In [17], the IWO algorithm was used as a parameterizer for the gains of a PID, focused on the speed control of a DC motor, in which improvements are evidenced in its stability characteristics such as the decrease of the settling time and over impulse, in comparison with the Bio algorithm inspired in particle swarm. This shows that the algorithm has favorable responses, however, the verification method is not deterministic, it could be added methodology such as the Wilcoxon test implemented in this work as shown in Tables 5 and 6, to determine more structured hypotheses with more experiments, to have a solid foundation.

In [18], the IWO strategy was used for the training of feedforward multilayer perceptron neural networks (FFAN), as a result, advantages were obtained in finding the values of weights and bias for the networks because the weeds and their large spread over the possible solutions are implemented, resulting in more optimal parameters reflected in the results; however, in the study does not focus on the control of a process, it focuses on data analysis. In the present research, training was performed for a DC motor speed control, which presents significant improvements in the stability characteristics as shown in Fig. 8.

Also, in [19], a neuro controller based on a wavelet network trained online by the gradient descent algorithm to control the speed of a DC motor, showed a better performance than a PI controller in speed control, if the NC had been tuned by IWO, possible solutions could be explored around the search space, thus having more optimal values, as is the case of the one developed in this research, having an adaptive and robust control, as can be seen in Fig. 6.

5 Conclusions

According to the experiments carried out, it was demonstrated that neuro controllers have better behavior than a PID, therefore, it has been possible to optimize the stability characteristics for the speed control of a DC motor, therefore, the industry would have efficient controllers allowing to reduce the energy consumption of its processes, as well as to maximize the production.

The IWO can be taken into account for adaptive control or tuning, since it sweeps through the entire search space until the optimal point is found, thus providing a more reliable response. However, this response depends on the number of weeds that can be spread over the search space, which represents a high computational cost.

The application of the Wilcoxon statistical method is very practical to evaluate intelligent controllers because with only 30 experimental tests it was possible to perform an analysis of sophisticated results with a confidence level of 95%, compared to other methods that require a greater number of physical experiments, leading to wear and tear on the elements of the control loop.

References

1. Quiros, A.R.F., Abad, A., Bedruz, R.A., Uy, A.C., and Dadios, E. P.: A genetic algorithm and artificial neural network-based approach for the machine vision of plate segmentation and character recognition. In: 8th International Conference on Humanoid, Nanotechnology, Information Technology, Communication and Control, Environment and Management, HNICEM 2015 (2016)
2. Gerardo, M., et al.: Neural networks applied to irrigation control using instrumentation and image analysis for a micro-greenhouse applied to the cultivation of basil. Res. Comput. Sci. **147**(5), 93–103 (2018)
3. Fuentes, M.S., Zelaya, N.A.L., Avila, J.L.O.: Coffee fruit recognition using artificial vision and neural networks. In: 5th International Conference on Control and Robotics Engineering, ICCRE 2020, pp. 224–228 (2020)
4. Riquelme, I.: Revisión de los Algoritmos Bio inspirados. *Universidad de Manchester*, no. June, pp. 1–31 (2014)
5. Crawford, B., Soto, R., Legue, I.F., Olguin, E.: Algoritmo Discreto de Optimización Hiebras Invasivas para el Set Covering Problem. In: Iberian Conference on Information Systems and Technologies, CISTI, vol. 2016 (2016)
6. Mehrabian, A.R., Lucas, C.: A novel numerical optimization algorithm inspired from weed colonization. Ecol. Inform. **1**(4), 355–366 (2006)
7. Anhui da xue et al.: Proceedings of the 32nd Chinese Control and Decision Conference (CCDC 2020), pp. 22–24 (2020)
8. R. Ib, I. Journal, and I. Systems.: No. E30 (2020)
9. Khalilpour, M., Razmjooy, N., Hosseini, H., and Moallem, P.: Optimal control of DC motor using invasive weed optimization (IWO) algorithm. In: Majlesi Conference on Electrical Engineering, no. January, pp. 1–7 (2011)
10. Adel, Z., Hamou, A.A., Abdellatif, S.: Design of real-time PID tracking controller using Arduino mega 2560 for a permanent magnet DC motor under real disturbances. In: Proceedings of 2018 3rd International Conference on Electrical Sciences and Technologies in Maghreb, CISTEM 2018, pp. 1–5 (2019)
11. Descripción y funcionamiento del Bus I2C I Robots Didácticos. https://robots-argentina.com.ar/didactica/descripcion-y-funcionamiento-del-bus-i2c/. Accessed 11 Jul 2022
12. Yadav, V., Tayal, V.K.: Tuner, pp. 442–445 (2018)
13. Danilo Rairán-Antolines, J., Fernando Chiquiza-Quiroga, D., Ángel Parra-Pachón, M.: Implementación de neurocontroladores en línea. Tres configuraciones, tres plantas, pp.1–12 (2011)

14. Diaz, A.L., Meza, J.E., Mecatrónica, Y.: Estudio Y Analisis De Neurocontroladores (2003)
15. Chen, Z., Wang, S., Deng, Z., Zhang, X.: Tuning of auto-disturbance rejection controller based on the invasive weed optimization. In: Proceedings - 2011 6th International Conference on Bio-Inspired Computing: Theories and Applications, BIC-TA 2011, vol. 2, no. 1, pp. 314–318 (2011)
16. MadhusudhanaRao, G., SankerRam, B.V.: A neural network based speed control for DC motor, Int. J. Recent Trends Eng. 2(6), 121–124 (2009)
17. Khalilpour, M., et al.: Optimal Control of DC motor using Invasive Weed Optimization (IWO) Algorithm Automatic Detection of Malignant Melanoma View project-Books View project Optimal Control of DC motor using Invasive Weed Optimization (IWO) Algorithm. https://www.researchgate.net/publication/221702286. Accessed 21 June 2022
18. Giri, R., Chowdhury, A., Ghosh, A., Das, S., Abraham, A., Snasel, V.: A modified invasive weed optimization algorithm for training of feed-forward neural networks. In Conference Proceedings - IEEE International Conference on Systems, Man and Cybernetics, pp. 3166–3173 (2010)
19. Institute of Electrical and Electronics Engineers, 2018 International Conference on Advancement in Electrical and Electronic Engineering (ICAEEE)

Abiotic Maize Stress Detection Using Hyperspectral Signatures and Band Selection

Pablo Carmona-Zuluaga[1]([⊠]), Maria C. Torres-Madronero[1], Manuel Goez[1],
Tatiana Rondon[2], Manuel Guzman[2], and Maria Casamitjana[2]

[1] Instituto Tecnológico Metropolitano, Medellín, Colombia
pablocarmona187539@correo.itm.edu.co
[2] Corporación Colombiana de Investigación Agropecuaria (AGROSAVIA), Centro de
Investigación La Selva, Rionegro, Colombia

Abstract. Identification of plant stress is fundamental for the improving crop efficiency, which is of economic and ecological interest around the globe. Passive remote sensing sensors measure emitted or reflected electromagnetic radiation, allowing the identification of present materials; this data is used for various plant analyses, including precision agriculture and stress detection. This paper uses hyperspectral signatures to classify of non-living negative factors (abiotic stress) in corn crops using hyperspectral signatures. The high dimensionality of hyperspectral data makes its processing highly complex, rendering dimensionality reduction essential. The two main approaches for reduction are feature selection and feature extraction; maintaining the physical meaning of data is important for interpretability, so feature extraction by band selection was used. Nitrogen deficiency was applied in a maize test field, collecting 337 samples in three nitrogen deficiency levels. Three unsupervised band selection methods were applied to the dataset. The reduced datasets obtained were classified using a Support Vector Machine, Random Forest, and a fully connected Neural Network. It was found that the low redundancy high information selected bands can equal or outperform the classification accuracy of the hyperspectral high dimensional dataset. This could allow the development of less complex multi-spectral equipment based on selected characteristics.

Keywords: Band Selection · Spectral Signature · Remote Sensing · Abiotic Stress · Machine Learning

1 Introduction

Remote sensing (RS) collects data about an event or object from a distance. RS sensors measure the electromagnetic radiation emitted or reflected by the measured object [18]. The spectral response or signature for different materials along the electromagnetic spectrum (usually visible, infrared, or microwave) varies,

F. R. Narváez et al. (Eds.): SmartTech-IC 2022, CCIS 1705, pp. 480–493, 2023.
https://doi.org/10.1007/978-3-031-32213-6_35

allowing RS to be applied to several applications [11]. RS systems include multispectral and hyperspectral sensors. These passive systems measure the energy reflected or emitted by a surface along tens or hundreds of spectral bands. The images captured by these sensors are seen as a cube: with two spatial dimensions and a third dimension that stores spectral information. Spectral imagery is used for various plant analyses [4,7,9,12], such as vegetation identification, plant growth monitoring, water monitoring, and precision agriculture.

The vegetation spectrum has a characteristic shape, with a huge potential to study a plant's phenological and health status [10]. However, the most used methods to study vegetation spectrum are based on vegetation indexes that are band ratios of two or three bands [15,16,19]. These widely used methods waste helpful information provided by the high resolution of hyperspectral imagery. An alternative is the application of machine learning algorithms that can use the full spectrum for vegetation characterization.

However, the high spectral resolution of hyperspectral images is challenging for machine learning. This is due to the large computational volume of this data, which implies a more significant number of labeled samples for training machine learning systems [5]. In addition, the spectral bands have redundancy between adjacent channels of the image, and a part of the spectral range of the sensor may not be relevant for a specific application. Therefore, the reduction of dimensionality becomes vital, where eliminating redundancy is wanted while its components maintain relevant features of the data [8]. Two possible approaches meet this objective. First is feature extraction; the original data is represented in a different characteristics space, modifying the initial data, which could complicate its final interpretation [14]. Second, band selection methods can be implemented; these techniques aim to choose the bands that contains most of the relevant information while ignoring those that present redundant information [20]. This last approach has advantages for the final interpretation since it does not alter the physical meaning of the data. There are several methods for band selection [13]; they can be grouped into six categories: 1) searching based, 2) ranking based, 3) sparsity-based, 4) clustering based, 5) learning based, and 6) hybrid-based methods. The most important techniques for this work are categories 2 and 4 due to the unsupervised approach taken in most previous works.

This paper will analyze the possibility of detecting abiotic stress in transitory crops, such as corn, from spectral data taken in the Colombian field in 2021. For this purpose, a methodology based on machine learning and dimensionality reduction by band selection is proposed. We use three reduction techniques for this purpose: first, [1], in which the difference between the data distribution of the lower dimensional subspace and the standard Gaussian distribution is maximized. Second, [17] in which an optimal clustering framework is proposed, which can obtain the optimal clustering result for a particular form of objective function under a reasonable constraint, and after that uses a rank on clusters strategy, which provides an adequate criterion to select bands on existing clustering structure. Furthermore, in [22], the optimal trade-offs between the amount of information and the redundancy contained in the dataset are explored to select the representative bands. Then, we use the resulting reduced datasets to classify the dataset according to three nitrogen deficiency levels. Support Vector Machines (SVM), Random Forest (RF), and a Fully connected neural network (NN) are used for this purpose.

2   Materials and Methods

2.1   Database

Location of Experiments and Experimental Design

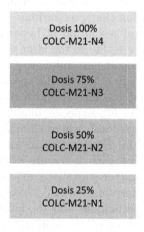

Fig. 1. Distribution of corn trials under different levels of nitrogen fertilization with respect to the optimal dose. Doses 100% (yellow color), 75% (blue color), 50% (red color) and 25% (gray color). (Color figure online)

The experiment was established at the AGROSAVIA research facility La Selva, located in the Llanogrande sector, municipality of Rionegro, Antioquia, Colombia. This area presents an average annual temperature of 17 °C, with precipitation of 1917 mm, relative humidity of 78%, solar brightness of 1726 h 1/year, and evapotranspiration of 1202 mm. It is in the Lower Montane Humid Forest (bh-MB) ecological life zone, on the soil of the Rionegro Association cartographic unit, on a low alluvial terrace of the Rionegro River, flat, with a slope of less than 3%, poorly drained.

The trials were established in the field on June 4, 2021. Three levels of nitrogen fertilization were evaluated. Nutrient deficiency levels correspond to 25%, 50%, and 75% of the optimal nitrogen dose for corn. In addition, we included a trial with 100% of the optimal fertilization for the corn crop according to its requirements Fig. 1. A soil fertility analysis was carried out to assert the optimal nitrogen level.

The experimental design corresponds to a randomized complete block with an arrangement of divided plots, where the main plot corresponds to the fertilization level. The 12.48 m2 experimental unit comprises three 5 m long rows or threads. The furrows are separated by 0.8 m, while the plants within the rows are spaced 0.2 m apart. This configuration leaves a plant density of 62,500 pl ha-1. The agronomic practices carried out corresponded to the conventional ones for cultivation. Soil preparation and planting were manual. Once sown, Glyphosate (Roundup, dose 2 L ha1) and 2-4-D (1.5 l ha-1) were applied as pre-emergent to the crop and post-emergent to weeds. At 30 days, plant thinning and weeding were carried out for one plant per planting point.

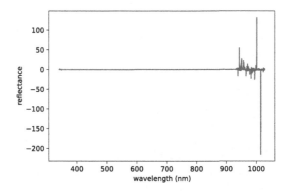

Fig. 2. Raw spectral signature.

Data Collection and Preprocessing

To collect spectral dataset, we used a FLAME spectrometer, model FLAME S VIS NIR from Ocean Insight, integrated with a 2-meter long QP600-2-VIR-NIR optical fiber and a Rasberry PI programmed by the manufacturer for data acquisition through WIFI control. The equipment is housed in a protective box to avoid exposure to moisture and dirt during field data collection. In addition, a fiber guide tube is attached, facilitating data collection in trees up to 2 m high, while protecting the optical fiber.

The spectrometer range is between 350 and 1000 nm, with a resolution of 1.33 nm; in total, 2049 bands are captured along the electromagnetic spectrum. Figure 2 presents a random example of a plant's raw spectral signature. Each signature is the result of averaging 10 samples; this is an automatic process presented by the manufacturer's software that improves the signal-to-noise ratio. In addition to plant signatures, we collected white and black spectra for calibration. Equation (1) describes the relation obtaining the reflectance. Figure 3 shows the reflectance for a corn plant obtained after calibration.

$$\frac{(PlantSignature - BlackPattern)}{(WhitePattern - BlackPattern)} \tag{1}$$

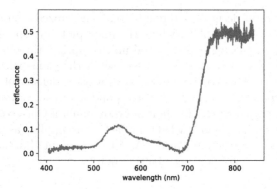

Fig. 3. Spectral signature without noisy bands.

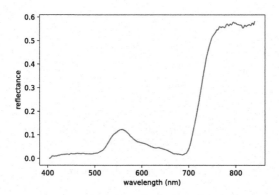

Fig. 4. Filtered spectral signature.

After this correction, the obtained signatures's spectral range is sliced because some sections's noise makes data analysis difficult. We ignored 798 bands, keeping 1251 bands from 404 nm to 840 nm. An example of an obtained signature is presented in Fig. 3. Subsequently, each spectral signature is applied to a sliding median filter with a 10-point window. As the last preprocessing step, median and standard deviation are calculated for each nutritional treatment class. The signatures outside ±2 standard deviation of the median are eliminated. After applying the previous preprocessing noise is reduced significantly; this can be seen in Fig. 4.

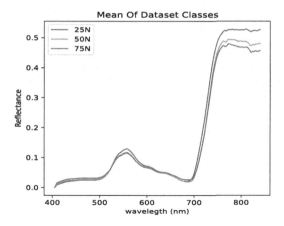

Fig. 5. Average signature for each of the classes.

We obtained 447 samples of tassel stage maize in the September 15-2021 data acquisition field trip, covering four distinctive classes based on the percentage of nitrogen nutrition presented in Fig. 1. However, a weather abnormality flooded the corn crop's 100% nitrogen nutrition section, which diminished its growth and altered the experiment-controlled environment. For the presented reasons, samples with an optimal dose of nitrogen were removed from the dataset, leaving 337 firms in three distinct labels as the final data used in the following experiments. The mean for each class is presented in Fig. 5 as a reference.

2.2 Band Selection Techniques

This section will deal with the description and detailing of band selection techniques that are further used in the result section.

SVD

The SVD method for hyperspectral band selection is an unsupervised linear algebra-based technique. Its principal goal is to search for a subset of sufficiently independent column rank revealing decompositions. Algorithm 1 summarized the main step for SVD subset selection

---

Algorithm 1. SVD

Require:

1: Construct a matrix representation of the hyperspectral cube as follows. Let $X = [x1, x2, ..., xN]$, where N is the number of pixels in the image. Notice that each image row corresponds to a band of the cube and each column corresponds to a measured pixel spectral signature.

2: Construct the normalized matrix $Z = [z1, z2, ..., zN]$ which is obtained by subtracting the mean from each pixel and normalizing each band to unit variance as follows:

$$z = \frac{D1}{2(x - \mu x)}$$

where $D = diag\{\sigma x21, \sigma x22, ..., \sigma x2d\}$ and $\sigma x2i$ is the variance of the ith band.

3: Compute the SVD of Z and determine its rank d (you can determine d in this form or use an a-priori value).

4: Compute the QR factorization with pivoting of the matrix $V1TP = QR$, where V1 is formed by the first d left singular vectors of X, P is the pivoting matrix of the QR factorization and Q and R are the QR factors.

5: Compute $X = PTX$, where P is the pivoting matrix from the QR factorization in step 4).

Ensure: Take the first b rows of X as the selected bands.

Optimal Clustering Framework

Optimal Clustering Framework [17] (OCF), estimates each band's contribution value toward different image data classes. The framework involves a ranking on clustering strategy where the desired clustering method, such as K-Means, clusters the input image into an arbitrary number of classes. Then, the bands contributions toward each cluster are ranked, using a selected objective function to determine the best-performing bands

For this experiment, the E-FDPC [6] was used as the ranking method to assess each band as a suitable cluster center. First, by determining whether it has a large local density, and second, by considering that it is not close to bands with higher local density. The clustering method used is presented in [21], and "top rank cut" (TRC) was selected as the objective function of the clustering section. It chooses the highest-ranking bands for each cluster and calculates the sum of their similarities, giving a score to each cluster.

Multi-objective Optimization Module

Zhang, Gong, and Chan proposed a multi-objective optimization model-based framework [22] (BOMBS), which explores trade-offs between redundancy and the amount of information in the spectral bands. One objective function is used to measure each of these two characteristics. Average formation entropy was used to measure the amount of information in a specific band. This is usually defined using of continuous random variables. However, it can also be a discrete problem with each band of the dataset as a discrete random variable X. The probability distribution $p(X)$ will be:

$$p(X) = \frac{h(X)}{Num} \qquad (2)$$

where $h(X)$ is the histogram of a band and Num is the totality of pixels in $h(X)$. This process gives a high score to clear images and a lower score to noisy bands.

The second aspect that needs to be measured is the correlation between bands. Cross entropy calculates the relative distance between the probability distributions of bands A and B. Its simplified equation would be:

$$H(A, B) = E_A(-log(B)) + E_B(-log(A)) \qquad (3)$$

where E_x is the expectation that obeys the probability distribution of x.

To find an optimal solution and trade-off between these two objective functions the authors proposed a novel multi-objective immune-system-inspired algorithm

2.3   Classification Techniques

Random Forest (RF)

RF is a well-known machine learning algorithm commonly used for classification or regression, where many of individual decision trees are used together. Scikit-learn RandomForestClassifier was used for this implementation with the following parameters: n_estimators = 100, criterion = "gini" and max depth = 6; all other parameters were left by default, and the random state was set to zero (0).

Fully Connected Neural Networks (NN)

This type of neural network consists of a series of layers where each node (neuron) is connected to every node in the next layer. It is a general-purpose network. Scikit-learn MLPClassifier was used for this implementation with the following parameters: hidden_layer_sizes = [100,200,50,20], activation = 'relu', solver = 'adam', and max_iter = 1000, all other parameters where left by default and the random state was set to zero (42).

Support Vector Machines (SVM)

SVM is a machine learning classical and commonly used algorithm that tends to work well for high dimensional spaces, and can be used for classification and regression. Scikit-learn SVC was used for this implementation with the following parameters: C = 100, kernel = 'poly', degree = 2, and cache_size = 10*1024, all other parameters were left by default, and the random state was set to zero (0).

3   Results

This section presents the classification performance using the selected bands by the methods above. Classification results help determine the effectiveness of identifying relevant bands for corn abiotic stress. In Fig. 5, the average of all the samples belonging to each of the classes given, #N refers to the percentage of nitrogen with respect to the healthy total of the nitrogen given to the plantation. It consists of 337 samples between three classes, as presented in Table 1.

Table 1. Corn dataset samples numbers for each class

Class	Samples	Training
25N	118	100
50N	110	93
75N	109	93

We compared 4, 8, 12, 16, 16, 20, 24, 28, and 32 relevant bands selected by the OCF, SVD, and Bombs methods. The classification will be performed using three machine learning commonly-used algorithms: Random Forest (RF), Fully connected Neural Network (NN), and Support vector machines (SVM).

3.1   Classification Results

Table 2 presents the results obtained with RF classifier. The higher accuracy for RF is 68.6% using 20 bands selected by Bombs and 32 bands selected by SVD. Note that the initial dataset benchmark of classification is 62.7% obtained using RF over the dataset with all bands.

Table 2. Random Forest classification results

Full dataset:			0.627
Bands	Bombs	SVD	OCF
4	0.510	0.608	0.569
8	0.608	0.608	0.569
12	0.549	0.667	0.647
16	0.608	0.647	0.588
20	**0.686**	0.608	0.608
24	0.627	0.667	0.608
28	0.608	0.608	0.647
32	0.627	**0.686**	0.627

Table 3 presents the results obtained by NN. In this case, we obtained a 68.6% accuracy using only 4 bands selected by SVD. In this case the classification benchmark was 68.6% using all bands.

Table 3. NN classification results

Full dataset:			0.686
Bands	Bombs	SVD	OCF
4	0.588	**0.686**	0.608
8	0.549	0.608	0.569
12	0.588	0.647	0.588
16	0.647	0.686	0.529
20	0.608	0.647	0.549
24	0.627	0.627	0.588
28	0.588	0.647	0.549
32	0.627	0.667	0.569

Table 4 presents the result for SVM classifier. The highest scoring results were archived with Bombs with 20 selected bands and SVD with 12 selected bands, reaching 76.5% accuracy. It is important to notice that the initial dataset benchmark of classification was matched, as the SVM classifier with the same parameters obtained 76.5% accuracy.

This algorithm has the best performance out of all three classifiers, Bombs 20 selected bands and SVD 12 selected bands will be further presented in the following section.

Table 4. SVM classification results

Full dataset:			0.765
Bands	Bombs	SVD	OCF
4	0.549	0.667	0.627
8	0.686	0.725	0.706
12	0.549	**0.765**	0.706
16	0.588	0.745	0.686
20	**0.765**	0.686	0.745
24	0.706	0.745	0.706
28	0.627	0.706	0.725
32	0.745	0.667	0.725

3.2 Best Selected Bands

A set of 20 bands selected using the Bombs algorithm and a set of 12 bands selected using the SVD algorithm is presented on their distribution across the electromagnetic spectrum. It is intended to see the overall difference or similarity since both reached the same high accuracy results with SVM classification.

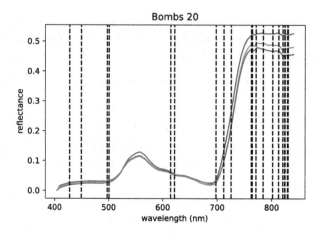

Fig. 6. 20 selected bombs bands over mean spectral firms

Table 5 and 6 show that a higher percentage of bands (close to 66.6%) is above 700 nm in a narrow range of 140 nm. This range corresponds to the electromagnetic spectrum's near-infrared and red edge sections. In the 296 nm range from 404 nm to 700 nm, fewer bands were deemed relevant by both selection algorithms (see Figs. 6 and 7).

Table 5. SVD 12

Band #	Wavelength
18	410.975
336	528.413
507	589.690
802	692.193
852	709.153
921	732.359
1018	764.580
1125	799.578
1162	811.546
1184	818.629
1222	830.804
1241	836.862

Table 6. Bombs 20

Band #	Wavelength
65	428.610
122	449.871
251	497.459
261	501.118
578	614.737
599	622.099
819	697.973
861	712.193
901	725.656
1013	762.932
1018	764.580
1039	771.494
1079	784.604
1133	802.172
1166	812.835
1190	820.556
1201	824.085
1203	824.724
1217	829.205
1221	830.484

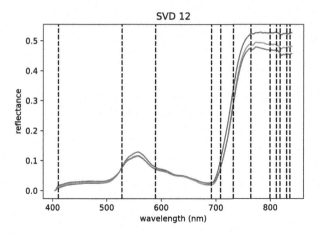

Fig. 7. 12 selected SVD bands over mean spectral firms

3.3 Discussion

To the best of our knowledge no studies that use band selection as a dimensionality reduction method for abiotic stress in corn. Most reviewed works used a preset subset of two or three bands to calculate vegetation indexes. For instance, in [3], approaches based on vegetation indexes are assessed to study water and nitrogen status. In [2] nitrogen deficiency for sweet maize is determined. Both studies use a variety indexes, based on bands NIR, RED-Edge, RED or Green. The spectral range used for indexes is related to this paper's selected wavelengths. However, our dimensionality reduction approach focuses on important sections by choosing a more significant number of bands in sections with low redundancy and high information value.

4   Conclusion

The results allow us to conclude that it is possible to considerably reduce the data collected to obtain an acceptable precision for abiotic stress in corn. This could create cheaper remote multispectral sensing systems to detect stress in plants based on the wavelengths found to be more discriminating.

It is considered that the results obtained could improve considerably since the current database is of minimal size and unplanned water stress made one of the classes unusable. Therefore, it is expected that by increasing the amount of data and ensuring regular conditions in the plants, it will be possible to increase the precision. Hyperparameter tuning of classification algorithms should be explored further.

Acknowledgments. This work was financed with resources from the Patrimonio autónomo fondo nacional de financiamiento para ciencia, tecnología e innovación Francisco José de Caldas through RC 80740-475-2020, supported by the Ministerio de

Ciencia, Tecnología e Innovación - Minciencias, Instituto Tecnológico Metropolitano - ITM, Corporación Colombiana de Investigación Agropecuaria - AGROSAVIA, and BLACKSQUARE S.A.S.

Data Availibility Statement. The data that support the findings of this study are available from the author, MCT (mariatorres@itm.edu.co), upon reasonable request.

References

1. Arzuaga-Cruz, E., Jimenez-Rodriguez, L.O., Velez-Reyes, M.: Unsupervised feature extraction and band subset selection techniques based on relative entropy criteria for hyperspectral data analysis. In: Algorithms and Technologies for Multispectral, Hyperspectral, and Ultraspectral Imagery IX, vol. 5093, no. 787, p. 462 (2003). https://doi.org/10.1117/12.485942
2. Burns, B.W., et al.: Determining nitrogen deficiencies for maize using various remote sensing indices. Precis. Agric. **23**, 791–811 (2022). https://doi.org/10.1007/S11119-021-09861-4/TABLES/7. https://doi.org/10.1007/s11119-021-09861-4
3. Colovic, M., et al.: Hyperspectral vegetation indices to assess water and nitrogen status of sweet maize crop. Agronomy **12**, 2181 (2022). https://doi.org/10.3390/AGRONOMY12092181. https://www.mdpi.com/2073-4395/12/9/2181/htm
4. Delalieux, S., van Aardt, J., Keulemans, W., Schrevens, E., Coppin, P.: Detection of biotic stress (Venturia inaequalis) in apple trees using hyperspectral data: nonparametric statistical approaches and physiological implications. Eur. J. Agron. **27**(1), 130–143 (2007). https://doi.org/10.1016/J.EJA.2007.02.005
5. Hook, S.J.: NASA 2014 the hyperspectral infrared imager (HyspIRI)-science impact of deploying instruments on separate platforms. HyspIRI group. Question Leads: CQ1-Kevin Turpie, CQ2-Sander Veraverbeke, CQ3-Robert Wright, CQ4-Martha Anderson, CQ5-Anupma Prakash/john "lyle" Mars, CQ6-Dale Quattrochi (2014)
6. Jia, S., Tang, G., Zhu, J., Li, Q.: A novel ranking-based clustering approach for hyperspectral band selection. IEEE Trans. Geosci. Remote Sens. **54**, 88–102 (2016)
7. Katsoulas, N., Elvanidi, A., Ferentinos, K.P., Kacira, M., Bartzanas, T., Kittas, C.: Crop reflectance monitoring as a tool for water stress detection in greenhouses: a review. Biosyst. Eng. **151**, 374–398 (2016). https://doi.org/10.1016/J.BIOSYSTEMSENG.2016.10.003
8. Lunga, D., Prasad, S., Crawford, M.M., Ersoy, O.: Manifold-learning-based feature extraction for classification of hyperspectral data: a review of advances in manifold learning. IEEE Signal Process. Mag. **31**, 55–66 (2014). https://doi.org/10.1109/MSP.2013.2279894
9. Mahlein, A.K., Steiner, U., Dehne, H.W., Oerke, E.C.: Spectral signatures of sugar beet leaves for the detection and differentiation of diseases. Precis. Agric. **11**(4), 413–431 (2010). https://doi.org/10.1007/S11119-010-9180-7
10. Schowengerdt, R.A.: Remote sensing: models and methods for image processing, p. 558 (2006)
11. Shanmugapriya, P., Rathika, S., Ramesh, T., Janaki, P.: Applications of remote sensing in agriculture - a review. Int. J. Curr. Microbiol. Appl. Sci. **8**, 2270–2283 (2019). https://doi.org/10.20546/IJCMAS.2019.801.238

12. Steddom, K., Bredehoeft, M.W., Khan, M., Rush, C.M.: Comparison of visual and multispectral radiometric disease evaluations of cercospora leaf spot of sugar beet. Plant Disease **89**, 153–158 (2007). https://doi.org/10.1094/PD-89-0153. https://apsjournals.apsnet.org/doi/abs/10.1094/PD-89-0153
13. Sun, W., Du, Q.: Hyperspectral band selection: a review. IEEE Geosci. Remote Sens. Mag. **7**, 118–139 (2019). https://doi.org/10.1109/MGRS.2019.2911100
14. Sun, W., et al.: UL-Isomap based nonlinear dimensionality reduction for hyperspectral imagery classification. ISPRS J. Photogramm. Remote Sens. **89**, 25–36 (2014). https://doi.org/10.1016/J.ISPRSJPRS.2013.12.003
15. Thorp, K.R., et al.: Proximal hyperspectral sensing and data analysis approaches for field-based plant phenomics. Comput. Electron. Agric. **118**, 225–236 (2015). https://doi.org/10.1016/J.COMPAG.2015.09.005
16. Ustin, S.L., et al.: Retrieval of foliar information about plant pigment systems from high resolution spectroscopy. Remote Sens. Environ. **113**, S67–S77 (2009). https://doi.org/10.1016/J.RSE.2008.10.019
17. Wang, Q., Zhang, F., Li, X.: Optimal clustering framework for hyperspectral band selection. IEEE Trans. Geosci. Remote Sens. **56**(10), 5910–5922 (2018). https://doi.org/10.1109/TGRS.2018.2828161
18. Weiss, M., Jacob, F., Duveiller, G.: Remote sensing for agricultural applications: a meta-review. Remote Sens. Environ. **236**, 111402 (2020). https://doi.org/10.1016/J.RSE.2019.111402
19. Xue, J., Su, B.: Significant remote sensing vegetation indices: a review of developments and applications. J. Sens. **2017** (2017). https://doi.org/10.1155/2017/1353691
20. Yang, H., Du, Q., Chen, G.: Particle swarm optimization-based hyperspectral dimensionality reduction for urban land cover classification. IEEE J. Sel. Top. Appl. Earth Obs. Remote Sens. **5**, 544–554 (2012). https://doi.org/10.1109/JSTARS.2012.2185822
21. Zelnik-Manor, L., Perona, P.: Self-tuning spectral clustering. In: NIPS (2004)
22. Zhang, M., Gong, M., Chan, Y.: Hyperspectral band selection based on multiobjective optimization with high information and low redundancy. Appl. Soft Comput. J. **70**, 604–621 (2018). https://doi.org/10.1016/j.asoc.2018.06.009

Optimal Energy Dispatch Analysis Using the Inclusion of Virtual Power Plants Based on Dynamic Power Flows

Darwin Canacuan[1] , Diego Carrión[1,2](✉) , and Iván Montalvo[2]

[1] Master's Program in Electricity, Universidad Politécnica Salesiana,
Quito 170525, Ecuador
dcanacuanq@est.ups.edu.ec
[2] Electrical Engineering Program, Universidad Politécnica Salesiana,
Quito 170525, Ecuador
{dcarrion,imontalvo}@ups.edu.ec
http://www.ups.edu.ec

Abstract. The growing manifestation of non-conventional renewable energies, in modern electrical power systems, creates a great challenge on the normal operation of the system and planning the dispatch of active power, in economic terms. In order to achieve the objective of economic dispatch and be competitive in the electricity market, the concept of virtual power plant (VPP) has been introduced. It considers electrical elements and equipment with the aim of working as a single set that generates economic and operational benefits to the electrical system, taking into account the features and restrictions for an energy dispatch scenari0. This paper proposes a case of study that considers the use of a virtual power plant in order to analyze the effects caused along the network. The optimal dynamic flow of AC power (ODFAC) uses a non-linear programming algorithm and how it is affected not only for the restrictions of the electrical elements and equipment but also for the restrictions of the topology and formation of the electrical power system. The IEEE 9-bar system is used to illustrate the efficiency of the method, comparing the results of the system with and without the integration of a virtual power plant.

Keywords: Economic dispatch · Energy management system (EMS) · Optimization · Planning · Power Flow · Renewable Energy Source (RES) · Virtual Power Plant (VPP)

1 Introduction

The study and research of non-conventional renewable generation technologies for a sustainable development with the environment, has started with the use of medium-scale of wind and photovoltaic generation into the electric power grid,

Universidad Politécnica Salesiana.

with the aim of reducing the use of fossil fuels and decreasing levels of environmental pollution [1]. Including non-conventional renewable energy sources in electrical power systems (EPS) it is not an easy job, because it has to be considered a complete analysis of the reliability and quality of the energy delivered, due to the fact that renewable energy is not a constant source of energy. In addition, the variation over a cycle of time of both demand and generation restricts the inclusion of a virtual power plant to maintain stability levels that allow continuous operation of EPS. One of the solutions to maintain the continuous operation of a virtual power plant is to add a thermal generation plant or use energy storage by creating a micro-network in a specific space of the EPS, which allows supplying the demand without any interruptions [2].

The progress on the information and data transmission technologies fields for smart grids allow these concepts to be applied on a larger scale for the management and operation of a set of non-conventional renewable power plants, and also let than other electrical elements or equipment can be incorporated to the electric power system as a set called virtual power plant, which permits the use as a clean energies within the electricity market [3]. Managing and operating an EPS allows planning and dispatching of electrical energy in an efficient way. Thus, in order to archive this aim, a mathematical optimization method have been used, where the most known are: linear programming, gradient method, non-linear programming, dynamic programming, etc. [4].

The optimal power flow is fundamental in the electrical power systems analysis because it shows how electricity generation must supply the energy demand based on the restrictions of the EPS topology and the properties or sizes of the electrical elements and equipment [5–7]. If restrictions about both time and energy generation are also added to the elemental problem of optimal power flow, the problem becomes a dynamic scenario, called optimal dynamic power flow (ODPF) [9], creating a more complex problem, but the method in order to find a solution for it is essential to obtain results that represent real operating conditions in the power systems which is been analyzed [10]. The objective of this article is to present the behavior of the optimal dynamic power flow in power systems that have a virtual power plant with high participation of non-conventional renewable energies.

The application of these methods on the optimization process of a variable of the electrical system requires large amounts of computational memory and high processing times due to the large number of equations and variables that exists in the modeling of the electrical power system [11]. Therefore, current research are now focus in the implementation of meta heuristic or evolutionary algorithms (EA), also methods such as Strategic Evolution (SE), Genetic Programming (GP), Genetic Algorithms (GA) and Evolutionary Programming (EP) can be used as well [12].

In the second section of the article, the concept of virtual power plant is explained. Section three discourses the mathematical model for optimal power dispatch in an EPS which integrates a virtual power plant using dynamic power flows. The four part integrates an analysis of the results obtained and finally, in the last section the conclusions of the current paper are showed.

2   Virtual Power Plant (VPP)

A virtual power plant is a set of elements that can be made up of conventional and non-conventional renewable generation sources (wind or solar), energy storage systems, controlled loads, communications system, management system (EMS) and system control, in order to carry out the economic energy dispatch on the electricity market compared to large conventional generation plants (hydroelectric, thermoelectric, gas) [13,14].

A virtual power plant must ensure the delivery of the right amount of power, for this reason it can be included a hydroelectric or thermal generation plants depending on the minimum dispatch capacity of the virtual power plant, thus the penalty by the electricity market regulator entity will be avoided [15,16]. Additionally, the inclusion of these conventional renewable energy sources allows the virtual power plant to have adaptability to face off stability problems that can occur in an electrical power system [17,18]. It is important mentioning that [19] perform a complete analysis of the energy dispatch in a virtual power plant taking into account two stages. The first one considers the electricity market restrictions and the second one reflects the topology and characteristics of operation of both the EPS and virtual power plant. Furthermore, it has to be considered that priority is given to the dispatch of energy by a virtual power plant because it is made up of non-conventional renewable energy sources, despite the high costs it represents in the electricity market [20,21].

In the model applied to a VPP it is important considered factors, such as energy producers, consumers and flexible consumers; because these ones have communication and control systems that allow shifting the electric power requirement to suitable periods of time for the operation of the VPP, without affecting the essential activities of the consumers or clients associated with this model. In [22,23] the optimal operation point of a virtual power plant is analyzed based on two facts, the benefits for investors and the technical conditions of the electric power system.

2.1   Economic Dispatch

The schedule for an energy dispatch along EPS must be carried out in a reasonable way for a specific period or moment of time, considering possible demand scenarios, economic and technical criteria, ensuring a safe and reliable electrical system [24]. The main aim in the problem of economic dispatch is to reduce generation costs, considering restrictions of the EPS, such as system topology, maximum and minimum limits, electrical elements and equipment features. Optimal values are calculated for independent or control variables (Active and reactive power in PV node, transformer tap, etc.). According with the results obtained, there are values in the state variables (magnitude and angle of the voltage at bars, reactive power generation, transmission line loads, etc.), thus the solution set of the optimization problem would indicate the stable and reliable operation of the EPS [25].

About the problem of economic dispatch, the literature classifies it into two segments; the first one is considered a static economic dispatch with a constant demand and defined restrictions. The second one defines the demand and some variable restrictions in certain periods of time, taking into account different types of operation, thus determining that minimum generation costs in both cases [26,27]. In [28] the virtual power plant is considered as a conventional power plant and the economic dispatch is carried out using the linear programming method. In [1] the energy dispatch of a virtual power plant is showed within a Smart Grid. In [12] the energy dispatch is carried out considering the demand variation and restriction of energy resources.

The algorithm presented in this paper allows obtaining information about line chargeability, voltage magnitude and angle in bars, active and reactive power dispatch. It has been considered 24 scenarios in which the energy demand is variable, conventional restrictions for synchronous machines, adjustable maximum limits on the virtual power plant and a continuous lower limit considering the contract that a virtual power plant must fulfill within the electricity market. In addition, the analysis ensures the total demand supply and compliance of technical restrictions along the network.

3   Problem Statement

This document presents an analysis of the energy economic dispatch in time intervals. By adding time constraints and due to the dynamic behavior of non-conventional renewable energy sources; the optimal power flow is converted into an optimal dynamic power flow (ODPF). These considerations end into a more complex problem that involves both the time variable and the network restrictions; therefore, method used for the implementation of the system is essential to obtain a solution that represents reliable operating conditions of the electrical system.

In [29,30] shows the measure of optimal dynamic stochastic power flow (DSOPF), in order to achieve an optimal power flows and consequently operate electrical energy networks that integrate non-conventional renewable energy sources.

The model selected to carry out the dispatch considers particular restrictions of the power electrical system, restrictions associated with elements and equipment, restrictions of maximum limits and minimum variables of non-conventional renewable electricity generation.

The optimal dispatch of energy allows obtaining active generation results that represent normal operating conditions for the EPS, depending on the availability of energy resource and the restrictions of the scenario, which is analyzed at that time, thus suppling the demand at a minimum cost [29,30].

To solve the dynamic dispatch of generation using a virtual power plant, the renewable resource available from wind and solar energy has to be integrated as a set in order to with the power system, where the conventional generators maintain their characteristics and restrictions [31,32].

3.1 Dynamic Optimal Dispatch Model Based on FOPAC

There are several solution models for economic dispatch, however for this solution method is based on the mathematical equations that represent the general AC power flow. Also is important to mention that an economic dispatch is developed in several periods of time considering the randomness and restrictions of the variables associated with the solution. The main component of the optimization problem is the objective function, which is displayed in Eq. (1):

$$OF = \sum_{i,t} b_g P_{i,t}^g + \sum_{i,t} BP_{i,t}^{sol+eol} \tag{1}$$

The objective function is subject to mathematical modeling of the AC power flow: power balance among generation, load and transmission (2) and (3), current flow along transmission elements (4), total power generated (5), active and reactive power at each node (6) and (7). All variables mentioned above are quantities that can change in order to balance the relation among generation, demand and losses [33].

$$P_{i,t}^g + P_{i,t}^{sol+eol} - P_{i,t}^L = \sum_{j \in \Omega_i^i} P_{ij,t} : \lambda_{i,t}^p \tag{2}$$

$$Q_{i,t}^g + Q_{i,t}^{sol+eol} - Q_{i,t}^L = \sum_{j \in \Omega_i^i} Q_{ij,t} : \lambda_{i,t}^q \tag{3}$$

$$I_{ij,t} = \frac{V_{i,t}\angle\delta_{i,t} - V_{j,t}\angle\delta_{j,t}}{Z_{ij}\angle\theta_{ij}} + \frac{bV_{i,t}}{2}\angle(\delta_{i,t} + \frac{\pi}{2}) \tag{4}$$

$$S_{ij,t} = (V_{i,t}\angle\delta_{i,t})I_{ij,t}^* \tag{5}$$

$$P_{ij,t} = \frac{V_{i,t}^2}{Z_{ij}}\cos(\theta_{ij}) - \frac{V_{i,t}V_{j,t}}{Z_{ij}}\cos(\delta_{i,t} - \delta_{j,t} + \theta_{ij}) \tag{6}$$

$$Q_{ij,t} = \frac{V_{i,t}^2}{Z_{ij}}\sin(\theta_{ij}) - \frac{V_{i,t}V_{j,t}}{Z_{ij}}\sin(\delta_{i,t} - \delta_{j,t} + \theta_{ij}) - \frac{bV_{i,t}^2}{2} \tag{7}$$

In the equation presented below, it can been seen variables restrictions, such as: active power (8), reactive power (9) and maximum limit of active power transmitted end to end lines (10).

$$P_i^{g,min} \le P_{i,t}^g \le P_i^{g,max} \tag{8}$$

$$Q_i^{g,min} \le Q_{i,t}^g \le Q_i^{g,max} \tag{9}$$

$$P_{ij}^{\min} \leq P_{ij,t} \leq P_{ij}^{\max} \tag{10}$$

The Algorithm 1 shows the methodology used to carry out the economic dispatch in an electrical power system that includes a virtual power plant using dynamic power flows, based on nonlinear programming.

Algorithm 1. Economical energy dispatch based on dynamic power flows

---

Step: 1 **Input data**

Electrical elements and equipment parameters to build the network topology
Z_{ij}, $P_{i,t}^L$, $Q_{i,t}^L$, $P_i^{g,max/min}$, $Q_i^{g,max/min}$, $P_{ij}^{g,max/min}$, b_g, B

Step: 2 **VPP**

$VPP = \sum_{i,t} P_{i,t}^{sol+eol}$

s.t.:

$P_{i,t}^{sol+eol,min} \leq P_{i,t}^{VPP} \leq P_{i,t}^{sol+eol,max}$

Step: 3 **Economic dispatch**

O.F.:

$OF = \sum_{i,t} b_g P_{i,t}^g + \sum_{i,t} B P_{i,t}^{sol+eol}$

s.t.:

$P_{i,t}^g + P_{i,t}^{sol+eol} - P_{i,t}^L = \sum_{j \in \Omega_i^i} P_{ij,t} : \lambda_{i,t}^p$

$Q_{i,t}^g + Q_{i,t}^{sol+eol} - Q_{i,t}^L = \sum_{j \in \Omega_i^i} Q_{ij,t} : \lambda_{i,t}^q$

$I_{ij,t} = \frac{V_{i,t}\angle\delta_{i,t} - V_{j,t}\angle\delta_{j,t}}{Z_{ij}\angle\theta_{ij}} + \frac{bV_{i,t}}{2}\angle(\delta_{i,t} + \frac{\pi}{2})$

$S_{ij,t} = (V_{i,t}\angle\delta_{i,t})I_{ij,t}^*$

$P_{ij,t} = \frac{V_{i,t}^2}{Z_{ij}}\cos(\theta_{ij}) - \frac{V_{i,t}V_{j,t}}{Z_{ij}}\cos(\delta_{i,t} - \delta_{j,t} + \theta_{ij})$

$Q_{ij,t} = \frac{V_{i,t}^2}{Z_{ij}}\sin(\theta_{ij}) - \frac{V_{i,t}V_{j,t}}{Z_{ij}}\sin(\delta_{i,t} - \delta_{j,t} + \theta_{ij}) - \frac{bV_{i,t}^2}{2}$

$P_i^{g,min} \leq P_{i,t}^g \leq P_i^{g,max}$

$Q_i^{g,min} \leq Q_{i,t}^g \leq Q_i^{g,max}$

$P_{ij}^{\min} \leq P_{ij,t} \leq P_{ij}^{\max}$

Step: 4 **Report optimization results by period**

$V_{i,t}$, $\delta_{i,t}$, $P_{i,t}^g$, P_{ij}, $Q_{i,t}^g$, Q_{ij},

---

where,

OF	Objective Function
b_g	Generation cost coefficient of unit g
$P_{i,t}^g$	Available active power of the generator g on bus i at time t
B	Cost coefficient of the Virtual Power Plant
$P_{i,t}^{sol+eol}$	Active power available from VPP on bar i at time t
$P_{i,t}^L$	Variable active load on bar i at time t
$P_{ij,t}$	Active power flow on transmission line which connecting bus i with bus j at time t

$Q_{i,t}^g$ Generator reactive power g on bus i at time t

$Q_{i,t}^L$ Variable reactive load on bar i at time t

$Q_{ij,t}$ Active power flow on transmission line which connecting bus i with bus j at time t

$I_{ij,t}$ Current flow on the element that connects bar i with bar j at time t

$V_{i,t}$ Voltage magnitude across bar i at time t

$\delta_{i,t}$ Voltage angle across bar i at time t

Z_{ij} Element impedance which connecting bar i with bar j

b Branch susceptance which connecting the bar y with the bar j

$S_{ij,t}$ Apparent power on transmission element that connects bar i with bar j at time t

$P_i^{g,max/min}$ Maximum/minimum power generation limit of unit g at time t.

4 Analysis of Results

The algorithm was developed in the MATLAB software R2018b, which is linked with GAMS software often used for solving optimization models. MATLAB allows handling input parameters and data for modeling of problems; while GAMS executes the model solution, storing input data and optimization results. The simulations are developed on a computer with an Intel (R) Core (TM) i7-4700MQ CPU @ 2.40 GHz, 8 GB of RAM and Windows 8. NLP solver is used for each period in GAMS.

4.1 Study Case

In order to observe the behavior of the algorithm used to obtain the economical dispatch of energy in a EPS that integrates a virtual power plant; some simulations are carried out with the data corresponding to IEEE 9-bar electrical system considering the data in Table 1 and thus the dispatch results obtained are examined as valid operating conditions.

Table 1. Generators and VPP data

Gen.	Bar (i)	c[$/MWh]	Pmax [MW]	Pmin [MW]
G1	1	11	200	5
G2	2	12	165	5
G3	3	10	85	5
VPP	5	9	20	0

Optimal dynamic power flows have been performed with and without the integration of the VPP in bar 5. The inclusion of VPP at bar 5 is used due to the fact that its voltages results in the AC optimal flow simulations produce the minimum value compared to the other bars of the power system. The active and reactive power demand of the system is variable on the particular bars in the 24 periods analyzed. In addition, due to the availability of the non-conventional renewable energy resource is dynamic, the virtual power plant has different active power capacity to deliver to the EPS in each period.

Figure 1 shows the results of angle variation of each generator considering the scenarios already mentioned previously, taking into account the generator of bar 1 as oscillating.

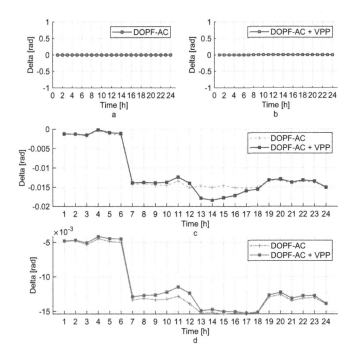

Fig. 1. Result of system angles. (a) and (b) Bar 1, (c) Bar 2, (d) Bar 3

According with the data obtained, it is evident that its value remain without any changes; however, the angles corresponding to the remaining synchronous machines decrease their value in each active power dispatch period for the interval between 7:00 and 18:00. For this case, the virtual power plant delivers the maximum amount of active power available, due to the stochastic nature of non-conventional renewable energy sources.

Also, some changes are detected at the bus associated with generator 2, which has the highest generation cost, mainly because at the interval in which the VPP delivers less power to the electrical system, there is variation in the value of the angle in generator 3, despite that it always delivers 85 MW in both cases. This result is due to the fact that state variables, such as the angles at the bars, not only depend on the generation at bar 3, since this result is associated with all the variables and equations that conform the mathematical method in the model of the electric power system.

Figure 2 shows the results of voltages at the bars of the IEEE 9 bar electrical system. It presents a simulation of the inclusion of a virtual power plant at bar 5 because the resulting voltage values at this bar, in comparison with the others ones, were the minimums values obtained along the electrical system, and thus improve the value of the voltage for each period.

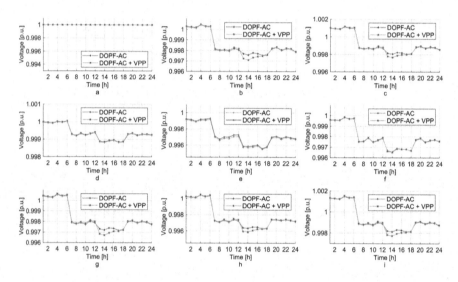

Fig. 2. Voltage results. (a) Node 1, (b) Node 2, (c) Node 3, (d) Node 4, (e) Node 5, (f) Node 6, (g) Node 7, (h) Node 8, (i) Node 9

As it was expected, bar 1 related with the slack generator maintains its value at 1 p.u. for each period analyzed in both scenarios. For the analysis of the remaining results, it will be developed in pairs since the bars are associated with a power transformer in each generation machine. At bars 3 and 9, a decrease in the voltage values is detected in the period between 1:00 p.m. and 4:00 p.m. For this specific case, the virtual power plant delivers the greatest amount of active generation power; therefore, the power transfer is modified in the transmission system, which changes the results obtained.

A similar situation exist at bars 2 and 7. In bar 4 there are no variations because it is connected to the transformer of the oscillating machine. In bars 6 and 8 that are associated with the EPS loads, the inclusion of VPP affects the bar that is feeding the highest load in the period analyzed. In bar 5, for each period analyzed, the voltage levels improve lightly despite the fact that this bar is connected with the highest load in the system.

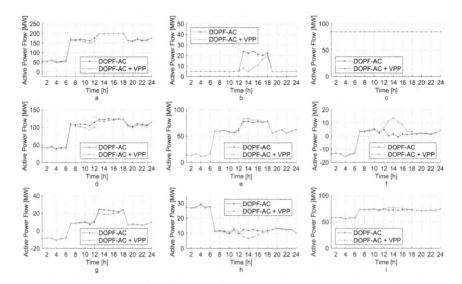

Fig. 3. Result of active power transfer along transmission lines and power transformers. (a) Trf 1-4, (b) Trf 2-7, (c) Trf 3-9, (d) LT 4-5, (e) LT 4-6, (f) LT 5-7, (g) LT 7-8, (h) LT 9-6, (i) LT 9-8

Figure 3 analyze the results of the active power with transmission elements and power transformers. The transformer associated with generator 1 has an average generation cost and its maximum and minimum power limits are adequate; also, it delivers most of the required active power to the system. For the interval between 8:00 a.m. and 12:00 p.m., due to the conditions and restrictions of the problems, it stops to deliver, to the electricity system, a minimum little quantity of active generation, approximately between 1 to 3 MW in each period.

For the transformer associated with generator 2, which has the highest generation cost, the active power flow through this electrical element, in most of the periods, is at a value of 5 MW; mainly, because this is the minimum restriction of active power associated with generator 2. In the period between 12:00 and 18:00, in which the load increases, this generator delivers the greater amount of active power to meet demand. In this same period with the inclusion of the virtual power plant, the transformer 2-7 transmits less power since the VPP assumes the increasing demand in the electrical power system due to its low production cost.

For the transformer associated with generator 3, the active power values transferred by this element do not change because the generation cost is the lowest after the generation cost of the VPP and it satisfies the solution for power flows. The results related with transmission lines 4–5, 5–7 and 7–8, have a greater influence over the income of the virtual power plant. For this scenario, the transfer of active power increases or decreases due to these elements; thus, the transmission line 5-7 is the one that has remarkable changes due to the fact that it is associated with the greater load of the electrical power system.

Likewise, for the remaining elements such as: transmission lines 4-6, 6-9 and 9-8, there are negligible changes in the active power flow, for a time interval between 12h00 to 16h00. This is a consequence that the additional generation source generates 19 MW, which is mostly consumed in bus 5; the rest of the active power is distributed to the electrical power system through different transmission lines to supply the load and at the same time satisfy the equations using for the mathematical model of AC power flow.

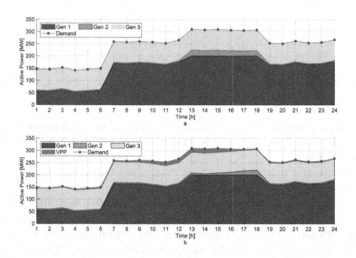

Fig. 4. Active Power Dispatch; (a) without PPV (b) with PPV

Figure 4 shows the effect of active power dispatch in generators with and without the integration of the virtual power plant. In both scenarios, the generation supplies the demand of the electric power system; consequently, the algorithm fulfills the objective of delivering results that represent effective operating conditions. Most of the active generation delivered by the virtual power plant is located between 9:00 a.m. and 5:00 p.m.; in the opposite hand, in the remaining periods the VPP delivers its minimum generation capacity restricted by the random and stochastic conditions of the non-conventional renewable energy sources used, such as solar and wind energy.

Keeping generation costs constant for a scenario without using a virtual power plant, there is a minimum value of demand for active power of 141 MW at 4h00; in which machine 2, with the maximum generation cost, delivers to the system only 5 MW which is the lower generation limit. Generator 3, with the lowest generation cost, delivers its maximum power of 85 MW due to the restriction values; meanwhile, machine 3 delivers the remaining power value to meet the supply of demand which is 51.1217 MW. Additionally the losses of the electrical power system, therefore the total active power that must be supplied in the IEEE 9 bus system for this case is 141.1217 MW.

According with previous consideration, the results achieved with the inclusion of VPP, in the period of 4:00 am are as follows. First, the values specified in machines 2 and 3 are preserved without the integration of VPP, because its minimum and maximum generation restrictions and the generation cost, both remain constant results. Second, the remaining load to feed the system would be 51 MW plus losses associated with this power dispatch schedule, for this the virtual power plant assumes approximately 3.2 MW, which is the maximum of its capacity at that moment, thus machine 1 dispatches 47.9197 MW to supply the total demand plus the associated losses.

Regarding with the information presented above, it is evident that the generation of active power in machine 1 changes, thus adapting itself to the insertion of the VPP. Additionally, the losses reduce along EPS, and exist a higher value of the total cost of generation without the integration of the VPP which is $ 1472.3, while the cost with VPP is $ 1465.9; therefore, there is a saving of $ 6 approximately.

At 2:00 p.m. is the time in which the VPP delivers its highest active power capacity to the system and there is a high demand for electrical energy. For this scenario without considering a VPP, the data is the same of Table 1. The cheapest machine is 3, so it delivers its maximum active power equal to 85 MW to the electrical system according to its maximum limits. Machine 2, according to its generation costs and its maximum generation power, it delivers 200 MW to the system. Therefore, generator 3 supplies to EPS the necessary active power in order to cover the remaining demand and losses; despite its high generation cost, it delivers 22,3115 MW.

For the analysis with the integration of the virtual generation plant exist equal conditions in the restrictions of elements and equipment as the previous scenario, so generator 3 is cheaper after the VPP, and it continues to deliver its maximum capacity to the system electricity, which is 85 MW. Due to the fact that generator 2 has the highest cost, now it delivers its minimum power, which is 5 MW. Finally, generator 1 delivers an active power of 199.0229 MW to the electrical system, while the VPP now assumes the remaining power to supply the demand including the losses associated with the active power dispatch schedule.

According with the previous results, it can be seen that only the active power generation, in machine 1, changes adapting according to the contribution of the VPP. Additionally, despite the fact that the losses increase, they are not relevant compared to the dispatch values that exist in the machines. There is a highest value of the total generation cost without the integration of the VPP which is $ 3317.7, while the cost with VPP is $ 3264, therefore there is an approximate saving of $ 53.7. The active power losses differ by 0.0114 MW, mainly because the current flow along ESP is not the same since generators have different active power values.

5   Conclusions

The results achieved show the efficiency and strength of the proposed methodology. It may allow the operator of a EPS to plan the dispatch of energy considering the use of non-conventional renewable energies in certain periods of the day, taking into account the structure and features of the EPS, allowing the reliable operation of EPS in scenarios of maximum or minimum demand.

The economic dispatch of energy using an optimal dynamic power flow considering the insertion of non-conventional renewable energies (wind and solar) based on the proposed methodology, allows the evaluation of results and restrictions that contribute in the formulation and solution of this problem. This provides a clear idea of the behavior of the active generation power compared with some simulation scenarios that reproduces the uncertain presence of the energy sources considered. All this process guarantees an economic dispatch that represents an operational and economical solution for the power electrical system.

The set of electrical elements and equipment known as virtual power plant (VPP), has the capability to join to the speculative and dynamic essence of non-conventional renewable energy sources. Due to the variability of energy demand and supply, the virtual power plant should be considered as a secondary type of generator, in the planning of the dispatch of active power. Thus, VPP can be integrated to participate in the electricity market in a competitive and efficient way depending on the requirements and conditions that requires EPS in a certain period of the day or throughout the day.

The proposed methodology shows a consistent and powerful behavior when considering several simulation scenarios with different demands and energy availability. This allows obtaining and analyzing results the whole day, noticing that do not exits convergence problems in the solution and the results are according with established ranges of normal operation of an EPS. Therefore, from technical point of view, it can assistance to the operator to find a perfect balance between demand and generation, especially in periods when the use of the virtual power plant is required.

References

1. Narkhede, M.S., Chatterji, S., Ghosh, S.: Optimal dispatch of renewable energy sources in smart grid pertinent to virtual power plant. In: Proceedings of the 2013 International Conference on Green Computing, Communication and Conservation of Energy, ICGCE 2013, Chennai, pp. 525–529. IEEE (2013)
2. Pandžić, H., Kuzle, I., Capuder, T.: Virtual power plant mid-term dispatch optimization. Appl. Energy **101**, 134–41 (2013)
3. Candra, D.I., Hartmann, K., Nelles, M.: Economic optimal implementation of virtual power plants in the German power market. Energies **11**(9), 2365 (2018)
4. Monoh, J.A., Ei-Hawary, M.E., Adapa, R.: A review of selected optimal power flow literature to 1993 Part II: newton, linear programming and interior point methods. IEEE Trans. Power Syst. **14**(1), 105–11 (1999)

5. Carrión, D., Palacios, J., Espinel, M., González, J.W.: Transmission expansion planning considering grid topology changes and N-1 contingencies criteria. In: Botto Tobar, M., Cruz, H., Díaz Cadena, A. (eds.) CIT 2020. LNEE, vol. 762, pp. 266–279. Springer, Cham (2021). https://doi.org/10.1007/978-3-030-72208-1_20
6. Quinteros, F., Carrión, D., Jaramillo, M.: Optimal power systems restoration based on energy quality and stability criteria. Energies **15**(6), 2062 (2022)
7. Masache, P., Carrión, D., Cárdenas, J.: Optimal transmission line switching to improve the reliability of the power system considering AC power flows. Energies **14**(11), 3281 (2021)
8. Chen, H., Chen, J., Duan, X.: Multi-stage dynamic optimal power flow in wind power integrated system. In: Proceedings of IEEE Power Engineering Society Transmission and Distribution Conference, 2005, pp. 1–5 (2005)
9. Chen, H., Chen, J., Duan, X.: Multi-stage dynamic optimal power flow in wind power integrated system. In: Proceedings of the IEEE Power Engineering Society Transmission and Distribution Conference 2005, pp. 1–5 (2005)
10. Xie, K., Song, Y.H.: Dynamic optimal power flow by interior point methods. IEE Proc. Gener. Transm. Distrib. **148**(1), 76–83 (2001)
11. Xie, J., Cao, C.: Non-convex economic dispatch of a virtual power plant via a distributed randomized gradient-free algorithm. Energies **10**(7), 1051 (2017)
12. Petersen, M.K., Hansen, L.H., Bendtsen, J., Edlund, K., Stoustrup, J.: Heuristic optimization for the discrete virtual power plant dispatch problem. IEEE Trans. Smart Grid **5**(6), 2910–2918 (2014)
13. Adu-Kankam, K.O., Camarinha-Matos, L.M.: Towards collaborative virtual power plants: trends and convergence. Sustain. Energy Grids Netw. **16**, 217–230 (2018)
14. Lemus, A., Carrión, D., Aguire, E., González, J.W.: Location of distributed resources in rural-urban marginal power grids considering the voltage collapse prediction index. Ingenius **28**, 25–33 (2022)
15. Zhou, B., Liu, X., Cao, Y., Li, C., Chung, C.Y., Chan, K.W.: Optimal scheduling of virtual power plant with battery degradation cost. IET Gener. Transm. Distrib. **10**(3), 712–725 (2016)
16. Tan, Z., et al.: Dispatching optimization model of gas-electricity virtual power plant considering uncertainty based on robust stochastic optimization theory. J. Clean. Prod. **247**, 119106 (2020)
17. Peikherfeh, M., Seifi, H., Sheikh-El-Eslami, M.K.: Optimal dispatch of distributed energy resources included in a virtual power plant for participating in a day-ahead market. In: 3rd International Conference on Clean Electrical Power: Renewable Energy Resources Impact, ICCEP 2011, pp. 204–210 (2011)
18. Narkhede, M.S., Chatterji, S., Ghosh, S.: Multi objective optimal dispatch in a virtual power plant using genetic algorithm. In: Proceedings - 2013 International Conference on Renewable Energy and Sustainable Energy, ICRESE 2013, pp. 238–242 (2014)
19. Gao, R., et al.: A two-stage dispatch mechanism for virtual power plant utilizing the CVaR theory in the electricity spot market. Energies **12**(17), 3402 (2019)
20. Toma, L., Otomega, B., Tristiu, I.: Market strategy of distributed generation through the virtual power plant concept. In: Proceedings of the International Conference on Optimisation of Electrical and Electronic Equipment, OPTIM, pp. 81–88 (2012)
21. Mosquera, F.: Localización óptima de plantas virtuales de generación en sistemas eléctricos de potencia basados en flujos óptimos de potencia. I+D Tecnológico **16**(2) (2020)

22. Wang, J., Yang, W., Cheng, H., Huang, L., Gao, Y.: The optimal configuration scheme of the virtual power plant considering benefits and risks of investors. Energies **10**(7), 968 (2017)
23. Yusta, J.M., Naval, N., Raul, S.: A virtual power plant optimal dispatch model with large and small- scale distributed renewable generation. Renew. Energy **151**, 57–69 (2019)
24. Yang, Y., Wei, B., Qin, Z.: Sequence-based differential evolution for solving economic dispatch considering virtual power plant. IET Gener. Transm. Distrib. **13**(15), 3202–3215 (2019)
25. Abdi, H., Beigvand, S.D., Scala, M.L.: A review of optimal power flow studies applied to smart grids and microgrids. Renew. Sustain. Energy Rev. **71**, 742–766 (2017)
26. Santillan-Lemus, F.D., Minor-Popocatl, H., Aguilar-Mejia, O., Tapia-Olvera, R.: Optimal economic dispatch in microgrids with renewable energy sources. Energies **12**(1), 181 (2019)
27. Soares, J., Pinto, T., Sousa, F., Borges, N., Vale, Z., Michiorri, A.: Scalable computational framework using intelligent optimization: microgrids dispatch and electricity market joint simulation. IFAC- PapersOnLine **50**(1), 3362–3367 (2017)
28. Kuzle, I., Zdrilic, M., Pandžić, H.: Virtual power plant dispatch optimization using linear programming. In: 2011 10th International Conference on Environment and Electrical Engineering, EEEIC.EU 2011 - Conference Proceedings, pp. 1–4 (2011)
29. Liang, J., Molina, D.D., Venayagamoorthy, G.K., Harley, R.G.: Two-level dynamic stochastic optimal power flow control for power systems with intermittent renewable generation. IEEE Trans. Power Syst. **28**(3), 2670–2678 (2013)
30. Liang, J., Venayagamoorthy, G.K., Harley, R.G.: Wide-area measurement based dynamic stochastic optimal power flow control for smart grids with high variability and uncertainty. IEEE Trans. Smart Grid **3**(1), 59–69 (2012)
31. Liu, Z., et al.: Optimal dispatch of a virtual power plant considering demand response and carbon trading. Energies **11**(6), 121693718 (2018)
32. Elgamal, A.H., Kocher-Oberlehner, G., Robu, V., Andoni, M.: Optimization of a multiple-scale renewable energy-based virtual power plant in the UK. Appl. Energy **256**, 113973 (2019)
33. Petersen, M., Bendtsen, J., Stoustrup, J.: Optimal dispatch strategy for the agile virtual power plant. In: Proceedings of the American Control Conference, pp. 288–294 (2012)

Routing Protocols Implementation for WSN Using Optimal Dimensioning

Jordi Castel(ID) and Juan Inga$^{(\boxtimes)}$(ID)

Universidad Politecnica Salesiana, Cuenca, Ecuador
jcastel@est.ups.edu.ec,
jinga@ups.edu.ec
https://ups.edu.ec/

Abstract. In a wireless sensor network (WSN), achieving efficient transmission in terms of energy consumption while guaranteeing low packet loss with the highest data transmission rate requires adequate processing in the analysis and calculation of the best routes to send the information from a source node to the data aggregation point.

On the other hand, the optimal sizing of a network seeks that the physical resources of the technologies used in wireless sensor networks can not only reduce implementation costs by considering, for example, capacity and coverage constraints but also seeks to ensure the connectivity of the nodes and the correct operation of the network.

Thus, this work aims to show through practical implementation, that the optimal planning and deployment of a wireless sensor network influence the routing protocols in this type of network since the correct location of the data concentrator nodes would allow optimizing the links between nodes so that the latency and packet loss rate is reduced. Routing algorithms such as LEACH and PEGASIS are considered as well as the implementation of routing based on the solution of the minimum spanning tree optimization problem using Dijkstra or PRIM. The implementation and evaluation are applied with ZigBee which allows the deployment of multiple network topologies for WSNs in a fast and flexible way.

Keywords: Optimization · Routing · Wireless Sensor Network · ZigBee

1 Introduction

Wireless sensor networks (WSN), due to their low cost and versatility in different application scenarios, have been the subject of interest in research and implementation for Internet of Things (IoT) deployment [1,2]. Furthermore, there is a wide range of technology related to WSNs where the development of heterogeneous technological solutions and interoperability between these technologies are important challenges. Thus, in the implementation of these networks, it is usually

F. R. Narváez et al. (Eds.): SmartTech-IC 2022, CCIS 1705, pp. 509–526, 2023.
https://doi.org/10.1007/978-3-031-32213-6_37

necessary to use gateways or gateways (called gateways) that allow interoperability between heterogeneous communication standards allowing an abstraction between hardware and user application layers [3]. In this way, information from any node in a WSN needs to be able to scale to Internet services. This interplay between layers allows things to connect to the Internet and is the basis of the IoT foundation. For example, [4] proposes a WSN that enables multi-hop through a hierarchical topology taking advantage of multi hops so that the information travels from a sensor node to a node considered as a data aggregation point (DAP) or also called "concentrator" of the network is very important in applications with these topologies identifying which is the origin node of the information.

IoT applications are diverse with various requirements, e.g., range distance, data rate, security level, power demand, latency, and reliability level. Thus, in WSNs, routing is a very challenging problem and of direct concern, because several issues or parameters must be considered to perform an efficient transmission reducing energy consumption and processing by the network nodes for the calculation of the best routes to route the information [5].

On the other hand, each technology has its key and unique features such as connectivity, coverage area, radio technology, channel capacity, power consumption, security, mobility, reliability, and latency. Thus, a real challenge is the successful coexistence of all available technologies. However, evaluating routing protocols for WSNs combined with optimal network sizing can ensure proper use of network resources and improve application characteristics in terms of cost and energy by guaranteeing minimum user coverage and allowing scalable and sustainable planning of the same over time [6–8]. Then, routing and dimensioning are shown to have a close relationship, therefore the objective of the present work is to analyze the effect of optimal sizing on latency metrics and packet loss rate of LEACH, PEGASIS, Dijkstra, and PRIM routing protocols implemented in a fixed WSN with ZigBee technology for example for Smart Grids. In the proposed scenario, packet transmission is performed with the data obtained from the smart metering system and evaluated with a WSN without sizing criteria and another one applying mathematical modeling of capacity and coverage. Finally, it should be noted that the technology to be used in the WSN network evaluated in this work is ZigBee because it allows the use of personal area network (PAN) routers and, since it is supported by the IEEE 802.15.4 standard, the working frequency corresponds to the industrial, scientific and medical (ISM) radio band, so the use of the radio electric spectrum is free.

In addition, it is a technology that presents a low-cost solution for energy savings that includes collision avoidance as it uses *spread spectrum* to avoid interference from data transmission in similar bands [7, 9, 10] and allows the use of various network topologies.

The paper is organized as follows: Sect. 2 presents a brief analysis related to WSN routing, as well as the mathematical formulation for the implemented optimization. Section 3 describes the methodology of the WSN implementation evaluated with ZigBee technology. The results are presented in Sect. 4 and finally, the conclusions are presented in Sect. 5.

2 Wireless Sensor Networks

To form a WSN, the nodes are distributed in a region to remotely transmit the data collected by a wireless medium [11], this distribution is specific according to the application of the network, allowing them to use different technologies and standards based on their application [11].

Among the most relevant characteristics of WSNs are the density of nodes deployed in the monitoring area, the flexibility to topology changes due to the loss of connectivity of the nodes [12]. Moreover, in the case of a large network, it is complicated to implement a global addressing scheme involving all nodes as it greatly increases the possibility of an overhead of maintaining the identification of each node [5,13–15].

On the other hand, routing protocols have the function of transmitting packets after establishing the most optimal routes for data delivery from a source node to the destination node, which will be the data concentrator. For this, in the context of WSN, the need to ensure energy efficiency [14,16,17], and in turn maintain communication between nodes even if some routes are disabled [16], takes more weight. In addition, the large number of sensor nodes that make up the network influences the routing problem [15].

As WSNs are a large network, it is not possible to perform a global addressing scheme involving all nodes as it would generate an overhead of maintaining the identification of each node [13,14]. Then, different algorithms have been developed that attempt to solve the routing problem [13,14]. For network resource management, especially node energy, routing protocols employ some techniques used in other types of networks and others designed only for this particular type [5,13,15].

2.1 Dimensioning for WSN

The purpose of sizing a WSN is to optimize resources and in this sense, we propose to optimize the number of candidate sites for the DAP location with the capacity and coverage restrictions [3,18]. In addition, to determine the influence of the network dimensioning on the operation of the routing protocols, the study of two scenarios is proposed, the first one considering deployment of the WSN nodes in locations considered for convenience, and the second one with the deployment of the WSN with the coordinator in a given location resulting from an optimization applied according to the aforementioned. Thus, 10 nodes were considered for the network design, of which one would be the coordinator of the ZigBee network and therefore would be considered the DAP node. The rest of the nodes will have the function of routers to be able to route the packet traffic according to the routing protocol implemented in the network.

Candidate sites are considered active sites if the DAP node is installed in that location and each DAP node works as a gateway. Within the network diagram, each coordinator has a capacity of sensor nodes connected in unison, after testing it was determined that this capacity is three nodes operating simultaneously and is denoted by the variable C. From the above details, the optimization problem aims to find the minimum number of active sites such that at least a percentage P of the sensors is covered. For this, it is necessary to define a set of M possible locations or candidate sites named $S = \{S_1, S_2, S_3, ..., S_M\}$ where the $i-th$ position is given by (xs_i, ys_i); and a set of N sensor nodes as $D = \{D_1, D_2, D_3, ..., D_M\}$ where the $j-th$ position is given by (xd_j, yd_j).

We define that a sensor node is covered if it is at a distance R from at least one coordinator. Haversine distance is used because a way that the curvature of the Earth between the georeferenced points [3] is considered. In addition, the quantity $\alpha_{j,i} \in \{0, 1\}$ is defined, which indicates that if sensor i has connection with coordinator j, then the value is 1; otherwise, the value is 0. Thus, for each candidate site, we define the quantity $Z_j \in \{0, 1\}$ which implies that the value is 1 when candidate site j is an active site. Similarly, for each sensor node d_i the quantity $Y_i \in \{0, 1\}$ is defined when the value is 1 the sensor node is covered by at least one candidate site. The optimization model for dimensioning is presented below [3]:

Objective Function:

$$min \sum_{j=1}^{M} Z_j, \tag{1}$$

Subject to:

$$Y_i = \sum_{j=1}^{M} X_{j,i}; \qquad \forall i \in D; \tag{2}$$

$$\sum_{i=1}^{N} X_{j,i} \leq C \cdot Z_j; \qquad \forall j \in S; \tag{3}$$

$$\sum_{i=1}^{N} Y_i \geq N \cdot P; \qquad \forall i \in D; \tag{4}$$

$$X_{j,i} \leq \alpha_{j,i} \cdot Z_j; \qquad \forall j \in S; \forall i \in D; \tag{5}$$

The presented model solves a linear optimization solution, mixed integer linear programming (MILP) is used to solve the optimization and in this sense, the tool used is LPSolve since it is a free software tool. It is worth mentioning that, in the case that the number of nodes could be very large, the sizing problem would become a combinatorial problem and in this case, it is recommended the division by zones to solve smaller sizing problems or even the use of a heuristic if the scenario becomes very large [19].

It is important to clarify that optimal sizing of networks seeks to ensure the characteristics of the physical layer of the technologies used in WSN so that the operation of the network is guaranteed under the extreme conditions that the designer considers for its network in response to each possible scenario. In this sense, optimal dimensioning allows identifying the appropriate number of concentrator nodes of a possible set of solutions.

3   ZigBee-Based WSN Implementation

For this work, considering the analyses presented in [3,18] and [20], an adequate number of nodes was chosen for the implementation so that the work of the different types of routing can be evaluated and to assess how at least a small resource optimization can improve the network operation. Therefore, the scenario to be optimized is framed in the conditions to be solved by MILP to obtain a fast solution. That is, two scenarios are studied: the first one considers the deployment of the WSN nodes in locations considered for "convenience", and the second one with the deployment of the WSN with the coordinator in a location determined from the mathematical models of capacity and coverage [3]. In both scenarios, the LEACH, PEGASIS, Dijkstra, and PRIM routing protocols are analyzed. The metrics analyzed are latency and packet loss.

Regarding the intelligence for the calculation and use of routing algorithms, each node has its microcontroller to which a ZigBee module is connected via UART for communication with the network. Table 1 summarizes the main characteristics of the microcontroller boards used in the study and summarizes which is the board for each node too. The reason for using these microcontrollers has been due to the ease of obtaining them in the market and their availability. The concentrator node has two communication modules since it operated as a gateway where it uses an XBEE module configured as a coordinator, and an Ethernet module to transmit data to a computer or the Internet if it is a remote network, and the data transfer to the computer is through messages in *sockets* format according to the user datagram protocol (UDP).

Table 1. Microcontroller/Development Boards used

Development Board	Nodos	Microcontroller	Memory	Clock
STM32F103C8T6	1, 2	- Core: ARM 32 bits Cortex - M3CPU - 72 MHz maximum frequency	- 128 KBytes Flash Memory - 20 KBytes SRAM	- 4-to-16 MHz crystal oscillator
STM32F401CxUx	3, 4	- Core: ARM 32-bit Cortex - M4 CPU with FPU - frequency up to 84 MHz	- 256 KBytes Flash Memory - 64 KBytes SRAM	- Internal 16 MHz factory-trimmed RC - 32 kHz oscillator for RTC with calibration
ARDUINO UNO	5, 6,7, 8, 9	- Core: ATMega328P - AVR CPU at up to 16 MHz/8bits microcontroller	- 32 KBytes Flash - 2 KBytes SRAM	- 0 to 16 MHz at 4.5 to 5.5
STM32F407VG	10 (coordinator/ gateway)	- Core: ARM 32-bit Cortex-M4 CPU with FPU - frequency up to 168 MHz	- 1 MBytes Flash Memory - 192+4KBytes SRAM	- Internal 16 MHz factory-trimmed RC (1% accuracy) - 32 kHz oscillator for RTC with calibration

The ZigBee modules used in each node of this network is the MikroE XBEE Click which uses an XBEE S2C device as it allows handling the ZigBee API mode and has a range of 60m indoors and up to 1200m outdoors with an absolute line of sight and transmission rate reaching 250,000 Kbps. Each of these modules has its own MAC address used for data routing. For the transmission of the data, the transmission request message (0x10) was used, so that the XBEE modules receiving the frame generated the packet reception message (0x90) as a response.

3.1 Routing Protocols for WSN Evaluated

For the programming of the routing protocols, a previous study of the existing links between each of the nodes was carried out, considering the maximum coverage radius provided by the modules used. Here a connectivity matrix G was determined, where the element $G_{i,j}$ corresponds to the connectivity of a pair of nodes i, j and is marked with 1 only if there is connectivity between them. The main diagonal keeps **0** to ensure that there are no loops.

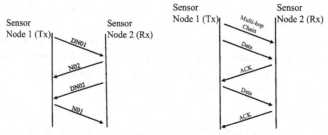

(a) Communication between nodes for Broadcast discovery.

(b) Communication between nodes for data transmission.

Fig. 1. Communication between nodes in the configuration and steady state phase.

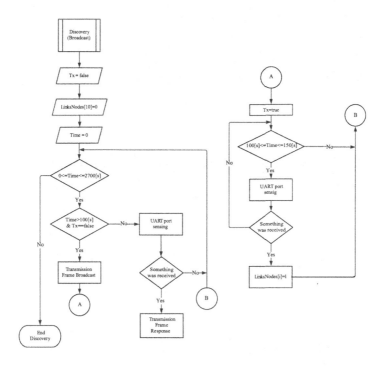

Fig. 2. Flowchart of the discovery process of sensor nodes in the network.

On the other hand, routing protocols in WSNs are composed of two stages or phases. The first phase is the configuration for a discovery of the network nodes is performed to establish the links between each node and organize groups in the case of a hierarchical routing protocol and is achieved through the transmission of broadcast messages (*broadcast*) summarized in Fig. 1(a). The second phase, also called the steady state phase, is when each of the packet transmissions from each node to the base station occurs, described in Fig. 1(b) [21]. This process consists of each sensor node having a time window to perform its discovery through a timer that is configured in each sensor node. In a vector called *LinksNodes*, each position represents a node in the network, each node stores the value of 1 if the receiving node sends the discovery response message. This process is summarized in Fig. 2.

Routing Based on the Dijkstra Algorithm: For the implementation of the Dijkstra algorithm in a sensor node, the two stages described above were established. After the configuration stage, a TDM multiplexing is established, where each sensor node has a time window to transmit its data. In this protocol, the input variables are a vector of distances between each node called *Dist* and a Boolean variable Tx to ensure that the nodes have only one space for the transmission of their data. Similar to the discovery process, after 100 s each node will start performing its data transmission, for which it must apply the Dijkstra algorithm and determine its next hop by considering the distances vector *Dist*.

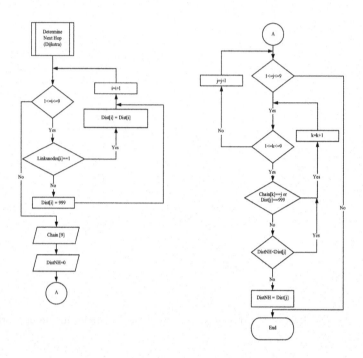

Fig. 3. Flowchart of Dijkstra's algorithm operation.

Figure 3 shows a flowchart with the operation of the algorithm based on Dijkstra's algorithm where the first phase establishes a very high distance for the nodes without a line of sight. This distance modification is done through the *LinksNodes* vector initialized in the discovery subprocess. Then the distances of nodes with active links are compared and at the same time, it is detected if the analyzed node is in the multihop chain. If the candidate node to be a receiver already belongs to the multi-hop chain, it means that this node was a solution of a previous node, so this node cannot be traversed twice. Once all the distances have been compared, the smallest one is stored in the variable *DistNH* and the next hop in the variable *NextHope*.

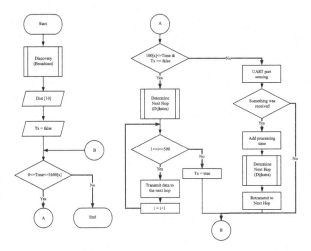

Fig. 4. Flowchart of the sensor node operation with the Dijkstra-based protocol.

Once this process is completed, the sensor node starts transmitting its data to the next node. The other nodes will remain in constant monitoring of the UART port to detect any packet coming from the other nodes. In case of receiving the multi-hop chain, it means that this node will belong to it and will have to perform the next hop calculation with Dijkstra to continue with the data transmission. This whole algorithm is summarized in the flowchart presented in Fig. 4. It should be noted that this process is repeated each time a node is in its assigned TDM window.

Routing Based on PRIM Algorithm: For routing based on the MST problem with undirected graphs solved by the PRIM algorithm (Fig. 5), it is established that the weight vector corresponds to the quality of the link that exists between the nodes and the calculation responds to the different constraints that may exist in a scenario using a weight matrix per link. A first approach to the weight matrix can be a distance matrix as a function of the connectivity matrix; but, it is also possible to establish a weight matrix where the lowest values correspond to the preferred routes. The dot product of the connectivity, weights, and distance matrices would result in an option for the calculation of PRIM routes.

To start the operation of this algorithm it is pertinent to perform a discovery of the nodes to subsequently determine the link with the best quality. After the configuration phase, the steady-state phase (Fig. 6) of the routing algorithm begins with a process similar to Dijkstra's with the particularity that the matrix of distances between nodes must be multiplied by the matrix of weights.

Low-Energy Adaptative Clustering Hierarchy (LEACH): In this protocol, after the discovery process each sensor node must determine whether that round has the function of Clusterhead (CH) or sensor node, for this a threshold is calculated which must be greater than a random number N ranging from

0 and 1 [21]. If the threshold is greater than the number N then the node is considered as CH, otherwise, the node will only transmit its data and will not perform the reception procedure. The flowchart of this protocol is presented in Fig. 7.

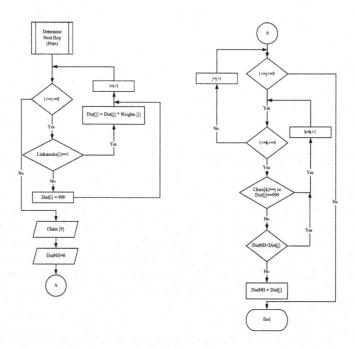

Fig. 5. Flowchart of the sensor node operation with the PRIM-based protocol.

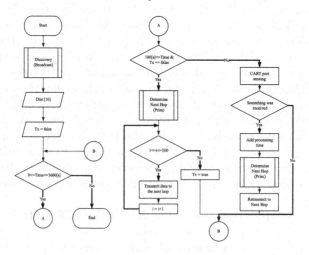

Fig. 6. Flowchart of the PRIM-based algorithm.

Power-Efficient Gathering in Sensor Information Systems (PEGA-SIS): For the programming of the PEGASIS [22] protocol, it must be considered that the nodes have a global knowledge of the network, therefore for the selection of the leader nodes of the multi-hop chain, the nodes that have a direct line to the network coordinator and that in turn have more than one node within their coverage and that share line of sight were taken into account.

The discovery process is maintained to know the leader of the chain or path to which each sensor node belongs and in turn determine the links with the rest of the sensor nodes until reaching the DAP. In the steady state phase, the sensor nodes will have the opportunity to transmit within their time window and perform a multi-hop chain through Dijkstra's algorithm described in Fig. 3. Also, the rest of the nodes monitor their links so that, when a packet reception event occurs, they can determine the next hop and retransmit the data. The leading nodes in the chain will perform their retransmission directly to the coordinator just as a CH does. Figure 8 shows how this protocol works in its entirety.

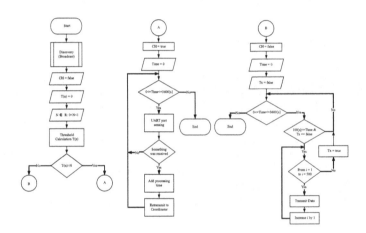

Fig. 7. Flowchart of sensor node operation with LEACH protocol.

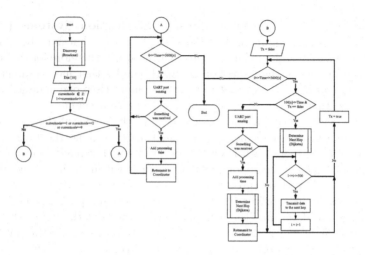

Fig. 8. Flowchart of the sensor node operation with the PEGASIS protocol.

4 Analysis of Results

For the transmission tests, each sensor node was to transmit a total of 500 packets in its time window omitting the discovery and multi-hop chain packets. Therefore, in the Dijkstra and Prim protocols, a total of 4500 packets were expected to be received, while in the LEACH and PEGASIS protocols 3500 packets since the nodes that had the CH function were to be omitted being this 20% of the total nodes. In the first scenario without optimal network sizing, two circumstances are considered, normal constant connection, Fig. 9(a) and connection with random disconnection events, Fig. 9(b). The latter intends to evaluate the behavior of the algorithms against randomly generated failures represented by the disconnection of nodes while the network is operating.

In the test without disconnection events, for the Dijkstra protocol the DAP received 3509 packets, with the 3564 protocol, with the PEGASIS protocol 2659, and with LEACH a total of 2719 packets were received. In the test with disconnection, the number of packets received in each protocol decreases because the number of possibilities to establish a path to reach the base station or the chain leader decreases. After this study, in Dijkstra-based routing, DAP managed to receive 2339 packets, with Prim 2457 packets, with LEACH a total of 1076 packets, and with PEGASIS 1076 packets. This reflects that the network is kept constantly busy with Dijkstra and PRIM-based algorithms and that the PRIM-based algorithm can receive more packets because the nodes prioritize the links with better quality and in turn can determine different routes despite the inactivity of certain nodes.

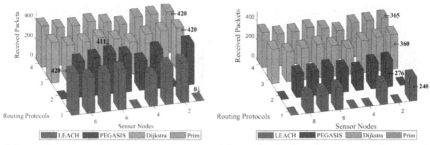

(a) Number of packets received by node. (b) Number of packets received per node versus node disconnection events.

Fig. 9. Packets received by node.

In the same scenario without sizing, the latency between packet transmission increases due to the number of multi-hops, so the Dijkstra, PRIM, and PEGASIS protocols have a higher latency compared to the LEACH protocol. Figures 10(a) and 10(b) show the average latency in the transmission process of each sensor node with the different routing protocols in operation, where Fig. 10(b) represents the scenario with disconnection of the nodes.

For the scenario analysis using network sizing, 7 candidate sites were selected (Fig. 11(a)), where, sites E, F, and G was at a height above the rest of the nodes of approximately 15 [m]. Therefore, the distance calculation for these nodes was performed using $d \approx \sqrt{2rh}$, where r is the radius of the earth 6371 [m] and h is the height difference between the sensor node and the candidate site. For the links between nodes that do not have a line of sight, an infinite distance was set in the distance matrix for the candidate sites to omit those connecting links.

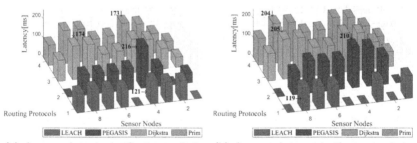

(a) Average latency in the transmission of each node. (b) Average latency in the transmission of each node with disconnection events.

Fig. 10. Average latency, scenario without dimensioning.

In this scenario, a simultaneous operational capability of 3 sensor nodes was considered due to the transmit stream, a coverage rate between 70–100%, and a coverage radius between 110 [m] and 170 [m]. It is known that the coverage radius of the XBEE module used is 1200 [m] in open spaces, but due to the density of the scenario its coverage reaches up to 180 [m], so for the mathematical modeling it was decided to reduce the coverage radius to ensure the reach of all nodes. The results obtained from the capacity and coverage analysis are presented in Table 2 which indicate that candidate sites A, B, and D are the optimal sites where a coordinator node should be implemented to achieve 70% and 80% coverage.

Table 2. Dimensioning Results

Coverage Radius	70%	80%	90%	100%
110	A — B — D	A — B — D	-	-
120	A — B — D	A — B — D	-	-
130	A — B — D	A — B — D	-	-
140	A — B — D	A — B — D	-	-
150	A — B — D	A — B — D	-	-
160	A — B — D	A — B — D	-	-
170	A — B — D	A — B — D	-	-

Figure 11(a) presents the original scenario of the study with the coverage radius of each sensor node. Figure 11(b) shows the optimal scenario with the links between the coordinators and the sensor nodes. The results shown consider a coverage radius of 170 [m] and a coverage percentage of 80%. No other results are presented since neither the links nor the optimal points of the network are modified. With this result, nodes 8 and 9 are determined to connect to candidate site A, nodes 1, 6 and 7 to candidate site B, and nodes 2, 3 and 5 to candidate site D. For the implementation of this scenario, the position of the coordinator was changed to that of node 1 and 2. In addition, the routing protocols were run to analyze the packet loss rate and latency.

When the coordinator was placed at the position of sensor node 1 the base station received 1652 packets when the LEACH algorithm was executed, 2919 packets with PEGASIS, 3593 packets with the Dijkstra algorithm and 3748 packets with PRIM, being the routing based on PRIM the one with the lowest packet loss rate managing to receive 83.28% of the transmitted packets. On the other hand, when placing the coordinator in the second position there is an increase of packets received by the base station, where with the LEACH protocol 1813 packets were received, with PEGASIS 3126, with the Dijkstra algorithm 3770 packets and with PRIM a total of 3969 packets, i.e. 51.8%, 89.31%, 83.77% and 88.2% of packets transmitted respectively. With this we observe that PEGASIS decreases the packet loss rate, inferring that the position of sensor node 2 is more centralized and therefore decreases the multi-hopping.

The amount of packets received from each sensor node in these scenarios is presented in Fig. 12(a) and 12(b) respectively, where the transmission of all sensor nodes is grouped according to the routing protocol. In addition, the labels point to the source sensor node of the largest number of packets received by the coordinator in each routing protocol.

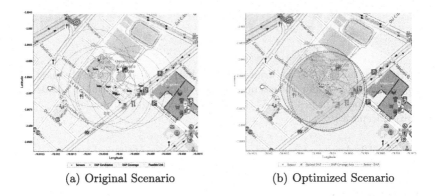

(a) Original Scenario   (b) Optimized Scenario

Fig. 11. Identification of locations for network optimization.

The benefits of the centralization of the coordinator are demonstrated by also verifying the latency analysis. In this sense, latency decreases as a function of the multi hops that must be performed for packet reception at the coordinator. The protocols that benefit the most are PEGASIS, Dijkstra, and PRIM, while LEACH maintains its hierarchical structure and therefore the number of multi hops. The comparison of the latency existing in each node according to the routing protocol in both tests is presented in Figs. 13(a) and 13(b) that show the average latency existing in the transmission of each sensor node according to the routing protocol implemented in the network showing that the highest latency existing in a sensor node according to the routing protocol.

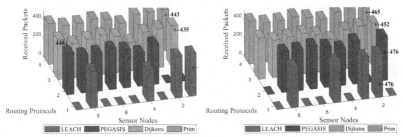

(a) Number of packets received per node (Coordinating Node at position A).

(b) Number of packets received per node (Coordinating Node at position B).

Fig. 12. Number of packets received under an optimized scenario.

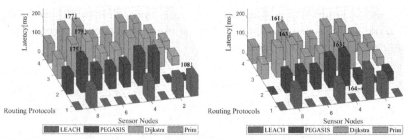

(a) Average latency in the transmission of each node under normal operation (Coordinator in position A). (Optimized Scenario)

(b) Average transmission latency of each node under normal operations (Coordinator in position B).

Fig. 13. Average latency at each node under an optimized scenario

5   Conclusions

Through the results shown, it was identified that the optimal sizing of networks can improve the performance metrics of a WSN such as the decrease in latency and packet loss rate. Therefore, it is correct to state that for the design of a WSN it is necessary to analyze the candidate sites to obtain the best location of the hubs or base stations, to optimize network resources and implementation costs. Since the objective of the WSN is the transmission of sensed data using the least amount of resources, network dimensioning becomes a tool to optimize these resources.

Considering the routing protocols analyzed for the application of a WSN in applications where several data have to be transmitted in hierarchical topologies, for example in the case of smart metering, the protocols recommended based on the study are PEGASIS and PRIM-based. These two routing protocols proved to have a lower packet loss rate and showed themselves as the best options as this is a key requirement for IoT-based systems. In addition, specifically with the Prim protocol, it was demonstrated that despite the loss of connection of the nodes, its transmission rate exceeds 50%, indicating that it is a stable and fault-tolerant protocol. Although multi-hop transmission protocols have latency problems, they manage to increase the network lifetime because they allow sensor nodes to use less power and therefore less energy consumption in each of their transmissions.

References

1. Atzori, L., Iera, A., Morabito, G.: From "smart objects" to "social objects": the next evolutionary step of the internet of things. IEEE Commun. Mag. **52**(1), 97–105 (2014)
2. Sendler, U.: The Internet of Things: Industrie 4.0 Unleashed. Springer, Heidelberg (2017). https://doi.org/10.1007/978-3-662-54904-9

3. Inga, E., Inga, J., Ortega, A.: Novel approach sizing and routing of wireless sensor networks for applications in smart cities. Sensors **21**(14), 1–17 (2021)
4. Lang, A., Wang, Y., Feng, C., Stai, E., Hug, G.: Data aggregation point placement for smart meters in the smart grid. IEEE Trans. Smart Grid **13**(1), 541–554 (2021)
5. Mahakalkar, N., Pethe, R.: Review of routing protocol in a wireless sensor network for an IoT application. In: 2018 3rd International Conference on Communication and Electronics Systems (ICCES), pp. 21–25. IEEE (2018)
6. Pinheiro, D.L., Garça, J.L., de Lima, O.A., Furtado, C.G.: Analysis of multi-hop strategies in leach protocol. In: 2019 IX Brazilian Symposium on Computing Systems Engineering (SBESC), pp. 1–8. IEEE (2019)
7. Ganán, C., Inga, E., Hincapié, R.: Óptimo despliegue y enrutamiento de UDAP para infraestructura de medición avanzada basada en el algoritmo MST Optimal deployment and routing geographic of UDAP for advanced metering infrastructure based on MST algorithm. Revista chilena de ingeniería **25**(1), 106–115 (2017)
8. Michael, R.A., Carlos, Z.P., Juan, I.O.: Optimum design and dimensioning model of a Mesh-WiFi network for emergency services in protected areas. In: 2017 IEEE 2nd Ecuador Technical Chapters Meeting, ETCM 2017, 2017-January, pp. 1–6 (2018)
9. Garcia, L., Jiménez, J.M., Taha, M., Lloret, J.: Wireless technologies for IoT in smart cities. Netw. Protocols Algorithms **10**(1), 23 (2018)
10. Digi International. XBee®/XBee-PRO® ZB SMT RF modules: ZigBee RF module datasheet (2010)
11. Sonthalia, M., Jha, A., Gupta, U., Thyagarajan, J.: A real time implementation of hierarchical routing protocol for IoT based wireless sensor network. In: 2019 International Conference on Wireless Communications, Signal Processing and Networking, WiSPNET 2019, pp. 512–516 (2019)
12. Zheng, J., Jamalipour, A.: Wireless Sensor Networks: A Networking Perspective. Wiley, Hoboken (2008)
13. Al-Karaki, J.N., Kamal, A.E.: Routing techniques in wireless sensor networks: a survey. IEEE Wirel. Commun. **11**(6), 6–27 (2004)
14. Raja, B., Rajakumar, R., Dhavachelvan, P., Vengattaraman, T.: A survey on classification of network structure routing protocols in wireless sensor networks. In: 2016 IEEE International Conference on Computational Intelligence and Computing Research, ICCIC 2016, pp. 4–8 (2017)
15. Shahraki, A., Taherkordi, A., Haugen, O., Eliassen, F.: A survey and future directions on clustering: from WSNs to IoT and modern networking paradigms. IEEE Trans. Netw. Serv. Manag. **18**(2), 2242–2274 (2021)
16. Sana, M., Noureddine, L.: Multi-hop energy-efficient routing protocol based on minimum spanning tree for anisotropic wireless sensor networks. In: Proceedings of International Conference on Advanced Systems and Emergent Technologies, IC_ASET 2019, pp. 209–214 (2019)
17. Nguyen, T.D., Khan, J.Y., Ngo, D.T.: A distributed energy-harvesting-aware routing algorithm for heterogeneous IoT networks. IEEE Trans. Green Commun. Netw. **2**(4), 1115–1127 (2018)
18. Machado, L., Inga, E.: Optimal placement of UDAP in advanced metering infrastructure for smart metering of electrical energy based on graph theory. Electronics (Switzerland) **11**, 1767 (2022)
19. Hochba, D.S.: Approximation algorithms for NP-hard problems. ACM SIGACT News **28**(2), 40–52 (1997)

20. Suárez, C., Inga, E.: Optimal performance and modeling of wireless technology enabling smart electric metering systems including microgrids. Sensors **21**, 7208 (2021)
21. Heinzelman, W.R., Chandrakasan, A., Balakrishnan, H.: Energy-efficient communication protocol for wireless microsensor networks. In: Proceedings of the Annual Hawaii International Conference on System Sciences, 2000-January(c), pp. 1–10 (2000)
22. Lindsey, S., Raghavendra, C.S.: PEGASIS: power-efficient gathering in sensor information systems. In: IEEE Aerospace Conference Proceedings, vol. 3, pp. 1125–1130 (2002)

Correction to: Design and Evaluation of a Prototype of Dual Channel Electrical Stimulator: Application in the Assessment of Current Perception Thresholds to Multiple Stimuli

D. A. Molina-Vidal⬛, P. Cevallos Larrea, L. Guambaña Calle,
D. Liquori, and C. J. Tierra-Criollo⬛

Correction to:
Chapter 25 in: F. R. Narváez et al. (Eds.): *Smart Technologies,*
Systems and Applications, **CCIS 1705,**
https://doi.org/10.1007/978-3-031-32213-6_25

In the original version of this chapter there is an error in the citation concerning the author names. This has been corrected.

The updated version of this chapter can be found at
https://doi.org/10.1007/978-3-031-32213-6_25

Author Index

Printed in the United States
by Baker & Taylor Publisher Services